Computer Forensics:

Computer Crime Scene Investigation

Computer Forensics:

Computer Crime Scene Investigation

John Vacca

CHARLES RIVER MEDIA, INC.
Hingham, Massachusetts

Publisher: David F. Pallai
Production: Tolman Creek Design
Cover Design: The Printed Image

CHARLES RIVER MEDIA, INC.
20 Downer Avenue, Suite 3
Hingham, Massachusetts 02043
781-740-0400
781-740-8816 (FAX)
info@charlesriver.com
www.charlesriver.com

This book is printed on acid-free paper.

John Vacca. *Computer Forensics: Computer Crime Scene Investigation.*

ISBN: 1-58450-018-2

Library of Congress Cataloging-in-Publication Data

Vacca, John R.
  Computer forensics: computer crime scene investigation / John Vacca.
    p. cm.
  ISBN 1-58450-018-2
  1. Computer security. 2. Computer networks—Security measures. 3.
Forensic sciences. I. Title.
  QA76.9.A25 V33 2002
  363.25'968—dc21

                    2002002583

Printed in the United States of America
02 7 6 5 4 3 2 First Edition

Contents

Part VI Appendixes 639

Acknowledgments

There are many people whose efforts on this book have contributed to its successful completion. I owe each a debt of gratitude and want to take this opportunity to offer my sincere thanks.

A very special thanks to my publisher, David Pallai, without whose initial interest and support would not have made this book possible; and, for his guidance and encouragement over and above the business of being a publisher. Thanks to production coordinator, Kelly Robinson, who provided staunch support and encouragement when it was most needed. Thanks to my copyeditor, Annette R. Pagliaro whose fine editorial work has been invaluable. And a special thanks to Michael Erbschloe, who wrote the foreword for this book. Finally, thanks to all the other people at Charles River Media whose many talents and skills are essential to a finished book.

Thanks to my wife, Bee Vacca, for her love, help, and understanding of my long work hours.

Finally, I wish to thank the organizations and individuals who granted me permission to use the research material and information necessary for the completion of this book.

I thank you all so very much.

To my mystery loving wife Bee

Foreword

Michael Erbschloe
Vice President of Research
Computer Economics, Carlsbad, California

Computer forensics is one of the largest growth professions of the 21st century. The soaring increase in the number of Internet users combined with the constant computerization of business processes has created new opportunities for computer criminals and terrorists. Study after study has consistently revealed that cyber attacks, hacking, and computer-based criminal activities are costing businesses and government organizations billions of dollars each year.

Law enforcement agencies around the world are starting to fight back. It has been a long, difficult struggle to train law enforcement personnel in computer-crime-related issues and recruit skilled computer professionals into law enforcement careers. These efforts are far from finished.

We need to train at least 50,000 more computer crime fighters in order to stem the global tide of computer attacks. Many computer professionals have asked me how they can get started in security and crime-fighting careers. My response has constantly been learn, study, train, and move forward. *Computer Forensics: Computer Crime Scene Investigation,* by John Vacca, is an excellent place to start establishing the required knowledge base to move into this fascinating new career field.

Computer Forensics is an excellent book for trained law enforcement personnel who desire to learn more about investigating and fighting computer crimes. *Computer Forensics* is also an excellent book for computer professionals who want to move into the rapidly growing security field and are considering shifting their career focus to law enforcement and criminal investigation.

It is also important that computer security personnel expand their understanding of forensic processes and keep their understanding of investigative and prevention procedures up to date. *Computer Forensics* is an excellent book for all levels of computer security personnel to further their professional development.

John Vacca has made an excellent contribution to the computer forensics field. I highly recommend *Computer Forensics* and congratulate John Vacca on a job extremely well done.

Introduction

Cyber criminals are wreacking havoc on computer systems—and are capturing front-page headlines in the bargain. It has made little difference that the Bush Administration pledged billions in additional federal funding to combat security breaches after the 9-11 terrorists attacks. The problem just keeps getting worse.

Fortunately, the computer security field is also progressing at a brisk rate. In particular, the field of computer forensics brings new ways of preserving and analyzing evidence related to cyber crime.

GROWING PROBLEM

The numbers are chilling. According to a recent industry survey, 91% of the survey respondents detected cyberattacks on their companies, and 384 organizations reported $376,690,051 in financial losses.

So what's going on? It doesn't take a computer engineer or computer scientist to learn hacking fundamentals. After spending a few nights on the Internet, high school students discover they can master hacking fundamentals by simply downloading software. Corporations and the federal government are just beginning to realize that securing their computer networks is critical. Equally frightening is that our national security has already been compromised. Colleges have finally started to offer courses and concentrations in computer security and forensics, but it remains difficult to find degree programs in these disciplines.

COMPUTER FORENSICS

Computer forensics involves the preservation, identification, extraction, and documentation of computer evidence stored as data or magnetically encoded information. The fascinating part of the science is that the computer evidence is often transparently created by the computer's operating system without the knowledge of the computer operator. The information may actually be hidden from view. To find it, special forensic software tools and techniques are required.

Emerging Field—But a Shortage of Experts

Most law enforcement agencies, especially those in large cities, are understaffed when it comes to having trained computer forensics experts. Industry, on the other hand, has been taking computer forensics seriously for several years. Sadly, it took a number of embarrassing computer break-ins by teenage hackers to put the spotlight on it. The problem is, industry doesn't know which computer forensics issues to focus on.

The biggest issue surrounding the computer forensics conundrum is a shortage of technologists who have a working knowledge of computer forensics. Academics are teaching the subjects, but most lack real-world experience, which is critical when training students. Also, many academics are not current with forensics trends and tools.

Times Are Changing

There's the old saying, "If you wait long enough, it's bound to change." The same can be said for computer forensics training. Not only will more techies be concentrating on computer forensics but also attorneys and judges will be taking courses in the subject. Learning forensics basics will help attorneys, especially, to determine the kinds of evidence that can be found by probing a computer's operating system and what techniques can be used to legally obtain it.

On the academic front, full-fledged degree tracks in computer forensics are being developed. Certification programs already exist.

Where are the jobs? Government agencies, such as the Department of Defense, FBI, CIA, NSA, and U.S. Postal Service need computer forensics specialists. State and local law enforcement departments are also hiring computer forensics specialists. On the corporate front, all companies (especially large and mid-size ones with a Web presence) will have serious computer forensics needs. Job titles differ, but, typically, these positions are advertised as Junior Computer Forensics Analysts for entry-level jobs and Senior Computer Forensics Analysts if you have a few years of experience in the field.

PURPOSE

The purpose of this book is to show experienced (intermediate to advanced) computer forensics, security, and law enforcement professionals how to analyze and conduct a computer forensics examination, and report the findings that will lead to the incarceration of the perpetrators. This book also provides the fundamental knowledge you need to analyze risks to your system and implement a workable security and forensics policy that protects your information assets from potential intrusion, damage or theft. Through extensive hands-on examples (field and trial experiments) and case studies, you will gain the knowledge and skills required to master the deployment of information warfare countermeasures to thwart potential attacks.

SCOPE

Throughout the book, extensive hands-on examples will provide you with practical experience in computer forensics evidence capture, analysis, and reporting, as well as information warfare countermeasures and future directions. In addition to advanced computer forensics technology considerations in commercial organizations and governments, the book addresses, but is not limited to, the following line items as part of the discovery of electronic evidence:

ON THE CD

- The CD-ROM that accompanies this book contains the latest and best computer forensics software tools.
- You will learn how to: Analyze your exposure to security threats and protect your organization's systems and data; manage risks emanating from inside the organization and from the Internet and extranets; protect network users from hostile applications and viruses; reduce your susceptibility to an attack by deploying firewalls, data encryption, decryption, and other information warfare countermeasures; and identify the security risks that need to be addressed in security and computer forensics policy.
- Chapters on how to gain practical experience in analyzing the security risks and information warfare countermeasures that need to be addressed in your organization also include: maintaining strong authentication and authenticity; preventing eavesdropping; retaining integrity of information; evaluating the strength of user passwords; selecting a firewall topology; and evaluating computer and hacker ethics.

This book leaves little doubt that the new and emerging field of computer forensics is about to evolve. This new area of knowledge is now being researched, organized, and taught. No question, this book will benefit organizations and governments, as well as their computer forensics and security professionals.

TARGET AUDIENCE

With regard to computer forensics, the book is primarily targeted at those in government and law enforcement who require the fundamental skills to develop and implement security schemes designed to protect their organizations' information from attacks, including managers, network and systems administrators, technical staff, and support personnel. This also includes those involved in securing Web sites, including Web developers; Web masters; and systems, network, and security administrators.

ORGANIZATION OF THIS BOOK

This book is organized into six parts, including the appendixes (which include a glossary of computer forensic and information warfare terms).

Part I: Overview of Computer Forensics Technology

Part One discusses computer forensics fundamentals; types of computer forensics technology; and vendor and computer forensics services.

- Chapter 1, "Computer Forensics Fundamentals," provides an overview of computer forensics types and techniques, and their electronic evidence and capture.
- Chapter 2, "Types of Computer Forensics Technology," covers the basic issues dealing with Windows NT, Windows 2000; and Windows XP and, their use within law enforcement computer forensic technology. In other words, it covers security and computer evidence issues associated with Windows NT, Windows 2000, and Windows XP.
- Chapter 3, "Types of Vendor and Computer Forensics Services," covers how a swift and measured forensic incident response—drawing on sound policies, vendor tools and support—allow an organization to contain the potential damage of an attack and effectively seek compensation or prosecution. In addition to the preceding, this chapter also covers the following computer forensic services: forensic incident response; evidence collection; forensic analysis; expert witness; forensic litigation and insurance claims support; training; and forensic process improvement.

Part II: Computer Forensics Evidence and Capture

The second part of this book discusses data recovery; evidence collection and data seizure; duplication and preservation of digital evidence; and computer image verification and authentication.

- Chapter 4, "Data Recovery," answers many questions about the ins and outs of data recovery as it relates to computer forensics.

- Chapter 5, "Evidence Collection and Data Seizure," points out the difficulties in collecting evidence and seizing data and what must be done to overcome them. Not everything is covered here—it should be used as a guide only, and you should seek further information for your specific circumstances.

- Chapter 6, "Duplication and Preservation of Digital Evidence," is a discussion on how to keep Murphy's law from ruining your case. When it comes to computer evidence processing, Murphy is always looking over your shoulder. He stands ready to strike at just the wrong moment.

- Chapter 7, "Computer Image Verification and Authentication," discusses the overall security of a computer image verification and authentication system and how it rests with the combination of security measures.

PART III: COMPUTER FORENSICS ANALYSIS

Part Three covers the discovery of electronic evidence; identification of data; reconstructing past events; and networks.

- Chapter 8, "Discovery of Electronic Evidence," addresses the consideration of the process of information discovery. The fact that information discovery only deals with logical evidence (electronic data), means that you can avoid much of the tedium required by search and seizure to ensure evidence integrity and the chain of custody.

- Chapter 9, "Identification of Data," specifically focuses on the long-recognized value of deterrence—through threat of retaliation—as an effective means of defense. The means for enabling deterrence in the cyberrealm will be introduced here.

- Chapter 10, "Reconstructing Past Events," illustrates the reconstruction of past events with as little distortion or bias as possible.

- Chapter 11, "Networks," introduces a solution to the dilemma of network forensics. Network forensics is the principle of reconstructing the activities leading to an event and determining the answer to "What did they do?" and "How did they do it?"

Part IV: Countermeasures: Information Warfare

Part Four discusses how to fight against macro threats—defensive strategies for governments and industry groups; the information warfare arsenal and tactics of the military; the information warfare arsenal and tactics of terrorists and rogues; the information warfare arsenal and tactics of private companies; the information warfare arsenal of the future; surveillance tools for information warfare of the future; and civilian casualties—the victims and refugees of information warfare.

- Chapter 12, "Fighting against Macro Threats: Defensive Strategies for Governments and Industry Groups," is an in-depth examination of the implications of IW for the U.S. and allied infrastructures that depend on the unimpeded management of information that is also required in the fight against macro threats–defensive strategies for governments and industry groups.

- Chapter 13, "The Information Warfare Arsenal and Tactics of the Military," focuses on two goals. First, you need to find a way to protect yourself against catastrophic events. Second, you need to build a firm foundation on which you can make steady progress by continually raising the cost of mounting an attack and mitigating the expected damage of the information warfare arsenal and tactics of the military.

- Chapter 14, "The Information Warfare Arsenal and Tactics of Terrorists and Rogues," recommends a number of specific steps that could better prepare the U.S. military and private companies to confront "the new terrorism" and its information warfare arsenal and tactics.

- Chapter 15, "The Information Warfare Arsenal and Tactics of Private Companies," deals with the IW tools and strategies of private companies and how they're used against the aggressors. It will also help to realistically guide the process of moving forward in dealing with the information warfare arsenal and tactics of private companies.

- Chapter 16, "The Information Warfare Arsenal of the Future," discusses how the increasing dependence on sophisticated information systems brings with it an increased vulnerability to hostile elements, terrorists among them, in dealing with the information warfare arsenal of the future.

- Chapter 17, "Surveillance Tools for Information Warfare of the Future," discusses the basic concepts and principles that must be understood and that can help guide the process of moving forward in dealing with the surveillance tools for the information warfare of the future.

- Chapter 18, "Civilian Casualties—The Victims and Refugees of Information Warfare," considers the application of civilian information operations (CIOs) to the conventional warfare environment. Although the array of CIO tools and techniques has been presented as discrete elements in a schematic diagram, the CIO environment is complex, multidimensional, interactive, and still developing.

Part V: Results and Future Directions

Finally, Part Five discusses advanced computer forensics, with a summary, conclusions, and recommendations.

- Chapter 19, "Advanced Computer Forensics," introduces numerous solutions for those of you who are in the process of conducting advanced computer forensics through the use of encryption for protection and hacking back with advanced hacker trackers.

- Chapter 20, "Summary, Conclusions, and Recommendations," No summary chapter on computer forensics would be complete without an examination of costs involved. This final chapter is concerned with how to conduct a relevant and meaningful review of computer forensic analysis software tools. It is also the intent of this chapter to initiate discussions to solidify the various computer forensics requirements. Finally, this chapter recommends the establishment of computer forensics standards for the exchange of digital evidence between sovereign nations and is intended to elicit constructive discussions regarding digital evidence.

Part IX: Appendixes

Five appendixes provide additional resources that are available for computer forensics. Appendix A is a list of frequently asked questions. Appendix B is a list of computer forensic resources. Appendix C contains links to computer forensics and related law enforcement Web pages. Appendix D contains more computer forensics case studies. Appendix E lists the CD ROM contents. The book ends with a glossary of computer forensics and information-warfare-related terms.

CONVENTIONS

This book uses several conventions to help you find your way around, and to help you find important sidebars, facts, tips, notes, cautions, and warnings. You see eye-catching icons in the left margin from time to time. They alert you to critical information and warn you about problems.

John R. Vacca
jvacca@hti.net

Overview of Computer Forensics Technology

1 Computer Forensics Fundamentals

Electronic evidence and information gathering have become central issues in an increasing number of conflicts and crimes. Electronic or computer evidence used to mean *the regular print-out from a computer*—and a great deal of computer exhibits in court are just that. But, for many years, law enforcement officers have been seizing data media; and, computers themselves, as they have become smaller and more ubiquitous.

In the very recent past, investigators generated their own print-outs, sometimes using the original application program, sometimes specialist analytic and examination tools. More recently, investigators have found ways of collecting evidence from remote computers to which they do not have immediate physical access, provided such computers are accessible via a phone line or network connection. It is even possible to track activities across a computer network, including the Internet.

These procedures form part of what is called *computer forensics,* though some people also use the term to include the use of computers to analyze complex data (for example, connections between individuals by examination of telephone logs and/or bank account transactions). Another use of the term is when computers are employed in the court itself, in the form of computer graphics, to illustrate a complex situation such as a fraud or as a replacement for large volumes of paper-based exhibits and statements.

So, what actually is computer forensics? Computer forensics is about evidence from computers that is sufficiently reliable to stand up in court and be convincing. You might employ a computer forensics specialist to acquire evidence from computers on your behalf. On the other hand, you may want one to criticize the work of others. The field is a rapidly growing one, with a solid core, but with many controversies at its edges.

WHAT IS COMPUTER FORENSICS?

Computer forensics, also referred to as computer forensic analysis, electronic discovery, electronic evidence discovery, digital discovery, data recovery, data discovery, computer analysis, and computer examination, is the process of methodically examining computer media (hard disks, diskettes, tapes, etc.) for evidence. A thorough analysis by a skilled examiner can result in the reconstruction of the activities of a computer user.

In other words, computer forensics is the collection, preservation, analysis, and presentation of computer-related evidence. Computer evidence can be useful in criminal cases, civil disputes, and human resources/employment proceedings.

Far more information is retained on a computer than most people realize. It's also more difficult to completely remove information than is generally thought. For these reasons (and many more), computer forensics can often find evidence of, or even completely recover, lost or deleted information, even if the information was intentionally deleted.

Computer forensics, although employing some of the same skills and software as data recovery, is a much more complex undertaking. In data recovery, the goal is to retrieve the lost data. In computer forensics, the goal is to retrieve the data and interpret as much information about it as possible.

USE OF COMPUTER FORENSICS IN LAW ENFORCEMENT

If there is a computer on the premises of a crime scene, the chances are very good that there is valuable evidence on that computer. If the computer and its contents are examined (even if very briefly) by anyone other than a trained and experienced computer forensics specialist, the usefulness and credibility of that evidence will be tainted.

Choosing a Computer Forensics Specialist for a Criminal Case

When you require the services of a computer forensics specialist, don't be afraid to shop around. There are an increasing number of people who claim to be experts in the field. Look very carefully at the level of experience of the individuals involved. There is far more to proper computer forensic analysis than the ability to retrieve data, especially when a criminal case is involved. Think about computer forensics just as you would any other forensic science and look for a corresponding level of expertise.

The bottom line is that you will be retaining the services of an individual who will likely be called to testify in court to explain what he or she did to the computer and its data. The court will want to hear that individual's own level of training and experience, not the experience of their employer. Make sure you find someone who not only has the expertise and experience, but also the ability to stand up to the scrutiny and pressure of cross-examination.

COMPUTER FORENSICS ASSISTANCE TO HUMAN RESOURCES/EMPLOYMENT PROCEEDINGS

Computer forensics analysis is becoming increasingly useful to businesses. Computers can contain evidence in many types of human resources proceedings, including sexual harassment suits, allegations of discrimination, wrongful termination claims, and others. Evidence can be found in electronic mail systems, on network servers, and on individual employee's computers. However, due to the ease with which computer data can be manipulated, if the search and analysis is not performed by a trained computer forensics specialist, it could likely be thrown out of court.

Employer Safeguard Program

As computers become more prevalent in businesses, employers must safeguard critical business information. An unfortunate concern today is the possibility that data could be damaged, destroyed, or misappropriated by a discontented individual.

Before an individual is informed of their termination, a computer forensic specialist should come on-site and create an exact duplicate of the data on the individual's computer. In this way, should the employee choose to do anything to that data before leaving, the employer is protected. Damaged or deleted data can be replaced, and evidence can be recovered to show what occurred. This method can also be used to bolster an employer's case showing the removal of proprietary information, or to protect the employer from false charges made by the employee.

Whether you are looking for evidence in a criminal prosecution, in a civil suit, or determining exactly what an employee has been up to, you should be equipped to find and interpret the clues that have been left behind. This includes situations where files have been deleted, disks have been reformatted, or other steps have been taken to conceal or destroy the evidence. For example, did you know:

- What Web sites have been visited?
- What files have been downloaded?
- When files were last accessed?

- Of attempts to conceal or destroy evidence?
- Of attempts to fabricate evidence?
- That the electronic copy of a document can contain text that was removed from the final printed version?
- That some fax machines can contain exact duplicates of the last several hundred pages received?
- That faxes sent or received via computer may remain on the computer indefinitely?
- That e-mail is rapidly becoming the communications medium of choice for businesses?
- That people tend to write things in e-mail that they would never consider writing in a memorandum or letter?
- That e-mail has been used successfully in criminal cases as well as in civil litigation?
- That e-mail is often backed up on tapes that are generally kept for months or years?
- That many people keep their financial records, including investments, on computers?[i]

COMPUTER FORENSICS SERVICES

No matter how careful they are, when people attempt to steal electronic information (everything from customer databases to blueprints), they leave behind traces of their activities. Likewise, when people try to destroy incriminating evidence contained on a computer (from harassing memos to stolen technology), they leave behind vital clues. In both cases, those traces can prove to be the *smoking gun* that successfully wins a court case. Thus, computer data evidence is quickly becoming a reliable and essential form of evidence that should not be overlooked.

A computer forensics professional does more than turn on a computer, make a directory listing, and search through files. Your forensics professionals should be able to successfully perform complex evidence recovery procedures with the skill and expertise that lends credibility to your case. For example, they should be able to perform the following services:

- Data seizure
- Data duplication/preservation
- Data recovery
- Document searches
- Media conversion
- Expert witness services
- Computer evidence service options
- Other miscellaneous services

Data Seizure

Federal Rules of Civil Procedure let a party or their representative inspect and copy designated documents or data compilations that may contain evidence. Your computer forensics experts, following federal guidelines, should act as this representative, using their knowledge of data storage technologies to track down evidence.[ii] Your experts should also be able to assist officials during the equipment seizure process. See Chapter 5, "Evidence Collection and Data Seizure," for more detailed information.

Data Duplication/Preservation

When one party must seize data from another, two concerns must be addressed: The data must not be altered in any way, and the seizure must not put an undue burden on the responding party. Your computer forensics experts should acknowledge both of these concerns by making an exact duplicate of the needed data. Because duplication is fast, the responding party can quickly resume its normal business functions. And, because your experts work on the duplicated data, the integrity of the original data is maintained. See Chapter 6, "Duplication and Preservation of Digital Evidence," for more detailed information.

Data Recovery

Using proprietary tools, your computer forensics experts should be able to safely recover and analyze otherwise inaccessible evidence. The ability to recover *lost* evidence is made possible by the expert's advanced understanding of storage technologies. For example, when a user deletes an e-mail, traces of that message may still exist on the storage device or media. Although the message is inaccessible to the user, your experts should be able to recover it and locate relevant evidence. See Chapter 4, "Data Recovery," for more detailed information.

Document Searches

Your computer forensics experts should also be able to search over 100,000 electronic documents in minutes rather than days. The speed and efficiency of these searches make the discovery process less complicated and less intrusive to all parties involved.

Media Conversion

Some clients need to obtain and interrogate computer data stored on old and unreadable devices. Your computer forensics experts should extract the relevant data from these devices, convert it into readable formats, and place it onto new storage media for analysis.

Expert Witness Services

Computer forensics experts should be able to explain complex technical processes in an easy-to-understand fashion. This should help judges and juries comprehend how computer evidence is found, what it consists of, and how it is relevant to a specific situation (see sidebar, "Provide Expert Consultation and Expert Witness Services").

Provide Expert Consultation and Expert Witness Services

Computers

EXPERT TESTIMONY
- Have testified multiple times as an Expert Witness in Computers/Computer Forensics in Circuit Court
- Regularly testify as an Expert Witness in Computers/Computer Forensics in Federal Court for U.S. Attorney's Offices

COMPUTER EXPERTISE
- Computer Crime Investigators Association
- Trained in the forensic examination of computers (PC & Mac), having conducted examinations in countless cases including: child exploitation, homicide, militia, software piracy, and fraud
- Testify in state and Federal Courts as an expert in computers, computer forensics, the Internet, and America Online; often as an Expert Witness for U.S. Attorney's Offices
- Is thoroughly familiar with both computer hardware and software, having written software and repaired and assembled computers
- Teach computer crime investigation, including computer search and seizure, for the Institute of Police Technology and Management
- Regularly consult with law enforcement officers in the search and seizure of computers
- Have provided forensic training to numerous law enforcement officers and corporate security officers
- Regularly consulted by other forensic examiners for advice in difficult cases

TRAINING GIVEN AS EXPERT IN COMPUTER CRIMES
- Law Enforcement and Corrections Technology Symposium and Exhibition
- Bureau of Justice Statistics/Justice Research Statistics Association

Electronic Surveillance

- Theft by employees or others
  - Time
  - Property
  - Propriety information/trade secrets
- Embezzlement
- Inappropriate employee actions
- Burglary

Your computer forensics expert's experience should include installing cameras in every imaginable location. This would include indoors/outdoors, offices, homes, warehouses, stores, schools, or vehicles; for every conceivable crime—theft, burglaries, homicides, gambling, narcotics, prostitution, extortion, or embezzlement (under every conceivable circumstance) controlled settings or hostage crisis or court-ordered covert intrusion.

If you need to know what your employees are doing on your time and on your premises, your computer forensics experts should be able to covertly install video monitoring equipment so that you can protect your interests. This even includes situations where employees may be misusing company computers. By using video surveillance to document employees that are stealing time, property, or secrets from you, you should protect yourself if you plan to take appropriate action against the employee.

Child Exploitation

- Child sexual exploitation
- Child pornography
  - Manufacture
  - Use
  - Sale
  - Trading
  - Collection
  - Child erotica
- Use of computers in child exploitation
- Search and seizure
- Victim acquisition
- Behavior of preferential and situational offenders
- Investigation
  - Proactive
  - Reactive[iii]

Computer Evidence Service Options

Your computer forensics experts should offer various levels of service, each designed to suit your individual investigative needs. For example, they should be able to offer the following services:

- Standard service
- On-site service
- Emergency service
- Priority service
- Weekend service

STANDARD SERVICE

Your computer forensics experts should be able to work on your case during normal business hours until your critical electronic evidence is found. They must be able to provide clean rooms, and ensure that all warranties on your equipment will still be valid following their services.

ON-SITE SERVICE

Your computer forensics experts should be able to travel to your location to perform complete computer evidence services. While on-site, the experts should quickly be able to produce exact duplicates of the data storage media in question. Their services should then be performed on the duplicate, minimizing the disruption to business and the computer system. Your experts should also be able to help federal marshals seize computer data and be very familiar with the Federal Guidelines for Searching and Seizing Computers.

EMERGENCY SERVICE

After receiving the computer storage media, your computer forensics experts should be able to give your case the highest priority in their laboratories. They should be able to work on it without interruption until your evidence objectives are met.

PRIORITY SERVICE

Dedicated computer forensics experts should be able to work on your case during normal business hours (8:00 A.M. to 5:00 P.M., Monday through Friday) until the evidence is found. Priority service typically cuts your turnaround time in half.

WEEKEND SERVICE

Computer forensics experts should be able to work from 8:00 A.M. to 5:00 P.M. Saturday and Sunday to locate the needed electronic evidence, and will continue working on your case until your evidence objectives are met. Weekend service depends on the availability of computer forensics experts.

OTHER MISCELLANEOUS SERVICES

Computer forensics experts should also be able to provide the following extended services:

- Analysis of computers and data in criminal investigations
- On-site seizure of computer data in criminal investigations
- Analysis of computers and data in civil litigation.
- On-site seizure of computer data in civil litigation
- Analysis of company computers to determine employee activity
- Assistance in preparing electronic discovery requests
- Reporting in a comprehensive and readily understandable manner
- Court-recognized computer expert witness testimony
- Computer forensics on both PC and Mac platforms
- Fast turnaround time

Recover Data That You Thought Was Lost Forever

Computers systems may crash. Files may be accidentally deleted. Disks may accidentally be reformatted. Computer viruses may corrupt files. Files may be accidentally overwritten. Disgruntled employees may try to destroy your files. All of these can lead to the loss of your critical data. You may think it's lost forever, but computer forensics experts should be able to employ the latest tools and techniques to recover your data.

In many instances, the data cannot be found using the limited software tools available to most users. The advanced tools that computer forensics experts utilize allow them to find your files and restore them for your use. In those instances where the files have been irreparably damaged, the experts' computer forensics expertise allows them to recover even the smallest remaining fragments.

Advise You on How to Keep Your Data and Information Safe from Theft or Accidental Loss

Business today relies on computers. Your sensitive client records or trade secrets are vulnerable to intentional attacks from, for example, computer hackers, disgruntled employees, viruses, and corporate espionage. Equally threatening, but far less considered, are unintentional data losses caused by accidental deletion, computer hardware and software crashes, and accidental modification.

Computer forensics experts should advise you on how to safeguard your data by such methods as encryption and back-up. The experts can also thoroughly clean sensitive data from any computer system you plan on eliminating.

Your files, records, and conversations are just as vital to protect as your data. Computer forensics experts should survey your business and provide guidance for improving the security of your information. This includes possible information leaks such as cordless telephones, cellular telephones, trash, employees, and answering machines.

Examine a Computer to Find out What Its User Has Been Doing

Whether you're looking for evidence in a criminal prosecution, looking for evidence in a civil suit, or determining exactly what an employee has been up to, your computer forensics experts should be equipped to find and interpret the clues that have been left behind. This includes situations where files have been deleted, disks have been reformatted, or other steps have been taken to conceal or destroy evidence.

As previously mentioned, your computer forensics experts should provide complete forensic services. These include: electronic discovery consultation; on-site seizure of evidence; thorough processing of evidence; interpretation of the results; reporting the results in an understandable manner; and court-recognized expert testimony.

Your computer forensics experts should also be able to regularly provide training to other forensic examiners, from both the government and private sectors. When other forensic examiners run into problems, they should turn to your experts for solutions.

Sweep Your Office for Listening Devices

In today's high-tech society, bugging devices, ranging from micro-miniature transmitters to micro-miniature recorders, are readily available. Automatic telephone-recording devices are as close as your nearest Radio Shack store. Your computer forensics experts should have the equipment and expertise to conduct thorough electronic countermeasures (ECM) sweeps of your premises.

High-Tech Investigations

Your computer forensics experts should have high level government investigative experience; and, the knowledge and experience to conduct investigations involving technology, whether the technology is the focus of the investigation or is required to conduct the investigation. The experts should be uniquely qualified to conduct investigations involving cellular telephone cloning, cellular subscription fraud, software piracy, data or information theft, trade secrets, computer crimes, misuse of computers by employees, or any other technology issue.

So, what are your employees actually doing? Are they endlessly surfing the Web? Are they downloading pornography and opening your company to a sexual harassment lawsuit? Are they e-mailing trade secrets to your competitors? Are they running their own business from your facilities while they are on your clock?

Your computer forensics experts should be uniquely qualified to answer these questions and many more. Don't trust these sensitive inquiries to companies that don't have the required expertise. *Trust No One!*

For a detailed discussion of the preceding computer forensics services, please see Chapter 3, "Types of Vendor and Computer Forensics Services." Now, let's examine how evidence might be sought in a wide range of computer crime or misuse, including but not limited to theft of trade secrets, theft or destruction of intellectual property, and fraud. Computer specialists can draw on an array of methods for discovering data that resides in a computer system, or for recovering deleted, encrypted, or damaged file information. Any or all of this information may help during discovery, depositions, or actual litigation.

BENEFITS OF PROFESSIONAL FORENSICS METHODOLOGY

The impartial computer forensics expert who helps during discovery will typically have experience on a wide range of computer hardware and software. It is always beneficial when your case involves hardware and software with which this expert is directly familiar. But fundamental computer design and software implementation is often quite similar from one system to another; and, experience in one application or operating system area is often easily transferable to a new system.

Unlike paper evidence, computer evidence can often exist in many forms, with earlier versions still accessible on a computer disk. Knowing the possibility of their existence, even alternate formats of the same data can be discovered. The discovery process can be served well by a knowledgeable expert identifying more possibilities that can be requested as possibly relevant evidence. In addition, during on-site premises inspections, for cases where computer disks are not actually seized or forensically copied, the forensics expert can more quickly identify places to look, signs to look for, and additional information sources for relevant evidence. These may take the form of earlier versions of data files (memos, spreadsheets) that still exist on the computer's disk or on backup media, or differently formatted versions of data, either created or treated by other application programs (word processing, spreadsheet, e-mail, timeline, scheduling, or graphic).

Protection of evidence is critical. A knowledgeable computer forensics professional should ensure that a subject computer system is carefully handled to ensure that:

1. No possible evidence is damaged, destroyed, or otherwise compromised by the procedures used to investigate the computer.
2. No possible computer virus is introduced to a subject computer during the analysis process.

3. Extracted and possibly relevant evidence is properly handled and protected from later mechanical or electromagnetic damage.
4. A continuing chain of custody is established and maintained.
5. Business operations are affected for a limited amount of time, if at all.
6. Any client–attorney information that is inadvertently acquired during a forensic exploration is ethically and legally respected and not divulged.[iv]

STEPS TAKEN BY COMPUTER FORENSICS SPECIALISTS

The computer forensics specialist should take several careful steps to identify and attempt to retrieve possible evidence that may exist on a subject's computer system. For example, the following steps should be taken:

1. Protect the subject computer system during the forensic examination from any possible alteration, damage, data corruption, or virus introduction
2. Discover all files on the subject system. This includes existing normal files, deleted yet remaining files, hidden files, password-protected files, and encrypted files
3. Recover all (or as much as possible) of discovered deleted files
4. Reveal (to the greatest extent possible) the contents of hidden files as well as temporary or swap files used by both the application programs and the operating system
5. Access (if possible and legally appropriate) the contents of protected or encrypted files
6. Analyze all possibly relevant data found in special (and typically inaccessible) areas of a disk. This includes but is not limited to what is called unallocated space on a disk (currently unused, but possibly the repository of previous data that is relevant evidence), as well as slack space in a file (the remnant area at the end of a file in the last assigned disk cluster, that is unused by current file data, but once again, may be a possible site for previously created and relevant evidence).
7. Print out an overall analysis of the subject computer system, as well as a listing of all possibly relevant files and discovered file data.
8. Provide an opinion of the system layout; the file structures discovered; any discovered data and authorship information; any attempts to hide, delete, protect, and encrypt information; and anything else that has been discovered and appears to be relevant to the overall computer system examination
9. Provide expert consultation and/or testimony, as required[v]

WHO CAN USE COMPUTER FORENSIC EVIDENCE?

Many types of criminal and civil proceedings can and do make use of evidence revealed by computer forensics specialists:

- Criminal prosecutors use computer evidence in a variety of crimes where incriminating documents can be found, including: homicides, financial fraud, drug and embezzlement record-keeping, and child pornography.
- Civil litigations can readily make use of personal and business records found on computer systems that bear on: fraud, divorce, discrimination, and harassment cases.
- Insurance companies may be able to mitigate costs by using discovered computer evidence of possible fraud in accident, arson, and workman's compensation cases.
- Corporations often hire computer forensics specialists to ascertain evidence relating to: sexual harassment, embezzlement, and theft or misappropriation of trade secrets and other internal/confidential information.
- Law enforcement officials frequently require assistance in pre-search warrant preparations and post-seizure handling of the computer equipment.
- Individuals sometimes hire computer forensics specialists in support of possible claims of: wrongful termination, sexual harassment, or age discrimination.

But there are concerns and problems with computer forensic evidence. So, let's examine some of those problems.

Problems of Computer Forensic Evidence

Computer evidence is like any other evidence; it must be:

- Authentic
- Accurate
- Complete
- Convincing to juries
- In conformity with common law and legislative rules (admissible)[vi]

However, there are also special problems:

- Computer data changes moment by moment.
- Computer data is invisible to the human eye; it can only be viewed indirectly after appropriate procedures.

■ The process of collecting computer data may change it—in significant ways. The processes of opening a file or printing it out are not always neutral.

■ Computer and telecommunications technologies are always changing so that forensic processes can seldom be fixed for very long.[vii]

Forensic Technician

Contrary to what is often thought, in many cases it is possible to produce reliable computer-derived evidence without recourse to specialist tools. The general principles are:

■ The scene of crime has to be frozen; that is, the evidence has to be collected as early as possible and without any contamination.

■ There must be continuity of evidence, sometimes known as chain of custody; that is, it must be possible to account for all that has happened to the exhibit between its original collection and its appearance in court, preferably unaltered.

■ All procedures used in examination should be auditable, that is, a suitably qualified independent expert appointed by the other side in a case should be able to track all the investigations carried out by the prosecution's experts.[viii]

Good results can be obtained by using the standard disk repair, network testing, and other utilities; however, very full records need to be kept. But for some purposes these may not be enough, for example, where it is hoped to recover previously deleted material or where a logic bomb or virus is suspected. In these circumstances, specialist tools are needed. However, special training is also required. The tools themselves don't address all of the problems of producing evidence that will stand up in court. Thus, the key features of the forensic technician are:

■ Careful methodology of approach, including record keeping
■ A sound knowledge of computing, particularly in any specialist areas claimed
■ A sound knowledge of the law of evidence
■ A sound knowledge of legal procedures
■ Access to and skill in the use of appropriate utilities[ix]

Legal Tests

The actual rules vary from legislation to legislation, but one can give a broad outline of what happens in those countries with a common law tradition—the UK, USA, and the so-called *old* Commonwealth. The law makes distinctions between real evidence, testimonial evidence, and hearsay. Real evidence is that which comes from an inanimate object that can be examined by the court. Testimonial evidence is that which a live witness has seen and upon which he or she can be cross-examined.

The hearsay rule operates to exclude assertions made other than those made by the witness who is testifying as evidence of the truth of what is being asserted. The pure hearsay rule is extremely restrictive and has been extensively modified by various statutory provisions. Thus, there are rules about the *proving* of documents and business books. Bankers' books have separate legislation. Some of the rules apply explicitly to computers, but many do not, although they can be (and have been) interpreted to cover many situations in which computers are involved.

For example, in the UK there have been situations where legal rules presumably designed to help the court may, in fact, hinder it. In practice, these issues may be circumvented. For instance, in a criminal case, evidence may be obtained by inadmissible methods. This evidence, however, then points investigators to admissible sources of evidence for the same sets of circumstances. An example of this could occur during a fraud investigation. In other words, computer search methods are often used to identify allegedly fraudulent transactions, but the evidential items eventually presented in court are paper-based invoices, contract notes, dockets, or whatever. In this manner, the prosecution can demonstrate to the jury the deception or breach of the Companies Act or other specific fraudulent act. Again, in civil litigation the parties may decide to jointly accept computer-based evidence (or not to challenge it) and instead concentrate on the more substantive elements in the dispute. A defendant may prefer to have a substantive defense rather than a technical one based on inadmissibility. Or, again, the legal team may not feel sufficiently competent to embark on a technical challenge.

In the United States, many practical problems exist around the actual seizure of computers containing evidence. Law enforcement officers must comply with the Fourth Amendment to the U.S. Constitution.

Subject Matter of Computer Forensics

The subject matter of computer forensics can, thus, not afford solely to concern itself with procedures and methods of handling computers, the hardware from which they are made up and the files they contain. The ultimate aim of forensic investigation is use in legal proceedings. At the same time, an obsession with common law and judicial rules is likely to inhibit many investigations. It might be a mistake for inquiries not to be commenced simply because of fear of possible inadmissibility. Furthermore, as we have already seen, a number of computer-investigatory methods may turn out not to be directly admissible, but may nevertheless be useful in locating noncomputer evidence that is admissible.

One may have to take a somewhat pragmatic view of the precise bounds of the subject matter, but it should still be possible to define its core activities. It might help to explore the way in which forensic science, in general, has developed and then see what expectations one might reasonably have of computer forensics.

Although forensic science had been established long before then and indeed forms a central feature of many of Conan Doyle's Sherlock Holmes stories published from 1892 onwards; up until the 1970s, each forensic scientist tended to develop his or her own methods and present them ad hoc to juries. Obviously, reliance was placed on descriptions of methods used by others, but for courts, the tests of whether to believe the forensic evidence were the manner of presentation—the supposed eminence of the forensic scientist and the skill of the opposition lawyer (and/or rival expert) who might be called. During the 1970s, a more formal checklist-based approach was introduced. This was partly to bring about standardization as between different laboratories and partly in response to the criticism (in the UK) that arose over such controversial cases as the Birmingham Six. In the UK Home Office Forensic Service, these checklists would be devised by senior staff. Obviously, such checklists are revised in the light of experience—the publication of new specialist research or adverse experience during a trial. An increasing feature of modern practice is quality control, which involves work being checked by an otherwise uninvolved coworker before being offered to external scrutiny. In any event, the broad tests for evidence include:

- *Authenticity:* Does the material come from where it purports?
- *Reliability:* Can the substance of the story the material tells be believed and is it consistent? In the case of computer-derived material, are there reasons for doubting the correct working of the computer?
- *Completeness:* Is the story that the material purports to tell complete? Are there other stories that the material also tells that might have a bearing on the legal dispute or hearing?
- *Freedom from interference and contamination:* Are these levels acceptable as a result of forensic investigation and other post-event handling[x].

Any approach to computer forensics would, thus, need to include the elements of:

- Well-defined procedures to address the various tasks
- An anticipation of likely criticism of each methodology on the grounds of failure to demonstrate authenticity, reliability, completeness and possible contamination as a result of the forensic investigation
- The possibility for repeat tests to be carried out, if necessary, by experts hired by the other side
- Checklists to support each methodology
- An anticipation of any problems in formal legal tests of admissibility
- The acceptance that any methods now described would almost certainly be subject to later modification[xi]

Divergences from Conventional Forensic Investigation

There will be divergences from the expectations of more traditional areas of forensic investigation. The main reason is the rate of change of computer technology. The devisor of a test for the presence of a prohibited drug, an explosive, fabric fibers, bodily tissues, and the like, can expect that over a period of time, the test may be improved or shown to be defective. But, the actual need for the test and most of its essential detail will probably not change. But, in computers, newness and obsolesce is the norm.

For example, a key feature of computer forensics is the examination of data media: New forms and techniques of methods of data storage occur at intervals of less than 5 years (the floppy disk of 10 years ago was in 5.25 in format and held 360k). The current equivalent is 3.5 inches and holds 1.44 MB; and much higher densities are expected soon. A typical hard-disk size on a PC of the same date was 20–30 MB, was in 5.25 inch form and used modified frequency modulation (MFM) controller technology. Today most PCs have hard-disks in excess of 350 MB in 3.5 inch or even 2.5 inch form using integrated development environment (IDE) or run length limited (RLL) technology. On minis and mainframes, data may be held on Redundant Array of Independent (or Inexpensive) Disks (RAID), where individual files may be split and spread over 8 or more separate disk surfaces. Similar changes have taken place in tape technology and the use of erasable programmable read-only memory (EPROMs).

Computer architectures have shown profound change in the same short period. PCs have become much more powerful, the large central mainframe is now a rarity and large companies are now served by a multiplicity of smaller computers that all interact via a complex network.

Computer peripherals keep changing as well. Modems and network routers have become *intelligent*, and digitizing scanners are fairly common devices. They can be subverted, for example, for forgery.

Wide-area telecoms methods are being used more and more. There are opportunities for both high-tech criminals and forensic investigators. The protocols they use also keep changing.

The foregoing simply lists technological changes. Similar changes that have taken place in computer applications; these, in turn, have affected the type of information one might expect to find held on a computer. For example, over the same 10 years, the following technological changes have taken place:

- The growth of e-mail, both locally within a large organization and worldwide
- The growth of client/server applications
- The software outcome of the more complex hardware architectures

- The client/server situation (software on)
- A PC or small local machine interacts with software and data held on other nonlocal machines and large mainframes, in a way that appears to be seamless to the user. One key effect of this is that a computer document often does not exist in some computer equivalent of a filing cabinet; but, rather, is assembled on demand by the activity of one computer drawing information from many others.
- The evidence of a transaction or event may, therefore, only be provable by the presentation of all the records from all the computers involved, plus an explanation of how the assembly of the report relied on took place.
- The greater use of EDIs and other forms of computer-based orders, bills of lading, payment authorizations, etc. EDIs have very complex structures, with some evidence being held in computers owned by the counter-parties and some by the EDI supplier/regulator.
- Computer graphics: computer-aided design (CAD) methods, particularly those that provide an element of autocompletion or filling-in of basic design ideas
- More extended, easier-to-use databases
- The greater use of computer-controlled procedures (sales, dispatch and emergency services, computer-controlled processes, traffic control, and manufacturing)
- The methods of writing and developing software have also changed. There is much greater use of libraries of procedures (of new computer language models). For example, object-oriented programming environments, and new, more formal methods of program development; standards, and methods of testing have also changed.[xii]

As a result, computer forensic methods may not have the time in which to establish themselves, nor the longevity, that more traditional chemistry and physics-based forensics enjoys. Nevertheless, the usual way in which specific forensic methods become accepted is via publication in a specialist academic journal. For example, a forensic scientist seeking to justify a methodology in court can do so by stating that it is based on a specific published method, which had not up to the point of the hearing been criticized.

NOTE

The rule of best practice refers to the use of best practice available and known at the time of the giving of evidence.

CASE HISTORIES

One of the fundamental principles of computer investigation is the need to follow established and tested procedures meticulously and methodically throughout the investigation. At no point of the investigation is this more critical than at the stage of initial evidence capture. Reproducibility of evidence is the key. Without the firm base of solid procedures, which have been strictly applied, any subsequent antirepudiation attempts in court will be suspect, and the case as a whole will likely be weakened.

There have been several high-profile cases recently where apparently solid cases have been weakened or thrown out on the basis of inappropriate consideration given to the integrity and reproducibility of the computer evidence. There are several reasons why this may happen. Lack of training is a prime culprit. If the individuals involved have not been trained to the required standards, or have received no training at all, then tainted or damaged computer evidence is the sad but inevitable result.

Another frequent cause is lack of experience. Not only lack of site experience, but also inappropriate experience of the type of systems, might be encountered. One of the most difficult on-site skills is knowing when to call for help. It is essential that a sympathetic working environment is created such that peer pressure or fear of loss of status and respect does not override the need to call for help. Easier said than done, perhaps, but no less essential for that reason.

Finally, sloppiness, time pressure, pressure applied on-site, tiredness, or carelessness have all been contributory factors in transforming solid computer evidence into a dubious collection of files. These totally avoidable issues are related to individual mental discipline; management control and policy; and selecting appropriate staff to carry out the work. There are issues with which one cannot sympathize. This is bad work, plain and simple.

Ultimately, anytime the collection of computer evidence is called into question, it is damaging to everyone who is a computer forensic practitioner; it is ultimately in everyone's best interest to ensure that the highest standards are maintained.

To use a rather worn phrase from an old American police series ("Hill Street Blues"): *Let's be careful out there!*

Taken for a Ride

A sad, but all too frequent story from prospective clients: I've just spent $5,000 on a Web site and got taken for a ride. I cannot find the con man now and all I have is an alias and a pay-as-you-go mobile number. Can you help me please?

WHAT CAN YOU DO?

It is strongly recommended that anyone dealing with entities on the Internet needs to make sure they know who they are dealing with before they enter into any transaction or agreement. If you cannot obtain a real-world address (preferably within the jurisdiction in which you live), then think twice about going any further. Always question the use of mobile phone numbers—they should set alarm bells ringing! This task is made easier in the UK now as all mobile numbers[xiii] start 077xx, 078xx, or 079xx. Pagers start 076xx. From April 28, 2001 on, all old mobile, pager (those that do not begin 07), special rate, and premium rate numbers stopped working.

If you feel you do want to proceed with the transaction, then use a credit card rather than a debit card or other type of money transfer; then at least you will have some protection and only be liable for $50 rather than having your entire bank account cleaned out. In terms of tracing a suspect like the one in the preceding, your computer forensic experts should be able to trace e-mails around the world; and, by acting quickly and in conjunction with legal firms, they should be able to track individuals down to their homes. An application for a Civil Search Order can then allow entry and the experts are thus able to secure all electronic evidence quickly and efficiently. Internet Cafés are sometimes more of a problem, but it is remarkable how many users go to the trouble of trying to disguise their tracks only to end up sitting in exactly the same seat every time they visit the same Café.

So, yes, your computer forensic experts can help, but by taking the proper precautions, you would not need to call them in the first place!

Abuse of Power and Position

This message is by no means new, in fact, it could be said that it has been repeated so many times in so many forums that it is amazing that management still falls foul of the following circumstances.

In recent months, investigators at Vogon International Limited[xiv] have been asked to examine computer data for evidence of fraud. On one occasion, the client was a charity, on the second, a multinational company.

In both cases, fraud, totaling hundreds of thousands of dollars (pounds) was uncovered. The modus operandi of the suspects was very similar in both cases. Bogus companies were set-up and invoices were submitted for payment. The fraudsters were in a position to authorize the payment of the invoices and had the power to prevent unwelcome scrutiny of the accounts.

In addition, one of the fraudsters was paying another member of staff to turn a blind eye to what was happening. On further investigation, this member of staff was obviously living beyond his means.

The message is simple, whether you are a multinational company or a small business, the possibility of fraud is ever present. And, while not wishing to fuel paranoia, traditional checks and balances must be in place to ensure that those trusted members of the staff who have power cannot abuse their position.

Secure Erasure

Now, let's touch on this *old chestnut* again, because it appears to be the source of considerable confusion and misinformation. Vogon's customer base seems to be polarized into two main camps:[xv] those who desperately want to retain their data and fail, often spectacularly, to do so; and the other camp who wish to irrevocably destroy their data, and frequently fail in a similarly dramatic manner.

The latter may be criminals who wish to cover their tracks from the police or legitimate business organization who wish to protect themselves from confidential information falling into the wrong hands. Fundamentally, the issues are the same. When considering the issues of the legitimate destruction of data, this is ultimately a matter of management responsibility, which requires a considered risk analysis to be carried out.

To the question *can data be securely erased?* The answer is, self-evidently, yes. If you were to ask: *Is it straightforward or certain?* It depends, would be the answer.

There are many systems in use for securely erasing data from a wide range of media. Some are effective, some completely ineffective, and some partially effective. It is the latter situation that causes concern, and, frequently, not an inconsiderable amount of embarrassment.

Those systems that absolutely destroy data do so in a manner that is total, unequivocal, and final; there can exist no doubt as to their effectiveness. Systems that are sold as being completely effective, but which are fundamentally flawed, are obviously flawed. With only cursory analysis, this is evident, and so these are (or should be) swiftly disregarded.

Vogon is regularly asked to verify the destruction of data by many of their large clients.[xvi] What they find is that frequently only a fraction of a sample sent is correctly or accurately deleted. RAID systems are a prime candidate for chaos. Certain revisions of drive firmware can present special challenges; in some cases, even the software used defeats the eraser. The list is long and growing.

Vogon is often asked for advice on this issue.[xvii] The answer is always the same. If the destruction of data has more value than the drive, physically destroy the drive. Crushing is good; melting in a furnace is better. If the drive had more value than the data, what are you worrying about?

CASE STUDIES

Over the years, Vogon's data-recovery laboratories have seen pretty much anything that can happen to a computer, no matter how incredible, whether it is a geologist who, in testing for minerals, inadvertently blew up his own laptop, or the factory worker who covered the computer running the production line in maple syrup. The list is now so long that the incredible has now become almost mundane.

Fortuitously, two in the latest of a long line of incredible recoveries recently arrived, so, it seemed appropriate to include them as case studies.

Case Study One: The Case of the Flying Laptop

Picture the scene: Police rushing into premises on the ninth floor of a building. Almost immediately thereafter, a laptop accelerates rapidly groundward out of the window of the aforementioned premises.

As long ago as 1687, Sir Isaac Newton predicted with uncanny accuracy the inevitable conclusion to this action: Namely, the laptop (or to be strictly accurate, large number of pieces of a former laptop) coming to rest with a singular lack of grace on the floor. Luckily, no one was injured by the impact. The resultant bag of smashed laptop components arrived at Vogon's laboratory for a forensically sound data recovery.[xviii]

The laptop computer had impacted the floor across its front edge at an angle, forcing the hard disk drive assembly to go completely through the screen of the laptop. The highly delicate spatial relationship between heads, flexures, platters, and spindle had become disturbed, and the bed of the drive unit was not concave. This imparted an oscillation in two dimensions during drive operation. The drive electronics were destroyed in the impact. After an evening's work by a highly skilled hardware engineer, it was determined that a full fix was possible, and a perfect image was taken. Vogon had no knowledge whether the chap was guilty; but, they bet he was in shock when the evidence was presented![xix]

Case Study Two: The Case of the Burned Tapes

This case does not involve true forensic investigation, but it does highlight the fact that it is important never to give up on a job, no matter how seemingly hopeless it appears.

Sets of digital audio tape (DAT) tapes were sent to Vogon from a loss adjuster.[xx] The DAT tapes were caught in a fire, which had engulfed a company's head office, and wiped out the primary trading infrastructure. The company's IT systems had been at the center of the blaze, and this had unfortunately raised the magnetic media on the surface of the servers hard drives past its curie point. The DAT tapes had, rather inadvisable as it turned out, not been stored off-site. They were, however, stored a little way from the center of the blaze.

Despite this, the DAT tapes arrived in a rather sorry condition. The plastic casing had melted to, around, and onto the tapes, and the whole mechanism was fused into a homologous glob. It is fair to say the tapes were sent to Vogon with the full expectation that they would be declared unrecoverable, and used as the basis from which to make a loss settlement.[xxi]

This recovery involved hours of work from both hardware and tapes recovery engineers. The tapes were carefully cut away from the molten mass, and treated for fire damage. The next stage was to rehouse the tapes and pass them forward to the tape recovery team. Following a number of complex stages, the recovery team was able to extract a stream of data from the tapes that accounted for some 95% of the original data stored on the company's tape backups.

The result was a company up and running in a matter of days rather than weeks, or, more likely, never. It also resulted in a significant reduction in the claims settlement by the loss adjuster, and business continuity for the unfortunate company concerned.

SUMMARY

Computers have appeared in the course of litigation for over 25 years. In 1977, there were 291 U.S. federal cases and 246 state cases in which the word *computer* appeared and which were sufficiently important to be noted in the Lexis database. In the UK, there were only 20. However, as early as 1968, the computer's existence was considered sufficiently important for special provisions to be made in the English Civil Evidence Act.

The following description is designed to give a summary of the issues rather than attempt to give a complete guide. As far as one can tell, noncontentious cases tend not to be reported, and the arrival of computers in commercial disputes and in criminal cases did not create immediate difficulties. Judges sought to allow computer-based evidence on the basis that it was no different from forms of evidence with which they were already familiar: documents, business books, weighing machines, calculating machines, films, and audio tapes. This is not to say that such cases were without difficulty; however, no completely new principles were required. Quite soon, though, it became apparent that many new situations were arising and that analogies with more traditional evidential material were beginning to break down. Some of these were tackled in legislation, as with the English 1968 Act and the U.S. Federal Rules of Evidence in 1976. But many were addressed in a series of court cases. Not all of the key cases deal directly with computers. But they do have a bearing on them as they relate to matters that are characteristic of computer-originated evidence. For example, computer-originated evidence or information that is not immediately readable by a human being, is usually gathered by a mechanical counting or weighing instrument. The calculation could also be performed by a mechanical or electronic device.

The focus of most of this legislation and judicial activity was determining the admissibility of the evidence. The common law and legislative rules are those that have arisen as a result of judicial decisions and specific law. They extend beyond mere guidance. They are rules that a court must follow; the thought behind these rules may have been to impose standards and uniformity in helping a court test authenticity, reliability, and completeness. Nevertheless, they have acquired a status of their own and in some cases prevent a court from making ad hoc common sense decisions about the quality of evidence. The usual effect is that once a judge has declared evidence inadmissible (that is, failing to conform to the rules), the evidence is never put to a jury; for a variety of reasons that will become apparent shortly. It is not wholly possible for someone interested in the practical aspects of computer forensics (that is, the issues of demonstrating authenticity, reliability, completeness, or lack thereof) to separate out the legal tests.

Now let's look at some of the more common questions that computer forensics can hope to answer. The following conclusions are not exhaustive, nor is the order significant.

Conclusions Drawn from Computer Forensics Situations

- *Documents:* To prove authenticity; alternatively, to demonstrate a forgery. This is the direct analogy to proving a print-based document
- *Reports:* Computer generated from human input. This is the situation where a series of original events or transactions are input by human beings, but where after regular computer processing, a large number of reports, both via print-out and on-screen can be generated. Examples would include the order/sales/ inventory applications used by many commercial organizations and retail banking.
- *Real evidence:* Machine-readable measurements and the like (weighing, counting, or otherwise recording events); the reading of the contents of magnetic stripes and bar codes and smart cards
- *Reports generated from machine-readable measurements, and the like:* Items that have been counted, weighed, and so on, and the results then processed and collated.
- *Electronic transactions:* To prove that a transaction took place, or to demonstrate a presumption that had taken place was incorrect. Typical examples would include money transfers, ATM transactions, securities settlement, and EDIs.

■ *Conclusions reached by search programs:* These are programs that have searched documents, reports, and so on, for names and patterns. Typical users of such programs are auditors and investigators.

■ *Event reconstruction:* To show a sequence of events or transactions passing through a complex computer system. This is related to the proving of electronic transactions, but with more pro-active means of investigation event reconstruction—to show how a computer installation or process dependent on a computer may have failed. Typical examples include computer contract disputes (when a computer failed to deliver acceptable levels of service and blame must be apportioned), disaster investigations, and failed trade situations in securities dealing systems.

■ *Liability in a situation:* This is where CAD designs have relied on autocompletion or filling-in by a program (in other respects, a CAD design is a straightforward computer-held document). Liability in a situation is also where a computer program has made a decision (or recommendation) based on the application of rules and formulae; where the legal issue is the quality and reliability of the application program, and the rules with which it has been fed.

The following occasions could arise in any of a number of forms of litigation:

■ Civil matters
■ Breach of contract
■ Asset recovery
■ Tort, including negligence
■ Breach of confidence
■ Defamation
■ Breach of securities industry legislation and regulation and/or Companies Acts
■ Employee disputes
■ Copyright and other intellectual property disputes
■ Consumer protection law obligations (and other examples of no-fault liability)
■ Data protection law legislation
■ Criminal matters such as:
    ■ Theft acts, including deception
    ■ Criminal Damage
    ■ Demanding money with menaces
    ■ Companies law, Securities industry, and banking offenses
    ■ Criminal offenses concerned with copyright and intellectual property
    ■ Drug offenses
    ■ Trading standards offenses
    ■ Official secrets

■ Computer Misuse Act offenses
■ Pornography offenses

As mentioned earlier, the most likely situations are that computer-based evidence makes a contribution to an investigation or to litigation and is not the whole of it.

An Agenda for Action in Computer Forensics Methods

The following is a provisional list of actions for some of the principle forensic methods. The order is not significant; however, these are the activities for which the research would want to provide a detailed description of procedures, review, and assessment for ease of use and admissibility. A number of these methods have been mentioned in passing already:

1. Safe seizure of computer systems and files, to avoid contamination and/ or interference
2. Safe collection of data and software
3. Safe and noncontaminating copying of disks and other data media
4. Reviewing and reporting on data media
5. Sourcing and reviewing of back-up and archived files
6. Recovery/reconstruction of deleted files—logical methods
7. Recovery of material from swap and cache files
8. Recovery of deleted/damaged files—physical methods
9. Core-dump: collecting an image of the contents of the active memory of a computer at a particular time
10. Estimating if files have been used to generate forged output
11. Reviewing of single computers for proper working during relevant period, including service logs, fault records, and the like
12. Proving/testing of reports produced by complex client/server applications
13. Reviewing of complex computer systems and networks for proper working during relevant period, including service logs, fault records, and the like
14. Review of system/program documentation for: design methods, testing, audit, revisions, and operations management
15. Reviewing of applications programs for proper working during relevant period, including service logs, fault records, and the like
16. Identification and examination of audit trails
17. Identification and review of monitoring logs
18. Telecoms call path tracing (PTTs or path-tracing telecoms and telecoms utilities companies only)
19. Reviewing of access control services—quality and resilience of facilities (hardware and software, identification/authentication services)

20. Reviewing and assessment of access control services—quality of security management

21. Reviewing and assessment of encryption methods—resilience and implementation

22. Setting up of proactive monitoring to detect unauthorized or suspect activity within application programs and operating systems, and across local area and wide area networks

23. Monitoring of e-mail

24. Use of special alarm or trace programs

25. Use of honey pots

26. Interaction with third parties (suppliers, emergency response teams, and law enforcement agencies)

27. Reviewing and assessment of measuring devices and other sources of real evidence, including service logs, fault records, and the like

28. Use of routine search programs to examine the contents of a file

29. Use of purpose-written search programs to examine the contents of a file

30. Reconciliation of multisource files

31. Examination of telecoms devices, location of associated activity logs and other records perhaps held by third parties

32. Event reconstruction

33. Complex computer intrusion

34. Complex fraud

35. System failure

36. Disaster affecting computer-driven machinery or process

37. Review of expert or rule-based systems

38. Reverse compilation of suspect code

39. Use of computer programs that purport to provide simulations or animations of events: review of accuracy, reliability, and quality

ENDNOTES

i "Computer Forensics," Rehman Technology Services, Inc., 18950 U.S. Highway 441, Suite 201, Mount Dora, Florida 32757, 2001. *(©Copyright 2002, Rehman Technology Services, Inc. All rights reserved), 2001.*

ii John R. Vacca, *The Essential Guide to Storage Area Networks*, Prentice Hall, 2002.

iii "Computer Forensics," Rehman Technology Services, Inc., 18950 U.S. Highway 441, Suite 201, Mount Dora, Florida 32757, 2001. *(©Copyright 2002, Rehman Technology Services, Inc. All rights reserved), 2001.*

iv Judd Robbins, "An Explanation Of Computer Forensics," National Forensics Center, 774 Mays Blvd. #10-143, Incline Village, NV 89451, 2001. *(©Copyright 2002, National Forensics Center. All rights reserved), 2001.*

v Ibid.

vi Peter Sommer, "Computer Forensics: An Introduction," Virtual City Associates, PO Box 6447, London N4 4RX, United Kingdom, 2001. *Academic URL: http//csrc.lse.ac.uk.*

vii Ibid.

viii Ibid.

ix Ibid.

x Ibid.

xi Ibid.

xii Ibid.

xiii John R. Vacca, *i-mode CrashCourse*, McGraw-Hill, 2001.

xiv Vogon Forensics Bulletin, Vol. 3, Issue 3, Vogon International Limited, Talisman Business Centre, Talisman Road, Bicester, Oxfordshire, OX26 6HR United Kingdom, 2001.

xv Ibid.

xvi Ibid.

xvii Ibid.

xviii Ibid.

xix Ibid.

xx Ibid.

xxi Ibid.

2 Types of Computer Forensics Technology

Defensive information technology will ultimately benefit from the availability of cyber forensic evidence of malicious activity. Criminal investigators rely on recognized scientific forensic disciplines, such as medical pathology, to provide vital information used in apprehending criminals and determining their motives. Today, an increased opportunity for cyber crime exists, making it imperative for advances in the law enforcement, legal, and forensic computing technical arenas. As previously explained, cyber forensics is the discovery, analysis, and reconstruction of evidence extracted from any element of computer systems, computer networks, computer media, and computer peripherals that allow investigators to solve a crime. Cyber forensics focuses on real-time, on-line evidence gathering rather than the traditional off-line computer disk forensic technology.

Two distinct components exist in the emerging field of cyber forensics technology. The first, computer forensics, deals with gathering evidence from computer media seized at the crime scene. Principle concerns with computer forensics involve imaging storage media, recovering deleted files, searching slack and free space, and preserving the collected information for litigation purposes. Several computer forensic tools are available to investigators. The second component, network forensics, is a more technically challenging aspect of cyber forensics. It gathers digital evidence that is distributed across large-scale, complex networks. Often this evidence is transient in nature and is not preserved within permanent storage media. Network forensics deals primarily with in-depth analysis of computer network intrusion evidence, because current commercial intrusion analysis tools are inadequate to deal with today's networked, distributed environments.

Similar to traditional medical forensics, such as pathology, today's computer forensics is generally performed postmortem (after the crime or event occurred). In a networked, distributed environment, it is imperative to perform forensic-like examinations of victim information systems on an almost continuous basis, in addition to traditional postmortem forensic analysis. This is essential to continued functioning of critical information systems and infrastructures. Few, if any, forensic tools are available to assist in preempting the attacks or locating the perpetrators. In the battle against malicious hackers, investigators must perform cyber forensic functions in support of various objectives. These objectives include timely cyberattack containment; perpetrator location and identification; damage mitigation; and recovery initiation in the case of a crippled, yet still functioning, network. Standard intrusion analysis includes examination of many sources of data evidence (intrusion detection system logs, firewall logs, audit trails, and network management information). Cyber forensics adds inspection of transient and other frequently overlooked elements such as contents or state of the following: memory, registers, basic input/output system, input/output buffers, serial receive buffers, L_2 cache, front side and back side system caches, and various system buffers (drive and video buffers).

Now, let's briefly look at specific types of computer forensics technology that are being used by the following computer specialists: military, law enforcement, and business. It is beyond the scope of this chapter to cover in detail every type of computer forensic technology. The rest of the chapters in this book as well as the appendices have been designed and created to do that specific task.

TYPES OF MILITARY COMPUTER FORENSIC TECHNOLOGY

The U.S. Department of Defense (DoD) cyber forensics includes evaluation and in-depth examination of data related to both the trans- and post-cyberattack periods. Key objectives of cyber forensics include rapid discovery of evidence, estimate of potential impact of the malicious activity on the victim, and assessment of the intent and identity of the perpetrator. Real-time tracking of potentially malicious activity is especially difficult when the pertinent information has been intentionally or maliciously hidden, destroyed, or modified in order to elude discovery. The Information Directorate's cyber forensic concepts are new and untested. The directorate entered into a partnership with the National Institute of Justice via the auspices of the National Law Enforcement and Corrections Technology Center (NLECTC) located in Rome, New York, to test these new ideas and prototype tools. The Computer Forensics Experiment 2000 (CFX-2000) resulted from this partnership. This first-of-a-kind event represents a new paradigm for transitioning cyber forensic technology from military research and development (R&D) laboratories into the hands of law enforcement. The experiment used a realistic cyber crime scenario specifically designed to exercise and show the value added of the directorate-developed cyber forensic technology.

The central hypothesis of CFX-2000 examined the possibility of accurately determining the motives, intent, targets, sophistication, identity, and location of cyber criminals and cyber terrorists by deploying an integrated forensic analysis framework. The execution of CFX-2000 required the development and simulation of a realistic, complex cyber crime scenario exercising conventional, as well as R&D prototype, cyber forensic tools.

The NLECTC assembled a diverse group of computer crime investigators from DoD and federal, state, and local law enforcement to participate in the CFX-2000 exercise hosted by the New York State Police's Forensic Investigative Center in Albany, New York. Officials divided the participants into three teams. Each team received an identical set of software tools and was presented with identical initial evidence of suspicious activity. The objective of each team was to uncover several linked criminal activities from a maze of about 30 milestones that culminated in an information warfare crime (Figure 2.1).[i]

The cyber forensic tools involved in CFX-2000 consisted of commercial off-the-shelf software and directorate-sponsored R&D prototypes. The SI-FI integration environment, developed under contract by WetStone Technologies, Inc.,[ii] was the cornerstone of the technology demonstrated. SI-FI supports the collection, examination, and analysis processes employed during a cyber forensic investigation. The SI-FI prototype uses digital evidence bags (DEBs), which are secure and tamperproof *containers* used to store digital evidence. Investigators can seal evidence in the DEBs and use the SI-FI implementation to collaborate on complex investigations. Authorized users can securely reopen the DEBs for examination, while automatic audit of all actions ensures the continued integrity of its contents. The teams used other forensic tools and prototypes to collect and analyze specific features of the digital evidence, perform case management and timelining of digital events, automate event link analysis, and perform steganography detection. The results of CFX-2000 verified that the hypothesis was largely correct and that it is possible to ascertain the intent and identity of cyber criminals. As electronic technology continues its explosive growth, researchers need to continue vigorous R&D of cyber forensic technology in preparation for the onslaught of cyber reconnaissance probes and attacks.

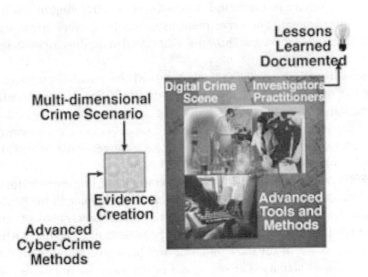

FIGURE 2.1 CFX-2000 schematic. *(©Copyright 2002, Associated Business Publications. All rights reserved).*

TYPES OF LAW ENFORCEMENT: COMPUTER FORENSIC TECHNOLOGY

As previously defined, computer forensics involves the preservation, identification, extraction, and documentation of computer evidence stored in the form of magnetically encoded information (data). Many times the computer evidence was created transparently by the computer's operating system and without the knowledge of the computer operator. Such information may actually be hidden from view and, thus, special forensic software tools and techniques are required to preserve, identify, extract, and document the related computer evidence.

Computer forensics tools and techniques have proven to be a valuable resource for law enforcement in the identification of leads and in the processing of computer-related evidence. Computer forensics tools and techniques have become important resources for use in internal investigations, civil lawsuits, and computer security risk management.

Forensic software tools and methods can be used to identify passwords, log-ons, and other information that is automatically dumped from the computer memory as a transparent operation of today's popular personal computer operating systems. Such computer forensic software tools can also be used to identify backdated files and to tie a diskette to the computer that created it.

Law enforcement and military agencies have been involved in processing computer evidence for years. This part of the chapter touches very briefly on issues dealing with *Windows NT™* and *Windows 2000™*, and their use within law enforcement computer forensic technology. In other words, security and computer evidence issues associated with *Windows NT* and *Windows 2000* will be covered in this part of the chapter.

Windows 95™ and *Windows 98™* are the predominant operating systems used on notebook and desktop computers in corporations and government agencies. Thus, they are currently the operating systems most likely to be encountered in computer investigations and computer security reviews. Be advised that this chapter does not cover the use of *Black Box* computer forensics software tools. Those tools are good for some basic investigation tasks, but they do not offer a full computer forensics solution. Furthermore, such approaches are all but useless in computer security risk assessments. Such assessments usually require that searches and file listings be conducted overtly or even covertly from a single floppy diskette.

Computer Evidence Processing Procedures

Processing procedures and methodologies should conform to federal computer evidence processing standards. Computer processing procedures have also been developed for the U.S. Treasury Department.

Training and certification programs have also been developed for the International Association of Computer Investigation Specialists (IACIS). For these reasons, computer forensic trainers or instructors should be well qualified to teach the correct computer-processing methods and procedures.

PRESERVATION OF EVIDENCE

Computer evidence is fragile and susceptible to alteration or erasure by any number of occurrences. Computer forensic instructors should try and expose their trainees to bit stream back-up theories that ensure the preservation of all storage levels that may contain evidence. For example, SafeBack software overcomes some of the evidence weaknesses inherent in *Black Box* computer forensics approaches (see sidebar, "Mirror Image Backup Software"). SafeBack technology can be purchased from Sydex, Inc.;[iii] and has become a worldwide standard in making mirror image back-ups since 1990, when it was developed based on requirements then established by the U.S. Treasury Department and the IACIS.

Mirror Image Backup Software

SafeBack is a sophisticated evidence-preservation tool that was developed specifically for use by federal law enforcement agencies in the United States in the processing of computer evidence. It is a unique piece of software that has become an industry standard in the processing of computer evidence around the world. SafeBack is currently the tool of choice for the Federal Bureau of Investigation and the Internal Revenue Service's Criminal Investigation Division. Both of these agencies lead the field in the federal government.

SafeBack can also be used covertly to duplicate all storage areas on a computer hard disk drive. Drive size creates essentially no limitation for this unique computer forensics tool. This unique tool has survived the test of time since 1990; and is used to create mirror-image back-ups of partitions on hard disks drives and also to make a mirror-image copy of an entire hard disk, which may contain multiple partitions and/or operating systems.

Back-up image files, created by SafeBack, can be written to essentially any writeable magnetic storage device, including SCSI tape backup units. SafeBack preserves all of the data on a backed-up or copied hard disk, including inactive or *deleted* data. Cyclical redundancy checksums (CRCs), distributed throughout the back-up process, enforce the integrity of back-up copies to ensure the accuracy of the process.

Back-up image files can be restored to another system's hard disk. Remote operation via parallel port connection allows the hard disk on a remote PC to be read or written by the master system. A date- and time-stamped audit trail maintains a record of SafeBack operations during a session, and software dongles are not involved or required for operation. From an evidence standpoint, SafeBack is ideal for the computer forensics specialist, because the restored SafeBack image can be used to process the evidence in the environment in which it was created. This is especially important when system configurations and/or application settings are relevant to the display or printing of the evidence.

This powerful software is designed for use by computer forensics experts and training is required in the use of this software. If you have not been formally trained in computer forensics or you don't have a strong background in computer hardware configurations, this software is not for you.

Primary Uses

The program is used to archive the image hard disk drives on *Intel*™-based computer systems. The program is also used to restore archived images on another computer hard disk drive of equal or greater storage capacity.

Program Features and Benefits

- DOS-based for ease of operation and speed
- Provides a detailed audit trail of the back-up process for evidence documentation purposes
- Checks for and duplicates data stored in sectors wherein the sector CRC does not match the stored data
- Copies all areas of the hard disk drive
- Allows the archive of non-DOS and non-Windows hard disk drives, (Unix on an Intel-based computer system)
- Allows for the back-up process to be made via the printer port
- Duplicate copies of hard disk drives can be made from hard disk to hard disk in direct mode
- SafeBack image files can be stored as one large file or separate files of fixed sizes. This feature is helpful in making copies for archive on CDs
- Tried and proven evidence-preservation technology with a 10-year legacy of success in government agencies
- Creates a noncompressed file that is an exact and unaltered duplicate of the original. This feature eliminates legal challenges concerning the potential alteration of the evidence through compression or translation.
- Fast and efficient. Depending on the hardware configurations involved, the data transfer rate exceeds 50 million bytes per minute during the back-up process.
- Makes copies in either physical or logical mode at the option of the user
- Copies and restores multiple partitions containing one or more operating systems
- Can be used to accurately copy and restore *Windows NT* and *Windows 2000* drives in a raid configuration
- Writes to SCSI tape back-up units or hard disk drives at the option of the user[iv]

Trojan Horse Programs

The need to preserve the computer evidence before processing a computer should be clearly demonstrated by the computer forensic instructor through the use of programs designed to destroy data and modify the operating systems. The participant should be able to demonstrate his (or her) ability to avoid destructive programs and traps that can be planted by computer users bent on destroying data and evidence. Such programs can also be used to covertly capture sensitive information, passwords, and network log-ons.

Computer Forensics Documentation

The documentation of forensic processing methodologies and findings is important. This is even true concerning computer security risk assessments and internal audits, because without proper documentation, it is difficult to present findings. In the event the security or audit findings become the object of a lawsuit or a criminal investigation, then documentation becomes even more important. Thus, the computer forensic instructor should also teach the participant the ins and outs of computer evidence processing methodology (which facilitates good evidence-processing documentation and good evidence chain of custody procedures). The benefits will be obvious to investigators, but they will also become clear to internal auditors and computer security specialists.

File Slack

The occurrence of random memory dumps in hidden storage areas should be discussed and covered in detail during workshops. Techniques and automated tools that are used to capture and evaluate file slack should be demonstrated in a training course. Such data is the source of potential security leaks regarding passwords, network log-ons, e-mail, database entries, and word processing documents. These security and evidence issues should also be discussed and demonstrated during the training course. The participants should be able to demonstrate their ability to deal with slack and should demonstrate proficiency in searching file slack, documenting their findings, and eliminating the security risk.

Data-Hiding Techniques

Trade secret information and other sensitive data can easily be secreted using any number of techniques. It is possible to hide diskettes within diskettes and to hide entire computer hard disk drive partitions. These issues should be discussed in any computer forensics training course from a detection standpoint, as well as from a security risk standpoint. Tools that help in the identification of such anomalies should be demonstrated and discussed (like *AnaDisk*™ {see sidebar, "Diskette Analysis Tool"}) in the training course. Participants should be required to demonstrate their understanding of such issues. This aspect of the training becomes especially important during the last day of the course when the participants are called on to extract their Certificate of Completion from a *special* floppy diskette. Data-hiding courses are only open to classified government agencies and businesses that have a demonstrated need to know of this kind of information as outlined in a company's training policies. This is because the information covered in a data-hiding course can be used to defeat government computer security review processes and techniques.

ANADISK DISKETTE ANALYSIS TOOL

AnaDisk turns your PC into a sophisticated diskette analysis tool. The software was originally created to meet the needs of the U. S. Treasury Department in 1991. It is primarily used to identify data storage anomalies on floppy diskettes and generic hardware in the form of floppy disk controllers; bios are needed when using this software. It works at a very low level and makes maximum use of the floppy diskette hardware. The software also has limited search capabilities and can be used to copy abnormal diskettes. It can also be used to write data at a physical sector level and to format diskettes using any number of combinations.

AnaDisk can be used to analyze floppy diskettes when doing computer evidence consulting work, which involves abnormal floppy diskettes or data storage issues tied to floppy diskettes. It can also be used in data-hiding courses to create data-hiding areas by adding extra sectors and/or tracks to floppy diskettes and in writing data to *unformatted* floppy diskettes. This unique software was also created at Sydex, Inc.[v]

Primary Uses

- Security reviews of floppy diskettes for storage anomalies
- Duplication of diskettes that are nonstandard or that involve storage anomalies
- Editing diskettes at a physical sector level
- Searching for data on floppy diskettes in traditional and nontraditional storage areas
- Formatting diskettes in nontraditional ways for training purposes and to illustrate data-hiding techniques

Program Features and Benefits

- DOS-based for ease of operation and speed
- Keyword searches can be conducted at a very low level and on diskettes that have been formatted with extra tracks. This feature is helpful in the evaluation of diskettes that may involve sophisticated data-hiding techniques.
- All DOS formats are supported as well as many non-DOS formats, (Apple Macintosh, Unix *TAR*™, and many others. If the diskette will fit in a PC floppy diskette drive, it is likely that *AnaDisk* can be used to analyze it.
- Allows custom formatting of diskettes with extra tracks and sectors
- Scans for anomalies will identify odd formats, extra tracks, and extra sectors. Data mismatches, concerning some file formats, are also identified when file extensions have been changed in an attempt to hide data.
- This software can be used to copy almost any diskette, including most copy-protected diskettes.[vi]

E-Commerce Investigations

A new Internet *forensic tool* has recently been introduced that aims to help educators, police, and other law enforcement officials trace the past World Wide Web activity of computer users. *Net Threat Analyzer™*, from Gresham, Oregon-based New Technology Inc. (NTI), can be used to identify past Internet browsing and e-mail activity done through specific computers. The software analyzes a computer's disk drives and other storage areas that are generally unknown to or beyond the reach of most general computer users.

Kids can figure out ways to prevent their parents from finding anything on their machine, but *Net Threat Analyzer* goes back in after the fact where things are easier to detect. New Technology Inc. has made its *Net Threat Analyzer* available free of charge to computer crime specialists, school officials, and police.

The program is booted from a floppy disk and uses filtering tools to collect data on users' basic browsing and e-mail history. It flags possible threats, like anything dealing with drugs, bombs, country codes, or pornography. Web sites are changing so often that it's difficult to keep up with which ones are porn or drug sites.

For example, http://www.whitehouse.gov, is the official White House Web site, and www.whitehouse.com is a pornography site. If Junior's been to whitehouse.com 300 to 500 times, it will make it through most Net Nanny's software. But that will cause a red flag with the *Net Threat Analyzer* product.

The software was designed to help prevent situations like the recent tragedies at Columbine High School in Littleton, Colorado, and the Thurston High School in Springfield, Oregon, where weapons were made by teenagers who had downloaded the instructions from the Internet.

New Technology Inc., which specializes in computer forensics tools and training, has posted order forms for its software on its Web site at http://www.forensics-intl.com. The tool is not available to the public, but a special version can be purchased by Fortune 500 companies, government agencies, military agencies, and consultants, who have a legitimate need for the software.

Dual-Purpose Programs

Programs can be designed to perform multiple processes and tasks at the same time. They can also be designed for delayed tasking. These concepts should be demonstrated to the training participants during the course through the use of specialized software. The participant should also have hands-on experience with these programs.

Text Search Techniques

New Technology Inc. has also developed specialized search techniques and tools that can be used to find targeted strings of text in files, file slack, unallocated file space, and *Windows* swap files. Each participant will leave their training class with a licensed copy of their *TextSearch Plus™* software and the necessary knowledge to conduct computer security reviews and computer related investigations (see sidebar, "*Text Search Plus*").

This search tool is approved for use in security reviews by some U.S. government classified agencies.

NOTE

TEXT SEARCH PLUS

TextSearch Plus was specifically designed and enhanced for speed and accuracy in security reviews. It is widely used by classified government agencies and corporations that support these agencies. The software is also used by hundreds of law enforcement agencies throughout the world in computer crime investigations.

This software is used to quickly search hard disk drives, zip disks, and floppy diskettes for key words or specific patterns of text. It operates at either a logical or physical level at the option of the user. TextSearch Plus has been specifically designed to meet the requirements of the government for use in computer security exit reviews from classified government facilities. The current version is approximately 25% faster than prior versions. It is also compatible with FAT 12, FAT 16, and FAT 32 DOS-based systems. As a result, it can be used on DOS, *Windows*, *Windows 95*, and *Windows 98* systems. Tests indicate that this tool finds more text strings than any other forensic search tool. It is sold separately and is also included in several of the NTI tool suites. As a stand alone tool, it is ideal for security risk assessments. When security spills are identified, they can easily be eliminated with NTI's *M-Sweep™* program.

Primary Uses

- Used to find occurrences of words or strings of text in data stored in files, slack, and unallocated file space
- Used in exit reviews of computer storage media from classified facilities
- Used in internal audits to identify violations of corporate policy

- Used by Fortune 500 corporations, government contractors, and government agencies in security reviews and security risk assessments
- Used in corporate due diligence efforts regarding proposed mergers
- Used to find occurrences of keywords strings of text in data found at a physical sector level
- Used to find evidence in corporate, civil, and criminal investigations that involve computer-related evidence
- Used to find embedded text in formatted word processing documents (*Word-Perfect*™ and fragments of such documents in ambient data storage areas)

Program Features and Benefits

- DOS-based for ease of operation and speed
- Small memory foot print (under 60k), which allows the software to run on even the original IBM PC
- Compact program size, which easily fits on one floppy diskette with other forensic software utilities
- Searches files, slack, and erased space in one fast operation
- Has logical and physical search options that maintain compatibility with government security review requirements
- User-defined search configuration feature
- User configuration is automatically saved for future use
- Embedded words and strings of text are found in word processing files
- Alert for graphic files (secrets can be hidden in them)
- Alert for compressed files
- High speed operation. This is the fastest tool on the market, which makes for quick searches on huge hard disk drives
- Screen and file output
- False hits don't stop processing
- Government Tested—Specifically designed for security reviews in classified environments
- Currently used by hundreds of law enforcement computer crime units
- Currently in use by all of the Big 5 accounting firms
- Currently used by several government military and intelligence agencies
- Currently used by numerous Fortune 500 corporations
- The current version allows for up to 120 search strings to be searched for at one time.[vii]

Fuzzy Logic Tools Used to Identify Unknown Text

NTI has also developed a methodology and tools that aid in the identification of relevant evidence and *unknown* strings of text. Traditional computer evidence searches require that the computer specialist know what is being searched for. However, many times not all is known about what may be stored on a given computer system. In such cases, fuzzy logic tools can assist and can provide valuable leads as to how the subject computer was used. The training participant should be able to fully understand these methods and techniques. They should also be able to demonstrate their ability to use them to identify leads in file slack, unallocated file space, and *Windows* swap files. Each training participant should also be able to leave the class with a licensed copy of NTI's *Filter_I*™ software (see sidebar, "Intelligent Forensic Filter").

INTELLIGENT FORENSIC FILTER

This enhanced forensic filter utility is used to quickly make sense of nonsense in the analysis of ambient computer data (*Windows* swap file data, file slack data, and data associated with erased files). This tool is so unique that process patents have been applied for with the U.S. Patent Office.

Filter_I relies on preprogrammed artificial intelligence to identify fragments of word processing communications, fragments of e-mail communications, fragments of Internet chat room communications, fragments of Internet news group posts, encryption passwords, network passwords, network log-ons, database entries, credit card numbers, social security numbers, and the first and last names of individuals who have been listed in communications involving the subject computer. This software saves days in the processing of computer evidence when compared to traditional methods.

This computer forensic tool can also be effectively used in computer security reviews as it quickly reveals security leakage and violations of corporate policy that might not be uncovered otherwise. Be aware that the software does not rely on keywords entered by the computer specialist. It is a pattern recognition tool that recognizes patters of text, letter combinations, number patterns, potential passwords, potential network log-ons, and the names of individuals. To avoid possible violation of privacy laws, this software should only be used with the approval of corporate legal counsel. For this reason, this software is not made available to the general public.

Primary Uses

- Used covertly to determine prior activity on a specific computer
- Used to filter ambient computer data, the existence of which the user is normally unaware of (memory dumps in file slack, *Windows* swap files, *Windows* DAT files and erased file space)
- The ideal tool for use by corporate and government internal auditors
- The ideal tool for use by corporate and government computer security specialists
- The ideal tool for use by corporate, military, and law enforcement investigators
- Perfect for covert intelligence gathering when laws permit and you have physical access to the subject computer

PROGRAM FEATURES AND BENEFITS

- DOS-based for speed. The speed of operation is amazing.
- Automatically processes any binary data object
- Provides output in an ASCII text format that is ready for import into any word processing application
- Capable of processing ambient data files that are up to 2 gigabytes in size[viii]

DISK STRUCTURE

Participants should be able to leave a training course with a good understanding of how computer hard disks and floppy diskettes are structured and how computer evidence can reside at various levels within the structure of the disk. They should also demonstrate their knowledge of how to modify the structure and hide data in obscure places on floppy diskettes and hard disk drives.

DATA ENCRYPTION

A computer forensics course should cover, in general, how data is encrypted; it should also be able to illustrate the differences between good encryption and bad encryption. Furthermore, demonstrations of password-recovery software should be given by the trainers to the participants regarding encrypted *WordPerfect, Excel, Lotus,* Microsoft *Word,* and *PKZIP* files. The participant should become familiar with the use of software to *crack* security associated with these different file structures.

MATCHING A DISKETTE TO A COMPUTER

NTI has also developed specialized techniques and tools that make it possible to conclusively tie a diskette to a computer that was used to create or edit files stored on the floppy diskette. Unlike some *special* government agencies, NTI relies on logical rather than physical data storage areas to demonstrate this technique. Each participant is taught how to use special software tools to complete this process.

DATA COMPRESSION

The participant should be shown how compression works and how compression programs can be used to hide and/or disguise sensitive data. Furthermore, the participant should learn how password-protected compressed files can be broken; this should be covered in hands-on workshops during the training course.

ERASED FILES

The training participant should be shown how previously erased files can be recovered by using DOS programs and by manually using data-recovery techniques. These techniques should also be demonstrated by the participant and cluster chaining will become familiar to the participant.

INTERNET ABUSE IDENTIFICATION AND DETECTION

The participant should be shown how to use specialized software to identify how a targeted computer has been used on the Internet. This process will focus on computer forensics issues tied to data that the computer user probably doesn't realize exists (file slack, unallocated file space, and *Windows* swap files).

THE BOOT PROCESS AND MEMORY RESIDENT PROGRAMS

The participant should be able to participate in a graphic demonstration of how the operating system can be modified to change data and destroy data at the whim of the person who configured the system. Such a technique could be used to covertly capture keyboard activity from corporate executives, for example. For this reason, it is important that the participants understand these potential risks and how to identify them.

TYPES OF BUSINESS COMPUTER FORENSIC TECHNOLOGY

Finally, let's briefly look at the following types of business computer forensics technology:

- Remote monitoring of target computers
- Creating trackable electronic documents
- Theft recovery software for laptops and PCs
- Basic forensic tools and techniques
- Forensic services available

Remote Monitoring of Target Computers

Data Interception by Remote Transmission (DIRT) from Codex Data Systems (CDS), Inc.[ix] is a powerful remote control monitoring tool that allows stealth monitoring of all activity on one or more target computers simultaneously from a remote command center. No physical access is necessary. Application also allows agents to remotely seize and secure digital evidence prior to physically entering suspect premises.

Creates Trackable Electronic Documents

Binary Audit Identification Transfer (BAIT) is another powerful intrusion detection tool from CDS[x] that allows the user to create *trackable* electronic documents. Unauthorized intruders who access, download, and view these *tagged* documents will be identified (including their location) to security personnel. BAIT also allows security personnel to trace the chain of custody and chain of command of all who possess the stolen electronic documents.

Theft Recovery Software for Laptops and PCs

If your PC or laptop is stolen, is it smart enough to tell you where it is? According to a recent FBI report, 97% of stolen computers are never recovered.

Also, according to Safeware Insurance, 756,000 PCs and laptops were stolen in 1997 and 1998, costing owners $2.3 billion dollars. And, according to a recent joint Computer Security Institute/FBI survey, 69% of the Fortune 1000 companies experienced laptop theft.

Nationwide losses of computer component theft cost corporate America over $8 billion a year. So, if your company experiences computer-related thefts and you do nothing to correct the problem, there is an 89% chance you will be hit again.

WHAT IS THE REAL COST OF A STOLEN LAPTOP OR PC?

When you lose your wallet, the last thing you think of is how much it is going to cost to replace your wallet. The same is true when equipment (especially a computer) is stolen.

Our mothers always told us, *"An ounce of prevention is worth a pound of cure."* They were right. Think about what it really costs to replace a stolen computer.

- The price of the replacement hardware
- The price of replacing the software
- The cost of recreating data. If possible at all, do you keep perfect back-ups?
- The cost of lost production time or instruction time

- The loss of customer goodwill (lost faxes, delayed correspondence or billings, problems answering questions and accessing data)
- The cost of reporting and investigating the theft; filing police reports and insurance claims
- The cost of increased insurance
- The cost of processing and ordering for replacements, cutting a check, and the like
- If a thief is ever caught (?), the cost of time involved in prosecution[xi]

So, doesn't it make sense to use an ounce of prevention? You don't have to be a victim!

With that in mind, CDS has a solution: *PC PhoneHome*[xii]—another software application that will track and locate a lost or stolen PC or laptop anywhere in the world. It is easy to install. It is also completely transparent to the user. If your *PC PhoneHome*-protected computer is lost or stolen, all you need to do is make a report to the local police and call CDS's 24-hour command center. CDS's recovery specialists will assist local law enforcement in the recovery of your property.

Basic Forensic Tools and Techniques

The *Digital Detective Workshop*' from CDS was created to familiarize investigators and security personnel with the basic techniques and tools necessary for a successful investigation of Internet and computer-related crimes. Topics include: types of computer crime, cyber law basics, tracing e-mail to source, digital evidence acquisition, cracking passwords, monitoring computers remotely, tracking on-line activity, finding and recovering hidden and deleted data, locating stolen computers, creating trackable files, identifying software pirates, and so on.

Forensic Services Available

Through *Forensic Evidence Acquisition Services*, CDS forensic experts can provide management with a potent arsenal of digital tools at its disposal. Services include but are not limited to:

- Lost password and file recovery
- Location & retrieval of deleted and hidden files
- File and e-mail decryption
- E-mail supervision and authentication
- Threatening e-mail traced to source
- Identification of Internet activity
- Computer usage policy and supervision
- Remote PC and network monitoring
- Tracking and location of stolen electronic files

- *Honeypot* sting operations
- Location and identity of unauthorized SW users
- Theft recovery software for laptops and PCs
- Investigative and security software creation
- Protection from hackers and viruses[xiii]

SUMMARY

Since the invention of the personal computer in 1981, new computer technologies have provided unintended benefits to criminals in the commission of both traditional crimes and computer crimes. Today computers are used in every facet of life to create messages, compute profits, transfer funds, access bank accounts, and browse the Internet for good and bad purposes. Notebook computers provide computer users with the benefits of portability as well as remote access to computer networks. Computer users today have the benefits of super computer speeds and fast Internet communications on a worldwide basis. Computers have increased productivity in business, but they also increase the likelihood of company policy abuses, government security breaches, and criminal activity.

In the past, documentary evidence was primarily limited to paper documents. Copies were made with carbon paper or through the use of a photocopy machine. Most documents today are stored on computer hard disk drives, floppy diskettes, zip disks, and other types of removable computer storage media. This is where potential computer evidence may reside and it is up to the computer forensics specialist to find it using sophisticated computer forensics tools and computer-evidence-processing methodologies. Paper documents are no longer considered the best evidence.

Computer evidence is quite unique when compared with other forms of documentary evidence. Unlike paper documentation, computer evidence is fragile and a copy of a document stored in a computer file is identical to the original. The legal 'best evidence' rules change when it comes to the processing of computer evidence. Another unique aspect of computer evidence is the potential for unauthorized copies to be made of important computer files without leaving behind a trace that the copy was made. This situation creates problems concerning the investigation of the theft of trade secrets (client lists, research materials, computer-aided design files, formulas, and proprietary software).

Industrial espionage is alive and well in the cyber age and the computer forensics specialist relies on computer evidence to prove the theft of trade secrets. Sometimes the unauthorized copying of proprietary files can also be documented through the analysis of ambient computer data. The existence of this type of computer evidence is typically not known to the computer user and the element of surprise can provide the computer forensics investigator with the advantage in the interview of suspects in such cases. Because of the unique features associated with computer evidence, special knowledge is required by the computer forensics specialist and the lawyers, who may be relying on the computer evidence to support their position in civil or criminal litigation.

Computer evidence is relied on more and more in criminal and civil litigation actions. It was computer evidence that helped identify the now infamous *Blue Dress* in the Clinton impeachment hearings. Oliver North got into some of his trouble with the U. S. Congress when erased computer files were recovered as computer evidence. Computer evidence is also used to identify Internet account abuses. In the past, much wasted government and company staff time was attributed to the playing of the *Windows Solitaire* game on company time. Thanks to the popularity of the Internet, *Windows Solitaire* has taken a backseat to unauthorized Internet browsing by employees of pornography Web sites. Internet access by employees has also created new problems associated with employees operating side businesses through the unauthorized use of company and government Internet accounts. These types of problems are becoming more frequent as more businesses and government agencies provide employees with Internet accounts. Computer forensics tools and methodologies are used to identify and document computer evidence associated with these types of computer abuses and activities.

Computer evidence is unique in other ways as well. Most individuals think that computer evidence is limited to data stored just in computer files. Most of the relevant computer evidence is found in unusual locations that are usually unknown to the computer users. Computer evidence can exist in many forms. On Microsoft *Windows* and *Windows NT*-based computer systems, large quantities of evidence can be found in the *Windows* swap file. In *Windows NT*-based computer systems, the files are called *Page Files* and the file is named PAGEFILE.SYS by the operating system.

Computer evidence can also be found in file slack and in unallocated file space. These unique forms of computer data fall into a category of data called ambient computer data. As much as 50% of the computer hard disk drive may contain such data types in the form of e-mail fragments, word processing fragments, directory tree snapshots, and potentially almost anything that has occurred in past work sessions on the subject computer. Ambient computer data can be a valuable source of computer evidence because of the potentially large volume of data involved and because of the transparent nature of its creation to the computer user.

Timelines of computer usage and file accesses can be valuable sources of computer evidence. The times and dates when files were created, last accessed, and/or modified can make or break a case.

Now let's look at some of the more common conclusions that computer forensics technology can hope to answer. The following conclusions are not exhaustive, nor is the order significant.

Conclusions Drawn from Types of Computer Forensics Technology

- As previously explained, the term *Computer Forensics* was coined back in 1991 in the first training session held by the International Association of Computer Specialists (IACIS) in Portland, Oregon. Since then, computer forensics has become a popular topic in computer security circles and in the legal community.
- Like any other forensic science, computer forensics deals with the application of law to a science. In this case, the science involved is computer science and some refer to it as Forensic Computer Science.
- Computer forensics has also been described as the autopsy of a computer hard disk drive because specialized software tools and techniques are required to analyze the various levels at which computer data is stored after the fact.
- Computer Forensics deals with the preservation, identification, extraction and documentation of computer evidence. The field is relatively new to the private sector but it has been the mainstay of technology-related investigations and intelligence gathering in law enforcement and military agencies since the mid-1980's.
- Like any other forensic science, computer forensics involves the use sophisticated technology tools and procedures which must be followed to guarantee the accuracy of the preservation of evidence and the accuracy of results concerning computer evidence processing.
- Typically, computer forensic tools exist in the form of computer software.
- Computer forensic specialists guarantee accuracy of evidence processing results through the use of time-tested evidence-processing procedures and through the use of multiple software tools developed by separate and independent developers.
- The use of different tools that have been developed independently to validate results is important to avoid inaccuracies introduced by potential software design flaws and software bugs.
- It is a serious mistake for a computer forensics specialist to put all of their eggs in one basket by using just one tool to preserve, identify, extract, and validate the computer evidence.
- Cross-validation through the use of multiple tools and techniques is standard in all forensic sciences. When this procedure is not used, it creates advantages for defense lawyers who may challenge the accuracy of the software tool used and, thus, the integrity of the results.
- Validation through the use of multiple software tools, computer specialists, and procedures, eliminates the potential for the destruction of forensic evidence.
- The introduction of the personal computer in 1981 and the resulting popularity came with a mixed blessing.

■ Society in general benefited but so did criminals who use personal computers in the commission of crimes.

■ Today, personal computers are used in every facet of society to create and share messages, compute financial results, transfer funds, purchase stocks, make airline reservations, access bank accounts, and a wealth of worldwide information on essentially any topic.

■ Computer forensics is used to identify evidence when personal computers are used in the commission of crimes or in the abuse of company policies.

■ Computer forensic tools and procedures are also used to identify computer security weaknesses and the leakage of sensitive computer data.

■ In the past, documentary evidence was typically stored on paper and copies were made with carbon paper or photocopy machines.

■ Most documents are now stored on computer hard disk drives, floppy diskettes, zip disks, and other forms of removable computer storage media.

■ Computer forensics deals with finding, extracting, and documenting this form of 'electronic' documentary evidence.

An Agenda for Action in Types of Computer Forensics Technology

The following is a provisional list of actions for some of the principle types of computer forensic technology. The order is not significant; however these are the activities for which the research would want to provide a detailed description of procedures, review, and assessment for ease of use and admissibility. A number of these technologies have been mentioned in passing already:

1. Documentary evidence has quickly moved from the printed or typewritten page to computer data stored on floppy diskettes, zip disks, CDs, and computer hard disk drives.

2. A new type of virtual evidence has been created as a result of e-commerce transactions and e-mail communications over the Internet.

3. The sharing of computer files over the Internet, when tied to the commission of a crime, creates a new and novel twist to the rules of evidence and legal jurisdiction.

4. Keep in mind that when criminal activities involve the use of the Internet, venue can be in different cities, counties, states, and/or countries. The evidence needed to prove such computer-related crimes potentially resides on one or more computer hard disk drives in various geographic locations.

5. The computer hard disk drives may also be the property of criminals as well as innocent third parties (Internet Service Providers). Such evidence is commonly referred to as computer evidence, but it is not limited to cases involving computer crimes.

ENDNOTES

i   John Feldman and Joseph V. Giordano, "Cyber Forensics," Air Force Research Laboratory's Information Directorate, Associated Business Publications, 317 Madison Avenue, New York, NY 10017-5391, 2001.

ii   WetStone Technologies, Inc., 273 Ringwood Road, Freeville, NY 13068, 2001.

iii   Sydex, Inc., P. O. Box 5700, Eugene, OR 97405, USA, 2001.

iv   "SafeBack Mirror Image Backup Software," New Technologies, Inc., 2075 NE Division St, Gresham, Oregon 97030, 2001. *(©Copyright 2002, New Technologies, Inc. All rights reserved), 2001.*

v   Sydex, Inc., P. O. Box 5700, Eugene, OR 97405, USA, 2002.

vi   "AnaDisk Diskette Analysis Tool," New Technologies, Inc., 2075 NE Division St, Gresham, Oregon 97030, 2001. *(©Copyright 2002. New Technologies, Inc. All rights reserved), 2001.*

vii   "Text Search Plus," New Technologies, Inc., 2075 NE Division St, Gresham, Oregon 97030, 2001. *(©Copyright 2002, New Technologies, Inc. All rights reserved), 2001.*

viii   "FILTER_1: Intelligent Forensic Filter," New Technologies, Inc., 2075 NE Division St, Gresham, Oregon 97030, 2001. *(©Copyright 2002, New Technologies, Inc. All rights reserved), 2001.*

ix   Codex Data Systems, Inc., 143 Main Street, Nanuet, New York 10954, USA, 2001.

x   Ibid.

xi   Ibid.

xii   Ibid.

xiii   Ibid.

3   Types of Vendor and Computer Forensics Services

Cyber crime potentially costs U.S. businesses millions, if not billions of dollars in unrealized profits and exposes organizations to significant risk. And it is on the rise. In 2001, the Computer Emergency Response Team (CERT) reported a fivefold increase on the number of computer security incidents reported in 2000.

As information technology and the Internet become more integrated into today's workplaces, organizations must consider the misuse of technology as a real threat and plan for its eventuality. When cyber crime strikes, the real issue is not the incident itself, but how the organization responds to the attack.

With that in mind, this chapter looks at how a swift and measured forensic incident response, drawing on sound policies, vendor tools, and support, allows an organization to contain the potential damage of an attack and effectively seek compensation or prosecution. In addition to the preceding, this chapter also covers the following computer forensic services:

■ Forensic incident response
■ Evidence collection
■ Forensic analysis
■ Expert witness
■ Forensic litigation and insurance claims support
■ Training
■ Forensic process improvement

OCCURRENCE OF CYBER CRIME

Cyber crime occurs when information technology is used to commit or conceal an offense. Computer crimes include:

- Financial fraud
- Sabotage of data and/or networks
- Theft of proprietary information
- System penetration from the outside and denial of service
- Unauthorized access by insiders and employee misuse of Internet access privileges
- Viruses, which are the leading cause of unauthorized users gaining access to systems and networks through the Internet[i]

Cyber crimes can be categorized as either internal or external events. Typically, the largest threat to organizations has been employees and insiders, which is why computer crime is often referred to as an 'insider' crime. For example, Ernst & Young's global research has found that 82% of all identified frauds were committed by employees, almost a third of which were committed by management.

Internal events are committed by those with a substantial link to the intended victim, for example, a bank employee who siphons electronic funds from a customer's account. Other examples include downloading or distributing offensive material, theft of intellectual property, internal system intrusions, fraud, or intentional or unintentional deletion or damage of data or systems.

However, as advances continue to be made in remote networks, the threat from external sources is on the rise. For example, in the 2001 *CSI/FBI Computer Crime and Security Survey*, 49% of respondents reported their internal systems as a frequent point of attack while 48% reported Internet connections as the most frequent point of attack.

An external event is committed anonymously. A classic example was the Philippine-based 1999 *"I Love You"* e-mail attack. Other types of external cyber crime include computer system intrusion, fraud, or reckless or indiscriminate deliberate system crashes.

Internal events can generally be contained within the attacked organization as it is easier to determine a motive and, therefore, simpler to identify the offender. However, when the person involved has used intimate knowledge of the information technology infrastructure, obtaining digital evidence of the offense can be difficult.

An external event is hard to predict, yet can often be traced using evidence provided by, or available to, the organization under attack. Typically, the offender has no motive and is not even connected with the organization, making it fairly straightforward to prove unlawful access to data or systems.

CYBER DETECTIVES

Computer forensics, therefore, is a leading defense in the corporate world's armory against cyber crime. Forensic investigators detect the extent of a security breach, recover lost data, determine how an intruder got past security mechanisms, and, potentially, identify the culprit.

A forensic expert needs to be qualified in both investigative and technical fields and trained in countering cyber crime. They should also be knowledgeable in the law, particularly legal jurisdictions, court requirements, and the laws on admissible evidence and production.

In many cases, forensic investigations leads to calling in law enforcement agencies and building a case for potential prosecution, which could lead to a criminal trial. The alternative is pursuing civil remedies as opposed to criminal prosecution, for instance, pursuing breach of trust, and loss of intellectual property rights.

The Legal Issues

The most common legal difficulty faced by organizations seeking to redress cyber crime in the courts is having digitally based evidence accepted. Notwithstanding the technical expertise of IT teams, most companies are ill-equipped to investigate cyber crime in a way that results in the collection of admissible evidence. For example, data collected for the purposes of evidence must be shown to be untampered with and accounted for at every stage of its life from collection to presentation in court. In other words, it must meet the requirements of the jurisdictions Law of Evidence.

Another issue is the lag time between legislation and the dynamic pace of change and improvements in technology. As a result, law enforcement organizations and computer forensic experts alike are often forced to use archaic and non-specific laws to fit unusual circumstances.

For example, to commit *theft*, a person must permanently deprive the victim of property. However, if a disgruntled employee copied an organization's database and sold to a rival company, the organization is not permanently deprived of the data, therefore, technically, no offense of *theft* has been committed. In addition, it is unclear whether *data* fits into the legal definition of property. However, even in cases where there is a clearly defined crime, corporations are often hesitant to pursue a criminal conviction because of the time, cost, and reputation risk involved in reaching a legal outcome.

FIGHTING CYBER CRIME WITH
RISK-MANAGEMENT TECHNIQUES

The rate of technological change, the spread of computer literacy, and the growth of e-commerce[ii] collaboration, such as alliances and marketplaces, make the challenge of restricting cyber crime damage daunting. With legislation lagging behind technology, businesses have had no choice but to absorb the responsibility for the security of their most valuable asset—their information. Risks range from expensive downtime; sales and productivity losses to corrupted data; damage to reputation and consumer confidence and loyalty; and hefty compensation payments or lawsuits for breaches of client information.

The best approach for organizations wanting to counter cyber crime is to apply risk-management techniques. The basic steps for minimizing cyber crime damage are creating well-communicated IT and staff policies; applying effective detection tools; ensuring procedures are in place to deal with incidents; and having a forensic response capability.

Effective IT and Staff Policies

Well-communicated and 'plain English' information technology policies educate staff about their rights and obligations in the workplace. The goal of these policies is to create a security solution that is owned by all staff, not only by those in the IT division.

To be effective, IT policies should make plain what an individual employee can and cannot do on the organization's systems, and the legal implications of misuse. It is also vital to make a continuing investment in policies, which must keep evolving and be supported by ongoing training initiatives.

Effective policies diminish the risk of internal attack, particularly unintentional attack. In addition, where attack does occur, these policies clearly define what constitutes a breach of security, making it easier to prosecute or seek compensation from the perpetrator.

Vendor Tools of The Trade

Although internal policies will not dissuade external cyber criminals, the right vendor tools will detect an external attack and alert the organization to the threat. These tools are programs that either analyze a computer system to detect anomalies, which may form the basis of an attack, or locate data that can be used as evidence supporting a crime or network intrusion.

Choosing the right cyber crime detection tools is essential for risk management in all organizations, but like most applications associated with an organization, the question is—what is the right tool? The right tools are those that deliver appropriate information that the forensic expert can interpret to achieve the best outcome. Ultimately, the evidence must withstand the rigors of legal proceedings. To deliver the information needed, software tools should be probing (without compromising the target of interrogation), concise, able to report findings fully, supported, and easy to use. Such tools will save forensic experts valuable time and allow them to concentrate on data interpretation.

The 2000 *CSI/FBI Computer Crime and Security Survey* shows a significant increase in companies using intrusion detection systems from 50% in 2000 to 58% in 2001 (see sidebar, "The Difficulties Of High-Speed Intrusion Detection"). Although some attacks will not be prevented, damage such as financial loss or negative publicity can be contained with early warning.

THE DIFFICULTIES OF HIGH-SPEED INTRUSION DETECTION

There's a persistent problem with today's new breed of gigabit-speed intrusion-detection systems (IDS): They simply cannot plow through IP traffic fast enough to provide blanket protection on networks running at gigabit speed, according to industry experts and at least three vendors who make such products.

When an IDS reaches its maximum processing capacity, it begins to drop large numbers of packets, thereby increasing the possibility of missing attacks. The newer gigabit-speed IDS products, delivered as an appliance or software customers load onto their own boxes, fall down on the job, according to lab tests conducted by Miercom, a network consultancy. Although IDS equipment can achieve near-gigabit throughput, in lab tests, they missed half the attacks thrown at them.

Miercom tested Intrusion's *SecureNet Gig*™ appliance to see how it stands up to a blitz of Web exploits, buffer overflows, port scanners, and the like. The test found the box could detect only 44% of the attacks when incoming traffic reached near-gigabit speed of 986.94M bit/sec.

Was it missing 60%? Yes! Like other IDS tools, *SecureNet Gig* recognizes suspicious activity based on attack *signatures*, and the challenge is finding a way to perform rigorous signature-based analysis at high speeds.

It's like sitting on a highway overpass trying to find autos with expired decals. It's much harder to do on a 10-lane highway than a country road. And gigabit speed is 10 lanes wide.

There is also a limit to the number of simultaneous connections an IDS can tolerate: 50,000 connections for HTTP, e-mail, or file transfer traffic—a number that should be higher. Intrusion benchmarked this 50,000 limit by beta-testing *Secure-Net Gig* at a large hosting facility for Web pornography sites in Colorado, chosen because of the large files, lengthy HTTP connections, and a lot of attempted hacker exploits.

In Miercom's lab tests, *Secure-Net Gig* recognized 88% of attacks thrown its way at 789.6M bit/sec and 98% at rates up to 690.86M bit/sec. According to Intrusion, it will release an upgrade of its gigabit IDS designed to overcome the first version's shortcomings.

IDS equipment from other vendors hasn't fared much better in lab tests. The higher the bandwidth, the more the IDS starts dumping packets.

However, two other Gigabit IDS vendors (Internet Security Systems [ISS] and Enterasys Networks), indicate their products have similar shortcomings. Although most vendors don't like to highlight the limitations of gigabit IDS in their marketing materials, they're straightforward about it if you ask.

According to Enterasys Networks, the company's gigabit IDS product, *Dragon Sensor™*, will not achieve optimum performance over 250M bit/sec. Enterasys added support for gigabit speed to *Dragon* so it could accept traffic over 100M bit/sec.

IDS works by copying IP traffic to analyze packet and packet flows in depth, so the more packets it needs to look at, the harder it is to perform that job. When an IDS pushes the limit, it just cannot look at the packets.

ISS, who sells *BlackIce Sentry Gigabit™*, indicates its IDS can perform attack monitoring at speeds up to 600M bit/sec. High performance has been a challenge to IDS for some time. The challenge is the packets per second. On a gigabit link, we could easily cover up to the full pipe. But if the packets are on the small side, ISS tends to drop packets because there are too many packets per second—1500-byte packets are easy, but 64-byte packets are hard. ISS is also working on a new high-speed sensor for release next year that is aimed at overcoming these limitations.

The lower-speed IDS product from ISS, *RealSecure Network Sensor™*, is designed to monitor 100M bit/sec segments. Some organizations, such as Johns Hopkins University, are harnessing multiple *RealSecure* sensors using load-balancing equipment (Top Layer Networks' *AppSafe™*) to achieve gigabit bandwidth coverage as their nets get faster. If you're dropping 50% or 60% of the packets in a full-gigabit network, you have to add more probes.

Load balancing is certainly a decent idea. It's a technique you can throw at the problem. Historically, you normally cannot handle more than 600M bit/sec with an IDS. Although *Top Layer* pushes its load-balancing equipment as specialized for IDS, balancing the load of IDS can be performed with switches from Arrow-Point

Communications (now Cisco), F5 Networks, and other vendors. However, costs rise when multiple IDS have to be used with load-balancing gear in lieu of gigabit IDS that cannot reliably handle the traffic stress. Load balancing is a crutch.

Gigabit ManHunt™ does not falter at high speeds, a claim backed by a Miercom lab test. But the product is designed differently from the signature-based offerings from ISS, Enterasys, and Intrusion. *ManHunt* spots *anomalies* or unusual traffic, but it doesn't provide nearly the level of detail about applications under attack as its competitor's products do.

Faster networks aren't the only challenge IDS vendors face. Their biggest fear may be new hacker tools with names such as *Stick, Snot,* and *Whisker* that generate bogus TCP traffic with the goal of interfering with routers and IDSs.

If you can plug tools such as these into the same hub as the IDS, you can deceive any network IDS. These hacker tools generate so many suspicious events that they can overwhelm any IDS sensor and let hackers sneak through in the process, or they can even cause an IDS to buckle completely.

These hacker tools work over T-3 or DSL connections to overwhelm IDS, although less effectively. For network managers who want to test how well their IDS is performing, professional engineering tools can generate a variety of attacks that might occur during Web sessions.

As with all of today's technology, detection tools date quickly as new threats emerge. Effective detection tools need to constantly evolve to counter these threats and must be engineered around best-practice risk management associated with vulnerabilities, system configurations, and viruses. Some on-line products and services currently in the market provide efficient, cost effective solutions by accessing computer vulnerabilities, specific to an organization's IT environment.

Effective Procedures

Even in an organization that has implemented the hardware, installed the software, produced the policies, and employed competent staff to run an effective IT environment, it is not possible to prevent an incident from occurring. However, the attack itself does not have the greatest impact on a company. How the business responds to that attack does have the greatest impact on a company. Without the appropriate procedures in place to counter detected attacks, an organization is exposed to the risks of lost data, financial loss, network damage, and loss of reputation.

Although many different types of attacks may occur, the majority requires the same basic steps of response. For example, the simple process of ensuring that

If you don't think you need a CFIR policy, try the following exercise: Do a mock incident (with the permission of your management), but don't let your security people know it is an exercise.

The difficult part of creating a CFIRP is that it has to be tailored for your site. You will need to take into consideration all the nuances of your particular site and get support and buy-in from upper management. Best of luck to you, it will be well worth the work.[iv]

Now, let's take a quick look at computer forensics investigative services. There are some underlying problems.

COMPUTER FORENSICS INVESTIGATIVE SERVICES

There are without doubt some very good experts in the field of Computer Forensics Investigations; however, there is a rise in the number of people purporting to be experts or specialists who produce flawed opinions or take actions which are just plain wrong.

The reasons for these errors are manifold but range from peer or management pressure, restricted timescales, and problems with software, to sheer lack of knowledge. Most investigations are basically the same in that they are either proving or disproving whether certain actions have taken place. The emphasis depends on whether the work is for the accuser or the accused.

In many companies, the forensic computer examiner is *king* because they have more knowledge of the subject than their peers. However, they are still subject to management pressures to produce results, and at times this can color their judgement. Time restrictions can cause them take short cuts that invalidate the very evidence they are trying to gather; and, when they do not find the evidence that people are demanding (even if it isn't there), they are subject to criticism and undue pressure.

Many of these *specialists* are well meaning, but they tend to work in isolation or as part of a hierarchical structure where they are the *computer expert*. The specialists management does not understand what they are doing (and probably don't want to admit it!), and often they are faced with the question: *Can't you just say this.....?* It takes a very strong-minded person to resist this sort of pressure, and it has been obvious that this has had an adverse effect in a number of cases.

This sort of pressure comes not only from within the organizations, but also from external sources. When you reply with: "*I'm sorry it's just not there or no the facts do not demonstrate that,*" you frequently end up with lengthy high-pressure discussions with the client, which appear to be designed to make you doubt your own valid conclusions.

Working in isolation is a major problem; apart from talking to yourself (first sign of madness), many people have no one else to review their ideas and opinions. This is where having recourse to a team of investigators, software engineers, hardware engineers, and managers who understand (not always a good thing, depending on your point of view!) any doubts or unusual facts, can be fully discussed and investigated to ensure that the correct answer is found.

Computer Intrusion Detection Services

Putting in technical safeguards to spot network intruders or detect denial-of-service attacks at e-commerce servers is a prudent idea. But if your staff doesn't have the time or skills to install and monitor intrusion-detection software, you might consider outsourcing the job.

Intrusion detection is the latest security service to be offered on an outsourced basis, usually by the types of ISPs or specialized security firms that have been eager to manage your firewall and authentication. Although outsourcing security means divulging sensitive information about your network and corporate business practices, some companies say they have little choice but to get outside help, given the difficulty of hiring security experts.

For example, Memorial Care of Los Angeles operates a private T-1 network for its five hospitals and gives doctors network access from their homes or offices using a VPN connection. Memorial Care hired Pilot Network Services to provide Internet access, VPN, router and firewall support, antivirus content filtering, plus intrusion detection.

Pilot apprises Memorial Care of all attacks occurring on their network address and any type of attempted intrusion through daily reports or notification. They see 100-plus incidents on a daily basis, mostly *kiddy hacker* attacks using the available tools. Although not sophisticated, someone is still rattling the doorknob.

Memorial Care outsourced this security guard function to Pilot primarily because it's hard to find skilled technicians with specialized knowledge about intrusion detection who will work round-the-clock. Outsourcing security costs Memorial Care *less than six figures* each year. Pilot doesn't monitor Memorial Care's internal network, but the hospital system has deployed its own homegrown intrusion-detection software on critical servers to issue alarms about unauthorized access attempts.

Allowing managed-security services deep into the network remains controversial. For example, Metromedia Fiber Network (MFN) opted not to go to managed security because you're forced to give away the keys to the castle in some respects. Sensitive information might include which employees or trading partners are allowed to use the intranet and where critical corporate data is stored. Instead of outsourcing, MFN is looking at deploying ISS intrusion-detection software, called *RealSecure*, on its intranet—thus staffing a round-the-clock data monitoring center on its own.

Although still in the intrusion-detection software business, ISS last year branched out into managed-security services by opening data centers in Atlanta and Detroit to provide managed firewall, VPN, and intrusion-detection services. ISS has centers in Sweden, Italy, and Brazil, and plans to open a center in Japan.

For the intrusion-detection managed service, corporations have to deploy the ISS *RealSecure Network Sensor* software in their internal network to remotely monitor traffic across LANs or behind the firewall. Each sensor's output, once encrypted, is transmitted across the Internet to consoles within the ISS data center, where employees watch for reports of suspicious activity or denial-of-service attacks.

ISS also plans to add host-based monitoring of servers, which would require users to buy into the *RealSecure Server Sensor* software. ISS often partners with telephone companies and Web-hosting providers, such as Exodus and network integrators or consultants, such as PricewaterhouseCoopers, to market its managed security services. Prices per month typically are between $1,800 to $3,000 per sensor. ISS claims to have 2,600 customers using its managed security services, which accounted for almost 11% of ISS' $192 million in revenue in 2000.

MyCIO.com, the Network Associates, Inc. (NAI) application service provider (ASP) division for antivirus and firewall software, has quietly begun managing its customers' intrusion-detection systems because the demand was there. The ASP technical staff is not going onto the customer site to manage only NAI's CyberCop intrusion-detection software, but also to manage competing products from companies such as ISS and Cisco.[v] It's a growth area for them. Also, outsourcing services typically cost a few thousand dollars per month.

The Yankee Group projects that managed-security services (of which intrusion detection is the latest phenomenon) more than doubled from $200 million in 1999 to $450 million in 2000. By 2006, the market is expected to reach $3.7 billion, fueled by the trend toward outsourcing internal LAN security to professional security firms as *virtual employees*.

Counterpane Internet Security, the managed-security services firm founded in 2000 by cryptography expert Bruce Schneier, has a distinctly different approach to intrusion monitoring than ISS. Counterpane built a *black box* device, called *Sentry*™, that it installs in the customer's network to aggregate data output from routers, servers, firewalls, and intrusion-detection software—including that from

ISS and Tripwire. Cisco routers and Unix servers are all very chatty, producing megabytes of information each day. *Sentry* collects all that information. *Sentry* then transmits that datastream in encrypted form to the Counterpane data center, which is staffed around the clock. Counterpane now has two centers in Mountain View, California, and Chantilly, Virginia. Counterpane does need information about the customer's network for this. If you went through a network expansion, Counterpane needs to know there's a change. Otherwise, they don't know what's happening in the network.

Counterpane then contacts the corporation to report suspicious findings or an attack in progress, but doesn't take further actions, such as shutting down access. Those steps are up to the corporation because Counterpane is there as a 24-7 remote monitoring alarm service. Cost typically runs $11,000 per month, and Counterpane services are offered through ISPs and Web host providers, including Exodus and Loudcloud.

Although the big fish, such as AT&T and IBM, are known to offer managed-security services that include intrusion detection, the water is becoming more populated with minnows. Sunnyvale, California, start-up eNet Secure provides intrusion detection for PBX equipment, charging $6,000 per month, with the Air Force and NASA as its first two customers.

Now, let's briefly look at digital evidence collection. For example, insurance companies that are interested in reducing fraudulent claims by discovered digital evidence can benefit from this computer forensic service.

Digital Evidence Collection

Perhaps one of the most crucial points of your case lies hidden in a computer. The digital evidence collection process allows you to not only locate that key evidence, but also maintains the integrity and reliability of that evidence. Timing during this digital evidence collection process is of the essence. Any delay or continuous use of the suspect computer may overwrite data prior to the forensic analysis and result in destruction of critical evidence (see sidebar, "Evidence Capture"). The following are some helpful tips that you can follow to help preserve the data for future computer forensic examination:

1. Do not turn on or attempt to examine the suspect computer. This could result in destruction of evidence.
2. Identify all devices that may contain evidence:

   ■ Workstation computers
   ■ Off-site computers (laptops, notebooks, home computers, senders and recipients of e-mail, PDAs, etc.)

- ■ Removable Storage Devices (Zips, Jaz, Orb, Floppy Diskettes, CDs, Sony Memory Sticks, Smart Media, Compact Flash, LS-120, Optical Disk, SyQuest, Bernouli, microdrives, pocketdrives, USB disk, firewire disk, PCMICA.)
- ■ Network storage devices (RAIDs, servers, sans, nas, spanned, remote network hard drives, back-up tapes, etc.)

3. Quarantine all in-house computers:
   - ■ Do not permit anyone to use the computers.
   - ■ Secure all removable media.
   - ■ Turn off the computers.
   - ■ Disconnect the computers from the network.
   - ■ Consider the need for court orders to preserve and secure the digital evidence on third party computers and storage media.

4. Forensically image all suspect media.[vi]

EVIDENCE CAPTURE

One of the fundamental principles of computer investigation is the need to follow established and tested procedures meticulously and methodically throughout the investigation. At no point of the investigation is this more critical than at the stage of initial evidence capture. Reproducibility of evidence is the key. Without the firm base of solid procedures that have been strictly applied, any subsequent antirepudiation attempts in court will be suspect and the case as a whole likely to be weakened.

There have been several high-profile cases recently where apparently solid cases have been weakened or thrown out on the basis of inappropriate consideration given to the integrity and reproducibility of the computer evidence. There are several reasons why this may happen. Lack of training is a prime culprit. If the individuals involved have not been trained to the required standards, or have received no training at all, then tainted or damaged computer evidence is the sad but inevitable result.

Another frequent cause of is lack of experience—not only lack of site experience but also inappropriate experience of the type of systems that might be encountered. One of the most difficult skills on-site is knowing when to call for help. It is essential that a sympathetic working environment is created such that peer pressure or fear of loss of status and respect does not override the need to call for help. Easier said than done perhaps, but no less essential for that reason.

Finally, sloppiness, time pressure, pressure applied on-site, tiredness, or carelessness have all been contributory factors in transforming solid computer evidence into a dubious collection of files. These totally avoidable issues are come down to individual mental discipline, management control and policy, and selecting appropriate staff to carry out the work. There are issues with which there is no sympathy. This is bad work, plain and simple.

Ultimately, anytime the collection of computer evidence is called into question, it is potentially damaging to everyone who is a computer forensic practitioner; it is ultimately in everyone's best interest to ensure that the highest standards are maintained. To use a rather worn phrase from a 1980s American Police Series ("Hill Street Blues"), *Let's be careful out there!*

Next, let's briefly look at drafting a comprehensive and effective computer forensics policy. This type of computer forensics service is used by countless organizations (banks, insurance companies, law firms, local governments, retailers, technology firms, educational institutions, charitable organizations, manufacturers, distributors, etc.).

Computer Policy

Often overlooked, detailed policies on the use of computers within an organization are an ever-increasing necessity. Corporations and government agencies are racing to provide Internet access to their employees. With this access, a Pandora's box of problems is opened. Paramount is loss of productivity; workers can easily spend countless hours on-line daily entertaining and amusing themselves at their employer's expense. A hostile workplace environment can be created through pornography, potentially exposing the organization to civil liability.

Although protecting your organization from outside threats is clearly important, protecting the organization from internal threats is at least as important, if not more so. According to the 2000 Computer Crime and Security Survey conducted by the Computer Security Institute and the FBI, 56% of the respondents reported unauthorized access to information by persons inside the organization, compared to just 31% who reported intrusions by outsiders. A quarter reported theft of proprietary information and 70% reported theft of laptop computers. Ninety-one percent (91%) reported virus contamination and a staggering 98% reported systems abuse by insiders (pornography, pirated software, inappropriate e-mail usage, etc.). According to Sextracker, an organization that tracks the on-line pornography trade, 71% of on-line pornography viewing occurs during the 9–5 workday.

Your computer forensics policy manual should, therefore, address all manners of computer-related policy needs. The content should be based on your corporation's years of experience in employment-related investigations, computer crime investigations, civil litigation, and criminal prosecutions.

Approximately half of the manual should consist of detailed discussions on each of the policy topic areas; the other half should be sample policies that can be readily customized for your organization. The discussions should include topics such as why policies are needed, potential liability, employee productivity considerations, and civil litigation. Safeguarding critical and confidential information should be discussed in detail. The policies should directly address the problems that you would typically find in organizations of all sizes.

Now let's look at another computer forensics service: Litigation support and insurance claims. As the risk increases, so will the interest in policies and the cost of premiums and litigation.

Litigation Support and Insurance Claims

Since its inception, cyberinsurance has been billed as a way for companies to underwrite potential hacking losses for things technology cannot protect. The concept of insuring digital assets has been slow in catching on because the risks and damages were hard to quantify and put a price tag on.

The 9-11-2001 terrorist attacks quickly elevated corporate America's interest in cyberinsurance, as industry magnates looked for ways to mitigate their exposure to cyberterrorism and security breaches. At the same time, it has become harder to find underwriters willing to insure multimillion-dollar cyberspace policies. For carriers willing to sell such paper, the premiums have skyrocketed.

Prior to 9-11-01, the focus, when it comes to information security, has been on critical infrastructure. Post-9-11-01, the focus has shifted to homeland defense and trying to understand whether financial institutions and other critical infrastructure such as telecommunications are vulnerable to cyberterrorism.

Insurance stalwarts such as Lloyd's of London, AIG, and Zurich now offer policies for everything from hacker intrusions to network downtime. The breadth of cyberinsurance policies is growing, from simple hacker intrusion, disaster recovery, and virus infection to protection against hacker extortion, identity theft, and misappropriation of proprietary data.

While the market was already moving to provide policies to cover these risks, many executives viewed cyberinsurance as a luxury that yielded few tangible benefits. Many risk managers buried their heads in the sand, believing they would never need anything like cyberinsurance.

There was a naivete on the part of senior management. IT managers were not willing to admit they had to fix something of that magnitude, because they are afraid to go ask for the money.

The aftermath of the 9-11-01 attacks illustrate the interconnectedness of all systems; financial services, information and communications, transportation, electrical power, fire, and police. They all relate in profound ways we are only now beginning to understand. Businesses are starting to think about what type of recovery position they would be in if something similar to the World Trade Center attack happened to them.

While the cyberinsurance market may reap growth in the wake of the 9-11-01 tragedy, carriers are tightening the terms and conditions of policies. Premiums are going up significantly, and underwriters are hesitating to sign big policies.

In the past, companies seeking a $25 million policy could find someone to cover them. Now, it's much more difficult. Underwriters who didn't blink at $5 million or $10 million policies, would rather insure $1 million policies. The marketplace is in transition, and there's undoubtedly a hardening of trading conditions for both traditional property and casualty insurance, as well as the emerging new e-commerce products.

Premiums on cyberinsurance are an easy mark for price hikes because there's little historical data on which to set premiums. It's difficult to pinpoint the losses if data is corrupted, a network is hacked, or system uptime is disrupted. The fear of bad publicity keeps many companies mum on hacking incidents, which makes it more difficult to collect data for projecting future losses.

To develop robust cyberinsurance, two major developments need to take place. First, sufficient actuarial data needs to be collected. Second, insurance carriers need to gain a better understanding of the IT systems in use and how they interact with other information and automated systems.

Industry analysts predict underwriters will push any changes in cyberinsurance offerings and the systems used by policyholders. The first indication of this trend came earlier in 2001, when J.S. Wurzler Underwriting Managers tacked a 5 to 15% surcharge on cyberinsurance premiums for users of *Windows NT* on IIS servers, citing their poor security track record, which makes them more expensive to insure. The underwriters are going to force the issue by saying: *Look, if you lose your whole business, if things like that happen, you can expect to pay a higher premium.*

Now, let's look at the computer forensic process improvement techniques. These techniques identify the threat to your systems by researching the apparent source of an attack.

FORENSIC PROCESS IMPROVEMENT

The purpose of this part of the chapter is to introduce the reader to a process that will enable a system administrator or information security analyst to determine the threat against their systems and networks. If you have ever wanted to know more about who might have attacked or probed your system than just the IP address that appeared in the *var/log/messages* of your machine, then this part of the chapter may help you. Although it is rare, some of these simple techniques may actually help you identify the perpetrator of an attack on your system. Although most system administrators are rightly concerned with first securing their hosts and networks from attack, part of doing that job correctly also demands that you also have an understanding of the threat against those systems and networks as. The risk any system connected to the net faces is a product of vulnerability and threat. The techniques covered in this part of the chapter will help you in determining possible actions and possible motivations of the attacker. If you can understand your attacker, than you can better defend and respond to attacks against your network. Of course, it is important to understand that hackers will loop through several systems during the attack phase. So why bother researching the apparent source of an attack? What if your system is the first system of many that the hacker will use in his or her attack against other systems? Could you be held liable for damage done by the attacker to someone else's systems downstream? What if he or she is operating from within a country that has no laws against hacking and can thus operate with impunity? Or, what if the hacker is just unskilled and has left clues behind that a skilled researcher could use to identify him or her? All of these reasons justify taking a small amount of time to research the apparent source of a serious attack or intrusion. Of course, all of these techniques should be used after you have secured your system and/or consulted with law enforcement personnel. This should be done if the level and seriousness of the attack justify such an action. Next, let's review the tools that are used in the threat identification process.

The Tools

The tools discussed here outline a step-by-step process that will help you to enumerate the attacking host and possible actors that may have used that host to attack your system. This section is not intended to be a tutorial for how to use each tool on its own. There are many sources of information that cover each tool by itself in more detail. Many of you are certainly familiar with or have used many of the tools discussed here at one time or another. Keep in mind that here we are talking about the overall process of characterizing the threat from a domain. The first steps in the threat identification process are simply to know who owns the IP used in the attack. For detailed switchology on the use of each tool, consult the main pages or other sources for each tool listed.

It is advisable to find a Web proxy or gateway Web site for conducting any type of intelligence collection operation against the attacking host itself. In this way, you do not run the risk of further antagonizing or scaring off a potential intruder who might be watching the connection logs from his or her victimized host. A good all-around site that contains most all the tools discussed here is http://www.samspade.org. This site also contains a brief description of each tool and its use. For instance, to learn more about "dig" command, simply hit the more information radio button listed beside the tool. Another useful site is http://network-tools.com/5/.

Dig –x /nslookup

The first step in the process is to reverse the offending IP address. The "dig –x ip" command will perform a reverse lookup on an IP address from its domain name server. The "-x" option will ensure that you receive all records possible about your host from the DNS table. This might include nameservers, e-mail servers, and the host's resolved name. The "nslookup" command, "nslookup ip," will also perform a reverse lookup of the host IP address, but will only return the resolved name.

Whois

The next step in the process is to perform a *whois* lookup on the IP address to see who owns or at least who the offending IP is registered to. This can be somewhat of a tricky operation. Use the resolved name previously mentioned to try to determine what country or region the IP address might be based in, and then be sure to use the proper *whois* gateway for that region of the world. The main gateways are ARIN (the American Registry), APNIC (the Asian Pacific Registry), and RIPE (the European Registry). There are dozens of others, but most addresses should be registered in one of the previously mentioned on-line centralized databases. If your *whois* data does not match your resolved name, for example the resolved name http://www.cnn.com and *whois* database ARIN indicates the registered owner is CNN network (a match), then you may have to do some more digging. *Whois* databases can contain outdated information. You may want to then research your IP with the country-specific *whois* database to determine the correct registered owner. A good collection of country-specific *whois* databases can be found at http://www.allwhois.com. For more information on conducting detailed *whois* queries check out http://www.sans.org/y2k/.

Ping

Conduct the "ping ip" command to determine if your attacking IP is currently on-line. Note that many administrators block ICMP traffic, so this is not conclusive evidence either way.

Traceroute

The next step in the process is to conduct a "traceroute ip" to determine possible paths from your proxy site to the target system. Traceroute may help you in two ways. If your IP does not resolve possible paths from your proxy site to the target system, there may be a clue as to its parentage. Look at the resolved host just before your target. This host's name may be the upstream provider for the attacking host, and thus a point of contact; or, it may in fact have the same domain as your attacking host, although that is not always true. Also, a traceroute might give you an important clue as to the physical location of the attacking box. Carefully look at the path the packets traveled. Do they tell you what city they are in? Oftentimes they will. If you can determine what city the attack came from, you have just narrowed down considerably the possible pool of candidates of who the attacker might be.

Finger

Conduct a "finger @ip" command to determine who is currently logged onto the system that attacked you. Now, to be frank, this command will rarely work, because most administrators wisely turn this service off. However, it does not hurt to try. Keep in mind that many systems that are compromised and used as lily pads to attack other hosts are poorly configured (that is why they were compromised in the first place!!). They may also have the finger service running. If it is running, finger root@ip sees the last time root was logged on and, more important, from where root was logged on. You might be surprised to see root logged on from a third system in another country. Keep following the trail as long as your commands are not refused. You should be able to trace back hackers through several countries using this simple, often-overlooked technique. Look for strange log-in names and for users logged into the system remotely. This may indicate where the host was compromised from and is the next clue as to where to focus your research.

Anonymous Surfing

Surfing anonymously to the domain from where your attacking IP is hosted, is the next step in the threat identification process. You will know this domain name by looking at the resolved name of the host and the *Whois* data. One technique that is useful is to use a search engine such as http://www.altavista.com with the specialized advanced search option of "+host:domain name and hack*." This query will return the Web links of possible hackers who operate from the domain name you queried. You can substitute warez or mp3, and the like, to focus in on terms of interest specific to warez or mp3 dealers. The number of Webpages returned by the query, as well as the details on those pages, gives you an indication of the level of threat to assess to a certain domain. For example, if you were investigating a host registered to demon.co.uk (Demon Internet), you would type "+host:demon.co.uk and hack*" in the Altavista query box. You may be surprised to see a return of some 22,000-plus hacking-related pages hosted on this domain. The Demon Internet seems to harbor many hackers and, as a domain, represents a viable threat to any organization. As a standard practice, you might want to block certain domains at your firewall, if you are not already blocking ALL:ALL. Another possibility to widen the search is to use "+link:domain name" in the Altavista search. This will show all Webpages that have a link to the domain in question listed on their Webpage. In other words, the ever-popular "here is list of my hacker friends and their c001 hacker sites" pages will appear via this search. You will also want to keep in mind the target of the attack. What were the hackers going after? Can you tell? Conduct searches for the resources targeted and combine these terms with Boolean operators such as "and espionage." Check newswires or other competitive intelligence sources to determine, if possible, who might be going after your companies' resources. A good site to use to conduct your searches anonymously is http://www.anonymizer.com.

USENET

The last step in the process of threat identification is to conduct a USENET traffic search on your domain. Sites such as http://www.deja.com are excellent for this. Search on the attacking IP address in quotes to see if other people are reporting activity from this IP in any security newsgroups. Search on the domain name or hacker aliases that you might have collected from your anonymous surfing, or from the returns of your finger queries. You can expand the headers of the postings by clicking on "view original posting." This may show you the actual server that posted the message, even if the hacker attempted to spoof his or her mailing address in the visible header. This method can reveal the true location of your hacker. Clicking on "author profile" can also give you valuable information. Look at the newgroups your hacker posts to and look at the number and sophistication of those postings. Pay attention to off-subject postings. A hacker will often let down his guard when talking about his favorite band or hobby, for example. You can also search sites such as http://www.icq.com if you have a hacker alias from a defaced Webpage or your Altavista search narrowed by the domain "+hacker" criteria previously noted.

Putting It All Together

Once you have completed the process previously outlined and gathered all the information from these tools, you should be able to reach an educated guess about the threat level from the domain that you are analyzing. Hopefully, you were able to collect information about the numbers and sophistication levels of the hackers who operate from the attacking domain, possible candidates for the attack (through finger or specialized Altavista searches), and what other CERTs may be seeing from that domain (via newsgroups or newswire searches). An excellent site to check for archived postings of recently seen attacks is both http://www.sans.org and http://www.securityfocus.com. Ask yourself were there thousands of hacker pages hosted on the domain that you were investigating? Likewise, did you find thousands of postings concerning hacking on USENET? Did you run a search on your organization's name plus "hack*"? Were there postings from other administrators detailing attacks from this domain? Were the attacks they mentioned similar to yours or different? Now you might be able to determine if that FTP probe, for example, was just a random probe that targeted several other companies as well as yours or targeted your company specifically. Could you tell from the logs that the attacker was attempting to find a vulnerable FTP server to set up a warez or mp3 site perhaps? Being able to provide an educated guess as to the motivation of your hacker is important. Knowing whether your company has been singled out for an attack as opposed to being just randomly selected, will change the level of concern you have with regard to assessing the threat. The process previously listed can be used to narrow down possible candidates or characterize the threat level from responsible domains. And, as a byproduct, it will also provide you with all the necessary names, phone numbers, and points of contact that may be useful when it comes time to notify the pertinent parties involved.

Finally, let's look at what is probably the most important computer forensics service: training! It has now been expanded to support U. S. Government and U. S. corporate needs, which became more of a priority after 9-11, 2001. It places priority on computer incident responses and now covers computer forensic binary data searches for foreign language (non-Latin based) computer data (Farsi, Chinese, Japanese, etc.).

Training

As has been previously explained, Computer Forensics involves the preservation, identification, extraction, and documentation of computer evidence stored in the form of magnetically encoded information (data). Many times the computer evidence was created transparently by the computer's operating system and without the knowledge of the computer operator. Such information may actually be hidden from view and, thus, special forensic software tools and techniques are required to preserve, identify, extract, and document the related computer evidence. It is this information that benefits law enforcement and military agencies in intelligence gathering and in the conduct of investigations.

Today computer forensics software tools and processing techniques have become important resources for use in internal investigations, legal electronic document discovery, computer security risk management, and computer incident responses. Computer forensic software tools and methods can be used to identify passwords, computer network log-ons, and other information that is transparently and automatically transferred from the computers memory to floppy diskettes, Iomega Zip Disks, and computer hard disk drives. Such computer forensic software tools and methods can also be used to identify backdated files and to tie a floppy diskette to a specific computer. These techniques should be taught in your specialized training course.

Law enforcement and military agencies have been involved in processing computer evidence for years. Therefore, computer forensics training courses should be taught by certified instructors (see sidebar, "Computer Forensics Certified") who are experienced computer crime experts (retired federal law enforcement computer evidence trainers and members of law enforcement computer crime units).

COMPUTER FORENSICS CERTIFIED

According to a Gartner Group study, certification of *InfoSec* computer-forensic-training professionals is becoming a common condition of employment. The research firm predicts that by 2005, *InfoSec* certification will be required for 70% of CISOs (chief information security officers) and associated training staff positions and for 30% of day-to-day technical operations positions in Global 2000 companies. Security is the No. 1 issue going forward in an on-line world, whether it's on-line voting or e-commerce.

The Demands of Security

It's bad enough when a certified IT employee doesn't possess claimed skills, but the skills gap is doubly worse in the security realm. What was once the near-exclusive purview of government agencies or companies involved in highly secret research, is now a mainstream discipline for the highly connected enterprise.

This market really didn't exist 10 years ago. The field has only matured in the last six years.

Protecting a company's most cherished assets (not just IT systems, but especially the digitally stored proprietary information on those systems) demands knowledgeable personnel, something not always easy to assess. Anyone can hang out a shingle and say: "I'm an *InfoSec* professional." Such people must be able to prove their credentials with *InfoSec* certification.

Good security demands a more proactive approach than the other traditional functions of a system administrator. Security is the system administrator area that requires the most constant learning and relearning.

Information security infrastructure, like the proverbial chain, is only as strong as its weakest link. The breadth of skills and management breadth required for strong information security puts unusual demands on organizations and professionals.

Another Game

A Certified Information Systems Security Professional (CISSP) isn't the only game in town. There's also CIW professional certification, coming on strong.

Perhaps the best known security certification player is System Administration, Networking, and Security (SANS) Institute, which sponsors the Global Information Assurance Certifications (GIAC). And, it's here where the line in the security sand is drawn. The CISSP is a broad top-down certification, whereas the LevelTwo GIAC is a series of specialized and technical certifications.

GIAC responds directly to the skills question. GIAC requires that candidates demonstrate content mastery before they sit for the exam. In intrusion detection, for example, a candidate must accurately analyze 10 real-world intrusion attempts before being allowed to take the exam. For firewalls, a candidate must design a perimeter that solves specific problems.

When comparing CISSPs to GIAC, the metaphor is an MBA (CISSP) versus a CPA (GIAC). You hire a CPA to do your accounting, but not to do your strategic business planning. Research indicates strategic business planning is what the industry desperately needs.

The principal difference is in the target. An analogy suggested by an (ISC)2 board member is that GIAC is for pilots and CISSP is for the managers who schedule the pilots.

SANS certification focuses on specific products. The product focus has limitations, because security professionals need to take into account the whole picture.

The short-term need is for the techie approach. Believe it or not, issues such as buffer overflows still form a large part of the action on security lists. In the long term, though, you need the big-picture view.

You cannot really say the technical issues are more important than management issues. But the technical issues are more solvable.

Indeed, whether approaching information security issues from a management or technical perspective, no one can escape political issues. Even if you had the best of the best techies on your payroll, you wouldn't be going anywhere unless the issues and policies around corporate standards, user awareness, remote/wireless access policies,[vii] acceptable authentication methods, and so forth have been decided. The critical success factors in most security jobs are being adept at the politics, possessing business skills and aptitude, good relationship management, and sales and negotiation skills, even in some lower-level jobs.

The product versus politics dilemma will eventually be moot with SANS' Security Essentials (LevelOne) certification. The basic GIAC certification now covers all the key knowledge sets covered by CISSP as well as additional, more current skills sets.

Growing a Profession

The information security profession draws people from diverse backgrounds into a cohesive group. Security pros may have backgrounds in law enforcement, the military, or traditional IT, each bringing their own jargon and argot. How do we learn to talk to each other? You need an agreed-on taxonomy. And that, certification advocates indicate, is what certification does: It creates a shared body of knowledge to encourage a cohesive professional body.

Such certification is also seen as a big asset to an employee's resume. CISSP is the gold standard in regards to security management and program development.

But a certification should be the beginning of a learning process, not an end in itself. Security is one area where yesterday's knowledge does not help today. The security threat is always changing, so security certification tests, more than any others, are out of date before the person even begins to study for them.

There's another problem: the SAT-prep-test phenomenon. Once (certifications) become widely accepted, some of their value will be lost. The more popular something is, the more likely there will be a "For Dummies" approach.

Although most computer forensics training courses do not answer all possible questions regarding computer evidence and computer security, they should cover most of the common issues and expose the participant to new state-of-the-art computer forensics techniques and computer forensics tools. Training should consist of a *Windows NT* Computer Forensics course and Restricted-Data-Hiding course. And an Expert Witness Testimony on Electronic Evidence course should fill in the gaps when the participant is ready for those advanced training courses. Training should not be focused on one specific computer forensics software tool or set of tools. This should not be a computer forensics 'paint by numbers' training course. Quality computer forensic software tools should be provided with the training course; but, it should be your company's mission to teach methodologies and the more technical aspects of computer evidence processing and computer incident responses.

The training course should be unique; the participants are expected to have a high degree of computer proficiency, know the difference between clusters and sectors, and have experience in the use of Norton *Utilities*, DOS, and Microsoft *Windows*. The course should not be an overview of computer forensics. It should be a technical hands-on training course that will tax your knowledge and computer skills. However, it should provide you with more information about computer security risks and evidence-processing information than can be found anywhere else.

Because the course should deal with computer security issues and computer risk management as well as computer evidence issues, it should be well suited for computer security specialists, computer incident response team members, and computer crime investigators. Most of your participants should be challenged by this course for it to be considered a success.

In special cases, a course like this should be taught at the training facilities of corporate and government sponsors.

NOTE

COURSE CONTENT

A typical Computer Forensics course should deal specifically with DOS, *Windows*, *Windows 95*, *Windows 98*, *Window 2000*, *Windows XP* and *Windows ME*. Concerning these operating systems, it should cover evidence preservation, evidence-processing methodologies, and computer security risk assessments in detail. It should touch briefly on issues dealing with *Windows NT*, *Windows 2000*, and *Windows XP*. However, you should have an advanced *Windows NT* training course that covers computer security and computer evidence issues associated with *Windows NT*, *Windows 2000*, and *Windows XP* in great detail.

Today, *Windows 98* and *Windows 2000* are the predominant operating systems used on notebook and desktop computers. Thus, they are the most likely operating systems to be encountered in computer investigations, internal audits, and computer security reviews. Most computer forensic courses do not cover the use of *Black Box* computer forensics software tools. Those tools are good for some basic investigation tasks, but they do not offer a complete and accurate computer forensics solution. Furthermore, such approaches are useless in computer security risk assessments. Computer security risk assessments usually require that searches and file listings be conducted overtly (or covertly) from a single floppy diskette.

Each participant in a computer forensics course who successfully completes the course, should receive some sort of a Certificate of Completion that is suitable fo framing. They should also leave the course with a good understanding of the following:

- Computer evidence processing
- Preservation of evidence
- Trojan horse programs
- Computer forensics documentation
- File slack
- Data-hiding techniques
- Internet-related investigations
- Dual-purpose programs
- Text search techniques
- Fuzzy logic tools used to identify previously unknown text
- Disk structure
- Data encryption
- Matching a floppy diskette to a computer
- Data compression
- Erased files
- Internet abuse identification and detection
- The boot process & memory resident programs

Computer-Evidence-Processing Procedures

The processing procedures and methodologies taught in a computer forensics course should conform to federal computer-evidence-processing standards. The tools that are used in the course, as well as the methods and procedures taught, should work with any computer forensics tools. The methods and many of the software tools should conform specifically to the computer-evidence-processing procedures followed by the FBI, U.S. Department of Defense and the U.S. Drug Enforcement Administration.

Preservation of Evidence

Computer evidence is very fragile and it is susceptible to alteration or erasure by any number of occurrences. The participant should be exposed to bit stream back-up procedures that ensure the preservation of all storage levels that may contain evidence.

Trojan Horse Programs

The need to preserve the computer evidence before processing a computer will be clearly demonstrated through the use of programs designed to destroy data and modify the operating systems. The participant should demonstrate his (or her) ability to avoid destructive programs and traps that can be planted by computer users bent on destroying data and evidence. Such programs can also be used to covertly capture sensitive information, passwords, and network log-ons. This should also be demonstrated during the course.

Computer Forensics Documentation

The documentation of forensic-processing methodologies and findings is important. This is even true concerning computer security risk assessments, computer incident responses, and internal audits, because without proper documentation it is difficult to present findings in court or to others. If the computer security or internal audit findings become the object of a lawsuit or a criminal investigation, then accurate documentation becomes even more important. The participant should be taught computer-evidence-processing methodology that facilitates good evidence-processing documentation and solid evidence chain of custody procedures. The benefits will be obvious to investigators, but they will also become clear to internal auditors and computer security specialists during the course.

File Slack

The occurrence of random memory dumps in hidden storage areas[viii] should be discussed and covered in detail during workshops. Techniques and automated tools used to capture and evaluate file slack should be demonstrated in the course. Such data is the source of potential security leaks regarding passwords, network log-ons, e-mail, database entries, and word processing documents. These security and evidence issues should be discussed and demonstrated during the course. The participants should be able demonstrate their ability to deal with slack from both an investigations and security risk standpoint. They should also be able demonstrate their proficiency in searching file slack, documenting their findings, and eliminating security risks associated with file slack.

Data-Hiding Techniques

Trade secret information and other sensitive data can easily be secreted using any number of techniques. It is possible to hide diskettes within diskettes and to hide entire computer hard disk drive partitions. These issues should be discussed from a detection standpoint as well as from a security risk standpoint. Tools that help in the identification of such anomalies should demonstrated and discussed (*AnaDisk*). Participants should be required to demonstrate their understanding of such issues. This aspect of the training becomes especially important during the last day of the course when the participants are called on to identify and extract their Certificate of Completion from a *special* floppy diskette.

Data-hiding issues should be covered in much more depth in a Data-Hiding course.

NOTE

Internet-Related Investigations

Issues and techniques related to the investigation of Internet-related matters should be covered in the course. This should include a demonstration of how Internet-related evidence differs from more traditional computer evidence. Emphasis should be placed on the investigation of Internet-based terrorist leads.

Dual-Purpose Programs

Programs can be designed to perform multiple processes and tasks at the same time. They can also be designed for delayed tasks and processes. These concepts should be demonstrated to the participants during the course through the use of specialized software. The participant should also have hands-on experience with such programs.

Text Search Techniques

Specialized search techniques and tools should be developed that can be used to find targeted strings of text in files, file slack, unallocated file space, and *Windows* swap files. Each participant should leave the class with the necessary knowledge to conduct computer security reviews and computer-related investigations. Because of the need to search for non-Latin words and word patterns tied to foreign languages, the course should also cover the search of such data tied to foreign languages (Farsi, Chinese, Japanese, etc.).

Fuzzy Logic Tools Used to Identify Previously Unknown Text

A methodology and special computer forensics tools should be developed that aid in the identification of relevant evidence and *unknown* strings of text. Traditional computer evidence searches require that the computer specialist knows what is being searched for. However, many times not all is known in investigations. Thus, not all is known about what may be stored on a targeted computer system. In such cases, fuzzy logic tools can assist and can provide valuable leads as to how the subject computer was used. The participant should fully understand these methods and techniques. They should also be able to demonstrate their ability to use them to identify leads in file slack, unallocated file space, and *Windows* swap files.

Disk Structure

Participants should leave the course with a solid understanding of how computer hard disks and floppy diskettes are structured and how computer evidence can reside at various levels within the structure of the disk. They should also leave the class with a good understanding of how easy it is to modify the disk structure and to hide computer data in obscure places on floppy diskettes and hard disk drives.

Data Encryption

A computer forensics training course should also cover how data is encrypted and illustrate the differences between good encryption and bad encryption. The participants should become familiar with the use of software to *crack* security associated with these different encryption file structures.

Matching a Floppy Diskette to a Computer

Specialized computer forensics techniques and computer forensics tools should also be developed that make it possible to conclusively tie a floppy diskette to a computer hard disk drive. Each participant should also be taught how to use special software tools to complete a unique computer storage data-matching process. Some computer forensics experts indicate that floppy diskettes are no longer popular. They are wrong! Actually, floppy diskettes are found to be a valuable source of computer evidence in some civil litigation cases that involve the theft of trade secrets.

Data Compression

The participant should be shown how data compression programs can be used to hide and/or disguise critical computer data. Furthermore, the participant should learn how password-protected compressed files can be broken.

Erased Files

Participants should be shown how previously erased files can be recovered using computer forensics processes and methods. Documentation of the process should also be covered in detail.

Internet Abuse Identification and Detection

The participant should be shown how to use specialized software to identify how a targeted computer has been used on the Internet. This process should focus on computer forensics issues tied to data that the computer user probably doesn't realize exists (file slack, unallocated file space, and *Windows* swap files). Participants should gain hands-on experience in using this unique technology and they should be given the opportunity to purchase the software for a nominal charge. Nevertheless, it should be provided free of charge to law enforcement computer crime specialists who attend the course. Law enforcement agencies are typically underfunded.

The Boot Process and Memory Resident Programs

Participants should be able to see how easy it is to modify the operating system to capture data and/or to destroy computer evidence. Such techniques could be used to covertly capture keyboard activity from corporate executives, government computers, and the like. For this reason, it is important that the participants understand these potential risks and how to identify them.

Finally, let's look at a couple of computer forensics case study scenarios. These scenarios will briefly cover planned forensics responses.

CASE HISTORIES

The following case study illustrates the organizational benefits of a planned forensic response:

Scenario One

An IT manager reviews a detection tool report that indicates a company employee is accessing restricted Internet sites and downloading objectionable material. After discovering the activity, the IT manager remotely accesses the employee's personal computer to obtain evidence. The employee is then dismissed, based on the evidence located and obtained.

Scenario Two

An IT manager reviews a detection tool report indicating a company employee is accessing restricted Internet sites and downloading objectionable material. After discovering this activity, the IT manager follows procedures, reporting his suspicions to the nominated computer incident response contact, in this case the Chief Information Officer (CIO).

The CIO then invokes the company's incident response plan by contacting the Incident Response Team, which includes computer forensic experts. This team isolates the *offending machine*; conducts a forensic examination of the computer system following methodologies known to be acceptable to criminal, civil, and arbitration courts or tribunals; and establishes where the material came from, how often, and who else knew about it. By following its effective policies and procedures, the organization (via the CIO) is in an excellent position to take immediate legal and decisive action based on all the available facts and evidence.

Which Scenario Works?

Only one of these scenarios illustrates a planned forensic response. In Scenario One, the evidence was obtained remotely. This fact alone may put the obtained evidence in doubt.

Any court of law would want to know whether there were policies and IT infrastructure for ensuring the IT staff member knew the correct PC was accessed. Other issues surround the need for evidence to prove that a particular employee's PC was responsible for downloading the objectionable material. Can it be proved that the objectionable material was viewed on a particular PC? Who else had access to that PC? It is likely that there is not adequate evidence in this scenario to answer these questions.

The IT manager detecting activity is only the first step in forming grounds for suspicion. If action is taken without proper policies, procedures, and processes in place, it is nothing more than an unplanned knee jerk reaction.

Unplanned reactions potentially expose an organization to risk. Clearly, any investigation must not only be thorough and methodical, but also staffs need procedures for reporting the activity, conducting the investigation, and appointing investigators.

In Scenario Two, the established policies let the organization clearly identify the incident and carry out appropriate immediate action. This places the organization in a comfortable position to resolve the situation, contain the potential damage, and effectively seek compensation or prosecution. The bottom line here is that without the appropriate procedures in place to counter detected attacks, an organization is exposed to the risks of lost data, financial loss, network damage, and loss of reputation.

SUMMARY

Don't react, respond! Cyber crime is rapidly increasing and is striking at the heart of many organizations. By ensuring measures such as effective policies and rapid response capabilities, excellent information technology security positioning and forensic support can exist. Businesses can respond quickly, minimizing the risks of lost data, financial loss, network damage, and loss of reputation.

Organizations wanting to counter cyber crime need to apply risk management techniques that allow a speedy response and minimize harm. Although organizations cannot prevent a cyberattack, they can have a planned response and even turn e-crime preparedness, or effective security, into a new competitive advantage.

Conclusions Drawn from Types of Vendor and Computer Forensics Services

- The technological revolution marches on at a frantic pace, providing the world with an immense availability of resources. The same technological revolution has also brought forth a new breed of investigative and legal challenges.
- Computers are now at the core of people's activities and evidence contained in them is being introduced with greater frequency in both civil and criminal judicial proceedings. Questions arise regarding location of evidence stored on digital media, analysis of that evidence, and authentication of that evidence in court. The field of computer forensics seeks to answer these questions and provide experts to introduce this digital evidence in court.
- Computer Forensic services include: digital evidence collection; forensic analysis of digital evidence (including analysis of hidden, erased, and password-protected files.); expert witness testimony; and litigation support.
- Who can benefit from Computer Forensic services: Attorneys involved in complex litigation that deals with digital evidence; human resource professionals involved in administrative proceedings such as wrongful termination claims, sexual harassment, or discrimination allegations, and employee violations of company policies and procedures, where key evidence may reside in e-mails, word processing documents, and the like; and company executives who are interested in confidentially auditing their employee computer usage concerning proprietary information, misuse of company resources, and trade secret issues.
- Insurance companies that are interested in reducing fraudulent claims by using discovered digital evidence.
- Documentary evidence has quickly moved from the printed or type written page to computer data stored on floppy diskettes, zip disks, CDs, and computer hard disk drives.
- Denial of service attacks have always been difficult to trace as a result of the spoofed sources.

- With the recent increasing trend toward using distributed denial of service attacks, it has become near impossible to identify the true source of an attack.
- ISPs need automated methods as well as policies in place to attempt to combat the hacker's efforts.
- Proactive monitoring and alerting of backbone and client bandwidth with trending analysis is an approach that can be used to help identify and trace attacks quickly without resource-intensive side effects.
- Subsequent detailed analysis could be used to complement the bandwidth monitoring.
- Timely communication between ISPs is essential in incident handling.
- Deleted computer files can be recovered.
- Even after a hard drive is reformatted or repartitioned, data can be recovered.
- In many instances, encrypted files can be decrypted.
- Forensic analysis can reveal: What Web sites have been visited; what files have been downloaded; when files were last accessed; when files were deleted; attempts to conceal or destroy evidence; and attempts to fabricate evidence.
- The electronic copy of a document can contain text that was removed from the final printed version.
- Some fax machines can contain exact duplicates of the last several hundred pages received.
- Faxes sent or received via computer may remain on the computer indefinitely.
- E-mail is rapidly becoming the communications medium of choice for businesses. People tend to write things in e-mail that they would never consider writing in a memorandum or letter; e-mail has been used successfully in civil cases as well as criminal cases; and e-mail is often backed-up on tapes that are generally kept for months or years.
- Many people keep their financial records, including investments, on computers.

An Agenda for Action in Types of Vendor and Computer Forensics Services

The following is a provisional list of actions for some of the principle types of vendor and computer forensic services. The order is not significant; however, these are the activities for which the research would want to provide a detailed description of procedures, review, and assessment for ease of use and admissibility. A number of these services have been mentioned in passing already:

1. Computer Forensics services should provide: Analysis of computers and data in criminal investigations; on-site seizure of computer data in criminal investigations; analysis of computers and data in civil litigation; on-site seizure of computer data in civil litigation; analysis of company computers

to determine employee activity; assistance in preparing electronic discovery requests; reporting in a comprehensive and readily understandable manner; court-recognized computer expert witness testimony; computer forensics on both PC and MAC platforms; and fast turnaround time.

2. Computers systems may crash. Files may be accidentally deleted. Disks may accidentally be reformatted. Computer viruses may corrupt files. Files may be accidentally overwritten. Disgruntled employees may try to destroy your files. All of these can lead to the loss of your critical data. You may think it's lost forever, but you should employ the latest tools and techniques to recover your data.

3. In many instances, the data cannot be found using the limited software tools available to most users. The advanced tools that you utilize should allow you to find your files and restore them for your use. In those instances where the files have been irreparably damaged, your computer forensics expertise should allow you to recover even the smallest remaining fragments.

4. Business today relies on computers. Your sensitive client records or trade secrets are vulnerable to such intentional attacks as computer hackers, disgruntled employees, viruses, and corporate espionage. Equally threatening, but far less considered, are unintentional data losses caused by accidental deletion, computer hardware and software crashes, and accidental modification. You should safeguard your data by such methods as encryption and back-up. You should also thoroughly "clean" sensitive data from any computer system you plan on disposing of.

5. Your files, records, and conversations are just as vital to protect as your data. You should survey your business and provide guidance for improving the security of your information. This includes such possible information leaks as cordless telephones, cellular telephones, trash, employees, and answering machines.

6. Always keep in mind that the IP you are investigating is only the apparent source of the activity you see on your logs. As mentioned earlier, this does not mean that you should ignore the IP address, only be cognizant of its limitations for determining the possible attribution of the event you are investigating. Although this process will educate the administrator on how to characterize the threat to his or her company from analyzing IP addresses that appear in the logs, a complete determination of the threat your organization faces is a more involved process.

7. What you can be sure of is that many threat entities will probe and attempt to intrude on your systems over time. These may range from Class I (privacy), II (industrial espionage), or Class III (terrorism) attacks. Attackers

may range from the script kiddy aimlessly probing the networks, to a dedicated industrial espionage hacker looking for your company's secrets. Depending on your company's resources and the value of those resources, you should also investigate the possibility of staffing a professional competitive intelligence cell in your company or in sponsoring an assessment of the threat to your company's systems from a group of intelligence and information security specialists.

8. The serious threat to your IT infrastructure is not a teenage hacker defacing your Web site. The true dangers are information and monetary theft, business disruption, and critical infrastructure failure. Perpetrators are likely to be professional criminals, hacktivists, competitors, or even foreign intelligence agencies. The most costly intrusions are likely to be those that you fail to detect. The bottom line, you need to know the threat against your systems as well as its vulnerabilities.

ENDNOTES

i "Computer Forensics: Response Versus Reaction," Ernst & Young Australia, The Ernst & Young Building, 321 Kent Street, Sydney NSW 2000, Australia (Ernst & Young LLP, 787 Seventh Avenue, New York, New York, 10019), 2001, p.3.

ii John R. Vacca, *Electronic Commerce: Online Ordering and Digital Money with Cdrom*, Charles River Media, 2001.

iii John R. Vacca, *Net Privacy: A Guide to Developing and Implementing an Ironclad ebusiness Privacy Plan*, McGraw-Hill Professional, 2001.

iv Katherine Bursese, "Computer Security Incident Response Procedures: Do You Need One? You Bet You Do!" Global Computer Operations, General Electric Company, 2690 Balltown Road, Bldg. 610, Schenectady, NY 12345 (SANS Institute, 5401 Westbard Ave. Suite 1501, Bethesda, MD 20816), 2002.

v John R. Vacca, *Planning, Designing, and Implementing High-Speed LAN/WAN with Cisco Technology*, CRC Press, 2002.

vi "Computers," Rehman Technology Services, Inc., 18950 U.S. Highway 441, #201, Mount Dora, Florida 32757, 2001.

vii John R. Vacca, *Wireless Broadband Networks Handbook, McGraw-Hill Professional*, 2001.

viii John R. Vacca, *The Essential Guide to Storage Area Networks*, Prentice Hall, 2002.

Computer Forensics Evidence and Capture

4 Data Recovery

Computers systems may crash. Files may be accidentally deleted. Disks may accidentally be reformatted. Computer viruses may corrupt files. Files may be accidentally overwritten. Disgruntled employees may try to destroy your files. All of these can lead to the loss of your critical data. You may think it's lost forever, but you should employ the latest tools and techniques to recover your data.

In many instances, the data cannot be found using the limited software tools available to most users. The advanced tools that you utilize should allow us to find your files and restore them for your use. In those instances where the files have been irreparably damaged, your computer forensics expertise should allow you to recover even the smallest remaining fragments.

With this in mind, data recovery is, of course, of potential interest to anyone who has lost data to the ravages of time, malice, or carelessness. But in forensic computing or analysis, it takes on a new meaning—suddenly what other people have thrown away can become an important component in understanding what has happened in the past, as burglary tools, data files, correspondence, and other clues can be left behind by interlopers.

This chapter covers the ins and outs of data recovery as it relates to computer forensics. But, before delving into the ins and outs, what is data recovery?

DATA RECOVERY DEFINED

Data recovery is the process in which highly trained engineers evaluate and extract data from damaged media and return it in an intact format. Many people, even computer experts, fail to recognize data recovery as an option during a data crisis.

Yet it is possible to retrieve files that have been deleted, passwords that have been forgotten, or to recover entire hard drives that have been physically damaged.

As computers are used in more important transactions and storage functions, and as more important data is stored on them, the importance of qualified data recovery experts becomes clear. Perhaps your information has been subjected to a virus attack, suffered damage from smoke or fire—maybe your drive has been immersed in water—the data recovery experts can help you. Or, perhaps your mainframe software has malfunctioned, or your file allocation tables are damaged—data recovery experts can help you.

So, what would happen to the productivity of your organization in the event of a system-wide data center failure? For most companies, the loss would be catastrophic. Hundreds, perhaps thousands, of employees would be rendered unproductive. Sales transactions would be impossible to complete. And customer service would suffer. The cost of replacing this data would be extraordinary—if it could be replaced at all.

DATA BACK-UP AND RECOVERY

We live in a world that is driven by the exchange of information. Ownership of information is one of the most highly valued assets of any business striving to compete in today's global economy. Companies that can provide reliable and rapid access to their information are now the fastest growing organizations in the world. To remain competitive and succeed, they must protect their most valuable asset—data.

Fortunately, there are specialized hardware and software companies that manufacture products for the centralized back-up and recovery of business-critical data. Hardware manufacturers offer automated tape libraries that can manage millions of megabytes of backed-up information and eliminate the need for operators charged with mounting tape cartridges. Software companies have created solutions that can back-up and recover dozens of disparate systems from a single console.

So why then, do industry experts estimate that over 45% of the data in client/ server networks is still not backed-up on a regular basis? It is often due to organizations' ever-shrinking back-up windows, inadequate network infrastructure, and a lack of system administration. Compounding the problem is an overall lack of experience in defining the proper features necessary for a successful back-up application. And finally, there is often a shortage of in-house expertise needed to implement sophisticated, enterprise-level back-up applications.

However, there are obstacles to backing-up applications. Let's look at a few.

Back-up Obstacles

The following are obstacles to backing-up applications:
- Back-up window
- Network bandwidth
- System throughput
- Lack of resources

BACK-UP WINDOW

The back-up window is the period of time when back-ups can be run. The back-up window is generally timed to occur during nonproduction periods when network bandwidth and CPU utilization are low. However, many organizations now conduct operations seven days a week, 24 hours a day—effectively eliminating traditional back-up windows altogether.

NETWORK BANDWIDTH

Many companies now have more data to protect than can be transported across existing LAN and WAN networks. If a network cannot handle the impact of transporting hundreds of gigabytes of data over a short period of time, the organization's centralized back-up strategy is not viable.

SYSTEM THROUGHPUT

There are three I/O bottlenecks commonly found in traditional back-up schemes. These are:

1. The ability of the system being backed-up to push data to the back-up server
2. The ability of the back-up server to accept data from multiple systems simultaneously
3. The available throughput of the tape device(s) onto which the data is moved[i]

Any or all of preceding bottlenecks can render a centralized back-up solution unworkable.

NOTE

LACK OF RESOURCES

Many companies fail to make appropriate investments in data protection until it is too late. Often, IT managers choose not to allocate funding for centralized data protection because of competing demands resulting from emerging issues such as e-commerce,[ii] Internet/intranet applications, and other new technologies.

These are just a few of the impediments that make implementation of an enterprise back-up and recovery solution a low priority for some organizations. Fortunately, there have been major advances in hardware and software technologies that overcome many or all of the traditional obstacles faced by IT professionals as they attempt to develop a comprehensive data-protection plan. In addition, companies such as StorNet[iii] provide specialized expertise in the deployment of complex, integrated storage solutions.

The Future of Data Back-up

Successful data back-up and recovery is composed of four key elements: the back-up server, the network, the back-up window, and the back-up storage device (or devices). These components are highly dependent on one another, and the overall system can only operate as well as its weakest link. To help define how data back-up is changing to accommodate the issues described earlier, let's take a look at each element of a back-up and recovery design and review the improvements being made.

THE BACK-UP SERVER

The back-up server is responsible for managing the policies, schedules, media catalogs, and indexes associated with the systems it is configured to back-up. The systems being backed-up are called *clients*. Traditionally, all managed data in an enterprise that was being backed-up had to be processed through the back-up server. Conversely, all data that needed to be restored had to be accessed through the back-up server as well. This meant that the overall performance of a back-up or recovery was directly related to the ability of the back-up server to handle the I/O load created by the back-up process.

In the past, the only way to overcome a back-up server bottleneck was to invest in larger, more powerful back-up servers, or data back-up and recovery, and divide the back-up network into smaller, independent groups. Fortunately, back-up-software developers have created methods to work around these bottlenecks. The most common workaround is to create *tape* servers that allow administrators to divide the back-up tasks across multiple systems, while maintaining scheduling and administrative processes on a primary or *back-up* server. This approach often involves attaching multiple tape servers to a shared tape library, which reduces the overall cost of the system. Figure 4.1 is an example of a back-up configuration such as this.[iv] The newest back-up architecture implements a serverless back-up solution that allows data to be moved directly from disk to tape, bypassing the back-up server all together. This method of data back-up removes the bottleneck of the back-up server completely. However, the performance of serverless back-up is then affected by another potential bottleneck—bandwidth. Figure 4.2 is an example of a serverless back-up.[v]

THE NETWORK DATA PATH

Centralization of a data-management process such as back-up and recovery requires a robust and available network data path. The movement and management of hundreds or thousands of megabytes of data can put a strain on even the best-designed networks. Unfortunately, many companies are already struggling with simply managing the existing data traffic created by applications such as e-commerce, the Internet, e-mail, and multimedia document management. Although technology such as gigabit Ethernet and ATM can provide relief, it is rarely enough to accommodate management of large amounts of data movement.

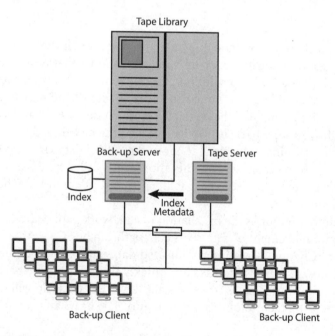

FIGURE 4.1 A back-up using a shared tape library. (*©Copyright 2002, StorNet. All rights reserved*).

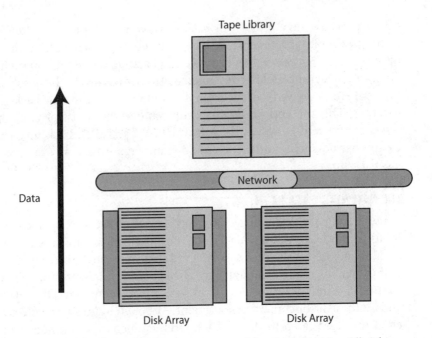

FIGURE 4.2 A serverless back-up system. *(©Copyright 2002, StorNet. All rights reserved).*

So, if there is not enough bandwidth to move all the data, what are the options? Again, it was the back-up-software vendors that developed a remedy. An enterprise-class back-up solution can distribute back-up services directly to the data source, while at the same time centralizing the administration of these resources. For example, if there is a 600GB database server that needs to be backed-up nightly, a tape back-up device can be attached directly to that server. This effectively eliminates the need to move the 600GB database across the network to a centralized back-up server. This approach is called a LAN-less back-up, and it relies on a remote tape server capability. Figure 4.3 demonstrates how this approach is configured.[vi]

Another option is the installation of a network path dedicated to the management and movement of data. This data path can be SCSI, Ethernet, ATM, FDDI, or Fibre Channel. Creating a dedicated data path is the beginning of a Storage Area Network (SAN).[vii] SANs are quickly dominating the back-up landscape, and applications such as serverless and LAN-less back-up will continue to push this emerging technology forward. Figure 4.4 shows an example of a dedicated SAN topology.[viii]

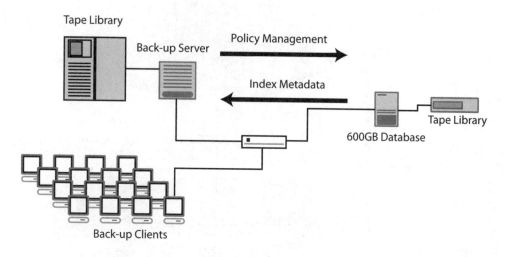

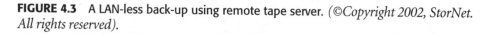

FIGURE 4.3 A LAN-less back-up using remote tape server. (*©Copyright 2002, StorNet. All rights reserved*).

THE BACK-UP WINDOW

Of all the parameters that drive the design of a back-up application, one remains an absolute constant, and that is time. A back-up window defines how much time is available to back-up the network. Time plays an important role in choosing how much server, network, and resource support needs to be deployed. Today, most companies are currently managing too much data to complete back-ups during these ever-shrinking back-up windows.

In the past, companies pressured by inadequate back-up windows were forced to add additional back-up servers to the mix, and divide the back-up groups into smaller and smaller clusters of systems. However, the back-up–software community has once again developed a way to overcome the element of time by using incremental back-ups, block-level back-ups, image back-ups, and data archiving.

Incremental Back-up

Incremental back-ups only transfer data that has changed since the last back-up. On average, no more than 5% of data in a file server changes daily. That means an incremental back-up may only require 5% of the time it takes to back-up the entire filesystem. Even then, a full back-up had to be made regularly, or restoration of the data would take too long. Fortunately, there are now back-up applications that

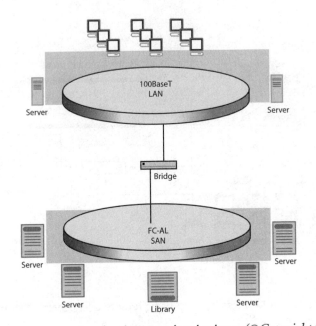

combine incremental back-ups together, thereby creating a *virtual* complete back-up every night without actually necessitating a full back-up during the limited back-up window.

Block-Level Incremental Back-up

Block-level incremental back-ups provide similar benefits as incremental back-ups, but with even more efficiency. Rather than backing-up entire files that have been modified since the last back-up, only the blocks that have changed since the last back-up are marked for back-up. This approach can reduce the amount of incremental data requiring back-up nightly by orders of magnitude.

However this benefit comes at a price. Often the filesystem of the client must be from the same vendor as the back-up software. Also, there are databases such as Oracle that allow block-level back-ups to be done, but the CPU requirements to do so may render the approach ineffective. Nevertheless, block-level back-ups may be the only viable option for meeting your back-up window.

Image Back-ups

Image back-ups are quickly gaining favor among storage administrators. This type of back-up creates copies or *snapshots* of a filesystem at a particular point in time. Image back-ups are much faster than incremental back-ups and provide the ability to easily perform a *bare bones* recovery of a server without loading the operating systems, applications, and the like. Image back-ups also provide specific point-in-time back-ups that can be done every hour rather than once a day.

Data Archiving

Removing infrequently accessed data from a disk drive can reduce the size of a scheduled back-up by up to 80%. By moving static, infrequently accessed data to tape, back-up applications are able to focus on backing-up and recovering only the most current and critical data. Static data that has been archived is easily recalled when needed, but does not add to the daily data back-up requirements of the enterprise. This method also provides the additional benefit of freeing up existing disk space without adding required additional capacity.

BACK-UP STORAGE DEVICES

In many cases, the single most expensive item in a back-up project is the back-up storage device itself. Therefore, it is important that the technical specifications of the storage device provide adequate capacity and performance to accommodate existing and planned data. Determining the tape format, number of tape drives, and how many slots are required is predicated on many variables. Back-up windows, growth rates, retention polices, duplicate tape copies, and network and server throughputs all affect which back-up storage device is best for your needs. Table 4.1 compares several different tape technologies.

TABLE 4.1 Comparison of various tape technologies.

Tape	Drive Capacity*	Data Transfer Rate*
4mm DDS-3 DAT	12 GB	1.0 MB per second
8mm Exabyte Mammoth	20 GB	3.0 MB per second
Sony AIT	25 GB	3.0 MB per second
Quantum DLT 7000	35 GB	5.0 MB per second
Quantum DLT 8000	40 GB	6.0 MB per second
IBM 3590 Magstar	10 GB	9.0 MB per second
StorageTek 9840	20 GB	10.0 MB per second

* native capacity

Tape libraries are sized using two variables: the number of tape drives and the number of slots; manufacturers of tape libraries continue to improve each of these elements. Tape libraries today are available with 5 to 50,000 slots and can support anywhere from 1 to 256 tape drives. Additionally, there are tape libraries available that support multiple tape formats.

When designing a centralized data back-up, take particular care selecting the right back-up storage device. Make sure that it can easily scale as your data rates increase. Verify that the shelf life of the media meets your long-term storage needs. Calculate the required throughput to meet your back-up window and make sure you can support enough tape drives to meet this window.

RECOMMENDED BACK-UP FEATURES

Today's global economy means that applications such as e-mail, relational databases, e-commerce, and ERP systems must be accessible and on-line 24 hours a day. Therefore, these applications cannot be shut down to perform administrative tasks such as back-up. A back-up vendor should provide agents for the most common database and e-mail applications that allow these databases to be backed-up without shutting down applications.

Data Interleaving

To back-up multiple systems concurrently, the back-up application itself must be able to write data from multiple clients to tape in an interleaved manner. Otherwise, the clients must be backed-up sequentially, which takes much longer.

Remote Back-up

Many remote systems are exposed to unrecoverable data loss. Off-site locations are often not backed-up at all due to the cost of deploying hardware and software remotely, and the lack of administrative support in these remote locations. Laptop computers are especially vulnerable to data loss. A back-up application should have a method to back-up systems across a WAN or over dial-up connections.

Global Monitoring

Companies are deploying applications that can be managed and monitored from any location in the enterprise. Back-up applications also need to be able to be accessed and administered from multiple locations. A robust back-up application should be able to support reporting and administration of any back-up system, regardless of location. It should also interface easily with frameworks such as *Tivoli* and *Unicenter*.

Performance

An enterprise back-up application should be able to benchmark back-up data rates exceeding one terabyte per hour. These benchmarks show that back-up performance is limited to the hardware and network and not to the application itself.

Now, let's explore some of the issues in the role of back-up in data recovery and some of the technologies that are available today. Then, let's take a look at what is still missing in the race to address fast recovery of these exponentially growing data repositories.

THE ROLE OF BACK-UP IN DATA RECOVERY

There are many factors that affect back-up. For example:

- Storage costs are decreasing.
- Systems have to be on-line continuously.
- The role of bBack-up has changed.

Storage Costs Are Decreasing

The cost per MB of primary (on-line) storage has fallen dramatically over the last several years and continues to do so as disk drive technologies advance. This has a huge impact on back-up. As users become accustomed to having immediate access to more and more information on-line, the time required to restore data from secondary media is found to be unacceptable.

Systems Have to Be On-line Continuously

Seven/twenty-four (7 x 24) operations have become the norm in many of today's businesses. The amount of data that has to be kept on-line and available (operationally ready data), is very large and constantly increasing. Higher and higher levels of fault tolerance for the primary data repository are a growing requirement. Because systems must be continuously on-line, the dilemma becomes that you can no longer take files off-line long enough to perform back-up.

The Role of Back-up Has Changed

It's no longer just about restoring data. Operationally, ready or *mirrored* data does not guard against data corruption and user error. The role of back-up is now taking on the responsibility for recovering user errors and ensuring that *good* data has been saved and can quickly be restored.

CONVENTIONAL TAPE BACK-UP IN TODAY'S MARKET

Current solutions offered by storage vendors and by back-up vendors focus on network back-up solutions. To effectively accomplish back-up in today's environment, tape management software is generally bundled with several other components to provide a *total* back-up solution. A typical tape management system consists of a dedicated workstation with a front-end interfaced to the network, and the back-end controlling a repository of tape devices. The media server is running tape management software. It can administer back-up devices across an enterprise and can run continuous parallel back-ups and restores.

An alternative to tape back-up is to physically replicate or mirror all data and keep two copies on-line at all times. Because the cost of primary storage is falling, this as not as cost-prohibitive as it once was. The advantage is that the data does not have to be restored, so there are no issues with immediate data availability. There are, however, several drawbacks to all the back-up and data availability solutions on the market today.

ISSUES WITH TODAY'S BACK-UP

Network back-up creates network performance problems. Using the production network to carry back-up data, as well as for normal user data access can severely overburden today's busy network resources. Installing a separate network exclusively for back-ups can minimize this problem, but even dedicated back-up networks may become performance bottlenecks.

Off-line back-up affects data accessibility. Host processors must be quiescent during the back-up. Back-up is not host-independent, nor is it nondisruptive to normal data access. Therefore, the time that the host is off-line for data back-up must be minimized. This requires extremely high-speed, continuous parallel back-up of the raw image of the data. Even in doing this, you have only deferred the real problem, which is the time to restore the information. Restoration of data needs to occur at the file level, not the full raw image, so that the most critical information can be brought back into operation first.

Live back-ups allow data access during the back-up process, but affect performance. Many database vendors offer *live* back-up features. The downside to the live back-up is that it puts a tremendous burden on the host. Redirection lives on the host, and journaling has to occur on the host. This requires local storage, host CPU cycles, and host operating system dependencies to consider. Up to 50% of all host CPU cycles may be consumed during the back-up process, severely impacting performance.

Mirroring doesn't protect against user error and replication of *bad* data. Fully replicated on-line data sounds great, albeit at twice the cost per megabyte of a single copy of on-line data. But synchronizing, breaking, and resynchronizing mirrors is not a trivial process and influences data access speeds while these activities are occurring. Also, duplicating data after a user has deleted a critical file or making a mirrored copy of a file that has been corrupted by a host process doesn't help. Mirroring has its place in back-up/recovery, but cannot solve the problem by itself.

NEW ARCHITECTURES AND TECHNIQUES ARE REQUIRED

Back-up at extremely high speed, with host-processor independence of the underlying file structures supporting the data, is required. Recovery must be available at the file level. The time that systems are off-line for back-up must be eliminated.

Mirroring, or live data replication for *hot* recovery also has a role. For data that must be always available, highly fault-tolerant primary storage is not enough, nor is a time-consuming back-up/restore. Remote hot recovery sites are needed for immediate resumption of data access. Back-up of critical data is still required to ensure against data errors and user errors. Back-up and mirroring are complementary, not competing technologies.

To achieve effective back-up and recovery, the decoupling of data from its storage space is needed. Just as programs must be decoupled from the memory in which they're executed, the stored information itself must be made independent of the storage area it occupies.

It is necessary to develop techniques to journal modified pages, so that journaling can be invoked within the primary storage device, without host intervention. Two separate pipes for file access must be created: one pipe active and the other dynamic. The primary storage device must employ memory-mapping techniques that enable the tracking of all modified information. Two copies of each change must be kept, with a thread composed of all old data stored in the journaled file.

Part of the primary storage area must be set aside for data to be backed-up. This area must be as large as the largest back-up block (file, logical volume, etc.). The point-in-time *snapshot* of changed data will be used for back-up, while the file itself remains in normal operation without impacting user access to data. To minimize this reserve storage area for back-ups, the storage device must support the reuse of this area by dynamically remapping.

Mechanisms must be put in place to allow for the back-up of data to occur directly from the primary storage area to the back-up area without host intervention. Host CPU bottlenecks and network bottlenecks are then eliminated. The net result will be faster user response times during *live* back-up, normal network performance levels throughout the process, and no back-up downtime.

What about restore times? Fast, nonrandom restoration of critical data assumes that the user can select at the file level exactly which information comes back on-line first. Here again, the primary storage and its back-up software must offload that burden from the host(s) and take on the responsibility for understanding the underlying file structures of multiple heterogeneous hosts. The necessary indexing of file structures can be done in the background subsequent to a high-speed back-up. Then, at the time of restore, the indices are accessible to allow selection at the file level for the recovery of the information from the back-up device.

How achievable is this scenario? Many back-up tools are available today. What have been missing are architectures that can support journaling within the primary storage area, to enable direct, *live* back-ups with high-speed file-level restores. A few storage vendors, mostly in the mainframe arena, are providing some of these types of solutions. Now vendors such as Storage Computer, with *Virtual Storage Architecture*[tm], provide an underlying structure to enable these back-up features in open systems environments. Thanks to this kind of progress on the part of storage vendors and their back-up partners, techniques to address continuous operations and fast data recovery in today's 7 x 24 business environment are now becoming both more cost-effective and more widely available.

THE DATA-RECOVERY SOLUTION

Availability once meant that an application would be available during the week, from 9 to 5, regardless of whether customers needed anything. Batch processing took over the evenings and nights, and most people didn't care because they were at home asleep or out having fun.

But the world has changed! It's now common to offer extended service hours in which a customer can call for help with a bill, inquiry, or complaint. Even if a live human being isn't available to help, many enterprise applications are Web-enabled so that customers can access their accounts in the middle of the night while sitting at home in their pajamas.

Shrinking Expertise, Growing Complexity

Increased availability is good, except for one fact: Many systems programmers, DBAs, and other mainframe experts are maturing. It takes a lot of *care and feeding* to keep applications ready for work, and the people who have maintained these environments for so long have other things they want to do. Many are starting to shift their sights toward that retirement community in Florida that they've heard so much about. Most of the bright youngsters who are graduating from college this term haven't had much exposure to mainframe concepts in their course work, much less any meaningful grasp of the day-to-day requirements for keeping mainframe systems running.

The complex systems that have evolved over the past 30 years must be monitored, managed, controlled, and optimized. Batch windows are shrinking down to almost nothing. Back-ups often take place while an application is running.

Application changes take place on the fly, under the watchful eye of the change-control police.

If an outage occurs, the company stands to lose tens of thousands of dollars an hour. In today's gloomy economy, stockholders don't want to hear that their favorite investment is having system availability problems.

Failures

Certainly, hardware failures were once more common than they are today. Disk storage is more reliable than ever, but failures are still possible.

More likely to occur, though, is a simple mistake made by an application programmer, system programmer, or operations person. Logic errors in programs or applying the wrong update at the wrong time can result in a system crash or, worse, an undetected error in the database—undetected, that is, until minutes, hours, or days later when a customer calls, a reconciliation fails, or some other checking mechanism points out the integrity exposure.

Finally, disasters do sometimes strike, and most often they occur without warning. Flooding doesn't always occur when it's convenient; tornadoes never do. Hurricanes and earthquakes are big-ticket events that ruin everyone's day. When they strike your data center, wipe out your processing power, or even destroy your basement-level back-up power supply, you have a lot of recovering to do.

Budgets and Downtime

Does anyone need a reminder that budgets are tight? You have fewer resources (people, processing power, time, and money) to do more work than ever before, and you must keep your expenses under control. Shrinking expertise and growing complexity cry out for tools to make systems management more manageable, but the tools that can save resources (by making the most of the ones you have) also cost you resources to obtain, implement, and operate.

Businesses today simply cannot tolerate availability problems, no matter what the source of the problem. Systems must remain available to make money and serve customers. Downtime is much too expensive to be tolerated. You must balance your data-management budget against the cost of downtime.

Recovery: Think Before You Back-Up

One of the most critical data-management tasks involves recovering data in the event of a problem. For this reason, installations around the world spend many hours each week preparing their environments for the possibility of having to recover. These preparations include backing-up data, accumulating changes, and keeping track of all the needed resources. You must evaluate your preparations, make sure that all resources are available in usable condition, automate processes as much as possible, and make sure you have the right kind of resources.

EVALUATE YOUR PREPARATIONS

Often the procedures that organizations use to prepare for recovery were designed many years ago. They may or may not have had *care and feeding* through the years to ensure that preparations are still sufficient to allow for recovery in the manner required today.

Here is a simple example: Say that an organization has always taken weekly image copies on the weekend and has performed change accumulations at midweek. Will this approach continue to satisfy their recovery requirements? Perhaps. If all of the resources (image copies, change accumulations, and logs) are available at recovery time, these preparations certainly allow for a standard recovery. However, if hundreds of logs must be applied, the time required for the recovery may be many hours—often unacceptable when the cost of downtime is taken into account.

This example illustrates the principle that, although your recovery strategy was certainly adequate when it was designed, it may be dangerously obsolete given today's requirements for increased availability. And what if a required resource is damaged or missing? How will you find out? When will you find out? Finding out at recovery time that some critical resource is missing can be disastrous!

DON'T LET YOUR RESOURCES FALL THROUGH THE CRACKS

The previous example was unrealistically simplistic. Many organizations use combinations of batch and on-line image copies of various groups of databases, as well as change accumulations, all staggered throughout the week. In a complex environment, how do you check to make sure that every database is being backed-up? How do you find out whether you are taking image copies (either batch or on-line) as frequently as you planned? How do you determine whether your change accumulations are taken as often as you wanted? What if media errors occur? Identifying these types of conditions is critical to ensuring a successful recovery.

AUTOMATED RECOVERY

Having people with the required expertise available to perform recoveries is a major consideration, particularly in disaster situations. For example, if the only person who understands your IBM Information Management System (IMS) systems (hierarchical database system) and can recover them moved far away, you're in trouble. However, if your recovery processes are planned and automated so that less-experienced personnel can aid in or manage the recovery process, then you're able to maximize all your resources and reduce the risk to your business.

Automation takes some of the human error factor and "think time" out of the recovery equation, and makes the complexity of the environment less of a concern. Creating an automated and easy-to-use system requires the right tools and some planning for the inevitable; but, compared to the possible loss of the entire business, it is worth the investment. With proper planning and automation, recovery is made possible, reliance on specific personnel is reduced, and the human-error factor is nearly eliminated.

Creating the recovery Job Control Language (JCL) for your IMS systems is not as simple as modifying existing JCL to change the appropriate names. In the event of a disaster, the IMS Recovery Control (RECON), data sets must be modified in preparation for the recovery. RECON back-ups are usually taken while IMS is up, which leaves the RECONs in need of many clean-up activities before they can be used to perform a recovery: deleting OLDS, closing LOGS, deleting SUBSYS records, and so on. This process often takes hours to perform manually, with the system down, equating to lost money. Planning for RECON clean-up is an important but often-overlooked step of the preparation process; discovering a deficiency in this area at disaster-recovery time is too late.

MAKE RECOVERIES EFFICIENT

Planning for efficient recoveries is also critical. Multithreading tasks shorten the recovery process. Recovering multiple databases with one pass through your log data certainly will save time. Taking image copies, rebuilding indexes, and validating pointers concurrently with the recovery process further reduce downtime. Where downtime is costly, time saved is money in the bank. Any measures you can take to perform recovery and related tasks more quickly and efficiently allow your business to resume faster and save money.

TAKE BACK-UPS

So after you've thought about and planned for your recoveries, it's time to think about executing your plan. Clearly the first step to a successful recovery is the back-up of your data.

Your goal in backing-up data is to do so quickly, efficiently, and usually with minimal impact to your customers. If you have a large window where systems aren't available, standard image copies are your best option. These clean copies are good recovery points and are easy to manage. If, however, you need to take back-ups while systems are active, you may need some help. You can take advantage of recent technological changes in various ways. You might need only very brief outages to take instant copies of your data, or you might have intelligent storage devices that allow you to take a snapshot of your data. Both methods call for tools to assist in the management of resources.

Back-up and Recovery Solution

If all of these challenges and preparations sound like a lot to keep up with, you're right. A lot of things can go wrong, and many of them can lead to major difficulties if you ever need to recover your data. Fortunately (and not surprisingly), for example, BMC Software has a solution to help with it all: the Back-up and Recovery Solution (BRS) for the IMS product.

IMAGE COPY

To assist you with your back-up needs, BRS contains an *Image Copy* component to help manage your image copy process. Image copies can be taken in a variety of ways, including methods that allow you to take the copy without taking the database off-line. Whether you elect to take batch, on-line (*fuzzy*), or incremental image copies; Snapshot copies; or Instant Snapshot copies, BRS can do it all. The *Image Copy* component of BRS is faster and easier to use than the IMS *Database Image Copy* utility and offers a variety of powerful features: dynamic allocation of all input and output data sets, stacking of output data sets, high-performance access methods (faster I/O), copying by volume, compression of output image copies, and database group processing—all while interfacing with DBRC and processing asynchronously. These features and more are available to help manage your image copy process more efficiently.

CHANGE ACCUMULATION

BRS also incorporates a *Change Accumulation* component, which replaces the functions of the IMS *Database Change Accumulation* utility. The BRS *Change Accumulation* component takes advantage of the multiple engines, large virtual storage resources, and high-speed channels and controllers that are available in many environments. Use of multiple task control block (TCB) structures enables overlapping of as much processing as possible, reducing both elapsed and CPU time. Use of state-of-the-art techniques reduces sort overhead and I/O, all while providing full DBRC support. Dynamic allocation makes it easy to use.

RECOVERY

The tools required both to perform the actual recoveries and to automate the recovery process are also included in BRS. The BRS *Recovery* component, which functionally replaces the IMS *Database Recovery* utility for full-function (DL/I) databases and data-entry databases (DEDBs), allows recovery of multiple databases with one pass of the log and change accumulation data sets while dynamically allocating all data sets required for recovery. And it is faster and easier to use than the native IMS utility. Multiple log readers can be used to maximize resource utilization and minimize elapsed recovery time. BRS also recovers multiple databases to any point in time, not just to times when the database is deallocated, eliminating the need for scheduled log switches and saving on the overall number of tapes that you must create, process, and manage. BRS can even determine the best choice for a Point-In-Time (PIT) recovery. Creating image copies concurrently with the database-recovery process, as well as concurrently checking database pointers, saves an additional job step and the time associated with it. You can use DBRC-registered secondary image copies and logs as input. Full DBRC support is included, of course.

Recovery Manager

The *Recovery Manager* component of BRS further automates a number of key functions that are associated with recovery. In a problem scenario, the time required to perform the recovery is a major issue and cost. By minimizing this recovery time, business can resume sooner. Because downtime is expensive, minimizing downtime lessens the financial impact of a problem. By creating meaningful groups of related databases and creating optimized JCL to perform the recovery of these groups, the *Recovery Manager* component lets you automate and synchronize recoveries across applications and databases.

Automatically issuing IMS commands and monitoring their results is also easier with the IMS Command utility of the *Recovery Manager* component, which provides a positive response for the IMS commands that are used to deallocate and start your databases. This utility is especially helpful in coordinating recoveries in a data-sharing environment.

The *Recovery Manager* component fully automates the process of cleaning the RECON data sets for restart following a disaster recovery. It captures allocation information about your IMS database data sets and builds IDCAMS delete/define control statements. The *Recovery Manager* component also allows you to test your recovery strategy. You can ensure that all assets that are necessary for a recovery exist, analyze logs, practice recoveries by creating sample recovery JCL, and create alternate databases for testing purposes. The *Recovery Manager* component also notifies you when media errors have jeopardized your recovery resources. All of these functions help you predict the impact that your recovery strategy may have on your databases, applications, users, and, ultimately, your business.

Pointer Checking

As part of your image copy or recovery process, wouldn't you like to verify the validity of database pointers as you go? For example, BRS offers this capability through the *Concurrent Pointer Checking* function for both full-function databases and Fast Path data-entry databases (DEDBs). By using the same I/O operation to read the database records, you'll save elapsed time and I/O. Reduced recovery time helps save resources, including money.

Index Rebuild

Rather than having to maintain image copies of your primary and secondary indexes, using the *Index Rebuild* function of BRS is another way you can save time and effort. If indexes are ever damaged or lost, this function allows you rebuild them rather than recover them.

Recovery Advisor

Last but not least, BRS contains the *Recovery Advisor* component that you can use to keep an eye on your recovery resources. The *Recovery Advisor* component allows you to monitor the frequency of your image copies and change accumulations. It helps you determine whether all of your databases are being backed-up. Finding out about a problem with your recovery resources, at the time you need to use those resources to solve a critical problem, is not a good thing; by then, it's too late. By identifying potential problems early, you can take steps to correct the situation before you need to recover. The tool can even take corrective action for you, if you like.

Finally, today's environment is complex and intolerant of unavailability. Many experts are leaving the field. It's becoming more difficult to manage this environment. Don't let your availability woes make the news. Plan for the worst, hope for the best, and make sure you can keep your business up and running. By using any number of back-up and recovery tools available, you can better manage your world and be ready to recover!

Finally, let's look at some disk and tape data-recovery case studies.

CASE HISTORIES

If there is any data, anywhere on your disk or tape, it can be recovered. Let's take a look at some of the more interesting disk-recovery case studies.

A Dog's Dinner

Late one afternoon, a phone call was received from a distraught customer who required data recovery from a couple of diskettes. The data was related to an important presentation. The customer was asked the nature of the problem and eventually confessed that the diskettes had suffered some *physical damage*. The problem involved one of his four-legged canine friends who had chewed the diskettes!

The damage to the disk cases was severe, with large tooth marks evident on the surface of the disks. Eventually both disks were imaged with only 15% sector damage and the File Allocation Tables (FATs) were rebuilt. All the files were successfully recovered and restored to the grateful customer.

Credit Card Monster

The customer was a well-known credit card company whose last few hours' transactions, for which there was no back-up, were stored on the failed system. It was a NetWare Server and RAID array in one large, very heavy metal box, containing 18 x 2.5GB wide SCSI drives and weighing nearly 200Kg.

There were three failed drives amongst the remaining batch of eight drives. One of the drives had suffered component failure on its electronics assembly, the other two had serious head/disk assembly (HDA) problems that needed work in a clean-room. Using a database of drive components and technical knowledge, the system administrator worked to correct the faults on the drives so he could take images.

When he finally finished, all 18 drives had been imaged with a total sector loss of just seven bad sectors. The total good sectors imaged that night was just under 88 million! The customer's valuable data was safe.

Flying Low

Having flown numerous times on business without a problem, one customer was surprised to find that his Toshiba laptop wouldn't boot. On contact with the system administrator, he finally mentioned that it had traveled in the cargo hold of a plane. The system administrator had a nagging suspicion that it had probably not only been thrown around by the baggage handlers, but also bounced its way down the carousel!

Luckily for him, it had not been swipe-damaged by any x-ray equipment at the airport. Hardware specialists opened the head disk assembly and found there was some speckle damage, confirming that it had been bounced around as the heads had dented the actual platters. Following a successful headstack swap, the drive was imaged and the system administrator found 112 bad sectors, of which he was finally able to read only 86 of them. The customer vowed always to take his laptop as hand luggage from then on.

Accounts Critical!

It was Easter Saturday and the system administrator had a critical tape data loss which another data-recovery company had failed to rectify. Within about four hours of receiving the first tape, the system administrator had several hundred megabytes of data from it. The tape was poorly recorded and had many areas where the recording had broken up.

The customer had a set of around 35 tapes in this condition, which the system administrator also needed to look at. By 6 A.M. on Sunday, the system administrator was recovering data from seven DAT tapes and had extracted images of each of the disks in the RAID.

A few hours later, most of the physical data had been recovered. The areas of missing data were being reprocessed to attempt to extract additional data from the tapes. However, the data of major importance was from the accounts system. About 48 hours later, the system administrator was still working on reading data from the damaged areas of the tapes. By the end of the following week, all the data had been successfully recovered—no mean feat considering the huge amount of data involved.

Sinking Ship

A seismic survey ship far away in a distant sea sent a system administrator an IBM 3590 tape. It contained the results of a number of geological surveys as part of a search for oil, but also contained a media flaw right at the start. If the data could not be recovered, they would have to send the ship back out to sea to repeat the tests–a rather costly operation!

At the time, the IBM 3590 drive was one of the fastest tape drives around. The 40kg monster is capable of storing 10GB of uncompressed data on a single cartridge and transferring that data at up to 9MB per second. At the heart of this mechanism is a read–writehead that records 16 data tracks at a time.

Gaining control of these various systems, finding the undamaged data on the tape, and then persuading the drive to read it was complex. However, after much perseverance, all the important data was safely on one of the systems, and the system administrator could call for a courier to take the data back to Singapore.

All Flooded Out

A business continuity firm had a customer with a big problem. A firm of automotive engineers had archived their important drawings and documents in a locked fireproof safe in their basement. Sadly, a flood had filled the basement with water and fine silt, and the engineers found that their archives and back-ups were soaked through and the media was coated inside and out with a thin layer of sediment.

In total, over 40 tape and optical cartridges of various different formats had been affected, and some of the tapes had started to dry while still in the safe. Each tape was extracted from its cartridge and installed in a special cleaning rig that removed any sediment. Once clean, the tape was then placed in a brand new cartridge assembly so that the data could be read. After a few hours, the system administrator was able to return the recovered files and folders on a total of 26 CD-ROMs; and, the engineers were grateful for the return of their archives.

A Concluding Case Study Example

As an almost real-life example, XYZ Corporation is an IMS shop with headquarters in Houston, Texas. Tropical Storm Allison visits the Texas Gulf coast and dumps three feet of rain on the city. XYZ, with its state-of-the-art data center located in the heart of the city, takes on a basement full of water. Their UPS system, network switches, and a portion of their direct access storage devices (DASD) are wiped out.

PREPARATIONS

Being good corporate citizens and experienced users of BRS, XYZ is in great condition to recover. They take weekly image copies, creating dual copies concurrently so that the second copy can be sent off-site. They run nightly change accumulations to consolidate their updates and send secondary CAs off-site each morning at 6 a.m.. Copies of logs are dispatched to off-site storage at 6 P.M. *Recovery Advisor* jobs are scheduled to make sure that image copies and change accumulations are performed at the specified intervals. They run the *Check Assets* function regularly to ensure that required assets are cataloged. Regular disaster-recovery drills let them practice, so their people know what to do.

PROOF

When disaster strikes, XYZ springs into action and the validity of their preparations is proved. They call their local disaster-recovery (DR) service provider, arrange for shipment of their tapes, and rush to the hot site. They IPL their system and bring up the *Recovery Manager* interface. They use the RECON cleanup utility to prepare the IMS RECONs for restart. They build the appropriate groups for their lost databases, and build appropriate recovery JCL. The recovery utility runs, calling in the appropriate image copy, change accumulation, and log data. Their data is restored without errors, their business resumes quickly, and everyone lives happily ever after, all with minimal expense and elapsed time.

SUMMARY

With ever-larger information sets being kept on-line, how quickly can data be restored and brought back into production? It is in addressing this requirement that the demand has arisen for new and more sophisticated data management and data-recovery techniques.

Back-up has never really been the problem. There have been a variety of back-up tools (both hardware and software) available for a number of years. Although data back-ups would seem to offer an effective shield against these threats, back-ups do not always provide comprehensive data protection. That is because the data back-up plans developed by many companies are not fully realized or, worse yet, not followed. What is more, individuals often fail to test the restore capabilities of their back-up media. If the back-ups are faulty, a simple data loss can quickly become a data disaster. Finally, even if back-ups are successful, they only contain data collected during the most recent back-up session. As a result, a data loss can potentially rob you of your most current data, despite your back-up attempts.

Conclusions Drawn from Data Recovery

- Data back-up and recovery has become the "killer application" of storage area networking.
- The ability to move data directly from disk to tape at 100 MB/second will offer performance levels that are unprecedented by today's standards.
- SAN-based back-up offers benefits such as higher availability, increased flexibility, improved reliability, lower cost, manageability, improved performance, and increased scalability.
- IT professionals face a number of challenges in today's marketplace. Whether your business is retail, health care, banking, manufacturing, public utility, government agency, or almost any other endeavor, one thing is common: your users expect more and more from your systems.
- Computer systems have grown to manage much of the business world. How does this growth affect your daily management of the data? What challenges do you face? If a problem occurs, how do you get your applications back to normal in the most efficient manner possible?
- Some files (especially on Linux systems) can and should be recovered with very little effort or time. And while it can take a great deal of time to actually recover something, wizardly skill is not really required.
- Ultimately, however, your odds at getting anything useful from the grave (dead storage) is often a question of personal diligence—how much is it worth to you? If it's important enough, it's quite possibly there.
- The persistence of data, however, is remarkable. Contrary to the popular belief that it's hard to recover information, it's actually starting to appear that it's very hard to remove something even if you want to.
- Indeed, when testing forensic software on a disk that had been used for some time on a *Windows 95, 98, 2000,* or *XP* machine, then reinstalled to be a firewall using Solaris, and finally converted to be a Linux system, files and data from the prior two installations are clearly visible. Now that's data persistence!
- Forensic data is everywhere on computers. You need to continue the examination, for you have simply scratched the surface.

An Agenda for Action in Data Recovery

The following is a provisional list of actions for data recovery. The order is not significant; however, these are the activities for which the research would want to provide a detailed description of procedures, review, and assessment for ease of use and admissibility. A number of these data-recovery topics have been mentioned in passing already:

1. Disasters really do happen! Floods, tornadoes, earthquakes, and even terrorism can and do strike. You must be ready.
2. To be ready, you must have a plan in place. Taking periodic image copies and sending them off-site is the first step.
3. Performing change accumulations reduces the number of logs required as input to the recovery, which saves time at the recovery site. However, performing this step consumes resources at the home site.
4. You should evaluate your environment to decide how to handle the change accumulation question.
5. Even with a plan, you need to check to make sure you can implement it.
6. Checking your assets to make sure they're ready should be part of your plan.
7. Building recovery JCL is tricky, and you need to get it exactly right. Data integrity and your business rely on this task.
8. Cleaning your RECON data sets can take hours if done manually, and it's an error-prone process. When your system is down, can you afford to make mistakes with this key resource?
9. Test your plan. Even with this simplistic example, there's a lot to think about. In the real world, there's much more. Make sure your plan works before you are required to use it!
10. You must deal with issues of increased availability, shrinking expertise, and growing complexity, failures of many types, and the costs of data management and downtime.

ENDNOTES

i Derek Gamradt, "Data Backup + Recovery," StorNet, Corporate Headquarters, 7074 South Revere Parkway, Englewood, CO 80112, 2001. (*©Copyright 2002, StorNet. All rights reserved*), 2001.

ii John R. Vacca, *Electronic Commerce: Online Ordering and Digital Money*, 3/E, Charles River Media, 2001.

iii StorNet, Corporate Headquarters, 7074 South Revere Parkway, Englewood, CO 80112, 2001. (*©Copyright 2002, StorNet. All rights reserved*), 2001.

iv Ibid.

v Ibid.

vi Ibid.

vii John R. Vacca, *The Essential Guide to Storage Area Networks*, Prentice Hall, 2002.

viii StorNet, Corporate Headquarters, 7074 South Revere Parkway, Englewood, CO 80112, 2001. (*©Copyright 2002, StorNet. All rights reserved*), 2001.

5 Evidence Collection and Data Seizure

Evidence is difficult to collect at the best of times, but when that evidence is electronic an investigator faces some extra complexities. Electronic evidence has none of the permanence that conventional evidence has, and it is even more difficult to form into a coherent argument. The purpose of this chapter is to point out these difficulties and what must be done to overcome them. Not everything is covered here—it should be used as a guide only, and you should seek further information for your specific circumstances.

No legal advice is given here—different regions have different legislation. If in doubt, always ask your lawyer—that's what they're there for.

WHY COLLECT EVIDENCE?

Electronic evidence can be very expensive to collect—the processes are strict and exhaustive, the systems affected may be unavailable for regular use for a long period of time, and analysis of the data collected must be performed. So, why bother collecting the evidence in the first place? There are two simple reasons—future prevention and responsibility.

Future Prevention

Without knowing what happened, you have no hope of ever being able to stop someone else (or even the original attacker) from doing it again. It would be analogous to not fixing the lock on your door after someone broke in. Even though the cost of collection can be high, the cost of repeatedly recovering from compromises is much higher, both in monetary and corporate image terms.

Responsibility

There are two responsible parties after an attack—the attacker, and the victim. The attacker is responsible for the damage done, and the only way to bring them to justice (and to seek recompense) is with adequate evidence to prove their actions.

The victim, on the other hand, has a responsibility to the community. Information gathered after a compromise can be examined and used by others to prevent further attacks. They may also have a legal obligation to perform an analysis of evidence collected, for instance if the attack on their system was part of a larger attack.

COLLECTION OPTIONS

Once a compromise has been detected, you have two options—pull the system off the network and begin collecting evidence or leave it on-line and attempt to monitor the intruder. Both have their pros and cons. In the case of monitoring, you may accidentally alert the intruder while monitoring and cause them to wipe their tracks any way necessary, destroying evidence as they go. You also leave yourself open to possible liability issues if the attacker launches further attacks at other systems from your own network system. If you disconnect the system from the network, you may find that you have insufficient evidence or, worse, that the attacker left a *dead man switch* that destroys any evidence once the system detects that it's off-line. What you choose to do should be based on the situation. The "Collection and Archiving" section later in the chapter contains information on what to do for either case.

OBSTACLES

Electronic crime is difficult to investigate and prosecute—investigators have to build their case purely on any records left after the transactions have been completed. Add to this the fact that electronic records are extremely (and sometimes transparently) malleable, and that electronic transactions currently have fewer limitations than their paper-based counterparts—and, you get a collection nightmare.

Computer transactions are fast, they can be conducted from anywhere (through anywhere, to anywhere), can be encrypted or anonymous, and have no intrinsic identifying features such as handwriting and signatures to identify those responsible. Any *paper trail* of computer records they may leave can be easily modified or destroyed, or may be only temporary. Worse still, auditing programs may automatically destroy the records left when computer transactions are finished with them.

Because of this, even if the details of the transactions can be restored through analysis, it is very difficult to tie the transaction to a person. *Identifying* information such as passwords or PIN numbers (or any other electronic identifier), does not prove who was responsible for the transaction—such information merely shows that whoever did it either knew or could get past those identifiers.

Even though technology is constantly evolving, investigating electronic crimes will always be more difficult due to the ease of alteration of the data and the fact that transactions may be done anonymously. The best you can do is to follow the rules of evidence collection and be as assiduous as possible.

TYPES OF EVIDENCE

Before you start collecting evidence, it is important to know the different types of evidence categories. Without taking these into consideration, you may find that the evidence you've spent several weeks and quite a bit of money collecting is useless.

Real Evidence

Real evidence is any evidence that speaks for itself without relying on anything else. In electronic terms, this can be a log produced by an audit function—provided that the log can be shown to be free from contamination.

Testimonial Evidence

Testimonial evidence is any evidence supplied by a witness. This type of evidence is subject to the perceived reliability of the witness, but as long as the witness can be considered reliable, testimonial evidence can be almost as powerful as real evidence. Word processor documents written by a witness may be considered testimonial—as long as the author is willing to state that they wrote it.

Hearsay

Hearsay is any evidence presented by a person who was not a direct witness. Word processor documents written by someone without direct knowledge of the incident is hearsay. Hearsay is generally inadmissible in court and should be avoided.

THE RULES OF EVIDENCE

There are five rules of collecting electronic evidence. These relate to five properties that evidence must have to be useful.

1. Admissible
2. Authentic
3. Complete
4. Reliable
5. Believable

Admissible

Admissible is the most basic rule (the evidence must be able to be used) in court or otherwise. Failure to comply with this rule is equivalent to not collecting the evidence in the first place, except the cost is higher.

Authentic

If you can't tie the evidence positively with the incident, you can't use it to prove anything. You must be able to show that the evidence relates to the incident in a relevant way.

Complete

It's not enough to collect evidence that just shows one perspective of the incident. Not only should you collect evidence that can prove the attacker's actions, but also evidence that could prove their innocence. For instance, if you can show the attacker was logged in at the time of the incident, you also need to show who else was logged in, and why you think they didn't do it. This is called *exculpatory evidence*, and is an important part of proving a case.

Reliable

The evidence you collect must be reliable. Your evidence collection and analysis procedures must not cast doubt on the evidences authenticity and veracity.

Believable

The evidence you present should be clearly understandable and believable by a jury. There's no point presenting a binary dump of process memory if the jury has no idea what it all means. Similarly, if you present them with a formatted, human-understandable version, you must be able to show the relationship to the original binary, otherwise there's no way for the jury to know whether you've faked it.

Using the preceding five rules, you can derive some basic do's and don'ts:

- Minimize handling/corruption of original data
- Account for any changes and keep detailed logs of your actions
- Comply with the five rules of evidence
- Do not exceed your knowledge
- Follow your local security policy
- Capture as accurate an image of the system as possible
- Be prepared to testify
- Ensure your actions are repeatable
- Work fast
- Proceed from volatile to persistent evidence
- Don't shutdown before collecting evidence
- Don't run any programs on the affected system

Minimize Handling/Corruption of Original Data

Once you've created a master copy of the original data, don't touch it or the original itself—always handle secondary copies. Any changes made to the originals will affect the outcomes of any analysis later done to copies. You should make sure you don't run any programs that modify the access times of all files (such as tar and xcopy). You should also remove any external avenues for change and, in general, analyze the evidence after it has been collected.

Account for Any Changes and Keep Detailed Logs of Your Actions

Sometimes evidence alteration is unavoidable. In these cases, it is absolutely essential that the nature, extent, and reasons for the changes be documented. Any changes at all should be accounted for—not only data alteration but also physical alteration of the originals (i.e., the removal of hardware components).

Comply with the Five Rules of Evidence

The five rules are there for a reason. If you don't follow them, you are probably wasting your time and money. Following these rules is essential to guaranteeing successful evidence collection.

Do Not Exceed Your Knowledge

If you don't understand what you are doing, you can't account for any changes you make and you can't describe what exactly you did. If you ever find yourself "out of your depth," either go and learn more before continuing (if time is available) or find someone who knows the territory. Never soldier on regardless—you're just damaging your case.

Follow Your Local Security Policy

If you fail to comply with your company's security policy, you may find yourself with some difficulties. Not only may you end up in trouble (and possibly fired if you've done something really against policy), but also you may not be able to use the evidence you've gathered. If in doubt, talk to those who know.

Capture as Accurate an Image of the System as Possible

Capturing an accurate image of the system is related to minimizing the handling or corruption of original data—differences between the original system and the master copy count as a change to the data. You must be able to account for the differences.

Be Prepared to Testify

If you're not willing to testify to the evidence you have collected, you might as well stop before you start. Without the collector of the evidence being there to validate the documents created during the evidence-collection process, the evidence becomes hearsay, which is inadmissible. Remember that you may need to testify at a later time.

Ensure That Your Actions Are Repeatable

No one is going to believe you if they can't replicate your actions and reach the same results. This also means that your plan of action shouldn't be based on trial-and-error.

Work Fast

The faster you work, the less likely the data is going to change. Volatile evidence may vanish entirely if you don't collect it in time. This is not to say that you should rush—you must still be collecting accurate data. If multiple systems are involved, work on them in parallel (a team of investigators would be handy here), but each single system should still be worked on methodically. Automation of certain tasks makes collection proceed even faster.

Proceed from Volatile to Persistent Evidence

Some electronic evidence (see below) is more volatile than others are. Because of this, you should always try to collect the most volatile evidence first.

Don't Shutdown before Collecting Evidence

You should never, ever shutdown a system before you collect the evidence. Not only do you lose any volatile evidence but also the attacker may have trojaned (trojan horse) the startup and shutdown scripts, Plug-and-Play devices may alter the system configuration and temporary file systems may be wiped out. Rebooting is even worse and should be avoided at all costs. As a general rule, until the compromised disk is finished with and restored, it should never be used as a boot disk.

Don't Run Any Programs on the Affected System

Because the attacker may have left trojaned programs and libraries on the system, you may inadvertently trigger something that could change or destroy the evidence you're looking for. Any programs you use should be on read-only media (such as a CD-ROM or a write-protected floppy disk), and should be statically linked.

VOLATILE EVIDENCE

Not all the evidence on a system is going to last very long. Some evidence is residing in storage that requires a consistent power supply; other evidence may be stored in information that is continuously changing.[i] When collecting evidence, you should always try to proceed from the most volatile to the least. Of course, you should still take the individual circumstances into account—you shouldn't waste time extracting information from an unimportant/unaffected machine's main memory when an important or affected machine's secondary memory hasn't been examined.

To determine what evidence to collect first, you should draw up an Order of Volatility—a list of evidence sources ordered by relative volatility. An example an Order of Volatility would be:

1. Registers and cache
2. Routing tables
3. Arp cache
4. Process table
5. Kernel statistics and modules

6. Main memory
7. Temporary file systems
8. Secondary memory
9. Router configuration
10. Network topology[ii]

Once you have collected the raw data from volatile sources you may be able to shutdown the system.

GENERAL PROCEDURE

When collecting and analyzing evidence, there is a general four-step procedure you should follow. Note that this is a very general outline—you should customize the details to suit your situation.

Identification of Evidence

You must be able to distinguish between evidence and junk data. For this purpose, you should know what the data is, where it is located, and how it is stored. Once this is done, you will be able to work out the best way to retrieve and store any evidence you find.

Preservation of Evidence

The evidence you find must be preserved as close as possible to its original state. Any changes made during this phase must be documented and justified.

Analysis of Evidence

The stored evidence must then be analyzed to extract the relevant information and recreate the chain of events. Analysis requires in-depth knowledge of what you are looking for and how to get it. Always be sure that the person or people who are analyzing the evidence are fully qualified to do so.

Presentation of Evidence

Communicating the meaning of your evidence is vitally important—otherwise you can't do anything with it. The manner of presentation is important, and it must be understandable by a layman to be effective. It should remain technically correct and credible. A good presenter can help in this respect.

COLLECTION AND ARCHIVING

Once you've developed a plan of attack and identified the evidence that needs to be collected, it's time to start the actual process of capturing the data. Storage of that data is also important as it can affect how the data is perceived.

Logs and Logging

You should be running some kind of system logging function. It is important to keep these logs secure and to back them up periodically. Because logs are usually automatically timestamped, a simple copy should suffice, although you should digitally sign and encrypt any logs that are important, to protect them from contamination. Remember, if the logs are kept locally on the compromised machine, they are susceptible to either alteration or deletion by an attacker. Having a remote syslog server and storing logs in a *sticky* directory can reduce this risk, although it is still possible for an attacker to add decoy or junk entries into the logs.

Regular auditing and accounting of your system is useful not only for detecting intruders but also as a form of evidence. Messages and logs from programs such as *Tripwire*™ can be used to show what damage an attacker did. Of course, you need a clean snapshot for these to work, so there's no use trying it after the compromise.

Monitoring

Monitoring network traffic can be useful for many reasons—you can gather statistics, watch out for irregular activity (and possibly stop an intrusion before it happens), and trace where an attacker is coming from and what they are doing. Monitoring logs as they are created can often show you important information you might have missed had you seen them separately. This doesn't mean you should ignore logs later—it may be what's missing from the logs that are suspicious.

Information gathered while monitoring network traffic can be compiled into statistics to define normal behavior for your system. These statistics can be used as an early warning of an attacker's actions.

You can also monitor the actions of your users. This can, once again, act as an early warning system—unusual activity or the sudden appearance of unknown users should be considered definite cause for closer inspection.

No matter the type of monitoring done, you should be very careful—there are plenty of laws you could inadvertently break. In general, you should limit your monitoring to traffic or user information and leave the content unmonitored unless the situation necessitates it. You should also display a disclaimer stating what monitoring is done when users log-on. The content of this should be worked out in conjunction with your lawyer.

METHODS OF COLLECTION

There are two basic forms of collection—*freezing the scene* and *honeypotting*. The two aren't mutually exclusive—you can collect *frozen* information after or during any honeypotting.

Freezing the scene involves taking a snapshot of the system in its compromised state. The necessary authorities should be notified (e.g., the police and your incident response and legal teams), but you shouldn't go out and tell the world just yet.

You should then start to collect whatever data is important onto removable nonvolatile media in a standard format. Make sure that the programs and utilities used to collect the data are also collected onto the same media as the data. All data collected should have a cryptographic message digest created, and those digests should be compared to the originals for verification.

Honeypotting is the process of creating a replica system and luring the attacker into it for further monitoring. A related method (sandboxing) involves limiting what the attacker can do while still on the compromised system, so they can be monitored without (much) further damage. The placement of misleading information and the attacker's response to it is a good method for determining the attacker's motives. You must make sure that any data on the system related to the attacker's detection and actions is either removed or encrypted; otherwise they can cover their tracks by destroying it. Honeypotting and sandboxing are extremely resource intensive, so they may be infeasible to perform. There are also some legal issues to contend with, most importantly entrapment. As previously mentioned— you should consult your lawyers.

ARTEFACTS

Whenever a system is compromised, there is almost always something left behind by the attacker—be it code fragments, trojaned programs, running processes, or sniffer log files. These are known as *artefacts*. They are one of the important things you should be collecting, but you must be careful. You should never attempt to analyze an artefact on the compromised system. Artefacts are capable of anything, and you want to make sure their effects are controlled.

Artefacts may be difficult to find—trojaned programs may be identical in all obvious ways to the originals (file size, MAC times, etc.). Use of cryptographic checksums may be necessary, so you may need to know the original file's checksum. If you are performing regular file integrity assessments, this shouldn't be a problem. Analysis of artefacts can be useful in finding other systems the attacker (or their tools) has broken into.

COLLECTION STEPS

You now have enough information to build a step-by-step guide for the collection of the evidence. Once again, this is only a guide—you should customize it to your specific situation. You should perform the following collection steps:

1. Find the evidence
2. Find the relevant data
3. Create an Order of Volatility
4. Remove external avenues of change
5. Collect the evidence
6. Document everything

Find the Evidence

Determine where the evidence you are looking for is stored. Use a checklist—not only does it help you to collect evidence but it also can be used to double-check that everything you are looking for is there.

Find the Relevant Data

Once you've found the evidence, you must figure out what part of it is relevant to the case. In general, you should err on the side of over-collection, but you must remember that you have to work fast—don't spend hours collecting information that is obviously useless.

Create an Order of Volatility

Now that you know exactly what to gather, work out the best order in which to gather it. The Order of Volatility for your system is a good guide, and ensures that you minimize loss of uncorrupted evidence.

Remove External Avenues of Change

It is essential that you avoid alterations to the original data, and prevention is always better than a cure. Preventing anyone from tampering with the evidence helps you

this point on; try not to get overwhelmed. Keep in mind that the degree of complexity in the search and seizure process can always be scaled back in accordance with an organization's investigation policies. (High-profile cases are given the full treatment; low-profile cases are given a less involved treatment.)

Searching and Seizing

The science of Computer Forensics is fast becoming a very necessary skill set for law enforcement departments, government entities, and corporations worldwide. As society becomes more digitized, the need for skilled personnel in this arena becomes more and more pressing. And as this shortage of skilled technicians becomes apparent, you will find more and more companies rushing in to fill the gap. You will see experts arise from all corners of the world. More on this later.

As it stands today, there is no one methodology for performing a computer forensic investigation and analysis. There are too many variables for there to be just one way. Some of the typical variables that first come to mind include operating systems; software applications; cryptographic algorithms and applications; and hardware platforms. But moving beyond these obvious variables spring other equally challenging variables: law, international boundaries, publicity, and methodology.

The intent of this part of the chapter is merely to put some ideas out there—to generate some interest, and, more important, stimulate thinking. As for evidence search seizure, some of these ideas already exist. However, the science of Computer Forensics is an exact science. It is tedious and meticulous. There is no room for error. However, does that not contradict what we, as humans, are. We error. We are not perfect. To sum up the intent here, it is hoped that you simply become more aware of the variables that are a part of computer forensics, and see that you must develop a methodology from which to work from. It is also very important for you to recognize that if you cannot be perfect and error free, then you must be exact in your methodology and make sure that you perform your investigations in check and to the standards you have developed. There are a few widely accepted guidelines for computer forensic analysis:

- A computer forensic examiner is impartial. Our job is to analyze the media and report our findings with no presumption of guilt or innocence.
- The media used in computer forensic examinations must be sterilized before each use.
- A true image (bit stream) of the original media must be made and used for the analysis.
- The integrity of the original media must be maintained throughout the entire investigation.

Before the Investigation

Long before the investigation begins, certain things need to be known. First, for sake of argument, let's say that you have skilled technicians in-house. They have acquired and analyzed a plethora of evidence during their tenure. Excellent. You are confident in their ability. Furthermore, you have a top notch lab—the right equipment, the right computer forensic analysis tools, and so on. You are set, right? Well, maybe.

All the equipment and talent will not help you if we are not in synchronization with your local District Attorney. *"Ah, we're sorry Capt. Solo, but this is not enough evidence for me to move this case forward and prosecute." Huh?* Well, perhaps your local DA requires such and such, and you only have such. Or, maybe the DA requires more documentation on the chain of evidence handling. You cannot go backwards and recreate the trail after you have already blazed it!

This may seem like a no-brainer. Maybe. But, you have asked around, and to your surprise, you have gotten this response more than a few times: *"Oh yeah, that is a good idea."* So, work with not only your local DA, but also your state DA. Network when you are not pushing a case to them. Learn what it is they require as a minimum, and tweak your methodology to meet this and go beyond. This way, when you have a case arise, you know what is required and can work the case from the inception in support of these requirements.

Methodology Development

Because there are so many variables in a Computer Forensics case, can anyone really develop the methodology from which to work from? Not really! However, there are two things that will lead to a solid analysis and case building: defining your methodology, and working according to this methodology. By definition, methodology implies a method, a set of rules: guidelines that are employed by a discipline.

The idea here is if you cannot defend how you work, nor why you work this way, the defending legal representation can drill you over and over again. Remember, the majority of jurors are not technical gurus. To sit there and explain to them that you have not defined the methodology your department uses is equivalent to admitting that you handle each case differently. Huh? Why not the same? Why is each case handled differently?

By defining your methodology, you are working from a guideline—a set of rules. This is what you do, this is how you do it, and here are the steps. It becomes a discipline. Your department has these guidelines and you follow them for each and every case. No, they are not exact. You use them as a point of reference and a focal starting point for each phase of every investigation. They cannot be exact because no two cases are identical. This car here is a Royals Royce, whereas that car there is a Yugo. You drive them differently because you have to. However, they are still both cars and so the basic mechanics are the same and you follow them. This is your methodology. You follow it. You open the door, you sit down, you start the engine, and so on. But, come time to drive, you drive differently! You have to because variables dictate this.

Document Everything

So important in computer forensic investigations is the chain of evidence. Who had custody at every step along the way? If resources allow, have two computer forensics personnel assigned to each case every step of the way. Specifically, having one person document what the other is doing and how they are doing it provides for a very detailed and accurate record of the handling of the evidence. Important in the documentation are the times that dates steps were taken; the names of those involved; and under whose authority were the steps taken?

If nothing else, by having this complete documentation you should be able to refute any claims of mishandling—especially if you have followed the steps defined within your methodology! Also, the documentation can provide a good point of reference for jogging the memories of the computer forensic examiners when case duration is lengthy and/or caseload is high.

Evidence Search and Seizure

Again, remembering that your specific needs will vary at some point in time, the steps listed here are not meant to be taken in a literal sense. They are not concrete, they may not be perfect for every case you work. Prior to search and seizure, you already have the proper documents filled out and paperwork filed as well as permission from the proper authority to search and seize the suspect's machine (PC, Server, Tapes, etc.).

Step 1: Preparation

Before the investigation, make sure you are prepared! You should sterilize all media that is to be used in the examination process. If you cannot afford new media for each case, then you must make sure that the reusable media is free of viruses and that all data has been wiped from the media. Document the wiping and scanning process. Also, check to make sure that all computer forensic tools (software) are licensed for use. And check to make sure that all lab equipment is in working order.

This is the time to make sure you have a good choice for your computer forensic examiner! Is the computer forensic examiner able to testify in court if necessary? Is the examiner able to explain the methodology used in real-world, simple to understand terminology? Or will the jurors be wondering what bytes, bits, slack space, and hidden files are? What is reasonable doubt in relation to something completely foreign? Better yet, there should be reasonable doubt when used in high-technology. It is reasonable to acquit, because some jurors would not understand, if a file is hidden, how someone else could find it!

When posed with the question of how to explain something so technical to a very nontechnical jury, give the analogy of comparing the computer to a library. The jurors know what a library is. Ask them if they would use the card catalog to look up a book in the library to find what shelf the book is located on. So, use the directory structure to find files on a piece of evidence. Furthermore, if you went through the library, would you not find books on the shelves that were not in the card catalog? The same on the computer. If you do a physical search, you will find data that is not cataloged.

Step 2: Snapshot

Your team needs to take a snapshot of the actual evidence scene. You should photograph the scene, whether it is a room in a home or in a business. Digital cameras seem to be the emerging standard here.

You should also note the scene. Take advantage of your investigative skills here. Note pictures, personal items, and the like. Later on in the examination, these items may prove useful (e.g., for password cracking).

Next, photograph the actual evidence. For simplicity, let us assume, for example, that the evidence is a PC in a home office. Take a photograph of the monitor. What is on the screen? Take a photograph of the PC. Remove the case cover carefully and photograph the internals.

In addition, document in your journal of the PC—the hardware, the internal drives, peripheral components, serial numbers, and so on. Make sure you document the configuration of the cables and connections as well (IDE, SCSI, etc.).

You should also label the evidence according to your methodology. And you should photograph the evidence again after the labels have been applied.

Remember to document everything that goes on (who did what, how, why, and at what time). Also make sure that you have your designated custodian for the chain of custody initial each item after double-checking the list you have created at the scene. So, you should now have noted the configuration, the components, and so on. The custodian of the evidence should double-check your list and put his/her initials next to yours while at the scene. It is imperative to do this checking at the scene so as to dispel the possibility of evidence tainting at a later date.

Finally, you should videotape the entry of all personnel. This may not always be possible, and in some cases or departments, this may be cost prohibitive. However, what you are doing here is taping the actual entrance of your team into the suspect's scene. By capturing your entrance and what you possess on tape, you are setting the stage for refuting any claims that evidence was planted at the scene, and so on.

However, where could the defense then point suspicion? The transport of the evidence? Right! So, by taping the entrance and the transport to the lab, you have a verifiable trail of what you did, when you did it, and how you did it. Is this overkill? Is this possible for every case you work? The taping process is a very solid means of supporting your work and may one day be required in your methodology.

Step 3: Transport

Assuming you have the legal authority to transport the evidence to your lab: You should pack the evidence securely. Be careful to guard against electrostatic discharge. Also, photograph/videotape and document the handling of evidence leaving the scene to the transport vehicle. Finally, you should also photograph/videotape and document the handling of evidence from transport vehicle to the lab examination facility.

Step 4: Examination

Now, you should prepare the acquired evidence for examination in your lab: This would involve unpacking the evidence and documenting according to your methodology (date, time, examiners, etc.). You should also visually examine the evidence, noting and documenting any unusual configurations (PC), marks, and so on. In other words, you should seize the PC from a home office. This PC usually has a hard drive of size 8GB.

Now, it is time to make an exact image of the hard drive. There are many options here on what tool to use to image the drive. You could use *EnCase*. You could use the Unix command *DD*. You could use *Byte Back*. You could also use *SafeBack*. This list could go on and on. It is wise to have a variety of tools in your lab. Each of these tools has its respective strengths. It is recommended here that you work with as many of them as you can. Become so familiar with them that you know their strengths and weaknesses and how to apply each of them. The important note to remember here is: Turn off virus-scanning software.

Next, you should record the time and date of the Complementary Metal Oxide Semiconductor (CMOS). This is very important, especially when time zones come into play. For example, the evidence was seized in California (PDT) and analyzed in Georgia (EDT).

It is crucial to remove the storage media (hard drives, etc.) prior to powering on the PC to check the CMOS!

NOTE

Do not boot the suspect machine! You can make the image in a number of ways. The key is that you want to do it from a controlled machine. A machine that you know works in a nondestructive/non-corrupt manner.

When making the bit stream image, note and document how the image was created. You should also note the date, time, and examiner. Note the tool used. Again, you are working from your methodology.

Also, when making the image, make sure that the tool you use does not access the file system of the target evidence media. You do not want to make any writes, you do not want to mount the file system, nor do you want to do anything that will change the file-access time for any file on that target evidence media.

After making the image, seal the original evidence media in a electrostatic-safe container, catalog it, and initial the container. Make sure that anyone who comes in contact with this container also inscribes his or her initials on the container. The container should be locked in a safe room upon completion of the imaging.

It may be a wise choice to then make a second bit stream image of your first image. You may need to send this to the suspect's residence or place of work—especially if the seized machine was used in the workplace. Finally, the examination of the acquired image begins.

SUMMARY

Companies are spending millions each year to ensure that their networks and data are properly protected against intrusion. Operating systems are hardened, firewalls are installed, intrusion detection systems are put in place, honeypots are implemented, security policies and procedures are established, security awareness programs are rolled out, and systems are monitored. This defense-in-depth approach is used because companies know that people will try to gain unauthorized access to their systems. When unauthorized access does occur, the last line of defense is legal action against the intruder. However, if evidence of an intrusion is not properly handled, it becomes inadmissible in a court of law. It is important to remember one of the basic rules of our legal system: If there is no evidence of a crime, there is no crime in the eyes of the law. Therefore, it is of paramount importance that utmost care is taken in the collection and seizure of data evidence.

Some of the most common reasons for improper evidence collection are poorly written policies, lack of an established incident response plan, lack of incident response training, and a broken chain of custody. For the purposes of this chapter, the reader should assume that policies have been clearly defined and reviewed by legal counsel, an incident response plan is in place, and necessary personnel have been properly trained.

Conclusions Drawn from Evidence Collection and Data Seizure

■ Admissible is the most basic rule (the evidence must be able to be used) in court or otherwise.

■ If you can't tie the evidence positively with the incident, you can't use it to prove anything.

■ It's not enough to collect evidence that just shows one perspective of the incident. Not only should you collect evidence that can prove the attacker's actions, but also evidence that could prove their innocence.

■ Your evidence collection and analysis procedures must not cast doubt on the evidence's authenticity and veracity.

■ The evidence you present should be clearly understandable and believable by a jury.

■ There are six fundamental rules to guide an investigator during a search and seizure. In essence, these rules are devised to help prevent the mishandling of evidence and encourage the documentation of search and seizure activities. In other words, the rules help to ensure an investigation's chain of custody, which is critical to the success of any case.

■ The preparation and team-structuring activities that take place help to ensure a successful investigation. Without these activities, the chain of custody is put at great risk.

■ The next three stages of the search and seizure process are: approach and secure the crime scene, document the crime scene, and search for evidence.

■ The crime scene security may range from locking doors to (for law enforcers) arresting trespassers.

■ The documentation can be rough, but must be adequate in its depiction of the crime scene layout, and the location of evidence.

■ The search for evidence can involve looking in a variety of places, but the legalities of searching must always be considered.

■ The virus protocol is a means of preventing and containing the threat to electronic evidence by computer viruses.

An Agenda for Action in Evidence Collection and Data Seizure

The following is a provisional list of actions for evidence collection and data seizure. The order is not significant; however, these are the activities for which the researcher would want to provide a detailed description of procedures, review, and assessment for ease of use and admissibility. A number of these evidence collection and data seizure topics have been mentioned in passing already:

1. Once you've created a master copy of the original data, don't touch it or the original itself—always handle secondary copies.
2. Sometimes evidence alteration is unavoidable. In these cases, it is absolutely essential that the nature, extent, and reasons for the changes be documented.
3. If you don't understand what you are doing, you can't account for any changes you make and you can't describe exactly what you did. If you ever find yourself out of your depth, either go and learn more before continuing (if time is available) or find someone who knows the territory.
4. No one is going to believe you if they can't replicate your actions and reach the same results. This also means that your plan of action shouldn't be based on trial-and-error.
5. The faster you work, the less likely the data is going to change.
6. Some electronic evidence is more volatile than others are. Because of this, you should always try to collect the most volatile evidence first. You should then proceed from volatile to persistent evidence.
7. You should never, ever shutdown a system before you collect the evidence.
8. Rebooting is even worse than shutting a system down and should be avoided at all costs. As a general rule, until the compromised disk is finished with and restored, it should never be used as a boot disk.
9. Because the attacker may have left trojaned (trojan horse) programs and libraries on the system, you may inadvertently trigger something that could change or destroy the evidence you're looking for. Any programs you use should be on read-only media (such as a CD-ROM or a write-protected floppy disk), and should be statically linked.
10. A planning stage must take place prior to any investigator arriving at the computer crime scene, including two ways to structure a team of investigators.
11. Good case management software can go a long way in easing the burden of carrying out a search and seizure.

ENDNOTES

i   John R. Vacca, *The Essential Guide to Storage Area Networks*, Prentice Hall, 2002.

ii   Matthew Braid, "Collecting Electronic Evidence After A System Compromise," Australian Computer Emergency Response Team (AusCERT (*http://www.auscert.org.au*), The University of Queensland, Qld 4072 Australia (*mdb©auscert.org.au*), ([SANS Institute, 5401 Westbard Ave. Suite 1501, Bethesda, MD 20816).], 2001.

6 Duplication and Preservation of Digital Evidence

Computer evidence is odd, to say the least. It lurks on computer hard disk drives, zip disks, and floppy diskettes at three different levels. Two of these levels are not visible to the computer user. Such evidence is fragile and can easily be destroyed through something as simple as the normal operation of the computer. Electromagnets and planted destructive Trojan horse programs are other hazards that can permanently destroy computer evidence within seconds. There is no other type of evidence that presents the investigator with as many potential problems and challenges. In the old days, defense lawyers didn't know much about computer evidence. As a result, cross-examination by the defense wasn't as strong a few years ago as it is today. However, things are changing because lawyers are becoming educated due to the current popularity of electronic document discovery in the legal community. Times have changed and it is all the more important to do things by the book.

PRESERVING THE DIGITAL CRIME SCENE

The computer investigator not only needs to be worried about destructive processes and devices being planted by the computer owner, he or she also needs to be concerned about the operating system of the computer and applications. Evidence is easily found in typical storage areas (spreadsheet, database, and word processing files). Unfortunately potential evidence can also reside in file slack, erased files, and the *Windows* swap file. Such evidence is usually in the form of data fragments and can be easily overwritten by something as simple as the booting of the computer and/or the running of Microsoft *Windows*. When *Windows* starts, it potentially creates new files and opens existing ones as a normal process. This situation can cause erased files to be overwritten and data previously stored in the *Windows* swap file can be altered or destroyed. Furthermore, all of the *Windows* operating systems (*Windows 95, 98, 2000*, and especially *XP*) have a habit of updating directory entries for files as a normal operating process. As you can imagine, file dates are important from an evidence standpoint.

Another concern of the computer investigator is the running of any programs on the subject computer. Criminals can easily modify the operating system to destroy evidence when standard operating systems commands are executed. Perpetrators could modify the operating system such that the execution of the *DIR* command destroys simulated evidence. Standard program names and familiar *Windows* program icons can also be altered and tied to destructive processes by a crafty high-tech criminal.

Even trusted word processing programs such as Microsoft *Word* and *WordPerfect*™ can become the enemy of the cyber cop. It works this way: When word processing files are opened and viewed, temporary files are created by the word processing program. These files overwrite the temporary files that existed previously and potential evidence stored in those files can be lost forever. There's a point to all of this. Computer evidence processing is risky business and is fraught with potential problems. Of course, any loss of crucial evidence or exculpatory material falls on the shoulders of the computer investigator. What will your answer be, if the defense attorney claims the data you destroyed proved the innocence of his or her client? You better have a good answer.

Many inherent problems associated with computer evidence processing vanish when tried and proven processing procedures are followed. The objective of this part of the chapter is to keep Murphy's law from ruining your case. When it comes to computer evidence processing, Murphy is always looking over your shoulder. He stands ready to strike at just the wrong moment.

Your first objective, after securing the computer, should be to make a complete bit stream back-up of all computer data before it is reviewed or processed. This should normally be done before the computer is operated. Preservation of evidence is the primary element of all criminal investigations and computer evidence is certainly no exception. These basic rules of evidence never change. Even rookies know that evidence must be preserved at all costs. As stated previously, evidence can reside at multiple levels and in bizarre storage locations. These levels include allocated files, file slack, and erased files. It is not enough to do a standard back-up of a hard disk drive. To do so would eliminate the back-up of file slack and erased file space. Without backing-up evidence in these unique areas, the evidence is susceptible to damage and/or modification by the computer investigator. Bit stream back-ups are much more thorough than standard back-ups. They involve the copying of every bit of data on a storage device and it is recommended that two such copies be made of the original when hard disk drives are involved. Any processing should be performed on one of the back-up copies. As previously recommended, the original evidence should be preserved at all costs. After all, it is the *best evidence.*

The need for forensic bit stream image back-ups was identified back in late 1989 during the creation of the first computer forensic science training courses at the Federal Law Enforcement Training Center. The first program created to perform this task was named IMDUMP and was developed by Michael White, who was employed by Paul Mace Software. That program proved to be helpful until approximately 1991, when most of the Paul Mace utilities were sold to another software company. Lacking the continued support for IMDUMP, Chuck Guzis at Sydex, Inc. in Eugene, Oregon, agreed to develop a specialized program that would meet law enforcement's bit stream back-up needs from an evidence standpoint. Chuck has come to be known as the father of electronic crime scene preservation; the resulting program, *SafeBack*, has become a law enforcement standard. In addition, it is used by numerous government intelligence agencies, military agencies, and law enforcement agencies worldwide. Unlike normal back-up programs, the *SafeBack* program copies and preserves all data contained on the hard disk. It even goes so far as to circumvent attempts made to hide data in bad clusters and even sectors with invalid Cyclic Redundancy Codes (CRCs). As of this writing, there are no other back-up programs that have these features—added specifically to help law enforcement deal with such issues.

NOTE

CRCs are a type of error detection codes commonly used on disk and tape storage devices. Data stored on a device using CRCs has an additional character added to the end of the data that makes it possible to detect and correct some types of error that occur when reading the data back. Direct memory access (DMA) is a technique that allows a peripheral device to transfer data directly to the main memory of the computer without first passing through an accumulator. This allows much faster transfer rates to and from memory. A value is calculated from a block of data to be stored or transmitted with the data block as a check item. CRCs are generated using a shift register with feedback and are described by the length of the register and the feedback terms used.

Another bit stream back-up program, called *SnapBack*, is also available and is used by some law enforcement agencies primarily because of its ease of use. It is priced several hundreds of dollars higher than *SafeBack* and its original design was not for evidence processing. It was designed as a network back-up utility for use by system administrators. *SafeBack* was designed from the ground up as an evidence-processing tool and is priced to fit law enforcement budgets. It has error-checking built into every phase of the evidence back-up and restoration process. Thus, the important thing is to make a bit stream back-up of all computer data before you begin processing. *SafeBack* and *SnapBack* seem to be the answer concerning computer hard disk drives.

The importance of bit stream image back-ups cannot be stressed enough. To process a computer hard disk drive for evidence without a bit stream image back-up is like playing with fire in a gas station. The basic rule is that only on rare occasions should you process computer evidence without first making an image back-up. The hard disk drive should be imaged using a specialized bit stream back-up product and the floppy diskettes can be imaged using the standard DOS *DISKCOPY* program. Directions should be followed exactly, regarding the use of the bit stream back-up software. When DOS *DISKCOPY* is used, it is recommended that the MS DOS Version 6.22 be used and the */V* (data verification) switch should be invoked from the command line. To avoid getting too technical for the purposes of this chapter, specifics regarding the uses of these back-up programs will be avoided. However, instruction manuals should be studied thoroughly before you attempt to process computer evidence. Ideally, you should conduct tests on your own computers beforehand and compare the results with the original computer evidence. Being comfortable with the software you use is an important part of computer evidence processing. Know your tools. Practice using all of your forensic software tools before you use them in the processing of computer evidence. You may only get one chance to do it right.

COMPUTER EVIDENCE PROCESSING STEPS

Computer evidence is fragile by its very nature and the problem is compounded with the potential of destructive programs and hidden data. Even the normal operation of the computer can destroy computer evidence that might be lurking in unallocated space, file slack, or in the *Windows* swap file. There really are no strict rules that must be followed regarding the processing of computer evidence. Every case is different and flexibility on the part of the computer investigator is important.

With that in mind, the following general computer evidence processing guidelines or steps have been provided. Please remember that these do not represent the only true way of processing computer evidence. They are general guidelines provided as food for thought:

1. Shut down the computer
2. Document the hardware configuration of the system

3. Transport the computer system to a secure location
4. Make bit stream back-ups of hard disks and floppy disks
5. Mathematically authenticate data on all storage devices
6. Document the system date and time
7. Make a list of key search words
8. Evaluate the *Windows* swap file
9. Evaluate file slack
10. Evaluate unallocated space (erased files)
11. Search files, file slack, and unallocated space for key words
12. Document file names, dates, and times
13. Identify file, program, and storage anomalies
14. Evaluate program functionality
15. Document your findings
16. Retain copies of software used[i]

CAUTION

If you are not trained and have had a computer incident or threat, see sidebar, "Emergency Guidelines."

EMERGENCY GUIDELINES

The popularity of desktop and notebook computers has come with a mixed blessing. These wonderful tools contribute to increased productivity and help to facilitate communications and file transfers worldwide over the Internet. However, they also provide opportunities for abuse of corporate policies and the commission of computer-related crimes. Internet viewing of pornography has become a serious problem for corporations and government agencies. Embezzlements using computers have become commonplace in small- and medium-size businesses.

Computer forensic tools and techniques can help to identify such abuses. They can also be used to find and document evidence in a civil or criminal case. However, the computer evidence must be preserved and protected. As a result, it is important that things are done correctly as soon as a computer incident is identified. By following the guidelines listed here, you stand a good chance of preserving the evidence:

1. Don't turn on or operate the subject computer.
2. Don't solicit the assistance of the resident 'computer expert.'
3. Don't evaluate employee e-mail unless corporate policy allows it.

Computer evidence is very fragile and can easily be altered or destroyed if the wrong things are done.

Don't Turn on or Operate the Subject Computer

The computer should first be backed-up using bit stream back-up software. When the computer is run, the potential exists for information in the *Windows* swap file to be overwritten. Internet activity and fragments of *Windows* work sessions exist in the *Windows* swap file. This can prove to be valuable from an evidence standpoint. In the case of a DOS-based system, the running of the computer can destroy *deleted* files. For that matter, the same is true of a *Windows* system. To save grief, don't run the computer.

Don't Solicit the Assistance of The Resident Computer Expert

The processing of computer evidence is tricky to say the least. Without proper training, even a world-class computer scientist can do the wrong things. Like any other science, computer science has its areas of specialty. Computer forensics investigators typically get calls *after the fact* and are informed that a computer-knowledgeable internal auditor or systems administrator has attempted to process a computer for evidence. In some cases, valuable evidence is lost or the evidence is so tainted that it loses its evidentiary value. For these reasons, seek the assistance of a computer specialist who has been trained in computer evidence processing procedures. Do this before you turn on the computer!

Don't Evaluate Employee E-Mail Unless Corporate Policy Allows It

New electronic privacy laws[ii] protect the privacy of electronic communications. If your corporate policy specifically states that all computers and data stored on them belongs to the corporation, then you are probably on safe ground. However, be sure that you have such a policy and that the employee(s) involved have read the policy. Furthermore, it is always a good idea to check with corporate counsel. Don't be in a hurry and do things by the book! To do otherwise could subject you and your corporation to a lawsuit.[iii]

Shut Down the Computer

Depending on the computer operating system, this usually involves pulling the plug or shutting down a network computer using relevant commands required by the network involved. At the option of the computer investigator, pictures of the screen image can be taken. However, consideration should be given to possible destructive processes that may be operating in the background. These can be in memory or available through a connected modem. Depending on the operating system involved, a password-protected screen saver may also kick in at any moment. This can complicate the shutdown of the computer. Generally, time is of the essence and the computer system should be shut down as quickly as possible.

Document the Hardware Configuration of the System

It is assumed that the computer system will be moved to a secure location where a proper chain of custody can be maintained and evidence processing can begin. Before dismantling the computer, it is important that pictures are taken of the computer from all angles to document the system hardware components and how they are connected. Labeling each wire is also important, so that it can easily be reconnected when the system configuration is restored to its original condition at a secure location.

Transport the Computer System to a Secure Location

This may seem basic, but all too often seized computers are stored in less than secure locations. War stories can be told on this one that relate to both law enforcement agencies and corporations. It is imperative that the subject computer is treated as evidence and stored out of reach of curious computer users. All too often, individuals operate seized computers without knowing that they are destroying potential evidence and the chain of custody. Furthermore, a seized computer left unattended can easily be compromised. Evidence can be planted on it and crucial evidence can be intentionally destroyed. A lack of a proper chain of custody can make a savvy defense attorney's day. Lacking a proper chain of custody, how can you say that relevant evidence was not planted on the computer after the seizure? The answer is that you cannot. Don't leave the computer unattended unless it is locked up in a secure location!

Make Bit Stream Back-ups of Hard Disks and Floppy Disks

The computer should not be operated and computer evidence should not be processed until bit stream back-ups have been made of all hard disk drives and floppy disks. All evidence processing should be done on a restored copy of the bit stream back-up rather than on the original computer. The original evidence should be left untouched unless compelling circumstances exist. Preservation of computer evidence is vitally important. It is fragile and can easily be altered or destroyed. Often such alteration or destruction of data is irreversible. Bit stream back-ups are much like an insurance policy and are essential for any serious computer evidence processing.

Mathematically Authenticate Data on All Storage Devices

You want to be able to prove that you did not alter any of the evidence after the computer came into your possession. Such proof will help you rebut allegations that you changed or altered the original evidence. Since 1989, law enforcement and military agencies have used a 32-bit mathematical process to do the authentication process. Mathematically, a 32-bit validation is accurate to approximately one in 4.3 billion. However, given the speed of today's computers and the vast amount of storage capacity on today's computer hard disk drives, this level of accuracy is no longer accurate enough. A 32-bit CRC can be compromised.

Document the System Date and Time

The dates and times associated with computer files can be extremely important from an evidence standpoint. However, the accuracy of the dates and times is just as important. If the system clock is one hour slow because of daylight-saving time, then file timestamps will also reflect the wrong time. To adjust for these inaccuracies, documenting the system date and time settings at the time the computer is taken into evidence is essential.

Make a List of Key Search Words

Because modern hard disk drives are so voluminous, it is all but impossible for a computer specialist to manually view and evaluate every file on a computer hard disk drive. Therefore, state-of-the-art automated forensic text search tools are needed to help find the relevant evidence. Usually some information is known about the allegations, the computer user, and the alleged associates that may be involved. Gathering information from individuals familiar with the case to help compile a list of relevant key words is important. Such key words can be used in the search of all computer hard disk drives and floppy diskettes using automated software. Keeping the list as short as possible is important and you should avoid using common words or words that make up part of other words. In such cases, the words should be surrounded with spaces.

Evaluate the *Windows* Swap File

The *Windows* swap file is a potentially valuable source of evidence and leads. In the past, this tedious task was done with hex editors, and the process took days to evaluate just one *Windows* swap file. With the use of automated tools, this process now takes only a few minutes. When *Windows 95, 98, 2000,* and *XP* are involved, the swap file may be set to be dynamically created as the computer is operated. This is the default setting, and when the computer is turned off, the swap file is erased. However, all is not lost because the content of the swap file can easily be captured and evaluated.

Evaluate File Slack

File slack is a data storage area of which most computer users are unaware.[iv] It is a source of significant *security leakage* and consists of raw memory dumps that occur during the work session as files are closed. The data dumped from memory ends up being stored at the end of allocated files, beyond the reach or view of the computer user. Specialized forensic tools are required to view and evaluate the file slack; file slack can prove to provide a wealth of information and investigative leads. Like the *Windows* swap file, this source of ambient data can help to provide relevant key words and leads that may have previously been unknown.

On a well-used hard disk drive, as much as 900 million bytes of storage space may be occupied by file slack. File slack should be evaluated for relevant key words to supplement the keywords identified in the previous steps. Such keywords should be added to the computer investigator's list of key words for use later. Because of the nature of file slack, specialized and automated forensic tools are required for evaluation. File slack is typically a good source of Internet leads. Tests suggest that file slack provides approximately 80 times more Internet leads than the *Windows* swap file. Therefore, this source of potential leads should not be overlooked in cases involving possible Internet uses or abuses.

Evaluate Unallocated Space (Erased Files)

The DOS and *Windows* 'delete' function does not completely erase file names or file content. Many computer users are unaware that the storage space associated with such files merely becomes unallocated and available to be overwritten with new files. Unallocated space is a source of significant *security leakage* and it potentially contains erased files and file slack associated with the erased files. Often the

DOS *Undelete* program can be used to restore the previously erased files. Like the *Windows* swap file and file slack, this source of ambient data can help to provide relevant key words and leads that may have previously been unknown to the computer investigator.

On a well-used hard disk drive, millions of bytes of storage space may contain data associated with previously erased files. Unallocated space should be evaluated for relevant key words to supplement the keywords identified in the previous steps. Such keywords should be added to the computer investigator's list of key words for use in the next processing step. Because of the nature of data contained in unallocated space and its volume, specialized and automated forensic tools are required for evaluation. Unallocated space is typically a good source of data that was previously associated with word processing temporary files and other temporary files created by various computer applications.

Search Files, File Slack, and Unallocated Space for Key Words

The list of relevant key words identified in the previous steps should be used to search all relevant computer hard disk drives and floppy diskettes. There are several forensic text search utilities available in the marketplace. Some of these tools are designed to be state-of-the-art and have been validated as security review tools by the federal government intelligence agencies.

It is important to review the output of the text search utility, and equally important to document relevant findings. When relevant evidence is identified, the fact should be noted and the identified data should be completely reviewed for additional key words. When new key words are identified, they should be added to the list and a new search should be conducted using the text search utility. Text search utilities can also be used effectively in security reviews of computer storage media.

Document File Names, Dates, and Times

From an evidence standpoint, file names, creation dates, and last modified dates and times can be relevant. Therefore, it is important to catalog all allocated and 'erased' files. The file should be sorted based on the file name, file size, file content, creation date, and last modified date and time. Such sorted information can provide a timeline of computer usage. The output should be in the form of a word-processing-compatible file that can be used to help document computer evidence issues tied to specific files.

Identify File, Program, and Storage Anomalies

Encrypted, compressed, and graphic files store data in binary format. As a result, a text search program cannot identify text data stored in these file formats. Manual evaluation of these files is required and, in the case of encrypted files, much work may be involved. Depending on the type of file involved, the contents should be viewed and evaluated for its potential as evidence.

Reviewing the partitioning on seized hard disk drives is also important. The potential exists for hidden partitions and/or partitions formatted with a non-DOS-compatible operating system. When this situation exists, it is comparable to finding a hidden hard disk drive; volumes of data and potential evidence can thus be involved. The partitioning can be checked with any number of utilities including the DOS *FDISK* program or *Partition Magic™*. When hidden partitions are found, they should be evaluated for evidence and their existence should be documented.

If *Windows 95, 98, 2000*, and *XP* are involved, it makes sense to evaluate the files contained in the Recycle Bin. The Recycle Bin is the repository of files selected for deletion by the computer user. The fact that they have been selected for deletion may have some relevance from an evidentiary standpoint. If relevant files are found, the issues involved should be documented thoroughly.

Evaluate Program Functionality

Depending on the application software involved, running programs to learn their purpose may be necessary. When destructive processes that are tied to relevant evidence are discovered, this can be used to prove willfulness. Such destructive processes can be tied to *hot keys* or the execution of common operating commands tied to the operating system or applications.

Document Your Findings

As indicated in the preceding steps, it is important to document your findings as issues are identified and as evidence is found. Documenting all of the software used in your forensic evaluation of the evidence, including the version numbers of the programs used, is also important. Be sure that you are legally licensed to use the forensic software. Software pirates do not stand up well under the riggers of a trial. Smart defense lawyers will usually question software licensing; you don't want to testify that you used unlicensed software in the processing of computer evidence. Technically, software piracy is a criminal violation of federal copyright laws.

When appropriate, mention in your documentation that you are licensed to use the forensic software involved. Screen prints of the operating software also help to document the version of the software and how it was used to find and/or process the evidence.

Retain Copies of Software Used

Finally, as part of your documentation process, it is recommended that a copy of the software used be included with the output of the forensic tool involved. Normally, this is done on an archive Zip disk, Jazz disk, or other external storage device (external hard disk drive). When this documentation methodology is followed, it eliminates confusion (about which version of the software was used to create the output) at trial time. Often it is necessary to duplicate forensic-processing results during or before trial. Duplication of results can be difficult or impossible to achieve if the software has been upgraded and the original version used was not retained.

There is a high probability that you will encounter this problem because most commercial software is upgraded routinely, but it may take years for a case to go to trial.

NOTE

LEGAL ASPECTS OF COLLECTING AND PRESERVING COMPUTER FORENSIC EVIDENCE

Some of the most common reasons for improper evidence collection are poorly written policies, lack of an established incident response plan, lack of incident response training, and a broken chain of custody. For the purposes of this chapter, the reader should assume that policies have been clearly defined and reviewed by legal counsel, an incident response plan is in place, and necessary personnel have been properly trained. The remainder of this chapter focuses on the procedure a private organization should follow in collecting computer forensic evidence to maintain chain of custody.

Definition

What is a chain of custody? In simple terms, a chain of custody is a roadmap that shows how evidence was collected, analyzed, and preserved in order to be presented as evidence in court. Establishing a clear chain of custody is crucial because electronic evidence can be easily altered. A clear chain of custody demonstrates that electronic evidence is trustworthy. Preserving a chain of custody for electronic evidence, at a minimum, requires proving that:

- No information has been added or changed
- A complete copy was made

- A reliable copying process was used
- All media was secured[v]

Proving this chain is unbroken is a prosecutor's primary tool in authenticating electronic evidence.

Legal Requirements

To collect evidence, certain legal requirements must be met. These legal requirements are vast, complex, and vary from country to country. However, there are certain requirements that are generally agreed on within the United States. U.S. Code Title 28, Section 1732 provides that log files are admissible as evidence if they are collected *in the regular course of business.* Also, Rule 803(6) of the Federal Rules of Evidence provides that logs, which might otherwise be considered hearsay, are admissible as long as they are collected *in the course of regularly conducted business activity.* This means you'd be much safer to log everything all the time and deal with the storage issues, than to turn on logging only after an incident is suspected. Not only is this a bit like closing the barn door after the horse has fled, it may also render your logs inadmissible in court.

Another factor in the admissibility of log files is the ability to prove that they have not been subject to tampering. Whenever possible, digital signatures should be used to verify log authenticity. Other protective measures include, but are not limited to, storing logs on a dedicated logging server and/or encrypting log files. Log files are often one of the best, if not only, sources of evidence available. Therefore, due diligence should be applied in protecting them.

One other generally accepted requirement of evidence collection is a user's expectation of privacy. A key to establishing that a user has no right to privacy when using corporate networks and/or computer systems is the implementation of a logon banner. CERT Advisory CA-1992-19 suggests the following text be tailored to a corporation's specific needs under the guidance of legal counsel:

- This system is for the use of authorized users only. Individuals using this computer system without authority, or in excess of their authority, are subject to having all of their activities on this system monitored and recorded by system personnel.
- In the course of monitoring individuals improperly using this system, or in the course of system maintenance, the activities of authorized users may also be monitored.
- Anyone using this system expressly consents to such monitoring and is advised that if such monitoring reveals possible evidence of criminal activity, system

personnel may provide the evidence of such monitoring to law enforcement officials.

Furthermore, security policy can play a key role in establishing a user's expectation of privacy. The Supreme Court ruling in O'Connor verses Ortega, 480 U.S. 709 (1987), implies that the legality of workplace monitoring depends primarily on whether employment policies exist that authorize monitoring and whether that policy has been clearly communicated to employees. To prove that the policy has been communicated, employees should sign a statement indicating that they have read, understood, and agreed to comply with corporate policy and consent to system monitoring.

Evidence Collection Procedure

When the time arrives to begin collection of evidence, the first rule that must be followed is *do not rush*. Tensions will probably be high and people will want to find answers as quickly as possible. However, if the investigators rush through these procedures, mistakes will be made and evidence will be lost.

The investigation team will need to bring certain tools with them to the incident site. They will need a copy of their incident-handling procedure, an evidence collection notebook, and evidence identification tags. Depending on the type of incident and whether the team will be able to retrieve an entire system or just the data, they may also need to bring tools to produce reliable copies of electronic evidence, including media to use in the copying process. In some cases, legal counsel will want photographs of the system(s) prior to search and seizure. If this is something your legal counsel wants as part of the evidence, then also include a Polaroid camera in the list of tools.

Policy and procedure should indicate who is to act as incident coordinator. When an incident is reported, this individual will contact the other members of the response team as outlined in the Incident Response Policy. Upon arrival at the incident site, this individual will be responsible for ensuring that every detail of the incident-handling procedure is followed. The incident coordinator will also assign team members the various tasks outlined in the incident-handling procedure and will serve as the liaison to the legal team, law enforcement officials, management, and public relations personnel. Ultimate responsibility for ensuring that evidence is properly collected and preserved, and that the chain of custody is properly maintained, belongs to the incident coordinator.

One team member will be assigned the task of maintaining the evidence notebook. This person will record the who, what, where, when, and how of the investigation process. At a minimum, items to be recorded in the notebook include:

- Who initially reported the suspected incident along with time, date, and circumstances surrounding the suspected incident
- Details of the initial assessment leading to the formal investigation
- Names of all persons conducting the investigation
- The case number of the incident
- Reasons for the investigation
- A list of all computer systems included in the investigation, along with complete system specifications. Also include identification tag numbers assigned to the systems or individual parts of the system
- Network diagrams
- Applications running on the computer systems previously listed
- A copy of the policy or policies that relate to accessing and using the systems previously listed
- A list of administrators responsible for the routine maintenance of the system
- A detailed list of steps used in collecting and analyzing evidence. Specifically, this list needs to identify the date and time each task was performed, a description of the task, who performed the task, where the task was performed, and the results of the analysis.
- An access control list of who had access to the collected evidence at what date and time[vi]

NOTE

A separate notebook should be used for each investigation. Also, the notebook should not be spiral-bound. It should be bound in such a way that it is obvious if a page or pages have been removed.

This notebook is a crucial element in maintaining chain of custody. Therefore, it must be as detailed as possible to assist in maintaining this chain.

Another team member (or members) will be assigned the task of evidence collection. To avoid confusion, the number of people assigned this task should be kept to a minimum. This member (or members) should also be highly proficient with the copying and analysis tools listed later in the chapter. This person will then tag all evidence and work with the person responsible for the evidence notebook to ensure that this information is properly recorded. Next, the person will also be responsible for making a reliable copy of all data to be used as evidence. The data will include complete copies of drives on compromised or suspect systems, as well as all relevant log files. Also, this can either be done on-site or the entire system can be moved to a forensics lab, as needs dictate.

A simple file copy is not sufficient to serve as evidence in the case of compromised or suspect systems. A binary copy of the data is the proper way to preserve evidence.

A reliable copy process has three critical characteristics. First, the process must meet industry standards for quality and reliability. This includes the software used to create the copy and the media on which the copy is made. A good benchmark is whether the software is used and relied on by law enforcement agencies. Second, the copies made must be capable of independent verification. Third, the copies must be tamperproof.

The Unix *dd* command and the product *Encase*™ are two examples of acceptable tools. Two copies of the data should be made using an acceptable tool. The original should be placed in a sealed container. One copy will be used for analysis and the other copy can be put back in the system so the system can be returned to service as quickly as possible.

In certain cases, it is necessary to keep the entire system or certain pieces of hardware as part of evidence. The investigation coordinator will work with the legal team to determine the requirements for a given case.

Once all evidence is collected and logged, it can be securely transported to the forensics lab. A detailed description of how data was transported and who was responsible for the transport along with date, time, and route, should be included in the log. It is required that the evidence be transported under dual control.

Storage and Analysis of Data

Finally, the chain of custody must be maintained throughout the analysis process. One of the keys to maintaining the chain is a secure storage location. If the corporation uses access control cards and/or video surveillance in other parts of the building, consider using these devices in the forensics lab. Access control cards for entering and exiting the lab will help verify who had access to the lab at what time. The video cameras will help to determine what they did once they were inside the lab. At a minimum, the lab must provide some form of access control; a log should be kept detailing entrance and exit times of all individuals. It is important that evidence never be left in an unsecured area. If a defense lawyer can show that unauthorized persons had access to the evidence, it could easily be declared inadmissible.

Pieces of evidence should be grouped and stored by case along with the evidence notebook. In an effort to be as thorough as possible, investigators should follow a clearly documented analysis plan. A detailed plan will help to prevent mistakes (which could lead to the evidence becoming inadmissible) during analysis. As analysis of evidence is performed, investigators must log the details of their actions in the evidence notebook. The following should be included as a minimum:

- The date and time of analysis
- Tools used in performing the analysis
- Detailed methodology of the analysis
- Results of the analysis[vii]

Again, the information recorded in the evidence notebook must be as detailed as possible to demonstrate the trustworthiness of the evidence. A trial lawyer well versed in the technological world, who knows how to ask the right questions, may find that the *method or circumstances of preparation indicate lack of trustworthiness* (under Fed. R. Evid. 803(6), to such a degree that a court will sustain, or at least consider, a challenge to the admissibility of the evidence). A properly prepared evidence notebook will help to defeat such a challenge.

Once all evidence has been analyzed and all results have been recorded in the evidence notebook, a copy of the notebook should be made and given to the legal team. If the legal team finds sufficient evidence exists to take legal action, it will be important to maintain the chain of custody until the evidence is handed over to the proper legal authorities. Legal officials should provide a receipt detailing all of the items received for entry into evidence.

SUMMARY

The latter part of the 20th century was marked by the electronic transistor and the machines and ideas made possible by it. As a result, the world changed from analog to digital. Although the computer reigns supreme in the digital domain, it is not the only digital device. An entire constellation of audio, video, communications, and photographic devices are becoming so closely associated with the computer as to have converged with it.

From a law enforcement perspective, more of the information that serves as currency in the judicial process is being stored, transmitted, or processed in digital form. The connectivity resulting from a single world economy, in which the companies providing goods and services are truly international, has enabled criminals to act transjurisdictionally with ease. Consequently, a perpetrator may be brought to justice in one jurisdiction while the digital evidence required to successfully prosecute the case may reside only in other jurisdictions.

This situation requires that all nations have the ability to *collect and preserve digital evidence* for their own needs as well as for the potential needs of other sovereigns. Each jurisdiction has its own system of government and administration of justice, but in order for one country to protect itself and its citizens, it must be able to make use of evidence collected by other nations.

Though it is not reasonable to expect all nations to know about and abide by the precise laws and rules of other countries, a means that will allow the exchange of evidence must be found. This chapter was a first attempt to define the technical aspects of these exchanges.

Conclusions Drawn from Duplication and Preservation of Digital Evidence

- The laws surrounding the collection and preservation of evidence are vast and complex.
- Even if local law enforcement does not have a computer forensics expert on staff, they will know the basic rules of evidence collection and should have contacts within the law enforcement community who are experts in computer forensics.
- A clearly documented plan is essential for an investigation team to be successful in collecting admissible evidence. The plan should be designed with the assistance of legal counsel and law enforcement agencies to ensure compliance with all applicable local, state, and federal laws.
- Once a plan has been drafted and the incident team is assembled, practice should begin.
- Configure a test network in a lab environment and invite members of the IT staff to attempt to circumvent the security measures installed in the lab network.
- Treat the intrusion as an actual incident and follow the incident handling and evidence collection procedures.
- Review the results with the team and evaluate whether evidence collected would be admissible, based on the procedures followed and the analysis results.
- When possible, include legal staff and local law enforcement in practice sessions.
- When in doubt, hire an expert.
- If resident security staff members are not equipped to perform the investigation, do not hesitate to bring in outside assistance.

- It is in the best interest of the company to ensure that the investigation is handled properly.
- The goal is to collect and preserve evidence in such a way that it will be admissible in a court of law.

An Agenda for Action in Duplication and Preservation of Digital Evidence

The following is a provisional list of actions for duplication and preservation of digital evidence. The order is not significant; however, these are the activities for which the researcher would want to provide a detailed description of procedures, review, and assessment for ease of use and admissibility. A number of these duplication and preservation of digital evidence topics have been mentioned in passing already:

1. Shut down the computer.
2. Document the hardware configuration of the system.
3. Transport the computer system to a secure location.
4. Make bit stream back-ups of hard disks and floppy disks.
5. Mathematically authenticate data on all storage devices.
6. Document the system date and time.
7. Make a list of key search words.
8. Evaluate the *Windows* swap file.
9. Evaluate file slack.
10. Evaluate unallocated space (erased files).
11. Search files, file slack, and unallocated space for key words.
12. Document file names, dates, and times.
13. Identify file, program, and storage anomalies.
14. Evaluate program functionality.
15. Document your findings.
16. Retain copies of software used.
17. A solid relationship should be established with local law enforcement, as they will be a valuable resource in the evidence collection process.

ENDNOTES

i   "Computer Evidence Processing Steps," New Technologies, Inc., 2075 NE Division St., Gresham, Oregon 97030, 2001. *(©Copyright 2002, New Technologies, Inc. All rights reserved). 2001*

ii   John R. Vacca, *Net Privacy: A Guide to Developing and Implementing an Ironclad ebusiness Privacy Plan,* McGraw-Hill Professional, 2001.

iii   "Computer Incident Response Guidelines," New Technologies, Inc., 2075 NE Division St., Gresham, Oregon 97030, 2001. *(©Copyright 2002, New Technologies, Inc. All rights reserved). 2001*

iv   John R. Vacca, *The Essential Guide to Storage Area Networks,* Prentice Hall, 2002.

v   Franklin Witter, "Legal Aspects Of Collecting And Preserving Computer Forensics Evidence," Branch Banking & Trust, 2501 Wooten Blvd., MC 100-99-08-25, Wilson, North Carolina 27893

vi   Ibid.

vii   Ibid.

7 Computer Image Verification and Authentication

As law enforcement and other computer forensics investigators become more familiar with handling evidential computer material, it is apparent that a number of more or less formalized procedures have evolved to maintain both the continuity and integrity of the material to be investigated. Although these procedures are extremely effective under the current rules of evidence, it is expected that alternative procedures will develop as technology advances. The current procedures, in use by both law enforcement and computer forensics investigators, work something like this:

At least two copies are taken of the evidential computer. One of these is sealed in the presence of the computer owner and then placed in secure storage. This is the master copy and it will only be opened for examination under instruction from the Court in the event of a challenge to the evidence presented after forensic analysis on the second copy. If the computer itself has been seized and held in secure storage by law enforcement, this will constitute *best evidence*. If the computer has not been seized, then the master copy becomes best evidence. In either case, the assumption is that while in secure storage, there can be no possibility of tampering with the evidence. This does not protect the computer owner from the possibility that secured evidence may be tampered with.

A growing practical problem with this method of evidential copying occurs not due to the security aspect or appearance of the situation, but because of the increasing sizes of fixed disks found in computers. A size of 2 Gigabytes is no longer unusual and it is common to find more than one fixed disk within a single machine. The cost of the media is decreasing slowly, but this is still significant when considering the quantity of information to be copied and stored (even though the system does allow for media re-use). There is also the problem of the length of time

How *Authenticode* Works with VeriSign® Digital IDs

Authenticode relies on industry-standard cryptography techniques such as X.509 v3 certificates and PKCS #7 and #10 signature standards. These are well-proven cryptography protocols, which ensure a robust implementation of code-signing technology. Developers can use the *WinVerifyTrust API*, on which *Authenticode* is based, to verify signed code in their own Win32 applications.

Authenticode uses digital signature technology to assure users of the origin and integrity of software. In digital signatures, the private key generates the signature, and the corresponding public key validates it. To save time, the *Authenticode* protocols use a cryptographic digest, which is a one-way hash of the document. The process is outlined below and shown in Figure 7.4 on page 171.[v]

1. Publisher obtains a Software Developer Digital ID from VeriSign
2. Publisher creates code
3. Using the SIGNCODE.EXE utility, the publisher:
   Creates a hash of the code, using an algorithm such as MD5 or SHA
   Encrypts the hash using his/her private key
   Creates a package containing the code, the encrypted hash, and the publisher's certificate
4. The end user encounters the package.
5. The end user's browser examines the publisher's Digital ID. Using the VeriSign® root Public Key, which is already embedded in *Authenticode*-enabled applications, the end user browser verifies the authenticity of the Software Developer Digital ID (which is itself signed by the VeriSign® root Private Key).
6. Using the publisher's public key contained within the publisher's Digital ID, the end user browser decrypts the signed hash.
7. The end user browser runs the code through the same hashing algorithm as the publisher, creating a new hash.
8. The end user browser compares the two hashes. If they are identical, the browser messages that the content has been verified by VeriSign, and the end user has confidence that the code was signed by the publisher identified in the Digital ID, and that the code hasn't been altered since it was signed.

NOTE *The entire process is seamless and transparent to end users, who see only a message that the content was signed by its publisher and verified by VeriSign.*

Timestamping

Because key pairs are based on mathematical relationships that can theoretically be "cracked" with a great deal of time and effort, it is a well-established security principle that digital certificates should expire. Your VeriSign® Digital ID will expire one year after it is issued. However, most software is intended to have a lifetime of longer than one year. To avoid having to resign software every time your certificate expires, a timestamping service is now available. Now, when you sign code, a hash of your code will be sent to VeriSign to be timestamped. As a result, when your code is downloaded, clients will be able to distinguish between code signed with an expired certificate, which should not be trusted, and code signed with a certificate that was valid at the time the code was signed, but which has subsequently expired. This code should be trusted.[vi]

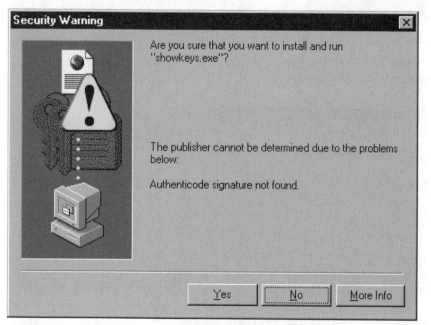

FIGURE 7.1   Security warning screen. *(©Copyright 2002. VeriSign. All rights reserved).*

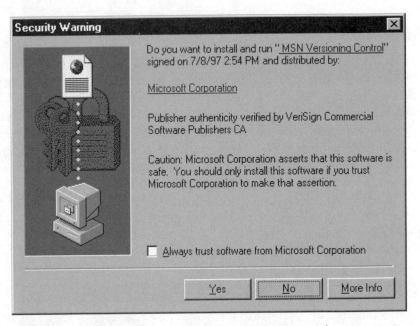

FIGURE 7.2 Client application security warning. *(©Copyright 2002. VeriSign. All rights reserved).*

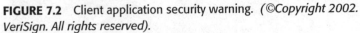

FIGURE 7.3 Inspect the certificate and verify its validity. *(©Copyright 2002. VeriSign. All rights reserved).*

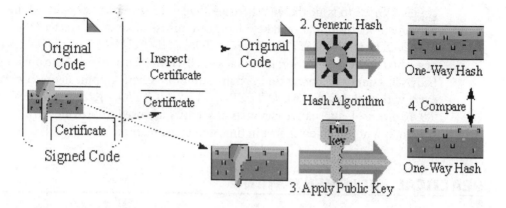

FIGURE 7.4 Authenticode–VeriSign® Digital IDs Process. *(©Copyright 2002. VeriSign. All rights reserved).*

PRACTICAL CONSIDERATION

It is useful to present some fundamental requirements of a forensic data collection system before considering how these can be securely protected. These requirements were chosen to reflect the experience of computer forensic investigators. Other forensic experts may argue against some or all of them:

1. Forensic data collection should be complete and non-software specific—thus avoiding software traps and hidden partitioning.
2. In operation, it should be as quick and as simple as possible to avoid error or delay.
3. It should be possible for anyone to use a forensic data collection system with the minimum amount of training.
4. Necessary costs and resources should be kept to a minimum.[vii]

To meet the conditions specified in items 2, 3, and 4 in the preceding list, the *DIGITAL INTEGRITY VERIFICATION AND AUTHENTICATION* protocol must be tailored to suit. For the collection phase to remain quick and simple, the *DIGITAL INTEGRITY VERIFICATION AND AUTHENTICATION* protocol must not add significantly to the time required for copying, nor should there be additional (possibly complex) procedures.

The time and effort required to introduce links with key management agencies, trusted third parties, key distribution centers, and similar paraphernalia of digital signatures and document authentication is not necessary. It would add to the cost and complexity with little increase to security. It might mean, for example, that only investigators issued with a valid digital signature would be able to complete copies. Who is to issue these? Where are they to be stored? How will each individual remember his or her own key? How can misuse of keys be detected?

The *DIGITAL INTEGRITY VERIFICATION AND AUTHENTICATION* protocol described in the next section is virtually a self-contained system. Quite obviously, a truly self-contained encryption system cannot be cryptographically secure. However, within the *DIGITAL INTEGRITY VERIFICATION AND AUTHENTICATION* protocol, alternative channels of security are used to provide a truly secure system, but at much lower cost in time and consumables.

PRACTICAL IMPLEMENTATION

The emphasis here is on a practical application of proven technology, such that a minimum amount of reliance is placed on the technical ability of the operator/investigator. It must be understood that during the copying process, procedures are implemented to trap and handle hardware errors, mapping exceptions where necessary. It must also be understood that procedures are implemented to verify that information is copied correctly.

Within the current *DIBS®* system, as well as the raw data content of the suspect disk drive, a copy is also taken of the high section of conventional memory (to include any on-board ROM areas) and the CMOS contents via port access. This information is stored on each cartridge within a copy series.

Also stored on each cartridge is a reference area containing copy-specific information—such as CPU type and speed; hardware equipment indicators; copying drive serial number; cartridge sequence number; exhibit details and reference comments; operator name together with a unique password; and the real date and time as entered by the operator. The remainder (in fact the bulk) of each cartridge contains the information copied from the suspect drive on a sector by sector basis.

For the purposes of the *DIGITAL INTEGRITY VERIFICATION AND AUTHENTICATION* protocol, the cartridge is divided into blocks of an arbitrarily chosen size. Blocks may contain reference, ROM, CMOS, or disk data depending on their location on the cartridge.

A prespecified area of each cartridge is set aside to store integrity verification information for the blocks on that cartridge. Using the analogy of a bank vault and safety deposit boxes—the storage area containing the integrity verification information pertaining to each block is referred to as a safe box. Also, the whole of the prespecified area where the safe boxes are stored is referred to as the vault.

Safe Boxes and the Vault

As each block is copied and verified, a hash value is generated such that a single bit change anywhere within the block would produce a different hash. The result is stored in the relevant safe box and copying proceeds to the next block.

Once all the blocks relevant to a particular cartridge have been copied and treated in this way, the whole group of safe boxes, collectively referred to as the vault, are treated as an individual block and a vault hash value is generated and stored in the final safe box. The vault is then copied to another area of the cartridge and this second copy is encrypted.

The vault hash value for each cartridge is stored in a separate area in memory and the operator is prompted to insert a new cartridge until the copy is completed. The final cartridge will contain similar information to the others in the series and in addition will have the accumulated vault hash values from all other cartridges in the series.

Once the final cartridge has been copied, the operator is prompted to insert a preformatted floppy disk into the drive used to start the *DIBS®* process. All of the accumulated vault hash values are then written to a floppy disk together with the reference details of the whole copy procedure. At least two (identical) floppy disks are created in this manner, although the operator may elect to generate more if he or she wishes.

The floppy disks are then sealed in numbered, tamperproof bags and both numbers are written on both envelopes. These are then shown to the owner of the computer or his or her legal representative and he or she chooses one of them. The computer owner is then given his or her chosen floppy and the other is placed in secure storage. The tamperproof envelopes are printed with instructions on their use and storage, such that the computer owner is aware of the protection that he or she is being given. If the computer owner or his or her legal representative is not available, then both disks are placed in secure storage.

Finally, for computer forensics investigators and senior technology strategists, IT security with regards to image verification and authentication is a study in contrasts. On the one hand, it's a topic that chief information officers (CIOs) repeatedly cite as one of their most important issues, if not the most important. Yet, despite the 9-11-2001 terrorist attacks, CIOs and senior IT executives still suggest that their non-IT colleagues simply do not share their sense of urgency. Perhaps that's because relatively few security breaches have hit their organizations—and most of those are of the *nuisance* variety, which doesn't cost a lot of hard dollars. Unfortunately, security is like insurance: You never know when you'll need it. With that in mind, let's take a look at why there isn't a sense of urgency in implementing image verification and authentication security considerations.

SUMMARY

The overall security of a computer image verification and authentication system rests in the combination of security measures. These can be summarized technically as follows:

- The block hash values are generated in conjunction with a one-time pad simulation. As well as providing continuity between blocks, this also negates the redundancy encountered when copying the type of data found on fixed disks (quantities of zeroes, ASCII text, and fixed structures). Thus, repeat hash values are avoided and a possible birthday attack is thwarted.
- The encryption of the vault, because it only occurs at the end of each section of the copy, can be accomplished using a secure encryption algorithm.
- Both the prosecuting and defending parties have a secure protection against the possibility of the evidence being tampered with as long as they retain the sealed floppies. In the event of a challenge, one or both envelopes can be opened in court and verified against each other and the cartridges. In the event of a mismatch with the cartridge, reference to the encrypted vault stored on the cartridge will show which block on the cartridge has been altered (or even the vault itself).[ix]

Finally, image verification and authentication security involves a relatively straightforward risk-management equation (the more security you put in place, the more onerous it is for end users), and until the technology arrives to make impenetrable security invisible to end users, it will remain that way. Most CIOs today clearly support increased security, and although they fault their non-IT cohorts for lack of security awareness, they appear to be realistic about the burden it puts on their companies' business units. But, CIOs aren't instituting enough of the high-profile risk-assessment measures that would increase awareness of the problem throughout their corporations.

Conclusions Drawn from Computer Image Verification and Authentication

- Having examined various alternative methods of copying suspect computers, a computer image verification and authentication concept with dedicated hardware remains the simplest, most secure, and most practical method currently available.
- Copying directly to CD-ROM is not possible without some buffer drive to enable correct data-streaming; this introduces a number of potential problem areas both with the increasingly complex hardware and evidential continuity.

- It should also be noted that CD-ROM technology was originally developed for audio requirements and the current reliability when storing digital data is extremely suspect.[x]

- Copying to tape is less expensive, but the viability of data stored for long periods (in many cases—years), particularly if unattended, is also extremely suspect. Both of these methods have additional problems of data verification during and after the copy process.

- Software-copying packages intended for use on nonspecific peripheral storage devices raise problems of technical support and hardware matching.

- The problems that were originally anticipated with rewriteable media have not materialized and the advantages of rewriteable media far outweigh the disadvantages.

- The process of copying fixed disks at BIOS level has enabled *DIBS®* to avoid problems with operating systems and access control mechanisms while the drive restoration process has proven capable of dealing with all currently available operating systems on the PC platform. In spite of these observations, no forensic copying system in current use offers equal protection to both the investigator and the computer owner. Note that this protection depends on neither how securely the copy cartridges are stored nor the relative security attending the storage of the floppy disks. Rather, it depends on the combination of all three and the technical security of the encryption mechanisms.

- *The DIGITAL INTEGRITY VERIFICATION AND AUTHENTICATION* protocol is not intended to supplant the existing dual-copy practice being used by most international law enforcement agencies. The intention here is to provide an equally secure alternative with due consideration of costs and resources.

- The presence of a cryptographically secure verification of the contents of each cartridge is a vital addition in this age of high-tech crime. It may even be considered useful by some operators to use both the dual-copy practice and the *DIGITAL INTEGRITY VERIFICATION AND AUTHENTICATION* protocol because this provides combined security of data contents with integrity verification and security for the computer owner.

- It is accepted that no security system can be 100% foolproof against subversion. However, careful consideration and detailed research have produced the *DIGITAL INTEGRITY VERIFICATION AND AUTHENTICATION* protocol previously described and this is considered to be as secure as is practically possible for the material being protected.

- When it comes to security readiness, company size doesn't matter. Larger companies (those with at least 1,000 employees) typically devote larger portions of their IT department's staff and budget to image verification and authentication security measures, but they are also more likely to have suffered security breaches, to have seen the number of security breaches increase from the previous year, and to have experienced more serious security problems.

■ Security breaches normally cost larger companies $79,000, compared with $56,000 for smaller companies.

■ Denial-of-service attacks are far more likely to occur at larger organizations.

■ Larger companies are also more likely to be hit with a virus than smaller companies, and more likely to have their Web sites defaced.

■ CIOs who place a high priority on security will spend an average of $647,000 in 2003 on security measures and technologies; whereas their counterparts who place a lower priority will spend an average of $432,000.

■ The role of senior business executives in beefing up security is significant, but CIOs continue to express concerns with their executives' approaches to security.

■ Indications are that CIOs often see their executives as paying lip service to aligning their companies' business practices with security concerns. At the same time, CIOs don't seem to be taking all the steps they could or should be taking to make security a higher priority for their companies.

■ There aren't many significant differences between CIOs who assign a high priority to security and those who don't, in terms of what security features they've put in place.

■ Antivirus software and firewalls are far and away the most frequently deployed technologies.

■ Desktop antivirus software is either already in place or in the process of being installed by the CIOs' companies.

■ Technologies not yet widely deployed include image verification and authentication, decoy services, risk-assessment software, and Public Key Information (PKI) document encryption.

■ The only significant divergence between CIOs who view security as a high priority and those who do not, is in the use of risk-assessment software, PKI document encryption, hybrid intrusion detection, and managed security services for firewall management.

An Agenda for Action in Computer Image Verification and Authentication

The following is a provisional list of actions for computer image verification and authentication. The order is not significant; however, these are the activities for which the research would want to provide a detailed description of procedures, review, and assessment for ease of use and admissibility. A number of these computer image verification and authentication topics have been mentioned in passing already:

1. To successfully subvert the *DIGITAL INTEGRITY VERIFICATION AND AUTHENTICATION* protocol, it would be necessary to: Alter the data on the cartridge—either in a manner that ensures that the relevant data block produces the same hash value or the relevant hash value is recalculated and inserted it into the vault; all the subsequent derivative hash values are recalculated; the relevant encrypted block is recalculated and rewritten; the seals on the relevant *DIGITAL INTEGRITY VERIFICATION AND AUTHENTICATION* floppy disks are broken; and the data is rewritten and the seals are repaired—without detection.

2. An alternative attack might be (if the machine in question was available) to alter the data on the machine and then re-*DIBS®* it. This would require: The original *DIBS®* drive; the original password known only to the copying officer (and severally encrypted on each cartridge in the series); exact knowledge of the date and time settings within the computer at the time of the original copy; and either a similarly numbered tamperproof bag on which the defendant's signature would be forged, or the original bag opened and resealed with the new floppy inside.

3. Any discrepancies between the defendant's floppy disk and that of the investigators should be examined and analyzed to determine whether such discrepancies disqualified any or all of the copied data. The digital integrity of the floppy disk and the physical integrity of the tamperproof bag are, in this case, the arbiters of whether such discrepancies were deliberately manufactured.

4. The inclusion of the encryption phase means that the digital integrity of any element in the chain (cartridges and floppies) should be verified independently of the others. It is, thus, useless for a defendant to destroy his or her floppy disk in the hope that its absence will assist any challenge to the *DIGITAL INTEGRITY VERIFICATION AND AUTHENTICATION* protocol.

5. Security-conscious CIOs should meet with their counterparts to: discuss security issues with their senior executives; have a dedicated chief security officer; perform a formal assessment of security risk; conduct simulated security breaches; force users to change passwords more frequently; and consult with vendors about their own security precautions.

6. CIOs should be taking all the steps they can to make security a higher priority for their companies.

with, or in exigent circumstances, without a search warrant, may enter the premises, examine records, and copy or seize them. They may use the computer system on the premises to search data and produce print-outs, which they may then seize for examination or copying.

Plaintiffs' lawyers and government investigators need to develop the knowledge and skill necessary to take advantage of the information residing in electronic form. This does not mean that they need to become computer specialists, but rather, that they need to understand enough about technology to ask the right questions and enlist the assistance of the forensic computer experts where necessary. Lawyers who choose to ignore these new opportunities could expose themselves to malpractice claims.

Lawyers representing parties with large amounts of electronic data need to understand that their clients' data will be targeted for such discovery and need to advise their clients on how to prepare. Defensive strategies that should be implemented prior to litigation include a proper document retention program, periodic purging of magnetic media, and the implementation of a document management system. Once litigation has commenced, defendants need to be better advised on how to preserve relevant electronic evidence adequately—to avoid possible sanctions or a negative inference at trial.

Now, let's begin the discussion of electronic document discovery. This is the process of viewing log files, databases, and other data sources on unseized equipment to find and analyze information that may be of importance to a computer crime investigation.

ELECTRONIC DOCUMENT DISCOVERY: A POWERFUL NEW LITIGATION TOOL

Other than direct testimony by an eyewitness, documentary evidence is probably the most compelling form of evidence in criminal and civil cases. Often, important communications are committed to writing and such writings can make or break a case. The same is true about documents used to conduct financial transactions. The *paper trail* has always provided a wealth of information in criminal and civil cases involving fraud. Traditional *paper* documents have been sought in the legal discovery process for hundreds of years in cases involving white collar crime (financial frauds, embezzlements). In more recent times, documentary evidence has become the keystone in civil cases involving wrongful employment dismissals, sexual discrimination, racial discrimination, stock fraud, and the theft of trade secrets. Today, judges and attorneys are very familiar with documentary evidence in *paper* form. Unfortunately, the legal process has not kept pace with computer technology and the document discovery rules have changed concerning the discovery of computer-created documents and related electronic data.

In years past, documentary evidence was limited to paper documents. Subpoenas and court orders were issued for the production of specific documents and the best evidence was typically considered to be the final draft of a document in paper form. Today, documents are rarely typed or handwritten. Most documents are created using personal computers with word processing applications or e-mail programs. Most professionals rely on personal computers to maintain diaries and to create their written communications. Most computer users have become prolific writers because of the convenience that computers provide. As a result, more documentary evidence exists today than ever before and it exists in a variety of electronically stored formats. However, you should keep in mind that a majority of computer-created documents are never printed on paper. Many are exchanged over the Internet and are read on the computer screen. Thus, the legal document discovery process has drastically changed as it relates to computer-created documents.

The best evidence rules also work differently today, because copies of computer files are as good as the original electronic document. From a computer forensics standpoint, this can be proven mathematically. There is no difference between the original and an exact copy. In addition, modern technology has created new types of documentary evidence that previously did not exist. This is especially true for the creation of documents on a computer word processor. When electronic documents are created, bits and pieces of the drafts leading up to the creation of the final document are written in temporary computer files, the *Windows* swap file, and file slack. The computer user is usually not aware of this situation. Furthermore, when computer-created documents are updated or erased, remnants of the original version and drafts leading up to the creation of the original version remain behind on the computer hard disk drive. Most of this data is beyond the reach or knowledge of the computer user who created the data. As a result, these forms of *ambient* data can become a valuable source of documentary evidence. Lawyers are just beginning to understand the evidentiary value of computer-related evidence and computer forensics in the document discovery process. It is becoming more common for lawyers to seek production of the entire computer hard disk drives, floppy diskettes, zip disks, and even cell phones and palm computer devices. These new forms of documentary evidence have broadened the potentials for legal discovery.

Electronic document discovery is clearly changing the way lawyers and the courts do business when it comes to documents created with personal computers. From a computer forensics perspective, computer data is stored at multiple levels on computer storage media. Some levels are visible to the computer user and others are not. When computer files are deleted, the data is not really deleted. Also, fragments of various drafts of documents and e-mail linger for months in bizarre storage locations on hard disk drives, floppy diskettes, and zip disks. Government intelligence agencies have relied on these secret computer storage areas for years, but the word is starting to get out. Electronic document discovery is making a difference in civil and criminal litigation cases. This is especially true in cases involving the theft of corporate trade secrets and in wrongful dismissal lawsuits. The trail of computer evidence left behind on notebook and desktop computers can be compelling.

A historical perspective helps one understand the evolution of computer forensics and its transition into the new field of electronic document discovery. When computer mainframe giant International Business Machines (IBM) entered the personal computer market in October of 1981, the event quickly captured the attention of corporations and government agencies worldwide. Personal computers were no longer thought of as toys; almost overnight they were accepted as reliable business computers because of the IBM endorsement. Since their introduction, IBM PCs and compatible computers have evolved into powerful corporate network servers, desktop computers, and portable notebook computers. They have also migrated into millions of households and their popularity exploded during the 90s when mankind discovered the Internet.

The worldwide popularity of both personal computers and the Internet has been a mixed blessing. Powerful personal computers are technology workhorses that increase productivity and provide portability. The Internet provides a conduit for the transfer of communication and computer files anywhere in the world via personal computers. However, essentially all personal computers lack meaningful security. This is because security was not factored into the design of the original personal computers or the Internet for that matter. The DOS operating system installed on the original IBM PC was never intended for commercial use. Security was never part of its design; in the interest of maintaining compatibility with the early versions of DOS, upgrades did not adequately address security. As a result, most popular desktop PCs and notebook computers lack adequate security. This situation creates an ideal environment for electronic document discovery of computer files, file fragments, and erased files. Some computer forensics specialists regard electronic document discovery as nothing more than the exploitation of the inherent security weaknesses in personal computers and the Internet.

You would think that the obvious security vulnerabilities of personal computers would be a wake-up call for government agencies and corporations. You would also think that individuals who carry *secrets* on their desktop and notebook computers would be more careful given these inherent security weaknesses. Lawyers, accountants, bankers, insurance agents, bankers, and health care professionals are particularly at risk because they are responsible for the *secrets* of others. It is likely that most lawyers don't even understand the potentials for attorney–client information to be compromised when computer files and data are exchanged with others.

These security issues should be of concern to computer users. However, they provide great benefits to lawyers concerning the potentials of electronic document discovery. Most computer users are unaware that their personal computers track their every move as it relates to documents created over time. This situation provides the technology savvy attorney with an edge when it comes to document discovery. Computer files, erased files, e-mail, and ambient computer data can be subpoenaed in civil and criminal cases. The attorney just needs to understand the potentials and the new twist in thinking that is required to reap the benefits of electronic document discovery.[ii]

SUMMARY

Computers should now be considered a primary source of evidence in almost every case. With businesses and individuals relying on computers for data processing, scheduling and communications, it is possible to discover anything from background information to the "smoking gun" document by investigating what is on your opponent's computer systems.

With that in mind, this chapter began the discussion with consideration of the process of information discovery. The fact that information discovery only deals with logical evidence (electronic data) means that you can avoid much of the tedium required by search and seizure to ensure evidence integrity and the chain of custody. Nevertheless, as you have seen, there are strong similarities between the two processes throughout their respective basic rules and planning stages.

For information discovery, where the basics are concerned, the investigator is occupied with safeguarding the chain of custody. During the planning stage, emphasis is given to understanding the information being sought after. Back-ups of discovered information files are critical to the overall process, and tools such as revision-control software can be very handy for this task.

Conclusions Drawn from Discovery of Electronic Evidence

- With regards to the basics of the information discovery process, establishing and protecting the chain of custody for logical evidence should be straightforward!
- The three basic rules of thumb should act as guides for any information discovery. Each rule has a parallel in the world of physical search and seizure.
- The notable difference between searching for physical evidence and searching for logical evidence is that, in the latter, there is much less structure.
- Because the format and location of information varies tremendously from case to case, how information is discovered depends on the circumstances of the case and the imagination of the investigator.

■ Once information is found, however, rigorous methods are applied to its handling and processing.

■ Computer forensics may be applied: search and seizure and information discovery. Although different in their implementations, both of these areas share a few prominent common principals. These include the important concept that evidence should always be backed-up and digitally authenticated prior to forensic work. Both approaches require that everything the investigator does be carefully documented. In addition, for both areas, the evidence preservation lab plays an important role as a secure, controlled environment for computer forensics work and evidence storage. Without such a facility, the investigator will have a difficult (if not impossible) time maintaining the chain of custody while examining and holding evidence.

■ The use of secure case-management software is highly desired because it lends structure, efficiency, and safety to the gathering and management of case notes and data.

■ In a venue where law enforcement authorities are investigating a computer crime, there is a measurable chance that a case could find its way to court. Within a corporation or other organization, however, things are vastly different.

■ Companies loathe being involved in litigation—even in situations where it appears the law is on their side!

■ It's no surprise that legal fees and bad publicity can take a mighty toll on the "bottom line." For this reason, much of what the corporate computer fraud and abuse investigator does is for naught.

■ It's easy for a corporate investigator to become frustrated and even disillusioned with his or her work when he or she sees good cases ending up on the wayside due to fears of bad PR. Such feelings must be contained, as they will quickly result in laziness and incomplete work on the part of the investigator.

■ Most of the computer crime cases handled by the corporate investigator won't end up in litigation; however, this does not apply to all cases!

■ Even a seemingly low-profile case can take a sudden twist and end up garnering the attention of the CEO.

■ Because practically any case can turn into a matter for litigation, the corporate investigator needs to treat all cases with a proper and reasonable amount of attention.

An Agenda for Action in Discovery of Electronic Evidence

The following is a provisional list of actions for discovery of electronic evidence. The order is not significant; however, these are the activities for which the research would want to provide a detailed description of procedures, review, and assessment for ease of use and admissibility. A number of these discovery of electronic evidence topics have been mentioned in passing already:

1. Do not alter discovered information.
2. Always back-up discovered information.
3. Document all investigative activities.
4. Accumulate the computer hardware and storage media necessary for the search circumstances.
5. Prepare the electronic means needed to document the search.
6. Ensure that specialists are aware of the overall forms of information evidence that are expected to be encountered as well as the proper handling of this information.
7. Evaluate the current legal ramifications of information discovery searches.
8. Back-up the information discovery file or files.
9. Start the lab evidence log.
10. Mathematically authenticate the information discovery file or files.
11. Proceed with the forensic examination.
12. Find the MD5 message digest for the original information discovery file or files.
13. Log all message digest values in the lab evidence log.
14. When forensic work is complete, regenerate the message digest values using the back-ups on which work was performed; log these new values along-side the hashes that were originally generated. If the new values match the originals, it's reasonable to conclude that no evidence tampering took place during the forensic examination of the information file(s)
15. Briefly compare the physical search and seizure with its logical (data-oriented) counterpart, information discovery.

ENDNOTES

i John R. Vacca, *The Essential Guide to Storage Area Networks*, Prentice Hall, 2002.

ii "Electronic Evidence Discovery: A Powerful New Litigation Tool," New Technologies Armor, Inc., 2075 NE Division St., Gresham, Oregon 97030, 2002.

9   Identification of Data

The Internet—friend or enemy? The popularity of the Internet has grown at incredible rates and today it reaches into the hearts of many corporations and households worldwide. The Internet gives computer users access to a wealth of information. It is also a wonderful mechanism for the exchange of e-mail communications and file attachments globally. International boundaries no longer exist when it comes to the exchange of information over the Internet. This new technology has proven to be ideal for international commerce and has the potential to be a valuable communications tool for exchange of law enforcement and government information. However, the Internet also provides the *crooks* with communication capabilities that did not exist previously. Through the use of a modem and with just a few clicks of a mouse, criminals can share information worldwide. It is sad but very true. Cyber crime has become a reality in our modern world.

More and more, law enforcement agencies are encountering computers at crime scenes. These computers are used to store the secrets of criminals and are also used in the commission of crimes. Internet-related crimes are clearly on the rise and abuses of corporate and government Internet accounts by employees are becoming commonplace. For example, one recent case involved an employee of a large corporation. He was using his corporate Internet account, on company time, to run his side business. What a deal—thanks to the Internet, he had two day jobs. To make matters worse, he was also using the corporate computers on company time to view and download pornographic images from the Internet. In another case, a law enforcement management official destroyed his 15-year law enforcement career when he was caught using a law enforcement computer to download pornography from the Internet. Just recently, law enforcement officials in Herndon, Virginia were requesting help in the investigation of the rape of a young girl. The girl had been lured from an Internet chat room to meet the rapist at a shopping mall. When the rapist was finally caught, his computer contained crucial evidence in the case.

The law enforcement community is starting to effectively deal with computer-related criminal investigations. Funding is finally being focused on the creation of local and state computer crime units. Law enforcement training organizations such as the National White Collar Crime Center, Search Group, International Association of Computer Investigation Specialists, and the Federal Law Enforcement Training Center are training hundreds of law enforcement computer specialists each year. Some of these training efforts are being directed at Internet-related crimes and more training emphasis will be placed on this important technology issue in the future.

Now, let's look at how keeping an accurate and consistent sense of time is critical for many computer-forensic-related activities such as data identification. In other words, being able to investigate incidents that involve multiple computers is much easier when the timestamps on files (identified data) and in logs are in sync.

TIME TRAVEL

It seems that, although every computer has a clock, none of them appear to be synchronized—unless the computer in question is running the Network Time Protocol (NTP). With NTP, you can synchronize against truly accurate time sources such as the atomic clocks run by NIST, the U.S. Naval Observatory, or counterparts in other countries around the world.

NOTE

NTP is a protocol built on top of TCP/IP that ensures accurate local timekeeping with reference to radio, atomic, or other clocks located on the Internet. This protocol is capable of synchronizing distributed clocks within milliseconds over long periods of time. It is defined in STD 12, RFC 1119. The package that implements the latest version of NTP is called xntp™, and was developed at the University of Delaware. You can obtain the latest version of xntp via anonymous ftp to terminator.rs.itd.umich.edu in the file /unix/xntp/xntp-src.tar.Z. You may also find binary distributions there. Filenames for binary distributions will be named xntp-VERSION-OSNAME.tar.Z, (the binary distribution for SunOS is named xntp-3.4h-sunos4.tar.Z).

File names and URLs can change without notice!

So, what does accurate timekeeping have to do with computer forensics? Keeping a consistent sense of time is critical for many computer-forensic-related activities.

Financial organizations rely on accurate timekeeping for their transactions. Many authentication systems, Kerberos being the most prominent example, use dated tickets to control access to systems and resources. Investigating incidents that involve multiple computers is much easier when the timestamps on files and in logs are in sync.

NTP began as a tool that permitted researchers to synchronize workstation clocks to within milliseconds or better. With the growth of the Internet, the mechanisms that enabled NTP clients and servers to securely exchange time data have gone from sufficiently secure to not nearly secure enough. A new version, NTP 4, seeks to fix that, while providing a model for automatic configuration and key exchange. Let's take a look at time-synchronization systems, and how you can securely use them to set all your clocks accurately.

Time Matters

Why bother having accurate clocks? Isn't the one that comes in your desktop PC or your Sun Enterprise server adequate? The answer is that accurate timekeeping is an advanced science, an avocation practiced by hundreds of scientists around the world, and the paltry clock chip you have in your PC or expensive server winds up being a bit less accurate than your Swatch watch for several reasons.

Computer clocks, like most electronic clocks, detect the oscillations of a quartz crystal and calculate the passing time based on these oscillations. Not all quartz crystals are the same to begin with, but put one inside of a nice, hot computer that's also cool whenever it's turned off, and the crystal's frequency tends to wander. Also, Unix systems base their notion of time on interrupts generated by the hardware clock. Delays in processing these interrupts cause Unix system clocks to lose time—slowly, but erratically. These small changes in timekeeping are what time scientists call *jitter*.

Over time, scientists and programmers have developed different techniques for synchronizing clocks over TCP/IP or other network protocols. The time protocol provides a server's notion of time in a machine-readable format, and there's also an Internet Control Message Protocol (ICMP) timestamp message. Though these remain available Internet standards, neither is currently sufficient for accurate timekeeping, and, hence, both are considered out-of-date. The *Unix r* commands include *rdate*, which permits setting a local clock based on a remote server. There are modem-based programs that contact NIST timeservers and fetch a time message (along with an estimate of round-trip time to account for latency), which you can still use today.

The NTP software includes drivers for a large number of devices—radios that listen to time signals such as WWV, Global Positioning System (GPS) receivers, and even atomic clocks—that serve as references for stratum-one servers. The University of Delaware site includes lists of stratum-one servers in the United States; you can also find stratum-one servers through Web search engines.

WWV is a radio station operated by NIST that maintains an atomic clock used by the scientific community.

NOTE

Below stratum-one servers are many stratum-two servers, and stratum-three servers are below that, and so on. NTP supports up to 15 different stratums, but being closer to the top implies being closer to the most accurate source of time. To improve each server's notion of time, servers in the same stratum may peer (that is, act as equals) and perform the same timestamp exchanges done by NTP clients. NTP servers and clients don't blindly accept another system's notion of time, even if it comes from a higher stratum. This was NTP's only security provision for a while.

Clock Filters

Automatically accepting another system's statement about the current time can be harmful: Suppose the timekeeping system has been taken over by an attacker who needs to *turn back the clock* so that a replay attack can function. NTP guards against this in several ways.

First, NTP assumes that time moves forward, not backward, although small backward changes are acceptable. Also, if a system has been using NTP, the NTP software assumes that changes in a local clock will be small, generally less than a second. This makes controlling a local clock or making large changes literally a time-consuming process—even a one-second change is a big deal.

NTP goes beyond this by collecting timestamps from many different servers (and peers, if appropriate). NTP maintains a queue comprised generally of eight samples and uses carefully crafted algorithms to compute the best approximation of exact time. For example, the outlyers in the sample (the timestamps with the largest divergence) are discarded. The remaining set of samples is then used to calculate what the local clock should read. On Unix systems, a special system call, *adjtime()*, makes small adjustments to system time. With multiple sources, the influence of a single, compromised timeserver (a falseticker, in NTP jargon) is completely avoided. You can modify the configuration of *ntpd* to label a timeserver as untrusted. You can also use the configuration to list trusted timeservers and peers.

By the late 1980s, version 2 had been released. NTP 2 included digital signatures based on a shared secret key so that servers and peers could sign NTP data and prevent an attacker from spoofing packets. NTP uses UDP packets (on port 123), which are easy to spoof because of their stateless nature (no connection setup, as in TCP).

Autokey

Version 4 of NTP is (most likely) still an Internet draft. Working versions of NTP 4 are being tested, and version 4 may have entered the IETF standards track by the time you read this book.

The most interesting aspects of version 4 are the security improvements. A system called the autokey uses public key algorithms combined with a list of one-way hashes. When a client contacts an NTP server, the client can collect a certificate that contains the server's public key and independently verifies it. Then, using the enclosed public key, the client can check the signature sent by the server containing a list of keyids. The keyids are used with session keys to perform a quick digital signature check based on MD5.

Using public key cryptography for signing timestamps is just too slow. Public key encryption algorithms aren't only slow (compared to private key algorithms such as RC4), they're also inconsistent in that the amount of time used to encrypt may vary by a factor of two—something very unpleasant for those obsessed with keeping accurate time. Using the list of keyids reduces the need for public key encryption to once an hour on average.

Version 4 also supports the Diffie-Hellman key exchange for peers, so that peers can exchange private session keys. Multicast updates of clients are also supported and use the client/server autokey for setting up security.

Next, let's look at how trade secret information and other sensitive data can easily be identified and secreted using any number of techniques. It is possible to hide diskettes within diskettes and to hide entire computer hard disk drive partitions.

FORENSIC IDENTIFICATION AND ANALYSIS OF TECHNICAL SURVEILLANCE DEVICES

It was one sentence among hundreds in a transcription of a dull congressional hearing on the environment, a statement anyone might have missed: Bristol-Myers Squibb Co. was looking to increase its harvest of the Pacific yew, a protected tree.

But, the competitive intelligence (CI) officer at arch rival SmithKline Beecham (SKB) Corp., happened to catch it, thanks to a routine search of competitors' activities on the Web.

The intelligence officer sprang into action. He knew Bristol-Myers' (BM) researchers had been testing a substance in the tree's bark as an experimental agent against breast cancer. But why was BM suddenly seeking to cut down 200 times as many yews? Was it ready to put its planned anticancer drug, Taxol, into production? Back at SmithKline headquarters in Philadelphia, the news was enough to trigger serious nail-biting in the boardroom. SKB was developing its own anticancer drug, Hycamtin, but it wouldn't be ready for another 18 months. Would it beat Bristol-Myers' drug to market? Or would SmithKline Beecham have to speed up its production schedule—and if so, by how much?

The intelligence officer's team wasted no time. It immediately began canvassing conferences and scouring on-line resources for clues. It tapped into Web sources on the environment and got staffers to work the phones, gathering names of researchers working for Bristol-Myers. It even zeroed in on cities where BM had sponsored experimental trials of the substance.

Sure enough, BM had had been taking out recruitment ads in those areas' newspapers for cancer researchers—a sure sign that Bristol-Myers was stepping up its hiring of oncologists specializing in breast cancer. The next clue? From data discovered on financial Web sites and in the comments of Wall Street analysts, the intelligence officer's team discovered that BM was increasing its spending on its oncology group.

That was all intelligence officer needed to hear: Senior R&D managers were ordered to speed things up, and ended up rushing Hycamtin to market in six months instead of 18—preserving SKB some $50 million in market share and millions in drug development costs. The CIA, the National Security Agency, and England's M15 used a form of CI to figure out what the Russians were doing. SKB used it too.

SmithKline Beecham's tale of how competitive intelligence saved a company millions is no longer unusual. Indeed, one of corporate America's worst-kept secrets these days is that more and more companies, from Burger King to Nutrasweet to MCI, are spying—and have in-house operations to keep tabs on rivals. The number of large corporations with CI units has tripled since 1995, and spending on CI is estimated to be around $14 billion annually—nearly double the amount spent just five years ago.

To be sure, data-diving isn't new. As far back as the 1970s, in a now-famous example of excess zeal, The Boeing Company discovered that a Russian delegation visiting one of its manufacturing plants was wearing crepe-soled shoes that would surreptitiously pick up metal shavings off the factory floor to determine the type of exotic metal alloys Boeing was using in its planes. And at Motorola Inc., the former chief of competitive intelligence used to work for the CIA.

But now, thanks to the Net and its ever-growing, low-cost reach and speed, nearly everybody's spying. In a May 2001 survey by marketing firm TR Cutler, Inc., 55% of U.S. manufacturing companies with fewer than 1,000 employees admitted to spying on competitors during the previous 12 months, using the Web and posing as potential customers to glean pricing and other competitive tidbits.

Cold War, Revisited

Now, here's a real secret: Until recently, most corporate gumshoeing was being outsourced to spy companies with 007-sounding names such as WarRoom Research Inc., many of which were founded by ex-CIA, National Security Agency, and Mossad operatives seeking work after the Cold War. Now, though, corporate snooping is increasingly being conducted in-house—and for the first time, Chief Information Officers (CIOs) are being forced to the frontlines. More and more CIOs are gaining responsibility for the intelligence function. And why not? Information is about technology, and information is increasingly a company's competitive edge.

To be sure, companies without the ability to pluck the juiciest scoops from a growing quagmire of data will increasingly lose market share to those companies that can. This is now a double-edged game. Those who get spied on are now also spying.

Case in point: The CIO of 3COM Corp., makers of Internet switches and hubs, now supplies employees with two toll-free numbers: one to report any intrusions into corporate secrets; the other to report what 3COM's rivals are up to. You've got to take the offensive these days, or you'll be clobbered in the marketplace. Stiffening competitive pressures of the current economy are only exacerbating the spy-versus-spy mentality.

What is competitive intelligence? Everything from illegal spying and theft of trade secrets to classic intelligence-gathering—whatever it takes to provide executives with a systematic way to collect and analyze public information about rivals and use it to guide strategy. At its best, competitive intelligence borrows tools and methods from strategic planning, which takes a broad view of the market and how a company hopes to position itself, and from market research, which pinpoints customers' desires. Its goal: to anticipate, with razor-sharp accuracy and speed, a rival's next move, plot new opportunities, and help avert disasters.

CI is hottest in the pharmaceuticals, telecom, petrochemicals, and consumer products industries, where consumers are the most fickle and where speed and flexibility are especially critical for success. Indeed, some companies, from Burger

Companies that ignore the CIO do so at their peril. Recently, that happened to a large telecom equipment maker with 10,000 home pages on its supply-chain intranet. Several hundred of the home pages were dedicated to the competition. But, there was no coordination between home pages. This was a situation where the CIO could have taken charge and made sure the information was in one spot. How many tens of millions of dollars were thrown at that intranet and wasted annually in inefficient man-hours?

Where to begin? Ideally, CIOs can help marketing and sales strategies turn on a dime. CI teams should spend one-third of their time gathering information on a project, one-third in analysis, and one-third discussing their findings. Instead, many companies spend 80% of their CI time on collection, most of the rest on analysis, and very little on communication that reaches everyone. CIOs can step in and devise ways to improve the ability of executives to focus on information that really matters to them, with filters that take out the junk nobody needs to be looking at.

CIOs also can help determine what the company considers junk. Often the best competitive information does not appear as highly structured data, such as financial information. More likely, it's something like an offhand comment in a press release, a photograph in a rival's advertisement, or a soundbite from a television news show.

Once the best data is tagged for collection, who gets access to it? If you search for data involving a two-in-one laundry soap and fabric softener, what terms do you classify, and which do you let everyone see? CIOs can help companies figure out how to tag, gather, store, and distribute a wide range of competitive data with differing levels of access and indexing—and with standards that are consistent throughout the company, domestically and abroad. Most companies are sloppy about this. They haven't marked documents as confidential. And nobody beyond a certain level knows what, specifically, they're trying to find. They just know they want something, and fast. And with a proliferation of business relationships these days (joint ventures, M&As, supply-chain collaborations, and so forth) you really need to do an information audit to make sure you know what you have and what you need.

Building Teams

You need to build teams with diverse membership. People who understand the concept of organizing information and indexing it could be paired with someone who understands different technology capabilities, such as a relational database showing connections between different terms or items. As managers, CIOs have to amass different strengths on a CI project *so you don't have an abundance of hammer holders who look only for nails.*

But, don't get carried away on the technology. A study conducted by Fuld & Company[i] found flaws with many of the 170 software packages with potential CI applications. None of them were able to take companies through the process of data identification, discovery, distribution, and analysis. Each did some part of the process, but not the whole thing. The thinking machine has not yet arrived. No company should buy a software package in the hope it will build an intelligence process for the corporation. CIOs need to help build that. It won't come off the shelf.

Still not convinced? CIOs confident that their rivals' intranet data is too safe to even try prying open should take a ride down Virginia's Dulles Corridor, a throughway outside Washington, D.C., which is lined with high-tech firms. If you have a laptop, slip a wireless card[ii] into it and drive down Route 7. You can actually pick up one wireless network after another, including the networks of a major credit clearinghouse; as well as Department of Defense contractors that store classified data on their servers. Instead of hacking from the Internet, people can hack from inside on the intranet, albeit from the road, and probably get to the accounting server or worse. Imagine the kind of damage that a terrorist organization could do!

But, for all the digital dumpster-diving out there, don't forget that even the most high-tech firms are still using plenty of old-fashioned snooping. For example, when Oracle Corp. got caught (in the summer of 2000) hiring a Washington, D.C.-based detective group to dig into the dealings of organizations sympathetic to Microsoft Corp., it didn't use even a byte of cybersleuthing. It did it the old-fashioned way—rummaging through the dumpsters of one of those groups by bribing janitors at its Washington office.

In other words, in this business, you need to be aggressive. Take the offensive. And always recall the words of ancient Chinese general Sun Tzu (6th–5th century B.C.): "*Be so subtle that you are invisible, be so mysterious that you are intangible; then you will control your rival's fate.*"

Finally, let's look at the concept of Strategic Cyber Defense as it relates to data identification. This is a complex and broad-ranging concept. Yet, despite this complexity, you can make some progress in developing your understanding by focusing on a few key elements of any good defensive strategy. This last part of the chapter will specifically focus on the long-recognized value of deterrence, through threat of retaliation, as an effective means of defense. The means for enabling deterrence in the cyber realm will be introduced briefly here. A much more detailed discussion of cyber realm deterrence is found in Chapters 12 through 18 of Part IV: "Countermeasures: Information Warfare."

DETERRENCE THROUGH ATTACKER IDENTIFICATION

Deterrence is a fundamental element of defensive strategy. However, for deterrence to be effective, potential antagonists must be convinced that they will be identified, and punished swiftly and severely. This is the essence of the three key causal variables of the General Deterrence Theory: certainty, severity, and celerity. Unfortunately, although the methods for identifying perpetrators of crimes in the law enforcement and military contexts are well developed, similar capabilities do not currently exist for the networked cyber realm. Thus, although deterrence is recognized as a highly effective defensive strategy, its applicability to defense against attacks on our nation's information infrastructures has not been clear, mainly due to the inability to link attackers with attacks.

A conceptual tool that can help to visualize and understand the problem is to think of a thread, or sequence, of steps (with requisite technologies) necessary to effect a deterrent capability. As with the *weak link* and *picket fence* analogies, if any one of these steps is missing or ineffective, the ability to achieve the desired result is compromised.

Looking at this thread, you can see that current intrusion detection technology is focused primarily on the first element in the sequence. Any *response* is generally limited to logging, reporting, and isolating or reconfiguring. What is missing is the ability to accurately identify and locate attackers, and develop the evidentiary support for military, legal, or other responses selected by decision makers. Although defensive techniques are important, it's critical not to *stovepipe* in such a way that you can't effectively link with the offensive component of an overall Strategic Cyber Defense.

In addition to detecting the attacks, perhaps you should also be developing a *forensic,* or identification of data capability, to pass the necessary *targeting* data on to the offensive components of the force, regardless of whether the response is through physical or cyber means. Such a capability is critical if your cyber defenses are to transcend beyond a merely reactive posture to one in which both offensive and defensive techniques can be effectively applied in tandem. This is in line with the established principles of war, which suggest that an offensive (and, therefore, deterrent) spirit must be inherent in the conduct of all defensive operations. Forensics could help to provide the bridge between the defensive and offensive elements of an overall cyber defense strategy. Accurate and timely forensic techniques would also enable the effective use of the three elements of deterrence. Otherwise, attackers can act with impunity, feeling confident that they need not fear the consequences of their actions.

Forensics is a promising area of research that could help to provide the identification and evidence necessary to support an offensive response against attacks on our information infrastructure, regardless of whether that response is executed through physical, information warfare (IW), or other means. Although forensic techniques are highly developed for investigations in the physical realm (and are being developed for application to computer crime), what is needed is an analogous capability for real-time distributed network-based forensic analysis in the cyber realm. It would seem appropriate to incorporate the collection of forensic data with the intrusion detection and response types of technologies currently being developed. Critical supporting technologies include those needed for correlation and fusion of evidence data, as well as automated damage assessment.

The importance of solid identification and evidence linking an attacker with an attack will be critical in the increasing complexity of the networked information environment. Cyber attacks against the United States and its allies may not have the obvious visual cues and physical impact typically associated with attacks in the physical realm. In these cases, the available courses of action will be heavily influenced by various political, legal, economic, and other factors. Depending on the situation, it may be necessary to have irrefutable proof of the source of the attack, the kind of proof typically developed through forensic types of methods.

For example, the RAND Corporation[iii] has recently recommended to DARPA some approaches that are both similar and complementary to those suggested in this part of the chapter, based on the results of its "Day after in Cyberspace" exercise. One suggested concept is for a *cyberspace hot pursuit* capability, to aid in the back-tracing of incidents to discover perpetrators. They also point out that use of such a capability implies the need for laws specifying authorization to conduct cyberspace pursuits, and cooperative agreements with foreign governments and organizations. A second suggestion is for the development of a tamperproof, aircraft-like *black box* recording device to ensure that when an incident occurs and is not detected in real time, the trail back to the perpetrator does not become lost.

Extending the aircraft analogy further, the need for effective identification during cyberspace pursuits, and for coordinating offensive IW response actions through intermediary *friendly* networks, may necessitate a type of *network IFF* capability, just as the introduction of fast-moving aircraft in the physical realm necessitated the need for secure Identification Friend or Foe (IFF). Although the need for IFF has traditionally been a concern at the tactical level of warfare, the failure to effectively deal with such issues could certainly have strategic implications.

One issue of concern at the strategic level of information warfare is the distinction between the military and private sector information infrastructures. It is clearly not feasible to require the private sector to secure its systems to the level required for military networks. The approach suggested in this part of the chapter may be applicable regardless of whether the networks attacked belong to the military. For example, in the physical realm today, if a civilian target is struck, the FBI and other Federal agencies are called in to assist and investigate the incident; when the identity of the attackers is determined, appropriate legal, political, or military actions are taken in response. From an organizational perspective, efforts are under way to develop the necessary coordination structures, such as the National Infrastructure Protection Center, between the private and commercial sectors. From a technical perspective, major elements of the commercial infrastructure could participate in a national-level monitoring system, whereas private entities could maintain their own in-house capabilities with the ability to provide necessary data to national authorities following an incident, just as would be the case with the FBI being called in to investigate a crime.

Another fundamental concern the suggested approach may help to address is the problem of malicious *insiders*. The security paradigm of enclaves separated by boundary controllers is most effective against attacks from the outside. Attacks initiated from within the enclave, possibly even by a *trusted* insider, have traditionally been much harder to defend against. Cyber forensics techniques may provide the type of capability needed to deal with this problem, which simply cannot be addressed by traditional security techniques based on privileges. These systems simply check whether a user is acting within the prescribed privileges, while remaining in complete oblivion regarding the abuse of these privileges.

SUMMARY

As previously explained, computer forensics involves the preservation, identification, extraction, and documentation of computer evidence stored in the form of magnetically encoded information (data).[iv] Many times the computer evidence was created transparently by the computers operating system and without the knowledge of the computer operator. Such information may actually be hidden from view and, thus, special forensic software tools and techniques are required to preserve, identify, extract, and document the related computer evidence. It is this information that benefits law enforcement and military agencies in intelligence gathering and in the conduct of investigations.

Computer forensic software tools and methods can be used to identify passwords, computer network log-ons, and other information that is transparently and automatically transferred from the computers memory to floppy diskettes, Iomega Zip Disks, and computer hard disk drives. Such computer forensic software tools and methods can also be used to identify backdated files and to tie a floppy diskette to a specific computer.

Trade secret information and other sensitive data can easily be secreted using any number of techniques. It is possible to hide diskettes within diskettes and to hide entire computer hard disk drive partitions.

The final part of this chapter discussed a deterrence-based approach as an element of an overall cyber defense strategy. The need for timely and unequivocal identification of attackers is essential for such an approach to be effective. Unfortunately, the technical basis for such identification has not received much attention to date from the research and development community. In addition, there may be some complicating factors for the implementation of the type of identification and forensics capability discussed in this chapter, such as the widespread move to encryption. However, until research and development resources are committed to investigation of the relevant issues, the extent of the challenge cannot be fully understood.

Conclusions Drawn from Identification of Data

- The hiding of data in computer graphic files (steganography)
- Detection of steganography and watermarks
- Steganography jamming techniques and theory
- Data written to 'extra' tracks
- Data written to 'extra' sectors
- Data written to hidden partitions
- Data stored as unallocated space
- Massive amounts of data written to file slack areas
- Data hidden by diffusion into binary objects, *Windows* swap, and *Windows* page files
- Hidden disks within disks
- Floppy diskette data storage anomaly detection
- Data scrubbing of ambient data storage areas. These security processes are especially helpful when computers are transferred from one user to another.
- Data scrubbing of entire storage devices using methods that meet current DoD security requirements
- Shadow Data issues are a potential risk.
- The appending of data to program files, graphics files, and compressed data files. This method is simple and very effective.
- Electronic eavesdropping techniques, threats, risks, and remedies
- Covert capture of keystrokes via hardware and radio interception
- Tempest issues regarding the capture of computer screen images remotely
- Electronic eavesdropping techniques concerning cellular telephones
- Electronic eavesdropping techniques concerning personal pagers
- Search methodologies for use in the identification of foreign language phrases in binary form stored on computer media

10 Reconstructing Past Events

The increase in computer-related crime has led to development of special tools to recover and analyze computer data. A combination of hardware and software tools has been developed using commercial off-the-shelf utilities integrated with newly developed programs. Procedures have been defined and implemented to protect the original computer data. Processes have been developed to recover hidden, erased, and password-protected data. To that end, all recovery and analysis work is performed on image copies of the original.

Because there is a wide variety of computers, peripherals, and software available, including many different forms of archival storage (Zip, Jaz, disk, tape, CD-ROM, etc.),[i] it is important that a wide variety of equipment be available for recovery and analysis of evidence residing on a computer's hard disk and external storage media. Recovered data must be analyzed, and a coherent file must be *reconstructed* using advanced search programs specifically developed for this work.

For example, these techniques were recently used to recover data from several computers that indicated a large check forgery ring was in operation throughout California and personal and business identities were being stolen without the knowledge of the victims. Case files going back over 5 years were cleared with the information obtained.

In another case, proprietary intellectual property was found on the suspect's computer and was being used for extortion. In the case of a murdered model, the murderer's computer address book was recovered and is now being used to determine if he might be a serial killer. Another case involved a stalker who had restricted pager information on his victim, which was recovered from the suspect's computer.

With the preceding cases in mind, the primary goal of this chapter is to illustrate the reconstruction of past events with as little distortion or bias as possible. Many analogies can be drawn from the physical to the virtual realms of detective work—anyone who has seen a slaying on a police show can probably give a reasonably good account of the initial steps in an investigation. First, you might protect and isolate the crime scene from outside disturbances. Next, comes recording the area via photographs and note taking. Finally, a search is conducted to collect and package any evidence found.

HOW TO BECOME A DIGITAL DETECTIVE

Recovering electronic data is only the beginning. Once you recover it, you need to determine how to use it in your case. In other words, how do you reconstruct past events to ensure that will be admissible as evidence in your case? What follows are some recommendations for accomplishing that goal.

If You Need Help, Get Help

When you receive the package of evidence containing a Zip disk and cover letter stating, "Enclosed and produced upon you please find," you may not know what to do with the disk. If you don't know, get help.

Help may be just down the hall. If you have an information services department, consider going there. They might not understand what you mean by a discovery request, but they may be able to help you convert the contents of the disk to a form you can look at. If you have a litigation support group, consider contacting them. They may have the tools you need to look at and start working with the data you just received. Even if there is no formal entity within your office dedicated to dealing with technological issues, there may be informal resources.

In addition, your client may have the resources you need. Your expert witnesses, assuming you have some, may be able to sort out the data for you. If you are using a litigation support vendor, that organization may be able to bring skills to bear. And, of course, don't forget the professionals, the ones who deal with electronic data recovery and reconstructing past events for a living.

Convert Digital Evidence

Before you can reconstruct past events and present the data, you need it on a medium and in a format you can work with. In other words, you need to get the data onto a medium you can use, if it is not already on one. Data can come on a variety of media, such as data tapes, Zip disks, CD-ROM disks, 3.5-inch floppy disks, and 5.25-inch floppy disks.

If you receive electronic evidence on an 8-millimeter data tape, chances are that you will not have an 8-mm tape drive at your desk. Even if you have a drive, it may not be able to read that specific tape. You need to get the data onto a medium your computer can read, which these days generally means a 3.5-inch floppy or a CD disk. How do you do this?

Well, for example, you could use Zip disks. Zip disks are simpler. The cost of Iomega Zip drives (http://www.iomega.com) is so low that you can keep one on hand just to copy data from Zip disks you receive (and to copy data to Zip disks when others request data from you on that medium).

CDs are even simpler, as CD drives have become commonplace on PCs. Similarly, 3.5-inch disks generally pose no problem.

Nevertheless, 5.25-inch floppy disks have started to become problematic, as fewer and fewer PCs have the drives in them. Older sizes of floppies can be even more difficult; when you receive electronic data on them, you usually have to engage outside vendors to move the data over to media you can work with.

Put the Evidence in a Useable Format

Having data on a useable medium is useless unless it also is in a useable format. At times this is not an issue. If the data comes in a format that you already use, then you can begin to work with it as soon as you get it off the media. The formats most likely to be useable without conversion are word processing files (principally *Word-Perfect* and *Word* files), spreadsheet files (principally *Excel* and *Lotus*), and presentation files (principally *PowerPoint* files).

USEABLE FILE FORMATS

Even if the data is in a format that appears to be one you already use, conversion still may be necessary. The format may be too new. For example, you will not be able to open an old *Word 97* file if you are using *WordPerfect 5.1* or even *Word 7.0*. The problem is a basic one. When those programs were written, *Word 97* did not yet exist. As a result, they do not have in them the pieces of code needed to read old *Word 97* files. You will need to find a machine with a word processing package capable of reading old *Word 97* files. Alternatively, you will need to get a program, such as *Word for Word*, that can recognize and work with many different file types. In a similar vein, you may have to get the data converted if it comes to you in a format that is too old or runs on a different operating system.

Finally, you may encounter problems of the *WordPerfect*-versus-*Word* kind. Although simpler files created with one company's software generally can be opened without a problem using a competitor's comparable product, this often

SUMMARY

Once the data has been successfully collected, it must be analyzed to extract the evidence you wish to present and to rebuild what actually happened. As for everything, you must make sure you fully document everything you do—your work will be questioned and you must be able to show that your results are consistently obtainable from the procedures you performed.

This is where logging utilities come in. Logging utilities are vital for forensics when reconstructing the sequence of events leading up to, during, and after an attack, provided the attacker doesn't delete the log files. Refining the firewall rules, keeping the IDS current, and reviewing the log files will be important to stay one step ahead of the bad guys.

Conclusions Drawn from Reconstructing Past Events

- Computer Forensics is the principle of reconstructing the activities leading to an event and determining the answer to "What did they do?" and "How did they do it?"
- Stored information can be volatile and persistent at the same time.
- As you can see, collecting electronic evidence is no trivial matter. There are many complexities you must consider, and you must always be able to justify your actions.
- Gathering electronic evidence is far from impossible though—the right tools and knowledge of how everything works is all you need to gather the evidence required.
- Audit trails can also be used to reconstruct events after a problem has occurred.

An Agenda for Action in Reconstructing Past Events

The following is a provisional list of actions for reconstructing past events. The order is not significant; however, these are the activities for which the research would want to provide a detailed description of procedures, review, and assessment for ease of use and admissibility. A number of these reconstructing past events topics have been mentioned in passing already:

1. To reconstruct the events that led to your system being corrupted, you must be able to create a timeline. This can be particularly difficult when it comes to computers—clock drift, delayed reporting, and differing time zones can create confusion in abundance.
2. One thing to remember is not to change the clock on an affected system.

3. Record any clock drift and the time zone in use as you will need this later, but changing the clock just adds in an extra level of complexity that is best avoided.

4. Log files usually use timestamps to indicate when an entry was added, and these must be synchronized to make sense.

5. You should also be using timestamps—you're not just reconstructing events, you yourself are making a chain of events that must be accounted for as well.

6. It's best to use the GMT time zone when creating your timestamps because the incident may involve other time zones than your own, so using a common reference point can make things much easier.

7. When analyzing back-ups, it is best to have a dedicated host for the job. This examination host should be secure, clean (a fresh, hardened install of the operating system is a good idea), and isolated from any network—you don't want it tampered with while you work, and you don't want to accidentally send something nasty down the line.

8. Once the system is available, you can commence analysis of the backups. Making mistakes at this point shouldn't be a problem—you can simply restore the back-ups again if required.

9. Remember the mantra—document everything you do.

10. Ensure that what you do is not only repeatable, but that you always get the same results.

11. Now that you have collected the data, you can attempt to reconstruct the chain of events leading to and following the attacker's break-in.

12. You must correlate all the evidence you have gathered (which is why accurate timestamps are critical), so it's probably best to use some graphical tools, diagrams, and spreadsheets.

13. Include all of the evidence you've found when reconstructing the attack—no matter how small it is, you may miss something if you leave a piece of evidence out.

14. The amount of damage that occurred with an incident can be assessed by reviewing audit trails of system activity to pinpoint how, when, and why the incident occurred.

ENDNOTES

i   John R. Vacca, *The Essential Guide To Storage Area Networks*, Prentice Hall, 2002.

11 Networks

As information systems become cheaper and cheaper, companies are rapidly automating not only their overhead processes such as purchasing, payables, hiring, and payroll, but also their value by adding processing such as marketing and sales. The result of this rush to automate and, with the explosion of the Internet, a rush to publish, is the highest level of dependency on information systems corporate America has ever seen. With this dependency comes a vulnerability: The ability of corporations to conduct their business is dependent on technology that was designed to be as *open* as possible and that only a minority of engineers and scientists understand.

When netted out, what managers need to do is create barriers that deter cyber-based or internal perpetrators from attacking their systems. The first way to do this is to analyze corporate resources for know vulnerabilities. That is, systems need to be checked that they are correctly configured and have the most up-to-date security patches in place. This is what security scanners do. Next, one needs to find out the perpetrator's methods of operation and alert when those methods are sensed. This is what intrusion detectors do. Next, one needs a mechanism to filter out suspected malicious activity, once it is identified. This is what firewalls do. However, even with all of these systems in place, there is a vulnerability to attacks that use new or unknown methods of attack.

What current Intrusion Detection Systems (IDS) do is monitor the network and watch for specific patterns. Once a pattern is recognized, IDS can alert the systems administrator, close the connection via the firewall, or record the activity for further analysis. However, if an attacker uses a method not previously known to the IDS, it will transpire unnoticed, the corporate Web site will be defaced, employee records will be retrieved, or client lists will be extracted. When the malicious act is

According to the court, the reasonable translation of electronic data into a usable form is an ordinary and foreseeable burden of litigation that the defendant should bear, absent a showing of extraordinary hardship.

And the fact that the electronic data may be duplicative of print documentation already produced in litigation is irrelevant. Thus, for example, when the insurance company in American Bankers Ins. Co. of Florida v. Caruth, et al., 786 S.W.2d 427 (Tex. Ct. App. 1990), failed to produce computer files despite already having produced approximately 30,000 boxes of material containing the same information, the court sanctioned the company by conclusively deeming each allegation against the company to be true, thereby precluding the company from contesting the allegations and leading to entry of default judgment against it.

Hitting the *delete* button on your keyboard is not a panacea either. Do you remember Oliver North, whose deleted e-mail messages from the White House were retrieved from a main frame back-up tape during the Iran-Contra investigation? If information that has been deleted has not yet been overwritten by the computer system or is stored on back-up tapes or archive tapes, the information may still be accessible.

Any attempts to destroy the e-mail will likewise be met with harsh consequences. For example, in Computer Associates International, Inc. v. American Fundware, Inc., 133 F.R.D. 166 (D. Colo. 1990), a developer of a computer program, over the course of years, destroyed prior versions of a source code, retaining only the current version. Although the court acknowledged that such destruction of older versions may be the standard industry practice, the court found that once the developer knew, or should have known that the source code would probably be critical evidence in pending or imminent litigation, a duty arose to preserve it. The court held that the developer had received a copy of the lawsuit filed by the holder of the copyright to the computer program; but continued to destroy older versions of the source code. Therefore, the developer had breached his or her duty to preserve the code. Accordingly, the court entered default judgment against the developer as an appropriate sanction.

Employers beware, for even prelitigation correspondence has been found sufficient to impose a duty to preserve relevant documents, electronic or otherwise (see the example of William T. Thompson Co. v. Gen'l Nutrition Corp., 593 F. Supp. 1443, 1446 [C.D. Cal. 1984]). Recently, one court imposed a $1 million sanction, as well as reimbursement of attorney fees, even though no willful destruction of electronic records was found (see the example of Prudential Insurance Co. Sales Practices Litigation, 169 F.R.D. 598 [D.N.J. 1997])!

To avoid these litigation nightmares, you should implement a consistent retention policy that includes one or more of the following: routinely archive all e-mail as it is received on your server for a certain period of time (say, 30–60 days); clear the archives after an additional specified time; physically segregate the back-up copies of the e-mail system from back-ups of the rest of the computer system; automatically erase e-mail from the computer system, including backups, after a short period (15-30 days); apply uniform retention and deletion standards and features outside the server to workstations and laptops; and formulate and distribute a statement that the automatic deletion of electronic records will be suspended and steps taken to preserve records in the event of investigation or litigation. With such a policy in place, you may not stay out of the courtroom, but at least you will be prepared if you ever find your company the target of a lawsuit or subpoena.

Now, let's look at the development of cross-disciplinary guidelines and standards for the recovery, preservation, and examination of digital evidence, including audio, imaging, and electronic devices with regards to the damaging of computer evidence. This part of the chapter proposes the establishment of standards for the exchange of digital evidence between sovereign nations and is intended to elicit constructive discussion regarding the damaging of digital evidence.

DAMAGING COMPUTER EVIDENCE

The latter part of the 20th century was marked by the electronic transistor and the machines and ideas made possible by it. As a result, the world changed from analog to digital. Although the computer reigns supreme in the digital domain, it is not the only digital device. An entire constellation of audio, video, communications, and photographic devices are becoming so closely associated with the computer as to have converged with it.

From a law enforcement perspective, more of the information that serves as currency in the judicial process is being stored, transmitted, or processed in digital form. The connectivity resulting from a single world economy in which the companies providing goods and services are truly international has enabled criminals to act transjurisdictionally with ease. Consequently, a perpetrator may be brought to justice in one jurisdiction while the digital evidence required to successfully prosecute the case may reside only in other jurisdictions.

This situation requires that all nations have the ability to collect and preserve digital evidence without damaging it, for their own needs as well as for the potential needs of other sovereigns. Each jurisdiction has its own system of government and administration of justice, but for one country to protect itself and its citizens, it must be able to make use of undamaged evidence collected by other nations.

Though it is not reasonable to expect all nations to know about and abide by the precise laws and rules of other countries, a means that will allow the exchange of undamaged evidence must be found. This part of the chapter also defines the technical aspects of these exchanges.

Standards

To ensure that digital evidence is collected, preserved, examined, or transferred in a manner safeguarding the accuracy and reliability of the evidence, law enforcement and forensic organizations must establish and maintain an effective quality system. Standard Operating Procedures (SOPs) are documented quality-control guidelines that must be supported by proper case records and use broadly accepted procedures, equipment, and materials.

The use of SOPs is fundamental to both law enforcement and forensic science. Guidelines that are consistent with scientific and legal principles are essential to the acceptance of results and conclusions by courts and other agencies. The development and implementation of these SOPs must be under an agency's management authority.

Rapid technological changes are the hallmark of digital evidence, with the types, formats, and methods for seizing and examining digital evidence changing quickly. To ensure that personnel, training, equipment, and procedures continue to be appropriate and effective, management must review and update SOP documents annually.

Because a variety of scientific procedures may validly be applied to a given problem, standards and criteria for assessing procedures need to remain flexible. The validity of a procedure may be established by demonstrating the accuracy and reliability of specific techniques. In the digital evidence area, peer review of SOPs by other agencies may be useful.

Procedures should set forth their purpose and appropriate application. Required elements such as hardware and software must be listed and the proper steps for successful use should be listed or discussed. Any limitations in the use of the procedure or the use or interpretation of the results should be established. Personnel who use these procedures must be familiar with them and have them available for reference.

Although many acceptable procedures may be used to perform a task, considerable variation among cases requires that personnel have the flexibility to exercise judgment in selecting a method appropriate to the problem. Hardware used in the seizure and/or examination of digital evidence should be in good operating condition and be tested to ensure that it operates correctly. Software must be tested to ensure that it produces reliable results for use in seizure and/or examination purposes.

In general, documentation to support conclusions must be such that, in the absence of the originator, another competent person could evaluate what was done, interpret the data, and arrive at the same conclusions as the originator. The requirement for evidence reliability necessitates a chain of custody for all items of evidence. Chain-of-custody documentation must be maintained for all digital evidence.

Case notes and records of observations must be of a permanent nature. Hand-written notes and observations must be in ink, not pencil, although pencil (including color) may be appropriate for diagrams or making tracings. Any corrections to notes must be made by an initialed, single strikeout; nothing in the handwritten information should be obliterated or erased. Handwritten signatures, initials, digital signatures, or other marking systems should authenticate notes and records.

As outlined in the preceding standards and criteria, evidence has value only if it can be shown to be accurate, reliable, and controlled. A quality forensic program consists of properly trained personnel and appropriate equipment, software, and procedures to collectively ensure these attributes.

International Principles against Damaging of Computer Evidence

The International Organization on Computer Evidence (IOCE) was established in 1995 to provide international law enforcement agencies a forum for the exchange of information concerning computer crime investigation and other computer-related forensic issues. Comprised of accredited government agencies involved in computer forensic investigations, IOCE identifies and discusses issues of interest to its constituents, facilitates the international dissemination of information, and develops recommendations for consideration by its member agencies. In addition to formulating computer evidence standards, IOCE develops communications services between member agencies and holds conferences geared toward the establishment of working relationships.

In response to the G-8 Communique and Action plans of 1997, IOCE was tasked with the development of international standards for the exchange and recovery of undamaged electronic evidence. Working groups in Canada, Europe, the United Kingdom, and the United States have been formed to address this standardization of computer evidence.

During the International Hi-Tech Crime and Forensics Conference (IHCFC) of October 1999, the IOCE held meetings and a workshop that reviewed the United Kingdom Good Practice Guide and the SWGDE Draft Standards. The working group proposed the following principles, which were voted on by the IOCE delegates present with unanimous approval. The international principles developed by IOCE for the standardized recovery of computer-based evidence are governed by the following attributes:

- Consistency with all legal systems
- Allowance for the use of a common language
- Durability
- Ability to cross international boundaries
- Ability to instill confidence in the integrity of evidence

- Applicability to all forensic evidence
- Applicability at every level, including that of individual, agency, and country[ii]

Furthermore, these international principles were presented and approved at the International Hi-Tech Crime and Forensics Conference in October 1999. They are as follows:

- Upon seizing digital evidence, actions taken should not change that evidence.
- When it is necessary for a person to access original digital evidence, that person must be forensically competent.
- All activity relating to the seizure, access, storage, or transfer of digital evidence must be fully documented, preserved, and available for review.
- An individual is responsible for all actions taken with respect to digital evidence while the digital evidence is in their possession.
- Any agency that is responsible for seizing, accessing, storing, or transferring digital evidence is responsible for compliance with these principles. [iii]

So, do you have a well-documented intrusion-detection response plan? In other words, if you are attacked, do you have the documentation tools that are needed to record the attack, so that you can make the proper response? Let's take a look.

DOCUMENTING THE INTRUSION ON DESTRUCTION OF DATA

It is very important to document and inventory the tools needed for intrusion response due to the destruction of data—including ID software, back-ups and file-system-recovery tools. There is also a need to have written requirements for training IT staff on how to deal with intrusions. This can be SANS courses, CERT's Software Engineering Institute, training offered for your intrusion detection tools, or even custom training developed in-house. Training should also include some form of regular fire drill.

Incident Reporting and Contact Forms

Documenting the intrusion (incident) on destruction of data is very important, not only as an aid for solving the intrusion problem, but also for an audit trail that may even be used in criminal proceedings. It is critical to capture as much information as possible and create forms enabling users who are not ID specialists to provide as much information as possible. Some of the important elements of incident reporting forms are:

- Contact information for person(s) discovering problem and/or responsible parties
- Target systems and/or networks. Know all about the systems under attack, including operating system versions, IP addresses, and so on.
- Purpose of systems under attack. Know which systems are used for (payroll, R&D, and so on), as well as some kind of a ranking of the importance of the system.
- Evidence of intrusion. Discover anything that is known about the intrusion, method of attacks used, source IP address of attacker, and network contact information for this address.
- List of parties to notify. This can include the technical contacts, internal legal contacts, and possibly the legal authorities.

Finally, when it comes to hardening your network against hackers, the best defense is to keep abreast of developing threats and test your system with due diligence. In other words, you need to seal off the leaks.

SYSTEM TESTING

It seems you can't open a newspaper or listen to the news these days without learning that yet another company's network has been broken in to. The Anna Kournikova worm and the "I Love You" virus are just two of the most notorious recent examples; the truth is that resilient new viral strains are popping up every day. Even worse, thanks to the advent of always-on DSL, ISDN, and cable modem connections, security breaches that were once limited to large corporations or government facilities are now finding their way into your homes as well.

Is your network vulnerable? If you do business on the Web or maintain a connection to an outside network, chances are that the answer is yes. Fortunately, it's not hard to decrease the odds of attack or intrusion. Statistics show that more than 80% of successful hacks occur because Web technicians fail to install patches for known and publicized bugs. In other words, a little effort can go a long way toward securing your network.

DNS: The Good, the Bad, the Ugly

If you've ever used a URL to represent an IP address, you've used DNS—a distributed database that provides translation capabilities between domain names and IP addresses. DNS also provides a standard Internet mechanism for storing and accessing other types of data, such as MX (mail exchange) records.

posture results in very large datasets that necessitate the use of data visualization techniques to reasonably analyze events.

■ Visualization software should be produced to present the IP sessions in a manner that enables visual data mining. This will consist of gaining an understanding of IP session attributes, mapping these attributes to visual resources (x-axis, y-axis, z-axis, color, shape, thickness, etc.), establishing the connections to the datasets, and constructing dynamic, data-driven visualization displays.

■ The resulting visualizations should allow an analyst with a cursory understanding of data networks to identify normal patterns of network traffic and therefore identify deviations from the norm.

■ The visualizations would allow an analyst to drill through the volumes of data from the global view down to individual events or transactions.

■ Different visualizations will be explored with ease of use and data density as the evaluation criteria.

■ Acquisition of digital evidence begins when information and/or physical items that are collected or stored for examination purposes.

■ The term "evidence" implies that courts recognize the collector of evidence.

■ The process of collecting is also assumed to be a legal process and appropriate for rules of evidence in that locality.

■ A data object or physical item only becomes evidence when so deemed by a law enforcement official or designee.

■ Data objects are objects or information of potential probative value that are associated with physical items.

■ Data objects may occur in different formats without altering the original information.

■ Digital evidence is information of probative value stored or transmitted in digital form.

■ Physical items are items on which data objects or information may be stored and/or through which data objects are transferred.

■ Original digital evidence are physical items and the data objects associated with such items at the time of acquisition or seizure.

■ Duplicate digital evidence is an accurate digital reproduction of all data objects contained on an original physical item.

■ Copy is an accurate reproduction of information contained on an original physical item, independent of the original physical item.

■ With forensic competency, there is a need to generate an agreement on international accreditation and the validation of tools, techniques, and training.

■ Issues need to be resolved that relate to practices and procedures for the examination of digital evidence.

■ The sharing of information that relates to hi-tech crime and forensic computing is needed—such as events, tools, and techniques.

- SNMP is an extremely useful feature for recording system error messages from servers and routers, but it can also reveal quite a bit of information about your network.
- With the volume of network traffic increasing every day, network security remains a top priority. Most instances of unauthorized access result from simple negligence; so if all your company does is pay attention and adhere to a few basic routines, you'll already be ahead of the game.

An Agenda for Action in Networks

The following is a provisional list of actions for networks. The order is not significant; however these are the activities for which the research would want to provide a detailed description of procedures, review, and assessment for ease of use and admissibility. A number of these network topics have been mentioned in passing already:

1. Provide expert data visualization techniques to the problem of network data pattern analysis
2. Apply standard research and analysis techniques to datasets provided by a company or organization
3. Apply the lessons learned from company-provided datasets to open datasets as the research advances
4. Provide initial datasets, project initiation, and training in network traffic datasets and analysis techniques
5. Provide expert network forensical rule-based algorithms for incorporation by researchers
6. Repeatedly test and verify new visualization techniques and procedures to ensure that new patterns are, in fact, accurate representations of designated activities
7. Develop a test database
8. Develop a design methodology for visualizing test data
9. Develop a query interface to the database
10. Map data structures to a visualization model
11. Build a prototype
12. Refine a prototype
13. Incorporate live Internet data
14. Test live Internet data
15. Deliver a final build
16. Produce new visualization techniques to streamline and enhance analysis of network forensic data
17. Produce a Web browser compatible prototype that demonstrates these techniques to visualize and query vast amounts of data. The resulting

interactive visualization interface will advance the usability of the system, solve the volumetric problem with analyzing these datasets, and advance the adaptation of the solution in the INFOSEC market.

18. Routinely archive all e-mail as it is received on your server for a certain period of time (say, 30–60 days)
19. Clear the archives after an additional specified time
20. Physically segregate the back-up copies of the e-mail system from back-ups of the rest of the computer system
21. Automatically erase e-mail from the computer system, including back-ups, after a short period (15–30 days)
22. Apply uniform retention and deletion standards and features outside the server to workstations and laptops
23. Formulate and distribute a statement that the automatic deletion of electronic records will be suspended and steps taken to preserve records in the event of investigation or litigation
24. All agencies that seize and/or examine digital evidence must maintain an appropriate SOP document
25. All elements of an agency's policies and procedures concerning digital evidence must be clearly set forth in this SOP document, which must be issued under the agency's management authority
26. Agency management must review the SOPs on an annual basis to ensure their continued suitability and effectiveness
27. Procedures used must be generally accepted in the field or supported by data gathered and recorded in a scientific manner
28. The agency must maintain written copies of appropriate technical procedures
29. The agency must use hardware and software that is appropriate and effective for the seizure or examination procedure
30. All activity relating to the seizure, storage, examination, or transfer of digital evidence must be recorded in writing and be available for review and testimony
31. Any action that has the potential to alter, damage, or destroy any aspect of original evidence must be performed by qualified persons in a forensically sound manner
32. Be alert. One of the best ways to ensure that your network is secure is to keep abreast of developing threats. Security experts agree that ignorance is the most detrimental security problem. Most hacks occur because some-

one wasn't paying attention. Web sites such as the CERT home page (http://www.cert.org) are excellent places to get current information.

33. Apply all service patches. Many companies will sit on patches rather than put them to use. Others are not diligent enough about searching for and downloading the latest virus definitions. Smart hackers bank on the negligence of others.

34. Limit port access. Although just about any application that uses TCP requires a port, you can minimize exposure by limiting the number of ports accessible through a firewall. NNTP (Network News Transport Protocol) is an excellent example: Unless your shop requires newsgroup access, port 119 should be shut down.

35. Eliminate unused user IDs and change existing passwords. Poor maintenance is almost as dangerous as ignorance.

36. System administrators should routinely audit and delete any idle user IDs.

37. To limit the likelihood of successful random guessing, all user and system passwords should be system-generated or system-enforced.

38. Avoid the use of SNMP across the firewall

39. Routers should be checked to make sure they do not respond to SNMP commands originating outside the network.

40. Secure remote access. Try to break into your own network. You can learn a lot by hacking into your own system.

41. If you can gain access to your systems from a workstation outside your network, you can easily test your packet-filtering scheme without any outside exposure. If you do spot a weakness, you'll be one step ahead of the hackers.

42. When in doubt, ask a consultant. If you don't have the technical wherewithal in-house or if your staff is too busy working on other projects, don't hesitate to call in a consultant. Many companies offer security assessment and training services.

43. Companies should assess their networking needs and shut down any ports that aren't necessary for day-to-day operations, such as port 53 for DNS access and port 119 for NNTP (Network News Transfer Protocol) services.

44. Be sure to eliminate unused user IDs and to avoid provisioning SNMP services through the firewall.

ENDNOTES

i   Advanced Visual System, World headquarters, 300 Fifth Avenue, Waltham, MA 02451, 2002.

ii U.S. Department Of Justice, Federal Bureau Of Investigation, J. Edgar Hoover Building, 935 Pennsylvania Avenue, NW, Washington, D.C. 20535-0001., 2002.

iii Ibid.

IV Countermeasures:
Information Warfare

12 | Fighting Against Macro Threats: Defensive Strategies for Governments and Industry Groups

Information warfare, or sneak electronic assaults, could easily crash power grids, financial networks, transportation systems, and telecommunications, among other vital services. The National Security Agency (NSA) traces the macro threat to hostile or potentially hostile governments as well as drug lords, criminal cartels, and increasingly computer-savvy guerrilla groups. Some of these rogue organizations are doing reconnaissance today on U.S. networks, mapping them, and looking for vulnerabilities.

Cyberblitzes like those that briefly knocked out major Web sites in February 2000 (including Yahoo! Inc.'s Internet gateway, eBay Inc.'s auction service, and Amazon.com Inc.'s retail site could easily be copied on a larger scale. Criminals, crackers, foreign governments—when President Bush reads that intelligence briefing, he had better move pretty fast!

Such warnings are not new for the agents at NSA, who have frequently conjured up a "digital Pearl Harbor"—a reference to the Japanese surprise attack that threw the United States into the Second World War. But the NSA and other U.S. officials seem to be stepping up a public awareness campaign, spurred by the spread of information technology, growing knowledge of malicious computer code, and ever-greater U.S. reliance on networked systems.

IS THE UNITED STATES GOVERNMENT PREPARED FOR INFORMATION WARFARE?

The answer to the preceding question is a resounding "no." A reasonable question that should be asked is "Why are we vulnerable?" In a recent report by the Defense

239

Science Board Task Force on Information Warfare, the task force unequivocally lays the blame at the U.S. government's own doorstep.

The reality is that the vulnerability of the Department of Defense (and of the nation) to offensive information warfare attack is largely a self-created problem. Program by program, economic sector by economic sector, the U.S. government has based critical functions on inadequately protected telecomputing services. In aggregate, the U.S. government created a target-rich environment and the U.S. industry has sold globally much of the generic technology that can be used to strike these targets. From the standpoint of psychological operations, it's not so much exploited technology as it is that the U.S. government has created a global information system it does not control and does not understand, and this in turn creates additional targets for exploitation. Most recently, this problem is being exacerbated by the growing emergence of "always-on" connections being made to individual homes and small businesses.

Recently, for example, a private security company alerted the FBI that it found a malicious program on some 3,000 computers that could be remotely activated to launch an attack on a site of choice—a Trojan. Many of these computers are privately owned and are on cable-modem or digital line subscriber (DSL) always-on connections. In addition to the technological risk posed by the fact that many of these computers have very limited or no security, the users of these computers often are attractive targets for social engineering efforts for a simple reason. The very thought that they would be targeted for an attack is foreign to the owners.

From an information warfare perspective, there are three primary target audiences for the attacker using psychological operations—PSYOPS. The attacker can focus on the enemy, those who are friendly to his or her cause, or the neutrals; with each target chosen for a specific purpose. If the attacker is simply a hacker/cracker/script-kiddy, it might be for nothing more than to grab a credit card number or prove to friends that he or she could do it. Unfortunately, the dangers the U.S. government faces are not limited to those groups. The government also faces the threat of multinational efforts to subvert their defenses and find an economic, diplomatic, or military advantage. These efforts might be aimed not only at the U.S. defense structure, but also at the U.S. utility infrastructure, transportation, communications, finance, and much more. The U.S. government also cannot discount the potential entrance of organized crime into the equation, not to mention political activists and disgruntled employees.

So, as more individuals (the neutrals) turn to the Internet to help them with tasks that have usually been served by personal service or other traditional means, tasks such as banking, tax filing, shopping, and personal communications, the Internet as a loci for commerce and communication becomes increasingly critical both to the individual and to the business and industries that serve the individual. And although the commercial sector is beginning to realize the importance of security, the information on the virtually unprotected personal machines may very well hold the key to a crippling attack on any sector simply because those sectors exist to allow the personal machines to connect to do business.

From a PSYOPS point of view, however, how is it done? In any attack, finding and exploiting a trust relationship can be a key to success for the attacker. Let's look at how a trust relationship can be exploited. One of the most often cited examples of a physical trust relationship that was exploited successfully is the Mitnick attack. Here Kevin Mitnick discovered a relationship between host A and host B. He was able to determine the probable response that host A would give to host B after receiving the initiating packet in a three-way handshake. He blocked host B with a Denial of Service attack and sent a packet to A crafted to look as if it came from B. He then sent the expected response along with a small payload that contaminated host A's .rhost file and caused host A at that point to completely trust Mitnick's computer. He dropped the attack on host B and simply accessed A as a trusted root user.

So, how might an attacker employ PSYOPS against a trust relationship? One of the more common examples used to explain trust exploitation is that of the over-worked call center. Imagine a worker at a large corporate call center. The caller has done some research and discovered that the CEO has hired a new personal report. He calls and identifies himself as Bert Jackson who has just been hired by the boss. He tells him he's been working all day researching a project that the CEO wants a report on in the morning and he needs access to the system to put the report together. Unfortunately, he's forgotten his password and it's already 11 P.M. Can he get a new password or should he call the CEO and have him call? In a shop with strong security that would be an easy call, but it's easy to see that, in many cases, the call center worker would simply trust that the caller is who he or she says he or she is and give out a new password. The net result? The attacker gets in and can probably hide his tracks before the real Bert Jackson complains.

If the company is also a prime contractor for the government, a public utility, or even a company whose success or failure can severely impact the stock market, then the attacker has gained a tremendous advantage by simply manipulating information he or she has gained by infiltrating the system. But, let's go back to Bert Jackson.

Assume, for this scenario, that a group wanted to create a deleterious impact on the stock market. That group, perhaps over a period of months, maps IP ranges that are known to belong to public Internet service providers (ISPs) providing high-speed, always-on access to individuals and small-businesses and they map for the Netbios ports. As they map, a second team begins the infiltration process, finding those machines that are unprotected and that contain information, such as passwords to personal investment accounts, banking, and the like. Even though these passwords may be encrypted, with modern cracking tools being what they are, at the end of the mapping period, they very well could have discovered thousands of accounts, including Bert Jackson's, that could be exploited. Choosing the time to strike, they simultaneously use these accounts to issue massive sell orders to the various brokers and close thousands of bank accounts with the money transferred to offshore accounts that they may or may not care about accessing. The distributed nature of this attack would make detection and prevention difficult, if not impossible, and would certainly sow an atmosphere of fear and distrust that would severely affect the general economy.

Again, the question is why? Let us look at the three basic types of attack—strategic, consolidation, and battlefield. If the preceding scenario were executed by organized crime, it would probably fall into the battlefield type because they probably would be looking to cause a drop in stock market prices where they could step in and buy cheaply, thus allowing them to see an impressive gain as confidence rebounded. If a foreign government perpetrated the attack, it might very well fall into one of the other two categories. The attackers might be trying to distract the attention of the current administration away from what they might be attempting elsewhere (strategic) or attempting to bring together the economic resources needed to launch a more serious battlefield attack against us later (consolidation).

But, what is it that causes you, as a whole, to make it easy for those who would want to abuse that trust? In a culture where the phrase "trust is earned" is a familiar maxim, it would seem that you would be more eager to challenge than you really are. However, trust also seems to be a social construct between two or more individuals. In both social and business milieu, as alluded to earlier, a need to trust develops out of the need to foster cooperation to achieve goals and objectives.

If that is, in fact, the case, then how does the U.S. government overcome this tendency and manage to protect their critical resources? Part of the difficulty they face here is that their focus tends to be on strengthening the security of their physical defenses, whether that be through encryption, perimeter-based defenses, host-based defenses, or, preferably, a combination of the three. Unfortunately, the U.S. government still has too few in system administrative positions who are security-aware enough to alter default installations on whatever machine they are setting up (whether it be Microsoft based or Unix based) to give an acceptable initial level of protection to their users. But these are technological trust defenses and likely will always be open to attack. And although hardening those physical defenses is undeniably important, the U.S. government often overlooks the most dangerous vulnerability (their users), and that is where they spend the least amount of time in education. Why do computer viruses such as the "I Love You" virus work? Because users, whether corporate, governmental, or private, haven't been taught how to protect themselves and change the paradigm of automatically trusting the e-mail that announces it comes from Aunt Barbara.

The U.S. government must begin focusing on the end user and on those who provide connections to the end users. When virtually all private connections to the

Internet were made over modems connecting to a Dynamic Host Configuration Protocol (DHCP) server where each session was served with a different IP address, it was much less likely for a private machine to be compromised and efforts to compromise machines tended to be focused on commercial, governmental, and educational systems. Today, however, that situation is rapidly changing and ISPs must accept the responsibility of advising or requiring their customers to install personal firewalls and give them the advice needed to properly configure and maintain those firewalls. They also must understand the need to properly filter their outgoing traffic to block and detect activity coming from within their networks that can be harmful to the general Internet community.

Educating the end user is going to be the most daunting task. The recent proliferation of e-mail-related viruses has certainly helped to awaken many to the dangers, but there must be a broader effort to educate and assist users in protecting themselves and the U.S. government from the bad guys. To do this, the security community needs to do a better job in educating first the media and then the public through the media. PSYOPS can work both ways. The difference between the U.S. government and the bad guys is that the government has permission—they have the intent to do what is right. So it is with perception management. The U.S. government can manage perception so that people will realize the risks they actually face and take steps to protect themselves. In helping them to protect themselves, the U.S. government also helps to protect the rest of the users on the Internet who could be attacked by their systems if they are compromised. Trust is wonderful when exercised in an environment where it is reasonable. In a global environment where criminals, unfriendly political forces, and people who just don't care about others have the same rights and access as anyone, trust can be dangerous.

Education, not legislation, is the key component. The U.S. government can pass all the laws it wishes, but it won't affect the traffic that is coming out of countries such as Korea, China, and Singapore. The government needs to be communicating these messages with intelligence. If the U.S. government knows what needs to be done and doesn't communicate it effectively, then whatever else it does is irrelevant. If the government scattershots their communications without filtering them through an understanding of the message they need to pass, then all they are sending out is noise.

ARE OTHER GOVERNMENTS PREPARED FOR INFORMATION WARFARE?

Are other governments ready to use information-age tricks to use against their adversaries? Yes, to some extent. Case in point is as follows:

At first, the urgent phone call from the U.S. Transportation Department confounded Cheng Wang, a Long Island-based Webmaster for Falun Gong, the spiritual

losses of more than $56 billion in 2000 from the theft of proprietary information—up from mid-1990s' estimates by the FBI that pegged the cost at roughly $24 billion a year. Tech companies reported the majority of those hacking incidents. The average tech company reported nearly 78 individual attacks, with the average theft resulting in about $26 million in lost business.

Following a string of attacks on federal systems, President Clinton in 2000 launched a $2 billion plan for combating cyberterrorism that included an educational initiative to recruit and train IT workers. The plan also included conducting federal agency vulnerability analyzes and developing agency-critical infrastructure protection plans. With the aftermath of the 9-11 terrorist attacks, the Bush administration is upgrading the preceding plan twenty-fold.

STRATEGIC DIPLOMACY AND INFORMATION WARFARE

Strategic diplomacy, according to the Department of Defense, is the "art and science of developing and using political, economic, psychological, and military forces as necessary during peace and war, to afford the maximum support to policies, in order to increase the probabilities and favorable consequences of victory and to lessen the chances of defeat." For most people, it is obvious that the political and economic aspects of the national security policies of the United States are developed by the national political authorities (the president and the Congress) and, in dealing with foreign states or groups, executed by the Departments of State, Commerce, Agriculture, and so on.

Policies for developing and using military forces are formulated by the national political authorities and conveyed to the armed forces through the secretary of defense. Few, however, have paid much attention to just how and by whom psychological forces are to be developed to support national policies. More important: What are psychological forces? Who will use these forces? With whose authority will this be done? To what ends?

New tools and technologies for communication have created the potential for a new form of psychological warfare to a degree imagined only in science fiction. This new form of warfare has become known as information warfare (IW). In other words, the United States armed forces need to develop a systematic, capstone concept of military knowledge diplomatic strategy. Such a strategy would include clear doctrine and a policy for how the armed forces will acquire, process, distribute, and project knowledge.

The U.S. military is expanding the concept of IW to include psychological operations aimed at influencing the emotions, motives, objective reasoning, and, ultimately, the behavior of others. Such an expansion would mirror the evolution of traditional warfare toward IW. It would also mirror the progressive steps of generating wealth from agriculture and natural resources in much earlier times, to the 19th- and early 20th century emphasis on industrial production, to the present emphasis on generating information products as a major new source of income.

As "first wave" wars were fought for land and "second wave" wars were fought for control over productive capacity, the emerging "third wave" wars will be fought for control of knowledge. And, because combat form in any society follows the wealth-creation form of that society, wars of the future will increasingly be information wars.

Currently, there is neither formal military doctrine nor official definitions of information warfare. Despite the computer jargon involved, the idea of information warfare has not only captured the attention of military analysts but also posed important policy questions.

Despite the lack of authoritative definition, "netwar" and "cyberwar" are emerging as key concepts in discussing IW. Originally, these ideas seem to have come from the science fiction community.

Netwar, is a societal-level ideational conflict waged in part through internetted modes of communication. That is, netwar is most likely to be a nation-against-nation strategic level conflict. Netwar is about ideas and epistemology—what is known and how it is known. It would be waged largely through a society's communication systems.

The target of netwar is the human mind. One could argue that certain aspects of the cold war had the characteristics of a dress rehearsal for future netwar. Consider, for example, Radio Free Europe, the Cominform, Agence France Presse, or the U.S. Information Agency. But netwar may involve more than traditional state-to-state conflict. The emerging of nonstate political actors such as Greenpeace and Amnesty International, as well as survivalist militias or Islamic revivalists, all with easy access to worldwide computer networks for the exchange of information or the coordination of political pressure on a national or global basis, suggests that the governments may not be the only parties waging Information War.

At first glance, netwar may appear to be a new word for old-fashioned propaganda. It would be comforting to believe that the tried and true methods (and limitations) of propaganda still worked. And the Gulf War showed that both Saddam Hussein and the Alliance were still of the old school. The war contained many elements of classic propaganda: accusations of bombed baby-milk factories and stolen baby incubators; inflated rhetoric and inflated stakes of the conflict; the future of the new world order and "the mother of battles" for the future of Islam; and the classic us or them polarization in which neutrality or unenthusiastic support was decried.

One element of traditional propaganda was absent, however, while Saddam Hussein became the new Hitler and President Bush Sr. was the Great Satan, there was little demonization or dehumanization of the opponent. Perhaps the multicultural nature of the American-led alliance precluded turning the Iraqi army into something subhuman. Indeed, there may have been a spark of netwar genius in treating the Islamic Iraqi soldiers as "brave men put into an impossible situation by a stupid leader." Under such conditions, there is no dishonor in surrendering. And there may have been a glimpse of future netwar—it is rumored that Baghdad Radio signed on one morning with *The Star-Spangled Banner*.

Traditional propaganda was usually targeted to influence a mass audience. Contemporary technologies have the potential to customize propaganda. Anyone who has received individually targeted advertising from a company specializing in niche marketing has had a momentary shudder upon realizing that some private companies seem to know everything about our tastes and buying habits.

Contemporary databases and multiple channels for information transmission have created the opportunity for custom-tailored netwar attacks. Computer bulletin boards, cellular telephones, video cameras tied to fax machines—all provide entry points and dissemination networks for customized assault.

A major new factor in information war results directly from the worldwide infosphere of television and broadcast news. Many people have begun to realize that governmental decisions are becoming increasingly reactive to a "fictive" universe created by CNN and its various international competitors. This media-created universe is dubbed fictive rather than "fictional" because although what is shown may be true, it is just not the whole, relevant, or contextual truth. And, of course, the close etymological relationship between fictive and fictional suggests how easy it is to manipulate the message.

Nevertheless, this fictive universe becomes the politically relevant universe in societies in which the government or its military is supposed to do something. Somalia gets in the news and the United States gets into Somalia despite the reality of equally disastrous starvation, disorder, and rapine right next door in Sudan. There were no reporters with skylink in Sudan because the government of Sudan issued no visas. The potential for governments, parties in a civil war such as Bosnia, rebels in Chiapis, or even nonstate interests to manipulate the multimedia, multi-source fictive universe to wage societal-level ideational conflicts should be obvious.

Fictive or fictional operational environments, then, whether mass-targeted or niche-targeted, can be generated, transmitted, distributed, or broadcast by governments or all sorts of players through increasingly diversified networks. The niche-manipulation potential available to states or private interests with access to the universe of internetted communications, such as the networks over which business, commercial, or banking information are transmitted to, suggests that Mexico is about to devalue the peso and that could easily provoke financial chaos. The target state would not know what had happened until too late.

Direct satellite broadcast to selected cable systems,[iv] analogous to central control of pay-per-view programs, again offers the potential for people in one province or region of a targeted state to discover that the maximum leader has decided to purge their clansmen from the army. To put it in the jargon of the infowarriors, info-niche attack in an increasingly multisource fictive universe offers unlimited potential for societal-level netwar.

Pictures Worth a Thousand Tanks

When the new, but already well understood, simulation technologies of the Tekwar and MTV generation are added to the arsenal of netwar, a genuinely revolutionary transformation of propaganda and warfare becomes possible. Traditional propaganda might have attempted to discredit an adversary's news media showing, for example, that as the official casualty figures were demonstrably false, all news from the government was equally false. The credibility of the opponent was the target and the strategic intention was to separate the government from the people.

Today, the mastery of the techniques of combining live actors with computer-generated video graphics can easily create a virtual news conference, summit meeting, or perhaps even a battle that exists in effects though not in fact. Stored video images can be recombined endlessly to produce any effect chosen.[v] Now, perhaps, pictures will be worth a thousand tanks.

Of course, truth will win out eventually, but by the time the people of the targeted nation discover that the nationwide broadcast of the conversation between the maximum leader and George W. Bush, in which all loyal citizens were told to cease fighting and return to their homes, was created in Hollywood or Langley, the war may be over. Netwar is beginning to enter the zone of illusion.

This is not science fiction; these are the capabilities of existing or rapidly emerging technologies. Here's how it might work: Through hitching a ride on an unsuspecting commercial satellite, a fictive simulation is broadcast. Simultaneously, various info-niches in the target state are accessed via the net. These info-niche targets, and the information they receive, are tailored to the strategic diplomacy needs of the moment: Some receive reinforcement for the fictive simulation; others receive the real truth; still others receive merely slight variations. What is happening here?

This kind of manipulation elevates the strategic potential of infopropaganda to new heights. This is not traditional propaganda in which the target is discredited as a source of reliable information. Rather, the very possibility of truth is being replaced with virtual reality; that is, information that produces effects independent of its physical reality. What is being attacked in a strategic level netwar are not only the

pirates are prowling the Internet, some in the employ of hostile commercial or intelligence services. The spy flap between France and the United States over alleged U.S. attempts to gather data on French Telecom may be indicative of the future.

Infosphere dominance (controlling the world of information exchange) may be as complex and elusive as escalation dominance appeared to be in nuclear strategy. It will certainly be expensive: The U.S. business community and the U.S. armed forces are required to devote ever more resources and attention to computer, communications, and database security. The resources and skills required for battlefield cyberwar are not insignificant, but the resources and skills required to wage information war at the national strategic level would be massive.

The second reason to doubt U.S. ability to prosecute an information war is that the political and legal issues surrounding info war are murky. What part does congressional oversight play in this? Would one declare information war in response, say, to an Iranian-originated computer virus assault on the FBI's central terrorist database? And what about preparing for it? How should the United States develop and implement a national capability for netwar?

Although theoretically a requirement to develop or implement a national information war strategy, analogous to the nuclear-era single-integrated operations plan, could be communicated from the president to the executive branch agencies. It is unclear whether there would be adequate congressional oversight. Which committees of the House or Senate would have control and oversight of policies attendant to information war, and which would have the power to inquire into the judgment of a local ambassador or military commander who wished to use the tools of cyberwar for a perception manipulation in peacetime that would shape the potential wartime environment?

The U.S. armed forces only execute the national military strategy—they do not control it. However, they are developing, quite appropriately, the tools and techniques to execute the national military strategy for operational-level cyberwar. They are simultaneously, albeit unintentionally, developing the tools and capabilities to execute a national strategic information war strategy. The former is their job under the Constitution; the latter may not be. Congressional oversight in the development of a national strategic-level information war capability is even more essential than oversight of the intelligence community.

The third reason to doubt U.S. capabilities in prosecuting an effective information war is that such a societal-level ideational conflict waged in part through internetted modes of communication may simply be beyond the competence of the executive agencies that would have to determine the substantive content to be communicated. Pluralism is a great strength of American society, but perhaps a drawback in waging information war.

Although diversity may make the formation and execution of domestic and even foreign policy more complex, the lack of a moral center or public philosophy in American society could render the political leadership incapable of building a consensus on strategic-level information war policies. And because there is no single view of what is morally acceptable, but simply a host of contending views, a national security strategy of information war could be developed by the national security decision makers who lacked a moral consensus.

The technological wizardry does not change the humanity of the target. Unless the goal of information war is merely to unhinge people from their ability to reason objectively, and thereby create an interesting problem for post-conflict reconstruction, any strategic-level netwar or information war would seem to require the ability to communicate a replacement for the discredited content of the target society.

If, say, an information war were to be mounted against China to disrupt its drive for regional hegemony, the goal would be to withdraw the Mandate of Heaven from the rulers and influence the Chinese leaders and people to adopt the policies or behavior the United States finds appropriate. Put in terms of such a concrete policy goal, the philosophically problematic nature of information war becomes outrageously obvious. Does anyone really believe that the U.S. national executive agencies, including the armed forces and the Central Intelligence Agency, know the substantive discourse of China sufficiently well to withdraw the Mandate of Heaven?

The final reason, then, can be stated in the form of a question: Does anyone really believe that anyone in the U.S. government has the philosophical sophistication to project an alternative discourse to replace the emotions, motives, reasoning, and behavior grounded in the Chinese reality that the United States proposes to influence? Would our fictive creation really have virtual effects? The United States might be able to use the armed forces or the CIA to destroy China's objective reasoning through a successful information war. Indeed, the United States might be able to lose anarchy in a society, but that is not usually the political goal of war.

Second Thoughts

The techniques being developed by the armed forces for a more narrowly constrained operational-level cyberwar was demonstrated in the Gulf War. Translated to the strategic level, however, netwar or information war is not a prudent national security or military strategy for the simple reason that neither the armed forces nor any other instruments of national power have the ability to exploit an adversary's society in a way that promises either advantageous or predictable results.

Societal-level ideational conflict must be considered with all the care given to the conduct of nuclear war, as the end state of a netwar may be total disruption of the targeted society. Conflict resolution, including ending wars this side of blasting people into unconditional surrender, assumes and requires some rationality—even if that rationality is the mere coordination of ends with means.

Moral reasoning and substantive communication may not be required; minimal reasoning and pragmatic communication are required. However, a successful all-out strategic-level information war may, however, have destroyed the enemy's ability to know anything with certainty and, thereby, his capacity for minimal reasoning or pragmatic communication.

In some exercises during the cold war decapitation of the Soviet military leadership in a hypothetical nuclear exchange, the intent was to defend the United States by preventing an escalatory or exploitative strike, nuclear or otherwise. Precisely how war termination would have been accomplished without an effective leadership will remain, hopefully, one of the great mysteries. The decapitation of the leadership is, however, often proposed as a key goal of an information war. That is, the credibility and legitimacy (even the physical ability to communicate) of the decision makers will be compromised or destroyed relative to their own population and in terms of their own worldview. And even if one merely seizes his or her communication system electronically and substitutes their reality into his or her society, with whom, then, does one negotiate the end of the conflict?

What confidence does the United States have that a call to surrender, even if communicated to the people by either the enemy leadership or our net warriors, would be accepted as real and not another virtual event? And, depending on the content, intensity, and totality of a strategic information war, personalities could be flooded with irrational or unconsciousness factors—the clinical consequence of which is generally acute psychosis. How does the United States accomplish conflict resolution, war termination, or postconflict reconstruction with a population or leadership whose objective reasoning has been compromised?

Just as the mutually destructive effects of nuclear war were disproportionate to the goals of almost any imaginable conflict, so may be the mutually destructive effects of a total information war exchange on the publics exposed and subsequent rational communication between the sides. And as the techniques of cyberstrike proliferate throughout the world, enabling small powers, nonstate actors, or even terrorist hackers to do massive damage to the United States, mutually assured cyber-destruction may result in a kind of infowar deterrence.

Information War, then, may be the central national security issue of the 21st century. Therefore, the United States must develop a coherent national-level policy on the military and strategic use of new information warfare technologies. To facilitate this objective, the U.S. armed forces are developing, under the rubric of command-and-control warfare, the technologies and systems that will provide the capability for cyberwar.

It may be possible to control and exploit information so as to generate stochastic chaos purposely, though there are some doubts. Many of the same technologies and systems can be used to develop a national-level capability for strategic netwar. Here, however, there are genuine doubts. It may not be possible to control and exploit information and information technologies to impose a form on the remnants of societies no longer capable of self-organization because their substantive universe of meaning has been destroyed or corrupted.

Few info-warriors would claim the ability to reorient the former Soviet Union into a liberal society, or to influence the far more ancient barbarism in that heart of darkness, Rwanda. Perhaps strategic-level information war is, indeed, like nuclear war: The capability is required for deterrence; its employment, the folly of mutually assured destruction. But if the United States is to develop the capacity for information war, in the sure and certain knowledge that the technologies have already proliferated to both state and nonstate potential rivals, a realistic national consensus must be built.

It is useless to pretend that the proliferation of these technologies will not provide capabilities that can do serious harm. It is useless to pretend that military-based command and control warfare capabilities will not be developed, and it is useless to pretend that cyberwar technologies could not be turned to netwar applications. It is almost universally agreed that these capabilities are essential on the contemporary battlefield. It is essential, then, that the president and the Congress give serious and sustained attention to cyberwar, netwar, and information war.

THE ROLE OF INTERNATIONAL ORGANIZATIONS

Information on countries with offensive IW initiatives is less authoritatively documented, but studies and foreign press reporting help point to international organizations that probably have such an initiative underway. A 1996 U.S. General Accounting Office (GAO) report on the threat to Defense D systems stated that the Department of Energy and the National Security Agency estimated that 120 countries had established computer attack capabilities. At the low end, June 1998 the Director of Central Intelligence stated that several countries are sponsoring information warfare programs, and that nations developing these programs recognize the value of attaching their country's computer systems—both on the battlefield and in the civilian arena. A March 1999 report by the Center for Strategic and International Studies (CSIS) identified Russia, China, the United Kingdom, France, Australia, and Canada as countries that have dedicated considerable resources toward developing IW capabilities. The March 1999 National Communications (NCS) report on the threat to U.S. telecommunications states that, among these, the National Intelligence Council reports that Russia, China, and France have acknowledged their IW programs. According to the NCS report, other countries, such as Bulgaria and Cuba, reportedly have initiatives focused on developing computer viruses (Table 12.1).

TABLE 12.1 Publicly identified foreign countries involved in economic espionage, information warfare: Initiatives and U.S. remediation.

Country	Economic Espionage	Information Warfare Initiative	Major Remediation Provider
Bulgaria	Yes*	—	—
Canada	Yes	Yes	—
Cuba	Yes*	Yes	—
France	Yes*	Yes	—
Germany	Yes*	Yes	—
India	Yes	Yes	Yes
Iran	Yes	Yes	—
Iraq	Yes*	Yes	—
Ireland	—	—	Yes
Israel	Yes*	Yes	Yes
Japan	Yes*	—	—
Pakistan	—	—	Yes
Philippines	—	—	Yes
Russia	Yes*	Yes	—
South Korea	Yes	—	—
Taiwan	Yes*	—	—

*Countries identified by NCS as using electronic intrusions usually for economic espionage purposes.

An independent review of international press reporting and military press articles on international organizations' initiatives points to three other countries among those engaged in economic espionage (Iran, Iraq, and Taiwan) that are involved in the development of IW technologies, programs, or military capabilities. All of these countries publicly acknowledge pursuing defensive IW initiatives goal of protecting their military information capabilities or national information infrastructure:

- India established a National Information Infrastructure-Defensive group several years ago, apparently in response to China's growing interest in IW.
- As recently as January 2001, the Israel Defense Forces (IDF) acknowledged the existence of an information warfare defense unit whose mission is to protect military systems, but noted that the electric utility had organized its own defense.
- Taiwan also recently announced creation of a task force to study ways to protect their information infrastructure from the growing IW threat from China.

Creation of national defensive information infrastructure program is a good (and probably necessary) indicator of an international offensive IW initiative. Defensive measures (deterrence, protection, and restoration) are difficult to implement without also developing an understanding of potential adversaries, investing in computer and software development, and creating a major operational capability—all steps directly applicable to creating an offensive IW capability. From a military strategic perspective, in an era when offensive IW has many technical advances over the complexities of cyber defense, a strong offensive IW capability provides both a defense and a virtually assured counter-strike capability against potential adversaries that is generally cost-effective.

The presence of a defensive IW initiative, however, is inadequate alone to assess that a foreign country is also developing its offensive counterpart. To judge that a country probably has an offensive IW initiative (including military theory, technology development, operational unit or individual training, or deployed forces) requires positive responses to at least one o following questions:

- Has a country been reliably identified as participating in offensive IW activities, especially in "preparation of the battlefield" activities (such as implanting and using trap doors) that would facilitate computer network attacks in a future conflict?
- Have authoritative, but unofficial, host country sources suggested that a country has an offensive IW program?

The case that India also has an offensive IW is more problematic. The 2000 ASIS survey report identifies Indian nationals as among the top five sources of economic espionage against the United States, but does not indicate whether these nationals use cyber techniques nor whether they targeted more commercial information.

Ranking the Risks

The results of this analysis point to a tiered set of foreign national risks to U.S. computing and network systems remediation involving the insertion of malicious code. For example, at the top, the United States, India, and Israel are the most likely countries to use the broad opportunity remediation in light of their historic involvement in economic espionage, and the likelihood that they have ongoing offensive IW initiatives.

On the other hand, France, Germany, Russia, and Taiwan comprise a second tier of countries that have been identified as participants in economic espionage against the United States and that have developed initiatives, but are not believed to be major foreign sources of U.S. remediation services. Although their efforts may have less impact on the national-level integrity of networks, companies and government agencies utilizing services provided by these countries are still at significant risk. Also, the governments and companies in the other countries that have engaged in economic espionage against the United States may also utilize this unique opportunity to take advantage of these espionage objectives.

Protecting and Responding

The ability to protect corporate or government systems and networks against these foreign (domestic) risks hinges on comprehensive testing and validation of the integrity of the remediation software by a *trusted* independent source before it is implemented. Analysis of the software and testing for trap doors and other accesses are key elements in this risk reduction.

Besides testing for intended performance analysis, the content of the program is most important. Evaluators should ensure that all the program code has a legitimate business purpose; any user code should be extracted. Often evaluators will have access to the object code (the applications-level information used to operate the software) rather than the program-language source code, which undermines the effectiveness of content analysis. Customers may wish that the source code be shared with the evaluator so its integrity can be examined. The evaluator needs to match the object code against what is actually used in the corporate application to validate the testing.

Preventing unauthorized access in the future is a second essential step in ensuring the integrity of the system or network. Evaluators can begin by using standard hacker tools to see if the software displays any access vulnerabilities. At a second level, a red team approach (actually trying the software) can be taken to explore more deeply whether trap doors exist. Special attention needs be paid to all authorized software accesses, such as those for remote system administration which could result in future introduction of malicious code. These software accesses should be protected and they should be able to identify and halt delivery of malicious code.

In the event malicious code is identified in testing or operation of the remediated software, specially trained FBI agents and computer specialists can preserve critical evidence that can be used in identifying and prosecuting the perpetrator. They can also use such evidence to compare similar events and facilitate the restoration of protected service to the system. Early FBI involvement in addressing criminal computer intrusions has helped smooth the national computing transition to the next millennium.

Proposed Cybercrime Laws Stir Debate within International Organizations

Lots of countries still haven't updated their laws to cover Internet-based crimes, leaving companies in many parts of the world without legal protections from malicious hackers and other attackers who are looking to steal their data. But corporate executives and IT managers may not necessarily like the laws that are starting to emerge in some regions. Of special concern is a proposed cybercrime treaty being developed by the 41-nation Council of Europe, which some business groups fear could affect corporate data-retention policies. For example, the Global Internet Project, an Arlington, Virginia-based organization that's trying to head off government regulation of the Internet, in November 2000, claimed that the proposed treaty could actually hamper efforts to stop cybercrime and to track down people who launch computer-related attacks. Those concerns were echoed by attendees at a forum on international cyberlaw sponsored by McConnell International LLC, the consulting firm that issued the new report on cybercrime laws.

Privacy advocates are also raising an alarm, arguing that the proposed European treaty may tread on privacy rights. They fear that they are going into an area where the problem is not too little law but too much law.

What's clear, however, is that many countries are beginning to wake up to the issue. There is competition among countries for leadership and excellence in the digital economy. There is a kind of a race to see which countries are going to be the leaders in this new way of doing business.

The European cybercrime treaty could be ready for approval by the middle of 2002, and is then expected to be adopted by the United States and other countries outside of Europe. Its intent is to help law enforcement officials track down malicious attackers and child pornographers by easing cooperation among police. The treaty also seeks to prevent data havens—areas in which laws governing cybercrimes are weak.

However, the treaty has left companies such as WorldCom Inc. uncertain about what its legal requirements or liability risks will ultimately be. There is so much gray area.

A key area of concern is data retention. Internet service providers are worried that they may face new obligations to hold onto data in response to requests from law enforcers. For example, the treaty as it now stands could enable countries to demand that companies keep data sought for use in investigations for as long as government officials deem necessary. Clarification on the data-retention issue is going to be needed.

France appeared on a list of legal laggards. But a recent court ruling in that country required Santa Clara, California-based Yahoo Inc. to prevent French citizens from trafficking in Nazi paraphernalia. The court action illustrates the point that there are too many laws on the books already.

THE ROLE OF THE GLOBAL MILITARY ALLIANCES

The following discussion highlights what actually constitutes global military alliances with regard to information operations. Three terms are examined: military, information, and operations).

Military

A look into the future of information warfare environment indicates an increasing role for information operations and the emergence of IW as a new paradigm of warfare. Global military planners must, therefore, prepare to develop information skills and strategies as part of their immediate capabilities and, ultimately, they must prepare their force for involvement in full-scale information wars through alliances with other countries. These global planners must also remember that IW is emerging as a paradigm of warfare, not a paradigm of information. Regardless of the extent that the IW paradigm influences the future warfare environment, war will still be war, and thus will still involve the human factors that have been associated with conflict since the dawn of time. Although there may be less bloodshed in an information war, human suffering will, in all likelihood, result. The legal and diplomatic consequences of war will also remain much the same. Information technology does not make war any more acceptable to a civilized society. Therefore, although the information systems, tools, techniques, and strategies of the military and civilian information warriors may be common, and, indeed, complementary, a nation as a whole, and the military profession in particular, must not forget the significance of the military.

Global Information

Although seemingly self-explanatory, understanding the nature of global information alliances is important. Information is the product of the processing of data, whereas data is simply the product of some observation. The processing of data into information involves placing the data into some form of context. This context can be the formation of a sentence or other human-readable form, a machine-readable sequence, or the classification of the data against some known measurement, such as time, height, weight, and the like. The result is information and this is created and manipulated to enable decisions to be made. Although most decisions are made by a human, increasingly decisions are being made by rules-based or knowledge-based systems, and, although currently limited in application, some artificial intelligence systems.

Information, or any developed form of the information, is only one part of an information technology system. An information technology system consists of data (both as an initial input and as stored in various parts of the information technology systems in the form of information), hardware, software, communications, people, and procedures. Any one of the individual elements of the information technology system, as well as the information technology system processes that convert the raw data into various forms of information, may provide a suitable target on which influence may be exerted. The information technology system as a whole, therefore, is the target of information operations, and not just the information itself or its associated technology.

Global Operations

Global information operations seek to influence the decision-making process. Global Military Information Operations (MIOs) alliances are not information technology support activities, such as system management and system administration. They are activities directly focused on warfare and include offensive and defensive activities aimed at all levels of the decision-making process. In the modern warfare environment, attacking and defending information technology systems is a vital combat task, and strategies must be considered in conjunction with the wider global military alliance plan. When correctly applied, offensive global information operations alliances can be just as lethal as the employment of conventional weapons. As an example, certain aircraft flight control systems may be shut down using MIO techniques. The resultant crash will destroy the aircraft, and generally kill the pilot and crew, just as effectively as the best air-to-air missile.

An MIO, therefore, is any activity that consciously targets or protects the elements of an information technology system in pursuit of global military alliances objectives.

NOTE

MARSHALL LAW AND CYBERSPACE

Realistically, there are a number of scenarios, each of varying degree, in which information warfare might be utilized in the future in cyberspace, and thus bring about Marshall Law. In the most apocalyptic scenario, information warfare will be waged in conjunction with conventional warfare, to determine the hegemon of the Information Age. Many scholars have put forth arguments concerning the formation and survivability of hegemonic powers. It is possible, that in this point in time, the instability of information technology requires the constancy only a hegemon can provide. Under this scenario, realist concerns run rampant, as the United States has a vested interest in becoming the hegemon for the next power cycle. However, a full-scale information war will be very costly, and it is highly unlikely that the hegemon will be able to salvage any value from the rubble of battle. A scenario where stability and consistency for information technologies are derived from cooperative international endeavors to promote and facilitate global prosperity is more likely. In the Information Age, Third Wave nations have legitimate aspirations to create a global information system that adds value to their existing information infrastructures. Information technology is cooperative by nature and tremendous benefits can be derived from greater interconnectivity. Therefore, nations will seek out ways to integrate their networks with the international network. Once that integration takes place, each connected nation will have an interest in maintaining the stability and survivability of the overall network. Each nation has a vested interest in preventing global information warfare and Marshall Law.

Despite collective interests, information terrorism will continue to be a viable national security concern for all Third Wave nations. Unfortunately, the U.S. options concerning terrorism are extremely limited. By increasing security and gathering intelligence regarding any plans that might be in consideration, the United States can ensure that the threat of terrorism is contained to isolated incidents from which this country can recover. Unfortunately, as the 9-11-2001 terrorist attacks on the WTC and Pentagon showed, the environment under which the

United States currently operates can make no such promise, therefore, it is essential that this issue be addressed now.

Other likely scenarios include the use of information warfare for blackmail or for limited short-term gains. These scenarios present other difficult political dilemmas that must be addressed at a global level. Will nations allow information warfare threats to be used as blackmail? Will the United States allow limited information warfare in order to pursue strategic or comparative political and economic gains? Or is the fear of escalation an adequate deterrent to such ambitions? These questions must also be addressed.

The Information Age promises to change many aspects of society. Life in cyberspace is more egalitarian than elitist, and more decentralized than hierarchical. It serves individuals and communities, not mass audiences. One might think of cyberspace as shaping up exactly like Thomas Jefferson would have wanted: founded on the primacy of individual liberty and commitment to pluralism, diversity, and community.

As a society, we have much to learn about ourselves through this new medium of communication. As a nation, the United States must make sure that the structure it is building has a strong foundation and that weaknesses in that structure are not used to destroy it. It is a difficult task, because the constitutionally guaranteed rights of U.S. citizens must be upheld in the process. However, it is a task the United States must undertake. These are issues the United States must address. If the United States does not address these issues now, the future of our country will be jeopardized. A handful of concerned citizens attempt to bring issues surrounding cyberspace to our attention every day. Some of these issues concern national security; others concern individual privacy.

Cyberspace has empowered the average person to explore and question the structure of our society and those that benefit from the way it is operated. Fundamental issues arise from hacker explorations. The United States must decide how, as a nation, it wishes to deal with these issues. Recent efforts in cloning produced a human fetus. The scientists that achieved this remarkable feat immediately halted research, arguing that a public debate must arise to deal with the ethical and moral issues surrounding this technology. They argued that before experimentation in cloning continued, the United States must decide as a society, which direction that the new technology will go, what ends it hopes to achieve, and what the limits on the use of this new technology should be. A similar debate on the issues of cyberspace must take place. There is no need to stop the technology, but the United States must decide what direction it wants the technology to take, and what rules will govern the use of this technology. The United States must do this now, before the technology starts dictating the rules—before it is too late to make changes in the basic structure of cyberspace without destroying the whole concept.

Rollout of Corporate Cybercrime Program

Recently, the FBI (or the other super cyber protection agency) officially announced the formation of its InfraGard program, a cybercrime security initiative designed to improve cooperation between federal law enforcement officials and the private sector (after completing the process of setting up InfraGard "chapters" at its 56 field offices). The National Infrastructure Protection Center (NIPC), an FBI affiliate that's based at the agency's headquarters in Washington, started the InfraGard program in 1996 as a pilot project in the Cleveland area. The last local chapter, comprised of information security experts from companies and academic institutions, was put in place in December, 2000, in New York.

According to FBI officials, InfraGard offers companies an intrusion-alert network based on encrypted e-mail messages plus a secure Web site for communicating with law enforcement agencies about suspicious network activity or attacks. The program allows law enforcement and industry to work together and share information regularly, including information that could prevent potential intrusions into the U.S. national infrastructure.

However, the NIPC has been criticized in the past for what some have called a fundamental inability to communicate with the rest of the national security community. The problem, according to sources, has been that the FBI treats all potential cybercrimes as law enforcement investigations first and foremost—a stance that effectively bars access to information by other government security agencies.

The timing of the announcement may be a sign that the FBI is jockeying for budget influence in the new Bush administration. The InfraGard program hasn't had much of an effect on corporate users thus far.

It seems like the different chapters are very personality-driven. But the FBI hasn't really institutionalized InfraGard or funded it to be anything very meaningful. The general feeling is that it is all input to the FBI and no output from them.

The InfraGard announcement is one of several rather belated efforts by the outgoing Clinton administration to create new security structures. For example, ex-President Clinton, before leaving office, also announced a plan to better coordinate federal counterintelligence efforts—a move partly aimed at improving the response of super cyber protection agencies such as the FBI and the CIA to information security attacks against companies.

However, InfraGard's prospects could still be very much in question during George W. Bush's administration. All of these initiatives could die if the Bush administration wants to place its own imprint on the issues or simply decides to take a different tack. These new programs will have a better chance of survival if they can demonstrate that they're already accomplishing useful objectives.

The FBI plans to expand and perfect InfraGard as it goes forward. But more than 600 businesses have already signed up to participate in the program, and the FBI is still getting applications daily from companies that want to be part of a chapter.

Finally, InfraGard does have its supporters. The program has had a beneficial impact because it lets companies share information on security vulnerabilities without creating the levels of hysteria that usually accompany highly publicized reports of hacking attacks and other cybercrimes.

It's actually working. There's an awful lot of industry support behind it. And there are no indications that the Bush administration is pro-crime.

SUMMARY

The United States has substantial information-based resources, including complex management systems and infrastructures involving the control of electric power, money flow, air traffic, oil and gas, and other information-dependent items. U.S. allies and potential coalition partners are similarly increasingly dependent on various information infrastructures. Conceptually, if and when potential adversaries attempt to damage these systems using IW techniques, information warfare inevitably takes on a strategic aspect.

There is no "front line." Strategic targets in the United States may be just as vulnerable to attack (as we all found out in the 9-11 terrorist attacks) as in-war zone command (such as Afghanistan, Iraq, etc. ...), control, communications, and intelligence (C3I) targets. As a result, the attention of exercise participants quickly broadened beyond a single traditional regional theater of operations to four distinct separate theaters of operation: the battlefield per se; allied "Zones of Interior" (for example, the sovereign territory of Saudi Arabia); the intercontinental zone of communication and deployment; and the U.S. Zone of Interior.

The post-cold war "over there" focus of the regional component of U.S. national military strategy is, therefore, rendered incomplete for this kind of scenario and is of declining relevance to the likely future international strategic environment. When responding to information warfare attacks of this character, military strategy can no longer afford to focus on conducting and supporting operations only in the region of concern. An in-depth examination of the implications of IW for the U.S. and allied infrastructures that depend on the unimpeded management of information is also required in the fight against macro threats—defensive strategies for governments and industry groups, as follows.

Conclusions Drawn from Fighting against Macro Threats

- Low entry cost: Unlike traditional weapon technologies, development of information-based techniques does not require sizable financial resources or state sponsorship. Information systems expertise and access to important networks may be the only prerequisites.
- Blurred traditional boundaries: Traditional distinctions (public versus private interests, warlike versus criminal behavior) and geographic boundaries, such as those between nations as historically defined, are complicated by the growing interaction within the information infrastructure.
- Expanded role for perception management: New information-based techniques may substantially increase the power of deception and of image-manipulation activities, dramatically complicating government efforts to build political support for security-related initiatives.
- A new strategic intelligence challenge: Poorly understood strategic IW vulnerabilities and targets diminish the effectiveness of classical intelligence collection and analysis methods. A new field of analysis focused on strategic IW may have to be developed.
- Formidable tactical warning and attack assessment problems: There is currently no adequate tactical warning system for distinguishing between strategic IW attacks and other kinds of cyberspace activities, including espionage or accidents.
- Difficulty of building and sustaining coalitions: Reliance on coalitions is likely to increase the vulnerabilities of the security postures of all the partners to strategic IW attacks, giving opponents a disproportionate strategic advantage.
- Vulnerability of the U.S. homeland: Information-based techniques render geographical distance irrelevant; targets in the continental United States are just as vulnerable as in-war zone targets. Given the increased reliance of the U.S. economy and society on a high-performance networked information infrastructure, a new set of lucrative strategic targets presents itself to potential IW-armed opponents.

An Agenda for Action in Preparing for Defensive Strategies for Governments and Industry Groups

The likely consequences of strategic information warfare point to a basic conclusion: Key national military strategy assumptions are obsolescent and inadequate for confronting the threat posed by strategic IW. As discussed next, major recommendations have emerged that address this shortcoming.

The U.S. government needs to set an agenda for action that goes beyond the work already done in preparation for the fight against macro threats—defensive strategies for governments and industry groups. Action steps should include, but not be limited to the following 16 areas:

1. Leadership: Who should be in charge in the government? An immediate and badly needed first step is the assignment of a focal point for federal government leadership in support of a coordinated U.S. response to the strategic IW threat. This focal point should be located in the Executive Office of the President, because only at this level can the necessary interagency coordination of the large number of government organizations involved in such matters—and the necessary interactions with the Congress—be effectively carried out.

2. This Executive Office should also have the responsibility for close coordination with industry, because the nation's information infrastructure is being developed almost exclusively by the commercial sector. Once established, this high-level leadership should immediately take responsibility for initiating and managing a comprehensive review of national-level strategic information warfare issues.

3. Risk assessment: The federal government leadership entity cited a previously explained, should, as a first step, conduct an immediate risk assessment to determine, to the degree possible, the extent of the vulnerability of key elements of current U.S. national security and national military strategy to strategic information warfare.

4. Strategic target sets, IW effects, and parallel vulnerability and threat assessments should be among the components of this review. In an environment of dynamic change in both cyberspace threats and vulnerabilities, there is no sound basis for presidential decision making on strategic IW matters without such a risk assessment.

5. In this context, there is always the hope or the belief that the kind of aggressive response suggested in this chapter can be delayed while cyberspace gets a chance to evolve robust defenses on its own. This is, in fact, a possibility—that the healing and annealing of an immune system that is under constant assault, as cyberspace is and assuredly will continue to be, will create the robust national information infrastructure that everyone hopes to use. But it may not, and we're certainly not there now.

6. Government's role: The appropriate role for government in responding to the strategic IW threat needs to be addressed, recognizing that this role (certain to be part leadership and part partnership with the domestic sector) will unquestionably evolve.

7. In addition to being the performer of certain basic preparedness functions (such as organizing, equipping, training, and sustaining military forces), the government may play a more productive and efficient role as facilitator

and maintainer of some information systems and infrastructure; through policy mechanisms such as tax breaks to encourage reducing vulnerability and improving recovery and reconstitution capability.

8. An important factor is the traditional change in the government's role as one moves from national defense through public safety toward things that represent the public good. Clearly, the government's perceived role in this area will have to be balanced against public perceptions of the loss of civil liberties and the commercial sector's concern about unwarranted limits on its practices and markets.

9. National security strategy: Once an initial risk assessment has been completed, U.S. national security strategy needs to address preparedness for the threat as identified. Preparedness will cross several traditional boundaries from "military" to "civilian," from "foreign" to "domestic," and from "national" to "local."

10. One promising means for instituting this kind of preparedness could involve the concept of a "minimum essential information infrastructure" (MEII), which is introduced as a possible strategic defensive IW initiative. The MEII is conceived as that minimum mixture of U.S. information systems, procedures, laws, and tax incentives necessary to ensure the nation continues functioning even in the face of a sophisticated strategic IW attack.

11. One facet of such an MEII might be a set of rules and regulations sponsored by the federal government to encourage the owners and operators of the various national infrastructures to take measures to reduce their infrastructure's vulnerability and/or to ensure rapid reconstitution in the face of IW-type attacks. The analog for this concept is the strategic nuclear Minimum Essential Emergency Communications Network (MEECN).

12. The MEII construct is conceptually very attractive even though there was some uncertainty as to how it might be achieved. An assessment of the feasibility of an MEII (or like concepts) should be undertaken at an early date.

13. National military strategy: The current national military strategy emphasizes maintaining U.S. capability to project power into theaters of operation in key regions of Europe and Asia. Because of the emerging theaters of operation in cyberspace for such contingencies, strategic IW profoundly reduces the significance of distance with respect to the deployment and use of weapons. Therefore, battlefield C3I vulnerabilities may become less significant than vulnerabilities in the national infrastructure.

14. Planning assumptions fundamental to current national military strategy are obsolescent. Consideration of these IW features should be accounted for in U.S. national military strategy.

15. Against this difficult projection and assessment situation, there is the ever-present risk that the United States could find itself in a crisis in the near term, facing the possibility of, or indications of, a strategic IW attack. When the president asks whether the United States is under IW attack (and, if so, by whom) and whether the U.S. military plan and strategy is vulnerable, a foot-shuffling "we don't know" will not be an acceptable answer.

16. It must be acknowledged that strategic IW is a very new concept that is presenting a wholly new set of problems. These problems may well yield to solution—but not without the intelligent and informed expenditure of energy, leadership, money, and other scarce resources.

ENDNOTES

i John R. Vacca, *Electronic Commerce, Third Edition*, Charles River Media, 2001.

ii John R. Vacca, *Net Privacy: A Guide to Developing & Implementing an Iron-clad ebusiness Privacy Plan*, McGraw-Hill, 2001.

iii John R. Vacca, *High-Speed Cisco Networks: Planning, Design, and Implementation*, CRC Press, 2002.

iv John R. Vacca, *The Cabling Handbook (2nd Edition)*, Prentice Hall, 2001.

v John R. Vacca, *The Essential Guide to Storage Area Networks*, Prentice Hall, 2002.

13 The Information Warfare Arsenal and Tactics of the Military

The growing reliance on computer networks makes the networks themselves likely sites for attack. What is more, civilian and military networks are becoming increasingly intertwined, and so the U.S. military's focus have shifted from protecting every network to securing mission-critical systems. Current efforts include software agent-based systems (for real-time detection and recovery from a cyberattack) and network-level early-warning systems (for monitoring suspicious on-line activity).

As tensions continue to mount in the Middle East, a different sort of pitched battle is being waged behind the scenes. With all the fervor of their comrades in arms, computer-savvy patriots on both sides have managed to infiltrate or disable enemy Web servers. And so the Hezbollah site was reprogrammed to play the Israeli national anthem, while Israeli government sites were slowed to a crawl by wave upon wave of hostile e-mail.

As displays of warlike aggression go, the bombs, bullets, and mortar fire that recently claimed the lives of some 600 Palestinians and Israelis were far more troubling. That said, the prospect of cyberwarfare, or information warfare, is a deadly serious matter in military circles. The electron is the ultimate precision-guided weapon. Indeed, the more heavily we come to rely on computer networks, the greater the fear that adversaries will attack the networks themselves. In the very worst case (what some have termed an electronic Pearl Harbor) a sudden, all-out network assault would knock out communications as well as financial, power, transportation, military, and other critical infrastructures, resulting in total societal collapse.

Civilian and military networks are increasingly intertwined. The advent of the Internet means there really isn't an outside anymore. Even when Air Force information warfare (IW) personnel are planning a mission, it coexists within the World Wide Web infrastructure.

Another concern is that the military's push toward commercial off-the-shelf technology is exposing vital networks to attack. A lot of important decisions are being made that will affect the future of information war, but they're being made in Washington State (home of Microsoft Corporation.), not in Washington, D.C.

Beyond the odd idiot or random rogue, military networks tend to be favored targets for hackers. The Pentagon figures it fends off something like a half-million attacks a year. Annoying and costly as that may be, it's not the chief worry. The odd idiot or random rogue trying to break in—that happens all the time. The Pentagon's primary concern is the government that's prepared to invest heavily in coordinated strategic attacks on the U.S.'s military and civilian networks. So, although the line between cyber crime and information warfare often blurs, what separates the two is that the latter is state-sponsored.

For the information warrior, the basic issues are protecting oneself from attack, identifying the attacker, and then responding. By far the most effort has gone into the first area, network security. Here, commercial firms have led the way, producing a host of off-the-shelf hardware, software, and services, from firewalls to intrusion sensors to encryption schemes. For the civilian world's take on information warfare, see Chapter 18, "Civilian Causalities: The Victims and Refugees of Information Warfare."

The U.S. military is generally regarded as being farthest along in its information warfare preparedness. A fairly recent recognition has been that it is not possible to simultaneously defend the myriad military, civilian, and commercial networks.

A further recognition has been that simply trying to "keep the bad guys out" is futile. No system is perfect—somebody's always going to get in.

Nowadays the focus is on keeping so-called mission-critical networks up and running, and detecting intruders early on, before any real harm gets done. Work is now going into developing early-warning systems for information networks, akin to the radar and satellites that watch for long-range missile attacks. A system administrator typically only has local knowledge of the health of his own system.

A bird's-eye view, by contrast, would allow analysts to correlate attacks from the same IP addresses, or from those having the same mode of operation, or from those occurring in a certain time frame. Achieving such a network-wide perspective is the aim of Cyberpanel, a new Darpa (Defense Advanced Research Projects Agency) program, as discussed in sidebar, "Renegotiating the Human–Machine Interface."

RENEGOTIATING THE HUMAN–MACHINE INTERFACE

Creating inherently secure and robust information technologies for the U.S. military is one of the chief aims of the information technology systems (ITS) office at the Defense Advanced Research Projects Agency (Darpa), in Arlington, Virginia. The work at the Darpa ITS office is defensive, rather than offensive, in nature. They're like the people who worry about seatbelts in cars, rather than the designers of large, fast engines.

Historically, Darpa not only was significant in generating technologies such as the Internet, but also in developing methods for protecting these systems. Fundamental protocols such as TCP/IP (transmission control protocol/Internet protocol) were meant for a very benign environment, and they're very leaky. Darpa spent the early to mid-'90s sort of patching the holes in these initial systems. They now need to start investing in the next-generation architecture.

One problem is that Darpa is making plans on moving ground. The sort of network attacks of two years ago were not nearly as sophisticated, serious, or numerous as what they are seeing now. In looking at the next-generation networks, they have to work iteratively so that functionality and security are negotiated in tandem.

Up until now Darpa didn't have any experience in designing for large-scale systems, in an operational environment. Their attitude was: They fund this work, which leads to commercial products, which the Department of Defense (DOD) then buys, and that's how they fulfill their defense mission. But DOD has problems that aren't addressed by the commercial world, such as having to deploy large, heterogeneous systems.

So Darpa plans to start working with the Pacific Command, which covers about 53% of the earth's surface. They're going to move out from the laboratory and develop their tools in their operational environment. Nothing will test what they do more than that.

Which Technologies Look Promising for Information Warfare?

Darpa sees great potential in optical networking. Eventually, an all-optical network might look like a telecommunications network, with a single switch from one person to you, and with a central hub. Thus, things like distributed denial-of-service attacks are ruled out. Also, it is almost impossible to detect the connection, because the signal is highly multiplexed over several wavelengths. It's clear they can do that for local-area networks (LANs). If Darpa can field these advanced systems for a DOD environment, which would involve maybe a hundred thousand nodes, they could be the precursors of what will enter the commercial market.

Right now, a typical defense analyst who wants to gain an understanding of the enemy will spend most of his or her time scouring databases, rather than doing what humans do best, which is using deep cognitive abilities. The defense analyst is not only looking for needles in a haystack but also pieces of needles. And as the world moves much faster, humans really can't keep up.

So Darpa has to start assigning to machines more of the job of searching data, looking for associations, and then presenting to the analyst something he or she can understand. It's like prosthesis, except it doesn't just assist the analyst, it lets the analyst do a 40-foot pole vault. It amplifies what the human is good at.

In the future, Darpa will be operating with increasingly heterogeneous forces—human soldiers alongside robotic forces. So how does a machine understand a commander's intent? To allow them to communicate, Darpa needs machine prosthesis to do the translation.

WetStone Technologies Inc., in Freeville, New York, a developer of information security products, is at work on a similar tool known as Synthesizing Information from Forensic Investigations (SIFI). Any given network will generate forensic data, and that data can come from any of a number of intrusion detection programs. Once that data is posted on SIFI's Web site, it is automatically synthesized so that analysts can examine, search, correlate, and graph information on attacks that have happened across many locations.

In regards to rapid recovery: In the summer of 2000, the computer network in one of the Department of Defense's (DOD's) battle management systems came under attack. Erroneous times and locations began showing up on screen; planes needing refueling were sent to rendezvous with tankers that never materialized, and one tanker was dispatched to two sites simultaneously. Within minutes, though, a recovery program installed on the network sniffed out the problem and fixed it.

The DOD itself staged the attack as a simulation, so as to demonstrate the first-ever "real-time information recovery and response" during an information warfare attack. In the demo, staged by Logicon, software agents were used to catch data conflicts in real time, allowing the system to remain on-line (see sidebar, "Agent-Based Systems").

AGENT-BASED SYSTEMS

Software agents are defined very broadly—enabling real machine-to-machine communications, allowing machines to understand content, send messages, do negotiations, and so on.

Darpa Agent Markup Language (DAML) is a fairly large project to create a next-generation Web language, a successor to extensible markup language (XML). It's aimed at semantic interoperability—to make more of what's on-line-machine-readable. Right now, when a machine gets to a Web page, it sees natural language, photos, and things like that, none of which are easy for machines to process. You can't ask it to do a content-based search for you, because it can't understand the content.

Making more readable content would involve anything from describing what's on the page ("this is a homepage," "this is an advertisement") all the way up to "this page is about such-and-such and it relates to the following facts." The more that machines can recognize content, the more they can share content, and the more agent-based systems can be built.

Military Applications of DAML

One of the military applications of DAML is in intelligence, which is used for collecting facts and, more important, for linking facts. Different communities have different terms for the same thing, or the same term for different things. One community may refer to a Russian fighter plane as a MIG 29A, and another group may call it a Hornet. On the current Web, you can't search on one term and find the other.

The other domain for DAML is command and control, where Darpa is trying to recognize what information relates to which entities. A famous failure of that system is the U.S. bombing of the Chinese embassy during Kosovo. An agent that could have said "this map is old" might have allowed the U.S. to recognize what was really going on.

But all that only works if Darpa's systems, which were built by different people talking different languages and using different approaches, can be integrated. In one of Darpa's other projects (control of agent-based systems [CoABS]), they're trying to set up middleware that makes it easy for systems, including legacy systems, to communicate. The ability to quickly throw together systems in a command center or on the battlefield is crucial. Both CoABS and DAML are aimed at creating that kind of infrastructure, for much richer machine-to-machine communication and understanding.

Broad Academic–Industry–Government Collaborations

In DAML, for example, Darpa is working very closely with the World Wide Web Consortium. They're also funding a group at Massachusetts Institute of Technology (MIT) who is helping refine the language. That group includes Tim Berners-Lee, one of the developers of hypertext markup language (HTML), and Ralph Swick, one of the developers of XML. They're making sure Darpa learns from their experiences.

That last step is key. One has to ensure the flow of information to the war-fighter. Network recovery also means preserving the so-called minimum essential data, the basic set of information one would need to regenerate a system should it be disabled.

New information technology will undoubtedly open up new attack routes, alongside whatever desirable features it may offer. Take wireless technology.[i] Jamming remains the tried-and-true mode of attack. But what if, instead of blocking signals, the enemy was to infiltrate communications links and send out false data? Just detecting such a RF attack is tricky.

Unlike the Internet protocol (IP) world, there are no virus checkers or intrusion detectors, and there are a lot of different types of radios and tactical data links. For example, Joint Tactical Radio System (JTRS) will support, in a single downstream box, all the legacy waveforms and provide interoperability among all existing and envisioned tactical radios. It also features software-defined cryptographic capabilities. Being computer-based, however, it introduces a whole new threat to radios that didn't exist before.

Of course, an offensive side of information warfare also exists: striking back. Given that you're able to determine the culprit, what is the appropriate response? Obviously, you'd have one response for a teenage hacker at a university in the United States, and quite a different one for somebody abroad who is working for a government.

Not surprisingly, the military is rather tight-lipped about its offensive IW capabilities. It's safe to assume, though, that the arsenal includes all the tactics deployed by ordinary hackers (worms, viruses, trapdoors, logic bombs), as well as surveillance technology for intelligence purposes.

Here it may be helpful to distinguish between weapons of mass destruction (which in the case of information warfare, would be a widescale assault on assorted military and civilian networks) and "weapons of precision disruption." The latter comprise lower-level strikes on specific targets, carried out over months or years by, say, an insider whose cooperation has been volunteered, bought, or coerced by a foreign state. That slow-drip mode of attack can be both harder to detect and more damaging over time. Pulling off an electronic Pearl Harbor, on the other hand, would mean not only bringing down vast and disparate networks, but also keeping them down long enough to inflict real harm.

Information warfare may also be waged as a social engineering campaign. Attacks on important, highly visible sites (the Nasdaq, say) might shake public confidence. If you could plant a lot of bogus earnings reports out there, so that you see a 50% sell-off in a single day, that would be enough to spook even long-term investors. Therefore, this type of attack is what the military is most vulnerable to, and should be their greatest concern.

So how vulnerable is vulnerable? Not all agree with the dire claims made about information warfare. Anyone still caught uttering 'electronic Pearl Harbor'... is either an ex-Cold Warrior trying to drum up antiterrorism funding through the clever use of propaganda, or a used-car salesman/white-collar crook of some type.

It's a problem, but not a crisis. Look, any time you institute a new technology, there are going to be downsides. You buy boilers, you get heat, but they may blow up. Thus, the way to have the positives and not the negatives is to attend to the safety and security issues. Computer networks are no different. If the national security of the United States were really on the line, there's a lot people could do that they haven't done yet. Diligent use of encryption and authentication, better policing of network activity, and air-gapping (keeping critical networks separate from noncritical ones) are all possible right now.

This is not to say that you shouldn't have a few cops on the beat to keep an eye out for anomalous on-line activity. But life is not risk-free.

Now, let's get down to specifics and look at the military tactics themselves.

OVERVIEW OF MILITARY TACTICS

The planning, security, and intelligence considerations of military information warfare tactics (MIWT) must be present in all aspects of the military information operations (MIO) development process, as previously discussed in Chapter 12, "Fighting against Macro Threats—Defensive Strategies for Governments and Industry Groups." These issues are fundamental to the success of MIWT.

Planning

MIWT operations, like most operations, can only be effective when adequate attention is given to the overall objective to which they are being applied. Developing an MIWT strategy requires careful adherence to planning philosophies, starting

This requires a close relationship between military and law enforcement. The FBI will have to help determine if any cyberattack (see sidebar, "Cyberoffense Mired in Cold War") suffered by U.S. military or business entities calls for a military or law enforcement response.

CYBEROFFENSE MIRED IN COLD WAR

The absence of a catastrophic cyberattack against the United States has created a false sense of cybersecurity and has allowed costly Cold War-era Pentagon programs to siphon money from critically needed information technology and security programs. The United States is still mired in a Cold War-era defense-spending mentality.

The rapid advance of IT has created real and potentially catastrophic vulnerabilities. The consequences of a cyberterrorist attack "could be devastating."

Eye of the Beholder

However, senior security officials are battling a perception problem, according to IW experts. Without a clear-cut example of an "electronic Pearl Harbor," where a surprise cyberattack cripples financial markets and other critical systems, it's difficult to convince top military and political leaders that IT research and development should be a bigger priority in the budget process.

Cyberterrorism is not an abstract concept. Although attacks historically have been labeled as "nuisances," that may not be the correct way to look at the problem. The government is dealing with an "enormous educational deficit" when it comes to IT security.

Part of the problem is the fact that the Defense Department remains committed to lobbying Congress for money to pay for programs such as the F-22 Joint Strike Fighter instead of increasing funding for IT programs. That is not affordable even in this age of surpluses. DOD's assumptions about future budget gains are "wrong."

More money should be spent on advanced sensors, precision-guided weapons, and other IT programs. That type of investment would preclude the need to buy costly systems such as the F-22.

But even events such as the outbreak of the "love bug," which reportedly cost the U.S. economy billions of dollars, have not convinced people in and out of government that the problem is real. Usually, when a major crisis costs people a lot of money, it leads to many visits to Capitol Hill and requests for help. But, that never happened after the love bug outbreak.

Some experts have questioned the government's liberal use of the term terrorism to describe acts of mass disruption on the Internet. However, when asked about the seeming lack of interest in cyberattacks by well-known terrorists such as Osama bin Laden, a senior White House official said the focus should not be on what bin Laden does or does not do, but on being proactive and understanding that a major attack may be coming.

The U.S. is attempting to be proactive. But, many believe that the U.S. is going to get seriously nailed.

The National Security Agency is one of the federal entities that has taken a proactive approach toward security cooperation between government and industry. But one of the biggest challenges facing the nation, highlighted during the love bug incident, remains to be convincing industry that security is as important as making money.

Vendors and users have to treat information assurance as a fundamental precept of doing business. It has to become part of the business case.

The Internet is ubiquitous. It allows attacks from anywhere in the world. Attackers can loop in from many different Internet providers.

NOTE

A cyberattack can include espionage using computer networks.

It could start across the street but appear to be coming from China. And something that might look like a hacker attack could be the beginning of cyberwarfare.

The growing bullets-and-guns conflict in the Middle East between Israel and the Palestinians, with Islamic supporters elsewhere, is being accompanied by cyberattacks from each side against the other. It's serious enough that the FBI issued an alert about it to the U.S. Space Command, giving U.S. forces warning that the action on the cyber front could affect them as well.

OFFENSIVE CONTAINMENT INFORMATION WARFARE TOOLS AND TACTICS

Of all the activities that have emerged with the evolution of IW and information operations, Command and Control Warfare (C2W) has attracted the most attention. The U.S.'s approach to C2W is comprehensive. This country has committed substantial resources to the development of technologies, doctrine, strategies, and organizations that will equip it to meet an information threat in any future conventional war. Countries like Australia, however, like most non-superpower nations of the world, will not be able to commit the substantial resources needed to follow the American model. Therefore, the general approach discussed in this chapter is tempered by the economic realities that will dictate the degree to which mid-level powers can invest in their own strategies.

Command and Control Warfare (C2W) is the approach to military operations that employs all measures (including but not limited to Electronic Warfare (EW), military deception, psychological operations (PSYOPS), operations security, and targeting), in a deliberate and integrated manner, mutually supported by intelligence and ITS, to disrupt or inhibit an adversary's ability to command and control his or her forces while protecting and enhancing our own.

C2W is the war-fighting or tactical application of MIWT and is usually aimed at a specific and defined battlespace, although it may be conducted in conjunction with other MIWT that may be focused on strategic information targets. There are five individual elements of C2W, covering both offensive and defensive applications.

- Operations security
- Military deception
- Psychological operations
- Electronic warfare
- Targeting

Operations Security

Operations Security (OPSEC) is a term that appears in many military documents in almost as many contexts, with several apparently different meanings. OPSEC is a process used for denying adversaries information about friendly disposition, intentions, capabilities, or limitations. It requires the employment of specialist equipment, including software, the adoption of suitable procedures, and most important, the development of a pro-security organizational culture. OPSEC is equally important as a defensive posture as it is in developing offensive strategies. By denying a potential enemy an understanding of the capabilities of friendly systems, possible hostile C2W will be more likely to miscalculate the friendly information capabilities and be ineffective.

Military Deception

Military deception is used to inject ambiguity and create false assessments in the decision-making process of the enemy. The objectives of employing military deception are to create a false deduction of friendly intentions, capabilities, and/or dispositions by the enemy. The target of deception is the enemy decision maker, that is, the individual who has the necessary authority to make a decision. There is no point influencing a decision if, in the event of ambiguity, the decision maker passes the decision to a higher authority. In this case, the higher authority must also be the target of deception.

Psychological Operations

Psychological Operations (PSYOPS) are operations that are planned activities in peace and war directed to enemy, friendly, and neutral audiences to influence attitudes and behavior affecting the achievement of political and military objectives. The objective of PSYOPS is to cause enemy, friendly, and neutral personnel to act favorably toward friendly organizations. PSYOPS have been used throughout history to influence adversary leaders and groups. The expansion and development of information technology (IT), and associated global media coverage, has enhanced modern PSYOPS opportunities.

Electronic Warfare

Electronic Warfare (EW) is the military action involving the use of electromagnetic energy to determine, exploit, reduce, or prevent hostile use of the electromagnetic spectrum. This action retains friendly use of the electromagnetic spectrum.

Targeting

Targeting is not just a process, nor is it just focused on destructive ends. Targeting is a capability that emphasizes the requirement to collect, process, and interpret information regarding decisive points in an enemy's command and control system; and, then selects the most effective option of incapacitating them. There are many hard- and soft-kill options available to a commander. Soft-kill options include the use of EW, strategic computer operations and information weapons, whereas hard-kill options refer to the various means of physically destroying targets.

Hard or soft destruction requires the capability to remove selected targets from an enemy's order of battle. These targets include vital communication nodes, national infrastructure, vital personnel, and specific military equipment. Any arm of the military may achieve destruction. Physical destruction has the highest risk associated with its application, and, unlike the other elements of C2W, physical destruction tends to be permanent, that is, buildings are destroyed and people are

The teams could be involved in a wide range of efforts, including enemy computer network attacks, defense of U.S. critical infrastructures, psychological operations, intelligence support, vulnerability assessments, and reviews of Pentagon Web sites for sensitive information.

The Pentagon expects 293 reserve officers and enlisted personnel to staff the five JRVIOs during fiscal 2002 and 2003 in Maryland, Virginia, and Texas. However, from 2004 to 2008, that number is expected to expand to more than 700.

The initiative is a result of a two-year Pentagon study called "Reserve Component Employment 2006." That study recommended the formation of a cyberdefense unit that would consist of people with IT skills who could work in different locations instead of at a single center. The study also urged the department to recruit high-tech savvy people from the private sector.

DEFENSIVE RESPONSIVE CONTAINMENT INFORMATION WARFARE TOOLS AND TACTICS

One of the more recent additions to the military commander's toolbox are defensive responsive containment information warfare tools. Computers and associated technology have helped change the face of modern information warfare tactics by providing the capabilities to generate and process massive amounts of data, and disseminate the resultant information throughout the battlespace. However, computers provide more than just an information-processing capability. They may also be used as weapons in their own right. The most common examples of computer operations include hacking, virus planting, and chipping. These techniques are primarily aimed at targeting the enemy's broad information environment. However, they may also be used to attack the enemy's computer-based weapon systems and computer-based platforms, such as "fly-by-wire" aircraft. Although generally strategic in nature, computer operations may be applied to the tactical and operational components of the conventional warfare environment, either in support of C2W operations or in direct support of air, land or sea operations. See sidebar, "Military Tests Digital Forces."

MILITARY TESTS DIGITAL FORCES

The Army has kicked off a major new warfighting experiment at Fort Polk, Louisiana, designed to test the effectiveness of infantry units armed with digitized information systems. The Joint Contingency Force Advanced Warfighting Experiment (JCF AWE) included about 5,000 soldiers. They took part in realistic combat scenarios against the Fort Polk Joint Readiness Training Center's opposing force.

The exercise was used to assess 58 technological and doctrinal initiatives, including the En Route Mission Planning and Rehearsal System (EMPRS), Land Warrior, and the Army Battle Command System. EMPRS is installed on aircraft and creates a wireless local-area network connecting all planes, thereby allowing commanders and soldiers to collaborate en route to their objective.

EMPRS allows airborne forces and light forces to do planning and mission rehearsal while they're on the way to the exercise. The Army really wants to disseminate that information down to the company commander, the platoon leader, and the individual soldier onboard those airplanes.

The Army Battle Command System will be instrumental for coordination between light and armored forces. The digital Army Battle Command System will go all the way from the platoon or to the brigade level; the Army wants to measure how those digital enablers allow that commander to fight differently.

The Land Warrior platoon conducted a nighttime ambush and a nighttime assault on a mock city. Some soldiers wore the latest version of the Land Warrior system, others an earlier version. The Army has reduced the Land Warrior system from about 65 pounds to 41. The JCF AWE is part of the Millennium Challenge, a major exercise conducted by Joint Forces Command, Norfolk, Virginia, in which the services interact and operate with one another.

Hacking

The term computer hacker is now synonymous with computer criminal although, arguably, this merging of terms is not justified. Someone who uses a computer to rob a bank is a criminal, not a hacker. The genuine computer hackers are still doing what the original computer hackers were doing 40 years ago—simply exploring the bounds of computer science.

Unfortunately, exploring today's computer science often means entering other people's systems. There are many computer hackers around the world who enter other people's systems on a daily basis. Most simply gain access to the systems, "snoop" around for a while, and leave. Some hackers like to explore the logic flow in systems. A few like to exploit these systems for either their own gain or simply to make life difficult for the users of that system. The genuine hackers, while invading system privacy, rarely damage the systems into which they have hacked. However, most users of systems understandably find it an unacceptable invasion of their privacy to have people intruding into their systems.

Hackers present a genuine problem to most organizations today, and a specific threat to military security. Hackers have historically found the challenge of breaking into so called "secure" military systems one of the more satisfying aspects of their hobby. Accordingly, the first and foremost aim of any information strategy for military forces must be to defend their own system integrity.

Once access is gained into a system, hackers can generally manipulate whatever files they wish. They will often set up personal accounts for themselves in case they wish to return again in the future. A hacker can, of course, collect very important information. In the business domain, intelligence can be gained about a competitor's product. In the government service domain, sensitive personal information can be obtained (or altered), which can later be used against individuals. In the military domain, classified information such as capabilities, vulnerability, strategies, and dispositions may be extracted or manipulated. A hacker can also change the file structure, amend the logic flow, and even destroy parts of the system.

Hacking is no longer simply a pursuit of misfits and computer scientists; it is now a genuine method of obtaining information by government agencies, criminals, or subversive organizations. There have been several reports about government sponsorship of such activity. Many of the world's secret security organizations are now passing industrial secrets to their nation's domestic businesses. The basic tool kit of today's industrial spy contains a PC and a modem. The industrial spy is simply a hacker who intrudes into someone else's computer system and then exploits the information obtained. Neither domestic nor international laws adequately address all of the issues surrounding hacking. Therefore, in the unlikely event that hackers are caught, in many situations prosecution is impossible.

The impact on those involved in developing MIWT is that hacking presents a genuine threat to the security and integrity of both military and civilian information systems. Defense against hacking can be successful to varying degrees. Most defensive strategies are system-dependent; therefore, listing them in this chapter would be pointless. However, defense against hacking needs to be considered by anyone who manages or operates an information technology system.

The other reason that national security forces should become involved in hacking is the potential benefits that can be derived by employing hacking techniques as an offensive tactic. Intelligence collection against information stored in an enemy's databases as well as the specific system capabilities, vulnerability, and architecture, can be accomplished successfully using hacking techniques. In future wars, information derived from hacking will form a large part of intelligence databases and, thus, manipulation of the enemy's decision-making support systems will become routine.

Viruses

A virus is a "code fragment that copies itself into a larger program, modifying that program." A virus executes only when its host program begins to run. The virus then replicates itself, infecting other programs as it reproduces. Protecting against computer viruses has become a part of using modern ITS. Viruses are passed from computer to computer via disks and reportedly via the more recent practice of electronic file transfer, such as e-mail. Although statistics concerning viruses are often difficult to substantiate, some specialists estimate that there are as many as 8,900 viruses currently existing on the Internet, with cures being available for only 1,250. Although virus screening software should prevent known viruses being brought into a system, they will not prevent all virus attacks. The most effective method of minimizing the risk of virus attack, and minimizing the damage caused by viruses in the event of an attack, is by employing sound and rigorous information-management procedures.

Isolating Internet systems from operating systems where practical is vital, and minimizing computer-to-disk-to-computer transfers, particularly if the origin of that data is the Internet, will reduce the chances of picking up a virus. The use of the most recent antivirus software and the screening of disks every time that they are placed in a computer will reduce the risk of disk infections being passed onto systems. Careful selection and management of passwords may deter a potential intruder from accessing a system and planting a virus, while the maintenance of comprehensive system back-ups can minimize the impact of viruses, should one find its way onto a system. Viruses, however, can also be backed-up and a dormant virus can infest any back-up files and can be reintroduced when a system is recovered. Accordingly, a layered back-up strategy is imperative. Antivirus strategies are aimed at minimizing the chances of getting a virus and minimizing the damage that viruses can cause if they are introduced. Users of today's ITS must be aware of the virus threat. Simple procedures will often be enough to avoid viruses, but a single failure to comply with antivirus procedures can result in systems becoming inoperable.

Virus planting is clearly a suitable and attractive weapon for military forces and is a valuable addition to the offensive information operations inventory. If a simple virus can be injected into the systems of a potential enemy, the need to expend effort in physically attacking that system may be eliminated.

Chipping

Most people are aware of the vulnerability of software to hostile invasions, such as a virus attack. Few, however, are aware of the risk to the essential hardware components of an ITS. Chipping is a term that refers to unexpected events that can be engineered into computer chips. Today's chips contain billions of integrated circuits that can easily be configured by the manufacturer so that they can initiate unexpected events at a specific time, or at the occurrence of specific circumstances. This may explain why some electronic goods fail a short time after the warranty has expired. There is almost no way of detecting whether a chip contained within a piece of equipment has been corrupted.

One way to minimize the risk of chipping is to self-manufacture all important chips, such as those that are used as part of an aircraft's flight control system. Economically, this is often not feasible. Most chips used within today's high-technology equipment are manufactured in countries where labor costs are low. Establishing an indigenous manufacturing capability would increase the cost of acquiring the equipment. A risk assessment must be made when purchasing vital equipment from overseas, by comparing the risk of vital equipment failing once hostilities commence to the cost of producing chips internally or developing rigorous quality control of imported chips.

Chipping represents a simple way to develop a conventional military advantage by those countries that regularly export military equipment. In the event of any hostilities with recipients of their "chipped" equipment, that equipment may be incapacitated without having to use conventional force. This makes economic as well as military sense. The legal and ethical aspects are a separate issue.

There are many other computer weapons that can be used in conjunction with or instead of chipping, viruses, and hacking. These weapons have many different descriptive names such as "worms," "trojan horses," and "logic bombs," and are commonplace in today's information society. They are all examples of computer operations that may be adapted to suit the information-warfare environment. A detailed description of all of these techniques is beyond the scope of this chapter. Suffice to say that computer weapons should be an integral part of any information-warfare operations strategy. They should be considered as valid alternatives to conventional weapons both in offense and defense.

COUNTERING SUSTAINED TERRORIST INFORMATION WARFARE TACTICS

Terrorism is, among other things, a weapon used by the weak against the strong. The United States has moved into the 21st century as a preeminent, global power in a period of tremendous flux within societies, among nations, and across states and regions. Terrorism will accompany changes at each of these levels, as it has in other periods of flux in the international environment. To the extent that the United States continues to be engaged as a global power, terrorism will have the potential to affect American interests directly and indirectly, from attacks on U.S. territory (including low-probability but high-consequence "superterrorism" with weapons of mass destruction) to attacks affecting the U.S.'s diplomatic and economic ties abroad, or the U.S.'s ability to maintain a forward military presence or project power in times of crisis. The United States will also have a unique, systemic interest in terrorism as a global problem (including acts of "domestic" terrorism confined within state borders that make up the bulk of terrorism worldwide) even where the United States is not directly or even indirectly targeted. In one way or another, terrorism can affect the U.S.'s freedom of action, not just with regard to national security strategy narrowly defined, but across a range of compelling issues, from drugs and money laundering to information and energy policy.

Many of the U.S.'s high-priority national objectives have been shaken by the recent experience of terrorism. The Oklahoma bombing, and World Trade Center and Pentagon 9-11 terrorist attacks, struck at the U.S.'s sense of security within its borders. Attacks against U.S. forces in Saudi Arabia raise questions about the U.S.'s strategy for presence and stability in an area of critical importance for world energy supply. The U.S. embassy bombings in Kenya and Tanzania, and the U.S.S. Cole in Yemen raise questions about the exposure that comes with active engagement in world affairs, and point to the risks of privately sponsored terrorism. The assassination of Prime Minister Rabin and the increased campaign of suicide bombings in Israel, has put the Middle East peace process in serious jeopardy, threatening a critical and long-standing U.S. diplomatic objective. Elsewhere, terrorism has destabilized allies (in Egypt and Turkey), and has rendered counternarcotics relationships difficult (in Colombia and Mexico). Where societies and regions are fundamentally unstable, and where political outcomes are delicately poised, terrorism will have a particular ability to affect strategic futures.

Overall Observations

Most contemporary analysis of terrorism focus on terrorist political violence as a stand-alone phenomenon, without reference to its geopolitical and strategic context. Similarly, counterterrorism policy is rarely discussed in terms of its place in broader national security planning. Prior to the specter of "superterrorism," using weapons of mass destruction (WMD), terrorism, however horrible, never posed an existential threat to U.S. security. With the important exception of WMD, terrorism still does not pose a grave threat to America's future as it does to many other societies around the world. But many types of terrorism do pose a threat to U.S. interests, from homeland defense to regional security and the stability of the international system. As a global power, the U.S. perspective on terrorism is bound to differ in substantial ways from that of others, including allies such as Britain, France, and Israel, whose experiences provide lessons, but not necessarily direction for U.S. counterterrorism policy. In light of the preceding IW arsenal and tactics analysis of the military, certain overall sustained terrorist information-warfare tactics observations stand out:

- Terrorism
- Geopolitics of terrorism
- Counterterrorism versus new terrorism

approach, emphasizing the monitoring and attack of key nodes in terrorist networks and the forcible apprehension of terrorist suspects—with or without the cooperation of local states. Future demands on air power may be driven as much by requirements for intercepting and extracting suspects as by the need to attack terrorist training camps and strike regimes supporting the export of terrorism.

Air and space power will help make terrorism (an inherently amorphous phenomenon) more transparent. The ability to identify and to target terrorist-related activity and to help expose terrorism and its sponsors for policy makers and international opinion will be key contributions of air- and space-based assets. As terrorism becomes more diffuse and its sponsorship increasingly hazy, finding the "smoking gun" will become more difficult, but essential to determine strategies and build a consensus for action. Space-based sensors, surveillance by UAVs, and signals intelligence (SIGINT) will facilitate the application of air power and other instruments in the service of counterterrorism.

Gaining leverage in addressing the new terrorism will be a key strategic and technical challenge. Future requirements for counterterrorism will be part of a broader need to tailor air and space power to challenges posed by nonstate actors, including networks of individuals. At the same time, policy instruments, including air and space power, will need to concentrate on detecting and preventing the use of weapons of mass destruction by terrorists—whether as a stand-alone apocalyptic act or as a low-tech delivery system in the hands of adversaries.

Much terrorism (and counterterrorism action) will focus on urban areas, with strong political and operational constraints. Terrorism is increasingly an urban phenomenon, worldwide. One explanation for this is that the political fate of most modern societies is determined by what happens in cities. Terrorists seeking to influence political conditions have many incentives to attack urban targets. Terrorists with transcendental objectives will, similarly, find symbolic and vulnerable targets in urban settings. The use of air power in a counterterrorist mode faces the more general problem of operating in an urban environment (the difficult Israeli experience in Beirut and South Lebanon is instructive). Terrorists and their facilities will be difficult to locate and target. Operations against them or to rescue hostages will pose severe challenges for the use of air power, not least the risk of placing uninvolved civilians in harm's way. The viability of air power as an instrument in such settings may depend on the capacity for discriminate targeting and the use of less-than-lethal technologies.

Air power's pervasiveness and speed are advantages in the face of transnational and transregional terrorism. In an era in which terrorist acts may take place across the globe and where sponsors cross national and regional lines, counterterrorism strategies will become "horizontal" in character. Where terrorists and their sponsors can be identified and attacked with purpose, the global sight and reach of air- and space-based assets will be valuable to national decision makers.

Air and space power will have a synergistic effect with other counterterrorism instruments. Air and space power can be used in concert with covert action, diplomacy, economic instruments, and joint military operations. The notion of "parallel warfare," developed in relation to attacks on infrastructure in war, will also be relevant to counterterrorism operations. Operations using a range of instruments can be designed to act, in parallel, on terrorist supporters, terrorist infrastructure and networks, and the terrorists themselves.

DEALING WITH RANDOM TERRORIST INFORMATION WARFARE

During the 1970s and 1980s, political extremism and terrorism frequently focused on 'national liberation' and economic issues. The collapse of the Soviet bloc, and the ending of its covert funding and encouragement of terrorism led to a decline in the militant and violent left-wing terrorist groups that were a feature of the age.

The 1990s through the present time have seen the development of a new terrorism: Random Terrorist Information Warfare. This is not to say that state-backed terrorism has ceased, but rather that the spectrum of terrorism has widened. This new extremism is frequently driven by religious fervor, is transnational, sanctions extreme violence, and may often be millennialist. The new terrorism may seek out military or government targets, but it also seeks out symbolic civilian targets, and the victims have mostly been innocent civilians (Alfred P. Murrah Building, Oklahoma City; World Trade Center, New York; AMIA Headquarters, Buenos Aires, etc.).

Growing concern about this new terrorism has been paralleled by concern about the employment of the new information and communication technologies (ICTs). ICTs offer a new dimension for political extremists and terrorists. They allow the diffusion of command and control; they allow boundless new opportunities for communication; and they allow the players to target the information stores, processes, and communications of their opponents. The sophistication of the modern nation-state, and its dependency on computer-based ICTs, make the state ever more vulnerable.

The use of ICTs to influence, modify, disrupt, or damage a nation-state, its institutions, or population by influencing the media, or by subversion, has been called "netwar." The full range of weapons in the cyberspace armory can be employed in netwar—from propaganda campaigns at one level to interference with databases and networks at the other. What particularly distinguishes netwar from other forms of war is that it targets information and communications, and may be used to alter thinking or disrupt planned actions. In this sense, it can be distinguished from earlier forms of warfare—economic wars that target the means of production, and political wars that target leadership and government.

Netwar is, therefore, of particular interest to those engaged in non-military war, or those operating at sub-state level. Clearly, nation-states might also consider it as an adjunct to military war or as an option prior to moving on to military war. So far, however, it appears to be of greater interest to extremist advocacy groups and terrorists. Because there are no physical limits or boundaries, netwar has been adopted by groups who operate across great distances or transnationally. The growth of such groups, and their growing powers in relation to those of nation-states, suggests an evolving power-based relationship for both. War in the future is more likely to be waged between such groups and states rather than between states.

Most modern adversaries of nation-states, in the realm of low-intensity conflict—such as international terrorists, single-issue extremists, and ethnic and religious extremists—are organized in networks, although their leadership may sometimes be hierarchical. Law enforcement and security agencies, therefore, often have difficulty in engaging in low-intensity conflict against such networks because they are ill-suited to do so. Their doctrine, training, and modus operandi has, all too often, been predicated on combating a hierarchy of command, like their own.

Only now are low-intensity conflict and terrorism recognized as "strategic" threats to nation-states, and countries that, until very recently, thought that terrorism was something that happened elsewhere, have become victims themselves. The Tokyo subway attack by the Aum Shinriko, the Oklahoma City bombing and the 9-11 terrorist attacks, would have been unthinkable a generation ago. Not only was the civil population unprepared but also the law enforcement population. And this was true despite clear warning signs that such attacks were in the offing.

Cyberspace is becoming a new arena for political extremists: The potential for physical conflict to be replaced by attacks on information infrastructures has caused states to rethink their concepts of warfare, threats, and national assets at a time when information is recognized as a national asset. The adoption of new information technologies and the use of new communication media, such as the Internet, creates vulnerabilities that can be exploited by individuals, organizations, and states.

Also, the arrival of the Internet has provided the first forum in history for all the disaffected to gather in one place to exchange views and reinforce prejudices. It is hardly surprising, for example, that the right-wing militias favorite method of communication is e-mail and that forums on the Internet are the source of many wild conspiracy theories that drive the media.

Preeminent amongst the extremists and terrorist groupings who have entered cyberspace faster and more enthusiastically than others, are the Far Right, that is white supremacists and neo-Nazis, and radical Islamists. Others, such as eco-extremists and the Far Left appear to be slower in seizing the opportunities available.

What characterizes these two groupings are their transnational natures. The Far Right is increasingly active in the USA and Europe, but, in contrast to its ideological roots in the 1920s and 1930s, it seeks now to unite a white Anglo-Saxon, or European-originating, entity in a rear-guard action to oppose centralized democratic government and return to some imagined past world in which an armed, racially pure, white man can live untroubled by the police, the Inland Revenue, and the world banking system. The Islamist diaspora, now spread worldwide, seeks a return to divine-ruled states (or even one transnational state) in which all Muslims will live under the norms and laws of the Saudi Arabian peninsula in the first and second centuries of the Common Era. These types of organizations make them ideal users of networks and proponents of netwar. Their ideas and their use of cyberspace will be further discussed in Chapter 14, "The Information Warfare Arsenal and Tactics of Terrorist Rogues."

Although the use of ICTs to enhance command and control and enhance communication is apparent among Islamist extremists and among the militia movement and Far Right in America, it is less so amongst Far Right and other extremists in other parts of the world. This clearly reflects the higher ICT access in North America. Fears by western governments that their national infrastructures may be a target for information warfare or cyberterrorism may be well-founded, but the evidence so far is that sub-state groups at least, use ICTs mainly for propaganda, secure communications, intelligence gathering, and funds management.

It has been noted by one observer that the Internet has not replaced other communications media for the Far Right, and that its largest use in this regard has been to advertise the sale of non-Internet-related propaganda, such as books, audiotapes, and videos. Nor has the Internet led to an increase in mobilization. The Seattle-based Coalition For Human Dignity observed that Far Right events in the United States, which were heavily promoted on the Internet only, were in fact failures.

For some on the American Far Right, the Internet has become an end in itself. Surfing the Net has replaced real action. It is a measure of how degenerate and weak the U.S.'s movement has become, that some people actually think this is a good thing. Not only do individuals want risk-free revolution, they now want people-free revolution. Here lies the great danger of the computer for everyone who uses it. It allows individuals to live and work interacting with a machine rather than with people.

However, it does not pay to be complacent; extremists and terrorists are increasingly information-technology literate. Unless law enforcement and national

a federal response other than the ad hoc overreactions and short-term task forces that have characterized U.S. counterterrorism policy. Such knee-jerk reactions have the potential to do much greater harm in IW than they have in countering terrorism: Heavy-handed, short-sighted, and hasty government measures in the information space might have unintended consequences ranging from stymied economic development to unconstitutional regulation to disastrous technical failures. Preempting an rogue IW attack with a multiagency policy of coordination could save the United States from their adversaries, and it might even save them from themselves.

Fighting against Random Rogue Information Warfare

History shows that terrorism more often than not has little political impact, and that when it has an effect it is often the opposite of the one desired. Terrorism in the 1990s and the present time is no exception. The 1991 assassination of Rajiv Gandhi as he campaigned to retake the prime ministership neither hastened nor inhibited the decline of India's Congress Party. Hamas' and Hezbollah's stepped-up terrorism in Israel undoubtedly influenced the outcome of Israeli elections, but although it achieved its immediate objective of setting back the peace process on which Palestine Authority President Yasir Arafat has gambled his future, is a hard-line Likud government really in these groups' best interests? On the other side, Yigal Amir, the right-wing orthodox Jewish student who assassinated Prime Minister Yitzhak Rabin in 1996, because he disapproved of the peace agreement with the Palestinians, might well have helped elect Rabin's dovish second-in-command, Shimon Peres, to a full term had the Muslim terrorists not made Israeli security an issue again.

Terrorists caused disruption and destabilization in other parts of the world, such as Sri Lanka, where economic decline has accompanied the war between the government and the Tamil Tigers. But in Israel and in Spain, where Basque extremists have been staging attacks for decades, terrorism has had no effect on the economy. Even in Algeria, where terrorism has exacted the highest toll in human lives, Muslim extremists have made little headway since 1993, when many predicted the demise of the unpopular military regime.

Some argue that terrorism must be effective because certain terrorist leaders have become president or prime minister of their country. In those cases, however, the terrorists had first forsworn violence and adjusted to the political process. Finally, the common wisdom holds that terrorism can spark a war or, at least, prevent peace. That is true, but only where there is much inflammable material: as in Sarajevo in 1914, so in the Middle East and elsewhere today. Nor can one ever say with certainty that the conflagration would not have occurred sooner or later in any case.

Nevertheless, terrorism's prospects, often overrated by the media, the public, and some politicians, are improving as its destructive potential increases. This has to do both with the rise of groups and individuals that practice or might take up terrorism and with the weapons available to them. The past few decades have witnessed the birth of dozens of aggressive movements espousing varieties of nationalism, religious fundamentalism, fascism, and apocalyptic millenarianism, from Hindu nationalists in India to neofascists in Europe and the developing world to the Branch Davidian cult of Waco, Texas. The earlier fascists believed in military aggression and engaged in a huge military buildup, but such a strategy has become too expensive even for superpowers. Now, mail-order catalogs tempt militants with readily available, far cheaper, unconventional as well as conventional weapons—the poor man's nuclear bomb, Iranian President Ali Akbar Hashemi Rafsanjani called them.

In addition to nuclear arms, the weapons of mass destruction include biological agents and man-made chemical compounds that attack the nervous system, skin, or blood. Governments have engaged in the production of chemical weapons for almost a century and in the production of nuclear and biological weapons for many decades, during which time proliferation has been continuous and access ever easier. The means of delivery (ballistic missiles, cruise missiles, and aerosols) have also become far more effective. While in the past missiles were deployed only in wars between states, recently they have played a role in civil wars in Afghanistan and Yemen. Use by terrorist groups would be but one step further.

Until the 1970s, most observers believed that stolen nuclear material constituted the greatest threat in the escalation of terrorist weapons, but many now think the danger could lie elsewhere. An April 2000 Defense Department report says that "most terrorist groups do not have the financial and technical resources to acquire nuclear weapons but could gather materials to make radiological dispersion devices and some biological and chemical agents." Some groups have state sponsors that possess or can obtain weapons of the latter three types. Terrorist groups themselves have investigated the use of poisons since the 19th century. The Aum Shinrikyo cult staged a poison gas attack in March 1995 in the Tokyo subway; exposure to the nerve gas sarin killed ten people and injured 5,000. Other, more amateurish attempts in the United States and abroad to experiment with chemical substances and biological agents for use in terrorism have involved the toxin that causes botulism, the poisonous protein rycin (twice), sarin (twice), bubonic plague bacteria, typhoid bacteria, hydrogen cyanide, vx (another nerve gas), and possibly the Ebola virus.

To Use or Not to Use?

If terrorists have used chemical weapons only once and nuclear material never, to some extent the reasons are technical. The scientific literature is replete with the technical problems inherent in the production, manufacture, storage, and delivery of each of the three classes of unconventional weapons.

The manufacture of nuclear weapons is not that simple, nor is delivery to their target. Nuclear material, of which a limited supply exists, is monitored by the U.N.-affiliated International Atomic Energy Agency. Only governments can legally procure it, so that even in this age of proliferation, investigators could trace those abetting nuclear terrorists without great difficulty. Monitoring can overlook a more primitive nuclear weapon: nonfissile but radioactive nuclear material. Iranian agents in Turkey, Kazakhstan, and elsewhere are known to have tried to buy such material originating in the former Soviet Union.

Chemical agents are much easier to produce or obtain, but not so easy to keep safely in stable condition; their dispersal depends largely on climactic factors. The terrorists behind the 1995 attack in Tokyo chose a convenient target where crowds of people gather, but their sarin was apparently dilute. The biological agents are far and away the most dangerous: They could kill hundreds of thousands of people whereas chemicals might kill only thousands. They are relatively easy to procure, but storage and dispersal are even trickier than for nerve gases. The risk of contamination for the people handling them is high, and many of the most lethal bacteria and spores do not survive well outside the laboratory. Aum Shinrikyo reportedly released anthrax bacteria (among the most toxic agents known) on two occasions from a building in Tokyo without harming anyone.

Given the technical difficulties, terrorists are probably less likely to use nuclear devices than chemical weapons, and least likely to attempt to use biological weapons. But difficulties could be overcome, and the choice of unconventional weapons will in the end come down to the specialties of the terrorists and their access to deadly substances.

The political arguments for shunning unconventional weapons are equally weighty. The risk of detection and subsequent severe retaliation or punishment is great, and although this may not deter terrorists, it may put off their sponsors and suppliers. Terrorists eager to use weapons of mass destruction may alienate at least some supporters, not so much because the dissenters hate the enemy less or have greater moral qualms, but because they think the use of such violence counter productive. Unconventional weapon strikes could render whole regions uninhabitable for long periods. Use of biological arms poses the additional risk of an uncontrollable epidemic. And although terrorism seems to be tending toward more indiscriminate killing and mayhem, terrorists may draw the line at weapons of super violence likely to harm both foes and large numbers of relatives and friends—say, Kurds in Turkey, Tamils in Sri Lanka, or Arabs in Israel.

Furthermore, traditional terrorism rests on the heroic gesture, on the willingness to sacrifice one's own life as proof of one's idealism. Obviously there is not much heroism in spreading botulism or anthrax. Because most terrorist groups are as interested in publicity as in violence, and because publicity for a mass poisoning or nuclear bombing would be far more unfavorable than for a focused conventional attack, only terrorists who do not care about publicity will even consider the applications of unconventional weapons.

Broadly speaking, terrorists will not engage in overkill if their traditional weapons (the submachine gun and the conventional bomb) are sufficient to continue the struggle and achieve their aims. But the decision to use terrorist violence is not always a rational one; if it were, there would be much less terrorism, because terrorist activity seldom achieves its aims. What if, after years of armed struggle and the loss of many of their militants, terrorist groups see no progress? Despair could lead to giving up the armed struggle, or to suicide. But it might also lead to a last desperate attempt to defeat the hated enemy by arms not tried before. Their only hope lies in their despair.

Post Apocalypse

Terrorist groups traditionally contain strong quasi-religious, fanatical elements, for only total certainty of belief (or total moral relativism) provides justification for taking lives. That element was strong among the prerevolutionary Russian terrorists and the Romanian fascists of the Iron Guard in the 1930s, as it is among today's Tamil Tigers. Fanatical Muslims consider the killing of the enemies of God a religious commandment, and believe that the secularists at home as well as the State of Israel will be annihilated because it is Allah's will. Aum Shinrikyo doctrine held that murder could help both victim and murderer to salvation. Sectarian fanaticism has surged during the past decade, and, in general, the smaller the group, the more fanatical the group.

As humankind survived the end of the second millennium of the Christian era, apocalyptic movements failed to rise to the occasion. Nevertheless, the belief in the impending end of the world is probably as old as history, but for reasons not entirely clear, sects and movements preaching the end of the world gain influence toward the end of a century, and all the more at the close of a millennium. Most of the preachers of doom do not advocate violence, and some even herald a renaissance, the birth of a new kind of man and woman. Others, however, believe that the sooner the reign of the Antichrist is established, the sooner this corrupt world will be destroyed and the new heaven and earth foreseen by St. John in the Book of Revelation, Nostradamus, and a host of other prophets will be realized.

Extremist millenarians would like to give history a push, helping create world-ending havoc replete with universal war, famine, pestilence, and other scourges. Those who subscribe to such beliefs number in the millions. They have their own subcultures, produce books, and CDs by the thousands, and have built temples and communities of whose existence most of their contemporaries are unaware. They

services makes it more and more difficult for organizations and individuals to control their own security environment.

Given this situation, you need to focus on two goals. First, you need to find a way to protect yourself against catastrophic events. Second, you need to build a firm foundation upon which you can make steady progress by continually raising the cost of mounting an attack and mitigating the expected damage of the information warfare arsenal and tactics of the military. The conclusions are as follows.

Conclusions Drawn from the Information Warfare Arsenal and Tactics of the Military

- Information warfare (IW) has become virtually synonymous with the revolution in information technologies and its potential to transform military strategies and capabilities.
- There is a growing consensus that national prosperity, if not survival, depends on one's ability to effectively leverage information technology. Without being able to defend vital information, information processes, and information systems, such a strategy is doomed to failure.
- Information warfare is often thought of as being defined by a particular target set of decision makers, information, information processes, and information systems.
- The "battlespace" associated with IW has been a constantly expanding one, moving far beyond traditional military situations.
- In some quarters, IW has even been associated with the leveraging of information technologies to achieve greater effectiveness and efficiency. This has stretched the meaning of IW to the breaking point and has sowed more confusion than enlightenment. For this reason, this treatment of the subject uses the term "information strategies" to refer to the recognition and utilization of information and information technologies as an instrument of national power that can be independent of, or complementary to, military presence and operations.
- The scope, or battlespace, of information warfare and strategy (IWS) can be defined by the players and three dimensions of the nature of their interactions, the level of their interactions, and the arena of their interactions.
- Nation states or combinations of nation states are not the only players. Non-state actors (including political, ethnic, and religious groups; organized crime; international and transnational organizations; and even individuals empowered by information technology) are able to engage in information attacks and to develop information strategies to achieve their desired ends.

- The term "war" has been used so loosely in recent times (War on Poverty, War on Drugs, War on Crime) that it should be no surprise that IW has evolved over the past several years to become a "catch-all" term that encompasses many disparate activities, some of which have long been associated with competition, conflict, and warfare, and others that are of more recent origin. These include activities that range from propaganda campaigns (including Media War), to attacks (both physical and nonphysical) against commanders, their information sources, and the means of communicating with their forces.

- Under this rather large umbrella that has become known as IW, one can find activities long associated with military concepts and operations, including deception, command and control warfare (C2W), and psychological operations (Psyops).

- Technological advances have added new forms such as electronic warfare (EW) and "hacker warfare."

- The term "defensive information warfare" (IW-D) is used here to refer to all actions taken to defend against information attacks, that is, attacks on decision makers, the information and information-based processes they rely on, and their means of communicating their decisions.

- Strictly speaking, nonmilitary groups, both foreign and domestic can launch these attacks during peace time at nonmilitary targets the term IW-D should be IWS-D. However, IW-D is currently in wide use.

- This overview of IW-D does not attempt to deal with the problems of defending against all of the different kinds of information attacks, but rather focuses its attention on the subset of IW that involves attacks against information infrastructure, including what has become known as "hacker warfare" and in its more serious form, "digital warfare."

An Agenda for Action in Preparing for the Information Warfare Arsenal and Tactics of the Military

The cornerstone of the military's efforts to combat IW will be the efforts of all global military organizations to protect their own systems and information. Some military organizations have been worrying about this for a long time and have developed and implemented plans to keep on top of this increasingly serious set of threats. Other military organizations have more work to do. It might be helpful, even for those military organizations that feel they are well prepared, to review the following list of suggested actions steps to determine what they need to do to be better prepared for the future.

The United States Government needs to set an agenda for action that goes beyond the work already done in preparation for the information warfare arsenal and tactics of the military. Action steps should include, but not be limited to, the following 10 areas:

1. The first suggested action involves a review of the military organization's mission in light of the emerging threat. A few military organizations may find that IW-D adds a mission or increases the importance of an existing mission.

2. New relationships with external organizations may be required, or perhaps existing relationships may need to be modified. Thus, a review of these relationships is in order.

3. Who is responsible for IW-D in the military organization? Perhaps the military organization has a Chief Information Officer (CIO) and it would be appropriate for the CIO to take on this responsibility. Perhaps the responsibility for IW-D is spread out among several individuals. In any event, a clear allocation of responsibilities is required.

4. Not all information or all systems should be considered equal with respect to the protection they merit. It is important, given resource constraints, to identify which information and systems (and functions of these systems) are critical and which are not critical.

5. How vulnerable are the information and systems? What is the specific nature of the vulnerabilities? Answers are needed to provide a basis for planning and developing defenses. It needs to be remembered that vulnerabilities are relative to the threat, the nature of which is constantly evolving. Thus, vulnerability analyzes are not a one-time task but must be part of a continuing effort.

6. Isolated actions to improve security are helpful, but they are no substitute for the development of a comprehensive IW-D strategy for a military organization.

7. Because it is not possible to avoid all the risks associated with IW, each military organization needs to develop a plan to manage these risks.

8. In the course of developing and articulating a military organizational IW-D strategy and risk-management plan, many issues will be raised and discussed. These discussions will create a greater awareness of the problem within the military organization and improve the organization's ability to meet the challenges associated with IW-D.

9. Combating IW is a long-term proposition. There are many long poles in the tent. A military organization's investment strategies need to be reviewed and investments in defenses and supporting technologies must be made.

10. Some reallocation of resources may be made necessary by changes in the operating costs associated with introducing new procedures and safeguards.

ENDNOTES

i   John R. Vacca, *Wireless Broadband Networks Handbook*, McGraw-Hill, 2001.

ii   John R. Vacca, *High-Speed Cisco Networks: Planning, Design, and Implementation*, CRC Press, 2002.

iii John R. Vacca, *Net Privacy: A Guide to Developing & Implementing an Ironclad ebusiness Privacy Plan*, McGraw-Hill, 2001.

iv   John R. Vacca, *"Satellite Encryption,"* Academic Press, 1999.

v   John R. Vacca, *The Essential Guide to Storage Area Networks*, Prentice Hall, 2002.

14 The Information Warfare Arsenal and Tactics of Terrorists and Rogues

The information warfare arsenal and tactics of terrorist and rogues have become increasingly transnational as the networked organizational form has expanded. When terrorism's mentors were the Soviet Union and the Eastern Bloc, they imposed their own rigid hierarchical structure on terrorist groups. Now that terrorism is increasingly substrate, or semidetached, networking and interconnectivity are necessary to find allies and influence others, as well as to effect command and control.

As discussed in Chapter 13, information and communication technologies (ICTs) have facilitated this, and have also enabled multiple leaders to operate parallel to one another in different countries. It, therefore, might be said that a shift is taking place from absolute hierarchies to hydra-headed networks, which are less easy to decapitate. An analogy, using the Palestinian example, may be that the more networked form of Hamas is replacing the hierarchical structure of the PLO. In many ways the Afghan War was a seminal event in promoting the networked form in that it showed that fluidly organized groups, driven in this case by a religious imperative, could defeat an experienced hierarchically structured army.

Geographical dispersion, both physical and in cyberspace, provides extra security. A rigid hierarchical structure is more easily penetrated and neutralized. Israel's admission that it had not yet found a way to deal with Hamas's decentralized and internationalized command and control structure, which uses encrypted Internet messages, suggests it has had difficulty in this matter. An investigation by the Federal Bureau of Investigation into terrorist activity in the United States indicated that part of Palestinian Islamic Jihad's command and control system was located in Tampa, Florida. Likewise, Hamas allegedly has some of its fundraising infrastructure in London and the USA, and publishes its main Arabic journal, *Filistin al Muslima*, in London.

Islamist terrorists may be said to fit the network ideal. Many supportive expatriate communities are based in sympathetic or neutral states enabling political activists and terrorists to operate within the safe haven that modern democracies provide.

It is not the intention here that the term "Islamists" should refer only to terrorist organizations, but rather to those Muslim militants who believe that Islam is incomplete without its own state, one in which Shariah provides the system of governance, and who campaign for its imposition.

Among Islamists, it is the Jihadists (religious warriors) who are of particular interest in this chapter. The followers of Hasan al Banna, Sayyid Qutb, and Abdul Ala Maududi, the organizations they founded, Ikhwan al Muslimoon and Jamaat Islami, and the ideological off-shoots these have spawned, give rise to the "Jihadist" ideology. And, although the concept of Jihad may be interpreted on different levels, it often incorporates violence when applied to Islamists.

The ultimate experience is, of course, Jihad, which for Islamists means armed battles against communists (Afghanistan) or Zionists (Palestine) or, for the radicals, against renegades and the impious.

Jihad in the modern Islamist sense knows no political space or state; its space is that of the Umma, the community of Muslims, wherever they may be. An example of the networked form amongst such Islamist organizations is that of the Algerian Armed Islamic Group, the GIA. Allegedly responsible for a bombing campaign in France, it appears to have had a command and control center in Britain for some years prior to the expulsion of some members by the British authorities. At the same time, sympathizers were also safe-housing some of its weapons and explosives in Belgium.

Algerian terrorists have been able to communicate with their sympathizers and members by use of the Internet and have used the services of Muslim news agencies, which republish their postings. Foremost amongst them is MSANEWS. On their site were published communiqués from the GIA, Front Islamique de Salut (FIS), and many other Islamists.

The MSANEWS also posts articles and communiqués from non-Islamist Muslim and non-Muslim sources, claiming that it has condemned terrorism, and that it no longer reposts communiqués of organizations that advocate terrorism.

The site of the Campaign for the Defense of Legitimate Rights (CDLR), the Saudi opposition group, also contains postings from groups not directly connected with it, as do London-net@Muslimsonline and the pro-Iranian Muslimedia International, which, like other sites, reposts interviews with Osama bin Laden, the exiled and wanted *dead or alive* Saudi terrorist leader (see sidebar, "Bin Laden Uses Web to Plan"). As with some other Islamists groups, Muslimedia International also promotes antisemitism and Holocaust denial and provides links with the American Holocaust denier, Michael Hoffman II, and his Campaign for Radical Truth in History, thereby highlighting the interconnectivity possibilities between totally different ideologies sharing a perceived common enemy.

BIN LADEN USES WEB TO PLAN

Osama bin Laden and other Muslim extremists are using the Internet to plan more terrorist activities against the United States and its allies. Recently, U.S. law enforcement officials and other experts disclosed details of how extremists hide maps and photographs of terrorist targets in sports chat rooms, on pornographic bulletin boards and other popular Web sites. Instructions for terrorist activities also are posted on the sites, which the officials declined to name. To a greater and greater degree, terrorist groups, including Hezbollah, Hamas, and bin Laden's al Qaeda group, are using computerized files, e-mail, and encryption to support their operations. According to various unnamed officials and investigators, the messages are scrambled using free encryption programs set up by groups that advocate privacy on the Internet. It's something the intelligence, law-enforcement, and military communities are really struggling to deal with. The operational details and future targets, in many cases, are hidden in plain view on the Internet. Only the members of the terrorist organizations, knowing the hidden signals, are able to extract the information.

An Islamist site that particularly aims its message to the outside world is that of Hizb-ut-Tahrir, the Islamic Liberation Party. Imperial College, London hosted their first UK-based site, but following complaints to the college authorities, the site was closed down. They now post in their own name as Hizb-ut-Tahrir, and as Khilafah, providing Internet-based access to their hard copy material, literature, and their regional activities. Al-Muhajiroun (the Emigrants) whose UK leader, Omar Bakri Mohammed, was the founding leader of Hizb-ut-Tahrir in Britain, and from which he split claiming differences with the Middle-East-based leadership, also provides details of its activities, as well as lists of its hardcopy publications and contacts. In 1998, Mohammed reported the communiqués of Osama bin Laden, for whom he claims to act as a spokesman. As a consequence of his endorsement of the bombings of the U.S. embassies in Dar-es-Salaam and Nairobi, his postings are no longer carried by MSANEWS.

Hamas and its supporters and sympathizers have been among the most prolific users of the Internet. MSANEWS provides a list of Internet resources about Hamas including copies of its covenant, its official communiqués (at Assabeel On-line), and communiqués of its military wing, the Izz al-Din Al-Kassam Brigades. Information about Hamas, in fact, may also be accessed in various different ways: via MSANEWS, the Palestine site, and the Islamic Association for Palestine. Hamas' own site, which posts in Arabic, is the Palestine Information Centre.

Religious luminaries from one country sometimes act as the higher legal and moral authority in another country. Sheikh Yusuf al-Qaradawri of the Egyptian Ikhwan al-Muslimoon (Muslim Brotherhood) lives in Qatar and serves as the Imam (religious leader) for the Palestinian Hamas. Sheikh Ibn Qatada, a Jordanian Palestinian living in London, serves as the Imam for the Algerian GIA. Sheikh Abu Hamza, an Egyptian national and former Afghan Jihad volunteer, serves as a propagandist for the Algerian GIA and Imam for the Yemeni Jihad group, but lives in London. Now, their messages of guidance and support find an outlet most frequently via ICTs.

Although some commentators have argued that modern cultural forces, such as ICTs, serve to undermine Islamisation in Muslim society, it is equally easy to argue that they provide a new and growing medium by which Islamism is disseminated. Even if they do not reach the poorer sections of Muslim society, they certainly reach many educated expatriate communities, among whom they find support. The growing number of advertisements, on the Internet and in Muslim papers and journals, for conferences to discuss the use of the Internet to promote Islam, or Islamism, supports the thesis that many activists and religious teachers see these developments as positive ones to be recommended and encouraged.

Combining religious injunctions with strategic commands is a noticeable feature of such Islamist leaders and their groups. Calls to carry out Jihad are frequently cloaked in religious and pseudo-religious language, but the implication is clear for the target audience. Thus, for example, Osama bin Laden's *Ladenese Epistle*, which was originally faxed to his London contact, Khalid al Fawaz, and then posted to MSANEWS in August 1996 by the London-based Saudi dissident groups CDLR and MIRA, is recognized as providing general guidance for anti-American terrorism.

For example, bin Laden's *Ladenese Epistle* reads:

The sons of the land of the two Holy Places had come out to fight against the Russian in Afghanistan, the Serb in Bosnia-Herzegovina, and today they are fighting in Chechenia and—by the Permission of Allah—they have been made victorious over your partner, the Russians. By the command of Allah, they are also fighting in Tajakistan.

I say: Since the sons of the land of the two Holy Places feel and strongly believe that fighting (Jihad) against the Kuffar in every part of the world, is absolutely essential; then they would be even more enthusiastic, more powerful and larger in number upon fighting on their own land.

The Nida'ul Islam site, based in Australia, promotes an uncompromising message of both Jihad and of suicide terrorism. A recent posting, *The Islamic Legitimacy of the Martyrdom Operations*, states that martyrdom is forbidden in Islam, but cites approvingly those martyrs who willingly gave their lives for Muslim causes and then transposes these causes to contemporary issues. It attempts to demonstrate with quotes from the Quran and the Sunnah that Islamic bombing assaults and martyrdom attacks are legitimate and fall within the framework of Islam.

Azzam Publications, named after Abdullah Azzam, a Palestinian who became a military leader in Afghanistan and who was assassinated in Pakistan in 1989, has also published calls for Jihad volunteers:

"The Saudi Government does not intend to help the Muslims in Kosova and it has prevented its nationals from going there to fight. This means that the Jihad in Kosova is now a greater responsibility on Muslims with western nationalities ... Redistribute this e-mail message all over the world ... telephone the nearest Saudi Embassy or Consulate to protest against this crack-down and tell everyone to do so until it jams the lines of the Saudi Consulates around the world ... e-mail the Saudi Embassy in Washington with messages of protest ... begin to prepare yourselves to go and fight in Kosova to make up for the lack of manpower that was heading there from Saudi Arabia. Wait for the Kosova bulletin from Azzam Publications."

Among the Far Right, the UK-based national revolutionary group, The International Third Position, illustrates graphically the adoption of ICTs to enhance a position. The group is tiny, but its foreign contacts are numerous, widespread and growing. In the space of just over one year its *Final Conflict* e-mail newsletter has grown in size and scope to reflect the news of, and messages from, its worldwide contacts.

Final Conflict also acts as a news agency for Holocaust deniers (in much the same way as MSANEWS does for Islamists), many of whom are also Far Right extremists. For example, the e-mail newsletter reposts communiqués from David Irving and Fredrick Toben's Australian Adelaide Institute, which like the California-based Institute for Historical Review, attempts to provide a scholarly veneer for denial. Some invitees to a conference held by the Adelaide Institute were refused permission to visit Australia by its Department of Immigration, but the easy access to the Internet and video links facilitated conference presentations that otherwise might not have taken place.

The Far Right has also used the Internet to post bomb-making manuals that are not otherwise available in Europe. The British neo-Nazi, David Myatt, of the National Socialist Movement posted his *Practical Guide to Aryan Revolution* at the end of November 1997 at the Web site of Canadian Bernard Klatt in order to evade police scrutiny. The chapter headings included: *Methods of Covert Direct Action, Escape and Evasion, Assassination, Terror Bombing, Sabotage, Racial War, How to Create a Revolutionary Situation, Direct Action Groups,* and so on. The contents provided a detailed step-by-step guide for terrorist insurrection with advice on assassination targets, rationale for bombing and sabotage campaigns, and rules of engagement. Although he may have committed no indictable offense in Canada, Klatt was forced to close down his site in April 1998. Myatt is currently the subject of a British criminal investigation for incitement to murder and promotion of race hatred.

Police forces in Britain and France also recently investigated an international neo-Nazi network that issued death threats against French celebrities and politicians from their British-based Internet site. Herve Guttuso, the French leader of the Charlemagne Hammer Skins, was arrested in Essex at the same time as eight members were arrested in the South of France. The French members of the network were charged with making death threats, and Guttuso was the subject of a French extradition request to the British courts. According to the French Interior Ministry, police in Toulon traced the London address of the Internet site, which was being accessed about 7,000 times a month. The investigation enabled the police to identify 3,500 people sympathetic to the neo-Nazi group in various countries including Britain, Greece, Canada, America, and Poland. The investigators found that the Charlemagne group appeared to be one of the largest and best organized neo-Nazi groups yet uncovered, with a coordinated international structure and logistical centers for disseminating violent racist propaganda, based principally in Britain and America. Although the group gave a postal address in London as their center, their material was disseminated via Klatt's FTC Net (as have been the postings of Marc Lemire, Paul Fromm, Doug Christie, The Heritage Front, and other neo-Nazi and white supremacist groups).

The British Far Right may have been slower to realize the command and control possibilities of ICTs than their U.S. or German co-ideologies, but they appear to be catching up. Although in recent years it is the violent skinhead music scene that has provided the main medium through which they promote liaison, it is clear that for some the future lies with ICTs.

In 1999, the Pentagon had to admit that there had been a major assault on its computer systems. Zionist Occupational Government (ZOG) observers have increasingly warned that the frequency and sophistication of the hack attacks will only increase as dissident groups realize that they can strike at the very heart of ZOG at the touch of a few buttons. It doesn't matter what government specialists invent to counter the techno-terrorist, there is always a way around their antihacker programs and the more ZOG relies on computers, the more damage can be done by attacking their systems. So all you techno-terrorists out there, get working on your "hack-attacks."

THE TERRORIST PROFILE

Sid-Ra, a 6-foot-4-inch, 350-pound giant of a man, paces between his "subjects" in the smoke-filled Goth club *Click + Drag*, located in the old meat-packing district of Manhattan. Inside the club are leather-clad, black-lipped females and young men dressed in women's underwear.

Sid is a hacker-terrorist and an acknowledged "social engineer" with curious nocturnal habits. There are thousands of people like him, who by day are system and network administrators, security analysts, and start-up cofounders. When night comes, they transform into something quite different.

But, is this the profile of a "wanna-be terrorist"? Perhaps!

These are the self-proclaimed freedom fighters of cyberspace. They've even got a name for it: hactivism. And political parties and human rights groups are circling around to recruit hactivists into their many causes.

Recently, for example, the Libertarian Party set up a table at the HOPE (Hackers on Planet Earth) conference. The San Francisco-based Electronic Frontier Foundation (EFF) collected donations. And members of civil-rights groups, including the Zapatistas, a Mexican rebel group, spoke up at one of two sessions on hactivism.

But even without such civil-liberties groups trying to organize them, hactivists have been busy on their own. They have formed privacy-related software companies such as ZeroKnowledge Systems USA Inc. in Montreal. They're developing anonymous, inexpensive e-mail and Web-hosting services through the DataHaven Project Inc. (http://www.dhp.com). And they're trying to get the Internet out to Third World human rights organizations through groups such as Cult of the Dead Cow Communications (cDc; http://www.cultdeadcow.com/hacktivismo.html).

URLs are subject to change without notice.

CAUTION

In fact, Sid feels hactivism's pull so strongly that he makes a dramatic claim: *"The Internet is the next Kent State, and we're the ones who are probably going to get shot."*

FROM VIETNAM MARCHES TO CYBERDISOBEDIENCE

Like any social engineer, Sid exaggerates. Except for the four-year jail terms handed down to Kevin Mitnick and Kevin Poulsen, sentencing for even criminal hacking in the past two years has been relatively light (mostly probation and fines) because of the suspects' young ages.

But the comparison to the psychedelic hippies of the 1960s who spoke out against the Vietnam War may not be so far off the mark. Only this time, the hackers are Goths and hedonists. And they're using the Internet to rid the world of tyranny.

The government tries to put electronic activism into the peg of cyberterrorism and crime with its Infowar eulogies. But E-Hippies, cDc, and others aren't criminals. The Internet just multiplies their voice.

Another group reaching out to hackers and technologists is the EFF. In 1999, the EFF successfully argued in the infamous Bernstein ruling, which stated that software code is protected as a form of speech.

Hackers question conventional models. They don't just look at technology and say, "This is how it works." They say, "How can I make it better?" They look at society that way too—their government, their schools, or their social situation. They say, "I know how to make this better," and they go for it.

In the MPAA case, staffers at 2600 Enterprises Inc., based in Middle Island, New York, were threatened with imprisonment if they didn't remove a link on the 2600 Web site to the code used to crack DVD encryption. Because the link was editorial content, it sets Sid off on another diatribe.

The Libertarian Party also recruits hackers and technologists. At HOPE, the party's New York State committee (http://www.cownow.com) handed out fliers, signed up recruits, and took a "sticker" poll of party affiliations. The poll got hacked, but about half the stickers were yellow—for libertarian, anarchist or independent.

Many party members are programmers. They're trying to rally hackers around encryption, privacy and freedom-of-communication planks. Hackers can offer them freedom, because the Internet routes around tyranny.

But hackers have ways beyond the Internet to electronically spread their message. Take a young dude named Alpha Underflow, for instance, who late one night broke the lock to a lit-up roadside-construction sign and reprogrammed it to read, "Hack Planet Earth" in support of the 2600 Magazine staff. But then again, he also likes to use his reprogrammed garage-door opener to pop open his neighbor's garage doors.

GROW UP

This moral confusion is typical of the younger hacking crowd. But most of the older hackers (30 years old and up) have grown up.

In the mid-1990s, there was more disillusionment as more bleeding-edge hackers ended up going to jail for cracking. That bummed out their whole theme. But now they've learned some limits, and they can still operate within them.

That means the older hackers do develop some scruples. For example, the EFF Web site (http://www.eff.org) was a popular target of punk hackers back in the mid-1990s, with hacks and defacements occurring weekly. Now, it's rarely being hacked. When the site did get hacked, a message was posted about it on 2600's bulletin board, and the hackers who responded called that hacker a lamer.

The process that turned the hippie of 1968 into the employed investor of 1985 is similarly going on here today. Hopefully, that the hippie-to-yuppie disillusionment that took place historically doesn't happen to hackers, too.

So, who are the real cyberterrorists? Are they for real?

Will The Real Cyberterrorists Stand-up

The debate over whether the United States faces imminent danger from cyberterrorist attacks took a new turn recently when the National Security Council declared that the term "terrorism" may be too strong a word when describing potential cyberthreats.

Although it would be a tough call to tell the difference between an attack by hackers and one launched by terrorists intent on disrupting national security, the administration's cyberdefense programs are battling a perception problem that stems from the misuse of the word "terrorism."

Maybe you shouldn't be saying "cyberterrorism." Maybe you should be saying "information warfare." In the end, you're going to know it when you see it—the difference between joy-riding hackers and state-sponsored cyberattacks.

Experts agree that, to date, most of the major cybersecurity incidents are best described as nuisance attacks, although many fear that a devastating surprise attack, sometimes referred to as an "electronic Pearl Harbor," is inevitable. Although the government tries to be proactive, the United States is going to get nailed seriously—sooner rather than later.

By not preparing for the worst-case scenario, the United States may be endangering the public's civil liberties. A lot of people are going to be willing to throw civil liberties out the window in an effort to recover from an attack that cripples large portions of the nation's critical infrastructure.

Preparation is crucial, and, in the current legal system, defensive measures are more "workable" than offensive ones. Overall, however, cyberdefense is not well understood and is not talked about sufficiently.

Pretending the threats are not there is not a solution. There are numerous efforts by rogue groups to acquire encryption algorithms and sophisticated tools. One presidential administration after another has lulled the American people into a false sense of security. Anyway, the Internet has become a new form of the "dead drop" (a Cold War-era term for where spies left information) for terrorists. And, bin Laden, the dissident and wanted Saudi businessman who has been indicted for the 1998 bombing of two U.S. embassies in East Africa; the 9-11 attacks in 2001; and, has been named as a possible suspect behind the bombing of the USS Cole destroyer in Yemen, has taken advantage of that Internet "dead drop" zone.

Four alleged bin Laden associates went on trial recently in federal court in New York for the embassy bombings. Officials say bin Laden began using encryption in 1996, but recently increased its use after U.S. officials revealed they were tapping his satellite[i] phone calls in Afghanistan and tracking his activities.

Thus, bin Laden meets the requirements for the new terrorist profile: He will use whatever tools he can (e-mails, the Internet, etc.) to facilitate jihad against the Israeli occupiers and their supporters, according to Ahmed Yassin, the founder of the militant Muslim group Hamas. Bin Laden (dead or alive) has the best minds working for him.

WHY TERRORIST AND ROGUES HAVE AN ADVANTAGE IN IW

Leaders from industry, government, and law enforcement recently hunkered down for a day of closed-door meetings in Menlo Park, California, to brainstorm about the difficult task of protecting the world's computer networks against cybercriminals. One theme to emerge early on at the event, billed as the Internet Defense Summit, was that governments have neither the financial resources nor the technical know-how to stay on top of hackers and computer terrorists. Therefore, this is why terrorist and rogues have an advantage in IW.

The private sector must (provide for) itself much of the action that is necessary to prevent attacks being made on the Internet. It's no longer possible for governments to provide the kind of resources and investment necessary to deal with these kinds of issues.

The summit, which recently took place at the Stanford Research Institute's (SRI) leafy campus, attracted more than 200 chief information officers and other top executives from companies and organizations including IBM, Microsoft, Visa International, the U.S. Postal Service, and the Los Angeles County Sheriff's Office. Meetings were held behind closed doors to encourage candid discussion about security problems and the ways participants have learned to cope with them. The event took place in the shadow of the "I Love You" virus, which emerged in 2000 and wreaked havoc in public and private computer networks the world over.

There are no cookie-cutter solutions; every network is different. At the top of CIOs' concerns here was denial of service (DoS) attacks, which recently brought Yahoo, Amazon.com, eBay, and other high-profile Web sites to their knees. DoS attacks are a key concern because the only way that is currently available to prevent them is to catch the perpetrators.

Second on the list of concerns was attacks that reach into networks to steal valuable corporate data. Firewalls are the best way to prevent data theft that originates outside of a network, whereas cryptography can help to protect data from internal theft.

Although the business leaders seemed focused on computer hackers, there is a "real danger" of terrorists and hostile rogue nations using computer networks to wage international warfare. In other words, most of the major terrorist organizations have their own Web sites, and, therefore, have the facility to carry out the same sort of action that was carried out with the release of the "I Love You" virus.

Cyberterrorism can be more effective and more costly to governments than the classic methods of bomb attacks and assassination. It is really a serious threat to everyone in all societies.

Solutions seemed harder to come by today than the problems just discussed. Governments, businesses, and research institutions must band together to find the best technologies and courses of action to defeat cybercrimes. And companies must be more willing to invest in security systems to protect their networks.

A few participants called on software companies and service providers to make their products more secure. Default settings for software products sold to consumers should be at the highest level of security.

You wouldn't build a swimming pool in the center of town and not put a fence around it. Basically, that's just what the software companies are doing.

Although security firms have financial incentives for promoting security issues, for the average corporation, the benefits of spending millions of dollars to bolster security in networks aren't immediately obvious, thus making them slow to act. If you have a choice of spending two million dollars on getting 360,000 new customers, or two million dollars on serving the ones you already have, that's a difficult value proposition. Most companies would take the additional customers.

But the severity of attacks could get worse, and businesses would be wise to make precautionary investments now. Most businesses have been lucky so far.

Cyberattack Risks if You're a Superpower

Information warfare and other security threats simply come with the territory when your country is the world's only remaining superpower. This is what is called a "superpower paradox." There is no other country that can challenge the United States directly. Instead, some countries look for indirect ways to challenge the United States. This challenge could come in the form of nuclear (see sidebar, "Stopping Nuclear Blackmail"), chemical or biological (see sidebar, "Chemical And Biological Terrorism"), or even cyberwarfare (see sidebar, "Hacker-Controlled Tanks, Planes, and Warships").

STOPPING NUCLEAR BLACKMAIL

Bill Clinton used to say that no Russian missiles are targeted at the United States. But there is every reason to believe that there are, or soon will be, North Korean missiles targeted at this country—missiles capable of delivering nuclear or chemical and biological warheads. In a few years, and without much warning, Iranian and Iraqi missiles could also be targeted at us and our allies. What can the U.S. do to stop such missiles once they are launched? Not a thing.

None of this was clear in 1998; it is undeniable now. The question is whether the U.S. government will build a missile defense system to protect their cities, military bases, and oil fields—and to block the kind of nuclear blackmail suggested by China's threat, during the Taiwan Strait crisis of 1996, to bomb Los Angeles.

A full warning came from a report in 1998 of the commission on missile threats headed by former Defense Secretary Donald Rumsfeld. This was a bipartisan commission, with members who have often disagreed on weapons issues. The panel had access to all U.S. intelligence sources, and its conclusion was unanimous: Rogue states could "inflict major destruction on the United States." within five years of deciding to do so, and with little or no notice to us.

This contradicted the Clinton administration line that the United States. would have plenty of notice of a missile attack. That conclusion was based on a 1995 national intelligence estimate that said there would be no threat to the 48 contiguous states for the next 15 years.

Evidently, the administration didn't think that the constitutional obligation to "provide for the common defense" applied to Alaska and Hawaii.

NOTE

The Rumsfeld report at first seemed to do little to change the views of President Clinton's top defense advisers. Five weeks after the report was released, Gen. Henry Shelton, the chairman of the Joint Chiefs of Staff, wrote that "the intelligence community can provide the necessary warning" of hostile missile development and added, "We view this as an unlikely development." A week after that, North Korea launched a 3,000-kilometer range, two-stage Taepo Dong 1 missile over Japan. The launch indicates that North Korea has made progress in building the Taepo Dong 2, whose 10,000-kilometer range includes not only Alaska and Hawaii but also much of the continental United States. No matter: All but four Senate Democrats blocked action on a bill sponsored by Thad Cochran, a Republican from Mississippi, and Daniel Inouye, a Democrat from Hawaii, that would have forced the administration to deploy a missile defense system as soon as technologically feasible.

A New World

The case against rapid deployment rests on three arguments: (1) the threat isn't real, (2) the technology is impossible, and (3) it is more important to maintain the antiballistic missile treaty signed with the Soviet Union in 1972, which bars most missile defense systems. The Rumsfeld report demolished Argument 1. Argument 2 is still raised by some who note that the United States has spent large sums on missile defense since Ronald Reagan proposed it in 1983, with disappointing results. But stopping a few rogue-state missiles with the computers of 2002 is much easier than stopping hundreds of Soviet missiles with the computers of 1983. As for Argument 3, the strategic environment in which the ABM treaty was adopted no longer exists. The argument for the treaty was that a missile defense system might provoke a Soviet or American first strike. However, the proximate missile threats now come from states that might risk such a strike.

CHEMICAL AND BIOLOGICAL TERRORISM

In "For Your Eyes Only," James Bond's irrepressible quartermaster, Major Boothroyd (a.k.a. Q) demonstrates his latest toy: a rather lethal umbrella. Using a faceless mannequin, one of Q's assistants illustrates how the umbrella looks and acts like it should until struck by water (as umbrellas are wont to do from time to time). Suddenly, sharp metal hooks extend all along the edge of the umbrella as it swiftly closes upon the victim's neck. The motion is quick and precise, but one can't help but imagine the far messier spectacle if a human being were caught under it in a rainstorm.

Unfortunately, the fictional version of MI6 portrayed in the James Bond films is not the only place one can find a deadly device masquerading as protection against the elements. In September 1978, the Bulgarian secret service shot a Bulgarian exile, Georgi Markov, with just such a device. Disguised as an umbrella, the surreptitious gun inserted a small pellet into Markov's thigh. The pellet contained only a few hundred millionths of a gram of the deadly poison ricin (supplied by the KGB), but it was enough. Markov died four days later in a London hospital. Another Bulgarian defector, Vladimir Kostov, was similarly attacked in Paris the month before. Kostov was shot in the back and suffered a high fever, but survived. He sought medical treatment after hearing of Markov's death and doctors removed from his back a small pellet identical to the one used to kill Markov.

Not satisfied with leaving such methods solely in the hands of the secret agent-types, the *Aum Shinrikyo* cult tried a simpler version during their chemical and biological escapades. In their infamous sarin gas attack on the Tokyo subway, *Aum* operatives chose the decidedly low-tech dissemination method of dropping bags of liquid sarin on the floor, puncturing them with the sharpened ends of their umbrellas, and then beating a hasty retreat as the nasty stuff spilled out onto the ground. Despite their primitive dissemination methods, *Aum* managed to murder 12 people, injure over a thousand, terrorize several thousand more, and spark a national weapons of mass destruction (WMD) counterterrorism industry in the United States.

Analysts have long commented on the copycat nature of terrorists and terrorist groups. Once a new method of attack (from car bombings to airplane hijackings to planes being used as bombs to hostage-taking for ransom money) has met with success, other terrorist groups are bound to emulate it. Given such a phenomenon among terrorists, is the United States witnessing any evidence of an increase in the use of umbrellas in terrorist operations—especially those involving chemical and biological weapons? Should the United States be calling for an international embargo on umbrella sales to Afghanistan to prevent Osama bin Laden and his al-Qaida organization from acquiring such dangerous, dual-use technology? Probably yes. For one thing, *Aum* has now inspired many follow-up attacks than many analysts had predicted shortly after their March 1995 attack. Although the jury is still out, *Aum* may have been unique. Even the Minnesota Patriots Council, which developed ricin because they believed it to be used by the CIA and the KGB, never conceived of using it in the same manner as the Bulgarian secret service. Rather than use an umbrella, the MPC experimented with using hand lotion as a means of dissemination.

For another, an umbrella (even one involving a chemical or biological weapon) simply does not offer the same level of destruction, the same "bang for the buck" as other terrorist methods. Not even the Weather Underground, whose name would seem to imply an interest in such methods, showed any evidence of ever considering using umbrellas in any of their attacks. Instead, they chose the symbolic bombing of the imperialist power structure. So the answer is yes, the standard terrorist arsenal is now the gun, the bomb, the plane bomb, box cutters and even the umbrella or anything else they can get their hands on. As all of us witnessed on 9-11, Osama bin Laden did try such a method of attack, and it brought a whole new meaning to his "umbrella terrorist network."

HACKER-CONTROLLED TANKS, PLANES, AND WARSHIPS

Army officials are worried that sophisticated hackers and other cybercriminals, including military adversaries, may soon have the ability to hack their way into and take control of major military weapon systems such as tanks and ships. The potential exists for hackers to infiltrate the computer systems used in tanks and other armored vehicles. Unlike in the past, today's modern tanks and ships are almost entirely dependent on computers, software, and data communications links for functions such as navigation, targeting, and command and control.

Although the Pentagon has always had computer security issues to deal with, they've never had computers in tanks and armored personnel carriers before. In fact, the Defense Department has already tested and proven that hackers have the ability to infiltrate the command and control systems of major weapons, including Navy warships. According to a training CD-ROM on information assurance, published by the Defense Information Systems Agency, an Air Force officer sitting in a hotel room in Boston used a laptop computer to hack into a Navy ship at sea and implant false navigation data into the ship's steering system.

Yes, this actually happened. The CD-ROM instructs military personnel taking the course. Fortunately, this was only a controlled test to see what could be done. In reality, only people's imagination and ability limit the type of crime and its objective.

Although there are well-known security gaps in the commercial systems that the Army plans to use on the battlefield, hacking into tanks and other weapons may prove to be too difficult for an enemy engaged in battle. The problem for the enemy is that computer security vulnerabilities will almost certainly prove fleeting and unpredictable. Such tactics would be nearly impossible to employ beyond the random harassment level.

It is imperative for the United States to study what it means to be a superpower in the Information Age. In addition to the two dozen countries known to be pursuing technologies that would enable them to produce weapons of mass destruction, threats to the nation's critical infrastructure from cyberattacks are also high on the present administration's list of things to prepare for.

Other countries are forming cells of professionals dedicated to finding ways to interrupt the U.S.'s information infrastructure. If you can shut down the U.S.'s financial system; if you could shut down the transportation system; if you could cause the collapse of energy production and distribution system just by typing on a computer and causing those links to this globalization to break down, then you're able to wage successful warfare, and the United States has to be able to defend against that. The United States is presently taking on those defense measures.

U.S. Government Agencies Shape Cyberwarning Strategy against Terrorists and Rogues

Under pressure from Congress to better coordinate the government's response to computer viruses and other cyberattacks by terrorists and rogue states, the National Security Council (NSC) has developed a plan outlining roles and responsibilities for federal cybersecurity organizations. Under the plan, the National Infrastructure Protection Center (NIPC), working with the General Services Administration's Federal Computer Incident Response Capability Office, will take the lead in alerting agencies to cyberattacks and will coordinate any immediate response.

The memo identifies the organizations and agencies to be involved in various kinds of attacks and defines the criteria for NIPC to call a meeting of the full cybersecurity community. The NSC will step in whenever a security response requires a broad policy decision, according to the plan.

This institutionalizes how the United States will share information both at an operations level and a policy level when cyberincidents occur. Many observers have called for coordination among organizations such as NIPC, the Critical Infrastructure Assurance Office (CIAO), and NSC itself.

NIPC, based at the FBI, was established in 1998 to serve as the government's central organization to assess cyberthreats, issue warnings, and coordinate responses. The CIAO was set up to help agencies develop and coordinate security policies and plans.

The proliferation of organizations with overlapping oversight and assistance responsibilities is a source of potential confusion among agency personnel and may be an inefficient use of scarce technical resources. The calls for coordination became louder after the "I Love You" virus affected almost every federal e-mail server and taxed many agencies' resources. The lack of formal coordination and communication led to many more agencies being affected by the incident than necessary, according to GAO.

Although the many warning and response organizations work together, the NSC memo lays out a standard process for coordination. In the past, that type of coordination happened on an ad hoc basis. Now, as laid out in the memo, the process is set so that it can last into the next administration in 2005.

Some of the formal mechanisms that existed were frankly ineffective in the tasks they were meant to do. For circumstances that are extraordinary, the U.S. now has a process where the NIPC will coordinate the operational response, and the National Security Council will head the policy response.

THE DARK WORLD OF THE CYBER UNDERGROUND

It was nearly Christmas (1998) when Dionne Smith received an alarming letter that dampened her holiday spirit—to say the least. The anonymous note warned Smith, 31, an employee of a Los Angeles parking company, that by opening the envelope she had just exposed herself to the biotoxin anthrax, livestock bacteria that can be fatal if inhaled. The 1998 Christmas incident was a horrible and frightening experience—which was one of approximately 220 nuclear, biological (see sidebar, "Bioterrorists On The Green"), and chemical scares (including some 140 anthrax false alarms) in this country alone.

BIOTERRORISTS ON THE GREEN

Will the next terrorist attack be against plants, not people? At the urging of the White House, the U.S. Department of Agriculture and the FBI are looking at the threat of agricultural bioterrorism—an assault on the country's efficient but fragile system of giant single-crop farms.

The fear is that if some party wanted to, they could damage a major crop—and the economy—by introducing a plant pathogen that doesn't normally exist here. Likely bioweapons include plant-killing fungi, such as soybean rust, or infectious microbes that induce plants to produce toxins. If the group were sophisticated enough, they could genetically engineer a highly pathogenic strain, produce it in large quantities, and sneak a lot of it in.

In wild plants, natural genetic diversity helps limit the spread of disease. Ninety-nine percent or more of the genes in crops are the same across the United States, and that uniformity makes an epidemic much more likely. Once unleashed here, a superbug could spread like wildfire before researchers identified it and figured out how to keep it in check. Even then, spores could survive and infect the next year's crop. They could also be spread by the wind, from field to field, or even state to state. It would be a continuing, recurring problem, like a permanent bomb going off.

Even though so far they've all been fakes, the feds are on edge. Their major worry is that terrorists are adding chemical and biological weapons to their arsenal of arms, and that, one day, they'll make good on their threats—thus, enter the dark world of the cyber underground. So, the government has begun taking precautions, and pours billions of dollars into creating a network of programs designed to respond to such attacks. The ambitious plans include amassing antidotes to potential bioagents such as anthrax and other bacteria and viruses, and to chemical weapons such as the nerve agent sarin. The government is training medical response, fire, police, and rescue teams; beefing up local health departments to handle civilians in case of a major attack; and gathering intelligence on terrorist groups believed to be interested in acquiring such weapons. These new programs have helped make counterterrorism one of the fastest-growing parts of the federal budget, even as terrorist acts plunged to a 30-year low prior to the 9-11 attacks, say congressional budget analysts. Total U.S. antiterrorism spending could exceed $60 billion in 2002, up from $10 billion in 2000. The question is whether it's money well spent.

A recent report by the General Accounting Office, Congress's watchdog, says no, claiming that lawmakers have dumped money into fighting a threat yet to be fully assessed. and probably less dangerous than widely believed, considering how tough it is to acquire, process, and use the deadly toxins. A growing number of government and private counterterrorism experts agree. They say that federal officials are so spooked by the possibility of a chemical or biological attack that they are deliberately hyping the threat to get Congress to cough up coveted cash for prevention programs. And most lawmakers are buying it wholesale. It's Mom, apple pie, and terrorism. In 1997, a jittery Congress ordered the Department of Defense to conduct multiagency training exercises in the nation's 120 largest cities against so-called weapons of mass destruction. Today, there are some 400 training courses run by myriad agencies, including the Energy and Justice Departments, the Environmental Protection Agency, and the Federal Emergency Management Agency. In just how many different ways is the United States going to set out to accomplish the same thing, because many of the programs are redundant?

The most eye-popping example of out-of-control spending, detractors say, is the Department of Health and Human Services (HHS). In 1996, HHS spent $7 million on its "bioterrorism" initiative. In 2001, it requested $452 million. Most notably, the department intends to create a national stockpile of millions of doses of vaccines and antibiotics, a potential boon for pharmaceutical companies that are among those eagerly lobbying for more antiterrorism measures. GAO investigators have repeatedly questioned the department's emphasis on vaccines for smallpox, pneumonic plague (airborne bacteria that cause respiratory failure), and tularemia (bacteria that cause a disabling fever in humans). None of these potential killers appear on the CIA's list of biggest germ threats from terrorist groups. Still, HHS is doing the right thing by focusing on them. Tularemia and pneumonic plague are very easy to develop. The easiest to develop is anthrax.

Other agencies are clamoring for a piece of the pie, leading to tremendous internecine fighting. FEMA wants a chunk of the training and equipment money, as does the Justice Department's Office of Justice Programs, whose mission is to dole out federal anticrime money to states and localities. The Department of Veterans Affairs wants to wrest stockpiling duties away from the Centers for Disease Control and Prevention. And the National Guard, a powerful lobby on Capitol Hill, is creating its own hazardous materials response teams, even though there are already more than 800 state and local hazardous material (HAZMAT) units, plus additional crews in the Army, Marine Corps, EPA, and Coast Guard. Then there's the Energy Department, which is pushing for $50 million to research palm-size bug and poison detectors and other antiterrorism products. Not to be left out, the United States Holocaust Memorial Museum and the Office of Personnel Management want $3 million apiece, and the Smithsonian Institution is asking for $4 million to bolster security against potential terrorist attacks.

When Congress first began considering this issue in 1995, the debate was driven by the belief that terrorists, although more likely to use guns and bombs, would eventually turn to lethal chemical and biological agents. The 1995 Tokyo subway gas attack by the cult Aum Shinrikyo was a shot across the bow. So were reports that Osama bin Laden—accused of masterminding the bombings of two U.S. embassies in East Africa—has tried to get his hands on unconventional weapons.

The only major case of bioterrorism in the United States was in 1984 by followers of the Indian guru Bhagwan Shree Rajneesh, who had set up a commune in Oregon. Hoping to sway a local election, they unleashed salmonella poisoning in 10 restaurants in a nearby town, sickening 751 people but killing none. Still, law enforcement officials are convinced that the risk merits whatever preventive measures the government can afford. This is not on the top 100 list of things you're going to die from. But if you're a national security expert, this is on the top 3 list of things to worry about.

One reason there have been no attacks is that it's so tough to effectively use biological weapons. But a dozen hostile nations now either possess or are actively pursuing bioweapons. Most counterterrorism and intelligence experts agree other countries would think hard before striking, because they know the United States would retaliate with stunning force. They also agree that terrorists cannot carry out large-scale lethal attacks without the backing of a foreign government. However, they can do damage. The question is: how much? Nobody knows, because few have bothered to assess how real the threats are. No one, though, wants to be caught asleep at the switch—just in case. It's one of those things it's hard to say no to. It's like fallout shelters in the 1950s. Was that wrong to do? You have to look at the world you're operating in.

THE CRIMINAL CAFÉ IN CYBERSPACE

Not long ago, if a terrorist wanted to cause a blackout in, say, New York, it would have taken some work. He or she might have packed a truck with explosives and sent it careening into a power plant. Or he or she might have sought a job as a utility worker so he or she could sabotage the electrical system. But now, intelligence experts say, it's possible for a trained computer hacker to darken Gotham from the comfort of home or a cybercafé (at a coffee house). Worse, his other home might be as far away as Tehran, Iran. Worse yet, he or she may enjoy the full backing and technical support of a foreign government.

In a closed briefing to Congress, the CIA reported that at least a dozen countries, some hostile to America, are developing programs to attack other nations' information and computer systems. China, Libya, Russia, Iraq, and Iran are among those deemed a threat, sources later declared. Reflecting official thinking, no doubt, the People's Liberation Daily in China notes that a foe of the United States only has to mess up the computer systems of its banks by hi-tech means. This would disrupt and destroy the U.S. economy. Although the specifics are classified, a new National Intelligence Estimate reports at least one instance to date of active cybertargeting of the United States by a foreign nation.

Officials are worried because so much of America's infrastructure is either driven or connected by computers. Computers run financial networks, regulate the flow of oil and gas through pipelines, control water reservoirs and sewage treatment plants, power air traffic control systems, and sustain telecommunications networks, emergency services, and power grids. All are vulnerable. An adversary capable of implanting the right virus or accessing the right terminal can cause massive damage.

In 1996, a Swedish hacker wormed his way through cyberspace from London to Atlanta to Florida, where he rerouted and tied up telephone lines to 11 counties, put 911 emergency service systems out of commission, and impeded the emergency responses of police, fire, and ambulance services. There have been many domestic cyberattacks as well. The number of pending FBI cases involving computer crimes (a category that includes computer infrastructure attacks and financial crimes) increased from 128 in 1996 to about 880 in 2001.

In 1997, intelligence officials got a glimpse of what's possible during an information-warfare exercise named "Eligible Receiver." The secret war game began with a set of written scenarios in which energy and telecommunications utilities were disrupted by computer attacks. In one scenario, the attackers targeted the 911 emergency phone system by telling Internet users there was a problem with the system. The scenario posited that people, driven by curiosity, would phone 911 and overwhelm the system.

"Eligible Receiver" culminated when three two-person "red teams" from the National Security Agency actually used hacker techniques that can be learned on the Internet to penetrate Department of Defense computers. After gaining access to the military's electronic message systems, the teams were poised to intercept, delete, and modify all messages on the networks. Ultimately, the hackers achieved access to the DoD's classified network (see sidebar, "Espionage By Keystroke?") and, if they had wished, could have denied the Pentagon the ability to deploy forces. In another exercise, the DoD found that 74% of test attacks on its own systems went undetected.

ESPIONAGE BY KEYSTROKE?

Forget about signal sites and dead drops (like the recent FBI Russian mole case of suspected spy Robert Phillip Hanssen). The classic tropes of the spy game have gone the way of the Model T. When an FBI computer jock finally hacked his way into Aldrich Ames's personal computer a few years ago, investigators were dumbfounded by the number of secrets he'd purloined from the CIA—hundreds of stolen documents and classified reports. FBI brass called Ames the worst case of treason in U.S. history.

But the preceding could be peanuts compared to the Wen Ho Lee case. Government officials confirmed that scientist Wen Ho Lee suspected of stealing classified data from a secret weapons laboratory downloaded reams of classified nuclear weapons information from a high-security computer system to one that could be accessed with relative ease.

Actually, reams don't begin to describe the dimensions of it. The FBI is talking about millions of lines of computer code here, data bits gathered during the course of 50 years of research and more than 2,000 nuclear tests—information that shows how the nation's most sophisticated nuclear weapons work. With a few simple computer strokes, in other words, someone made America's national-security crown jewels available to any reasonably sophisticated person in possession of a computer, a modem, and the file names under which the information was stored. It is flabbergasting. There's just no other word for it.

The someone in question is Wen Ho Lee, a Taiwan-born scientist employed, until recently, at the Department of Energy's weapons laboratory in Los Alamos, New Mexico. Lee was dismissed from his job in 1999 for security breaches after it was disclosed that he was the subject of an FBI espionage investigation. Prosecutors have not charged Lee with spying, and he has asserted his innocence. But when FBI agents searched Lee's computer after his dismissal, officials say, they discovered that he had transferred an incredibly large amount of nuclear data from the Energy Department's high-security computers to the more accessible network, dumped the information under bogus file names, then tried to erase the evidence from his hard drive. The transfers occurred between 1983 and 1995, but accelerated in 1994 and 1995, when Los Alamos began installing a new system designed to impede such transfers. He was really racing right there at the end.

The evidence gathered to date does not show that the security breach resulted in damage on a massive scale. But it is huge nonetheless. The FBI is still investigating whether anyone accessed the data from the low-security network to which Lee transferred the information. Some officials say that may never be known for sure.

Like every espionage investigation, the Lee case is rife with peculiarities. Lee first came under suspicion in 1996, after the CIA obtained a document showing that China's military had obtained classified information about the size and shape of America's newest miniaturized nuclear warhead, the W-88. The FBI was slow to investigate Lee, in part because Lee's wife was working as a confidential informant for the bureau. But there were other problems. When agents in the FBI's Albuquerque field office pressed for a search warrant in Washington, lawyers at the Justice Department rebuffed the request. The Foreign Intelligence Surveillance Court has almost never rejected a search warrant request, and bureau officials indicate the rejection here was unwarranted. In any case, by that time the damage was done.

In 1998, the FBI raided the homes of two California high school sophomores. Their hacker assaults on the Pentagon, NASA (which was very easy), and a U.S. nuclear weapons research lab were described as "the most organized and systematic attack" on U.S. computers ever discovered. To make the Pentagon attack hard to trace, the hackers routed it through the United Arab Emirates. A teenage hacker in Israel directed them.

To help industries fend off hacker attacks, both foreign and domestic, the government has created the National Infrastructure Protection Center, to be staffed by 458 people from the FBI, other agencies, and industry. Recent events make clear that tighter defenses are needed. In 1997, a 13-year-old boy with a home computer disabled control-tower communications at a Worcester, Massachusetts, airport for nine hours. The loopholes the teenager exploited have been closed. But no computer environment is totally secure. Preventing hacker attacks is like a never-ending journey. You will never get to your destination.

Chinese Cyber Criminal Cafe Hacktivists Spin a Web of Trouble at Home

In the university district of Beijing, a bunch of 20-year-olds calling themselves the "Web Worms" slouch around in an apartment stacked with old issues of *PC* magazine. Chinese computer networks are so easy to break into nowadays. Ninety-three (93%) percent of them are not secure.

From the moment in 1995 that a commercial Internet provider first gave Chinese citizens access to the Web, the government has tried to maintain what some cybersurfers derisively call "the Great Firewall of China." This elaborate control system is supposed to block sites that the Communist Party considers morally or politically degenerate, from Penthouse to Amnesty International and CNN. But with a few simple tricks, ordinary Internet users are now making a mockery of the Great Firewall, tapping easily into forbidden foreign sites.

Sabotage

Sophisticated hackers, meanwhile, are breaking into sensitive Chinese computers (see sidebar, "Cyberspace Incidents on the Rise in China"). Members of the Hong Kong Blondes, a covert group, claim to have gotten into Chinese military computers and to have temporarily shut down a communications satellite last year in a "hacktivist" protest. The ultimate aim is to use hacktivism to ameliorate human rights conditions.

CYBERSPACE INCIDENTS ON THE RISE IN CHINA

Intelligence and security experts are warning foreign firms in China of a growing threat of Internet-related crimes, government surveillance, and loss of proprietary data. But some U.S. companies said they view those threats as exaggerated.

The latest warning comes from a report published in 2000 by a network security firm founded by two former U.S. Navy intelligence officers. The report, released by Dublin, Ohio-based LogiKeep Inc., cautions companies that the government-controlled Internet environment in China could put the integrity of their networks at risk.

The most important consideration is that, in one way or another, the government is involved in the operation, regulation, and monitoring of the country's (China) networks. As a result of this and other factors, such as tensions with Taiwan, U.S. companies could see an increase in scans, probes, and attacks that could be aimed at gaining technical information.

But representatives from companies with major operations in China indicate that they have never had problems and don't plan to run scared now. The companies discount most of the alarmist reports.

The real focus of their control efforts is what the Chinese call "black and yellow," or political and pornographic material. How serious an issue economic espionage is depends on who you are and what business you're in. And economic espionage isn't unique to China.

Nevertheless, there are other companies who are not convinced that the Chinese government is overtly (or, for that matter, covertly) engaging in corporate espionage via the Internet. Yet, U.S. intelligence experts warn that China's vast intelligence-collecting apparatus has a voracious appetite for any U.S. technology that could help speed the People's Republic's military modernization and boost the country's economy. That puts high-tech vendor companies particularly at risk.

Businesses operating in China are up against a national government that has essentially unlimited resources and a long track record of industrial and economic espionage. The government runs every business in China; any effort to develop intelligence and promote those industries is a national effort. Scans, probes, and attacks against U.S. firms in China are statistically confirmed and growing, and could be Chinese tests of offensive information warfare tactics or the work of Chinese virus writers.

The U.S. firms that may be at the greatest risk of losing proprietary data include companies that have set up development laboratories in China. But those companies, eager to gain a foothold in China's burgeoning IT market, don't necessarily share the fears of intelligence experts.

Nonetheless, there are more controls in place in China than in some other countries, but they have not been put in place to foster espionage. Although the Chinese view controls and regulations as necessary to facilitate an orderly Internet market and to protect the country from subversion and other Internet crimes, the controls are partially the result of political rigidity and bureaucratic inertia.

Human nature is the same everywhere in the world. The thought that there are lots of people with time on their hands to explore what the 20 million Internet users in China are doing is totally impractical.

Free speech also is proliferating. A political journal called *Tunnel* (http://www.geocities .com/SiliconValley/Bay/5598) is said to be edited secretly in China and sent by e-mail each week to an address in the United States, where it is then e-mailed anonymously back to thousands of Chinese readers. *Big Reference* (http://www .ifcss.org) is another on-line challenge to the authorities. One recent issue extolled individualism and paid tribute to the mother of a student killed when troops crushed the pro-democracy protest in Tiananmen Square in 1989.

The Internet provides not only speed and efficiency but also cover. If you tried to do a traditional newsletter promoting democracy in China, you'd surely get arrested. If only the authorities were smart enough to realize what's going on, all the political activities on the Internet would really have them scared.

Perhaps they are smart enough. New regulations introduced in 1997 imposed stiff penalties (including jail sentences) for using the Internet to damage state interests, spread rumors, or publicly insult others. Nonetheless, China's wired population has grown to 4.408 million, according to government figures. Although that is a tiny portion of an overall population approaching 3 billion, China's Internet users are virtually by definition the country's most educated and modern elite. To watch over them, a new force of more than 500 "Internet security guards" has been assigned to patrol computer networks at state companies and ministries. What the Chinese government is really afraid of is political infiltration. The government's goal is to have a security guard in every work unit.

Perhaps most worrisome to the authorities, young Chinese are using the Net to coordinate political campaigns. On August 17, 1998, Indonesia's independence day, hackers in China broke into Indonesian government Web sites and posted messages protesting violence against ethnic Chinese there. Chinese security officials ignored the demonstration until it reached the streets. That day, about 200 students rallied outside the Indonesian Embassy, carrying photographs of rape and murder victims that they had downloaded from the Web. The incidents weren't written up in the Chinese news, but were posted on the Web.

Recently, the government has taken even more drastic action. In Shanghai, a computer engineer named Lin Hai faces charges of inciting the overthrow of state power by providing 60,000 e-mail addresses to *Big Reference*. And at the end of 2000, the publishers of *Tunnel* went into hiding.

THE SUPER COMPUTER LITERATE TERRORIST

During the next 20 years, the United States will face a new breed of Internet-enabled terrorists, super computer literate criminals, and nation/state adversaries who will launch attacks not with planes and tanks, but with computer viruses and logic bombs. American adversaries around the world are hard at

They don't understand how much security costs. Mark has to provide a clear return on investment statement. It's the same problem an insurance agent has. Mark has to identify the probability that something will happen—it's the down-stream effect.

To devise a security plan for a client, Mark makes a technical assessment of a network and combines it with his own interviews and observations. He assesses a company's "pain threshold," or how much security risk it can endure before the business would shut down. Once completed, a security plan can be 600 pages long. Mark then either implements the plan or recommends how the client can enact it.

HOW THEY WATCH AND WHAT THEY KNOW

Palestinian supporters are using a combination of hacking tools and viruses to gain what appears to be the upper hand in the Middle East's ongoing cyber war. How Palestinians hackers watch and what they know will determine the success of this cyber war for them.

They are distributing the tools and viruses for destroying Israeli sites using a recently created attack site. Visitors to the site are greeted with the message, "I swear that I will not use these programs on anyone but Jews and Israelis." The site comes complete with a list of directions on how to use the attack tools.

LoveLetter, CIH, and the Melissa Virus (along with 12 *Word* macro viruses) form the arsenal for attacking Israeli sites. Apparently, it's an effective system.

According to sources at iDefense, an international security firm monitoring the situation, pro-Palestinian hackers are using a variety of tools to orchestrate a well-organized attack against the 100 or more Israeli Web sites that have been hit during the conflict. It is hard to say for sure who is winning. But it appears that the pro-Palestinian hackers have successfully affected more sites.

The pro-Palestinians have been much more aggressive in scope. Instead of just targeting specific sites, they've been methodically working through all the sites, thus broadening their agenda.

Over 226 Web sites have been targeted by both sides for denial-of-service attacks, attempts to gain root access, system penetrations, defacements, and a variety of other attacks. Many sites have been indirectly affected, due to the strain that the attacks have placed on the Net infrastructure in the Middle East.

The conflict began on October 6, 2000, when pro-Israeli hackers created a Web site to host FloodNet attacks. Since then, both sides have sustained blows to vital-information and financial-resource sites such as the Palestinian National Authority site and the Tel Aviv Stock Exchange.

Sixteen tools have been identified as those actively distributed among attackers, with many others being discussed or suspected of already being deployed. One such tool is called the *EvilPing*, believed to have been created especially for this war. The tool launches a "ping of death attack" that, when utilized by several users against the same target, crashes the system.

Then there is *QuickFire*, an attack tool that sends 32,000 e-mails to the victim from what appears as the same address. Used simultaneously by multiple attackers, the tool crashes an e-mail server.

QuickFire strength is that it does not relent, continually firing off thousands of e-mails until the server is shut down and the address blocked. It is believed to be the tool used for hack attacks on the Israeli Foreign Ministry site and its Webmaster's e-mail address.

A group called "Hackers of Israel Unite" originally used another popular tool called *WinSmurf*, which also uses mass pinging to bring down a site. Borrowing amplifying power from broadcast sites, the hackers send out pings that are boosted 10,000-fold, or more. According to the group, they were able to shut down Alma-nar.org using one computer with a 56K modem and an ADSL line.

According to Netscan.org, a site that provides a list of broadcast sites with an average amplification of times five, a dial-up user with 28.8 Kbps of bandwidth, using a combination of broadcast sites with an amplification of 40, could generate 1152.0 Kbps of traffic, about two-thirds of a T1 link. With tools like these, a 56K can become a powerful weapon and your bandwidth is irrelevant.

Netscan.org creators call themselves a small group of concerned network administrators who got fed up with being smurfed all day. But they recognize the fact that their site has also become a hacking tool.

Pro-Palestinians recently turned the tables by using broadcast-site attack tools against Israeli sites. Although the leaders in the war (groups such as UNITY, DoDi, and G-Force Pakistan) remain in the limelight, many previously unknown hackers are taking the cyberwar to another level.

Hackers are making moves to gain root access to Israeli computers and servers. Root access is the ultimate possession, it means doing whatever you want with a system. In essence, a hacker who gains root access control of a computer can scan, delete, and add files, use it as an attack tool against others, and even view and hear users whose computers are equipped with cameras and microphones.

With no end in sight to the Middle East cyberwar, talk of targeting U.S. interests on the Web has been popping up in chat rooms and IRC channels frequented by pro-Palestinian hackers. Recent aggression against Lucent.com, coupled with hits on cnn.com in 2000 and other mainstream sites, has many high-profile companies watching their backs for the next wave of attacks.

Hackers such as DoDi have come out and said that the current war isn't just against Israeli, but the U.S. as well. But Arab activists such as Mustapha Merza believe the American media continues to portray Arabs as terrorist aggressors, even in cyberspace.

The irony of the matter is that the number of times that Israelis have targeted U.S. government sites are more numerous than those times they were targeted by pro-Palestinians. Yet, the American media fails to identify its real perpetrators and victimizes the Arabs as usual. For its part, the National Infrastructure Protection Center (a division of the FBI concerned with cyberwarfare, threat assessment, warning, and investigation) lists both Israeli and Arab sites that promote the cyberwar.

How Israelis Watch and What They Know Too

A group of self-described ethical hackers are taking the reins of the Israelis' Web networks into their own hands in the Middle East's cyberwar. Known as the Israeli Internet Underground, the coalition of anonymous on-line activists from various Israeli technology companies has set up a Web site to disseminate information concerning the ongoing battle in cyberspace.

According to the IIU mantra, they are dedicated to the Israeli spirit and united to protect Israel on the Internet against any kind of attacks from malicious hacking groups. The site claims to provide a comprehensive list of sites that were hacked by Arab attackers since the cyberwar went into full swing in October 2000.

Listed are over 50 Israeli sites that have been defaced and vandalized by various hacking groups. The number coincides with estimates provided by officials at iDefense, an international private intelligence outfit in Washington that is monitoring the ongoing war. IIU also provides a list of Israeli sites that they believe run services with commonly known security holes such as BIND NXT overflow, IIS 4 holes, and FTP format string bugs.

Examples of defacements by Arab hackers such as the one perpetrated on the homepage of Jerusalembooks.com, one of the largest Jewish booksellers on the Web, serve as a warning to those Israeli sites with suspect security.

The Jerusalembooks.com text and graphics were recently replaced with the word "Palestine" in flaming letters and with text asking Israelis if the torah teaches them to kill innocent kids and rape women. The site is currently under construction due to the attack.

Taking credit for the attack is the group "GForce Pakistan," a well-known activist group that has joined forces with Palestinians and other Arab hackers in fighting the cyberwar against Israeli interests.

Working alongside the group is the highly skilled Arab hacker named DoDi. On November 3, 2000, DoDi defaced an Israeli site and stated he could shut down the Israeli ISP NetVision, host of almost 80% of the country's Internet traffic.

Though petty defacements and racial slurs have been the norm on both sides of the battle, Arab hackers like DoDi have promised to kick the war into high gear in the coming years, implementing what they refer to as phases three and four of their "cyber-jihad."

The Muslim extremist group "UNITY," with ties to "Hezbollah," laid out a four-part plan for destroying the Israeli Internet infrastructure at the onset of the cyberwar. Phase four culminates in blitzing attacks on e-commerce sites, causing millions of dollars of losses in transactions. IIU said there is already evidence of phase-four attacks, such as the destruction of business sites with e-commerce capabilities, which they believe caused a recent 9% dip in the Israeli stock exchange.

The current onslaught of cyberattacks against Israel's key Web sites is perhaps the most extensive, coordinated, and malicious hacking effort in history. ISPs and ebusinesses must recognize the need to install protection that goes beyond firewalls to provide real security against application-level assaults.

In order to thwart future attacks, IIU has created what they call the "SODA project" (sod is Hebrew for secret). The stated goal of the project is to inform and provide solutions wherever the IIU can and, therefore, protect their sites against political cyber-vandalism. It lists those Web sites with security vulnerabilities, making them susceptible to future attacks by Islamic groups.

The SODA project formed an alliance with the Internet security firm 2XS Ltd., which is linked to the site and agreed to provide security advice for casualties of the cyberwar. 2XS Ltd., however, does not accept responsibility for IIU actions. On November 3, 2000, IIU contacted 2XS Ltd. to share their idea of creating a site for publishing vulnerability alerts.

Another link on the SODA project is the Internet security information forum SecurityFocus.com, a resource guide to on-line security links and services based in San Mateo, California. The site is not taking any sides in the Middle Eastern war.

Typically, the odds are heavily in the attackers' favor—the attacker can launch attacks against any number of sites for little to no cost. They only need to find one vulnerable victim to succeed, perhaps after checking thousands of potential victims.

Because both Arabs and Israelis are launching volley after volley against the others' sites, neither faction gets to play the victim in this war. The victims end up being citizens and businesses in the affected area. Unfortunately, that's not uncommon in that part of the world.

HOW AND WHERE THEY GET THEIR TOOLS

Despite increasing concern about cyberterrorism, the tactics and goals of the world's terrorist organizations remain low-tech. Although the terrorist's toolbox has changed with the advent of the Information Age, the objectives of the world's terrorist organizations have not.

A growing percentage of terrorist attacks are designed to kill as many people as possible. Guns and conventional explosives have so far remained the weapons of choice for most terrorists.

However, terrorists are adopting information technology as an indispensable command-and-control tool. Raids on terrorist hideouts, for example, are increasingly likely to result in the seizure of computers and other IT equipment. Instead of just finding a few handwritten notebooks and address books, counterterrorism authorities are faced with dozens of CD-ROMs and hard drives. Likewise, terrorists' increasing use of advanced encryption tools often delays the process of finding key files and information.

Terrorists groups, such as the Osama bin Laden organization, have yet to demonstrate that they value the relatively bloodless outcome of a cyberattack on the nation's critical infrastructure, but the threat remains real. There are warning signals out there. If the United States fails to recognize this, then the United States will pay another high price like they did on 9-11.

Information Weapons

There are several weapons or tools currently available that can negate, destroy, or incapacitate information systems, with many more being rapidly developed. Within this part of the chapter, these are broadly grouped into three main types: High Energy Radio Frequency (HERF) guns, Electro-Magnetic Pulse (EMP), and other information weapons.

HERF Guns

A HERF gun (as discussed briefly in Chapter 12) is a device that directs high-power radio energy at an electronic target. Electronic circuits are vulnerable to overload; a HERF gun simply overloads particular circuits to disable specific pieces of equipment that are dependent on that circuit. A HERF gun can be designed to cause varying degrees of damage from simply shutting a system down to physically destroying equipment. Pointed at a computer, a HERF gun may either permanently or temporarily terminate its operations. A HERF gun pointed at a "fly-by-wire" aircraft may trigger a catastrophic failure.

Although currently limited in range and destructive capacity, in the near future, HERF guns are likely to be substantially more capable and freely available and, therefore, must be taken seriously. HERF guns represent an excellent addition to the offensive military inventory of a nation, and also a significant threat if possessed by an enemy. The defensive measures that can be employed to reduce the risks of

HERF attacks are not well developed at this stage, but include using Gaussian shielding, gaseous discharge devices, and the maintenance of physical separation.

Electro-Magnetic Pulse

Electro-Magnetic Pulse (EMP) has been described as "the next great weapon to evolve in modern warfare." Initially discovered as a side effect of nuclear tests, the phenomenon has now been extended to non-nuclear generators. Such generators can create an EMP that will disable unshielded electronic systems. A development beam generator with a one gigawatt capacity could be used to develop a line of sight EMP that would knock-out most unshielded electronic devices within a radius measurable in tens to hundreds of meters, depending on the employment method. High power microwaves, communications, computers, navigation, and data processing systems would be most affected by such weapons. The current limitations of these weapons are power generation and capacitor storage capability, but these can be expected to be overcome in the future.

Research is well advanced with EMP warheads recently being fitted on USAF air-launched cruise missiles. EMP weapons are less discriminatory than HERF guns and could be used to shut down a general area rather than a specific system. Again, with the exception of screening techniques such as Gaussian shielding, defensive measures are not common.

Other Information Weapons

There are several weapons that are currently being developed that do not fit in the HERF or EMP categories. Some already are in service with various military forces, others remain on the drawing board. The following weapons are described in a variety of freely available publications and give an indication of the technologies being developed and the possible capabilities that may result.

Low-Energy Lasers

These lasers can be used to damage the optical systems of sensors (including data collection devices), thus attacking the information systems at the data collection level. Low-energy lasers have already been fitted on rifles and armored vehicles and were deployed during the Gulf War. A number of systems are reported to be under further development in the United States and United Kingdom.

Electrical Power Disruption Technologies

An electric power disruption munition was first used during the Gulf War in 1991. The technology originated after an accident on the U.S. West Coast when chaff cut power supplies to the city of San Diego in 1985. The weapon uses light conductive carbon fibers that wrap around transmission lines and distribution points to

CHINA GRABS U.S. TECHNOLOGY TO MODERNIZE ITS MILITARY

The request, to a Massachusetts defense contractor, seemed innocent enough: China needed fiber-optic gyroscopes, the latest in navigation equipment, for a new high-speed rail system, the buyers allegedly said. The deal might have gone through if not for a small hitch: The manufacturer recalled that the men, using a different company name, had tried earlier to get a U.S. license to export the gyroscopes to China—and had been turned down.

In 1999, U.S. Customs agents in San Diego arrested a Chinese national named Yao Yi for criminal export violations. Yi has pleaded not guilty; as well as his co-conspirator, Collin Shu, a Canadian, who was also arrested and pleaded not guilty. The two are accused of conspiracy to illegally export items designed for military purposes. The gyroscopes are generally used for guiding missiles or maneuvering fighter jets. To put these in a train, is like putting an F-14 engine in a Cessna.

Intense Debate

The gyroscope case is one of the latest incidents illuminating Beijing's voracious appetite for high-end U.S. technology that has military capabilities. Also in 1999, a man was arrested in Detroit for allegedly trying to illegally ship to China a riot-control vehicle. A report by a panel chaired by Rep. Christopher Cox (R-Calif.), in 1999, suggested that China may have married U.S. computer technology with nuclear weapons designs it stole in the 1980s from U.S. labs. The report presented no hard evidence of this. But it will almost certainly add fuel to an already intense debate over exports of high-speed computers to Beijing.

Proponents of the sale of high-tech goods to China say they help open the country to influences like American television shows beamed off U.S.-manufactured satellites. And, they add, U.S. electronics firms need foreign markets like China if they are to stay healthy in the face of stiff foreign competition.

The present and past administrations have generally supported this view. But in 1999, in a surprising turnaround, past Clinton advisers blocked California satellite maker Hughes Electronics Corp. from sending two $670 million satellites to be launched in China. Various officials offered different explanations for the decision, but the government told Hughes the launches could transfer too much militarily significant know-how.

Critics of high-tech exports to China say they have other concerns as well: The same technology that is already turning China into a land of ATM machines and cell phones could help the People's Liberation Army begin to master information warfare. Pentagon officials counter that nobody is assessing the impact of the fiber-optic lines, electronic-switching gear, computers, and satellites pouring into China. Some examples:

In March 1996, as Beijing was threatening Taiwan with missiles, the State and Defense departments approved the export of two satellite receiving stations worth $7.3 million. The recipient, documents show, was China Electronic Systems Engineering Company, part of China's military. The stations came equipped with ports to plug in Chinese-made encryption devices. The National Security Agency signed off on the deal, but congressional critics say the sale deserves a second look.

China buys nearly half of the supercomputers exported to high-risk countries. Experts point out that the Chinese can evade U.S. export controls by harnessing together less powerful machines—or buying high-capacity machines on a Russian Internet site. Industry groups plan to lobby Congress to allow more powerful machines to be exported, arguing that 1995 limits are already outdated. The Cox report calls for greater scrutiny, including spot checks in China to ensure the best machines are used only for civilian purposes. There are two trains rushing down the track directly at each other on this.

Experts say China's rapidly modernizing military is still years from catching up with the United States, at best. But some worry that China will put high-tech imports to their best military uses and turn into a surprising adversary.

The most sensational charge in the 872-page report—that China has obtained secret data on every warhead in the U.S. nuclear arsenal—is based on a single document that a Chinese agent deliberately fed the CIA in 1995. Why would China's spy masters tip their hand? Maybe they bungled, giving away too much in an effort to plant a double agent. Maybe they were warning Washington to butt out of China's touchy relationship with Taiwan. Or, maybe, they were just following the 1,500-year-old advice of the military philosopher Sun Tzu to "sow confusion in the enemy's camp."

The release of the bipartisan Cox report in 1999 certainly did that. Its overall conclusions are chilling. For two decades, it says, China has used spies, front companies, and scientific exchanges to filch some of America's most precious secrets. But on closer reading, it is still unclear how much damage has been done to U.S. national security. In most cases, it seems, Beijing got helpful hints, not blueprints.

Democrats on the congressional panel, which was led by Republican Rep. Christopher Cox of California, unanimously approved the report. But they also questioned its alarmist tone. There are, unfortunately, a number of places where the report reaches to make a point and, frankly, exaggerates.

On the other hand, concrete advances from spying sometimes don't show up in weapon systems until years later. It's possible, as Cox and some Pentagon officials argue, that the sum of China's technological thievery is even larger than its parts. So how worried should Americans be? Here's what the report does and does not say:

Nuclear Warheads

China stole classified design data on the W-88, a miniaturized nuclear warhead that is the most advanced in the U.S. arsenal. The CIA discovered this in 1995 when a Chinese "walk-in" (an agent who came forward voluntarily) handed over a Chinese document stamped "secret." The unclassified version of the report does not reveal the contents of the document, but an administration official at the time said it contained two "quite specific and detailed" bits of data on the W-88. One was the size of the "package" containing the nuclear device, whose yield (explosive power) was already available from open sources. Although useful, that knowledge is a far cry from a detailed plan for a nuclear weapon. It's more like looking at a car's engine compartment and knowing how much horsepower the block can produce.

Because the CIA later determined that the "walk-in" was a double agent acting on the orders of China's intelligence service, it is unclear whether the Chinese had already milked the information or never considered it all that important. The Chinese document, dated 1988, also described the size and yield of four other U.S. warheads. But that may have come from publicly available sources.

Why does China covet America's nuclear secrets? The Cox committee concluded that U.S. technology would help China build smaller warheads to sit atop a new generation of lighter, mobile missiles. But the upgrade has been in the works for 23 years. And most experts think that its goal is to ensure China's "second-strike capability"–the ability to retaliate for a nuclear attack, not to launch a first strike. Beijing's leaders have good reason to worry about the reliability of their current strategic-missile force: fewer than 20 aging, 1950s-era rockets.

The first of the new missiles, the DF-31, won't be able to reach most of the territory of the United States. But could it intimidate China's neighbors or make the United States hesitate to defend Taiwan in a crisis? Definitely!

Rocket Technology

The Cox panel was established partly to look into allegations that two U.S. aerospace firms, Hughes and Loral, helped China to improve the reliability of its Long March booster rockets. The report says that the two companies ignored restrictions on technology transfers and gave away sensitive information while helping China investigate a series of failed attempts to launch the firms' satellites into space.

What, exactly, did Chinese scientists learn? How to build better "fairings," the nose cone that protects the satellite during launch. How to compensate for the violent winds that buffet rockets in flight. How to fix the Long March 3B's guidance system. How to better investigate failed launches. This information has improved the reliability of Chinese rockets useful for civilian and military purposes.

Still, it is unclear how quickly China will be able to make those improvements. In the past, China has sometimes had difficulty absorbing Western technology. The spying and technology transfer is of enormous concern. But, having it in your hand doesn't mean you know how to use it or effectively deploy it.

Computers

There is no mystery about how China got advanced computers. The question is what it does with them. Under relaxed export rules, China has legally bought 903 high-speed, American-made computers since 1996. The Cox report says that they have been used in nuclear weapons applications, such as modeling hypothetical explosions rather than conducting real ones after Beijing signed the Comprehensive Test Ban Treaty in 1996. But the congressional panel recommended spot checks to monitor the use of U.S. computers in the future, rather than cutting off sales.

Radar

The Cox report also asserts that classified U.S. radar research stolen by the People's Republic of China could be used to threaten U.S. submarines. But the White House produced a letter from the Navy to the Justice Department stating, "It is difficult to make a case that significant damage has occurred" from the alleged disclosure.

China has never aspired to a large nuclear arsenal. One possible explanation for Beijing's disclosure of its own espionage is that Chinese leaders wanted the world to know they could build a large, modern arsenal—if they wanted to. It's deterrence on the cheap. If that was the plan, it just might have worked.

WHY TOOLS ARE EASY TO GET AND USE

Why are hacking and information warfare tools and weapons of mass destruction easy to get and use? Easy answer: They can be stolen!

For example, investigators at Los Alamos National Laboratory, in 2000, discovered that computer hard drives containing nuclear weapons data and other highly sensitive material stored in a vault at the laboratory had disappeared, according to several United States Government officials. The hard drives were stored in locked containers inside a vault in the nuclear weapons division of the national laboratory. Officials reported that the hard drives were missing on June 1, 2000 after officials went to search for them following the forest fires in the area. The containers remained in the vault, but the hard drives were gone.

talkative terrorist has a record of shifting loyalties and admits to lying to investigators in the past.

El-Hage, a naturalized U.S. citizen, certainly seems to be feeling the pressure. Five days after Mohamed's testimony, he suddenly also attempted to plead guilty. The plea, offered without consulting with prosecutors, was thrown out because el-Hage told the judge he was acting not out of guilt, but because he wanted to escape the humiliation of a trial. Should el-Hage decide to flip with prosecutorial blessing, his testimony could offer a trove of information. Court documents place the 40-year-old el-Hage within a rogues' gallery of terrorists. The Lebanese native is allegedly tied not only to the embassy bombs but also to a string of criminal acts, including attempted arms sales to those later convicted in the 1990 murder of radical Rabbi Meir Kahane and the 1993 World Trade Center bombing.

Further revelations may come from Ali Mohamed, who is cooperating with the FBI. Terrorism experts already are pondering his assertion that through the mid-1990s, bin Laden's al-Qaeda maintained close ties to Hezbollah, the Iranian-backed militia, and to Iranian security forces. Al-Qaeda and its allies received explosives training at Hezbollah camps in Lebanon, Mohamed claimed, and received bombs disguised to look like rocks from the Iranians. The implications are troubling. Iran is an untold story in this. How many elements have they kept out of this indictment?

Perhaps several. Ties to the USS Cole bombing may well emerge from trial testimony. And a further indictment in New York (this one under seal) names even more alleged bin Laden conspirators. Clearly, the trial will be but one act in an ongoing and altogether grim play.

In November, 2000, for instance, authorities in Kuwait, who thought they had radical Islamists under control, got a nasty shock. They uncovered a tiny terrorist cell plotting to bomb U.S. and Kuwaiti facilities, and quietly called in the CIA, which helped trace the plot beyond Kuwait's borders. A suspect, Mohammed al-Dosary, led investigators to a desert weapons cache that held 293 pounds of high explosives, 1,450 detonators, and, for good measure, five hand grenades. They were in the final stages of casing targets, claims a U.S. official. Even more worrisome, the plotters had helpers in Kuwait's government, one of the closest U.S. allies in the Persian Gulf.

Publicly, the face of the adversary is bin Laden's. But focusing on one man misses the full picture. Bin Laden has tapped into what U.S. officials sardonically call the "Afghan Veterans" Association, Arabs who answered the call to holy war against the Soviets two decades ago—at the time, with backing from the CIA. The threat posed by the Jihadist network didn't become clear until five years ago, with the U.S. arrests of those behind the 1993 World Trade Center bombing. That case sounded the first broad alarms that thousands of Arab veterans from the Afghan war had now trained their sights on the West.

Terror Inc.

Bin Laden finances and motivates a "network of networks," co-opting homegrown terrorist groups, from Egyptian Islamic Jihad to the Abu Sayyaf group in the Philippines to the Islamic Movement of Uzbekistan. It's like you're winding up little dolls and sending them back to their own countries and letting them create their own movements. The United States was slow as a government to recognize what bin Laden was doing. Bin Laden was doing something much more than spreading the money around.

Without fanfare, Washington in 1999 opened a new front in the war. The strategy: Go on the offensive, and hound and disrupt terrorist cells wherever they can be found. U.S. intelligence agencies routinely tip off local security services to a problem they didn't even know they had. Cells are placed under surveillance or, using a legal process called "rendition," suspects are forcibly returned to their home country. In Albania, Algeria, Pakistan, Syria, and elsewhere, bin Laden devotees have been booted out, often on immigration charges and with little publicity. More than two dozen suspects have been brought to justice. The war on terror is fought down in the weeds. It's guys talking to their sources, pulling people in for questioning, and digging for telephone records. It's the slow, dirty, grunt police work that goes on every day.

In 2000, the CIA launched the largest counterterror operation in U.S. history, working with counterparts in Jordan and other countries to thwart a multicontinent "terrorist spectacular" during the millennium celebrations. CIA operatives in more than 60 countries pressured, pleaded, and paid local authorities to crack down on Islamic radicals. The message was: It's crunch time. This cost the agency a great deal of money and resources.

But like battling the mythical Hydra, an eliminated terrorist cell only seems to regenerate, sometimes in the same place. Bin Laden and his organization, al-Qaeda, are still itching to pull off an attack in pro-Western Jordan. And though U.S. and Kenyan authorities busted up an al-Qaeda operation in Nairobi in early 1998, the victory was only temporary. They immediately came back in. They were able to use the infrastructure that was in place, spin up a new cell, and go after the target. The August 7, 1998 blasts at the U.S. embassies in Nairobi and Dar es Salaam, Tanzania, killed more than 220 people.

Just as sobering is what officials call the "mujahideen underground railroad," a vast effort to move young recruits to terrorist training camps in Afghanistan. An estimated 40,000 recruits have gone to Afghanistan since 1996. Using professionally forged documents and Hotmail Internet accounts to keep in touch, network members move people through Italy, the Balkans, Turkey, and Dubai.

Recruitment

The Finsbury Park Mosque sits in a gritty part of London, not far from the Arsenal soccer stadium. Inside, the only sign of Islamic activism is a hand-made sign protesting Russia's war in Muslim Chechnya. But U.S., British, and Yemeni officials say the mosque is a recruitment station for terror camps and that its fundamentalist imam, Abu Hamza al-Masri, has ties with terror groups abroad.

Often, the process begins when a potential recruit visits a local mosque and makes a small donation. While some of the funds may go to legitimate Islamic charity work, bin Laden receives a steady stream from mosques, charities, and schools. The way to get rich is to come up with a scheme to get everyone to pay you 5 cents a month. That's what he's done. The United States has tried to block the money flow but has made little progress.

Despite the nature of the quarry, progress is being made in the war on terrorism. The U.S. is certainly holding their own. There's a chance that the U.S. is gaining ground, but not very much. Bin Laden's very success (due to the 9-11 attacks) has spurred unprecedented international law enforcement cooperation. Jordanian officials alerted U.S. agencies to the millennium threat. Even Russia, which fears radical Islam in Chechnya and Central Asia, now works regularly, if quietly, with U.S. counterparts. This is a dramatic turnaround. Nevertheless, some U.S. agencies still *dropped the ball* in not being able to prevent the 9-11 terrorist attacks.

Through eavesdropping and, increasingly, informants, Western spy agencies are gaining a clearer picture of the structure of bin Laden's network and his inner circle. But penetrating the distinct cultures in which the terrorists operate is difficult. The CIA has begun a special program to recruit Muslims, in hopes of worming its way inside. One advantage: the terrorist networks' decentralized structure. They are vast, but they're not real tight. The CIA is more aggressive but is hampered by 1995 regulations restricting recruitment of sources with unsavory backgrounds. The CIA claims the rules don't block operations.

Nor have the terror fighters been able to get bin Laden himself, who still moves between homes, residences, and underground bunkers in Afghanistan or in neighboring Pakistan. He is protected by what a Pentagon official calls "double walls of security." One is provided by his dwindling Taliban hosts, and his own personal security detail includes an elder son who is said to rarely leave his side, but now is presumed dead.

NOTE

Recently, terror fighters were further embarrassed by the elusiveness of bin Laden, when he showed up at his elder son's wedding in full view of international media cameras.

The terrorists do their own spying. They do exploit our weaknesses. The Cole attackers slipped through a small window (four hours every other month) as U.S. ships refueled in Yemen. They hit U.S. in exactly the right place. Sometimes, terrorists dispatch walk-ins, "informers" who proffer false information to U.S. agents. Bin Laden previously used an INMARSAT satellite telephone—on which U.S. spy agencies eavesdropped and quickly established his role in the East Africa bombings. When that fact became public, he switched to a system of mule messengers and code words.

Still, U.S. high-tech wizardry plays a key role in combating terrorists who are increasingly high-tech themselves. When Khalil Deek was arrested in Pakistan in December 1999, U.S. and Jordanian officials weren't sure how much of the millennium plot they'd unraveled. Deek (who denies involvement) had computer files locked with a commercially available encryption program. U.S. agents rushed the computer to the Fort Meade, Md., campus of the code-breaking National Security Agency. It was a race against time. NSA had to know whether Deek had operational information such as where and how the attacks were planned.

That threat was thwarted, but others keep coming: an average of 40 each week, according to the FBI. Fighting terrorism is like being a soccer goalie. You can block 99 shots, but you miss one and you lose the game.

WHAT THEY WILL DO NEXT—THE INFORMATION WARFARE GAMES

Finally, the number of cyberattacks and intrusions into Pentagon computer networks in 2001 is expected to top off at 35,000, an increase of 6% compared to the number of intrusions that occurred 2000, according to the Department of Defense. However, the overwhelming majority of those intrusions are due to known vulnerabilities and poor security practices. Ninety-nine percent of the successful attacks and intrusions can be attributed to known vulnerabilities and security gaps that have gone unfixed and poor security practices by defense agencies.

Malicious hackers and other criminals penetrated Pentagon network security at least 25,160 times during the first seven months of 2000. Hackers stung the Pentagon at least 22,144 times in 1999 and 5,844 times in 1998.

These incidents will have served a constructive purpose if the Pentagon is willing and able to learn from them. By exposing and highlighting vulnerabilities, the attacks can actually help to inoculate the system during times of crisis—but only if the appropriate lessons are learned now.

The number of successful attacks raises questions about the Pentagon's preparedness to withstand more skilled adversaries. The Pentagon is currently operating in a relatively benign international environment, yet they were hard pressed to deal with the detected hacks. The Pentagon has a raging case of technological hubris and is ready to be taken to the cleaners by a savvy adversary.

In addition to weak security practices by Defense of Department (DoD) network administrators, the increase in the number of attacks can be attributed to the greater availability of sophisticated hacker tools on the Internet. Someone with a very limited amount of computer skills can do a lot of damage. The increase in the number and the sophistication of the attacks pose a significant threat to DoD plans to use computer networks as part of its overall strategy to fight future conflicts, a concept known throughout the Pentagon as "network-centric warfare."

Despite claims by senior officials that DoD's classified systems are immune from attack, there are several connections between the Pentagon's top secret and secret networks and the unclassified network that connects to the global Internet that make them vulnerable. However, sophisticated encryption devices designed by the National Security Agency protect the classified networks. All of the Pentagon's various layers of networks are connected. Regardless of classification, there are connections and you are dependent on that infrastructure.

However, legal restrictions have hampered the DoD's ability to respond to attacks and track down hackers. Due to legal and privacy[iii] restrictions, the department is prohibited from pursuing hackers beyond its networks. The agency can take defensive measures to stop a hacker, but to actively catch and prosecute a hacker, it must go through the FBI. The agency doesn't go outside of their firewalls, but they'd like to.

One solution that the department is working on is a concept called "legal hot pursuit." Pentagon criminal investigators are searching for a legal framework that would enable them to use one search warrant to track hackers back through the multitude of Web sites they often use as launching pads for their attacks. Today, these investigations require separate search warrants for every system used as part of a distributed denial-of-service attack.

How Other Countries Are Getting into the IW Games

According to the CIA, other countries are developing cyberattack capability. The United States could become a target of cyberattacks from a growing list of terrorists and foreign countries, including Russia, China, and even Cuba (see sidebar, "Has Cuba Joined the IW Games?"

HAS CUBA JOINED THE IW GAMES?

These must be jittery times for anyone in the military who uses the Internet. Not only do they have to guard against Love Bug worms and security holes in Microsoft *Outlook* but also they've got to worry about Fidel Castro hacking into their computers.

According to the Defense Intelligence Agency, the 75-year-old communist dictator may be preparing a cyberattack against the United States. Castro's armed forces could initiate an "information warfare or computer network attack" that could disrupt the military.

One can say there is a real threat that Cuba might go that route. There's certainly the potential for Cuba to employ those kinds of tactics against the U.S.'s modern and superior military. Cuba's conventional military might is lacking, but its intelligence operations are substantial.

In addition to Cuba, terrorists such as Osama bin Laden are now using the Internet and encryption to cloak communications within their organizations. So, you know, you recruit people on Internet sites, and you use encryption. You move your operational planning and judgments over Internet sites' use of encryption. You raise money.

Bin Laden allegedly uses encryption (and a variant of the technology, called steganography) to evade U.S. efforts to monitor his organization. Also, bin Laden and his global network of lieutenants and associates remain the most immediate and serious threat to America.

And what about Castro? It might seem odd to view a country best known for starving livestock, Elian Gonzalez, and acute toilet paper shortages as a looming threat, but the Pentagon seems entirely serious. Cuba is not a strong conventional military threat. But, their ability to ploy asymmetric tactics against the U.S.'s military superiority would be significant. They have strong intelligence apparatus, good security, and the potential to disrupt the U.S.'s military through asymmetric tactics. Asymmetric tactics is military-ese for terrorist tactics when your opponent has a huge advantage in physical power.

The CIA is detecting with increasing frequency, the appearance of doctrine and dedicated offensive cyberwarfare programs in other countries. They have identified several (countries), based on all-source intelligence information, that are pursuing government-sponsored offensive cyberprograms.

behind terrorism's rising lethality, presumably justified in the terrorists' minds by the transcendent cause.

- In 1996, for example, the year of the Khobar Towers attack, religiously motivated terror accounted for 10 of the 13 extremely violent and high-profile acts that took place worldwide.
- Counterterrorism today requires diverse responses to an increasingly diverse challenge.
- Mainstream ethnic, separatist, or ideological groups will deviate little from established patterns. They will largely rely on the gun and the bomb, as they have for a century. The sophistication of their weapons will be in their simplicity: clever adaptation of technology and materials that are easy to obtain and difficult to trace.
- State-sponsored terrorism has been the most conservative in terms of tactics; almost without exception these acts have been carried out with a conventional arsenal of weapons. But new entities with systemic, religious, or apocalyptic motivations and greater access to weapons of mass destruction may present a new and deadlier threat.
- High-tech weapons and nuclear materials from the former Soviet Union are increasingly available, and chemical or biological warfare agents are easily manufactured.
- Amateurs, in particular, who may be exploited or manipulated by professional terrorists or covert sponsors, may be willing to use these weapons.
- In addition to becoming more lethal, the terrorist threat is changing in another dimension as well—one driven by computer and communication networks. The most striking development here is not attacks on America's information infrastructure. It is the way that terrorists are organizing themselves into new, less hierarchical networks and being sponsored by secret, private backers. This change, enabled by the information revolution, makes detecting, preventing, and responding to terrorist activity more difficult than ever before.
- Analysis of terrorist organizations in the Middle East also suggests that the more active and lethal of these make extensive use of information warfare techniques.
- Future terrorism may often feature information disruption rather than physical destruction. PAF found that many terrorist entities are moving from hierarchical toward information-age network designs.
- Terrorists will continue using advanced information technology to support these organizational structures.
- More effort will go into building arrays of transnationally internetted groups than stand-alone organizations. And this is likely to make terrorism harder to fight.
- Hierarchies in general have a difficult time fighting networks. There are examples across the conflict spectrum, including the failings of governments to defeat

transnational criminal cartels engaged in drug smuggling and narco-terrorism, as in Colombia.

■ The persistence of terrorist movements, as in Algeria, in the face of unremitting state opposition, also shows the robustness of the network form, including its ability to spread to bases in Europe.

■ Arrests in the United States just before New Year's Eve 1999 suggest the ability of such networks to operate across regions. The study notes that this change is part of a wider move away from formally organized, state-sponsored groups to privately financed, loose networks of individuals and subgroups that may have strategic guidance but enjoy tactical independence.

■ Conventional counterterrorism techniques may not work well against such groups.

■ Retaliation directed at state sponsors, for example, may be effective against traditional terrorist groups, but will be likely to fail against an organization with multiple, dispersed leaders, and private sources of funding.

■ Implications for the Air Force: How can the United States respond to more lethal, more diverse, and increasingly privatized patterns of terrorism?

An Agenda for Action in Preparing for the information Warfare Arsenal and Tactics of Terrorist and Rogues

The United States needs to formulate a clear, realistic, and realizable national strategy that can evolve with the changing terrorist threat. The PAF team identified four core elements to that strategy: reducing systemic causes, deterring terrorists and their sponsors, reducing the risk of "superterrorism" such as attacks involving weapons of mass destruction, and retaliating where deterrence fails. This strategy leads to key implications for the use of air- and space-based assets:

With its increasing lethality, possible access to weapons of mass destruction, and the shift to flexible and robust network organization, terrorism is a more formidable problem than ever before. Air and space power will be critical elements in defending U.S. interests—including USAF forces—against this evolving threat.

The United States government needs to set an agenda for action that goes beyond the work already done in preparation for defending against the information warfare arsenal and tactics of terrorist and rogues. Action steps should include, but not be limited to the following 14 areas:

1. Default settings for software products sold to consumers should be at the highest level of security.
2. Nations developing information strategies should consider investment, both intellectually and financially, across the gamut of information operations.

3. Air power's pervasiveness and speed are advantages in the face of transnational and transregional terror. In an era when terrorism may take place across the globe and sponsors may cross national and regional lines, the global sight and reach of Air Force assets should be valuable to national decision makers.

4. Air and space power should not always be the instruments of choice in the U.S. counterterrorism arsenal. They can, however, play an important role in intelligence and covert action.

5. Air and space power should rarely be used independently; instead, they will have a synergistic effect with other counterterrorism instruments such as covert action, diplomacy, economic instruments, and joint military operations. And the same instruments may be used in parallel against terrorist supporters, terrorist infrastructure and networks, and terrorists themselves.

6. Air power in the service of counterterrorism should include, but also go beyond, surveillance and punishment of state sponsors.

7. Deterrence and response should probably evolve in the direction of a more "personalized" approach emphasizing the monitoring and attack of key nodes in terrorist networks and the forcible apprehension of individual terrorist suspects.

8. Demands on air power should be driven as much by the requirement to intercept and extract suspects as by the need to attack training camps or strike supporting regimes.

9. Air and space power should help make terrorism—an increasingly amorphous phenomenon—more transparent.

10. The ability to identify and target terrorist-related activity and help expose terrorism and its sponsors for policy action and international censure should be key contributions of Air Force assets.

11. As terrorism becomes more diffuse and its sponsorship increasingly hazy, finding the "smoking gun" should become more difficult but essential to building a consensus for action.

12. Space-based sensors, surveillance by unmanned air vehicles, and signals intelligence should facilitate the application of air power and other counterterrorist capabilities.

13. Counterterrorism should increasingly focus on urban areas and thus face strong operational constraints. For political reasons, terrorists find key targets in cities. The use of air power for counterterror, therefore, faces the more general problem of operating in urban environments, a situation where the difficult Israeli experience in Beirut and south Lebanon is instructive.

14. The value of air power here should depend on its capacity for discriminate targeting and less-than-lethal technologies.

ENDNOTES

i John R. Vacca, *Satellite Encryption*, Academic Press, 1999.

ii John R. Vacca, *Electronic Commerce, Third Edition*, Charles River Media, 1999.

iii John R. Vacca, *Net Privacy: A Guide to Developing & Implementing an Iron-clad ebusiness Privacy Plan*, McGraw-Hill, 2001.

and growing activities of criminal enterprises. These enterprises include everything from arms traders and drug cartels, which will provide and use existing and new weapons in terrorist campaigns as a part of their pursued profit and political power.

In sum, present and future terrorists and their supporters are acquiring the capabilities and freedom of action to operate in the international jungle. They move in what has been called the "grey areas," those regions where crime control has shifted from legitimate governments to new half political, half criminal powers. In this environment, the line between state and rogue state, and rogue state and criminal enterprise will be increasingly blurred. Each will seek out new and profitable targets through terrorism in an international order that is already under assault.

NOTE

There is an appreciation that the multinational corporation shares a common characteristic with terrorists, that is (to a certain extent) a rejection of this state-centric system. This rejection is, by no means, complete (both corporations and terrorists exists at a substrate level in some degree). The corporation may seek the protection of the law of a state, and many terrorist organizations will rely on the protection and assistance of states—whether it's overt, or semiovert, or more covert.

Although some might argue that multinational corporations and terrorists groups stand at either end of a spectrum, the spectrum would still be that of a movement away from "state-centrism" and the concentration of coercive power in the state—with the danger that they each move so far away from one another and that they meet up again. Any ambivalence in allegiance or identification on the part of a nonstate quasi-criminal or terrorist organization toward a corporation could easily find its way into violent activity directed at the multinational corporation. Such an ambivalence (and an appreciation of the vulnerability of a corporation) would be brought to the fore, were a corporation to hire the same cyberterrorists to undermine its competitors. A corporation willing to use such agents and to expose its insides to them, puts itself at their mercy should the flow of money dry up or should the cyberterrorists then sell their services to another competitor or organization that bids higher. In addition, the multinational corporation, through its existence on many planes of definition at one time, can at any time be seen to be on a similar plane with a substrate or nonstate actor, as well as being on a nation-state plane—thus attracting criticism and violence that would have been directed toward the identifiably "official" organs of the nation-state in previous times.

As potential targets continue to be hardened in urban areas, the visible aspects of multi-national corporations are strengthened and protected. At this point, activities may then move to rural and/or less protected areas.

Many multinational corporations have now "desegregated their operations" (to borrow a term from another context) and have placed various aspects of that operation in different geographical areas (and even different countries). A failure to strengthen and protect a particular part of that operation may cause incalculable damage to a multinational corporation's network should a weak network node be attacked and disabled.

OVERVIEW OF DEFENSIVE TACTICS PRIVATE COMPANIES CAN TAKE

This part of the chapter deals with some technical issues relating to attacking computer and information networks, and defensive tactics that private companies can take in stopping or hindering attacks. This part of the chapter will also very briefly deal in passing with some discrete problems that may be encountered in applying traditional forms of risk treatment to what is essentially a new form of risk, and it will then discuss the need for perhaps a new or revised approach to the risk-management system of a corporation in respect of the new form of threat represented by computer terrorism. It will also discuss what has become known as "information peace-keeping" (IP). The three elements of IP are:

- Open source intelligence
- Information technology
- Electronic security and counter intelligence

Interestingly, IP must rely almost entirely on the private sector for sources and services that will require the development of a new national intelligence and secure approach to take into account what has hitherto been an area in which the private sector has not participated. Perhaps the most important aspect of information operations in the 21st century is that it is not inherently military; instead, civilian practitioners must acquire a military understanding and military discipline in the practice of information operations if they are to be effective. This is known as the enmeshing phenomenon.

Information peacekeeping is the act of exploitation of information and information technology to achieve national policy objectives.

NOTE

Common to all aspects of information operations (IP, IW, and all source intelligence) is open source intelligence. This means that the involvement of the private sector will become more clinical in defense terms in the 21st century. Along with this must go an increasing identification of the private sector with the defense establishment, both in its own perception and in the perception of outsiders. IP is not:

- Application of information or information technology in support of conventional military peacekeeping operations (contrary to what some may consider revolution in military affairs [RMA] thinking)
- Traditional psychological operations or deception operations
- Covert media manipulation
- Clandestine human intelligence operations or overt research operations

Attempts to avoid the enmeshing phenomenon or to protest that private corporations are essentially that, private, and rely on this as a defense is unwise. It may also be futile. In any event, what is also important is the perception of the other entities with which the private corporation may come face to face (such as substrate and nonstate terrorist groups, the military forces of other nation-states, and also against other corporate competitors).

Defensive Tactics to Thwart the Threat of Business Spies

Threats to the security of business information are numerous and they come from all directions, including organized crime syndicates, terrorists, and government-sponsored espionage, and most global high-technology companies have little idea of the array of hostile forces targeted against them. U.S. businesses that are increasingly expanding their operations into foreign lands are finding the situation challenging because the nature of such threats and how to protect against them is not taught in business school.

Some of the threats might be obvious, as well as the strategies that companies can mount against them, but others might not be so cut and dried. In a world in which countries measure themselves in terms of economic might, many intelligence services around the world are shifting their emphasis and targets to business. Government-sponsored intelligence operations against companies seek information about bids on contracts, information that affects the price of commodities, financial data, and banking information.

Furthermore, government intelligence services want technological production and marketing information, and they usually share what they get with their country's companies. To get this sensitive information, government intelligence services use many of the techniques developed during the Cold War. That includes bugging telephones and rifling through papers left in hotel rooms by visiting businessmen and businesswomen. In addition, government intelligence services are known to plant moles in companies and steal or surreptitiously download files from unsecured computers. Several also have highly sophisticated signal intelligence capabilities to intercept even encrypted company communications. Messages that are not encrypted with the latest technology are especially vulnerable. These include telecom and computer communications, including e-mail.

Though the French intelligence service is probably the most egregious offender, it is far from alone. Russia, China, South Korea, India, Pakistan, Germany, Israel, and Argentina all have some type of intelligence-gathering operation for the benefit of companies in their countries, and many more countries are doing the same. The United States, however, is not among them.

No American intelligence agency conducts industrial espionage against foreign companies for the advantage of U.S. companies. What the U.S. intelligence community (CIA, NSA, etc.) does is support the efforts of their own government, and that information is not shared with American companies.

Reports originating in Europe, especially France, that the United States is using signal intelligence capabilities as part of a program called "Echelon" to attack European companies for the economic advantage of U.S. companies is simply not true. Another threat comes from the dozens of intelligence services in developing countries that have profited from the training they received from the Soviet Union, Eastern European countries, and the CIA during the Cold War. The result of this history is that the reservoir of professionally trained intelligence mercenaries is growing.

Other threats include terrorism, organized crime and inside operations carried out by disgruntled employees and hackers. Some of these groups are looking for the greatest amount of destruction, and an attack on the critical information infrastructure of the United States would satisfy that goal.

Business needs to understand that the criminal and terrorist threat worldwide is changing and is now both more sophisticated and more dangerous than anyone would have thought. Vulnerabilities that all the different types of attackers exploit include open systems, plug-and-play systems, centralized remote maintenance of systems, remote dial-in, and weak encryption. Companies could provide substantial information security protection for relatively low cost.

Companies should review security measures in sensitive areas of their operations such as research and development, talk to traveling executives who carry company laptops about using precautions to prevent theft, and examine communications with overseas facilities with an eye toward installing commercially available encryption that is all but impossible to crack. The new algorithm recently approved by the Department of Commerce, for example, is so strong that it would take an estimated 149 trillion years to unscramble.

Company executives should also limit physical access to sensitive data and programs and regularly change computer passwords. It's all obvious, but every one knows how many companies are lax in their actual implementation.

A basic rule is to take time to identify company critical information, whether it is technology, a production technique, basic research and development, financial information, or marketing strategy, and take steps to protect it. What is required first is simply awareness by CEOs and boards of directors that there is a threat and then, second, response using a common-sense way to protect themselves. These are measures that make good business sense even if you are not a target of a government intelligence service, a competitor, a criminal organization, a terrorist, or a hacker.

Cybersecurity Progress in the Private Sector

Many companies have made significant progress since 2000 to protect their infrastructures from attack, but others still face an uphill battle. Nevertheless, the government and private firms must work together to bolster cybersecurity.

The banking and energy industries remain ahead of many other sectors in security preparedness. Other sectors, including telecommunications, transportation, and waterways, face difficult challenges stemming from a vast array of factors such as deregulation and market fluctuations.

However, progress hasn't proceeded at the same pace in all sectors. There are some sectors that are ahead of others. Nonetheless, private companies accept the challenge that the government has given them to protect the networks that run their infrastructure.

Obstacles

The IT sector has been moving very aggressively. Any perceived slowness is due to a genuine desire by industry to protect proprietary and sensitive information on behalf of their companies, shareholders, and clients.

Corporate concerns regarding shareholder value and increased competition may be getting in the way of security progress at some banks, airlines, and telecommunications companies. Despite the banking industry's perceived success in the area of security, a recent spate of money laundering schemes in the banking industry, including a $2.5 billion scam against Citigroup Inc. and Commercial Bank of San Francisco that lasted ten years, raises serious questions about the status of security in the industry.

Likewise, the airline and telecommunications sectors have come "under siege" as a result of deregulation and the current climate of mergers and acquisitions. Years of a systematic underinvestment in electric power grid capacity, combined with the effects of wholesale deregulation, have created a potentially perilous security situation.

But security protections against cyberattacks in natural gas and electric industries are being addressed constantly, although the national effort lacks a useful gauge for how much security is enough. If you don't have any attacks, it's easy to let the program slip.

SURVIVING OFFENSIVE RUINOUS INFORMATION WARFARE

The principal actors in any cyberterrorist attack on a corporation, and the levels on which the attack may be made have already been discussed. This part of the chapter deals with surviving offensive ruinous information warfare by looking at the mechanics of attack and defense.

The United States General Accounting Office (GAO) has produced a report on information security and computer attacks at the Department of Defense. It identifies the following means of attack:

■ Installation of a malicious code in an electronic mail message sent over a network machine—as the *sendmail* program scans the message for its address, you will execute the attacker's code. *Sendmail* operates at the systems root level and, therefore, has all privileges to alter passwords or grant access privileges to an attacker.

■ Password cracking and theft is much easier with powerful computer-searching programs that can match numbers or alphanumeric passwords to a program in a limited amount of time. The success depends on the power of the attacking computer.

■ Packet Sniffing: An attacker inserts a software program at a remote network or host computer that monitors information packets sent through the system and reconstructs the first 125 keystrokes in the connection. The first 125 keystrokes would normally include a password and any log-on and user identification. This could enable the attacker to obtain the password of a legitimate user and gain access to the system.

■ Attackers who have gained access to a system can damage it from within, steal information, and deny service to authorized users.

■ Trojan Horses: An independent program that when called by an authorized user performs a useful function but also performs unauthorized functions, which may usurp the user's privileges.

■ Logic Bomb: An unauthorized code that creates havoc when a particular event occurs (for example, the dismissal of an employee).

It is becoming increasingly impossible for "low knowledge" attackers to use relatively cheap, "high-sophistication" attack tools to gain access to what was, historically, a relatively impregnable system. The addition to this ready availability of high-technology attack tools of an increasingly networked global economy, and the integration of corporations within that networked global economy, expedientially increases the risk of attack and the ability of any attacker to cause damage.

Surviving a Misbehaving Enemy

Article 99 of the Uniform Code of Military Justice defines misbehavior in the face of the enemy as any person who, before or in the presence of the enemy:

1. Runs away
2. Shamefully abandons, surrenders, or delivers up any command, unit, place, or military property that it is his or her duty to defend
3. Through disobedience, neglect, or intentional misconduct endangers the safety of any such command, unit, place, or military property
4. Casts away his arms or ammunition
5. Is guilty of cowardly conduct
6. Quits his place of duty to plunder or pillage
7. Causes false alarms in any command, unit, or place under control of the armed forces
8. Willfully fails to do his utmost to encounter, engage, capture, or destroy any enemy troops, combatants, vessels, aircraft, or other thing, which it is his or her duty to encounter, engage, capture, or destroy
9. Does not affect all practical relief and assistance to any troops, combatants, vessels, or aircraft of the armed forces belonging to the United States or their allies when engaged in battle
10. Shall be punished by death or such punishment, as a court-martial shall direct

Now, you're wondering what this has to do with network security, information warfare, or yourself—because you are not at war. Let me assure you that it does apply to network security, information warfare, and to you—and you most certainly are at war.

Every day, someone from a subculture other than your own is waging a battle against you and your systems. As network professionals, you are the propagators of your own doom. You are guilty of misbehavior in front of the enemy by not admitting your own fallibility, by not passing critical information to your own team, and from your sheer arrogance in thinking that you can't be bested by some punk kid.

Remember; misbehavior in the face of the enemy. True, it is not life or death and hacked systems aren't really your enemy, but the concept is the same. In neglecting to raise the alarm and warn the others, you are guilty of this cowardly act. Open communication is your enemy's greatest advantage and your greatest weakness.

SURVIVING OFFENSIVE CONTAINMENT INFORMATION WARFARE

Surviving offensive containment IW with layered biometric tools to boost security is now part of the latest arsenal and tactics of private companies. In the race to improve security infrastructures faster than hackers can invent methods to penetrate firewalls, it is important to ascertain a user's identity before permitting access to protected data. Given the pervasive use of passwords and personal identification number codes for user authentication across all aspects of our daily life, attackers have developed powerful password-cracking tools.

New technologies that aim to directly strengthen user authentication include the use of tokens and smart cards combined with digital certificates. The most compelling and intriguing authentication technologies involve biometrics matching the measurement of physical and behavioral characteristics such as facial structures, voice patterns, and fingerprints.

In the past few years, biometrics technology has rapidly pushed through barriers that have slowed its adoption in mainstream environments. Performance, accuracy, and reliability have increased among all types of biometrics methods, and prices for capture devices have plunged, making biometrics an attractive addition to security systems. The remaining challenge for biometrics is to address the requirements for large-scale deployments in complex governmental, institutional, and commercial systems.

To gain widespread acceptance in businesses, multiple individual biometrics methods must coexist in a single-system solution, and the underlying architecture must better support the conditions of interoperability, scalability, and adaptability that govern total cost of ownership calculations. A multitiered authentication system built around these notions is one solution.

At the center of the authentication system, a server orchestrates interaction among clients devices, an authentication validation policy system, multiple authentication matching engines, and databases housing user information. Applications and transaction systems request a centralized authentication server to confirm or deny a user's identity. The server receives incoming requests for authentication and directs actions to gather appropriate user credentials and evaluate them against a set of validation criteria.

The policy system might maintain extensive rules to meet security requirements that may differ depending on the user, application, or transaction task. The authentication security policy may require many biometrics for validation. Thus, the validation system must be able to layer biometrics approaches, balance matching scores from each matching process, and interpret these results in light of preset policies. This process is computationally expensive. It's critical that companies scale with system demand. Because each biometrics method requires a different matching-process engine, the authentication system should distribute the matching task to the correct algorithm and thread the processes across a farm of processors.

The user-interaction tier collects credentials from live users in real time. To collect a new biometric sample, a prompting system must request a specific user action, such as presenting a particular finger for scanning or repeating a voice phrase in a microphone. Many types of point-of-service access devices, such as desktops and laptop computers, mobile phones,[i] wireless pocket devices,[ii] and airport kiosks, may be used at any time by end users. Each device may have limited capabilities to request and gather a specific biometric from the user. Therefore, the authentication server must dynamically determine what biometric to request, based on the client device.

To complete the process, a user's credentials must be evaluated against a stored pre-enrolled user information profile, such as biometrics templates, digital certificate keys, and text passwords. Repositories of this information may be centralized in protected databases or decentralized within personal tokens or smart cards. With the use of a smart card that contains the enrollment data, the authentication server would also prompt users to present their template cards instead of accessing them from a central database.

Although there are advantages to using biometrics, authentication should not forego other methods as part of the overall authentication solution. Even old-fashioned PIN codes and passwords provide an extra layer of protection and may be preferable in lower-risk security systems. Other security technologies, such as public-key infrastructure, also perform critical roles in an overall security model.

PARTICIPATING IN DEFENSIVE PREVENTIVE INFORMATION WARFARE PLANNING

A congressionally appointed panel of national security experts recently recommended the creation of a National Homeland Security Agency (NHSA) to oversee government and private sector IW planning efforts to protect the nation's critical infrastructure from cyber- and physical attacks. The U.S. Commission on National Security, headed by former senators Gary Hart and Warren B. Rudman, urged the Bush administration to form the new agency and to include a National Crisis Action Center as a focal point for monitoring emergencies and for coordinating federal support in a crisis to state and local governments, as well as to the private sector.

It is doubtful, however, whether a proposal for a new security agency would fly, given the large number of agencies and organizations seeking the same funds and authority. Central to the new agency would be a directorate of critical infrastructure protection (CIP) that would manage cyberdefenses for the various sectors of the economy, including banking and finance, telecommunications, transportation, and utilities. Most of the nation's critical infrastructure is owned and operated by private sector companies.

An attack on any one of several highly interdependent networks can cause collateral damage to other networks and the systems they connect. Some forms of disruption will lead merely to nuisance and economic loss, but other forms will jeopardize lives. One need only note the dependence of hospitals, air-traffic-control systems, and the food-processing industry on computer controls to appreciate the point.

According to the U.S. Commission on National Security's recommendations, the CIP directorate would have two primary responsibilities. The first would be to oversee the physical assets and information networks that make up the U.S. critical infrastructure. The second would be to coordinate government and private sector efforts to address the nation's vulnerability to electronic or physical attacks.

In partnership with the private sector, where most cyberassets are developed and owned, the Critical Infrastructure Protection Directorate would be responsible for enhancing information sharing on cyber- and physical security, tracking vulnerabilities, proposing improved risk-management policies, and delineating the roles of various government agencies in preventing, defending, and recovering from attacks.

That effort is now done through a maze of different agencies and private sector partnerships, such as the National Infrastructure Protection Center, the Critical Infrastructure Assurance Office, and the various information-sharing centers formed in the private sector. As a result, the commission recommended that the Bush administration consolidate these efforts. To do this, the government needs to better institutionalize its private sector liaison across the board with the owners and operators of critical infrastructures; hardware and software developers; server and service providers; manufacturers and producers; and applied technology developers.

Stopping DoS Attacks Together

The most recent round of denial-of-service (DoS) attacks shows that cyberterrorism is alive and well, and that ebusinesses and their service providers aren't doing enough to stop it. Unfortunately, all corporate America and ISPs seem to be focused on is who to blame. After the recent attack on Microsoft shut off access to everything from Expedia to Hotmail, the company attributed the problem to one employee's misconfiguration of a router. Yet experts noted a failure to distribute DNS servers made the company vulnerable to begin with.

If a private company is going to minimize the number and effect of DoS attacks, what's required is a spirit of cooperation between companies and their ISPs, as well as among the ISPs themselves. ISPs are starting to tackle the subject of networkwide security, but they're doing it by laying out requirements for their corporate customers. In many cases, customers either follow the ISP's security guidelines or find themselves a new ISP there's no room for negotiation. It's high time ISPs and their clients start sharing information about what works (and doesn't work) in terms of network architecture, data access, and security systems.

ISPs must ask themselves whether they're doing everything possible from a network monitoring and warning perspective. They should be giving serious thought to the latest security tools that can stop DoS attacks at their routers. After all, once an attack gets through the ISP, it's a lot tougher for an individual site to fend it off.

Everyone along the ebusiness food chain has something to lose when a DoS attack succeeds. The site that's been hit loses traffic, revenue, and customer loyalty. The ISP loses customer confidence and significant resources in combating the attack. Ultimately, every site that relies on the ISP must spend time and resources rethinking its security levels.

ISPs must communicate the types of attacks they're experiencing. They also must be prepared to notify one another of attacks, and even coordinate their responses when they do get hit. With so much at risk, it's hard to imagine why these conversations haven't been taking place all along.

Approaching IW Planning with IW Games

It's Independence Day, 2003. Glitches in air-traffic-controller screens cause a deadly mid-air collision above Chicago's O'Hare Airport killing over 345 people in both planes, and over 1,200 people on the ground when the planes plunge into a nearby crowded shopping center. Four weeks later, California Independent System Operator Corp., which controls California's power grid, somehow misplaces an electrical energy order to Northern California Edison, leaving three-fourths of

Sacramento in the dark. Then in October, a high-power microwave burst fries the electronics at an e-bola virus lab research building at Fort Deterick (Frederick, Maryland).

Hypothetical "information warfare" (IW) planning exercises like these are being played out around the country in preparation for what politicians, the military, and law enforcement officials fear will be an orchestrated cyberattack on critical U.S. private infrastructure companies (see sidebar, "Five Easy Steps to Planning and Launching a Cyberattack"). The theory goes that if a well-funded, organized series of cyberattacks were to strike at a target's economic and structural nerve centers, it would send the target society into chaos and make it difficult for the military to communicate and move troops.

FIVE EASY STEPS TO PLANNING AND LAUNCHING A CYBERATTACK

Here's how a computer invader plans and launches an attack on information systems:

1. Recon: Invader uses information-gathering programs and techniques to sniff traffic at the network gateway, then scans ports or vulnerable services.
2. Profile target: Invader gets passwords, then identifies machines and software running on the network.
3. Attack: Invader gains root or administrative privilege of unclassified systems, then seeks and modifies information.
4. Cover tracks: Invader hides the evidence trail and slips away.
5. Wait for results: Invader watches CNN to see what damage he or she wrought.

The weak areas of the preceding scenario are in predicting when someone is gathering information for a later attack. And, once a company has been attacked, the problem is in recovery.

Researchers are working on ways to tie an algorithm into other technologies also in research, including advanced forensics and a tracking system to follow a live evidence trail. Don't be surprised if algorithms eventually wind up in the private sector.

This particular information war game was played out among 86 IT executives attending an IW workshop at NSA Headquarters in Fort Meade, Maryland. In the worst-case scenario, every major industry sector would be affected.

Most of the targets in the NSA IW games are private-sector companies.

NOTE

When you're talking about information warfare, you're talking about information technology systems used to cripple the government and economy. Close to 92% of those critical infrastructure companies are privately owned and operated.

Since 1999, IW preparedness has moved forward the fastest in the highly regulated and well-organized financial, energy, and telecommunications sectors. But IT leaders in the private sector say they're hesitant to report incidents to agencies such as the NSA and the FBI. Still, the agencies need this information for intelligence and predictive analysis.

Although the impact of IW bears the same uncertainty as Y2k did, many IW experts say cyberterrorism and cyberwarfare are inevitable. In 2000, hacking hobbyists have shown how easy it is to propagate viruses throughout Internet-connected mail systems. They've also shown they can hack armies of unwitting computers and make those computers do their bidding. Now, the U.S. government is thinking about what terrorists with more resources could accomplish. And so are countries such as China and Russia, which are developing their own IW capabilities.

Yet, in spite of these indicators, IW thinkers say a cyberwar is years away. Clearly, the eventuality of such an attack is present. That's what motivated the Bush administration to move forward with a national plan. But, it's doubtful that anyone has the cybercapability today to launch an attack that would cripple the nation's infrastructure. The presidential directive predicts such a scenario is still years away.

BENEFITING FROM AND SURVIVING DEFENSIVE RUINOUS INFORMATION WARFARE

Users are drowning in computer passwords. Let's count them: At the office, they need one to log-on to their computer. They need still another to access their corporate e-mail. Users also need three for separate databases within their company, one for a legal research database (a corporate lawyer), and two to get information on retirement plan and benefits. When they get home, they need a password to log-on to their home computer, and a handful more to use on-line services. Amazon.com and other on-line merchants also require a password to make purchases. To get cash from an ATM, they need their personal identification number.

With as unique a fingerprint as a password, corporations can be sure that a person logging-on to a computer network is who he or she claims to be. As previously discussed in the chapter, you can benefit from and survive defensive ruinous IW by using biometric technology (which uses unique human characteristics such as fingerprint, voice, face, or iris patterns to verify a person's identity), which is making rapid inroads into corporate America. According to Gartner Group, within three or four years about 55% of all corporations will use fingerprint readers or some other kind of biometric device.

The scramble to commercialize biometrics stems primarily from changes in how companies organize their information technology. The 1990s switch to network computing, which moved important data from mainframe computers to servers, increased the flow of information within a company. But in the process, it made that information more vulnerable to theft and tampering. A recent FBI survey found that system penetration by corporate outsiders and unauthorized access by corporate insiders are both on the rise.

Corporate networks are not the only potential commercial application for biometrics. Credit card issuers want to reduce losses from fraud. In recent small tests, MasterCard began using fingerprints as a substitute for a signature. Biometrics holds the ultimate security key to future payment systems. The explosion of e-commerce[iii] has also created a gigantic need to authenticate the identity of buyers.

The price of biometric devices has plummeted. In 1994, the smallest fingerprint reader sold by Identicator Technology was the size of a telephone and cost $2,000; today it's the size of one sugar cube and sells for $97. In five years, a similar fingerprint reader may cost $13.

It's likely that more than one biometric technology will emerge. Fingerprinting will snag the lion's share in the fast-growing corporate computer network market. But technology using voice identification can be easily integrated into already existing telephone services such as automated call centers that answer queries about credit cards, bank accounts, and benefits. Facial recognition technology also has its advantages. When Mr. Payroll Corp. (now called innoVisions) wanted to automate its check-cashing kiosks in 1997, it chose facial recognition developed by Miros over fingerprinting because of the latter's law enforcement connotations.

The ultimate goal for biometrics manufacturers is to get into the homes of millions of consumers, with the PC being the likely point of entry. About 8% of all new PCs, including some laptops, are already equipped with cameras, a harbinger that facial recognition may eventually play a role on the Web.

But privacy concerns are a big hurdle. Consumers may decide that using a face or a fingerprint as a password will jeopardize privacy more than protect it.

when it comes to e-commerce. Ultimately, companies that want ISPs to deliver any service at all (even a simple pipe to the Net) will pay more in hard costs, internal policy changes, infrastructure, and business processes.

How much more companies will pay depends on how secure the ISP thinks its customers' network should be. But the ISP is, in many cases, dictating the terms. And whether the customer buys the needed security technology from the ISP or elsewhere, this technology will have to be bought before network services begin. This could mean a huge cash outlay before service even starts.

Fighting Back

IT managers may be told to spend more on security prerequisites, but there's still room for negotiation. This is an emerging trend, not a government regulation. So it's entirely fair for IT managers to bark back, particularly when many ISPs still can't deliver the security services they're asking customers to have up front.

For example, security is something companies must buy from security-management companies, not ISPs. So if a company must go elsewhere for security, it then begs this question: What level of security does the ISP itself offer corporate customers? And if ISPs are demanding that customers walk into the relationship with higher levels of security, corporate customers can turn the tables and demand the same of the ISPs.

Corporate customers should be encouraged to push back. When an ISP tells you to open up your system so they can look around and see if you meet their standards, tell them you want them to do the same.

The ISPs must either ensure that their security mechanisms will work or be responsible for damages, so ask about their network-monitoring tools and alert mechanisms. Once companies open up the conversation to include both sides, it becomes more of a negotiation, and less of an ultimatum.

Before a company gives an ISP access to its entire network for inspection, it should ask the ISP if it's actually going to manage every aspect of the network. If they're not going to manage a certain aspect of your network, like a certain server, then they don't need access.

It may prove to be more trouble for ISPs to deliver security if parts of a potential customer's network are unknown to them. But that's the ISP's problem. Besides, it's the ISP's responsibility to monitor a customer's outgoing traffic, so the ISP already has access to what it needs to know to protect itself. If the ISP's monitoring tools aren't robust enough to give it intelligent reporting, traffic analysis, and alerts to red flags, that's something corporate customers should try to get the ISP to deliver.

The best way to protect the company is to handle these issues in the service level agreement (SLA). The ISPs have the leverage to force customers to implement security, but customers also have a certain leverage. The ISP market is more competitive than ever.

According to Gartner Group, there are now thousands of full-service ISPs, up from less than 1,000 since 1999. The competition means it's in the ISP's best interest to offer corporate customers as much value-add as possible.

But there's one caveat: The idea is to get the ISP to concede some points—for example, help with making the company's network compatible with the ISP's and/or on-site tech support.

The reality is that even if ISPs can dictate security policies, they will be eager to offer value-added services. If you do the negotiating in the context of drafting an SLA agreement, it shows the ISP you're a serious customer and gives them an opportunity to offer you fee-based services over the long term.

A good SLA won't get the company out of paying more for ASP and ISP services in the end. In fact, it can end up costing more—but it will at least get the company the most bang for the buck. The truth is that ISPs will dictate how much security customers will have because they can. They are the conduits to the networks.

IT managers should understand that pushing back at the ISPs will only do so much. This is a trend that's here to stay. The ISPs started the trend, but it won't end with them. Business partners and regulators will step in and give the security push even more teeth, including standards such as best practices and default security requirements.

For example, Visa's approach to surviving defensive responsive containment of information warfare offers some insight. Visa's new policy requires merchants that want to accept Visa on-line to follow a Visa-condoned list of 10 best practices. The rules are nothing earth-shattering. Companies have to have a firewall, up-to-date antivirus software, and SSL encryption. What does this have to do with the ISP security trend? Simply that there's support for the ISPs' position in the financial world. So, if IT managers think they can push back at the ISPs for their demands, they'll find they can only push so far.

Ultimately, the ISPs will protect themselves from outgoing traffic by shutting Web sites down that have been commandeered for DoS and other attacks. The ISPs that survive will start offering security services. It's only during this interim period that the onus will be on companies that use ISPs to pick up the slack. Whether the time period is six months or six years is hardly important. Companies that want to do business with top-tier providers had better get serious about security.

PROTECTION AGAINST RANDOM TERRORIST INFORMATION WARFARE TACTICS

Are application service providers (ASPs) and hosting providers selling customer information? How can private companies protect their data against random terrorist information warfare tactics? The answer lies between the implementation of data-protection techniques and firewalls—both are briefly covered in this part of the chapter.

An information security officer for the New York State Office of Mental Health is mulling the application service provider (ASP) model. But he's afraid that patient data could end up in the wrong hands.

Data security concerns, too, tarnish ASPs' allure for government clients. Think of the commercial windfall if any of these hosting companies started selling social services data or any other government agencies' data. It's unacceptable, but it could happen. And indeed it is.

According to a recent industry survey, it was found that 30% of application-hosting providers were selling their customers' data. What is most disturbing is that the hosting companies all had privacy policies in place, which they were violating.

The would-be gatherers of the stolen data aren't always advertising agencies or marketing firms. They could be random terrorists seeking out corporate data (any data) to destroy as part of an IW tactic. For example, one ASP executive reported software vendors asking him to host their applications for vertical market customers so they could mine the customers' databases. At least, that's what they claimed to be doing. The vendors wanted to act as a purchasing agent between the members of those vertical markets, enabling them to sift through the members' databases for information to cross-sell between the member companies.

If the customers agree, it could be great. But that is a big if. Most companies don't want anyone mining their data.

Selling customer data is taboo for most ASPs, whose executives cringe at the prospect and chalk it up to a few bad apples who will soon be out of business. If it is happening, it could have terrible implications on the rest of the industry. But most ASPs view their customers' data as their sacred asset and would never consider selling it. An ASP should also be bound to a privacy policy as part of the service contract.

Prevent your data from being sold up front by making them sign a contract that says they can't sell it. And make sure you take a close look at the wording to see what constitutes a sale or transfer of data (see sidebar, "Data Protection Measure Tips").

DATA PROTECTION MEASURE TIPS

Application-Hosting Providers

1. Consider working with a lawyer or auditing firm when writing a privacy contract
2. Limit staff access to data and set up multiple levels of security
3. Require employees to sign a statement that they will abide by security and privacy policies
4. Separate the data center from corporate offices
5. Have one-door access to the data-center
6. Install security cameras in the data center

Customers

1. Examine a privacy policy's wording to understand what constitutes a sale or transfer of data
2. Keep the "what-ifs" in mind: If providers go bust or are acquired, what happens to the data?
3. Do a background check on the provider and check references
4. Look for seals of approval

What if the hosting provider goes out of business? Is it permissible to sell its customers' information as an asset (as on-line retailer Toysmart.com tried before being rebuffed by the Federal Trade Commission)? Or what if the ASP is acquired? Will the acquirer stick to the same privacy agreement (see sidebar, "Privacy Agreements")? An ASP should be able to answer all these questions.

PRIVACY AGREEMENTS

What's stopping hosting providers from selling their customers' data? Ethics and little else, according to industry watchdogs.

Companies are being tempted to sell valuable information at their disposal because there are no set legal ramifications against doing so. Right now, a lot can be bought and sold rather freely.

And that includes the business sector. The pressure right now to sell data applies to business information as well as to consumer data. People tend to overlook that.

Hosting providers can be held accountable if they violate their privacy policies, as the Federal Trade Commission suit against e-tailer Toysmart.com shows, but privacy policies often are more vaporware than reality. Privacy policies have more holes than Swiss cheese.

Customers must take some of the blame for flimsy privacy policies because many only skim over privacy statements in their rush to sign on with an ASP. A lot of ASPs are offering free services. They say, "Sign up now and get the first few months free." And in their rush to sign on, customers don't even look at the privacy policy.

However, the ASP industry aims to police itself. The ASP Industry Consortium is working with the World Intellectual Property Organization to establish dispute resolution procedures between ASPs and their customers, covering such areas as copyright/proprietary rights infringement and loss of data or data integrity.

Companies hosting data also should take measures to prevent internal and external "marauders" from gaining access to customer information. Many ASPs, for example, check the backgrounds of the data center staff and restrict their access to data. Often, the customer, not the ASP, chooses who gets access.

Another safeguard is making data center employees pass through several security levels, including physical security guards, key-card door access, and even biometric hand scans. A common mistake made by ASPs is housing the data center in the same facility as a corporate office.

For example, it's too easy to say, "I work with the company," flash an ID and walk right in. It's easier to be able to bypass external data center security measures by pretending to be a member of a nightly cleaning crew and telling a security guard that he or she was with a group already in the building.

To test an ASP's privacy policy and security measures, customers should hire an outside auditing firm. Privacy group TrustE, for example, uses seeding to make sure that companies live up to their privacy policies. Global Integrity probes hosting providers' networks to find out if it can bypass their security schemes.

Customers should test an ASPs' security measures up front and use an auditing firm to test them on an ongoing basis. Some ASPs are even getting in on the auditing act. Breakaway Solutions, for instance, recently formed its own managed security practice. The Boston-based ebusiness integrator and ASP conducts security audits, builds security architectures, and performs ongoing security breach tests for customers.

Another data safety avenue for ASPs are seals of approval from such organizations as the Better Business Bureau and TrustE. TrustE, San Jose, California, gives out privacy seals of approval, called "trustmarks," to Web sites. It's also considering expanding the program to include software companies. To get a privacy seal of approval, software companies have to disclose their data-gathering and dissemination practices.

And that might become more common. ASP clients are sharpening their scrutiny of data privacy. Customers of ASPs are taking a long look at privacy policies. And most won't work with ASPs that don't have a solid one in place.

WHAT TO DO WHEN TERRORISTS KEEP ATTACKING

At 9:15 A.M. on Feb. 7, 2000, AT&T researcher Steve Bellovin walked up to the podium at the North American Network Operators' Group and started a talk. His topic: How a relatively unknown type of Internet attack couldn't be stopped by current technology. Less than an hour later, Yahoo seemingly dropped off the Internet, as the company's servers were targeted with the very attack that Bellovin had warned about.

Today, e-commerce and information sites worldwide remain vulnerable because there are (still) no strong defenses deployed—thus, terrorists keep attacking. The DDoS (distributed denial of service) attack that knocked out Yahoo used a host of hacked servers (dubbed "slaves" or "zombies") to inundate a Web site or Internet-connected server with data, effectively stopping the server's ability to respond to Web page requests or other access attempts. The attack could not be easily pinpointed, as data seemingly came from 100 or more points across the Internet. Simple DoS (denial of service) attacks only come from one source, although attackers can make data appear to come from multiple sources.

Two days later, eBay, Amazon.com, Buy.com, ZDNet, CNN.com, E*Trade, and MSN.com joined Yahoo, dropping off the Web for hours at a time. The attacks affected other sites as well. Overall, Internet traffic slowed by as much to 37%, according to Net performance watcher Keynote Systems.

Although repeated attacks have increased awareness of the problem, and technologies for dealing with a DoS attack are seemingly on their way, 2000's messes are only the tip of the iceberg, there is a lot more to come. Also, the attacks have become more sophisticated.

Recently, Microsoft became the latest proof when it suffered a router glitch and two DoS attacks that left access to the company's Web properties spotty at best. The outage followed attacks on worldwide Internet Relay Chat (IRC), servers that collapsed parts of the service for hours at a time.

And the problem is not going away. At least one tester of anti-DoS technology (a major Internet provider) has estimated that anywhere from 6 to 11% of the traffic on its networks is, in reality, data sent by vandals intent on a DoS attack.

COUNTERING SUSTAINED ROGUE INFORMATION WARFARE

In 2000, the Yahoo message boards were full of postings that insinuated that Titan Corp.'s stock was headed south. According to one message board, "A very very bad earnings surprise is coming today." Titan was getting nailed with huge sell orders! "Jump the sinking ship," said another, posted by someone with the screen name "CCRibber."

If the goal was to scare investors and drive the stock price even lower, it worked. Messages like that (plus a fake analyst report criticizing Titan) sent Titan's shares plummeting from $45 on June 20, 2000 to $20 on Aug. 22, 2000. It was a staggering 56% loss in market value, totaling $1.4 billion.

Sustained Retaliation

The San Diego-based high-tech company filed suit on Aug. 30, 2000 angrily charging that the posters were "unscrupulous short sellers" who conspired to depress the stock for their own profits. The company got a subpoena to "smoke out" the people behind the three dozen screen names that had torpedoed Titan's stock.

The case hasn't wrapped up, but it's yet another episode in which corporate reputations have taken a real sustained beating from rogue Internet messages, fake press releases, and "gripe sites." Of course, critical opinions are legally protected as free speech, but when the messages are false, defamatory, or trying to manipulate the stock, corporate America is fighting back.

To do that, companies are hiring Internet IW monitoring firms that use software that scans the Internet to find out what's being said about business clients. They're also hiring private investigators to track the perpetrators. But it's not something you want to do if you're just aggravated [about the messages], because the investigation can be very expensive—say, $40,000 to $50,000.

The investigations usually turn up former employees, disgruntled insiders, or stock manipulators. The big challenge is identifying the people behind the anonymous screen names. A flurry of messages may actually be the work of only one or two people who use different handles to make it look like they're a crowd.

One approach is to file a "John Doe" lawsuit and use subpoena power to obtain the identity of the mischief maker from his or her Internet service provider. That's what Titan is doing, but it's a strategy that has to be used with caution. It should be a serious lawsuit, based on a cost/benefit analysis.

Another technique employs "forensic psycholinguists" (the same folks who analyze hate mail sent to the White House), who look for signs that the messages came from the same poison keyboard. In one recent case, a psycholinguist studied 40 messages from three screen names and concluded that they came from the same writer because they had the same format: a question in the headline and the answer in the body. The messages also used the same vulgarities.

Based on the analysis, the psycholinguist surmised that the writer was probably 40, white, professional, and, perhaps, a day trader. Furthermore, the analysis indicated that he or she suffered from low self-esteem and felt his or her regular job was threatened by the acquisitions of the company he or she was berating.

Private detectives can also engage suspects in on-line conversations to seek clues about their identities, but there's a danger that the undercover gumshoe could tip his or her hand or cross the line into entrapment. There are even better investigation tricks. For example, perpetrators may have left some electronic footprints behind by filling out a Web site guest book with the same cybersignature they use later for derogatory messages.

Sometimes the text of a message itself provides clues. If they say it's snowing outside, you can check [weather records] to find out where on the planet it's snowing right now, to narrow the suspect pool. If they say they have a blue Jaguar and live in Ohio, you can get a database that lists every blue Jaguar owner in the state.

Apparently, private companies are willing to go to great lengths to identify Internet content that besmirches their corporate reputation or infringes on their intellectual property. For example, Nintendo of America Inc. in Redmond, Washington, retained Cyveillance to identify pornographic Web sites that use its video-game brands such as Pokemon or Mario Bros. to draw visitors to their sites.

Cyveillance uses both human and artificial intelligence to monitor on-line brand abuse for clients. First, the company's Web crawler looks for information that meets customer-defined criteria. Then a team of e-commerce analysts studies the automated reports and recommends a plan of action. The cost ranges from $90,000 to $500,000 per year.

But such services can be used for much more than just defending against countering sustained rogue information warfare in the form of defamation and piracy. Clients start off having a defensive mindset, but then they transition to more of an offensive approach.

In other words, they begin to use Internet surveillance for benchmarking and competitive intelligence, such as finding out when a competitor adds a new feature, such as on-line customer chat, to its Web site. Internet surveillance can even help companies gather soft information such as "marketing buzz" from the world's largest focus group.

NetCurrents, Inc. in Burlingame, California, uses artificial-intelligence technology that scans Internet message traffic to provide a real-time graphical display of public sentiment about a company. Positive messages show up as a green bar, and negative ones as a red bar. But NetCurrents may not stop there. Theoretically, the technology could be used to gauge customer reaction to a new product or voter reaction to a presidential debate.

Law enforcement's new weapons for protection against random rogue information warfare, with regards to electronic detection, spurs privacy proponents to strike back. But will these shifting tactics by law enforcement agencies really protect private companies? Let's take a look.

PROTECTION AGAINST RANDOM ROGUE INFORMATION WARFARE

The growing availability of powerful encryption has, in effect, rewritten the rule book for creating, storing, and transmitting computer data.[iv] People everywhere rightly regard confidentiality as essential for conducting business and protecting against random rogue information warfare and personal privacy.[v] But governments worldwide have been sent into a spin, for fear secret encryption keys will add to the weapons of terrorists and other criminals. Some nations have even attempted to control the technology by constructing a maze of regulations and laws aimed at blocking its import, export, and/or use. Such bans have largely failed, however.

In recent years, the war over encryption has moved beyond controlling the technology itself. Now, some governments are granting law enforcement agencies new powers and funding the development of new tools to get at computerized data, encrypted or otherwise. Rising to that challenge, privacy proponents are striking back with new techniques for hiding data and preserving anonymity in electronic communications.

Confess up!

One legal tactic being used by states is to require owners of encrypted files to decrypt them when asked to by authorities. So far, only Singapore and Malaysia have enacted such laws, with Britain and India about to follow suit.

In Britain, two recent bills would give law enforcement officers the authority to compel individuals to decrypt an encrypted file in their possession under pain of a two-year jail term. Further, anyone given such a command would have to keep the giving of the notice, its contents, and the things done in pursuance of it secret—on penalty of a six-year jail term. The bills broadly define encryption, even including what some consider to be mere data protocol.

Straightforward though it seems, the approach is technically flawed. After all, a suspect may truly be unable to decrypt an encrypted file. He or she may have forgotten or lost the key. Or, if public-key encryption was used, the sender of a file will have the key used to encrypt the file, but rarely, if ever, the decryption key, which remains the exclusive property of the intended recipient. If symmetric key encryption was used, and the sender's hard disk crashes, the key will likely be wiped out along with all the other stored data. This flaw in the legislation was demonstrated by a British group, which mailed an ostensibly incriminating document to a government official and then destroyed the decryption key, making it impossible for that official to decode the file, even if "compelled."

Moreover, according to the latest version of the Cyberspace Electronic Security Act (CESA), police would be at liberty to present a text in court and claim it was the decrypted version of an encrypted file, without revealing to the defendant exactly how they arrived at the plain text. This means that the defendant can have a hard time defending himself, and makes it a lot easier for the police to fabricate evidence. The ability to receive a fair trial could be at stake.

Escrowed Encryption

Another controversial scheme for letting law enforcement in on encrypted data is known as escrowed encryption. Here, a third party is appointed by the state to keep a copy of the decryption keys (in escrow, as it were) for the state to use to decrypt any file sent to or by any user. In other words, encrypted files would be protected—except from the state.

Needless to say, many people abhor the mere idea. Even if a sound case could be made for revealing the decryption key to government personnel, what is to prevent them from reusing that key in the future, to look at other documents by the same user? Furthermore, drug traffickers, terrorists, and others of most concern to law enforcement are the least likely to use encryption that is openly advertised as readable by the government.

Then, too, given the transnational nature of the Internet, a global key-escrow system would need to be established. Sovereign states, with their own interests to protect, would object to such a system; this, in fact, happened with the escrow scheme known as the "Clipper Chip," which was heavily promoted by the U.S. government but largely dismissed by other states. The logistics of who keeps the escrowed keys, who has authority to demand their release, under what conditions, and so on, becomes unwieldy when vast numbers of encryption keys, states, and legal systems are involved. In view of such concerns, official support for escrowed encryption has all but died in the United States and elsewhere.

Global Surveillance

The ineffectiveness of legal constraints on encryption appears to have persuaded many governments to change direction. They are instead seeking to capitalize on the unencrypted nature of most digital traffic and to derive information by monitoring that traffic. Even encrypted messages tend to leave unencrypted who is communicating with whom and when.

Officially, most states deny the existence of electronic surveillance networks. But extensive claims of their existence persist. Echelon and FIDNet are two such alleged intelligence-gathering efforts that have been frequently described in the mainstream press and debated in official hearings by government legislatures.

Echelon is, according to the Washington, D.C.-based Federation of American Scientists, a global network that searches through millions of interceptions for pre-programmed keywords on fax, telex, and e-mail messages.

The same sort of public inquiries have been made about the Federal Intrusion Detection Network (FIDNet) that the U.S. National Security Council has proposed creating. It would monitor traffic on both government and commercial networks, with the stated goal of safeguarding the critical U.S. information infrastructure. Although the House Appropriations Committee did away with funding for it last summer, FIDNet supporters continue to push the program, arguing that it would not intrude on individuals' communications. Meanwhile, a number of civil rights groups, including the Electronic Privacy Information Center (EPIC), in Washington, D.C., and the American Civil Liberties Union, based in New York City, have challenged FIDNet's constitutionality. The plan demonstrates that privacy concerns are being swept under the carpet.

Computer Forensics

As society relies increasingly on computers, the amount of crime perpetrated with the machines has risen in kind. To law enforcement's delight, electronic records have proved to be a fertile ground for detectives. Indeed, in their present shape, computers, the Internet, and e-mail are the most surveillance-friendly media ever devised.

This development has given rise to an entirely new industry: computer forensics. Its purpose is not only to find out what files are stored in a computer, but also to recover files that were created with, stored in, sent by, received from, or merely seen by that computer in the past, even if such files were subsequently "deleted" by the user.

The ability to resurrect electronic paper trails from supposedly deleted files stems, in large part, from the features built into many computer programs. For example, the delete command in most software does not delete. It merely marks the space that such a file occupied in a disk as being available in the future to be overwritten.

If it was really deleted, then undelete commands would not work.

NOTE

Also, many Windows applications save temporary versions of a file being worked on, just in case the computer crashes. Even if a user were to deliberately overwrite the original file, the temporary version still lurks in some part of the disk, often with an unrecognizable name and occasionally even invisible from the conventional directory.

Electronic paper trails are also left behind by the fast save function, which saves the latest version of a word-processing document as the original plus the sequence of changes made to it. A recipient of the electronic end result can see how the document evolved over time—not the kind of information most people care to share.

Internet-related applications, like many other software programs, do a lot of internal housekeeping that involves writing information onto the hard disk. For example, the popular Web browser *Netscape Navigator* creates a file called *netscape.hst*, which gives a chronological listing of almost everything its user has done with the browser since it was installed.

Simply surfing the Web pushes other data into computer memory, in the guise of "cookies" and as documents "cached" on one's disk. Web sites visited can also learn the visitor's Internet service provider, Web browser, and a lot more. A remote Web site could even gain full access to a visitor's hard disk, depending on how aggressive that remote site elects to be and how extensive the protective measures taken by the visitor are.

Software tools now make it fairly straightforward to get a computer to cough up information that its owner may not realize is there. Not to be outdone, computer programmers have developed numerous tools that can defeat most computer forensics tools. Although such counter-forensics programs will remove most traces of sensitive data from a computer, it is extremely difficult to remove all traces that may have been left behind. In the absence of a thorough schooling in the esoteric details of computers, the odds favor the competent computer forensics investigator.

Also favoring the forensics expert are new laws legalizing the accessing of computers by law enforcement agencies. In December 1999 for example, the Australian Parliament passed a bill giving the Australian Security Organization the power to obtain warrants to access computers and telecommunications services, and, if necessary, to delete or alter other data in the target computer and conceal the fact that anything had been done under the warrant. As of February 2000, the Dutch authorities are now permitted to use bugging devices in computers to retrieve text.

Countermeasures

The various legal roadblocks and technical wizardry contrived by governments and law enforcement to block encryption's spread have, of course, curbed neither the need for the technology nor the ingenuity of privacy-loving programmers. As a result, a number of countermeasures have been engineered to augment or replace encryption. Among them are anonymizers, which conceal the identity of the person sending or receiving information, and steganography, which hides the information itself.

The need for anonymity in a democratic society has long been recognized, to shield whistleblowers and political dissenters from retaliation, to protect the records of medical patients, and so on. Less dramatic situations also justify anonymity, such as placing a personal ad or seeking employment through the Internet without jeopardizing one's current job. To be sure, anonymity can be exploited by sociopaths seeking to avoid accountability for their actions. But, in general, it serves a useful social function.

Anonymous and pseudonymous remailers are computers that are accessible through the Internet that launder the true identity of an e-mail sender. Most are operated at no cost to the user. A pseudonymous remailer replaces the sender's e-mail address with a false one and forwards the message to the intended recipient. The recipient can reply to the sender's pseudonymous address, which, in turn, forwards the response to the sender's true address.

Anonymous remailers come in three flavors: cypherpunk, mixmaster, and Web-based. Cypherpunk remailers strip away the message header, which describes where the message came from and how it got there, before forwarding the message to the recipient. Conceivably, someone with physical access to such a remailer's phone lines could correlate the incoming and outgoing traffic and make inferences.

Mixmaster remailers avoid that problem by using stronger encryption and tricks for frustrating traffic analysis, such as padding messages to disguise their true length. But even mixmasters can be compromised. For example, through a concerted effort, it would be possible to detect a correlation between Mr. A sending an encrypted message through a remailer, and Ms. B receiving a message at some variable time afterwards.

Web-based anonymizers range from sites offering conventional anonymizer services, to others where the connection between the user's computer and the anonymizer is itself encrypted with up to 128-bit encryption. The job is done using the standard Secure Socket Layer (SSL) encryption, built into all Web browsers of recent vintage.

For extra privacy, a message may be routed through a series of remailers. Two popular remailer software packages, *Private Idaho* and *Jack B. Nymble*, enable the sender to do this automatically.

The Onion Router project (see the site at http://www.onion-router.net) of the Naval Research Laboratory in Washington, D.C., offers another way to string together remailers. What's more, it allows anonymized and multiply encrypted Web browsing in real time.

Onion routing is a two-stage process. The initiator instructs router W (in this case, a proxy server at the firewall of a secure site) to create an onion, which consists of public-key-encrypted layers of instructions. Router X peels off the first layer of the onion, which indicates the next step in the path and supplies a symmetric decrypting key for use when the actual message comes through later.

The onion then goes to Routers Y and Z, depositing keys at each stop. Once the connection is established, the encrypted message is sent through and successively decrypted, arriving at the recipient as plaintext. To respond, the recipient sends the message to Router Z, which encrypts the text, onion-style, and sends it back through the already established path.

Hiding Data

The microdot used by German spies during World War II to transmit strategic information is an example of steganography, used to hide data in plain view. The microdot consisted of a greatly reduced photograph of a page of text, which was pasted over a period in an otherwise innocuous document. A more modern application is the digital watermark, for identifying official copies of copyrighted images and recordings. Unlike encryption, which hides the content of a message in an obvious manner, steganography hides the mere existence of anything hidden. The commercially available computer-based steganography programs popular today rely on three techniques:

1. Merging the information to be hidden into a "cover" sound file by changing the least significant bit of each digitized sample of the file. The resulting file sounds the same to the human ear and is the same length as the original file.

2. Merging the information to be hidden into a cover image file by changing the least significant bit of the digitized value of the brightness of each pixel. Typical images use 256 levels of brightness, with 8 bits per pixel for black-and-white images and 8 bits for each of the three primary colors (red, green, and blue) per pixel for color images. A lot of data can lurk in a 1024-by-768-pixel image.

3. Hiding data in the areas of a computer floppy disk or hard drive that are normally not accessed. A computer disk is divided into clusters, each of which holds from 512 bytes to over 32,000 bytes. When a file is saved, it uses a portion of one or more clusters; because DOS and Windows store only one file per cluster, the space left over between the end of a file and the end of the cluster (called the slack) is available to hide data in. This scheme is extremely easy to detect, however.

The most commonly used commercial steganography software tools are *Hide and Seek, Steganos, StegoDos, White Noise Storm, S-Tools for Windows, Jpeg-Jsteg,* and *Stealth.* For Unix computers, there is *SFS* (Steganographic File System).

Steganography does have some weaknesses. For one thing, sending or storing many seemingly harmless images or sound files can in itself raise a red flag, unless the sender's normal routine as, say, a musician or photographer warrants such conduct. And although image and sound files hiding information may seem natural to the eye or ear, the difference may still be detectable by techniques devised to spot such aberrations.

Interestingly, the extent to which hidden information can be detected is related to the popularity of the steganography software used. Law enforcement agencies treat steganography much like a computer virus: Once a program hits the market in a big way, tools are developed to detect it. The more extensive the program's use, the more resources are devoted to detecting its footprint.

The Future of Encryption

Encryption today is as strong as it is because there is no need for it to be any stronger. Of course, the underlying mathematical assumptions might be challenged by a breakthrough, such as a solution to factoring large numbers into their prime-number components. Meanwhile, an encryption method can be strengthened by merely adding bits to the encryption key.

Nevertheless, several schemes under development may eventually find use for electronic communication and storage: elliptic curve encryption; voice encryption (already freely available and used worldwide over the Internet); quantum cryptography; and DNA cryptography.

Few microprocessors have been specially designed to run encryption software. Most personal computers can accommodate the hardware and software requirements of modern encryption, but most hand-held devices, such as 3Com's Palm Pilot, cannot. For these devices, a new class of algorithms, known as elliptic curve encryption, is claimed to provide encryption strength equal to that of the standard algorithms in use today, while using a smaller key and arithmetic that is easier on microprocessors and that needs much less memory. Being a new type of encryption, its security has yet to withstand the concerted scrutiny of experts.

Voice encryption is a response to the increasing flow of audio traffic over the World Wide Web, which has led, among other things, to the merging of strong encryption with Internet telephony. Given appropriate software, anyone today can carry on fully encrypted conversations with any other user connected to the Internet.

Perhaps the most advanced such software is *SpeakFreely*, which is available worldwide free of charge (see http://www.speakfreely.org). Some mainstream voice-over-the-Internet services do not offer encryption, though. Instead, they route the data through the company's servers, thereby opening up a security weakness.

Quantum cryptography is not in itself an encryption algorithm. Rather, it is a means for creating and securing the distribution of private keys. Based on the Heisenberg uncertainty principle, the idea is that communicating photons cannot be diverted from the intended recipient to the unsought-for interceptor without creating an irreversible change in the quantum states of the system.

The precepts of quantum cryptography date from the early 1970s, and research has been ongoing for the last decade at universities such as Johns Hopkins University, in Baltimore, Maryland, and the University of Geneva in Switzerland; at U.S. national laboratories such as Los Alamos; and in the corporate sector, at British Telecom and elsewhere.

In DNA cryptography, each letter of the alphabet is converted into a different combination of the four bases that make up human deoxyribonucleic acid (DNA). A piece of DNA spelling out the message to be encrypted is then synthesized, and the strand is slipped into a normal fragment of human DNA of similar length. The end result is dried out on paper and cut into small dots. As only one DNA strand in about 30 billion will contain the message, the detection of even the existence of the encrypted message is most unlikely.

Shifting Attitudes

If, as seems likely, encryption and related products will continue to develop for personal and commercial uses, countries will have to rethink their policies toward the technology. In what may be a sign of things to come, the German government announced in May 1999, that it would fund the development and free distribution of open-source encryption software that the government itself will be unable to break (see http://www.gnupg.org). The Federal Ministry of Economics and Technology released a report stating that Germany considers the application of secure encryption to be a crucial requirement for citizens' privacy, the development of e-commerce, and the protection of business secrets.

Also in 1999, French Prime Minister Lionel Jospin announced a similar shift, saying that his country would scrap any key escrow plans in favor of free use of cryptography. In both cases, the motivation seems to have been the realization that protecting data from foreign parties outweighs any law enforcement concerns, and that the use of strong encryption furthers, rather than hinders, national security.

Independently, the Canadian government announced in October 1999 that it would not seek to regulate the domestic use of encryption. The significance of such trends is clear: The global reach of the Internet has made it extremely easy for encryption software to travel between countries, with or without controls, and if one or more major countries elects not to enforce controls, the technology will spread even more easily. Society's transformation into a computer-based economy makes protecting corporate and personal information not only desirable but also necessary.

How then does one balance privacy and confidentiality with security? Governments are undoubtedly obligated to protect their citizens from terrorism and out-and-out criminality. A partial solution may be to criminalize the use of encryption only in the commission of generally recognized serious crimes and to encourage its use elsewhere.

Attempting to control encryption, however, has proved to be an ineffective means of preventing crime and may actually hurt vital national interests. Similarly, the granting of new policing powers to law enforcement agencies will do less to protect a country's critical infrastructure than building better security technology. And if greater security is truly what governments are after, then much can be done with the tools already in hand: Encrypting all important data and communications makes their illegal retrieval and interception useless to the thief.

KEEPING THE AMATEUR ROGUE OUT OF THE CYBER HOUSE

Finally, how do you keep amateur rogues out of the cyberhouse? Today, you probably can't; but, tomorrow (see Chapter 16, "The Information Warfare Arsenal of The Future")—well, that's another matter.

Today however, motivated amateur rogue "hacktivists" have grabbed headlines, announcing they've collected credit card and other personal data on some 2,500 business and political leaders by breaking into the database of the recent World Economic Forum. Increasingly, these amateur social activists have turned to hacking to make their point, breaking into computer systems and wreaking havoc on organizations they oppose. The Internet has turned out to be a remarkable tool for nonviolent protest on a scale activists could only dream of before.

As previously explained, the term "hacktivist" was first applied to supporters of the Zapatista rebels in Mexico's southern state of Chiapas, who have sabotaged Mexican government Web sites since 1998 and held "virtual sit-ins" designed to overload servers. More recently, the tactic has been used in Serbia, Pakistan, and India—and by both Palestinians and Israelis in the Middle East. In one case, Palestinian sympathizers broke into a Web site operated by a pro-Israel lobbying group in the United States, stealing credit card information and e-mail addresses.

However, the theft of private data is a relatively new tactic, which goes beyond defacing Web sites and electronic bombardment of servers. Antiglobalist protesters contend the WTO's trade treaties benefit big corporations and rich countries at the expense of the environment and workers. They consider the World Economic Forum, which holds its high-profile annual meetings in the Swiss resort of Davos, to epitomize the elitist dealmaking they oppose.

Protesters who showed up in person were largely stymied by a heavy police presence at the recent Davos meeting. On-line, however, they effectively surmounted physical barriers.

Another Frontier

The Net is another frontier for people to engage in these types of activities. The attacks against forum organizers showed just how far hacktivists could reach. They obtained the travel itineraries (including flight numbers) of politicians from around the world, and published them on the Web. This poses operational security problems, and goes beyond what's been seen before.

Almost every major corporation and organization has been hit at one time or another by hacking, with McDonald's, Starbucks, and the WTO being favorite targets of hacktivists. During the WTO's last major meeting, in Seattle in December 1999, the organization faced attempts to shut down its system.

There were millions of bits of spam thrown at the WTO, but they had a good defense which bounced these right back like junk e-mail. People are still being misled by a copycat Web site that uses the WTO's old name (GATT) and looks nearly identical to the real WTO site.

In some respect, it is really quite clever and quite funny. But it is less funny when people believe it (as has been the case) and go to a lot of trouble and then are deceived.

SUMMARY

It can be seen that the development of the Internet presents serious threats to the security of private companies, in addition to the much-touted opportunities it provides. It may also be that the more extreme scenarios discussed in this chapter may never eventuate—the possibility that they may, however, must be appreciated. It is not advisable for any risk-management approach to merely disregard the threats previously discussed on the basis that they are far-fetched and fanciful. In addition to the threats being technically feasible, either now or in the next two decades or so, the ability of intruders to gain entry to computer systems and disguise the very fact of entry makes this a peculiarly difficult threat to appreciate. Undetectability of many attacks per se may lead private companies to a false sense of security, and leave the companies vulnerable to serious disruption of total disablement in the event of an attack.

16 Information Warfare: Arsenal of the Future

Terrorists take control of the New York Stock Exchange? Terrorism over the Internet? Computer viruses in the arsenal of Hizballah? As discussed in preceding chapters, such possibilities are currently being discussed by strategic analysts under the catch-all title of "Information Warfare." To date, the defense establishment has yet to agree on the exact definition of the term "information warfare."

Only the entertainment industry, in the form of films and novels, has popularized the notion of an electronic doomsday scenario in which covert terrorist groups manage to penetrate critical nodes of the National Information Infrastructure (NII) and Defense Information Infrastructure (DII) and are able to, variously, launch nuclear weapons, crash the telephone system, cause mayhem on the railways or in the air, or bring the financial sector to a catastrophic halt (see sidebar, "Will The Real La Femme Nikita Stand Up"). Warnings also come from more sober sources. In 1996 the U.S. Joint Chiefs of Staff concluded that the convergence of vulnerable information infrastructures with traditional critical infrastructures had created a tunnel of vulnerability previously unrealized in the history of conflict. In other words, the one thing that everyone agrees on, in the digital age, information, and its dissemination, has achieved the status of a vital strategic asset.

WILL THE REAL *LA FEMME NIKITA* STAND UP

Section One (in USA's *LA Femme Nikita*) is the most covert antiterrorism organization on the planet. Section One is a skilled team of operatives responsible for protecting human life around the globe from chaos and destruction.

Sound implausible? Maybe. But the creation of such covert antiterrorism organizations are currently in the planning stages by the National Security Agency (NSA) and the CIA.

NSA and the CIA realize that conventional IW tactics will not be enough in the future to thwart the very dangerous and often suicidal world of covert terrorist organizations. Like the character Nikita (USA's *LA Femme Nikita*), who "transforms into a highly trained agent dedicated to fighting global terrorism by any means necessary—legal or otherwise," today's agents will have to do the same.

In the very near future, agents trained and armed with an arsenal of futuristic high-tech weapons, and trained in the most sophisticated techniques on how to carry out successful assassinations will swoop down upon deadly terrorist operatives. Like Nikita, they will all have to be the perfect weapon. They will also have to keep their wits about them, as well as ingenuity to keep themselves alive, where a single mistake could mean death. This will be their most vital weapon—and the best hope for the future of all that is good in the world.

If the response of the American defense establishment is any indication, strategic analysts are taking the possibilities of infowar seriously. The first global cyberwar will be like no other war ever fought before—where the enemy is invisible, the battles virtual, and the casualties all too real. Special committees in every branch of the U.S. armed forces are studying the potential of infowar, both as a defensive and an offensive weapon. The National Security Agency (NSA) is reportedly studying a rather imaginative arsenal of "info-weapons." Among the current possible offensive weapons are:

- Computer viruses, which could be fed into an enemy's computers either remotely or by "mercenary" technicians.
- Logic bombs, another type of virus which can lie dormant for years, until, upon receiving a particular signal, it would wake up and begin attacking the host system.
- "Chipping," a plan (originally proposed by the CIA, according to some sources) to slip booby-trapped computer chips into critical systems sold by foreign contractors to potentially hostile third parties (or recalcitrant allies?).

- Worms, whose purpose is to self-replicate ad infinitum, thus eating up a system's resources. An example is the infamous worm that crashed the entire internet network in 1994.

- Trojan horses, malevolent code inserted into legitimate programming to perform a disguised function.

- Backdoors and trapdoors, a mechanism built into a system by the designer, to give the manufacturer or others the ability to "sneak back into the system" at a later date by circumventing the need for access privileges.

A few other goodies in the arsenal of information warfare are devices for disrupting data flow or damaging entire systems, hardware and all. Among these, as explained in earlier chapters, are High Energy Radio Frequency (HERF) guns, which focus a high power radio signal on target equipment, putting it out of action; and, Electro-Magnetic Pulse (EMP) devices, which can be detonated in the vicinity of a target system. Such devices can destroy electronics and communications equipment over a wide area.

All of the preceding current and future offensive and defensive IW weapons arsenal will be discussed in specific detail next. Let's take a look.

YOU HAVEN'T SEEN ANYTHING LIKE WHAT IS COMING

Body count: 796. Cause: midair collision. The air traffic control system was "cybotagged." News reports indicate that FAA personnel complained that their radar screens were freezing, and were switching data tags (such as aircraft altitude data) between close-flying planes. Series of near-misses in skies throughout the country—and one head-on collision between passenger jets in a thunderstorm over New York, resulting in the deaths of all aboard. It's suspected that the automated route and altitude management program's collision-avoidance algorithm was damaged.

Body count: 1,807. Cause: midair collision with a structure. The navigation system of another passenger jet was taken over by hackers, leaving the pilots helpless as the jet nose-dived into the Sears Towers in Chicago. No reports yet on how the hackers got in. A couple of hit sites have posted theories, some of them pretty good.

A message posted to 60,000 newsgroups from a group known as "The Vulture of Jihad" claimed credit for the attack. As they're an obscure Sunni sect known for abjuring the use of any technology, their claim, made during prayers in a mosque in Aleppo, was disregarded. Other Islamic splinter groups also claimed credit, along with a white supremacist faction and an anarchist syndicate. These claims were swiftly dismissed, too: All were missing the digital signature which the Islamic Liberation Army (ILA) had in both previous site hacks. The most outrageous theory as to the identity of the people responsible for the attack came on a hit site called the

"Hit Theorist." It says the whole thing is a CIA, NSA, and DOD plot to generate support in Congress for increased spending of military and Black Ops operations.

Do these scenarios sound like spin-offs from Fox's *X-Files*: "The Lone Gunmen"? Perhaps! But could it happen? You bet!

The E-Bomb: A Weapon of Electrical Mass Destruction

Perhaps the most dangerous of all of defensive and offensive weapons in the IW arsenal of the future is the E-Bomb. High Power Electro-Magnetic Pulse generation techniques and High Power Microwave (HPM) technology have matured to the point where practical E-Bombs (Electromagnetic bombs) are becoming technically feasible, with new applications in both strategic and tactical information warfare. The development of conventional E-Bomb devices allows their use in non-nuclear confrontations. This part of the chapter discusses aspects of the technology base, weapon delivery techniques and proposes a foundation for the use of such devices in warhead and bomb applications.

The prosecution of a successful Information Warfare (IW) campaign against an industrialized or post-industrial opponent will require a suitable set of tools. The efficient execution of an IW campaign against a modern industrial or post-industrial opponent will require the use of specialized tools designed to destroy information systems. E-Bombs (also popularized by USA's futuristic sci-fi show "Dark Angel") built for this purpose, can provide, where delivered by suitable means, an effective tool for this purpose.

The EMP Effect

The ElectroMagnetic Pulse (EMP) effect was first observed during the early testing of high-altitude airburst nuclear weapons. The effect is characterized by the production of a very short (hundreds of nanoseconds) but intense electromagnetic pulse, which propagates away from its source with ever-diminishing intensity, governed by the theory of electromagnetism. The ElectroMagnetic Pulse is, in effect, an electromagnetic shock wave.

NOTE

EMP stands for electromagnetic pulse. The source can be a nuclear or a non-nuclear detonation. It can be used by special forces teams who infiltrate the enemy's and detonate a device near their electronic devices. It destroys the electronics of all computer and communication systems in a quite large area. The EMP bomb can be smaller than a HERF gun to cause a similar amount of damage and is typically used to damage not a single target (not aiming in one direction) but to damage all equipment near the bomb.

This pulse of energy produces a powerful electromagnetic field, particularly within the vicinity of the weapon burst. The field can be sufficiently strong to produce short-lived transient voltages of thousands of Volts (kiloVolts) on exposed electrical conductors, such as wires, or conductive tracks on printed circuit boards, where exposed.

It is this aspect of the EMP effect that is of military significance, as it can result in irreversible damage to a wide range of electrical and electronic equipment, particularly computers and radio or radar receivers. Subject to the electromagnetic hardness of the electronics, a measure of the equipment's resilience to this effect, and the intensity of the field produced by the weapon, the equipment can be irreversibly damaged or, in effect, electrically destroyed. The damage inflicted is not unlike that experienced through exposure to close proximity lightning strikes, and may require complete replacement of the equipment, or at least substantial portions thereof.

Commercial computer equipment is particularly vulnerable to EMP effects, as it is largely built up of high-density Metal Oxide Semiconductor (MOS) devices, which are very sensitive to exposure to high-voltage transients. What is significant about MOS devices is that very little energy is required to permanently wound or destroy them; any voltage typically in excess of ten volts can produce an effect termed "gate breakdown," which effectively destroys the device. Even if the pulse is not powerful enough to produce thermal damage, the power supply in the equipment will readily supply enough energy to complete the destructive process. Wounded devices may still function, but their reliability will be seriously impaired. Shielding electronics by equipment chassis provides only limited protection, as any cables running in and out of the equipment will behave very much like antennae, in effect, guiding the high-voltage transients into the equipment.

Computers used in data processing systems; communications systems; displays; industrial control applications, including road and rail signaling; and those embedded in military equipment, such as signal processors, electronic flight controls, and digital engine control systems, are all potentially vulnerable to the EMP effect.

Other electronic devices and electrical equipment may also be destroyed by the EMP effect. Telecommunications equipment can be highly vulnerable, due to the presence of lengthy copper cables between devices.[i] Receivers of all varieties are particularly sensitive to EMP, as the highly sensitive miniature high-frequency transistors and diodes in such equipment are easily destroyed by exposure to high-voltage electrical transients. Therefore, radar and electronic warfare equipment, satellite, microwave, UHF, VHF, HF, and low-band communications equipment and television equipment are all potentially vulnerable to the EMP effect. It is significant that modern military platforms are densely packed with electronic equipment, and unless these platforms are well hardened, an EMP device can substantially reduce their function or render them unusable.

Because UE occurs at relatively low power levels, the use of this detection method prior to the outbreak of hostilities can be difficult, as it may be necessary to overfly hostile territory to find signals of usable intensity. The use of stealthy reconnaissance aircraft or long range, stealthy Unmanned Aerial Vehicles (UAV) may be required. The latter also raises the possibility of autonomous electromagnetic-warhead-armed expendable UAVs, fitted with appropriate homing receivers. These would be programmed to loiter in a target area until a suitable emitter is detected, upon which the UAV would home in and expend itself against the target.

The Delivery of Conventional Electromagnetic Bombs

As with explosive warheads, electromagnetic warheads will occupy a volume of physical space and will also have some given mass (weight) determined by the density of the internal hardware. Like explosive warheads, electromagnetic warheads may be fitted to a range of delivery vehicles.

Known existing applications involve fitting an electromagnetic warhead to a cruise missile airframe. The choice of a cruise missile airframe will restrict the weight of the weapon to about 340 kg (750 lb), although some sacrifice in airframe fuel capacity could see this size increased. A limitation in all such applications is the need to carry an electrical energy storage device (a battery), to provide the current used to charge the capacitors used to prime the FCG prior to its discharge. Therefore, the available payload capacity will be split between the electrical storage and the weapon itself.

In wholly autonomous weapons such as cruise missiles, the size of the priming current source and its battery may well impose important limitations on weapon capability. Air-delivered bombs, which have a flight time between tens of seconds to minutes, could be built to exploit the launch aircraft's power systems. In such a bomb design, the bomb's capacitor bank can be charged by the launch aircraft enroute to target, and after release a much smaller onboard power supply could be used to maintain the charge in the priming source prior to weapon initiation.

An electromagnetic bomb delivered by a conventional aircraft can offer a much better ratio of electromagnetic device mass to total bomb mass, as most of the bomb mass can be dedicated to the electromagnetic-device installation itself. It follows, therefore, that for a given technology an electromagnetic bomb of identical mass to an electromagnetic-warhead-equipped missile can have a much greater lethality, assuming equal accuracy of delivery and technologically similar electromagnetic device design.

A missile-borne electromagnetic warhead installation will comprise the electromagnetic device, an electrical energy converter, and an onboard storage device such as a battery. As the weapon is pumped, the battery is drained. The electromagnetic device will be detonated by the missile's onboard fusing system. In a cruise missile, this will be tied to the navigation system; in an antishipping missile, the radar seeker; and in an air-to-air missile, the proximity fusing system. The warhead fraction (ratio of total payload [warhead] mass to launch mass of the weapon) will be between 15% and 30%.

An electromagnetic bomb warhead will comprise an electromagnetic device, an electrical energy converter, and an energy storage device to pump and sustain the electromagnetic device charge after separation from the delivery platform. Fusing could be provided by a radar altimeter fuse to airburst the bomb, a barometric fuse or in GPS/inertially guided bombs, the navigation system. The warhead fraction could be as high as 85%, with most of the usable mass occupied by the electromagnetic device and its supporting hardware.

Due to the potentially large lethal radius of an electromagnetic device, compared to an explosive device of similar mass, standoff delivery would be prudent. Although this is an inherent characteristic of weapons such as cruise missiles, potential applications of these devices to glidebombs, antishipping missiles and air-to-air missiles would dictate fire and forget guidance of the appropriate variety, to allow the launching aircraft to gain adequate separation of several miles before warhead detonation.

The recent advent of GPS satellite[iii] navigation guidance kits for conventional bombs and glidebombs has provided the optimal means for cheaply delivering such weapons. Although GPS-guided weapons without differential GPS enhancements may lack the pinpoint accuracy of laser- or television-guided munitions, they are still quite accurate (CEP \(~~ 40 ft), cheap, and autonomous all-weather weapons (see sidebar, "Helping Hackers Take Control of Military Satellites").

HELPING HACKERS TAKE CONTROL OF MILITARY SATELLITES

Defense contractor Exigent International Inc. recently disclosed that an unknown number of hackers broke into a U.S. Navy computer system and made off with source code that controls dozens of military and commercial satellite systems around the world. The Melbourne, Florida-based company indicated that the incident, which occurred December 24, 2000, may have compromised a small portion of an older version of its OS/COMET software that was stored on a computer at the Naval Research Laboratory in Washington. OS/COMET is commercial software that allows ground station operators to monitor satellite systems and communicate commands to those systems.

Only a portion of an older version of the source code was downloaded. Because one of Exigent's government customers was the target of this cyber crime, Exigent is working closely with, as well as domestic law enforcement and international organizations to remedy the breach of security.

However, experts agree that it is unclear how much damage the compromise has done to the security of dozens of military navigation and commercial communications satellites that use the software. Although the FBI has declined to comment on the investigation, the incident has been traced to systems in Sweden and a university in Kaiserslautern, Germany.

Hypothetically, the source code might allow an adversary to identify flaws that could be exploited at a later date to disrupt communications. But that's a lot easier said than done.

Although the OS/COMET software is now a commercial product, it started as a classified defense program in the 1980s. If the control systems using it left themselves open to penetration, possession of the source code could help figure out how to write malicious commands that could be sent to the satellites.

In addition to the Air Force's 24 NAVSTAR global positioning system (GPS) satellites, OS/COMET is used by the entire constellation of more than 70 satellites owned by Iridium LLC. The software is also used by several NASA programs, direct broadcast, and Internet satellite systems operated by DACOM, one of the largest telecommunications companies in Korea, and Food Automation-Service Techniques Inc., a Stratford, Connecticut-based manufacturer of electronic controls to major restaurant chains and commercial appliance manufacturers.

Word of the theft comes after the national Counterintelligence Center recently issued its annual report to Congress on foreign industrial espionage operations targeted at U.S. high-tech companies involved in military contracts. The report identified satellite communications systems technology as among the top four technologies most often targeted by foreign espionage efforts.

Countries with less developed industrial sectors often prefer older off-the-shelf hardware and software. They will also seek military technologies that are at least a generation old because such technologies cost less, are easier to procure, and are more suitable for integration into their military structures.

There's a tremendous amount you can learn from the code. Although military and commercial satellite control links are typically protected by encryption, companies should still be concerned about having a portion of this source code out in the open.

Clearly, it could help a hacker take control of a system. You want to control this information because all of a sudden hackers have all sorts of new tricks to exploit systems.

The companies and agencies affected by the theft should begin to "carefully consider" how this software is used and how the systems connect. They need to review what the access mechanisms to these systems look like. However, it doesn't seem that these are easily accessible Internet systems.

Still, a major software revision may be necessary if the investigation uncovers more damage than originally thought. Because the intruder was detected, that should make it possible to minimize the practical consequences of the incident by revising the source code if necessary. This is probably just another case of cyber-vandalism. It's aggravating, but it's a fact of life.

The USAF has recently deployed the Northrop GPS-Aided Munition (GAM) on the B-2 bomber, and will then deploy the GPS/inertially guided GBU-29/30 Joint Direct Attack Munition (JDAM) and the AGM-154 Joint Stand-Off Weapon (JSOW) glidebomb. Other countries are also developing this technology. For example, the Australian BAeA Agile Glide Weapon (AGW) glidebomb is achieving a glide range of about 140 km (75 nmi) when launched from that altitude.

The importance of glidebombs as delivery means for HPM warheads is three-fold. First, the glidebomb can be released from outside the effective radius of target air defenses, therefore minimizing the risk to the launch aircraft. Second, the large standoff range means that the aircraft can remain well clear of the bomb's effects. Finally the bomb's autopilot may be programmed to shape the terminal trajectory of the weapon, such that a target may be engaged from the most suitable altitude and aspect.

A major advantage of using electromagnetic bombs is that they may be delivered by any tactical aircraft with a nav-attack system capable of delivering GPS-guided munitions. As you can expect GPS-guided munitions to be become the standard weapon in use by Western air forces in the 21st century, every aircraft capable of delivering a standard guided munition also becomes a potential delivery vehicle for an electromagnetic bomb. Should weapon ballistic properties be identical to the standard weapon, no software changes to the aircraft would be required.

Because of the simplicity of electromagnetic bombs in comparison with weapons such as Anti Radiation Missiles (ARM), it is not unreasonable to expect that these should be both cheaper to manufacture and easier to support in the field, thus allowing for more substantial weapon stocks. In turn, this makes saturation attacks a much more viable proposition.

Defense against Electromagnetic Bombs

The most effective defense against electromagnetic bombs is to prevent their delivery by destroying the launch platform or delivery vehicle, as is the case with nuclear weapons. This however may not always be possible, and, therefore, systems that can

Computer Viruses

A virus is a code fragment that copies itself into a larger program, modifying that program. A virus executes only when its host program begins to run. The virus then replicates itself, infecting other programs as it reproduces.

Viruses are well known in every computer-based environment, so that it is not astonishing that this type of rough program is used in information warfare. One could imagine that the CIA (or Army, Air Force, etc.) inserts computer viruses into the switching networks of the enemy's phone system. As today's telephone systems are switched by computers, you can shut them down, or at least causing massive failure, with a virus as easy as you can shut down a "normal" computer.

Worms

A worm is an independent program. It reproduces by copying itself in full-blown fashion from one computer to another, usually over a network. Unlike a virus, it usually doesn't modify other programs.

Also, if worms don't destroy data, they can cause the loss of communication by merely eating up resources and spreading through the networks. A worm can also easily be modified so that data deletion or worse occurs. With a "wildlife" like this, you could imagine breaking down a networked environment such as a ATM and banking network.

Trojan Horses

A Trojan horse is a code fragment that hides inside a program and performs a disguised function. It's a popular mechanism for disguising a virus or a worm.

A Trojan horse could be camouflaged as a security-related tool, for example, like SATAN (Security Administrating Tool for Analyzing Networks). SATAN checks UNIX system for security holes and is freely available on the Internet. If someone edits this program so that it sends discovered security holes in an e-mail message back to him (Let's also include the password file? No problem.), the Cracker learns much information about vulnerable hosts and servers. A cleverly written Trojan horse does not leave traces of its presence and, because it does not cause detectable damage, it is hard to detect.

Logic Bombs

A logic bomb is a type of Trojan horse, used to release a virus, a worm, or some other system attack. It's either an independent program or a piece of code that's been planted by a system developer or programmer.

With the overwhelming existence of U.S.-based software (MS Windows or UNIX systems), the U.S. Government, or whomever you would like to imagine, could decide that no software would be allowed to be exported from that country without a Trojan horse. This hidden function could become active when a document with "war against the USA" exists on the computer. Its activation could also be triggered from the outside. An effect could be to format the computers hard disks or to mail the document to the CIA.

Trap Doors

A trap door, or a back door, is a mechanism that's built into a system by its designer. The function of a trap door is to give the designer a way to sneak back into the system, circumventing normal system protection.

As previously mentioned, all U.S. software could be equipped with a trap door that would allow IW agencies to explore systems and the stored data on foreign countries. This could be most useful in cases of military strategic simulations and plans and would provide the DoD's intelligence with vital information.

Chipping

Just as software can contain unexpected functions, it is also possible to implement similar functions in hardware. Today's chips contain millions of integrated circuits that can easily be configured by the manufacturer so that they also contain some unexpected functions. They could be built so that they fail after a certain time, blow up after they receive a signal on a specific frequency, or send radio signals that allow identification of their exact location—the number of possible scenarios exceeds, by far, the scope of this chapter. The main problem with chipping is that the specific (adapted) chip be installed in the place that is useful for the information warrior. The easiest solution is to build the additional features into all the chips manufactured in the country that is interested in this type of IW.

Nano Machines and Microbes

In the future, Nano machines and microbes will provide the possibility to cause serious harm to a system. Unlike viruses, you can use these to attack not the software, but the hardware of a computer system. Nano machines are tiny robots (smaller than ants) that could be spread at an information center of the enemy. They crawl through the halls and offices until they find a computer. They are so small that they enter the computer through slots and shut down electronic circuits.

Another way to damage the hardware is a special breed of microbes. It is known that this special breed of microbes can eat oil, but what about if they were bred for eating silizium? They would destroy all integrated circuits in a computer lab, a site, a building, a town, and so on. Anyway, nano technology and microbes will be discussed in much greater detail later in the chapter.

Electronic Jamming

In the old days (and even today) electronic jamming was used to block communications channels at the enemy's equipment so that they couldn't receive any information. The next step is not to block their traffic, but, instead, overwhelm them with incorrect information—otherwise known as disinformation.

NEW TOYS FOR BIG BROTHER AND THE BOYS

GPS receivers: One of the newest and probably most important of the IW toys for Big Brother and the boys, will be everywhere soon—in cars, boats, planes, backpacks, briefcases, purses, jackets, and pants pockets. The good news is, you'll always know exactly where you are. The bad news is, so will everyone else.

Most humans who have ever lived have known roughly where they were, day-by-day, year-by-year. Not in abstract terms, of course, but in the terms of experience and familiarity—by neighborhood, not map. For eons, we've known things about ourselves that could be expressed in a statement like "I'm standing on the threshing floor in the village of my birth." or "I'm walking across the mid-morning shadow cast by Notre Dame." Or even "I'm in a part of town I've never seen before." Whether one utters it or not, this awareness of "whereness" is part of the meaning of being human. But for centuries, a dedicated band of mapmakers, navigators, astronomers, inventors, and mathematicians has tried to turn this innate sense of place into a more precise determination of position that is intelligible to anyone, not only to locals. On one level, this is like the difference between knowing you're coming to the corner where you always turn left on your way to the grocery store and knowing the names of the streets that cross at that intersection. On another level, however, the pursuit of pure position is about to lead us into a world that none of us has ever seen. The agent of change will be GPS—the Global Positioning System, which, like so many tools of the modern world, is both familiar and misunderstood at the same time.

Until recently, not a single human-made object has ever known where it was. Even a venerable tool of navigation such as a sextant knows nothing more about its location than does the *Mona Lisa* or the pigments of which she is painted. So imagine a world in which man-made objects know where they are and can communicate that information to other self-locating, communicating objects. This sounds as strange and surprising as the Marauder's Map in the "Harry Potter" novels for children.[iv] The Marauder's Map shows the position and movement of every animate creature at the school of wizardry called Hogwarts. A Marauder's Map of the world would be even stranger. It would show the position and movement (even a history of movements) of man-made objects as well. This would be an ever-changing map or a world filled with artifacts busily announcing something significant about themselves to each other and to anyone else who cared to listen.

That world is nearly here. In August 2000, a company called SiRF Technology based in Santa Clara, California, announced that it had developed an advanced GPS chip no bigger than a postage stamp. SiRF's vision is to bring location awareness to virtually everything that moves. This is a subtle but profound change in the history of GPS technology—a change driven, like everything else these days, by increasing miniaturization and declining prices for sophisticated circuitry. In the past few years, consumers have grown used to the sight of hand-held GPS receivers, which have been marketed as individual positioning devices for anglers, hunters, hikers, and cyclists. But what SiRF and other companies have in mind, is conferring upon objects a communicable sense of place. One day soon, most GPS devices will not be stand-alone receivers used by those of us who venture off the beaten path, but integral components of everyday objects.

Some of these objects, especially the big ones, are easy enough to imagine, because they exist now. Boats and ships of every kind already incorporate GPS technology as do some automobiles made by Toyota, Honda, Lexus, and Cadillac. So do the newest farm implements, such as combines that allow farmers to map crop yields in precise detail. But some uses of GPs that are not yet widely available will soon be common in smaller devices. Beginning in 2002, for instance, the Federal Communications Commission will require cellular-phone service providers to be able to identify the location of a cell-phone caller who dials 911. This means that most cell phones will likely include a tiny GPS chip. So will beepers and watches and hand-held digital assistants and, who knows, Game Boy Colors, Tamagotchis (virtual game animals), dog collars, and, probably, handguns as well.

The spreading of a technology such as GPS is easy enough to predict, but it's much harder to foresee what the effect of that spreading may be. There's always a limit to how far one can see into the future of the tools being used, especially into a future where those tools become interlinked. There was a time (only as long ago as Bill Gates's first book) when the value of computers was believed to lie mainly in their stand-alone power, not in the networks they might form when linked together. Now there's the Internet and the World Wide Web, whose far-reaching implications are only dimly visible, but which have already transformed the way countries all over the world do business.

The development of GPS technologies may follow a similar pattern. It's already obvious how useful GVS is in discrete applications: for surveying and mapmaking, the tracking of commercial vehicles, maritime and aeronautic navigation, and for use by emergency rescue crews and archaeologists. But there is simply no telling what it will mean when, on a planet full of location-aware objects, a way is found to coordinate all the data they send out. Awareness may be a metaphor when applied to inanimate objects, but the potential of that metaphor is entirely literal.

In the meantime, for most of us, there is still a more basic question to be answered: Where did GPS technology come from and how does it work?

GPS depends on an array of 27 satellites (24 in regular use, plus spares) flying some 11,000 miles above Earth. They were put there by the Department of Defense, which began the NAVSTAR global positioning system program in 1973. A version of GPS was first tested in 1964, when the Navy deployed a five-satellite prototype, called "Transit," for submarines. It could take an hour and a half for a Transit satellite to saunter above the horizon and then another 10 or 15 minutes to fix the submarine's position. The current generation of satellites was built by The Boeing Company and Lockheed Martin, and each one orbits the planet in about 12 hours, cutting across the equatorial plane at an angle of roughly 55 degrees. The U.S. Air Force tracks the satellites from Colorado Springs, Hawaii, and three other islands: Ascension in the South Atlantic, Diego Garcia in the Indian Ocean, and Kwajalein in the South Pacific. These ground stations provide the satellites with navigational information, which the next generation of satellites will be able to supply to each other. Ordinary users can track this constellation of satellites with one of several Web sites or with an appealing public-domain software program called "Home Planet," which can map any satellite you choose, GPS or not, against a projection of the Earth's surface. Or you can track the satellites with a GPS receiver.

In the world of GPS, knowing where you are, give or take a few meters, depends on knowing precisely when you are. Just as longitude couldn't be effectively calculated until 1764, when John Harrison's chronometer was tested on a voyage to Barbados, so GPS couldn't be created until there was a way to mount highly accurate clocks in stable orbits. The problem with finding longitude in Harrison's era was making a chronometer that could keep accurate time at one location (Greenwich, England) even while the ship carrying that chronometer was halfway around the globe. The chronometer provides a constant frame of reference for the celestial events that shift as a ship moves eastward or westward.

GPS satellites effortlessly provide a constant frame of reference. Each carries three or four ultra-precise clocks synchronized to GPS time—which is, essentially, Coordinated Universal Time (UTC) without the leap seconds. The satellite clocks are accurate to within one-millionth of a second of UTC as kept by the U.S. Naval Observatory. The GPS receiver translates the time that the satellites transmit into local time. In fact, as far as most civilian users are concerned, GPS is more accurate for time than it is for position. And, in most cases, GPS is far more accurate for position than it is for altitude. In 1764, Greenwich time was available only in Greenwich (on the meridian running through England, if you knew where that was) and in the presence of a properly maintained chronometer, of which there were two. Now, GPS time is available globally to anyone with a receiver.

When you turn on a GPS receiver, it tunes itself to a radio signal called "L_1," which comes from any GPS satellite—usually one of four to eight—coasting above the horizon. The American military and other authorized users also receive two encrypted signals—one from L_1, another from a frequency called "L_2." Those extra signals are one of the reasons military users can fix their location more precisely than civilian users can. By measuring the time it takes a signal to reach it, a GPS receiver calculates what is called the pseudo-range to the transmitting satellite. With at least four satellites in view, and, hence, four pseudo-ranges (the minimum for determining accurate location plus time), a GPS receiver can compute its position using basic trigonometry. It can also calculate velocity by comparing location readings taken at different points in time.

The real value of GPS begins to emerge when you consider a GPS receiver's ability to compare where it is now with where it was moments or hours or days ago. When you begin to move, a GPS springs to life. It announces your directional bearing, average speed, approximate altitude, the estimated time to get to a named destination, the degree to which you're adhering to a planned path, and the distance to your destination—in short, it calibrates the dimensions of your dynamism or the dynamism of anything you attach it to, from a delivery truck to an outcropping of the Earth's crust. A navigator's task has always been to plot his current position, compare it with his previous day's position, and deduce from those two points some idea of tomorrow's position. These are the functions inherent, and almost instantly accessible, in a dynamic tracking system such as GPS. It's no wonder GPS has rapidly made its way into the navigation stations of recreational boats and commercial ships alike, replacing older electronic navigation systems as well as celestial navigation.

But for civilian GPS users, there is a catch. The system is purposely compromised, its accuracy intentionally degraded. GPS was designed, as the responsible federal agencies are careful to remind us, to serve "as a dual-use system with the primary purpose of enhancing the effectiveness of U.S. and allied military forces." One way to do that is to de-enhance everyone else's effectiveness—to deny nonmilitary users and foreign adversaries the kind of accuracy that military users enjoy, which in all kinds of targeting weapons is a difference of dozens of feet. This has been done by selectively and intermittently introducing error into the information GPS satellites dispense to receivers lacking access to the military's encrypted signals—in other words, to the receivers nonmilitary users and foreign adversaries can buy. One of the many ironies of GPS, however, is that a system designed mainly for military use and developed through the Department of Defense at a cost of more than $10 billion has been engulfed by the commercial market. The result is that "Selective Availability," as GPS's intentional error is called, will most likely be phased out within the next decade.

Under many networking protocols, data that you transmit gets split into small segments, or packets, and the Internet Protocol address of the destination computer is written into the header of each packet. These packets then get passed around by routers and eventually make their way to the network segment that contains the destination computer.

As each packet travels around that destination segment, the network card on each computer on the segment examines the address in the header. If the destination address on the packet is the same as the IP address of the computer, the network card grabs the packet and passes it on to its host computer.

Promiscuous Network Cards

Packet sniffers work slightly differently. Instead of just picking up the packets that are addressed to them, they set their network cards to what's known as "promiscuous mode" and grab a copy of every packet that goes past. This lets the packet sniffers see all data traffic on the network segment to which they're attached—if they're fast enough to be able to process all that mass of data, that is. This network traffic often contains very interesting information for an attacker, such as user identification numbers and passwords, confidential data—anything that isn't encrypted in some way.

This data is also useful for other purposes—network engineers use packet sniffers to diagnose network faults, for example, and those in security use packet sniffers for their intrusion detection software. That last one is a real case of turning the tables on the attackers: Hackers use packet sniffers to check for confidential data; companies use packet sniffers to check for hacker activity. That has a certain elegant simplicity to it.

The thing that worries most people about *Sniffit* is how easy it is to install. It takes about three commands and three minutes to get this thing installed and running on a Linux machine. It even has a GUI (not exactly pretty, but it is free).

Like *Nmap*, *Sniffit* is easy to use and does exactly what it says it does: It sniffs your network and shows you what sort of data is getting passed around.

It is recommended that you install a packet sniffer and have a look at what sort of data you can see on your local network. Better still, get one of your network engineers to install it for you. They probably know of better, more professional sniffers and will be able to talk you through some of the data that you see going past. It's an interesting look into exactly what's going on within your network.

Sniff

A recent report submitted by the Illinois Institute of Technology's Research Institute (IITRI) in Lanham, Maryland, has not convinced security experts that Carnivore (the software created by the U.S. Federal Bureau of Investigation [FBI] to tap into Internet communications) is either ready to be used safely (without abuse) or can gather information that would be legally admissible in court.

Although *Carnivore* is the best software available for the job today, it is perhaps not as good as it could be. *Carnivore*'s source code should be made available for open review.

Such a review would provide confidence in *Carnivore*'s ability to gather information accurately and fairly—confidence needed to make it a publicly accepted crime-fighting instrument. Unless it is demonstrated that *Carnivore* will enable surveillance personnel to obtain the information they are authorized to see, and not draw innocent bystanders into its net, it will remain an object of public suspicion (see sidebar, "Privacy Concerns Remain").

PRIVACY CONCERNS REMAIN

Despite winning a favorable review by an outside group, the FBI's *Carnivore* Internet wiretap system continues to raise strong concerns about privacy and the legal limits of government surveillance.[v] The new report could mean further trouble for a system that has drawn criticism since its existence was first revealed in July 2000.

The new report responds to a review of *Carnivore* by the Illinois Institute of Technology's Research Institute, which released a draft report on November 17, 2000. While lauding the Justice Department and the Illinois group for a good-faith effort to examine the Internet wiretap system, the study was designed too narrowly to answer the most pressing questions.

The limited nature of the analysis described in the draft report simply cannot support a conclusion that *Carnivore* is correct, safe, or always consistent with legal limitations. Serious technical questions still remain about the ability of *Carnivore* to satisfy its requirements for security, safety, and soundness.

The Illinois review should have included a thorough search for programming flaws, and should have more deeply explored whether the system provides the kind of precise records that wiretapping calls for—especially in systems that can be operated remotely, such as *Carnivore*.

Carnivore is a modified version of a common piece of software known as a packet sniffer that is used by Internet service providers to maintain their networks.

The *Carnivore* version is installed during criminal investigations at the office of the suspect's Internet service provider.

The system has been used dozens of times in criminal and national security cases under federal wiretap authority. It is designed to be adjustable so that it can skim only some information from the flood of data that make up on-line communication. Law enforcement officials assert that it provides a tool for the Internet similar to "pen register" and "trap and trace" devices, which capture the telephone numbers of criminal suspects and those who call them.

What worries privacy advocates and lawmakers critical of *Carnivore* is that the Justice Department wants to follow the rules for pen registers in using the device. Those rules are far less restrictive than the regulations governing wiretaps. Justice Department officials confirmed that the system has been used, in most cases, under the less-restrictive rules.

Because the system can be used to collect much more than Internet addresses, lawmakers and civil liberties advocates contend that the government should not be able to use the less-stringent standards of proof. Another review of the Illinois report from the Privacy Foundation, which is based in Denver, sounded similar notes of concern about auditing *Carnivore*'s use and its place in the legal system.

Carnivore is, potentially, an appropriate law enforcement tool. But there are technical deficiencies that have to be addressed, as well as legal questions.

The legal framework for wiretapping must be revised for the digital age, and that the system must undergo continuing review. Software is a moving target, and a one-time review doesn't tell you what you need to know about future versions.

The FBI publicly admitted the existence of *Carnivore* in July 2000, after it had been in use for over a year at numerous Internet service providers (ISPs) and rumors of its existence began to surface. Congress and privacy advocates then called for full disclosure of the software. Replying that such disclosure would only help criminals get around the system, the FBI offered to let it be reviewed by an outside technical group selected by the Bureau. Illinois Institute of Technology's Research Institute (IITRI) was chosen after accepting the review limits proposed by the FBI, a stipulation other institutions such as the San Diego (California) Supercomputing Center (SDSC) would not accept.

The IITRI report does not address significant technical issues. Although it looks at how *Carnivore* worked when it was used as intended, the report failed to look at "the larger issue,": its system requirements. They did not look at the interaction between *Carnivore* and its host operating system or the interaction between *Carnivore* and the ISP's setup. Thus, the vulnerability of the system to hackers is still not clearly established.

Carnivore runs on Windows and, to control it, the person who is using it must be logged on at the highest level: administrator. At that level, the operator (meant to be an FBI agent) has a great deal of freedom. For instance, he or she can access the content of all communications, and change and edit files at will. What is more, anyone logged in as administrator can hide any evidence of the activity. Thus, it would be possible for an agent or someone who hacked into the system to tamper with evidence, plant false leads, or extract confidential information for bribery, extortion, fraud, and so on.

Failure to examine the interaction between *Carnivore* and an ISP's systems may be a gap in the report. The limited nature of IITRI's review cannot support a conclusion that *Carnivore* is accurate, safe, or always consistent with legal requirements. The scope of IITRI's review was dictated by the FBI, and any additional effort would have invalidated the contract under which the work was performed.

BEWARE: E-MAIL WIRETAPS LIKE CARNIVORE CAN STEAL SENSITIVE CORRESPONDENCE

Recently, the Privacy Foundation (see sidebar, "The Privacy Foundation") announced that a simple, hidden JavaScript code segment in HTML-formatted e-mail messages can effectively allow someone to monitor all succeeding messages that are forwarded with the original message included. Clearly, this can cause confidential internal communications to be compromised. Here's a look at how to identify wiretaps and protect yourself from them.

THE PRIVACY FOUNDATION

The Privacy Foundation at the University of Denver conducts research into communications technologies and provides the public with tools to maintain privacy in the information age. You can read the Foundation's report and commentary on e-mail wiretaps. The report cites the following possible uses for this security breach:

- The wiretaps can provide the ability to monitor the path of a confidential e-mail message and the written comments attached.
- In a business negotiation conducted via e-mail, one side can learn inside information from the other side as the proposal is discussed through the recipient company's internal e-mail system.
- A bugged e-mail message can capture thousands of e-mail addresses as the forwarded message is sent around the world.
- Commercial entities, particularly those based offshore, may seek to offer e-mail wiretapping as a service.

This security problem is a particularly dangerous one for organizations that conduct conversations containing sensitive internal information via e-mail. The usual scenario for such communication is that a message from an outside source is forwarded from executive to executive within a company, and it includes each person's comments. If there's an e-mail wiretap on the original external document, each time someone forwards the message to someone else, a copy of their message is automatically and invisibly e-mailed to the original sender of the external message (or someone designated by them).

This problem affects only HTML-enabled e-mail readers that have JavaScript turned on by default, such as Microsoft *Outlook, Outlook Express,* and *Netscape Communicator 6.1. Eudora* and *AOL 6.0* are not affected, nor are Web mail services such as *Yahoo* and *Hotmail.*

Snuff

As hackers obtain ever more dangerous and easy-to-use tools, they are being countered by novel defense strategies. The Pentagon envisions a war in the heavens, but can it defend the ultimate high ground? You bet! Witness the experimental idea of setting up a decoy network separate from your real one to fool intruders as they try to fool you.

Deception Network

This so-called "deception" network is envisioned as more than just a single server set up to be a "honeypot," where hackers may break in, find a dead-end, and have their activities recorded with an eye toward prosecution. Rather, the decoy net is an entire fake network, complete with host computers on a LAN with simulated traffic, to convince hackers for as long as possible that it's real.

Experts debate whether such nets will be worth the effort, but agree they can be a way to slow hackers long enough to sort the curious from the truly destructive "snuff." A group calling itself "The Honeynet Project" has quietly begun testing decoy networks on the Internet.

The Honeynet Project is not intended to prosecute intruders who haplessly wander into their elaborate decoys, but to study hacker responses in depth to devise the best decoy defenses. There are only a few commercial honeypot-style products on the market, including Network Associates *CyberCop Sting* and (from Recourse Technologies) *ManTrap.*

Other decoy networks do slow intruders with an eye toward collecting evidence to prosecute them. To collect evidence, you need to divert the hacker to a deception network. The idea is to feed back information about what hackers do to a kind of "deception central" for network administrators. The time the hackers are dealing with a deception environment, is time they're not in your network.

It is possible to create a deception network that has the same IP network address as your real network. Deception nets carry obvious administrative burdens, such as the need to generate realistic traffic to fool a hacker and maintain a network no one really uses.

There is a risk that administrators will lose track of what's real and what's not.

NOTE

These deception techniques have doubters. It's not clear yet if you can fool a lot of people with this deterrent. Meanwhile, hackers continue to learn new tricks.

The year 2000 has seen the emergence of a new breed of distributed port scanners and sniffers that make it easier for attackers to hide their intent. There's now a kernel-level root-kit for Linux, called *Knark*, which when installed by hackers changes the operating system to hide files and present false information to administrators. And another new one, called *Dsniff*, can be used to capture traffic on Ethernet switches and inject traffic into a network to direct traffic to itself, known as the man-in-the-middle attack.

It's pretty nasty stuff. For very sensitive networks, you may want to activate port-level security on your switches.

Many tools that let hackers carry out surveillance are now Web-based. Why Web-based? It's easy. No complicated downloads or zip files. They can hack from anywhere, and it's anonymous.

Although a talented few among hackers actually make attack tools, many of these tools today are freeware. And they're posted on dozens of techie sites, not the secret underground.

The tool, which involves launching an attack to determine operating system weakness, was given solely to vendors, but somehow ended up posted on the Packetstorm site in its depository for tools. In the wrong hands this tool is dangerous. But that version isn't as dangerous as other versions that will be released.

The New IW Space Race

The war was not going well. Serbian forces were sowing terror across Kosovo. NATO pilots squinting through clouds could do little to stop them. Errant NATO bombs had killed dozens of civilians and shaken support for the alliance. Then the Pentagon saw it had another problem. A Colorado outfit, called "Space Imaging," was about to launch a picture-taking satellite with clarity nearly as good as that of U.S. spy satellites. The company could have sold photos of NATO air bases or troop encampments to, say, Serbian operatives. That had to be stopped. But how?

The brass canvassed its experts for recommendations. The U.S.-licensed firm could simply be ordered not to take pictures over a broad swath of Europe. A similar ban could be issued for a few key areas, such as northern Albania. In the end, however, no order was issued. A malfunction sent Space Imaging's satellite plunging into the Pacific Ocean 30 minutes after it lifted off.

Fortune may not be so kind next time. Space Imaging launched another satellite and started selling pictures from it. Several other companies are right behind it. Before too long, an international bazaar for high-quality satellite imagery will be open for business. And potential foes are making headway with their own satellite capabilities. There's a new proliferation of space-based capabilities. Plus, the U.S.'s Cold War-era capabilities have atrophied.

That's pushing the Pentagon into a whole new kind of warfare. In the future, the U.S. military will be responsible for countering space systems and services used for hostile purposes. That's a nice way of saying the Pentagon needs to be prepared to defend the ultimate high ground by attacking hostile satellites. The new policy also directs the Space Command to start developing tactics and doctrine for conducting warfare in the heavens. It must also come up with plans for deploying space-based lasers or other weapons that could be used against targets anywhere on Earth or above it. If the United States ultimately deploys such weaponry, not only would it break one of the great taboos of the past 50 years, but it could also transform the way America structures its military and fights wars.

But aggressive "space control," as the military calls its quest for dominance in the sky, could backfire. The military view is that it would be the neatest thing in the world to have a death ray in space. But will deploying it lead to a war with somebody?

Very possibly, some critics say. Developing space weapons would be a mistake of historic proportions that would trigger an arms race in space. Imagine scenarios in which other nations follow the U.S. example and scramble to launch their own space weapons while frantic generals, unable to tell exactly who has put what into orbit, plead for extravagant countermeasures. In Pentagon war games, just trying to defend U.S. satellites causes problems. If you defend the satellite, you often widen the war. The activity ends up being the problem and not the solution.

SPY DUST BALLS AND MECHANICAL DRAGONFLIES

Now, let's look at some really "far out" IW arsenals of the future: spy dust and tiny mechanical robots. Let's look first at spies the size of a mote of dust. This will be followed by tiny robotic insects that may soon serve as military scouts.

Spy Dust Balls

"If only these walls could talk" may not be an idle plea much longer. Kris Pister, expectant father of an invention he calls "smart dust," thinks that in a few years almost anything, from a wall to a mote floating in the air, may have a story to tell. Thousands of these gossipy particles, each a tiny bundle of electronic brains, laser communications system, power supply, sensors, and even a propulsion system, could lurk all around, almost undetectable. One or more of the remote sensors would fit inside the letter "O."

Pister exemplifies the surging confidence of the leaders in a new field called "MEMS," which stands for microelectrical and mechanical systems. The idea is to build complex gadgets so small one needs a microscope to see the parts, using fabrication methods invented by the electronics industry for making silicon chips. He talks big and earnestly, even though the best his prototypes (an undustlike inch or so across) can do is exchange laser signals with a counterpart on a tennis court visible 600 yards away through his fifth-floor office window at the University of California-Berkeley. But that's enough to show that the components work. Miniaturizing them is well within current technology.

Tracking Tots

Cheap, dispersed sensors may tell farmers the exact condition of their acreage; manufacturers, the precise humidity and temperature history of their raw materials; parents, the locations and conditions of their small children all the time. Climate-control systems in buildings would know exactly where it is too cold, humid, hot, or drafty. In five years, smart dust could be linked by satellite. Eventually, you could log-on to readings from smart dust almost anywhere. One dream of Pister: explore outer space with smart dust. NASA could scatter smart dust sensors into the Martian atmosphere and they'd settle all over the planet (like in the recent movie "Red Planet").

But they could also be used as tiny spies. In 1992, as a new associate professor at the University of California-Los Angeles, Pister attended a RAND Corp. workshop in Santa Monica sponsored by the Pentagon's Defense Advanced Research Projects Agency. The topic was miniaturization of novel battlefield surveillance methods. The question was whether tiny electronic sensors could be scattered in contested territory to relay vital information back to commanders. You could find out, say, if a tank had gone by, or whether there was anthrax in the air. The concept sent his imagination racing.

Poppy Seeds

He coined the label "smart dust" in 1996 and expects to produce by mid-2002 the first complete smart-dust particle, about 1 millimeter on a side, or roughly between a poppy seed and a grape seed in size. None of the unit's components seems to present major fabrication obstacles. Before building the first fully small versions, however, the team wants to be sure it can get oversize prototypes to work. One of the students is working on a variant that will sport a thin, winglike extension, like that of a maple seed, so that a modest breeze will keep it aloft. Another student is designing a solid rocket micromotor, visible with a good magnifying glass, carved out of silicon. If a smart dust particle detects a tank going by, it could hop up and hitch a ride like a little spy. Some smart dust may be equipped with solar cells for power. Others might alight on vibrating machinery to soak up energy from the motion, or charge batteries off electromagnetic pulsations leaking from power lines. Sensors, at first, would be simple (such as for temperature, humidity, a few targeted chemicals, etc.) but eventually microphones and camera systems should be possible.

Pister tells the grad students and postdocs in the engineering school's smart dust group that above all, they must have a passion for new ideas and teamwork. He warns them against giving in to the "dark side," (Big Brother) against becoming stealth researchers whose distrust of others makes them, in his words, roach motels for information. Love of freely flowing communication is appropriate from a man who expects a tomorrow suffused with tiny snoops. He knows his ideas may occasionally serve nefarious ends, invading privacy or monitoring citizens of authoritarian governments. His reply to nervous objections is simple. "Information is good, and information flow reinforces democracy and not tyranny." Well, maybe!

Mechanical Dragonflies

The military calls it "situational awareness": the ability to detect how many hostile tanks await in the next valley, or if bombed-out buildings are filled with snipers. And it is an advantage that has proved difficult to attain: Spies, satellites, and U-2s have all failed to keep commanders from blundering into ambushes and mismatches. The worst thing is just not knowing where the enemy is. It's having the sense that somebody's out there trying to get you but having no idea of where the enemy might be.

Military researchers are working to free future American troops from the terror of the unknown. The researchers envision tomorrow's soldiers coming to a hill, halting, and reaching into their packs for cigar-shaped tubes. From every tube emerges a robotic spider, or a robotic dragonfly, each no longer than 3 inches. Equipped with cameras or acoustic sensors, the mechanical insects range forward and provide data on the hazards that lie in wait on the other side: the number of machine gun nests and the position of artillery.

Robotic Conundrum

Backed by $4.7 million from the Pentagon's Defense Advanced Research Projects Agency (DARPA), military researchers are designing such insect-inspired spies. Recently, the researchers built their first crawling bug prototypes, and they aim to perfect the design within two years. Insect-shaped "micro aerial vehicles" are next on the slate. Along with providing the military with state-of-the-art scouts, the researchers hope their project alters the way engineers approach the long-vexing problem of robotic locomotion.

In most robotic systems today, people think that if you want to move one joint, then you need to attach a motor at that joint. That makes for large, bulky, energy-hog robots. It also reduces robots to the ranks of expensive toys. Motors are only about 70% efficient in turning electrical power into movement. So, although robots may impress with their futuristic looks, most motor-driven devices have ranges limited to only a few dozen yards, rendering them useless for practical applications.

In the initial design, piezoelectric ceramics—thin, ceramic-coated metal wafers that bend when an electrical current is applied to their surfaces—were proposed. Such materials already are used commercially to make silent pagers vibrate or to make zoom lenses move strips (built from lead, zirconium, and titanium) that are sandwiched together, a structure known as a bimorph actuator. When charged, one half of the actuator expands while the other contracts, causing it to curve. When the brief energy pulse ends, the structure snaps back to its original form and then can begin the cycle anew. The researchers attached titanium legs to these vibrating strips. Vibration is translated into motion, as the crawler takes 2-millimeter-long forward strides in response to each oscillation.

Because piezoelectrics require only occasional energy boosts to keep up the vibration, the bugs promise to be up to 60% more energy efficient than traditional robots. If you're in a weight room and you lift 100 pounds up and down 10 times, that takes a lot of energy from a person (illustrating the principle behind the design). The same work could more easily be accomplished by hooking that weight to a spring on the ceiling, then displacing it a bit and letting it bounce up and down by itself. Another common analogy is a child on a swing set; once in motion, very little pumping action is required to keep moving. The bugs' energy efficiency should give them ranges of almost 600 yards, and allow them enough juice to carry such intelligence-oriented payloads as chip-size infrared detectors and quarter-size video cameras.

Natural Efficiency

The engineers' decision to model their robots after bugs was a natural choice: Biological systems are far more energy efficient than anything cooked up in the laboratory. Most things biological sort of oscillate as they walk. If you look at humans walking and the way our legs act as pendulums off our hips and swing back and forth, that's a cyclic motion. They were also impressed by the shape of daddy longlegs, whose low-slung bodies and inverted-V legs create a stable configuration—important for robots that will have to scamper across uneven, sometimes treacherous terrain. Additional hardiness comes from the solid-state legs, which are free of bearings, rods, or shafts that could get jammed by pebbles or dust. They probably won't survive being stomped on, but short of that they're pretty tough—they could actually survive four-story falls.

Before the bugs can be unleashed on the battlefield, however, a few major hurdles remain. Chief among them is a power problem; though the robots will require around 60 volts to start vibrating, the watch-size batteries being considered can provide only 3 to 6 volts. To get the bugs moving without the aid of chargers, circuitry must be developed to amplify the current, and it must be small enough to fit the 2-by-?-inch bugs. Still, the design's voltage requirement is impressively low; rival efforts to create locomotive robots of comparable size have needed well over 1,000 volts.

Another lingering question is how a robotic swarm can be controlled. With thousands of bugs roving at once, commanding each individual unit would be close to impossible. So, a battalion leader, outfitted with a remote control, would only have to control a "mother ship," an insect at the fore that would then relay instructions to other members of the swarm. In the event of the mother ship's destruction, the leadership role could be shifted to a surviving robot. The exact details of this control, however, have yet to be worked out.

Nevertheless, DARPA officials and the researchers are optimistic that the kinks can be worked out and that assembly-line production of the bugs is nearing. Along with the crawling prototype, the researchers have already managed to construct a piezoelectrically actuated thorax for the flier. Once all design issues are resolved, the researchers believe, the insects could cost as little as $10 per unit. The required metals are readily available, and the bimorph strips and legs can be cheaply pressed from large sheets.

The low price makes the insects potential candidates for a variety of uses, including delivering lethal toxins on the battlefield or aiding police SWAT teams. Or perhaps 40,000 of the mechanical creatures could be dropped on the Martian surface to probe the nooks and crannies Pathfinder missed. But those missions are far distant; the bugs' first and foremost duty will be to give American troops an upper hand and to save them from stumbling into situations too perilous to survive.

Finally, let's look at how machines the size of molecules are creating the next industrial revolution in information warfare.

NANOTECHNOLOGY

In 2000, a group of scientists from the University of Michigan's Center for Biologic Nanotechnology traveled to the U.S. Army's Dugway Proving Ground in Utah. The purpose of their visit: to demonstrate the power of "nano-bombs." These munitions don't exactly go "Kaboom!" They're molecular-size droplets, roughly 1/5000 the head of a pin, designed to blow up various microscopic enemies of mankind, including the spores containing the deadly biological warfare agent anthrax.

The military's interest in nano-bombs is obvious. In the test, the devices achieved a remarkable 100% success rate, proving their unrivaled effectiveness as a potential defense against anthrax attacks. Yet their civilian applications are also staggering. For example, just by adjusting the bombs' ratio of soybean oil, solvents, detergents, and water, researchers can program them to kill the bugs that cause influenza and herpes. Indeed, the Michigan team is now making new, smarter nano-bombs so selective that they can attack E. coli, salmonella, or listeria before they can reach the intestine.

If you're a fan of science fiction, you've no doubt encountered the term *nanotechnology*. Over the past 20 years, scores of novels and movies have explored the implications of mankind's learning to build devices the size of molecules. In a 1999 episode of *The X-Files* titled "S. R. 819," nanotechnology even entered the banal world of Washington trade politics, with various nefarious forces conspiring to pass a Senate resolution that would permit the export of lethal "nanites" to rogue nations.

Yet since 1999, a series of breakthroughs have transformed nanotech from sci-fi fantasy into a real-world, applied science, and, in the process, inspired huge investments by business, academia, and government. In industries as diverse as health care, computers, chemicals, and aerospace, nanotech is overhauling production techniques, resulting in new and improved products—some of which may already be in your home or workplace.

Silicon Fingers

Meanwhile, nearly every week, corporate and academic labs report advances in nanotech with broad commercial and medical implications. In 2000, for example, IBM announced it had figured out a way to use DNA to power a primitive robot with working silicon fingers 1/50 as thick as human hair. Within a decade or so, such devices may be able to track down and destroy cancer cells. Over at Cornell University, researchers have developed a molecular-size motor, built out of a combination of organic and inorganic components, that some dub nanotech's "Model T." In tests announced in 2000, the machine's rotor spun for 40 minutes at 3 to 4 revolutions per second. When further developed, such motors will be able to pump fluids, open and close valves, and power a wide range of nanoscale devices.

These inventions and products are just the beginning of what many observers predict will be a new industrial revolution fostered by man's growing prowess at manipulating matter one atom, or molecule, at a time. Because of nanotech, all of us will see more change in our civilization in the next 30 years than we did during all of the 20th century.

> *Nanotech takes its name from the nanometer, a unit of measurement just one billionth of a meter long.*

NOTE

Imagine the possibilities. Materials with 10 times the strength of steel and only a small fraction of the weight. Shrinking all the information housed at the Library of Congress into a device the size of a sugar cube. Or detecting cancerous tumors when they are only a few cells in size.

To build such objects, engineers are employing a wide range of techniques, borrowed from bioengineering, chemistry, and molecular engineering. Such feats include imitating the workings of the body, where DNA not only programs cells to replicate themselves but also instructs them how to assemble individual molecules into new materials such as hair or milk. In other words, many nanotech structures build themselves.

Atom by Atom

The inspiration for nanotech goes back to a 1959 speech by the late physicist Richard Feynman, titled "There's Plenty of Room at the Bottom." Feynman, then a professor at the California Institute of Technology, proposed a novel concept to his colleagues. Starting in the Stone Age, all human technology, from sharpening arrowheads to etching silicon chips, has involved whittling or fusing billions of atoms at a time into useful forms. But what if we were to take another approach, Feynman asked, by starting with individual molecules or even atoms, and assembling them one by one to meet our needs? The principles of physics, as far as Feynman could see, did not speak against the possibility of maneuvering things atom by atom.

Four decades later, Chad Mirkin, a chemistry professor at Northwestern University's $45 million nanotech center, used a nanoscale device to etch most of Feynman's speech onto a surface the size of about 10 tobacco smoke particles—a feat that Feynman would no doubt have taken as vindication. But the course science took to achieve such levels of finesse has not always been straightforward. Nor has it been lacking in controversy.

Indeed, some scientists are alarmed by nanotechnology's rapid progress. In 2000, the chief scientist at Sun Microsystems, created a stir when he published an essay in *Wired* magazine warning that in the wrong hands, nanotech could be more destructive than nuclear weapons. Influenced by the work of Eric Drexler, an early and controversial nanotechnology theoretician, the scientist predicted that trillions of self-replicating nanorobots could one day spin out of control, literally reducing the earth's entire biomass to "gray goo."

Most researchers in the field don't share that type of concern. They are compelled to keep going. Researchers are knocking on the door of creating new living things, new hybrids of robotics and biology. Some may be pretty scary, but they have to keep going.

The early payoffs have already arrived. Computer makers, for example, use nanotechnology to build "read heads," a key component in the $45-billion-a-year hard disk drive market, which vastly improve the speed at which computers can scan data. Another familiar product, Dr. Scholl's brand antifungal spray, contains nano-scale zinc oxide particles—produced by a company called Nanophase Technologies—that make aerosol cans less likely to clog. Nanoparticles also help make car and floor waxes that are harder and more durable and eyeglasses that are less likely to scratch. As these examples show, one huge advantage of nanotech is its ability to create materials with novel properties not found in nature or obtainable through conventional chemistry.

What accounts for the sudden acceleration of nanotechnology? A key breakthrough came in 1990, when researchers at IBM's Almaden Research Center succeeded in rearranging individual atoms at will. Using a device known as a scanning probe microscope, the team slowly moved 35 atoms to spell the three-letter IBM logo, thus proving Feynman right. The entire logo measured less than three nanometers.

Soon, scientists were not only manipulating individual atoms but also "spray painting" with them. Using a tool known as a molecular beam epitaxy, scientists have learned to create ultrafine films of specialized crystals, built up one molecular layer at a time. This is the technology used today to build read-head components for computer hard drives.

One quality of such films, which are known as giant magnetoresistant materials, (GMRs), is that their electrical resistance changes drastically in the presence of a magnetic field. Because of this sensitivity, hard disk drives that use GMRs can read very tightly packed data and do so with extreme speed. In a few years, scientists are expected to produce memory chips built out of GMR material that can preserve 100 megabits of data without using electricity. Eventually, such chips may become so powerful that they will simply replace hard drives, thereby vastly increasing the speed at which computers can retrieve data.

Natural Motion

The next stage in the development of nanotechnology borrows a page from nature. Building a supercomputer no bigger than a speck of dust might seem an impossible task, until one realizes that evolution solved such problems more than a billion years ago. Living cells contain all sorts of nanoscale motors made of proteins that perform myriad mechanical and chemical functions, from muscle contraction to photosynthesis. In some instances, such motors may be re-engineered, or imitated, to produce products and processes useful to humans.

Animals such as the abalone, for example, have cellular motors that combine the crumbly substance found in schoolroom chalk with a "mortar" of proteins and carbohydrates to create elaborate, nano-structured shells so strong they can't be shattered by a hammer. Using a combination of biotechnology and molecular engineering, humans are now on the verge of being able to replicate or adapt such motors to suit their own purposes.

How are these biologically inspired machines constructed? Often, they construct themselves, manifesting a phenomenon of nature known as self-assembly. The macromolecules of such biological machines have exactly the right shape and chemical-binding preferences to ensure that, when they combine, they will snap together in predesigned ways. For example, the two strands that make up DNA's double helix match each other exactly, which means that if they are separated in a complex chemical mixture, they are still able to find each other easily.

This phenomenon is potentially very useful for fabricating nanoscale products. For instance, in 1999, a team of German scientists attached building materials such as gold spheres to individual strands of DNA and then watched as the strands found each other and bound together the components they carried, creating a wholly new material.

Similarly, the 1996 Nobel Prize in chemistry went to a team of scientists for their work with "nanotubes"—a formation of self-assembling carbon atoms about 1/50,000 the width of a human hair. Scientists expect that when they succeed in weaving nanotubes into larger strands, the resulting material will be 100 times stronger than steel, conduct electricity better than copper, and conduct heat better than diamond. Membranes of such fibers should lead to rechargeable batteries many times stronger, and smaller, than today's.

In 2000, a team of IBM scientists announced that they had used self-assembly principles to create a new class of magnetic materials that could one day allow computer hard disks and other data-storage systems[vi] to store more than 100 times more data than today's products. Specifically, the researchers discovered certain chemical reactions that cause tiny magnetic particles, each uniformly containing only a few thousand atoms, to self-assemble into well-ordered arrays, with each particle separated from its neighbors by the same preset distance.

Other scientists have discovered important new self-assembling entities by accident. In 1996, Samuel Stupp, a professor at Northwestern University, was in his lab trying to develop new forms of polymer when he inadvertently came upon "nanomushrooms." He saw the potential right away. The molecules he had been experimenting with had spontaneously grouped themselves into supramolecular clusters shaped like mushrooms. Soon afterward, Stupp discovered, again accidentally, that he could easily program these supramolecules to form film that behaves like Scotch tape.

Meanwhile, researchers at UCLA and Hewlett-Packard have laid the groundwork for the world's first molecular computer. Eventually, the researchers hope to build memory chips smaller than a bacterium. Such an achievement is essential if computing power is to continue doubling every 18 to 24 months, as it has for the past four decades. This is because the more densely packed the transistors on a chip become, the faster it can process, and we are approaching the natural limit to how small transistors can be fabricated out of silicon.

Future Phenomena

Finally, where will it all end? Many futurists have speculated that nanotech will fundamentally change the human condition over the next generation. Swarms of programmable particles, sometimes referred to as "utility fog," will assemble themselves on command. The result could be a bottle of young wine molecularly engineered to taste as if it had aged for decades, or a faithful biomechanical dog with an on/off switch.

Meanwhile, new, superstrong, lightweight nanomaterials could make space travel cheap and easy and maybe even worth the bother, if, as some scientists predict, nanotech can be used to create an Earth-like atmosphere on Mars. And space colonization could well be necessary if the new science of "nanomedicine" extends life indefinitely, manufacturing new cells, molecule by molecule, whenever old cells wear out. It all seems hard to imagine; yet nanotech has already produced enough small wonders to make such big ideas seem plausible, if not alarming—at least to the high priests of science and the IW military strategists.

SUMMARY

Information technology is being developed by strategic planners both as an offensive battlefield weapon, and as a weapon for "logistics attack," as a means to disrupt the civilian infrastructure on which an enemy's military apparatus depends. Technology has already been used effectively by American forces in the Gulf War and in the conflict in Haiti.

However, information warfare is a double-edged sword. Those countries most capable of waging it are also the ones most vulnerable to it. The increasing dependence on sophisticated information systems brings with it an increased vulnerability to hostile elements and terrorists. The following are conclusions drawn from the information warfare arsenal of the future

Conclusions Drawn from the Information Warfare Arsenal of the Future

- Even though the anticipated national security threats of the coming decades involve less-developed countries, the CVW threat and other methods of intrusion and disruption are not necessarily beyond their reach.
- Opportunities to deceive and confuse through an elaborate misinformation scheme along a myriad of information paths are available to anyone.
- The information warfare arsenal of the future provides a new avenue to employ deception techniques through the use of multiple paths that create the perception and validation of truth.
- There exists the prospect of an intelligence analyst manipulating an adversary's command-and-control system so that reality is distorted
- Tomorrow's soldier will depend more than ever on the very well-known and trusted factors of mobility.
- Imagine a scenario depicting a "left hook" in the Iraqi desert that fails because the systems in use were successfully attacked by CVW, or some other intrusion method, with the resulting disruption putting U.S. troops in a flailing posture—facing the unknown and losing confidence in their operation.
- One thing is sure. An Iraqi "left hook" will be difficult to repeat.
- One can assume that Iraq, and others, will exploit the GPS to their own advantage. The information warfare arsenal is coming of age!
- World War II set the stage, but only with today's technology can we expect action in this sphere of warfare on a grand scale.
- The necessity to prevent irresponsible groups and individuals from getting access to nanotechnological manufacturing capability is a prime concern in the near future.
- The chapter has shown how this quest for containment has shaped many aspect of society, most notably via the institution of a global surveillance network.

An Agenda for Action in Preparing for the Information Warfare Arsenal of the Future

In the United States, where the threat is most immediately recognized, debate is currently going on to decide what part government can and should play in protecting civilian networks. On the one hand, the civilian networks are controlled by private interest groups, some of them internationally owned. Government regulation would seem to be interference or even repression. On the other hand, the vulnerability and ease of manipulation of some networks are weak links in modern society, and their exploitation by hostile elements threatens all elements of society, and not just the direct controllers of the networks. One solution is to require organizations with a dependence on sensitive information technology to fulfill certain security criteria before being issued a government license. Something like this has been done in Israel already, with the legislation of the "Computer Laws" of 1994.

The United States government needs to set an agenda for action that goes beyond the work already done in preparation for defending against the information warfare arsenal of the future. Action steps should include, but not be limited to the following 12 areas:

1. Identify substrate groups who have embraced the information revolution, as has the rest of society. Going a stage further and attacking the NII can certainly be an attractive option for substrate groups. However, as the PIRA case shows, to inflict even a portion of the disruption that the doomsday mongers suggest would require a tremendous investment in IPB, not to mention actually implementing the assault. More technology-savvy groups such as environmental protesters may, in fact, be the first to use offensive IW techniques but they will have limited aims and not pose a national security threat. It is likely to be some time yet before professional cyberterrorists become a significant IW threat.

2. Institute a review of national vulnerabilities to a IW arsenal of the future. This prospect leaves governments with a window of opportunity that needs to be seized. In the past, states have tended to react to changing terrorist threats rather than pre-empting them, and the substrate group usually retains the initiative. This may also be the case with cyberterrorism. As yet, though, there has not been national leadership of the sort provided by the White House and the Congress.

3. Proactively monitoring the threat, doing a holistic assessment of national vulnerabilities, and creating a rigorously enforced information assurance program can meet this new threat. Although it is obvious that the American NII is far more vulnerable to the IW arsenal of the future than the British NII, due to the far higher level of connectivity, there is little room for complacency. For once, the British government, in conjunction with its European partners, has the opportunity of staying ahead of an emerging threat from terrorist and other substrate groups. It will not be long before substrate groups graduate from exploiting the Internet for propaganda to using it offensively.

4. Conduct strategic IW campaigns. The introduction of non-nuclear electromagnetic bombs into the IW arsenal of a modern air force considerably broadens the options for conducting strategic campaigns. Clearly, such weapons are potent force multipliers in conducting a conventional war, particularly when applied to electronic combat, OCA, and strategic air attack operations.

5. Develop the use of IW weapons responsibly. The massed use of such IW weapons would provide a decisive advantage to any nation with the capability to effectively target and deliver them. The qualitative advantage in capability so gained would provide a significant advantage even against a much stronger opponent not in the possession of this capability.

6. Commit to strategic IW campaigns. Electromagnetic weapons however, open up less conventional alternatives for the conduct of a strategic campaign, which derive from their ability to inflict significant material damage without inflicting visible collateral damage and loss of life. Western governments have been traditionally reluctant to commit to strategic campaigns, as the expectation of a lengthy and costly battle, with mass media coverage of its highly visible results, will quickly produce domestic political pressure to cease the conflict.

7. Develop a strategy of graduated response. An alternative is a strategy of graduated response (SGR). In this strategy, an opponent who threatens escalation to a full-scale war is preemptively attacked with electromagnetic weapons, to gain command of the electromagnetic spectrum and command of the air. Selective attacks with electromagnetic weapons may then be applied against chosen strategic targets, to force concession. Should these fail to produce results, more targets may be disabled by electromagnetic attack. Escalation would be sustained and graduated, to produce steadily increasing pressure to concede the dispute. Air and sea blockades are complementary means via which pressure may be applied.

8. Develop advanced electromagnetic weapons. Because electromagnetic weapons can cause damage on a large scale very quickly, the rate at which damage can be inflicted can be very rapid, in which respect such a campaign will differ from the conventional, where the rate at which damage is inflicted is limited by the usable sortie rate of strategic air attack capable assets.

9. Implement a full-scale conventional strategic air attack campaign. Should blockade and the total disabling of vital economic assets fail to yield results, these may then be systematically reduced by conventional weapons, to further escalate the pressure. Finally, a full-scale conventional strategic air attack campaign would follow, to wholly destroy the hostile nation's warfighting capability.

10. Use the strategy of graduated response. Other situations where electromagnetic bombs may find useful application is in dealing with governments that actively implement a policy of state-sponsored terrorism or infoterrorism, or alternately choose to conduct a sustained low-intensity land warfare campaign. Again, the strategy of graduated response, using electromagnetic bombs in the initial phases, would place the government under significant pressure to concede.

11. The central theme here is the need to regulate nanotechnology because of its immense abuse potential.

12. Advanced nanotechnology should not be used to build small self-replicating machines that can feed on organic matter—a bit like bacteria but much more versatile, and potentially more destructive than the H-bomb.

ENDNOTES

i John R. Vacca, *The Cabling Handbook (2nd Edition)*, Prentice Hall, 2001.

ii John R. Vacca, *i-mode Crash Course*, McGraw-Hill, 2002.

iii John R. Vacca, *Satellite Encryption*, Academic Press, 1999.

iv J. K. Rowling, *Harry Potter and the Chamber of Secrets (Book 2)*, Scholastic Trade, 1999.

v John R. Vacca, *Net Privacy: A Guide to Developing & Implementing an Iron-clad ebusiness Privacy Plan*, McGraw-Hill, 2001.

vi John R. Vacca, *The Essential Guide to Storage Area Networks*, Prentice Hall, 2002.

17 Surveillance Tools for Information Warfare of the Future

Wireless systems capable of monitoring vehicles and people all over the planet (basically everything) are leaving businesses and the military aglow with new possibilities, and some privacy advocates deeply concerned. Companies seeking to tap the commercial potential of these technologies are installing wireless location systems in vehicles, hand-held computers, cellphones—even watchbands. Scientists have developed a chip that can be inserted beneath the skin, so that a person's location can be pinpointed anywhere.

For example, the owner of a small company in Dallas that installs automobile alarms, uses a wireless tracking service to monitor his fleet of six Dodge Dakota pickup trucks, and the equipment alerted him recently when one of his trucks turned up in the parking lot of the Million Dollar Saloon, a strip club. When he signed up for this service, he told his guys, "Big Brother's keeping an eye on you, and I'm Big Brother." After he fired that one fellow, you bet they all believed him.

These technologies have become one of the fastest-growing areas of the wireless communications industry. The market for location-based services is already estimated at nearly $700 million and is forecast to approach $6 billion by 2004.

MONITORING EVERYTHING

A federal effort to make it easier to pinpoint the location of people making emergency 911 calls from mobile phones means that by 2002, cell-phones sold in the United States will be equipped with advanced wireless tracking technology. Various plans already under way include alerting cell-phone users when they approach a nearby McDonald's, telling them which items are on sale, or sending updates to

469

travelers about hotel vacancies or nearby restaurants with available tables. One Florida company wants to provide parents with wireless watchbands that they can use to keep track of their children.

Although the commercial prospects for wireless location technology may be intriguing, and the social benefits of better mobile 911 service are undisputed, privacy-rights advocates are worried. By allowing location-based services to proliferate, you're opening the door to a new realm of privacy abuses. What if your insurer finds out you're into rock climbing or late-night carousing in the red-light district? What if your employer knows you're being treated for AIDS at a local clinic? The potential is there for inferences to be drawn about you based on knowledge of your whereabouts.

Until recently, location-based services belonged more in the realm of science fiction than to commerce. Although satellite-based Global Positioning System technology has been commercially available for some time for airplanes, boats, cars, and hikers, companies have only recently begun manufacturing GPS chips that can be embedded in wireless communications devices.[i] GPS uses satellite signals to determine geographic coordinates that indicate where the person with the receiving device is situated. (GPS monitoring technology will be discussed in much greater detail later in the chapter.)

Real-life improvements in the technology have come largely from research initiatives by start-up companies in the United States, Canada, and Europe as well as from large companies like IBM, which recently formed a "pervasive computing" division to focus on wireless technologies such as location-based services.

Location technology is a natural extension of ebusiness. It's no surprise that a whole new ecology of small companies has been formed to focus on making it all more precise.

For instance, Peter Zhou helped to create a chip called "Digital Angel" that could be implanted beneath human skin, enabling his company to track the location of a person almost anywhere using a combination of satellites and radio technology. After all, he reasoned, wouldn't the whereabouts of an Alzheimer's patient be important to relatives? Wouldn't the government want to keep track of paroled convicts? Wouldn't parents want to know where their children are at 10 P.M., 11 P.M., or any hour of the day?

A review of Digital Angel's commercial potential, though, revealed concern over the possibility of privacy abuses.[ii] So Professor Zhou, the chief scientist for Applied Digital Solutions, a company in Palm Beach, Florida, which makes embedded devices for tracking livestock, altered his plans for Digital Angel, which is about the size of a dime, so that instead of being implanted it could be affixed to a watchband or a belt.

Embedding technology in people is too controversial. But that doesn't mean a system capable of tracking people wherever they go won't have great value."

Although Digital Angel is still in the prototype stage, Applied Digital Solutions is planning to make it commercially available in 2002.

That Professor Zhou found himself in the middle of the privacy debate is no surprise, given the growing interest in location-based services. Through the use of existing cellular communications technology or the Global Positioning System, researchers' ability to track wireless devices more precisely is growing.[iii]

Some of the world's largest wireless carriers, such as Verizon Wireless, Vodafone of Britain, and NTT DoCoMo of Japan are promoting the technology, in addition to dozens of small companies in the United States and Europe.

The SignalSoft Corporation, based in Boulder, Colorado, develops software that allows tourists or business travelers to use their mobile phones to obtain information on the closest restaurants or hotels in a given city.[iv] Meanwhile Cell-Loc Inc., a Canadian company, is already testing a wireless service in Austin, Texas, and in Calgary, Alberta, that, after determining a caller's location, delivers detailed driving directions.

Some companies are even more ambitious. Webraska, a French company that recently secured $60 million in financing from investors in the United States and Europe, plans to map every urban area in the world and allow these maps to be retrieved in real time on wireless devices.

Yet while businesses around the world seek to improve the quality of location-based services, the biggest impetus behind the advancement of the technology has come from the federal government, through its effort to improve the precision of locating wireless 911 emergency calls. Nearly a third of the 260 million 911 calls made in 2000 came from cell phones, according to the National Emergency Number Association.

With the number of wireless users growing, the Federal Communications Commission has determined that by the end of 2002, carriers will need to begin equipping either cell-phones or their communications networks with technology that would allow authorities to determine the location of most callers to within 300 feet, compared with current systems that can locate them within about 600 feet. For example, Verizon Wireless and Western Wireless have chosen to develop a network-based system that pinpoints the signal on a handset using the existing cellular network to determine the location, whereas other carriers including Sprint PCS, Alltel, and Nextel favor handsets equipped with GPS chips. Supporters of the initiative, called "E-911" for "enhanced 911," expect the technology's precision to be even better than the federally mandated 300-foot radius.

If your cell-phone is on while you're driving, you'll be able to tell which intersection you're at. Although the E-911 initiative has driven wireless carriers in the

United States to improve their location technology, industry groups have started to grapple with privacy issues. The Wireless Advertising Association, a group of carriers, advertising agencies and device manufacturers, encourages companies to allow consumers to choose whether they want location-based services. The association will endorse companies that adhere to the policy.

And, late in 2000, the Cellular Telecommunications Industry Association, a Washington group that represents several hundred wireless companies, submitted a proposal for privacy guidelines for location-based wireless services to the Federal Communications Commission. The principles of the proposal suggested that companies inform each customer about the collection and use of location-sensitive information, provide customers with the opportunity to consent to the collection of location information before it is used, ensure the security of any information collected, and provide uniform rules and privacy expectations so consumers are not confused when they travel in different regions or use different kinds of location-based services.

People are justifiably concerned with the rapidity with which this technology is being deployed. They need to be assured that there is no conspiracy to use this information in an underhanded way.

CYBER SURVEILLANCE

Nicodemo S. Scarfo, the son of Philadelphia's former mob boss, was almost paranoid enough. Scarfo, who has been charged with masterminding a mob-linked loan sharking operation in New Jersey, reportedly used the popular PGP encryption software to shield his computer's secrets from prying eyes or cyber surveillance.

But when the feds learned of Scarfo's security measures, they decided to do something that would bypass even the best encryption software: FBI agents sneaked into Scarfo's office in Belleville, New Jersey, on May 10, 1999, and installed a keyboard-sniffing device to record his password when he typed it in.

A seven-page court order authorized the FBI and cooperating local police to break into Scarfo's first-floor "Merchant Services of Essex County" office as many times as necessary to deploy, maintain, and then remove recovery methods that will capture the necessary key-related information and encrypted files. The case, which is still awaiting trial, appears to be the first in which the U.S. government used such aggressive surveillance techniques during an investigation; some legal observers say the FBI's breaking-and-entering procedures go too far. This case has the potential to establish some very important precedents on this issue.

Scarfo's prosecution comes at a time when the FBI's *Carnivore* surveillance system (previously discussed) is under increasingly heavy fire from privacy groups, and the use of data-scrambling encryption products appears to be growing.

Recently, for instance, news leaked out about Yahoo's encrypted Web-based e-mail service it introduced through a deal with Zixit, a Dallas firm.

Scarfo has been charged with supervising "an illegal gambling business" in violation of state and federal law and using extortionate loan shark tactics, according to a three-count indictment filed in federal court in June 2000. He has pleaded not guilty.

The elder Scarfo, who once ran the Philadelphia mob that also dominated the Atlantic City gambling racket, was imprisoned in 1991 on racketeering charges. The spring 1999 investigation of the younger Scarfo, who is 35 years old, may be what prompted the previous Clinton administration to recommend changing federal law to allow police to conduct electronic "black bag" jobs.

The idea first publicly surfaced in mid-1999, when the Justice Department proposed legislation that would let police obtain surreptitious warrants and "postpone" notifying the person whose property they entered for 30 days. After vocal objections from civil liberties groups, the administration backed away from the controversial bill. In the final draft of the Cyberspace Electronic Security Act submitted to Congress, the secret-search portions had disappeared.

In January 2000, the previous Clinton administration seemed to change its mind. When criminals such as drug dealers and terrorists use encryption to conceal their communications, law enforcement must be able to respond in a manner that will not thwart an investigation or tip off a suspect.

The feds didn't need a new law—and would instead rely on "general authorities" when asking judges to authorize black bag jobs. A related "secret search" proposal resurfaced in May 2000 in a Senate bankruptcy bill.

In the Scarfo case, the FBI in May 1999 asked for authority to search for and seize encryption-key-related pass phrases from his computer as well as install and leave behind software, firmware, and/or hardware equipment that will monitor the inputted data entered on Nicodemo S. Scarfo's computer by recording the key related information as they are entered. Although the government has refused to release details, this appears to indicate the FBI was using either a hardware device (inserted into the keyboard or attached to the keyboard cable) or a software program that would quietly run in the background and record keystrokes. With the PGP private key and Scarfo's secret password, the government could then view whatever documents or files he had encrypted and stored on his computer.

Ruling that normal investigative procedures to decrypt the codes and keys necessary to decipher the 'factors' encrypted computer file have been tried and have failed, U.S. Magistrate Judge G. Donald Haneke granted the FBI's request. Haneke did not, under federal law, have the authority to grant such an order. The interesting issue is that they in those (court) documents specifically disclaim any reliance on the wiretap statute. If they're on record saying this isn't communications (and it isn't), then that extraordinary authority they have under the wiretap laws does not apply.

If the government is now talking about expanding (black bag jobs) to every case in which it has an interest, where the subject is using a computer and encryption, the number of break-ins is going to skyrocket. Break-ins are going to become commonplace.

However, the government could successfully argue that break-ins are constitutional. There's nothing in the Constitution that prohibits this kind of anticipatory search. In many respects, it's no different from a wiretap.

A lawyer for Scarfo told the Philadelphia Inquirer that he would file a motion challenging the legality of the FBI's black bag job. The FBI's got everything that Scarfo typed on that keyboard (a letter to his lawyer, personal or medical records, legitimate business records, etc.).

Finding a mentally impaired relative, a lost child, or a criminal in a sprawling metropolitan area would be simple if the person were equipped with a personal locator device. The next part of the chapter will take a close look at these IW tracking devices.

THE CYBER FOOT PRINT AND CRIMINAL TRACKING

At 10:00 A.M. one morning in 1999, an elderly woman in Osaka, Japan, became alarmed. Her 74-year-old husband, who suffers from dementia, had left four hours earlier and had not yet returned. She did not panic, but contacted the provider of her personal locator service, Life Service Center. Within a minute, the provider found him on the second floor of a department store, simply by paging a miniature locator device secured to the man's clothes. Forty minutes later, when the man's son arrived at the department store, his father had already left. Fortunately, the service provider continued tracking the elderly man and was able to direct the son to the fourth floor of an Osaka hotel. At 1:10 P.M., the two were reunited. Locus Corp. provided the system that made this possible.

The belief that it should be easy to find anyone, anywhere, at any time with a few pushes of a button has caught on with the advent of the global positioning system (GPS). People imagine a miniature device, attached to one's person, that reports one's whereabouts almost instantaneously. Add the highly practical need to find missing persons promptly, and the personal locator system (PLS) industry is born.

Systems of this nature, whether based on the GPS or some other technology, are being tested throughout the world. Some, in fact, are already being deployed in Japan. The service alone can be sold by cellular companies, which base it on their wireless infrastructure. But several companies looking into the technology options plan to offer a broad array of services to the public and to businesses.

In Japan, location services are now commercially available to 74% of the nation's population, inclu1ding Tokyo, Osaka, Kyoto, Yokohama, Nagasaki, and Hiroshima. Initially designed to support the mentally handicapped, personal locator services have expanded to serve children, the elderly, tourist groups, and security patrols, as well. They may also be used to track valuables and recover stolen vehicles. Not surprisingly, service areas coincide with wireless infrastructure deployments, which personal locators have exploited since their beginning in 1998.

In the United States, two further factors encourage the adoption of these geolocation systems. One is the need to effectively monitor offenders on parole and probation. Tagging offenders with locator devices would tighten their supervision and enhance public safety, and could even reduce the prison population. The other is the wish to provide wireless callers with enhanced 911 (E-911) emergency services. For land-line telephony, the location of a phone from which a 911 call is made appears automatically on the 911 operator's computer screen. But callers using cellular phones could be anywhere and unlocatable, unless location technology were applied to the wireless telephone system.

Of course, wireless services for locating vehicles have been thwarting car theft and managing fleets of cars since the mid-1980s. But unlike vehicular locators, which are less constrained by size and power, locators borne on the person have to be the size of a pager, and their power output has to be less than 1 W, because they can only carry a small battery that cannot be continuously recharged. Most challenging of all, personal locators have to be able to operate in RF-shielded areas such as buildings, because people spend a lot of their time indoors.

One PLS Architecture

A personal locator system is likely to involve a service provider, a location center, and a wireless network. In this setting, three scenarios, each involving a different operating mode, are possible. The person bearing a locator device is either being sought by a subscriber to the service, or is seeking help from the subscriber, or, as in the case of a parolee, is having his or her whereabouts monitored continuously.

Consider again the introductory example, but from a system architecture perspective. It is representative of the first scenario, based on the paging mode, wherein the person with the locator device is sought. In this instance, the subscriber calls the service provider, giving the operator there a password and the "wanted" person's identification (user) number (ID). The operator enters the ID into a computer, which transmits it to another computer at the location center. That machine calls the locator device, in effect paging it to establish communication through the PHS wireless telephone switching office (where PHS stands for personal handy phone systems). Immediately the office forwards the call to the wireless base station nearest the locator.

Once communication is established between the center and the device, the center asks the device for the signal strength data and IDs of any base stations in its vicinity. The locator replies, and from those inputs, plus RF database information on the base stations, the center computes the locator's coordinates. Details of the geolocation technology behind this architecture follow in subheading: "Enhanced Signal Strength."

These coordinates are transmitted to the service provider's computer, which displays the missing person's position on a street map for the service operator to report to the subscriber. The user's location is continuously updated on the service provider's map as long as the location center maintains its call connection to the locator device.

In a second scenario, surrounding the emergency mode, the user of the locator is lost or in dire straits of one sort or another, and presses the device's panic button. The locator calls the location center, which computes the user's position and alerts the service provider, which in turn alerts the subscriber to the user's situation.

The system can employ either packet data or voice channel communications. If a data channel is used, the service takes about 8 seconds to obtain a geolocation fix. But if a voice channel is used, the wait could last up to 33 seconds because of processing differences between the two channel types.

Several minutes may be added by communication between the service's operator and the subscriber. Such a human interface may be necessary given the complexity of Japanese (as explained in the Japanese example earlier) city-addressing schemes. Otherwise, subscribers using personal computers may obtain the information directly from the computer of either the service provider or location center.

Both the emergency and paging operating modes of personal locator systems are characterized as intermittent. In addition, a continuous automatic mode, in which the system polls the locator nonstop, is possible. Strictly speaking, the polling is periodic rather than continuous, but the latter term is more common.

Of the three locator modes, this last requires the most RF bandwidth and battery power. If it were implemented with a continuous voice call between the system and the locator, the expense would be beyond the reach of most applications. Assuming a minimal cost of 4 cents per minute for airtime, such a connection would cost US $57.60 a day—and also drain the locator battery within a few hours.

Packet data calls between the locator and the rest of the system are far more economical. In the packet version, the locator is likely to be polled every few minutes, exchanging 100 bytes or so with the system in a fraction of a second.

Given a 3-minute polling interval and a 1-cent-per-poll cost, the daily cost per locator would be only $4.80.

For most of the time, the locator would be in standby mode, conserving valuable battery charge. Another plus, upcoming third-generation mobile wireless telephony will increase the availability of packet data communications.

NOTE

Six Technologies

A personal locator system could use any of several technologies. Among the most common methods are angle and time difference of the signal's arrival, global positioning system (GPS) and the more recent assisted GPS, enhanced signal strength, and location fingerprinting.

Signal Direction

The simplest is based on measuring the direction of a signal received from an RF transmitter at a single point. This can be done by pointing a directional antenna along the line of maximum signal strength. Alternatively, signal direction can be determined from the difference in time of arrival of the incoming signals at different elements of the antenna. A two-element antenna is typically used to cover angles of ±60 degrees. To achieve 360-degree coverage, a six-element antenna can be used.

A single mobile directional antenna can give only the bearing, not the position, of a transmitting object. The single bearing can be combined with other information, such as terrain data, to provide location. Such an antenna is generally used to approach and locate objects up to several kilometers away. A common use of this technique is tracking RF-tagged wildlife. The same basic technique is used by LoJack Corp., of Dedham, Massachusetts, in its system for finding stolen vehicles.

With two directional antennas spaced well apart, however, the position of a transmitting device in a plane can be computed. In this method, also known as the angle of arrival (AOA) method, transmitter position is determined from the known (fixed) position of the receivers' antennas and the angle of arrival of the signals with respect to the antennas.

Angle measurement precision affects the accuracy of positioning calculations, as does the geometry of the transmitting device and receiving antennas. For example, if a transmitter is too near a line drawn between two receiving antennas, its measured position could be off by more than the distance between the antennas. Fortunately, multiple receiver antennas distributed throughout the area of coverage enable the cellular system to select those antennas that introduce the smallest error.

GPS satellites and other data that enable the mobile receiver to synchronize and match its pseudo-random noise code replicas with those of the satellites. Within about a second, the GPS receiver collects sufficient information for geolocation computation and sends the data back to the server. The server can then combine this information with data from the satellites' navigation message to determine the position of the mobile device.

With the assisted GPS approach, the mobile receivers conserve power by not continuously tracking the satellites' signals. Moreover, they have only to track the pseudo-random noise code and not extract the satellites' navigation message from the signal, in effect, becoming sensitive enough to acquire GPS signals inside most buildings.

In addition, the assisted version of the technology attains greater accuracy. Because the actual position of the stationary GPS receiver is known, the difference between that and its measured position can be used to calculate a correction to the mobile receiver's position. In other words, assisted GPS is inherently differential GPS (DGPS), which counters some of the inaccuracy in civilian GPS service.

The most accurate GPS service is reserved for military use.

NOTE

In June of 2000, Lucent Technologies Inc., of Murray Hill, New Jersey, announced that its wireless assisted GPS had attained an accuracy of better than 5 meters outdoors—an achievement attributable to the differential GPS capability of assisted GPS. More good news in this field was announced by SiRF Technology Inc., of Santa Clara, California, in the form of a postage-stamp-sized chipset (Star II) with built-in DGPS. In addition to providing improved GPS capability, it also offers reduced power consumption and greater accuracy, as well as performing well at handling weak signals.

Enhanced Signal Strength

If no obstructions are present, computing the position of a mobile locator is straightforward for both the signal timing and signal strength methods. When timing is used, the speed of light is multiplied by the time a signal takes to propagate between the two points gives the distance between them.

For the signal strength method, the distance between two points can be determined from the signal attenuation between the points. However, direct line contact seldom exists inside buildings, where signal attenuation is usually unknown and many indirect paths between transmitter and receiver are likely. Although techniques exist for reducing this multipath effect, the effect cannot be eliminated, and the errors it produces are difficult to predict. Multipath effects impede signal timing methods somewhat, but affect signal strength methods even more.

In addition, signal strength is very sensitive to antenna orientation, attenuation by obstructions, and other operating conditions. In contrast, signal timing is unaffected by antenna orientation and is less sensitive to attenuation.

Nonetheless, an enhanced signal strength (ESS) method that overcomes such impediments as multipath effects, attenuation, and antenna orientation has allowed the deployment of personal locator systems in PHS service areas in Japan. Such a system takes in three-dimensional information on the lay of the land, buildings, elevated highways, railroads, and other obstructions, and uses it to simulate the RF signal propagation characteristics of every PHS wireless transmitting antenna in the area of interest. The location system center stores the results in an RF database.

The position of a mobile locator is determined by getting it to measure the signal strength of preferably three to five base stations. From this input plus information from the base stations' databases, the system can calculate the position of the locator. The mean accuracy of the ESS is 40–50 meters. Inside large public buildings, with a PHS base station on every floor, the system can indicate a specific floor level. In subway and railroad stations, the availability of base stations makes it possible to find an individual on a specific track.

The stand-alone locator used by Locus Corp.'s enhanced signal strength method weighs only 58 grams and can operate for 16 days on a single battery charge. The ESS geolocation capabilities are also available in a standard PHS phone handset, in which the firmware has been modified. Presently, researchers in Japan are investigating how to apply ESS technology to other wireless phone systems.

Location Fingerprinting

Instead of exploiting signal timing or signal strength, a new technique from U.S. Wireless Corp., of San Ramon, California, relies on signal structure characteristics. Called "location fingerprinting," it turns the multipath phenomenon to surprisingly good use: By combining the multipath pattern with other signal characteristics, it creates a signature unique to a given location.

U.S. Wireless's proprietary *RadioCamera* system includes a signal signature database of a location grid for a specific service area. To generate this database, a vehicle drives through the coverage area transmitting signals to a monitoring site. The system analyzes the incoming signals, compiles a unique signature for each square in the location grid, and stores it in the database. Neighboring grid points are spaced about 30 meters apart.

To determine the position of a mobile transmitter, the RadioCamera system matches the transmitter's signal signature to an entry in the database. Multipoint signal reception is not required, although it is highly desirable. The system can use data from only a single point to determine location. Moving traffic, including vehicles, animals, and/or people, and changes in foliage or weather do not affect the system's capabilities.

What's PLS Good For?

In the United States, the need to provide wireless phone users with emergency 911 services has been one of the spurs to the development of location technologies. Today, an enhanced 911 (E-911) emergency call made over a land line is routed to a public safety answering point (PSAP), which matches the caller's number to an entry in an automatic location information database. When the match is made, this database provides the PSAP with the street address plus a location in a building— maybe the floor or office of the caller handset. So quickly is the caller located that the emergency crew can respond within 5 to 7 minutes on average.

But the very mobility of wireless handsets rules out a simple database relationship between phone number and location. In fact, the response to a wireless call can be 10 times longer than for a land-line call—far from ideal in an emergency.

Accordingly, the U.S. Federal Communications Commission (FCC) in Washington, D.C., directed operators of wireless phone services to enable their E-911 services to locate callers. The directive specified two phases. The first required an accuracy of several kilometers by April 1998 and the second required an accuracy of 125 meters with 0.67 probability by 2002. Whereas the first phase needed only software changes to the system, the second required the adoption of new location technologies.

The original FCC directive for Phase II also required support for existing handsets, which implied that only network upgrades would be acceptable. Yet a network-only solution would preclude the use of emerging technologies, such as assisted GPS, because that would require handset modification in addition to any network infrastructure and software changes. All users might not bring in their handsets for modification, severely complicating support for handsets already in service.

To ease the introduction of new technologies, in September 1999, the FCC modified its original Phase II directive to permit handset-enabled solutions and also to tighten the accuracy required. In addition to the many technical roadblocks to implementing the E-911 directive, an even greater obstacle is cost. Upgrading all the wireless networks will cost billions of dollars. Cost recovery is the central issue for cellular service providers. Although wireless subscribers are the most likely source of recouping the cost, the government has made no formal decisions yet.

Presently, only the U.S. government requires its wireless companies to add caller geolocation to their E-911 services. But as the United States is a major telecommunications market, many manufacturers of wireless telecommunications equipment elsewhere are developing approaches to meet the commission's directive.

In an international development, a working group of the European Telecommunications Standards Institute (ETSI), based in Sophia Antipolis, France, is currently drafting a standard for supporting location services for the Global System for Mobile Communications (GSM). Currently, GSM is the most common mobile wireless system in the world and is available in more countries than any other wireless system.

Monitoring Tops Services LIST

Wireless E-911 just helps the individual. But monitoring the mentally impaired and criminals could have even greater impacts on society at large. With the changing demographics of the developed world, the percentage of individuals over age 65 will soar over the next several decades. So will the number of elderly afflicted with age-related mental impairments. Most of the five million or so U.S. patients diagnosed with Alzheimer's disease are over age 65.

Recall how personal locator technology helped a family find a mentally impaired elderly man, fortunately within 50 minutes or so. But what if many hours passed before anyone noticed that the man was missing? What if he had run into some kind of difficulty during that time? Being mentally impaired, he would be unlikely to press the panic button. An automatic polling system could solve this problem by checking whether the man was within a defined polygonal area or not—the location service and the family would be alerted whenever the man went out of this area.

As the population ages, the need for and cost of long-term care are likely to increase, too. Today it costs over $40,000 per year in the United States to care for a patient in a nursing home. Systems that monitor the whereabouts of the mentally impaired elderly could help them live longer in their communities and spend less time in institutions.

Criminal justice is another area of social concern where personal locators could intervene. The United States leads industrial nations in the percentage of its population incarcerated. In 2000, according to U.S. Department of Justice statistics, almost 5.2 million people were serving time in U.S. jails and prisons, and a further 8 million were in parole and probation programs. In comparison, in Japan in 2000, only 135,000 were serving prison terms while 180,000 were on parole or probation.

The high human and monetary cost of corrections could be cut by new technologies, such as personal locator systems, that would reduce prison populations and improve the monitoring of parolees and persons on probation. First-generation monitoring systems, introduced in the mid-1980s, track the location of the offender in a very confined area, such as the home. They enable the corrections system to verify that a parolee stays there during specified periods, 6 P.M. to 6 A.M., say.

But by day, when the offender is presumably at work, these systems can do nothing.

Second-generation monitoring systems do better. A tamperproof personal locator is fastened on the offender and tracked continuously and automatically over a wide area. The newer system compares the actual with the supposed positions of the offender, as stored in a database. If any violation or tampering with the locator occurs, the system alerts the appropriate corrections or law enforcement agencies.

The goal is to verify that parolees and probationers comply with the directives imposed by the corrections system as to where and when they should and should not be by day and night. For example, a child molester is excluded from school areas, and a stalker is excluded from areas near the home and workplace of the victim.

Storage of the offender's ongoing whereabouts in an electronic file benefits law enforcement agencies in other ways.[v] The record can be used to exclude or include a monitored offender as a suspect in a crime by comparing events at the crime scene with the file entries.

In 1996, two companies, Advanced Business Sciences Inc. (ABS) of Omaha, Nebraska (http://www.abscomtrak.com), and Pro Tech Monitoring Inc., located in Palm Harbor, Florida (http://www.ptm.com), were the first to introduce GPS-based continuous monitoring systems for criminal offenders. These systems are deployed in, among other places, Michigan, Minnesota, Florida, Colorado, Wisconsin, Pennsylvania, South Carolina, Arizona, Ohio, Texas, and Nebraska. More recently, BI Inc., headquartered in Boulder, Colorado (http://www.bi.com), the leading manufacturer of first-generation offender monitoring systems, began testing its version of a GPS-based system.

The Pro Tech Monitoring, ABS, and BI systems all include a personal locator, a wireless telephone interface, and a location center. The personal locator has two parts, a GPS unit and an ankle bracelet. The ankle bracelet, which employs tamper-detection circuitry, uses a low-power transmitter with a range of about 50 meters. The GPS unit consists of a GPS receiver, a wireless phone component, and a receiver to detect the bracelet signal. The offender carries the GPS unit by hand, or in the case of the ABS system, wears it on a belt.

Should the GPS unit fail to detect the bracelet signal (probably because it is out of range) or should the bracelet circuitry detect tampering, the unit will alert the location center through its wireless interface. What's more, the unit monitors its own position by means of its GPS receiver whenever the satellite signals are detectable, primarily outdoors.

The GPS unit can operate in either of two modes: autonomous or continuous. In autonomous mode, it logs the offender's location in its internal memory. It compares this position with an on-board database of exclusion and inclusion zones for the offender. When it detects a zone or other violation, it alerts the location center with a wireless call. In this mode, once or twice a day the GPS unit dials the location center and updates it with the logged data.

Operation in autonomous mode, of course, avoids the costly continuous voice-type wireless connections. Using the far less expensive, packet-based, cellular digital packet data (CDPD) wireless phone connection, the GPS unit can maintain continuous real-time contact with the location center—the second operating mode. Unfortunately, however, CDPD is unavailable in many areas.

Splitting the locator in two (into a bracelet and GPS unit) offers a simple recharging strategy. The unit's batteries usually require a daily recharging to power the GPS unit. At night, when the offender is typically required to be at home, the unit is placed in a docking station for recharging, while maintaining contact with the location center all the while and sending information whenever appropriate.

Privacy, Security Still Issues

Confidentiality of information about a person's whereabouts is a serious concern for location technology. Databases already store large amounts of personal information, including medical data, marketing preferences, and credit information. Lax security could lead to serious abuse of this data. Access to a database of location information could aggravate this situation by further exposing a person's movements. Moreover, it can have real-time implications. For example, someone could find and harm a victim.

The location information stored in databases needs to be secured, as does the tracking and locating process itself. Because RF communications are used, eavesdropping is a possibility. To reduce this risk, location information can be encrypted or transmitted using coded signals employing such spread-spectrum technology as CDMA.

Privacy protection can also depend on the technology used. For example, in GPS or the enhanced-signal-strength method, the location system uses information captured and transmitted by the locator. Some devices are equipped with an option to block such transmissions, preventing the system from locating the device. But in network-based locator systems that measure the locator's signal characteristics without requiring its cooperation, the only safe way for users to keep their locations secret is to turn off the device.

More Work To Be Done

Despite the strides made in recent years in personal locator technologies, much work remains to be done on their accuracy, locator miniaturization, battery life, multipath effects, ability to penetrate buildings, and the economical use of RF

same site. On many sites, this badgering can include multiple cookies per page, cookies that change gratuitously even once accepted, and cookies on pages that don't even require cookies for any apparent reason.

As feedback from users reaches the designers of browser software, look for browsers to add the following features to help users cope with this overuse of cookies:

■   Reject all cookies option
■   Better choices when asked
■   Cookie management tools

Reject All Cookies Option

Today, browsers present only the annoying false choice between "Accept all cookies without asking" and "Ask about each cookie." Users should expect to see these choices expanded to include a third "Reject all cookies without asking" option.

Better Choices When Asked

For users who choose notification, browsers should offer a more flexible set of choices regarding what happens after a cookie has been accepted or rejected. Specifically, the user should be able to say "I want to accept/reject this cookie, and then don't ask me again..."

■   About this particular cookie on this Web site integrated platform
■   About any cookie on this Web site integrated platform
■   About any cookie on this page

Cookie-Management Tools

Finally, expect to see browsers offer a mechanism that lets users view and manage the set of cookies they've collected. Certain browsers, such as the most recent release of Microsoft *Internet Explorer*, have begun to add these or similar cookie-management features. Until a majority of common browsers have incorporated these options, integrated platform designers should plan to minimize the number and type of cookies a visitor encounters on a site.

WINTEL INSIDE, OR HOW YOUR COMPUTER IS WATCHING YOU

A previously discussed, the Privacy Foundation has discovered that it is possible to add "Web bugs" to Microsoft *Word* documents. A "Web bug" could allow an author to track where a document is being read and how often. In addition, the author can watch how a "bugged" document is passed from one person to another or from one organization to another. Some possible uses of Web bugs in *Word* documents include:

- Detecting and tracking leaks of confidential documents from a company
- Tracking possible copyright infringement of newsletters and reports
- Monitoring the distribution of a press release
- Tracking the quoting of text when it is copied from one *Word* document to a new document

Web bugs are made possible by the ability in Microsoft *Word* of a document to link to an image file that is located on a remote Web server. Because only the URL of the Web bug is stored in a document and not the actual image, Microsoft *Word* must fetch the image from a Web server each and every time the document is opened. This image-linking feature then puts a remote server in the position to monitor when and where a document file is being opened. The server knows the IP address and host name of the computer that is opening the document. A host name will typically include a company name if a computer is located at a business. The host name of a home computer usually has the name of a user's Internet Service Provider (ISP).

An additional issue, and one that could magnify the potential surveillance, is that Web bugs in *Word* documents can also read and write browser cookies belonging to Internet *Explorer*. Cookies could allow an author to match up the computer viewer of a *Word* document to their visits to the author's Web site.

Web bugs are used extensively today by Internet advertising companies on Web pages and in HTML-based e-mail messages for tracking. They are typically 1-by-1 pixel in size to make them invisible on the screen to disguise the fact that they are used for tracking.

Although the Privacy Foundation has found no evidence that Web bugs are being used in *Word* documents today, there is little to prevent their use. Short of removing the feature that allows linking to Web images in Microsoft *Word*, there does not appear to be a good preventative solution. However, the Privacy Foundation has recommended to Microsoft that cookies be disabled in Microsoft *Word* through a software patch. In addition to *Word* documents, Web bugs can also be used in *Excel 2000* and *PowerPoint 2000* documents.

Detailed Description

Microsoft *Word* has, from the beginning, supported the ability to include picture files in *Word* documents. Originally, the picture files would reside on the local hard drive and then be copied into a document as part of *Word* .doc file. However, beginning with *Word 97*, Microsoft provided the ability to copy images from the Internet. All that is required to use this feature is to know the URL (Web address) of the image. Besides copying the Web image into the document, *Word* also allows the Web image to be linked to the document via its URL. Linking to the image results in smaller *Word* document files because only a URL needs to be stored in the file instead of the entire image. When a document contains a linked Web image, *Word* will automatically fetch the image each time the document is opened. This is necessary to display the image on the screen or to print it out as part of the document.

Because a linked Web image must be fetched from a remote Web server, the server is in a position to track when a *Word* document is opened and possibly by whom. Furthermore, it is possible to include an image in a *Word* document solely for the purpose of tracking. Such an image is called a Web Bug. Web bugs today are already used extensively by Internet marketing companies on Web pages and embedded in HTML e-mail messages.

When a Web bug is embedded in a *Word* document, the following information is sent to the remote Web server when the document containing the bug is opened:

- The full URL of the Web bug image
- The IP address and the host name of the computer requesting the Web bug
- A Web browser cookie (optional)

This information is typically saved in an ordinary log file by Web server software.

Because the author of the document has control of the URL of the document, they can put whatever information they choose in this URL. For example, a URL might contain a unique document ID number or the name of the person to whom the document was originally sent.

These tracking abilities might be used in any number of ways. In most cases, the reader of a particular document will not know that the document is bugged, or that the Web bug is surreptitiously sending identifying information back through the Internet.

One example of this tracking ability is to monitor the path of a confidential document, either within or beyond a company's computer network. The confidential document could be "bugged" to "phone home" each time it is opened. If the company's Web server ever received a "server hit" from an IP address for the bug outside the organization, then it could learn immediately about the leak. Because the server log would include the host name of the computer where the document was opened, a company could know that the organization that received the leaked document was a competitor or media outlet, for example.

All original copies of a confidential document could also be numbered so that a company could track the source of a leak. A unique serial number could be encoded in the query string of the Web bug URL. If the document is leaked, the server hit for the Web bug will indicate which copy was leaked.

A serial number could be added to a Web bug in a document either manually (right before a copy of a document is saved) or automatically through a simple utility program. The utility program would scan a document for the Web bug URL and add a serial number in the query string. A Perl script of less than 20 lines of code could easily be written to do this sort of serialization.

Another use of Web bugs in *Word* documents is to detect copyright infringement. For example, a publishing company could "bug" all outgoing copies of its newsletter. The Web bugs in a newsletter could contain unique customer ID numbers to detect how widely an individual newsletter is copied and distributed.

A third possible use of Web bugs is for market research purposes. For example, a company could place Web bugs in a press release distributed as a *Word* document. The server log hits for the Web bugs would then tell the company what organizations have actually viewed the press release. The company could also observe how a press release is passed along within an organization or to other organizations.

In an academic setting, Web bugs might be used to detect plagiarism. A document could be bugged before it is distributed. An invisible Web bug could be placed within each paragraph in the document. If text were to be cut and pasted from the document, it is likely that a Web bug would be picked up also and copied into the new document

To place a Web bug in a *Word* document is relatively simple. These are the steps in *Word 2000*:

1. Select the Insert | Picture | From File... menu command.
2. Type in the URL of the Web Bug in the "File name" field of the Insert Picture dialog box.
3. Select the "Link to File" option of the "Insert" button.

Access to the sender's server logs is required to monitor the movement of such Web bugs. The Privacy Foundation ran simple experiments with Excel and PowerPoint files and found that these files can also be "bugged" in Office 2000. The Privacy Foundation continues to investigate this issue with regard to other software programs.

The Privacy Foundation has set up a demonstration of a Web bug in a *Word* document. The demo document can be downloaded from the University of Denver Privacy Center Web site at this URL: http://www.privacycenter.du.edu/demos/ bugged.doc

The document contains a visible Web bug. When the document is opened, the Web bug will show the host name of the computer that fetched the image. In addition, a non-identifying Web browser cookie will be set on your computer. The cookie is nonidentifying because everyone gets the same cookie value, which is simple test string. Demonstrations of "bugged" *Excel* and *PowerPoint* files are also available for download from the Privacy Center Web site: http://www.privacycenter.du.edu/demos/bugged.xls or http://www.privacycenter.du.edu/demos/bugged.ppt

The use of Web bugs in Word does point to a more general problem. Any file format that supports automatic linking to Web pages or images could lead to the same problem. Software engineers should take this privacy issue into consideration when designing new file formats.

This issue is potentially critical for music file formats such as MP3 files where piracy concerns are high. For example, it is easy to imagine an extended MP3 file format that supports embedded HTML for showing song credits, cover artwork, lyrics, and so on. The embedded HTML with embedded Web bugs could also be used to track how many times a song is played and by which computer, identified by its IP address.

DATA MINING FOR WHAT?

The use of data mining for information warfare is growing rapidly. The number of data-mining consultants, as well as the number of commercial tools available to the "nonexpert" user, are also quickly increasing. It is becoming easier than ever to collect datasets and apply data-mining tools to them. As more and more nonexperts seek to exploit this technology to help with their business, it becomes increasingly important that they understand the underlying assumptions and biases of these tools. There are a number of factors to consider before applying IW data mining to a database. In particular, there are important issues regarding the data that should be examined before proceeding with the data-mining process. Although these issues may be well-known to the data-mining expert, the nonexpert is often unaware of their importance.

Now let's focus on three specific issues. Each issue is illustrated through the use of brief examples. Also, insight is provided for each issue on how it might be problematic, and suggestions are made on which techniques can used for approaching such situations.

The purpose here is to help the nonexpert in IW data mining to better understand some of the important issues of the field. Particular concern is also established here with characteristics of the data that may affect the overall usefulness of the IW data-mining results. Some recent experiences, and the lessons learned from them, are described. These lessons, together with the accompanying discussion, will help to both guide the IW data-collection process and better understand what kinds of results to expect.

One cannot blindly "plug-and-play" in IW data mining. There are a number of factors to consider before applying data mining to any particular database. This general warning is not new. Many of these issues are well-known by both the data mining experts and a growing body of nonexpert, data "owners." For instance, the data should be "clean," with consistent values across records and containing as few errors as possible. There should not be a large number of missing or incomplete records or fields. It should be possible to represent the data in the appropriate syntax for the required data-mining tool (attribute/value pairs).

As previously mentioned, this part of the chapter will discuss three specific, but less well-known, issues. Each will be illustrated through real-world experiences. The first is the impact of *data distribution.* Many IW data-mining techniques perform class or group discrimination, and rely on the data-containing representative samples of all relevant classes. Sometimes, however, obtaining samples of all classes is surprisingly difficult. The second issue is one of *applicability and data relevance.* High-quality data, combined with good data-mining tools, does not ensure that the results can be applied to the desired goal. Finally, this part of the chapter will discuss some of the issues associated with using *text* (narrative fields in reports) in data mining. The current technology cannot fully exploit arbitrary text, but there are certain ways text can be used.

These three issues are not new to the field. Indeed, for many IW data-mining experts, these are important issues that are often well understood. For the nonexpert, however, these issues can be subtle or appear deceivingly simple or unimportant. It is tempting to collect a large amount of clean data, massage the representation into the proper format, hand the data tape to the consultant, and expect answers to the most pressing business questions. Although this part of the chapter does not describe all of the potential problems one might face, it does describe some important issues, illustrate why they might be problematic, and suggest ways to effectively deal with these situations.

Two Examples

The discussion of data distribution, information relevance, and use of text will be illustrated with examples from two current projects. The first involves a project with the Center for Advanced Aviation Systems Development (CAASD) in the domain of aviation safety. In this project, one of the primary goals is to help identify and characterize precursors to potentially dangerous situations in the aviation world. One particular way to do this is to mine accident and incident reports involving aircraft for patterns that identify common precursors to dangerous situations. For any type of flight—commercial, cargo, military, or pleasure—accidents (and often less serious incidents) are investigated. A report is filed containing a variety of information such as time of day, type of aircraft, weather, pilot age, and pilot experience. These reports often include the inspector's written summary. One task involves using collections of these reports to try to identify and characterize those situations in which accidents occur. A source of such reports is the National Transportation Safety Board (NTSB).

The second project involves targeting vehicles for law enforcement. In this particular instance, vehicles (mostly passenger vehicles and small trucks) arrive at an inspection stop. At this primary stop, a brief inspection is conducted to decide if further examination is necessary. There is typically a constant flow of cars to be processed, so excessive time cannot be taken. This first inspection typically takes 20 to 30 seconds. If the primary inspector feels it is warranted (and there are any number of reasons that justify this), any vehicle can be pulled out for secondary inspection. This secondary inspection and background check is more thorough. If the driver/vehicle is found to be in violation of the particular laws under consideration, then various information concerning both driver and vehicle is collected and entered into the "violators" database. The goal of this project is to find a way to better profile these violating drivers and vehicles, so that the primary inspectors can more accurately identify likely suspects and send them for secondary inspection.

Data Distribution

Let's first discuss the issue of data distribution. Of particular concern is the situation in which the data lacks certain types of examples. Consider the aviation safety domain. One goal of the project in this domain is to characterize situations that result in accident flights. An obvious source of information is the NTSB's database of accident reports.

This database does not contain records about uneventful flights (the NTSB is an accident investigation agency). That is, the data are unevenly distributed between records of accident flights and records of uneventful flights.

NOTE

This lack of reports about uneventful flights has important consequences for a significant class of data-mining techniques. When given the data containing only accident flights, each of the approaches in this class concludes that all flights contain accidents. Such a hypothesis is clearly incorrect. The majority of the flights are uneventful. Also, such a hypothesis is not useful because it does not offer any new insight on how to differentiate the accident flights from the uneventful ones. Furthermore, some of the most popular IW data-mining tools, including decision tree inducers, neural networks, and nearest neighbor algorithms, fall into this class of techniques. (They assume that the absence of uneventful flights in the data implies that they do not exist in the world.)

To continue this discussion, it is necessary to first define some terms used in data mining. The "target concept" is that concept you are trying to learn. In the aviation domain, the target concept is accident flights. Consequently, each example of an accident flight (each accident report in the database) is called a member of the target concept, and each uneventful flight is a nonmember of the target concept. The NTSB data do not contain records of uneventful flights. That is, there are no descriptions of non-members of the target concept. The problem of learning to differentiate members from nonmembers is called a "supervised concept learning problem."

It is called supervised because each example in the data contains a label indicating its membership status for the target concept.

NOTE

For example, a supervised concept learner uses a training sample as input. A training sample is a list of examples, labeled as members or nonmembers, which is assumed to be representative of the whole universe. The supervised concept learner produces hypotheses that discriminate the members and nonmembers in the sample. Many IW data-mining tools use supervised concept learners to find patterns.

Let's say that a supervised concept learner makes the closed-world assumption that the absence of nonmembers in the data implies that they do not exist in the universe. Why do some of the popular learners make the closed-world assumption? The case of decision tree learners provides a good illustration. These learners partition the training sample into pure subsamples, containing either all member or all nonmembers. The partitioning of the training sample drives the rule generation. That is, the learners introduce conditions that define partitions of the training sample; each outcome of a condition represents a different subsample. Ultimately, the conditions will become part of the discrimination rules. Unfortunately, if the input sample contains only data that are members of the target class, the training sample is already pure and the decision tree learner has no need to break-up the sample further. As a consequence, the rules commit to classifying all new data as members of the target class before conducting any tests. Thus, in the aviation project, all flights would be classified as accident flights, because the learner never saw any uneventful flights. This is not to say that learners employing the closed-world assumption are inappropriate in all, or even most situations. For many problems, when representative data from all the concepts involved is available, these learners are both effective and efficient.

Applicability and Relevance of Data

Even when collected data is of high quality (clean, few missing values, proper form, etc.) and the IW data-mining algorithms can be successfully run, there still may be a problem of relevance. It must be possible to apply the new information to the situation at hand. For instance, if the data mining produces typical "if...then..." rules, then it must be possible to measure the values of the attributes in the condition ("if" part) of those rules. The information about those conditions must be available at the time the rules will be used. Consider a simple example where the goal is to predict if a dog is likely to bite. Assume data are collected on the internal anatomy of various dogs, and each dog is labeled by its owner as either "likely" or "unlikely" to bite. Assume further that the data-mining tools work splendidly, and it is discovered that the following (admittedly contrived) rules apply: Rule 1—If the rear molars of the dog are worn, the dog is unlikely to bite; and, Rule 2—If the mandibular muscles are over-developed, the dog is likely to bite.

These may seem like excellent rules. However, if faced with a strange, angry dog late at night, these rules would be of little help in deciding whether you are in danger. There are two reasons for this: First, there is a time constraint in applying the rules. There are only a few seconds to check if these rules apply. Second, even without such a constraint, the average person probably can't make judgments about molar wear and muscle development. The lesson here is that just because data are collected about biting (and nonbiting) dogs, it does not mean one can predict whether a dog will bite in every situation.

In the vehicle-targeting task described earlier, a similar situation occurred. The initial goal was very specific: develop a set of rules, a profile, that the primary inspectors could use to determine which vehicles to pull out for secondary inspection. As mentioned, much more information is collected concerning actual violators than for those that are just passed through the checkpoint. Thus, the initial goal was to profile likely violation suspects based on the wealth of information about that group. The problem, noticed before any analysis was done, was that the information that would make up the profiles would not be applicable to the desired task. As mentioned, the primary inspectors have only a short amount of time to decide whether a particular vehicle should be pulled out for secondary inspection. During that time, they have access to only superficial information. That is, the primary inspectors don't have quick access to much of the background knowledge concerning the driver and vehicle. Yet this is precisely the knowledge collected during seizures initially chosen to build profiles. Thus, they have no way to apply classification rules that measure features such as "number of other cars owned," "bad credit history," or "known to associate with felons" (types of data collected on violation vehicles and drivers).

The problem here is not that the data is "bad," or even that the data is all from the target concept. The problem is that the data cannot be applied to the initially specified task. How does this situation come about in general? The answer involves a fairly common situation. Often, IW data mining begins with data that has been previously collected, usually for some other purpose. The assumption is made that since the collected data is in the same general domain as the current problem, it must be usable to solve this problem. As the examples show, this is often not the case. In the vehicle-targeting task, the nature of the law enforcement system is such that a great deal of information is collected and recorded on violators. No one ever intended to use this information as a screening tool at stop points. Thus, it is important to understand the purpose for which a set of data was collected. Does it address the current situation directly? Similarly, when data is collected for the specific task at hand, careful thought must go into collecting the relevant data.

There are two primary ways to address this problem of data irrelevancy. The most obvious is to use additional data from another source. It may be that different data already exists to address the primary question. For instance, returning to the dogs example, general aggressiveness characteristics for different breeds of dogs have been determined. Using this data, rather than the original data, deciding how likely a dog is to bite is reduced to the problem of determining its breed (often done by quick visual inspection). When the necessary data does not already exist, it may be necessary to collect it. Some of this data collection will likely take place in the vehicle-targeting project. In this case, data must be collected that relates directly to the information available to the inspectors at the initial inspection. For example, the demeanor of the driver may be an important feature. Of course, collecting new data may be a very expensive process. First, the proper attributes to collect must be determined. This often involves discussions and interviews with experts in the field. Then the actual data-collection process may be quite costly. It may be that an inordinate amount of manpower is required, or that certain features are difficult to measure.

If additional data cannot be obtained, there is another, often less desirable way to address this issue. It may be possible to alter the initial goals or questions. This will clearly require problem-specific domain expertise to address a few simple questions: Is there another way to address the same issue? Is there another relevant issue that can be addressed directly with this data? In the vehicle-targeting domain, only those attributes that were directly accessible to the inspector were used. A good example would be looking at simple statistical patterns for time of day, weather, season, and holidays. This is not a deep analysis and doesn't quite "profile" likely violators, but it makes progress toward the initial goal. Another alternative is to use the violator database to profile suspects for other situations. It may be that profiles of certain types of violators bear similarities to other criminal types. Perhaps this information can be used elsewhere in law enforcement. Admittedly, this latter solution does not address the initial issue: helping the primary inspectors decide who to pull out for secondary inspection. However, it may not be possible to achieve that goal with this data and the given time constraints. It is important to understand this potential limitation early in the process, before a great deal of time, effort, and money has been invested.

Combining Text and Structured Data

IW data mining is most often performed on data that is highly structured. Highly structured data have a finite, well-defined set of possible values, as is most often seen in databases. An example of structured data is a database containing records describing aircraft accidents that includes fields such as the make of an airplane and the number of hours flown by the pilot. Another source of valuable yet often unused information is unstructured text. Although more difficult to immediately use than structured data, data mining should make use of these available text resources.

Text is often not used during IW data mining because it requires a preprocessing step before it can be used by available tools such as decision trees, association rule methods, or clustering. These techniques require structured fields with clearly defined sets of possible values that can be quickly counted and matched. Such techniques sometimes also assume that values are ordered and have well-defined distances between values. Text is not so well behaved. Words may have multiple meanings depending on context (polysemy), multiple words may mean the same thing (synonymy), or may be closely related (hypernymy). These are difficult issues that are not yet totally solved, but useful progress has been made and techniques have been developed so that text can be considered a resource for data mining.

One way to exploit text, borrowed from information retrieval, is to use a vector-space approach. Information retrieval is concerned with methods for efficiently retrieving documents relevant to a given request or query. The standard method for doing this is to build weight vectors describing each document and then compare the document vector to the query vector. More specifically, this method first identifies all the unique words in the document collection. Then this list of words is used to build vectors of words and associated weights for the query and each of the documents. Using the simplest weighting method, this vector has a value of 1 at position x when the xth vocabulary word is present in the document; otherwise it has a value of 0. Every document and query is now described by a vector of length equal to the size of the vocabulary. Now each document vector can be compared to every other document by comparing their word vectors. A cosine-similarity measure (which projects one vector along another in each dimension) will then provide a measure of similarity between the two corresponding documents. Surprisingly, although this approach discards the structure in the text and ignores the problems of polysemy and synonymy altogether, it has been found to be a simple, fast baseline for identifying relevant documents.

A variant of this vector-space approach was used on the airline safety data to identify similar accidents based on a textual description of the flight history. The narrative description of each accident was represented as a vector and compared to all other narratives using the approach described earlier. One group of accidents identified by this technique can be described as planes that were "veering to the left during takeoff." The following accident reports were found to be similar in this respect:

- MIA01LA055: During takeoff roll he or she applied normal right rudder to compensate for engine torque. The airplane did not respond to the pilot input and drifted to the left.
- ANC00LA099: Veered to the left during the first attempt to take off.
- ANC00LA041: Pilot added full power and the airplane veered to the left.

Identifying this kind of a group would be difficult using fixed fields alone. This technique can also be used to find all previous reports similar to a given accident, or to find records with a certain combination of words. This can be a useful tool for identifying patterns in the flight history of the accident so that the events leading up to different accidents can be more clearly identified.

The information stored in text can be extracted in other ways as well. A collection of documents and a taxonomy of terms are combined so that maximal word or category associations can be calculated. It could also be used in the airline safety domain to calculate, for example, which class of mechanical malfunctions occurred most often in winter weather.

Another approach very relevant to IW data mining from text is information extraction (IE). Information extraction is interested in techniques for extracting specific pieces of information from text and is the focus of the DARPA Message Understanding Conference (MUC). The biggest problem with IE systems is that they are time-consuming to build and domain specific. To address this problem a number of tools have (and continue to be) developed for learning templates from examples such as CRYSTAL, RAPIER, and AutoSlog. IE tools could be used in the airline safety data to pull out information that is often more complete in the text than in the fixed fields. This work is geared toward filling templates from text alone, but often the text and structured fields overlap in content.

An example of just such an overlap can be found in the NTSB accident and incident records. The data in the NTSB accident and incident records contains structured fields which together allow the investigator to identify human factors that may be important to the accident scene. However, it was found that these fields are rarely filled out completely enough to make a classification: 95% of the records that were identified as involving people could only be classified as "unknown." IE methods could be used to reduce this large unknown rate by pulling information out of the narrative, which described if a person in the cockpit made a mistake. Such an approach could make use of a dictionary of synonyms for "mistake" and parser for confirming if the mistake was an action made by the pilot or copilot and not in a sentence describing, for example, the maintenance methods.

Although IW data mining has primarily concerned itself with structured data, text is a valuable source of information that should not be ignored. Although automatic systems that completely understand the text are a still a long way off, one of the surprising recent results is that simple techniques, which sometimes completely ignore or only partially address the problems of polysemy, synonymy, and complex structure of text, still do provide a useful first cut for mining information from text. Useful techniques, such as the vector-space approach and learned templates from information extraction, can allow IW data miners to make use of the increasing amount of text available on-line.

THE INTERNET IS BIG BROTHER

How prepared is your business for the future? As the Internet expands its reach to the farthest corners of the globe, companies will find themselves dealing with increasingly complex challenges such as Big Brother.

In the Internet of tomorrow you can be sure of at least three things. First, the experience will not be anything like what we're familiar with. Second, despite Point One, little will change in the next 10 years. And third, the business environment of the future will be much less forgiving, so companies that do not take the new technologies seriously are putting themselves at risk.

A High-Fiber Diet

During the 1990s we all heard about fiber-optic technology's potential for increasing bandwidth and enhancing performance. Recently, better installation techniques and a wider range of fiber-compatible equipment have made fiber both easily available and less expensive than it used to be.

Although fiber will remain a good choice for backbones and carrier-class interconnections, most companies will probably continue to run copper, at least for the foreseeable future. After all, few businesses want to bear even slightly higher costs for fiber installation and networking gear. Instead, expect to see more companies upgrading their existing copper technology. Expect them to get away with it, too, because for most practical purposes, copper can handle the load.

Let Them Eat Broadband

High-speed Internet connections, especially the cable modem[vi] and DSL technologies lumped together under the "broadband" heading, are increasing in number at an astonishing rate, at least in First-World countries such as the U.S. and within the European Union. The biggest problem the providers face seems to be keeping up with demand. The current waiting list of DSL and cable access orders probably won't be caught up until 2006. Even then, North America will be home to wide swaths of rural territory without high-speed access.

This scenario isn't likely to change in the next decade, either. Unless governments (Big Brother) insist that Internet carriers supply rural service at a loss (as American telephone companies were ordered to do with voice service), broadband providers will have little incentive to deploy their technologies on a wide scale.

The increasing availability of broadband wireless connections is another revolution that's already under way, although it won't make a serious difference anytime soon either. In its infant state, broadband wireless, with its ability to support certain ebusiness applications, is best suited to a LAN-like role. It will be a while before we see a device that combines the size of the cell-phone with the power of the laptop.

What about IPv6?

In the next decade, we'll probably also see a wider implementation of IPv6 (IP version 6) which already has a foothold. IPv6 addresses many of the limitations of today's IP (version 4), such as address shortages, quality-of-service issues, and security. A dedicated backbone, the "6bone" is already in place. Moreover, to ease the task of changing fundamental IP protocols, IPv6 is designed for backward compatibility with IPv4.

Network equipment vendors have also been building IPv6 support into their products, which increases the likelihood that IPv6 will conquer the backbones first, trickling down to the desktop via OS upgrade cycles. Ten years out, it's safe to assume that most of the devices on the Internet will be using IPv6 from end to end.

A Truly Global Internet

The days of Americans (Big Brother) ruling the Internet are not over by a long shot. Even so, the next decade will bring an explosion of Internet usage in places such as Asia and Africa. As the Internet becomes more pervasive, businesses will face an even greater shortage of skilled employees. American businesses that have traditionally relied on a foreign labor market may be caught short when those workers can find jobs at home.

As always, the spoils will go to those businesses that think ahead. We are going to see big changes, so start preparing yourself for a world ruled by broadband, culturally neutral, easily maintained wireless access. That means considering technical issues and different standards of civil rights, conduct, and privacy. The companies that do will have a head start on the competition for the next decade and maybe the next century.

THE WIRELESS INTERNET—FRIEND OR FOE?

The wireless networking engineer was working her way through the information warfare test range when she stopped and looked at her computer screen. Another unsecured access point, she noted. She was actually testing the roaming capabilities of 802.11b network devices; but as she moved their portable computers through the areas covered by the devices, other access points popped up.

This isn't surprising, because one of the nice things about wireless Internet is the ability to install the products quickly and easily, with a minimum amount of configuration. Clearly, some people around her test site (which is being kept nameless to protect the guilty) took advantage of the ease of installation but never got around to protecting their internetworks.

If Internetwork managers don't pay attention to the fact that the default condition of wireless access points is to let anyone into the network, then they may be doing just that. Those people who constitute "anyone" can include people across the street, your competitors parked outside, and malcontents who want to use your network to shield their activities. It's like installing a network port on the lamppost outside your building and asking anyone who walks by to plug in.

Fortunately, if you plan accordingly, securing your wireless Internet isn't very difficult. It just requires network administrators to take a few simple steps.

First, turn off the broadcasting of your access point's extended service set identification, which lets anyone with a wireless Internet card know the address of your wireless Internet access point. Having that ID makes logging-in even easier than it already is.

Second, turn on encryption. All 802.11b access points support the wireless encryption protocol (WEP), which can handle 40- and 128-bit encryption.

Third, turn on your ability to use access control lists, available in some access points. This allows you to keep a list of acceptable users according to the MAC address of their network card.

These steps will keep most wireless networks reasonably secure. It's convenient that these capabilities are built into most wireless Internet access points—the only exception being some early Apple AirPorts, which can be upgraded.

You must also deal with the fact that wireless access points are inexpensive, and that getting them running is a no-brainer. This means that pretty much anyone on your network can pick up a wireless access point at Best Buy, plug it into the corporate network, and use it. You'd then have an entry point into your network that's open to anyone with a wireless Internet card. Fortunately, if you already have a wireless Internet, you probably also have the management software that lets you locate all access points, including those that aren't authorized, and can either take them off the network or secure them.

Another problem is that, without limits on what users are allowed to do and where they're allowed to go, you lose control. So even more security is needed.

One solution is to move to a third-party provider of wireless security products, such as WRQ, whose *NetMotion* product requires a log-in that's authenticated through Windows NT. It uses much better encryption than is available under WEP, and it offers some security management features, such as the ability to remotely disable a wireless Internet card's connection to the network. Such capabilities require a bit more attention from managers, but the result can be a wireless Internet that's more secure than the wired one it's attached to.

Stories abound of employees who bought their own wireless access points, installed them, and claimed they were "just testing" when they were discovered. Meanwhile, these employees opened their companies' networks to anyone (friend, foe, hacker, or spy) who cared to enter.

So how do you find these people who would expose your network? Oddly enough, the easiest way is for your company to start using wireless Internet-working—in an organized fashion. That eliminates the need for employees to buy their own access points, and it gives the IT department the tools it needs to detect and eliminate them.

SUMMARY

Attacks on information technology are unsettling and easy to carry out. The means are relatively inexpensive, easy to smuggle, virtually untraceable, and completely deniable. This, coupled with the fact that the civilian networks, which are most attractive to terrorists, are also the most vulnerable, makes infowar the perfect weapon in the terrorist arsenal of the future.

Currently, the security solutions lag far behind the potential threat. This situation is likely to continue until the threat becomes reality, forcing a reassessment of preventive measures. The basic concepts and principles that must be understood and can help realistically guide the process of moving forward in dealing with the surveillance tools for the information warfare of the future are as follows.

Conclusions Drawn from the Surveillance Tools for Information Warfare of the Future

- Fortunately, the U.S. military senior leadership is becoming involved in IW, and, in many cases, taking the lead on this perplexing issue. With this emphasis, they must carefully assess the vulnerabilities of the systems they employ.

- Systems proposals must be thoroughly evaluated and prioritized by highest value payoff. This needs to be accomplished through a more balanced investment strategy by the U.S. military that conquers our institutional prejudices that favor killer systems weapons.

- Offensive systems will be at risk if the U.S. military does not apply sufficient defensive considerations in this process.

- The electromagnetic spectrum will be their 'Achilles heel' if the U.S. military does not pay sufficient attention to protecting their use of the spectrum and, at the same time, recognize that they must take away the enemy's ability to see themselves and to control his or her forces.

- Interdict opportunities exist for adversaries to intrude on U.S. military systems.

- Other nations have realized the value of offensive applications of the information warfare arsenal of the future; therefore, the U.S. military must attack. The issue from two directions, offensively and defensively, with almost equal accentuation.

- The information warfare arsenal of the future adds a fourth dimension of warfare to those of air, land, and sea. When the Soviets developed a nuclear program after World War II, the United States was caught by surprise. In this new dimension, the U.S. military must stay ahead.

- As with so many other design issues, taking the user's experience into account suggests how to proceed with implementing cookies.

- If the data contains examples of only a single class, extra work may be involved as some popular types of data-mining methods may not be appropriate.

- Although automated understanding of natural language is not available, an increasing number of techniques can be used for exploiting text data.

- An important feature of bandwidth/packet management technology is its stealthy wireless internet security features that render complete invisibility and protection for end users from network hackers and other wireless users sharing the same access points.

An Agenda for Action in Preparation of Surveillance Tools for Information Warfare of the Future

It must be pointed out that although such IW preparation measures can provide a minimum level of protection against tampering, there is no such thing as 100% security. What is more, the solutions are sure to lag behind the potential threat until the threat becomes reality. At present the cost of protection is higher than the cost of attack, and until an attack on a major system actually happens, organizations are unlikely to take security measures as seriously as they could, or should.

The United States government needs to set an agenda for action that goes beyond the work already done in preparation for defending against the surveillance tools for information warfare of the future. Action steps should include, but not be limited to the following 11 areas:

1. Use electromagnetic devices. As a punitive weapon, electromagnetic devices are attractive for dealing with belligerent governments. Substantial economic, military, and political damage may be inflicted with a modest commitment of resources by their users, and without politically damaging loss of life.

2. Use cookies wisely and visitors will appreciate their value. Use them gratuitously and visitors will resent the intrusion. It's up you to help keep cookies from being the most unpalatable junk food on the Web.

3. Short of getting rid of the ability to link to Web images from Word documents, there really is no solution to being able to track Word documents using Web bugs. Because this linking ability is a useful feature, the Privacy Foundation does not recommend its removal.

4. The Privacy Foundation does believe that the Web browser cookies should be disabled inside of *Word* documents. There appears to be very little need for cookies outside of a Web browser. In general, the Foundation believes that cookies should be disabled by default any time *Internet Explorer* is reused inside of other applications such as *Word, Excel,* or *Outlook.* Hopefully Microsoft will make this change in the next release of *Internet Explorer.*

5. Users concerned about being tracked can use a program such as *ZoneAlarm* (http://www.zonelabs.com) to warn about Web bugs in *Word* documents. *ZoneAlarm* monitors all software and warns if an unauthorized program is attempting to access the Internet. *ZoneAlarm* is designed to catch Trojan Horses and Spyware. However, because *Word* typically does not access the Internet, *ZoneAlarms* can also be used to catch "bugged" *Word* documents.

6. The data to be mined should have a direct connection to the goal task, and the new information should be directly applicable to the task situation.

7. Collect appropriate data. Think first about what kind of information is needed and how it will be used.

8. If the data already exist, understand their strengths and limitations as they relate to the task specification and the available data-mining techniques.

9. If necessary, consider alternative data sources.

10. It may be possible to augment the existing data with additional data.

11. If no additional data can be obtained, and the existing data is inadequate for the original task specification, consider altering the objectives.

ENDNOTES

i John R. Vacca, *Satellite Encryption, Academic Press*, 1999.

ii John R. Vacca, *Net Privacy: A Guide to Developing & Implementing an Iron-clad ebusiness Privacy Plan*, McGraw-Hill, 2001.

iii John R. Vacca, *Wireless Broadband Networks Handbook*, McGraw-Hill, 2001.

iv John R. Vacca, *i-mode Crash Course*, McGraw-Hill, 2002.

v John R. Vacca, *The Essential Guide to Storage Area Networks*, Prentice Hall, 2002.

vi John R. Vacca, *The Cabling Handbook (2nd Edition)*, Prentice Hall, 2001.

18 Civilian Casualties—The Victims and Refugees of Information Warfare

National information infrastructures are becoming an important vehicle for the generation of national wealth throughout the developed world. National information systems are, among other things, already used to conduct commerce and regulate and control national production. Nations are becoming increasingly dependent on their information infrastructure as the information age evolves. Accordingly, this infrastructure may now be considered to be representing an extension of national sovereignty and any attacks on national information systems may be perceived as attacks on the nation itself. This has resulted in civilian casualties (the victims and refugees of information warfare).

A further argument may be that the national security implications of information attacks make the defense against such attacks a military task. If this is the case, the vast majority of the world's military forces require a significant review of their current doctrine and capabilities. Most are presently not capable of operating in a hostile information environment. An alternative argument may be that attacks against national information systems are criminal in nature and are, therefore, the responsibility of national police forces. Again, most police forces are incapable of defending against such attacks. Indeed, there is probably no organization in the world that can adequately defend national information infrastructures as of yet. Regardless of the capabilities of the various organizations, a clear observation is that the jurisdiction boundaries that separate civilian and military security responsibilities are blurring as the information age evolves.

Separating military and civilian information operations, particularly as they pertain to defending national information systems, is also complicated by the military dependence on the civilian information infrastructure. Significant elements of

The U.S. government should face the ethical consequences of the new global bat-tleground now before a crisis arises by having a declarative policy concerning IW attacks. During the Cold War, the United States used a policy of strategic nuclear deterrence, warning that any attack on the United States could expect total destruc-tion in return. It is commonly believed that this policy of deterrence was successful but is impossible to prove. By analogy, analysts have wondered if a similar strategy might deter IW attacks on the U.S. National Information Infrastructure (NII). For a strategy of deterrence to work the following must hold:

- The incident must be well defined.
- The identity of the perpetrator must be unambiguous.
- The will and ability to carry out a deterrence strike must be believed.
- The perpetrator must have something of value at stake.
- The deterrence strike must be controllable.

This strategy of deterrence must be measured in the context of the inherent vul-nerability of large technologically based systems. In what has been called the "com-plex-system issue," there are axioms:

1. Complex systems fail in unpredictable ways from causes that seem to be minor and, often, obvious flaws in retrospect.
2. The failure of a complex system may be exceptionally difficult to discover and repair.
3. Complex systems fail at inopportune moments—usually during demand-ing system use when the consequences of failure are highest.

It must be possible to determine if an "event" involving one of the United States' vital infrastructures is the result of an accident, criminal attack, isolated terrorist inci-dent, or an act of war. The damage to the cyber masses from an event may be the same regardless of the cause, but the cause of the event will determine the jurisdic-tion and nature of the response from the U.S. Government. Possible jurisdictions include private industry, the FBI/Department of Justice, CIA/NSA, or DoD; possible responses range from doing nothing to a nuclear retaliatory strike.

Ethical Challenges of IW to Prevent Cyber Masses Losses

This part of the chapter analyzes the most significant ethical questions of IW as a new form of warfare. Many of the questions have been raised before in previous contexts, but the unique characteristics of IW bring urgency to the search for new relevant answers.

It should be noted that this analysis is also pertinent to other military situations generally referred to as operations other than war (OOTW), such as peacekeeping missions, preludes to conflict, alternatives to conflict, sanctions, and blockades. For example, in an IW analogy to the U.S. blockade of Cuba during the Cuban missile crisis, there are IW techniques (jamming and denial of service attacks) that could be used to block and, thus, isolate rogue nations from international communications without circumventing physical sovereignty—much in the same way the British decided to sever all transatlantic telegraph cables that linked Germany to international communications at the outset of World War I.

What Constitutes an Act of War in the Information Age?

The nation-state combines the intangible idea of a people (nation) with the tangible construct of a political and economic entity (state). A state under international law possesses sovereignty, which means that the state is the final arbiter of order within its physical geographical borders. Implicit to this construct is that a state is able to define and defend its physical geography. Internally, a state uses dominant force to compel obedience to laws, and externally, a state interacts with other states, interaction in either friendly cooperation, competition, or to deter and defeat threats.

At the core view of any nation-state's view of war should be a national information policy that clearly delineates national security thresholds over which another nation-state must not cross. This national information policy must also include options that consider individuals or other non-state actors who might try to provoke international conflicts.

Increasingly, the traditional attributes of the nation-state are blurring as a result of information technology. With IW, the state does not have a monopoly on dominant force, nor can even the most powerful state reliably deter and defeat IW attacks. Non-state actors are attacking across geographic boundaries, eroding the concept of sovereignty based on physical geography. With the advent of the information age, the United States has lost the sanctuary that it has enjoyed for over 200 years. In the past, U.S. citizens and businesses could be protected by government control of our air, land, and sea geographical borders, but now, an IW attack may be launched directly through (or around) these traditional geographical physical defenses.

War contemplates armed conflict between nation-states. Historically, war has been a legal status that could be specified by declaration and/or occur by way of an attack accompanied by an intention to make war. The modern view of war provides a new look at just war tradition, "jus ad bellum," (when it is right to resort to armed force) and "jus in bello," (what is right to do when using force). The six require-ments of "jus ad bellum" were developed by Thomas Aquinas in the 13th century:

1. The resort to force must have a just cause.
2. It must be authorized by a competent authority.
3. It is expected to produce a preponderance of good over evil.
4. It must have a reasonable chance of success.
5. It must be a last resort.
6. The expected outcome must be peace.

There are two requirements for "jus in bello": The use of force must be discriminate (it must distinguish the guilty from the innocent), and the use of force must be pro-portional (it must distinguish necessary force from gratuitous force). The applica-tion of just war reasoning to future IW conflicts is problematic, but there is a growing voice that there is a place for the use of force under national authority in response to broader national security threats to the values and structures that define the international order.

Looking at one aspect of the application of just war reasoning to IW is the problem of proportionality. It is impossible to respond to every IW action, because there are too many. At what threshold in the lives of the cyber masses and their money, should the United States consider an IW attack an act of war? How many cyber masses live for a certain IW attack or what is the threshold in monetary terms or physical destruction.

Article 51 in the United Nations Charter encourages settlement of interna-tional disputes by peaceful means. However, nothing in the Charter impairs the inherent right of individual or collective self-defense if an armed attack occurs.

Infringement of sovereign geographical boundaries by itself is not considered an "armed attack." Experts do not equate "use of force" with an "armed attack." Thus, certain kinds of data manipulation as a result of IW that are consistent with "use of force" would not constitute an "armed attack" under Article 51.

On the other hand, Article 41 of the United Nations specifically states measures that are not considered to be an "armed attack": complete or partial interruption of eco-nomic relations and of rail, sea, air, postal, telegraphic, radio, and other means of communications. IW might still be considered an Act of War, however, if fatalities are involved.

If data manipulation is such that the primary effects are indistinguishable from conventional kinetic weapons, then IW may be considered an "armed attack." The paradigm shift is that weapons are devices designed to kill, injure, or disable people or to damage and destroy property, and have not traditionally included electronic warfare devices.

So, what are the ethical implications of the blurring distinction between acts of war from acts of espionage from acts of terrorism? Let's take a look.

Ethical Implications

It is important to be precise in what the cyber masses identify as a crime and what they identify as an act of war. An "armed attack" as stated in Article 51 contemplates a traditional military attack using conventional weapons and does not include propaganda, information gathering, or economic sanctions. Espionage is a violation of domestic and not international law.

The threat analysis section of the 1997 Defense Science Board Report indicates that a significant threat includes activities engaged on behalf of competitor states. This introduces the new concept of low-intensity conflict in the form of economic espionage between corporations. In the age of multinational corporations that view geographical boundaries and political nation-states as historical inconveniences, should economic warfare between multinational corporations involve the military?

The new IW technologies make it difficult to distinguish between espionage and war. If espionage is conducted by computer to probe a nation's databanks and military control systems, when is it an act of war versus an act of espionage? Does it depend on whether the intelligence was passively read versus information actively destroyed in battle and/or manipulated? Does it depend on whether the intelligence was used for military advantage or for political or criminal advantage? Does the answer depend on whether a state of war exists?

A different scenario is modifying internal computer software (via viruses, Trojan horse, or logic bomb) or hardware (chipping) before shipment to cause an enemy's computer to behave in a manner other than they would expect. If during peacetime, gaining entry to a computer's internal operating system could be considered a criminal offense or act of espionage, despite the fact that the action in question took place before the enemy had acquired ownership of the computer. Is this prudent preparation for IW or is this a hostile action that could precipitate a war? If the computer hardware "chip" is commercially manufactured and altered, what are the legal and ethical implications for a company inserting internal hardware hooks as specified in cooperation with national security at the "request" of the government—especially if the company has international sales? Finally, is IW a potential step that might lead to an escalated conventional military conflict that could have been avoided by other means?

Can IW Be Considered Nonlethal?

Nonlethal weapons are defined as weapons whose intent is to nonlethally overwhelm an enemy's lethal force by destroying the aggressive capability of his or her weapons and temporarily neutralizing their soldiers. Nonlethal most often refers to immediate casualty counts, not on downstream collateral effects.

In response to the power of cyber masses opinion and instant global media coverage, the U.S. military has begun to develop a new kind of weaponry designed to minimize bloodshed by accomplishing objectives with the minimum use of lethality. This weaponry includes sticky foam cannons, sonic cannons, and electromagnetic weapons—which effectively temporarily paralyze the enemy without killing them.

Is it more ethical to use a sophisticated smart bomb precisely targeted to kill 30–40 soldiers immediately or is it more ethical to choose a nonlethal weapon that has the same tactical effect with no immediate casualty count, but an indirect collateral effect of 300–400 cyber mass deaths? Ethically, the function of the target against which the weapon is used and the existence or lack of a state of war determines one ethical framework for analysis. For instance, disabling the electronics of a fighter plane or air defense radar during wartime is the goal of a large investment in electronic warfare equipment by the United States, and is considered fair and ethical. However, disabling the electronics of a civilian airliner or air traffic control, during either peacetime or wartime, violates the principles of discrimination of combatants and proportionality of response, and is considered unethical and a act against the cyber masses.

Is It Ethical to Set Expectations for a "Bloodless War" Based on IW?

As nonlethal weaponry of all types (especially IW weapons) advance from novelty to norm, however, many potential pitfalls will need to be faced. The most important of these is the expectation that such weapons will ultimately allow wars to be fought without casualties.

Nonlethal military capabilities are not new, although IW weapons are the newest weapons in the nonlethal arsenal. Military forces have used riot-control chemical agents, defoliants, rubber bullets, and electric stun weapons for decades. As U.S. military forces are involved in missions that require extended direct contact with civilians (Somalia, Bosnia), force can no longer be viewed as either on or off, but rather as a continuum with nonlethal weapons on one end and nuclear devices on the other end. In more traditional conventional warfare, IW attacks to disrupt, deny, and destroy C4I capabilities (command, control, communication, and computer intelligence) are a core part of military tactics and strategy. If IW weapons can be used to remotely blind an opponent to incoming aircraft, disrupt logistics support, and destroy or exploit an adversary's communications, then many of the problems associated with the use of ground forces for these missions can be avoided.

It is important to point out that although nonlethal weapons are not meant to be fatal, they can still kill if used improperly or against people particularly susceptible to their effects. Because these technologies are potentially lethal in these circumstances, the term "nonlethal" has not been universally accepted within the U.S. military. For example, the U.S. Marines Corps uses the term "less lethal" to imply that there is no guarantee of nonlethality.

Asserting that IW will ultimately allow future wars to be fought without a casualty is a widespread misconception likely to prove counterproductive and even potentially dangerous to the cyber masses. First, all nonlethal weapons are not equally applicable to all military missions. Second, overselling of nonlethal capabilities without providing a context can lead to operational failures, deaths, and policy failure. Third, unrealistic expectations about nonlethal weapon capabilities inhibit their adoption by military forces that need to build confidence in these weapons.

There is a large asymmetry in global military power when comparing the United States to other nation-states. In 1994, the U.S. DoD budget exceeded that of Russia, China, Japan, France, and Great Britain combined. This asymmetry makes it unlikely another nation-state would challenge the United States in a direct high-technology conventional war, except in circumstances that cyber masses should not depend on (incredible miscalculations and/or ignorant dictators, which were both present in the Gulf War.

Despite the luxury of a bumbling opponent, the success of the Gulf War has lead the U.S. citizenry to expectations of low casualties in all future conflicts. These expectations go against two cardinal rules of military strategy: (1) you do not plan to refight the last war and (2) the future battlefields cannot be dictated by the United States. The next battlefield for which the U.S. DoD is preparing is a global battlefield with weapons of information warfare targeting the civilian infrastructure. Even in this scenario, military and civilian casualties will be likely from either primary or secondary effects from IW attacks.

Is It Ethically Correct to Respond to IW Tactics with IW Tactics?

If the United States is attacked by IW weapons, how should the U.S. government respond? By changing perspectives from defense to offense, what is in the U.S. arsenal to wage IW against an adversary:

- Offensive software (viruses, worms, trojan horses)

- Sniffing or "wiretapping" software (enabling the capture of an adversary's communications)
- Chipping (malicious software embedded in systems by manufacturer)
- Directed energy weapons (designed to destroy electronics & not humans/buildings)
- Psychological operations (sophisticated and covert propaganda techniques)

A strategy that uses these weapons in various combinations has the potential to replace conventional military forces. The questions remains: Is it ethically correct for the United States to defend its security interests by resorting to the same IW tactics that are being used against it? Should information attacks be punished by information counterattacks? The options include maintaining the United States' superpower status at all costs; covertly listening to their adversaries, but not actively disrupting operations; or contracting mercenaries, who are not officially affiliated with the U.S. government, to do their dirty work.

Cracking computers to deter and punish computer cracking erodes any moral basis the United States has for declaring the evils of IW warfare. It is also harder to predict secondary effects due to the globalization of systems. Retaliation may produce effects ranging from nothing to being counterproductive through destruction of U.S. interests. A nation-state or nonstate actor that sponsors an attack on the United States. NII might lack an NII of their own for the United States to attack in punishment, and, thus, not be intimidated by a U.S. IW deterrence strategy.

Short of an official declaration of war, nation-states may seek UN Security Council action authorizing "all necessary means" even in the absence of an "armed attack" in cases of any threat to peace, breach of peace, or act of aggression. Every breach of international law creates a duty to pay for loss or damages; nation-states may seek recompense under "state responsibility doctrine." In additional to recompense, retribution in the form of proportional countermeasures is authorized when an IW attack that does not involve the use of force violates international law. IW may violate multiple international laws depending on the scenario including the following:

- UN Convention on Law of the Sea (prohibits unauthorized broadcasts from the high seas)
- International Telecommunications Convention of 1982 (requires nations to avoid "harmful interference")
- INTELSAT Convention (satellite communications for nonmilitary purposes)[i]
- INMARSAT (maritime satellite communications for "only peaceful purposes")
- Chicago Convention (refrain from endangering safety of flight)

According to DoD policy Directive 5100.77, U.S. military forces are bound by law to follow the rules of engagement of the specific conflict as follows: "The Armed Forces of the United States shall comply with the law of war in the conduct of military operations and related activities, however such conflicts are characterized." The problem is that there are no characterized rules of engagement for IW conflicts, which can take the form of isolated operations, acts of retribution, or undeclared wars.

The most serious problem for using IW retaliation to counter IW attacks is that adversaries could counter and/or copy IW capabilities. Every breakthrough in offensive technology eventually inspires a matching advance in defensive technology, thus escalating an IW weapons race.

A last issue related to retaliation is the ethical dilemma faced by the intermingling of the military and civilian sides of society. Given the uncertainty of deterrence and identifying the enemy, the strategy that is the most ethical for retaliation is a strategy that attempts to separate the military from civilians and, in so doing, having a diminished impact, which potentially prolongs the duration of the conflict; or a strategy that attempts to minimize lethality and duration, but deliberately targets civilian systems?

Can Protection from IW Take Place in the United States Given Our Democratic Rights?

How much government control of the U.S. NII is permissible in a free society? Most of the IW technology is software—which is easy to replicate, hard to restrict, and dual-use by nature (uses for both civilian or military). In the 1997 Defense Science Board report, it states that the DoD is "confused" about when a court order is required to monitor domestic communications. This raises basic questions about the constitutional and ethical balance between privacy[ii] and national security in a new IW context.

A "Big Brother" approach that places all of a nation's telecommunications under a single government jurisdiction is improbable given the diffusion and complexity of technology and the shrinking size of government. Most systems were built to serve commercial users who will vehemently object to unfunded mandates (taxes) and new requirements not driven by business demand (CLIPPER chip encryption and key escrow accounts). Regardless, it is critical to the future security of the United States that the cyber masses find a way to protect their infrastructure from IW attack and have contingency plans for potential IW crises. If the IW attack is detected and the enemy identified, but the United States is unable to react promptly due to bureaucratic inefficiency or indifference from private industry, it may be too late to react at all.

Current political discussion has floated tax incentives and direct subsidies to promote industry cooperation. In a related matter that may provide a precedent, the government has pledged to provide telephone companies with at least $900 million to ensure that FBI officials can access telephone conversations over digital circuits (as opposed to accessing telephone conversations over analog circuits, which is technically much easier).

Now, let's take a look at how much damage and/or destruction cyberattacks actually cause.

THE DESTRUCTION OF PERSONAL ASSETS IN INFORMATION WARS

The Mounties always get their man—or, when it comes to hackers, their boy. In 2000, Canadian cops announced the arrest of a Montreal-area 15-year-old for disabling CNN's Web site. His father was also nabbed, on unrelated charges of plotting to assault a business associate. The teen suspect, who was identified only by the hacker handle "Mafiaboy," allegedly bragged about his exploits in on-line chats. He was not what one would call a genius. Mafiaboy was charged with two counts of "mischief to data" and faces two years' detention plus a $786 fine. While awaiting trial, he could not enter any public space that hosts networked computers.

The CNN.com incident was part of a rash of "denial of service" attacks that crippled Yahoo!, eBay, and other Internet titans, leading to a manhunt that stretched throughout the United States, Canada, and Germany. The international dragnet was spurred by damage and/or destruction of personal and corporate assets estimates ranging up to $2.3 billion (see sidebar, "Widespread Break-in by Crime Groups Cause Damage").

WIDESPREAD BREAK-IN BY CRIME GROUPS CAUSE DAMAGE

The FBI recently disclosed it has launched 50 separate investigations into alleged hacking incidents by Eastern European organized crime groups that are believed to have stolen more than 2 million credit card numbers from e-commerce[iii] and on-line finance Web sites powered by *Windows NT* servers. The break-ins have occurred in 30 U.S. states and are thought to be part of a systematic effort by crime syndicates in Russia and Ukraine to break into vulnerable Web servers. Estimated financial losses since the FBI's National Infrastructure Protection Center (NIPC) issued an initial warning about the threat in December 2000 total as much as hundreds of millions of dollars.

But the figure could be much higher. The NIPC hasn't been able to determine an exact damage amount. The agency, which is based at FBI headquarters in Washington, released an advisory saying the hacking activities are continuing. The advisory reiterated a recommendation that systems administrators should check their *Windows NT*-based servers to make sure patches designed to fix several known security holes have been installed.

To date, the NIPC spokeswoman claimed that e-commerce sites across the country have failed to heed the warnings about the holes in Microsoft Corp.'s operating system software. This a public service announcement meant to urge companies to bolster the security of their Web sites by downloading the patches made available by Microsoft.

These organized crime groups have hit on these sites using known vulnerabilities for months now, and people are not heeding the warnings. Microsoft discovered and patched many of the vulnerabilities in NT as early as 1998. But until companies take the appropriate steps, the attacks are "not going to stop."

Federal investigators have identified several different groups of hackers that they believe are responsible for the incidents. It's national in scope and at a point that the FBI felt it was appropriate to let a wider audience know what is going on. The threat posed by the hackers is a serious impediment to public confidence in e-commerce.

There's no way of knowing how widely the NT patches have been applied. Download rates are a poor indicator because a single download can be applied "an infinite number of times." Conversely, the fact that a user has downloaded a patch doesn't guarantee it will actually be applied. Still, it is clear that not enough users are installing patches.

The crime syndicates are targeting customer data, specifically credit card information, according to the FBI. In many cases, the attacks go on for several months before the company being hit discovers the intrusion.

After the attackers steal the data from a Web site, they often contact the victimized company by fax, e-mail, or telephone and make a veiled extortion threat by offering Internet-based security services that would protect the targeted server from other attackers. Federal investigators also believe that, in some instances, the credit card information is being sold to other organized crime groups. The NIPC's advisories or warnings about the attackers list the vulnerabilities that are being exploited and provide links to bulletins issued by Microsoft about the relevant patches.

A lot of malicious hacking activity, including widescale probing of Web servers, is originating in Eastern Europe. Anything that gets plugged in to the Internet gets probed. It's not a question of if, but when.

The SANS Institute, a Bethesda, Maryland-based research organization for systems administrators and security managers, and recently released an alert about the

FBI's ongoing investigations that called the hacking incidents the largest criminal Internet attack to date. The alert added that the SANS-affiliated Center for Internet Security plans "within a day or two" to release a software tool that can be used to check NT servers for the vulnerabilities and to look for files found by the FBI on many compromised systems. The center's tools are usually limited to its members, but SANS indicated this one will be made available on a widespread basis because of the importance of this problem.

The NIPC wouldn't identify any of the Web sites that have been hit by attacks. But in December 2000, Creditcards.com, a Los Angeles-based company that has since changed its name to iPayment Technologies Inc., confirmed that about 66,000 credit-card numbers had been stolen from its Web site. More than 36,000 of the numbers were exposed on the Internet after the company ignored a $200,000 extortion attempt believed to have come from a Russian hacker.

Recently, Bibliofind.com, an on-line marketplace for rare and hard-to-find books that's owned by Amazon.com Inc., disclosed that a malicious hacker had compromised the security of credit-card data for about 109,000 users of its Web site. The intrusions began in October 2000, and weren't discovered until recently.

Egghead.com Inc. in Menlo Park, California, was also hit by an intrusion late in 2000. The on-line technology retailer's CEO said recently that an internal investigation showed that no customer data had been compromised. But some Egghead users claimed that their credit-card numbers had, in fact, been stolen, with one saying her card was debited for a charge to a fraudulent Web site in Russia.

Critics charge that companies and prosecutors regularly inflate such numbers and that the Mafiaboy case is no exception. If you're a law enforcement organization, it makes the crime look more serious. If you're a company, it allows you to get more money from insurance (see sidebar, "Hacker Insurance"). And if you're the press, it makes the story more sensational."

HACKER INSURANCE

In the increasingly competitive hacker insurance market, American International Group is making an offer it hopes prospective clients won't refuse—a free, comprehensive security assessment. AIG, the largest commercial insurance underwriter in the United States, hopes the free on-site security check—which ordinarily can cost tens of thousands of dollars—will encourage more companies to buy insurance coverage from it. AIG is one of the biggest players in a swarm of underwriters and brokers who are rushing into the hacker insurance market, a sector that the Insurance Information Institute estimates could generate $3.6 billion in annual premiums by 2006.

The insurers' sales efforts are being aided by highly publicized events such as the assault on Microsoft's Web site in January and the more recent "Anna Kournikova" worm that tied up mail servers around the world. Insurance industry officials indicate their business is doubling every 7 to 13 months, as worries about hacking increase and more information technology professionals realize their companies' standard insurance policies don't cover risks incurred by their Internet-based businesses.

Cyber masses aren't used to spending money on this. The cost of the insurance application in the past included (for almost everyone) an on-site security assessment that would cost upward of $30,000, regardless of whether you bought the insurance.

To help convince qualified prospects (applicants must be seeking $6 million or more in coverage) to buy insurance, AIG will pay independent security firms Global Integrity and Unisys to do the on-site assessments. The firms will do external probes and "ethical hacking" of a prospect's Web site, as well as perform a three-day, on-site analysis to determine what types of security problems the company faces.

At the end of the assessment, if a prospect decides not to buy AIG's coverage, the company can keep the security report and assessments as AIG's gift. Although AIG's assessment is free, some competitors expressed skepticism. AIG's offer may create a false sense of security among insurance buyers. Security is not a product; it's a process.

What's Covered

Companies interested in hacker insurance can buy coverage either as a package or a la carte. Some policies only pay for risks associated with loss or misuse of intellectual property. Others cover liability for misuse of a company's site by a third party, or damage caused by an outside hacker.

Premiums are generally based on a company's revenue, as well as the type and amount of coverage being sought. Rates vary. A package policy that covers a range of risks, including liability, loss of revenue, errors and omissions, and virus protection, can cost from $7,000 to $21,000 per year (or more) for each million dollars of coverage in the policy.

Given the range of costs and coverage, industry officials warn potential buyers to be wary. Some policies cover only the amount of net income lost due to hacking. A better choice for some companies may be coverage for lost revenue.

Numerous variables can affect premiums. Just as a buyer of auto insurance can choose a high dollar deductible to lower the premium, hacker insurance buyers can choose different waiting periods before coverage begins. For instance, a policy that begins paying for business losses just four hours after a hacker shuts down a site may cost more than a policy that begins paying after 24 hours of downtime. These waiting periods, called "time element deductibles," are variable and depend on the kind of business being covered and the amount of risk a business may face.

Companies can also get substantial discounts on their policies if they have managed service contracts with an insurer-certified security firm. Security assessments are critically important for both insurers and insurance buyers. Hacker insurance is such a new product that there are no reliable actuarial tables to determine rates. Therefore, insurance companies rely heavily on the assessments to help them determine the amount of risk they are taking on with a given company. For the companies seeking insurance, assessments should help them find (and immediately fix) holes in their defense systems.

Stiff Competition

Underwriters competing with AIG (the Chubb Group, Fidelity and Deposit Companies, St. Paul Companies, Lloyd's of London and Wurzler) are rolling out a fleet of new products and alliances to help them gain market share. Chubb recently announced new coverage designed for on-line banks, brokerages, and insurance companies. Wurzler has joined with Hewlett-Packard to market its products to a select group of HP's clients.

Insurance brokers and security firms are teaming up to sell branded products and services. Marsh & McClennan Companies, the world's largest insurance brokerage, is selling insurance provided by AIG, Chubb and Lloyd's. The brokerage relies on internet security systems to do its security assessments. Counterpane Internet Security has allied with brokers Safeonline and Frank Crystal & Co. to provide its clients with special policies underwritten by Lloyd's.

It's a wildly growing market, and its primary underwriters are AIG, Fidelity and Deposit, and Wurzler. Hacker insurance has been a small market because people were waiting for e-commerce to hit. Well, now e-commerce has hit.

Insurers are finding a ready market for their products, because companies with Internet operations are increasingly under attack. A survey done in 2000 by the Federal Bureau of Investigation and the Computer Security Institute, an association of computer security personnel from the private and public sectors, found that from March 1999 to March 2000, 29% of the 752 governmental agencies and businesses that responded indicated that they experienced denial-of-service attacks. Viruses are also wrecking havoc. Losses from 2000's "Love Bug" virus were estimated to be as high as $20 billion.

AIG's move to lower the cost of obtaining hacker insurance shows the market is beginning to mature, according to industry experts. And security analysts hope it will encourage more Net companies to get insurance coverage.

Companies need to understand that getting hacked is not only an inconvenience. Anything Internet-facing is a point of vulnerability. Companies can be attacked directly or they can be used to attack someone else. There's real exposure and liability. They need to reduce their risk, and the only way to do that is through proper insurance.

Pricing cyberintrusions is pretty much a guessing game. If a burglar steals your television set, you know what its replacement value might be. But what's the value of the time of all the people who had to drop their work and deal with this hacker nonsense? More tangential costs are also often tabulated; the $2.3 billion figure associated with recent attacks, calculated by the Yankee Group, includes the expense of security upgrades, consulting fees, and losses in market capitalization from tumbling stock prices.

The implication is that companies wouldn't have had to spend the money if they never had a problem. That's like saying you don't need to get a lock for your front door unless somebody breaks in.

Fair Punishment

Inflated estimates can skew jail terms. A formula should be devised to calculate the severity of hacks. The question is, how serious a societal harm has been done in the hands of these companies, without any real check or balance? If the FBI is going to punish somebody by sending them to prison, they probably don't want to send them to prison for something that's just a nuisance.

In one famous case, an editor at the computer-security webzine *Phrack* was charged with publishing a document stolen from BellSouth's network. Prosecutors valued the 13-page paper at $80,550, which included the $42,000 cost of the computer it was typed on, $7,000 for the printer, and $7,300 for a "project manager." It was revealed at trial, however, that BellSouth sold a nearly identical document to the public for just $14 per copy.

SHORT- AND LONG-TERM PERSONAL ECONOMIC IMPACT ON CYBER CITIZENS

Cyberattacks cost U.S. organizations and their cyber citizens $377 million in 2000—more than double the average annual losses for the previous three years. The study, released by the San Francisco-based Computer Security Institute (CSI) and the San Francisco FBI Computer Intrusion Squad, found that 92% of survey respondents detected some form of security breach in 2000.

Based on information from 384 of CSI's member organizations, 72% reported serious security attacks, including theft of proprietary information, financial fraud, system penetration from outsiders, denial-of-service attacks, and sabotage of data or networks. This figure, up from 64% in 1998, didn't include data from common security problems caused by computer viruses, laptop theft, and abuse of Internet access by employees.

According to the report, 76% of respondents confirmed that they sustained financial losses due to security attacks, but only 44% said they were willing and able to quantify these costs. The figures are based on responses from 754 computer security practitioners in 384 U.S. corporations, government agencies, financial institutions, medical institutions, and universities.

The $377 million in verifiable losses claimed by respondents was more than twice the average annual total of $140 million reported from 1998 to 2000. Seventy-seven respondents reported $77.8 million in losses from theft of proprietary information and 64 organizations listed $67 million in losses from financial fraud.

CSI indicates a continuing trend in the study—that computer security threats to large corporations and government agencies come from both inside and outside the organization. Whereas media reports often focus on outside computer crackers, 82% of respondents were worried about disgruntled employees. Sixty-two respondents indicated that they suffered $28 million in damages from sabotage of data or networks, compared to a combined total of $32 million for previous years.

For the third consecutive year, 60% of respondents identified their Internet connection as a frequent point of attack, compared with 39% who cited internal systems as the target. The short- and long-term personal economic impact on cyber citizens continues to be staggering.

Unauthorized access and security attacks are widespread. The private sector and government organizations must increase their focus on sound security practices, deployment of sophisticated defensive technology, and adequate training and staffing of security managers.

Next, let's take look at why corporations are mobilizing against the threat of a federal Internet privacy-protection law, which violates the privacy of their employees during the onset of information warfare.

THE VIOLATION OF PRIVACY DURING INFORMATION WARS

Privacy—who could possibly be against it? Not IBM, which has vowed to yank all its ads from Web sites that fail to post a clear privacy policy. Not America Online, which promises never to disclose information about members to "outside companies."

And certainly not Microsoft, which in 1999 threw its weight behind a plan that could one day let people skip automatically past sites that don't meet their privacy standards. The biggest collectors of information, it seems, are suddenly in the forefront of the campaign for our right to be let alone.

Privacy protection is good for business (see sidebar, "Cyberattack Protection Plan"). But it may not be quite that simple. True, millions of Americans are wary of the Internet, and surveys suggest that many are hanging back because of confidentiality concerns.

CYBERATTACK PROTECTION PLAN

Privacy advocates in 2000 raised red flags before a U.S. Senate Judiciary Subcommittee looking into privacy implications of a plan to safeguard critical systems against cyberattacks. Critics of the plan charged specifically that it relies too heavily on monitoring and surveillance, instead of simply focusing on making systems more secure.

Called the "National Plan for Information Systems Protection," the plan will eventually loop in critical systems for communications, transportation, and financial services. There is disagreement as to whether an intrusive, government-directed initiative that views computer security as almost solely defending cyberspace from foreign assault is the right way to go.

The Electronic Privacy Information Center (EPIC) especially took exception to the plan's inclusion of a Federal Intrusion Detection Network (FIDNet). Under the plan, a single government agency would be allowed to monitor communications across all federal networks.

FIDNET would require notification to all users of federal systems, including government employees and the public, or would break various privacy statutes including wiretapping guidelines. EPIC officials indicated that the government's security policy overall has been inconsistent because it has prevented availability of some encryption and security tools.

The plan is designated Version 1.0 and subtitled "An Invitation to a Dialog" to indicate that it is still a work in progress and that a broader range of perspectives must be taken into account if the plan is truly to be national in scope and treatment. Part of the unfolding plan calls for a partnership between Fortune 500 companies and all levels of government to work out details for safeguarding computers.

Privacy must play a key part in any efforts to hone details of the plan. The government is just now digging itself out of the many mistakes that were made over the past decade with computer security policy. This is not the best time to be pushing an outdated approach to network security.

However, the recent frenzy of corporate initiatives is only partly about building public trust. It's also about fending off legislation. Corporate America is mobilizing against the threat of a broad federal privacy-protection law. In particular, businesses are disturbed by one likely element of such a law: a subject access provision that would allow citizens to find out what companies know about them and how the information is being used.

To comply with such a measure, corporate information systems would have to be retrofitted to serve a purpose for which they weren't designed—a vastly expensive undertaking that worried executives liken to the year 2000 problem. The technological costs, however, could be exceeded by the psychological costs.

Junkbusters

If subject access becomes law, Americans will be stunned to discover how much data large corporations have on them. People are going to be horrified.

So far, the United States has addressed the subject on a case-by-case basis. The confidentiality of video rentals is protected, for example, because a reporter got hold of Robert Bork's rental records during the fight over his failed nomination to the Supreme Court. Otherwise, corporate lobbyists have sold Republican and Democratic leaders alike on their view of the Internet economy as a tender, if vital, young thing needing protection from the regulatory mechanisms of the past.

The market can do the job. In addition, companies are banding together to develop privacy guidelines, hoping to show that they can regulate themselves. That premise, however, is under mounting attack on two fronts, domestic and foreign.

The immediate pressure is coming from Europe. A European Union privacy directive that took effect in October not only includes subject access but also requires that, when soliciting information from people, companies clearly spell out what they intend to do with it. This concept is anathema to many large U.S. companies. Accustomed to collecting data for hazy purposes (a "personalized experience"), businesses reserve the right to discover more specific uses or sell the information later on.

But the most annoying element of the EU directive, as far as U.S. corporations are concerned, is a ban on transborder shipment of data to countries that don't offer "adequate" privacy guarantees. The Sabre Group, a Texas-based airline-reservation network, is fighting in Swedish court for the right to maintain in its global data bank such facts as a passenger's wheelchair use or preference for kosher meals. Prodded by Sabre and other large information-oriented companies, the U.S. government is trying to convince European officials that the argument isn't really over the degree of privacy protection, but over two different "cultural perspectives." The Europeans have gone to ridiculous extremes, creating privacy commissions and "privacy czars" to deal with such trivialities as L. L. Bean's decision to send out a catalog of their home products as opposed to their clothing products." Literally interpreted, the EU directive would bar a traveling American business executive from flying home with the names and phone numbers of European clients in his laptop.

Double Standard

Such fears are overwrought. But the European officials point to deep historical reasons (including Nazism) for their view of privacy as a basic human right. The White House is not in any position to cut deals on that, any more than the British are in a position to cut deals on the U.S.'s First Amendment. But if Washington has to make concessions, U.S. multinationals could find themselves in the ticklish position of explaining why they have granted rights to Europeans that they are trying to withhold from Americans. The self-regulation concept has already suffered a series of embarrassments at home. In 1999, Microsoft was discovered to be collecting data on users who had expressly requested anonymity.

Privacy advocates agree that there are informal and technological fixes for many of the problems. On-line privacy protection has the potential to become a significant industry in itself. But it will grow much faster with legal incentives. In the absence of sanctions, the privacy commissioner of Hong Kong claims that self-regulation amounts to putting Count Dracula in charge of the blood bank.

Oddly enough, the concept of subject access originated in the United States, with the Fair Credit Reporting Act of 1971. Credit companies have been living quite profitably with the rule for over 30 years.

Many of the same companies that have been battling against a federal privacy law, have pressed Congress to enact more stringent copyright and patent laws. They're only against regulation when it's something they don't like.

Exposed on-line? On the Web, your personal life is merely marketable data. Learn how to protect your personal information on-line next.

THE INDIVIDUAL EXPOSED

On the Internet, goes the saying, nobody knows you're a dog. If that ode to on-line anonymity was once true, the notion seems laughable today. The Internet is now more like an unlocked diary, with millions of consumers divulging marketable details of their personal lives, from where they live to what they eat for dinner. Operators of sites on the World Wide Web collect and sell the information, or use it to lure advertising. Software tracks the sites you visit and the pages that catch your eye. If you were a dog, on-line snoops would soon learn that you're a collie who plays a mean game of Frisbee catch and likes your kibble moist.

No one is immune. On-line databases bulge with facts on millions of Americans. "Spammers" cram your e-mailbox with ads. And continuous loopholes in *Netscape Navigator* and Microsoft *Explorer* are giving Web administrators direct access to the hard disk of any browser user visiting their site.

Businesses recognize the Web's potential as a "shopping mall," but because of concern over consumer privacy, many stores in that "shopping mall" were forced out of business. It doesn't help matters that many Web sites don't reveal how they intend to use the information collected or whether it might be shared. In a recent survey by the Boston Consulting Group, more than 74% of on-line users worried more about offering up private facts on-line than they did via phone or mail—so they often refused or gave false information. Mounting user fears prompted the Federal Trade Commission to hold a four-day public workshop recently to determine whether the government should step in. Congress is examining the issue, too; several measures to govern the use and sale of personal data, such as Social Security numbers, are pending.

Facing possible regulation, on-line companies vowed during the workshop to help individuals preserve their anonymity and decide whether to reveal personal details. After all, a pro-consumer stance is good for business. It is estimated that on-line consumer commerce will grow from 1996's $500 million to as much as $78 billion by the year 2002—if privacy is addressed, that is.

There have been recent attempts to do so. Recently, *Netscape* and about 100 other Internet companies proposed a privacy-oriented Open Profiling Standard (OPS). Also, Microsoft and 80 other businesses recently signed on. Under OPS, you would no longer be asked to register your name, age, ZIP code, and other facts at each site. Rather, you would store them in an encrypted file on your hard drive. A site could grab any part of the file only after you had approved how the data would be used. The explanation would pop up when you clicked on an independent auditor's logo authenticating the claims. The World Wide Web Consortium, which develops various standards for the Web, is mulling the proposal and working on its own privacy standard. It should be completed within the year 2002.

Of course, you can avoid keying in anything you consider private. But that would bar you from using quite a few sites, and abstinence is not always foolproof. Using a technology called "cookies," some sites, unbeknownst to you, can pick up the address of the site you most recently visited and the Internet service provider (ISP) or on-line service used, and can log your movements within the site. Even companies that advertise there can also drop cookies on your hard drive without your knowledge; some expire only after the year 2002.

Web users do have a few ways to deal with the cookie problem. Surfing through the *Anonymizer* hides your identity but slows you down to some degree. You can also program most popular Web browsers to accept or reject cookies before they are downloaded to your hard disk. Many shareware programs, which can be tried out before being purchased, can help you manage cookies (you might want to permit cookies from a personalized news product, for example) or cut them out entirely; *Cookie Crusher, Cookie Pal,* and *CookieMaster* can all be downloaded.

You're Everywhere! You're Everywhere!

None of these tools, however, will wipe out details about you that are stored in on-line databases ranging from telephone books such as *Switchboard* and *WorldPages* to commercial reference services such as *Lexis-Nexis, CDB Infotek,* and *Information America.* Résumé banks, professional directories, alumni registries, and news archives can all be harvested, as well.

Resourceful thieves can exploit these on-line caches. The Delaware State Police nabbed a couple recently who had obtained birth certificates and drivers' licenses in others' names (thus enabling them to open bank accounts and get credit cards) using information gleaned from sources that included the Internet. Going on-line made it much easier to get at some of the more personal information.

Eight major reference services announced an agreement at the FTC workshop to prevent the misuse of nonpublic data, such as the name, address, and Social Security number found at the top of a credit report. A law enforcement agency, for example, might see all of the data, but a commercial enterprise might not see the Social Security number.

> *The Fair Credit Reporting Act restricts dissemination of data in the body of a credit report (such as credit card accounts, car loans, or mortgages), but does not cover the material at the top.*

NOTE

Much of the material in on-line databases is culled from public files such as property tax records and drivers' license rolls. That raises questions about the quality of the data. It's a known fact that databases are notoriously inaccurate. Yet major institutions use such services to judge, say, fitness for jobs and insurance. Privacy advocates say consumers should be told if any personal facts are being sold, and should have the right to dispute errors in the databases. In their proposed privacy guidelines, however, reference services agreed merely to tell people the "nature" of the data held on them.

Privacy advocates also argue that consumers should be able to opt out of junk e-mail, or spam. America Online, the largest on-line service, says that up to 34% of the 19 million e-mail messages its members receive each day are junk, and that spamming is members' No. 1 complaint. Although all major on-line services and

ISPs prohibit spamming and use filtering programs to weed it out (several have won injunctions barring spammers from their networks), the filters don't always work. Sleazy marketers often also use fake return addresses that are nearly impossible to track down. The FTC recently vowed to prosecute perpetrators of fraud and deception, soliciting the assistance of the new Internet E-Mail Marketing Council.

The FTC recently gave on-line businesses and organizations six months to a year to make good on their promises to protect the privacy of on-line consumers. If that does not happen, the FTC will consider taking stronger steps to enable people to browse and buy in confidently as if they were shopping at the local mall.

Stolen identity? It can ruin your credit. And that's just the beginning.

UNCOVERING SECRET IDENTITIES

When Melanie Banks (named changed to protect her privacy) and her husband went to the bank in December to refinance their home, they thought it would be routine. After all, the couple, who live in Topeka, Kansas, were refinancing with their existing mortgage lender, and they prided themselves on their credit history. So it was quite a shock when the bank officer turned them down, pointing to their credit report, which listed numerous accounts in arrears.

It turns out that a woman in New Mexico had applied for credit 22 times using Bank's name and Social Security number. In all, she had made purchases totaling $90,000, leaving a trail of unpaid debt that Banks is desperately trying to prove is not hers: a $38,000 loan for a mobile home, three car loans, credit card bills, and charges for a cellular phone and other services. The perpetrator torched her credit to the point where even the perpetrator herself was denied.

Banks is a victim of a crime of the 21st century—identity theft. It happens when one individual uses another's personal identification (name, address, Social Security number; date of birth; mother's maiden name) to take over or open new credit cards and bank accounts; apply for car and house loans; lease cars and apartments; and, even take out insurance. The perpetrators don't make the payments, and the victim is left to deal with the damage—calls from collection agencies and creditors; the endless paperwork that results from trying to expunge fraudulent accounts from a credit record; and, the agony of waiting to see if more phony accounts pop up. Meanwhile, the proliferation of black marks on a credit report can be devastating. Victims of identity theft are often unable to get loans; some run into trouble applying for a job. A few have even been arrested after the thief committed a crime in the victim's name.

Many identity thieves use stolen personal information to obtain driver's licenses, birth certificates, and professional licenses, making it easier to get credit. Most victims don't even know how the criminals pulled it off. Data have been stolen from desk drawers in the workplace, mailboxes, job application forms, and the Internet. False identification cloaks a thief in anonymity, and the impostor can often use the alias for a prolonged period of time. Thieves typically have the bills sent to an address that is not the victim's, concealing the scheme for months, even years. Most victims aren't aware that their credit has taken a nose-dive until, like Banks, they apply for credit themselves or receive a call from a bill collector.

Proof Positive

In the 1980s, criminals who wanted free plastic simply made up counterfeit credit cards with the correct number of digits. To thwart them, the industry instituted sophisticated security measures involving holograms and algorithms. Now criminals are taking advantage of what some see as the weakest link in the credit system: personal identity. There is nothing in the system that demands proof that you are the person you say you are. Personal identifiers are now, more than ever, a valuable commodity to criminals.

Although no single agency tracks identity fraud, statistics collected by the GAO point to a growing problem. Trans Union, for example, one of the three major credit bureaus, indicates three-fourths of all consumer inquiries relate to identity fraud. Those inquiries numbered 35,235 in 1992; in 2000 there were 855,255. The costs of identity fraud can be very high: The Secret Service indicates losses to victims and institutions in its identity-fraud investigations were $1.8 billion in 2000, up from $442 million in 1995. It's a problem that Congress has to address.

Identity fraud is a relatively new phenomenon, and it's not a crime, except in a handful of states, such as Arizona and California, which have recently made it illegal. Legislation is pending to make it a federal crime.

Most victims call the police. But in states with no statute, some police departments refuse to take a report because the law sees the victim in a case of identity fraud as the party that granted the credit (the bank or the merchant, for example), and not the person impersonated. That's frustrating to the victims because they often need a report to prove they are not the bad guys.

Victims need proof because the attitude they often encounter when dealing with creditors is guilty, guilty, and guilty. Every person Mike Smith (name changed to protect privacy) talks to has been skeptical, condescending, and hostile, and he is still trying to clean his credit report of 23 bounced checks, written to stores in Arizona in 1994 on a bank account opened fraudulently in his name. That really aggravates Smith who has already been turned down for a mortgage. Victims often have to play detective, coming up with clues, leads, and even the basic evidence that a fraud has been committed. You have to do all the footwork yourself.

Even the Kitchen Sink

Typically, creditors ask an identity-theft victim to fill out an affidavit certifying he or she did not incur the debt. Some require much more: One collection agency told Banks it needed a copy of her driver's license, her Social Security card, her birth certificate, and any lease or mortgage contract for the past five years—all for a $54 cable bill. In the end, Banks neither paid the bill nor sent the copies to prove her innocence, opting to explain the $54 item on her credit report to future creditors. As with many victims of identity theft, sensitive documents were the last thing she wanted to send to a stranger.

The belligerence that victims encounter from some creditors is particularly irksome to those who suspect a creditor's negligence in the first place. Many creditors do not take the proper steps to verify the identity of the credit applicant. Dorothy Helus (name changed to protect privacy) of Reston, Virginia, points to a credit-card application that started an impostor on a crime spree in her name: The application was preprinted with the impostor's name and address, but the impostor had crossed off her own name (leaving her address) and written in Helus's name, Social Security number, and occupation. The bank gave the impostor a credit card with a $20,000 credit line, leading Helus to ask: "Wouldn't a reasonable person say something is fishy here?" Bankers, meanwhile, insist they are on the ball. All the banks have systems that detect fraud. They have to modify them for every new scheme that comes up.

Dialing for Dollars

To make matters worse, two weeks after Helus notified the bank that the account was fraudulent, the bank sold it to a collection agency, and she and her children started receiving threatening phone calls and letters. It didn't stop there. The card triggered an avalanche of preapproved credit offers to the phony Helus's mailbox: One different address on a credit account was all it had taken for one of the credit bureaus to switch Helus's credit-file address to the impostor's. They came to Helus like candy. Some credit bureaus won't change a file address until three creditors report a new address, but a criminal on a spree can quickly cross that threshold.

It's not easy getting a credit report back on track. The credit bureau says contact the creditor, the creditor says contact the credit bureau, and the consumer just gets ping-ponged back and forth. The bureaucracy can be maddening: Banks recently received a letter from the credit bureau Experian saying it was reinserting a disputed item. The letter did not say which of the 22 accounts it referred to.

One of the few weapons victims have to protect them is a "fraud alert," which credit bureaus will put in consumer credit files. This notifies anyone who pulls the report that the subject is a victim of fraud and that he or she should be called to verify any credit application. The alert isn't foolproof.

Credit bureaus might want to step up their efforts at finding a solution before more aggrieved consumers turn to the courts. Recently, in Clarksdale, Mississippi, a man won a lawsuit against Trans Union for failing to clean up his credit report. The award: $7.8 million.

Meanwhile, the credit-reporting industry has formed a taskforce to tackle identity theft. Among solutions being considered are taking files of theft victim's off-line and sharing fraud alerts among credit bureaus more quickly. Individual creditors are also taking steps to stem their losses and prevent future ones. In San Francisco, Cellular One routinely flags suspect applications and compares details with credit reports. That's how Irene Cole (named changed to protect privacy) in San Francisco found out her identity had been compromised: Recently, a woman applied for service using Irene Cole's identity, but Cellular One's fraud department thought the application looked suspicious and phoned her to check. Moreover, it alerted competitors in the area that they might be the next targets.

Identity theft is a crime that comes back to haunt its victims, and many are taking determined measures to prevent its recurrence. Banks and her husband have taken an unusual vow: When they have children, they will not get them Social Security numbers—even though that means no tax deduction. To her way of thinking, safeguarding her children's identity is far more valuable.

Service providers have largely solved the cloning problem, but the monitoring of private affairs in cyber space is still an issue, and e-commerce has barely been addressed. Cellular security is better, but foes still lurk.

THE MONITORING OF PRIVATE AFFAIRS IN CYBER SPACE

Not being Prince Charles or Newt Gingrich, most of us give little thought to cell-phone eavesdropping. After all, who cares if someone overhears you telling your husband or wife you're stuck in traffic. Of course, if the conversation is of a sensitive nature, then one of your concerns is (or should be) the security of your phone.

Cellular service providers have a different security problem. Their great concern is service theft, through which criminals succeed in using a cell-phone without paying for it.

In the early days of cellular telephony, service theft mostly meant cloning. People with radio scanners would simply "sniff" the cellular frequency bands, pick up cell-phone identification numbers, and program them into other phones. That problem has been reduced by almost two orders of magnitude through the application of some thoughtful technology. But it has been replaced by other problems: subscription fraud (the same problem that bedevils issuers of credit cards) and the misapplication of service provider subsidies on handsets.

Subscription fraud has several forms: pretending to be another, real person; pretending to be a nonexistent person; and even just being yourself and pretending you intend to pay your bill. Subsidy fraud involves taking a phone whose cost has been heavily subsidized by a cellular carrier and activating it on a different carrier's network.

Solutions to these problems exist. However, the newest and best of them cannot be implemented on old handsets, so the technical situation is not without interest. Some of the solutions, particularly those used to fight subscription fraud, tend by their very nature to inhibit sales (after all, the idea is to eliminate deadbeats), which presents the executives of cellular companies with a dilemma. On the one hand, many of them need the revenue stream from a large number of subscribers to help them pay off the huge investments they made when they bid wildly for spectrum space back in 1995. On the other, they have no desire to be cheated.

As the practice of conducting serious business over the Internet continues to grow, other security issues will arise. In particular, someone conducting business on a cell-phone needs to be confident of the identity of the other instrument's user. The technical solutions to be discussed here, such as RF fingerprinting and authentication, do a good job of guaranteeing that the handset is what it claims to be, but they guarantee nothing about the person using it.

Several approaches are being pursued to user identification. The problem, in fact, is not finding solutions, but getting everyone to agree on which to use. To do banking over a cell-phone, your bank, your cellular service provider, and your phone must agree on the same end-to-end solution. And the phone companies, as an industry, must standardize that solution to drive mass-market end-user accessibility.

Biometrics may play a role here. In fact, one company, AuthenTec Inc., in Melbourne, Florida, is developing a fingerprint sensor that can be integrated into a cell-phone without adding noticeably to the phone's weight, price, or energy consumption (see sidebar, "Checking Fingerprints").

CHECKING FINGERPRINTS

As everyone knows, the time-tested way to verify a person's identity is through his or her fingerprints. For the present application, the question is can it be done quickly, without expert assistance, when the person is out in the field somewhere using a cell-phone?

The answer, according to the people at AuthenTec Inc., Melbourne, Florida, is yes. All it takes is the company's FingerLoc fingerprint sensor, its accompanying software, and a microprocessor on which the software can run.

Finding a microprocessor is no problem. Modern digital handsets contain quite powerful processors that have nothing to do when a cell call is not in progress.

The FingerLoc sensor is a monolithic silicon chip comprising a sensing array and its associated circuitry, all covered by a fairly thick (75 µm) proprietary coating. It can be easily embedded in the surface of a cell-phone, where the robust coating will protect it from the rigors of normal usage.

FingerLoc's key advantage over other (optical) fingerprint sensors, is that it ignores the external fingerprint, which is often dirty or damaged or has even disappeared. Instead, it senses the fingerprint in a buried layer of living cells, where fingerprints are created, and where they are found in pristine condition.

What it does is apply a low-voltage AC signal to the fingertip and then measures how the resulting electric field varies in amplitude over the fingertip surface. The signal is applied by means of a conductive epoxy ring surrounding the sensor area. It is defined and measured with respect to a reference plane within the chip.

The electric field is set up between the reference plane and a thin layer of highly conductive saline liquid that resides at the interface of the living skin tissue and the dead skin. The saline layer has the same shape as the living tissue—the shape of the fingerprint. Being highly conductive, it imposes its shape as a boundary condition on the field, thereby spatially modulating the field into an analog of the fingerprint.

An array of tiny antennas arranged in a square matrix of 96 rows and columns does the actual sensing. Located above the reference plane, the array measures about 6.5 mm on a side, giving the sensor a linear resolution of about 15 pixels per millimeter.

The sensed analog electric field values are scanned from the sensor matrix a row at a time, digitized, and sent from the FingerLoc chip to the cell-phone's microprocessor for further processing. In the cell-phone, a module from AuthenTec's software suite analyzes the fingerprint pattern and extracts information from it, which it converts into a unique representation of the fingerprint's owner. To "enroll" a user, that representation, called a "template," is stored in nonvolatile memory for future use. To authenticate a user, it is compared with all of the stored templates to determine his or her identity.

What happens next depends on how the cell-phone manufacturer and service provider have set things up. If the handset does not recognize the applicant, service will probably be denied. It gets more interesting when the system does recognize the fingerprint, because each user can have a stored profile, which personalizes the phone for him or her.

For example, a child may have the phone set so that it can do nothing but call home, no matter which button it presses. Older users may have their personal phone books automatically loaded, and certain calling privileges activated or blocked. And, of course, with the right standards in place, the sensor can be part of a verification and authentication system for e-commerce.

Analog Yes, Digital No

When it comes to eavesdropping, the situation is pretty simple. Analog phones are easy to bug; digital phones are hard. Although it is illegal to sell scanners in the United States today that are capable of receiving the frequency bands used for cellular telephony (824-849 MHz, 869-894 MHz, 1.85-1.91 GHz, and 1.93-1.99 GHz), older units that can receive them are readily available. Moreover, it is hardly rocket science to modify a new, compliant receiver to add the extra bands.

The scanners are inherently capable of receiving at least the lower bands; they have just been rigged to block them.

NOTE

Lest anyone think that analog cellular telephony is an old, dead technology, as of June 1999, over 70% of the subscribers in the United States still used analog handsets, according to Boston's Yankee Group. And many who have dual-mode phones (capable of analog and digital operation) turn to the analog mode when roaming, especially in rural areas.

The latest figures from the Cellular Telecommunications Industry Association (CTIA), Washington, D.C., indicate merely that digital penetration today exceeds 50%. But the CTIA counts dual-mode handsets as digital, so its number may not be so different from the Yankee Group's. Whatever the precise numbers, the message is clear: Eavesdropping is not of only historical interest.

Digital phones, be they of the time- or code-division multiple-access (TDMA or CDMA) variety, are, unlike analog units, quite foolproof against eavesdropping by ordinary mortals. Would-be listeners-in, for one thing, has to know what system they are trying to tap into, because TDMA and CDMA are utterly different. For TDMA, what can be snatched out of the ether is a digital data stream representing one side of each of three multiplexed conversations. Eavesdroppers need to lock onto the correct time slot to get the conversation they want.

In the case of CDMA, what they wind up with is an even thornier problem—a mishmash of half a dozen conversations, each modulated by a different pseudorandom code, all occupying the same band. So, the signal has to be decoded with the same code, which has been obtained in some mysterious fashion.

Plus, in digital systems, voice is vocoded. The sound is not only digitized, but also compressed. As before, someone interested in decompressing it needs to know the compression algorithm used.

In short, eavesdroppers need to build what amounts to the receiving part of a cellular phone base station to have a chance of "overhearing" a call. Small wonder that none of the system operators or phone manufacturers regards eavesdropping on digital cell-phones as a problem.

Ethereal Signatures

The fight against cloning analog handsets has gone a lot better than efforts to combat eavesdropping. Conceived in innocence, early analog phones were almost comically vulnerable to security attacks. For one thing, the signaling between handset and base station takes place in the clear, so anyone with a suitable RF scanner can simply listen-in and learn the phone numbers (called "mobile identity numbers," (MINs) of handsets in the vicinity and the electronic serial numbers (ESNs) that go with them. To program those numbers into another handset is the work of a minute, and behold, another cloned phone is ready for use.

Once the problem manifested itself, service providers began taking steps to protect themselves. Working with the U.S. Secret Service, they persuaded Congress in 1998 to amend the law pertaining to "fraud and related activity in connection with access devices" (Title 18, Section 1029, of the U.S. Code), so as to make it a federal crime to own a scanning receiver or a cell-phone programmer with intent to defraud. That same law also makes it a crime knowingly, and with intent to defraud, to use a counterfeit phone, to traffic in such phones, or to possess 15 or more of them. The law is serious, specifying maximum prison terms of 10 or 15 years (for first-time offenders), depending on the exact nature of the crime.

The service providers also instituted the use of personal identification numbers (PINs) that a user had to key in before a call could be completed. PINs certainly made it tougher for thieves to use stolen phones. But because the PINs were transmitted in the clear, they were not very effective against cloning.

What did help was a technology pioneered by the military for keeping track of enemy troop movements, namely, RF fingerprinting. Corsair Communications Inc., Palo Alto, California, is currently the only company active in the field. The technology involves measuring several (unspecified) parameters associated with RF signals and characterizing them (again, in a proprietary manner) to produce a signature unique to the transmitter being studied. Even nominally identical transmitters, manufactured on the same assembly line to the same specifications, have slight differences, which are sufficient for PhonePrint (as Corsair named its product) to tell them apart.

PhonePrint is a combination of hardware and software that cellular operators install in base stations in high-fraud areas. Once installed, it characterizes all the handsets that ask it for service (by monitoring the reverse control channel) and creates a database of their RF signatures, or fingerprints. The database soon acquires entries for almost all of the active users in the area. On subsequent service requests, PhonePrint compares the stored signature with the live one. If they fail to match, the call is torn down—that is, broken before it can be completed.

PhonePrint had its origins at TRW Inc., from which Corsair spun off in 1994. The Cleveland, Ohio, company developed similar systems for military use. Such systems can tell that an enemy unit supposedly stationed at position X has, in fact, moved to position Y by recognizing the RF signatures associated with the unit's radios. Obviously, as this feat implies, RF fingerprinting will work with any phone, and indeed, with any transmitter. It is, therefore, particularly suitable for legacy analog cell-phones, which have no built-in fraud-fighting provisions.

How effective is it against cloning fraud? Corsair to date has torn down over 400 million calls.

Authentication Secrets

With the advent of digital and more advanced analog phones, an even more effective fraud-fighting technology came into use—authentication. A sort of handshaking process, authentication makes use of secret numbers that are stored in the phone and known to the network, but never passed over the air. Every time a call is made, the network sends the handset a random number, which the handset then combines with its secret number using an algorithm designed for the task. The result is another random number that the handset sends back to the network, which has meanwhile performed the same calculations. If the numbers match, the call is completed; if not, it is not.

The algorithm is designed to avalanche very quickly. If the input numbers are off by even a single bit, the resulting number will not even be close to the right answer. Because a different random number is used for each challenge, an eavesdropper would have a hard time figuring out a phone's secret number. This is not to suggest that sophisticated code crackers could not do it (the experts at the National Security Agency would probably consider it a warm-up exercise), but even high-level criminals rarely have access to the required expertise or equipment.

Criminals, by the way, generally clone cell-phones not for economic reasons, but rather in the pursuit of anonymity. Eighty percent of narcotics dealers arrested in 1998 were found to be in possession of cloned phones, according to testimony from the Drug Enforcement Administration, Arlington, Virginia.

Call counting is another technique that can be used instead of (more often, in addition to) authentication. Like authentication, it requires a phone capable of performing its part of the process. With call counting, both the handset and the network track the number of calls made by the handset. Those numbers are compared whenever a call is made. If they do not match or if they disagree by more than a specified amount (generally one call), then the call is not allowed. Obviously, if someone has cloned a phone, then both he or she and the legitimate users will be making calls, so the network will have their combined number, whereas each handset will have only its own.

RF fingerprinting and authentication between them have proven extremely effective. Cloning fraud has dropped about 96% over the past four to five years. It has been replaced, however, by another kind of fraud called "identity theft" (as previously discussed), also known as subscription fraud.

Who Are You?

Criminals, like electrons, tend to take the path of least resistance. Make it really hard to steal what they want one way, and they find a different way to get it. In the case of cell-phones (or, more accurately, cell-phone service), the defenses in place against cloning have motivated criminals to adopt the various techniques used by credit-card thieves, which are all lumped together under the rubric of subscriber fraud.

As with cloning, the industry's first defensive move was to persuade Congress to strengthen the relevant statute (in this case Title 18, Section 1028 of the U.S. Code, "fraud and related activity in connection with identification documents and information"). As the law now stands, it is a federal crime merely to steal someone's identity information with intent to defraud. Previously, the government had to wait until fraud was committed before it could act.

The industry became particularly susceptible to subscriber fraud when it started pursuing new customers through such nontraditional channels as telemarketing and the Internet. Previously, cell-phone service was mostly purchased in face-to-face transactions in company-owned stores, and clerks could do things like check photo IDs to verify a customer's identity. Now companies are finding they will have to get back to the basics if they are to keep subscriber fraud losses at a tolerable level. They are going to have to verify addresses against credit-card databases, for example. But, there are legitimate reasons for discrepancies, because people may have just moved or they may maintain multiple residences. Therefore, methods must be developed for screening out bad risks without turning off legitimate customers.

Technology as such is of limited value in this area. One thing computers are being used to do is keep track of subscriber calling patterns—the numbers they tend to call or receive calls from. If a subscriber is terminated for nonpayment of bills, and if a "new" subscriber shows up with pretty much the same calling pattern, then an alarm can be raised calling attention to the possibility that this may be the same person, and the company can look more closely at him.

Subsidy Loss

A major problem, especially in Latin America, are cell-phones moving sideways through the distribution channels. Cellular handsets are often heavily subsidized by service providers, who supply them to subscribers on condition that the subscribers remain with the company for a specific period, typically a year. But what sometimes happens is that the phones wind up being activated on some other carrier's network.

A distributor, for example, who has purchased a batch of subsidized handsets at a low price from one carrier may find that he or she can sell them at a handsome profit to a dealer who is not affiliated with that carrier. In Latin America, that dealer may not even be in the same country as the distributor. As a result, the carrier loses the money it invested in subsidizing the phone.

As with subscriber fraud, the remedy is mostly a matter of running a tighter ship. But some sort of technological fix will also be developed, which can be described as an authentication kind of approach for the activation process. This technology is foreseen as showing up in some second-generation phones, and it will be part of any third-generation deployment.

THE NEW ORDER AND STATE MEDICAL ID CARDS

The recent hacking of 6,000 administrative patient files from one of the country's top hospitals underscores the lack of firm, clear, universal standards to ensure the security of on-line medical records (see sidebar, "Patient Files Copied by Hacker"). But although officials are crafting regulations governing electronic patient records for the health care industry, some analysts and industry players are skeptical about how effective these specifications will be.

PATIENT FILES COPIED BY HACKER

A major university hospital in Seattle recently confirmed that a hacker penetrated its computer network in 2000 and made off with files containing information about 6,000 patients. Officials at the University of Washington Medical Center indicated the hacker (who calls himself "Kane") stole user passwords and copied thousands of files while he had access to the hospital's systems. The hacker slipped into the network through a server in the hospital's pathology department.

The medical center suspected at the time that its network had been infiltrated and took steps to cut off the hacker's access. But the hospital was unaware that the files had been pilfered until Kane provided information about the intrusion to SecurityFocus.com, a San Mateo, California-based Web site that focuses on security issues.

Kane, who indicated he lives in the Netherlands, shared some of the copied files with SecurityFocus.com to verify that he had accessed the sensitive data. Kane views himself as an ethical hacker and indicated that he simply wanted to expose the vulnerability of the hospital's network. He portrays himself as more of a whistle-blower than an outlaw.

But after being informed of the file copying, officials at the medical center reported the hacking incident to the FBI for investigation The hospital also beefed up its firewalls in an effort to better protect its network, and it began notifying all of the patients whose personal information was in the files copied by Kane.

In a statement, the hospital indicated the copied information wasn't directly related to the delivery of care to its patients. Instead, it added, the information was stored in administrative databases and was used for patient tracking and for following up on research studies.

The hospital indicated that there is no evidence that anyone has breached their main electronic medical records system. They have assured patients and the public that this system remains fully protected by the highest levels of security possible.

Kane used sniffer software to steal the electronic identifications of a number of hospital employees from an exposed server and then used those credentials to access thousands of files related to patients in the medical center's cardiology and rehabilitation departments. The hospital plans to comply with the Health Insurance Portability and Accountability Act (HIPAA), a set of privacy and security guidelines that the federal government is close to finalizing.

The hacking incident wasn't that unusual and appears to have been relatively minor compared with the amount of damage that a malicious attacker could have inflicted. Kane's intrusion is a classic penetration of a secondary system that was running a personal application with collected data, rather than an attack on the hospital's main database server.

Academic medical centers are prone to this, as part of the spirit of academic freedom that creates pressure for open access. The only major impact from the hacking incident might be to get policymakers in Washington to push through the HIPAA as quickly as possible.

In an attempt to remedy the situation, the U.S. government is finalizing and releasing the security and privacy portions of the Health Insurance Portability and Accountability Act (HIPAA), which will define interface and security standards and policies. Unless it is derailed by the new administration, both the regulatory commissions that accredit hospitals and the federal agencies that receive complaints will enforce the HIPAA privacy regulations.

Bumpy Road Ahead

But the industry has a long way to go. The privacy provisions are a quagmire. A lot of it is onerous and expensive, and a lot of it hard to interpret (see sidebar, "New Medical Privacy Rules").

NEW MEDICAL PRIVACY RULES

Before President Clinton left office, he announced a sweeping set of federal rules aimed at protecting the privacy of medical records and other personal health information, establishing the potential for penalties to be imposed on executives at health care businesses that breach the new standards.

The regulations, which were prepared by the U.S. Department of Health and Human Services (HHS), are the final version of proposed rules that were issued in 1999 after Congress failed to pass comprehensive medical privacy legislation as required by the 1996 Health Insurance Portability and Accountability Act (HIPAA).

Oral, paper-based, and electronic communications are all covered by the measures. That casts a wider net than the original proposal, which applied to electronic records and to paper ones that at some point had existed in electronic form.

Under the regulations, health care providers are prohibited from releasing most information about individual patients without getting their consent in advance. But in another change from the proposed rules, HHS indicates doctors and hospitals will be given full discretion in determining what personal health information to include when sending patients' medical records to other providers for treatment purposes.

However, the final rules also tighten the consent requirement, mandating that approval be secured from patients for even routine use and disclosure of health records for purposes such as bill payments. Patients also must be given detailed written information about their privacy rights and any planned use of their personal information.

In addition, HHS is calling on hospitals, health insurers, and health care clearinghouses to establish procedures for protecting the privacy of patients, including the appointment of executives to oversee their internal privacy procedures. And companies are prohibited from accessing health records for employment purposes.

Under the HIPAA, civil fines of $100 per violation can be imposed, up to a total of $25,000 per year. Criminal penalties of up to $250,000 and 10 years in prison could also be targeted at individuals who try to profit from the sale of health information. Most health care companies will be given two years to comply with the regulations.

Nothing is more private than someone's medical or psychiatric record. And, therefore, if the government is to make freedom fully meaningful in the Information Age, when most of the stuff is on some computer somewhere, then the government has to protect the privacy of individual health records. The regulations were made necessary by the great tides of technological and economic change that have swept through the medical profession over the last few years.

HHS estimates that complying with the HIPAA rules will cost the health care industry $17.6 billion. But in the long run, government officials claim, the regulations will help achieve savings of almost $30 billion over the next 10 years, as a result of related rules that eliminate paperwork by issuing standards for electronic communication of health insurance claims.

The government is expected to receive a lot of backlash regarding the inclusion of paper and oral communications in the new rules. Originally, the HIPAA was intended to apply solely to electronic communications. It could be virtually impossible to monitor written and oral messages.

One of the problems is that the HIPAA is supposed to offer specifications to cover all privacy implementations, from one-doctor offices to giant health care organizations. It's too strict in many respects and too loose in others to offer adequate regulations across the board.

Nevertheless, some health organizations are already prepared for the HIPAA. One such organization is CareGroup Healthcare System, a Boston-based health provider network that includes Beth Israel Deaconess Medical Center.

For security, 128-bit Secure Sockets Layer (Web encryption) is fine, along with auditing, strong authentication, and role-based access. CareGroup has two full-time employees who monitor the security and confidentiality of patients' on-line medical records. CareGroup also lets patients access their medical records through secure e-mail messages.

Lessons to Learn

However, there is a whole range of institutions that must be educated on any guidelines to be implemented, including third-party companies that offer electronic patient-record hosting or storage.[iv] For instance, MOMR Inc. in Darien, Illinois, offers patients access to their own records via its secured Web site. It has yet to sign on any institutional customers, but it claims that it will be compliant with the HIPAA.

But, with start-ups, patients face the risk that companies that store their records on-line will go out of business. A bankrupt company could sell its data to a company with a different privacy policy.

However, one security professional who stores his private health data on-line indicated that the security problem is really more a perception than a reality. Bill Schneider, director of business development at Presideo Inc., a biometric authentication company in St. Louis, uses MOMR to store his own health data and is confident that the company has adequate security. MOMR requires users to sign-in with a password, and it transmits data with 128-bit encryption.

On the other hand, there are companies such as PointShare Corp., a Bellevue, Oregon based firm that handles networking services for medical providers, including the transmission of patient data, but only over secure private lines. The company is not comfortable using the public Internet, although there has been a lot of good work with virtual private networks and public-key infrastructure technology.

Despite the obstacles, on-line medical records will eventually gain more general acceptance. The biggest resistance is fear. Once fear is behind the patients and the companies that store their records, on-line medical records can really take off.

For privacy experts, the beginning of the 21st century is looking more like 1984. Big Brother is watching and listening, and he won't go away anytime soon.

BIG BROTHER IS HERE AND IS STAYING

Workplace surveillance was the leading privacy concern in 2000, according to an analysis recently released by the Privacy Foundation, a Denver-based nonprofit group that performs research and educates the public on privacy issues. In 2000, millions of Americans were watched at work, as employers became increasingly concerned about employee productivity and their use of the Internet. Three-fourths of major U.S. companies now perform some type of in-house electronic surveillance, according to the American Management Association, and 28% of all companies surveyed now monitor e-mail.

The Big Brother tactic has led to some people losing their jobs. Dow Chemical fired 35 employees and disciplined 346 others in 2000 for allegedly storing and sending sexual or violent images on the company's computers. Xerox, The New York Times Co., and the CIA were others that fired or disciplined employees because of alleged bad behavior.

Employers may be rightly concerned about security and productivity issues, or legal liability arising from e-mailed sexual banter. But pervasive or spot-check surveillance conducted through keystroke monitoring software, reviewing voice-mail messages, and using mini-video cameras will undoubtedly affect morale and labor law, as well as employee recruitment and retention practices.

In the future, the Privacy Foundation predicts that employers, especially so-called "New Economy" companies, may offer "spy-free" workplaces as a fringe benefit. But only as fringe benefit. Big Brother is here and staying—and, it's only going to get worse. "You ain't seen nothing yet!"

Big Brother Is Watching and Listening

"How the United States Spies on You," read the afternoon headline in Le Monde, enough, certainly, to jolt Parisians on their commute home. Across Europe recently, politicians and the press were in full cry over a vast Anglo-American electronic surveillance system named "Echelon." The system scans billions of private e-mails, faxes, and telephone conversations each hour, according to a report debated by the European Parliament. Echelon, said Parliament President Nicole Fontaine, is "a violation of the fundamental rights" of European Union citizens.

The most incendiary charge is that Echelon represents economic espionage nonpareil, helping the United States and its English-speaking allies steal trade (and jobs) from non-Anglos. But charges cited are mostly old, well-known cases: In 1994, U.S. intelligence discovered that French companies were offering bribes to Saudi Arabia and Brazil for multibillion-dollar contracts. Washington complained, and U.S. firms got the deals.

U.S. officials insisted last week that American intelligence does not steal trade secrets for U.S. firms. Even if it tried, the National Security Agency, which oversees Echelon, is drowning in data thanks to the global communications revolution. In some ways, people's communications have never been safer from becoming intelligence. And France is certainly not a slouch in the industrial espionage arena.

Although it has the added spice of Internet-age privacy concerns, the Echelon flap revealed anew how Europe and the United States are increasingly at odds over matters from defense cooperation to genetically engineered "frankenfoods." Just a few days earlier, a French intelligence report suggested the NSA helped create Microsoft to eavesdrop around the world. The loser this time may be the United Kingdom, whose special intelligence-sharing accord with Washington looks to some like disloyalty to the EU. George Orwell, after all, was English.

Speaking of Orwell, he would be either shocked or pleased on how close his book *1984* is to reality. Meet John Norseen: He's going to read your mind and inject you with smart thoughts.

BioFusion

Buck Rogers, meet John Norseen. Like the comic-strip hero, a 20th century man stuck in the 25th century, Norseen feels he's not quite in the right time: His brain-research ideas are simply too futuristic. And he admits his current obsession seems to have been lifted from a Rogers saga. The Lockheed Martin neuroengineer hopes to turn the "electrohypnomentalophone," a mind-reading machine invented by one of Buck's buddies, from science fiction into science fact.

Norseen's interest in the brain stems from a Soviet book he read in the mid-1980s, claiming that research on the mind would revolutionize the military and society at large. The former Navy pilot coined the term "BioFusion" to cover his plans to map and manipulate gray matter, leading (he hopes) to advances in medicine, national security, and entertainment. He does not do the research but sees himself as the integrator of discoveries that will make BioFusion a reality and the ultimate IW weapon for Big Brother.

BioFusion would be able to convert thoughts into computer commands, predicts Norseen, by deciphering the brain's electrical activity. Electromagnetic pulses would trigger the release of the brain's own neurotransmitters to fight off disease, enhance learning, or alter the mind's visual images, creating what Norseen has dubbed "synthetic reality."

The key is finding "brain prints." Think of your hand touching a mirror. It leaves a fingerprint. BioFusion would reveal the fingerprints of the brain by using mathematical models. Just like you can find one person in a million through fingerprints, you can find one thought in a million.

It sounds crazy, but Uncle Sam is listening and watching. The National Aeronautics and Space Administration, the Defense Advanced Research Projects Agency, and the Army's National Ground Intelligence Center have all awarded small basic research contracts to Norseen, who works for Lockheed Martin's Intelligent Systems Division. Norseen is waiting to hear if the second stage of these contracts (portions of them classified) comes through.

Norseen's theories are grounded in current science. Mapping human brain functions is now routine. By viewing a brain scan recorded by a magnetic resonance imaging (MRI) machine, scientists can tell what the person was doing at the time of the recording–say, reading or writing. Emotions from love to hate can be recognized from the brain's electrical activity.

Thought Police

So could the murderous thoughts of a terrorist be compromised: applying neuroscience research to antiterrorism? Norseen has submitted a research-and-development plan to the Pentagon, at its request, to identify a terrorist's mental profile. A miniaturized brain-mapping device inside an airport metal detector would screen passengers' brain patterns against a dictionary of brain prints. Norseen predicts profiling by brain print will be in place by 2006.

A pilot could fly a plane by merely thinking, indicates Norseen. Scientists have already linked mind and machine by implanting electrodes into a paralyzed man's brain; he can control a computer's cursor with his mind. Norseen would like to draw on Russian brain-mimicking software and American brain-mapping breakthroughs to allow that communication to take place in a less invasive way. A modified helmet could record a pilot's brain waves. When you say right 090 degrees, the computer would see that electrical pattern in the brain and turn the plane 090 degrees. If the pilot misheard instructions to turn 090 degrees and was thinking "080 degrees," the helmet would detect the error, then inject the right number via electromagnetic waves.

Finally, if this research pans out, you can begin to manipulate what someone is thinking even before they know it. But Norseen feels he is "agnostic" on the moral ramifications, that he's not a mad scientist—just a dedicated one. The ethics don't concern him, but they should concern someone else.

SUMMARY

This chapter has considered the application of civilian information operations (CIO's) to the conventional warfare environment. Although the array of CIO tools and techniques has been presented as discrete elements in a schematic diagram, the CIO environment is complex, multidimensional, interactive, and still developing. Accordingly, the introduction of a CIO capability into an existing military force requires careful consideration and adherence to a series of principles espoused within this chapter. These principles are defined within a framework of concepts including Information Assurance, Information Superiority and Information Dominance. This framework can be applied to both the introduction of a CIO capability and the application of CIO's in information warfare.

CIO's will change the nature of future wars and will eventually evolve into a separate paradigm of warfare—IW. However, CIOs can be applied to today's conventional environment and it is within this context that more urgent attention from military planners is required. CIO's offer both a support capability to existing arms of the military and also an additional dimension to conventional warfare. They may be used to strike enemy systems, control the overall information environment, deter enemy aggression, or support either themselves or other military strategies. Regardless of which tasks they are employed for, CIO's offer a significant addition to the conventional inventory and should be developed as a matter of priority as an essential Joint Force operational capability in dealing with the civilian casualties of information warfare, as follows.

Conclusions Drawn from Civilian Casualties of Information Warfare

- Information warfare (IW) is the latest development in a long list of revolutions in military affairs based on new technology (other examples include the introduction of airplanes, the atom bomb, and long-range missiles).

- IW is defined as an attack on information systems for military advantage using tactics of destruction, denial, exploitation, and/or deception.

- Information systems are so critical to military operations that it is often more effective to attack an opponent's information systems than to concentrate on destroying its military forces directly.

- In the civilian context, the U.S. economic, social, and political structures are increasingly dependent on complex and extensive systems for financial transactions, telecommunications, electric power, energy distribution, and transportation. Because these systems rely on each other, a serious disruption in any one system will cascade quickly through the other systems potentially causing a national security crisis. Under these circumstances, the ability of the government to respond will be interrupted and severely constrained.

- In addition to outages caused by natural disasters and accidents, these systems present a tempting target for IW attack to those contemplating an action against U.S. interests.

- IW provides a new context for the application of ethical theories.

- The ethical questions about IW are not meant to be a complete set of ethical questions, but rather a subjective assessment of what are the ethical questions derived from the most important issues exposed by IW.

- New unforeseen ethical questions will inevitably arise from IW in the near future.

- It is hoped that this research will begin a dialog on the issues and lay a framework for more substantive work by ethicists.

- IW and its complement (protection from IW) require important new research efforts from both the technology and ethics research communities.

- The threat of IW raises the following ethical challenges: (1) What constitutes an act of war in the information age? (2) What are the ethical implications of the blurring distinction between acts of war from acts of espionage from acts of terrorism? (3) Can IW be considered nonlethal? (4) Is it ethical to set expectations for a "bloodless war" based on IW? (5) Is it ethically correct to respond to IW tactics with IW tactics? (6) Can protection from IW take place in United States, given our democratic freedoms?

An Agenda for Action in Preparing for Civilian Casualties of Information Warfare

Three policy questions dominate the issue of critical infrastructure protection for civilian casualties of information warfare—how limited should the government's role be; what is adequate infrastructure security and how will appropriate standards be determined; and what data does the government need from business and why. None seems fundamentally settled if only because policy continues to develop. There are more questions than answers. Nonetheless, a few basic principles are emerging that should guide infrastructure protection efforts.

The United States government needs to set an agenda for action that goes beyond the work already done in preparation for civilian casualties of information warfare. Action steps should include, but not be limited to the following 6 areas:

1. General or centralized monitoring of communications need not and should not be a chief or central component of the government 's response to computer security. There are other activities (notably the identification and closing of existing vulnerabilities) that should be given higher priority.
2. Authority for increased monitoring of information systems is not required and should be rejected. Rather, the underlying laws for monitoring communications systems and accessing stored data should be strengthened.
3. The role of the FBI and the NSA in computer security should be carefully limited: it has been demonstrated that their surveillance agendas trump their protective missions, and their activities are often so cloaked in secrecy as to generate understandable suspicion.
4. Oversight of infrastructure protection should be institutionalized within the Executive Branch and should be accessible to the public. There should be established within the Executive Branch appropriate mechanisms for oversight of computer security issues, involving both industry representatives and privacy advocates.
5. Congress must follow this issue carefully, and should insist on periodic reports on the status, scope, and effectiveness of critical infrastructure activities, with special focus on monitoring and intrusion detection initiatives and the protection of privacy.
6. Although the cyber masses acknowledge the need for government participation, especially in educating society about what is at stake, the government's role in private sector infrastructure protection should be limited and largely advisory. The private sector should set information security standards, and the government should clearly define and limit what information it seeks from businesses and how that information will be used.

ENDNOTES

i John R. Vacca, *Satellite Encryption*, Academic Press, 1999.

ii John R. Vacca, *Net Privacy: A Guide to Developing & Implementing an Iron-clad ebusiness Privacy Plan*, McGraw-Hill, 2001.

iii John R. Vacca, *Electronic Commerce, Third Edition*, Charles River Media, 2001.

iv John R. Vacca, *The Essential Guide to Storage Area Networks*, Prentice Hall, 2002.

V Results and Future Directions

19 Advanced Computer Forensics

T he rise of the so-called information economy, borne along by proliferating computers, sprawling telecommunications, and the Internet, has radically transformed how people do business, govern, entertain themselves, and converse with friends and family. Private documents that in the past would have been committed to paper and hand-delivered or stowed under lock and key are now routinely created, sent, and stored electronically.

But the very things that allow such speed and ease of communication have also made it far more difficult to ensure one's privacy.[i] In an electronic age, an interloper can intercept and alter messages far more easily now than when face-to-face exchanges were the norm.

Mounting concern over the new threats to privacy and security has led to widespread adoption of cryptography. Once the purview of professional spies, strong encryption is now available worldwide to any amateur with a PC and inexpensive, off-the-shelf software.

Over the past two decades, individuals and businesses alike have embraced the technology, using it for everything from sending e-mail and storing medical records and legal contracts to conducting on-line transactions. Cryptographic algorithms are written into all the most popular World Wide Web browsers and can be readily incorporated into most e-mail programs.

But if ordinary individuals can now encrypt a message in all but unbreakable form, then so can criminals, terrorists, and other troublemakers. That prospect has governments on edge. In the past, armed (or not) with a court warrant, police could readily get at hidden documents by, say, forcing a safe. But physical force is of no use in decoding computer-encrypted data.

This turn of events has led many governments worldwide to view the technology as a grave threat to social order and to seek to control its spread. Repressive regimes fear that dissident groups will use encryption to promote their subversive ideas. Democratic governments, too, fret over the possibility that encryption will be used to further the activities of drug dealers, militant dissenters, and assorted enemies of the state. Indeed, the U.S. government once categorized encryption technology as a controlled munition, on a par with nuclear weapons, and until very recently it banned the export of the most advanced encryption products.

State controls have met with fierce protests, pitting governments against an unlikely confederacy of privacy rights advocates, cryptography experts, and corporations with a financial stake in promoting encryption's use. The ensuing battle over encryption has taken on several dimensions—technical, legal, ethical, and social. At times, the arguments have assumed the same rigidity and polarization as certain religious debates.

With the rise of hard-to-crack encryption, sensitive data is easier to protect—and criminal activity tougher to monitor. This part of the chapter will review the advanced encryption techniques now available worldwide and discuss the legal campaigns that governments have mounted in response, including the changes recently proposed to U.S. export laws.

ADVANCED ENCRYPTION: THE NEED TO CONCEAL

On German television several years ago, a stunned audience looked on as an unsuspecting Web surfer had his computer scanned while he was visiting a site. The site operators determined that a particular on-line banking program was installed on his computer, and they remotely modified a file in it so that the next time the user connected to his bank on-line, he also directed his bank (unbeknownst to him) to send a payment to the owners of that Web site.

The vulnerability of computer data affects everyone. Whenever a computer is connected to a network, be that a corporate intranet or the Internet, unless proper precautions are taken, the data residing in the machine can be accessed and otherwise modified by another knowledgeable user. Even computer data that the user may believe to be deleted or overwritten can be retrieved. Courts now routinely subpoena individuals' and companies' magnetic media as evidence; forensic experts can reconstruct data files that have been erased. In these cases, possession is not nine-tenths of the law. The best way to protect electronic data is to encrypt it.

The purpose of encryption is to render a document unreadable by all except those authorized to read it. The content of the original document, referred to by cryptographers as "plaintext," is scrambled using an algorithm and a variable, or key. The key is a randomly selected string of numbers; generally speaking, the longer the string, the stronger the security.

Provably unbreakable encryption has been around since the dawn of recorded history, and although computers have made encryption more accessible, they are certainly not a requirement. One precomputer method is the conceptually simple, yet very strong, encryption scheme known as the one-time pad, developed in 1926 by Gilbert S. Vernam (see sidebar, "Computer-Free Encryption").

NOTE

The term "unbreakable encryption" is somewhat misleading. In many cases, the plaintext has a limited lifespan, and so the protection afforded by encryption need not last forever. Tactical data, for example, often requires encryption that takes only slightly longer to break than the useful life of that data. This truism is often forgotten in debates about the relative strengths of encryption methods.

COMPUTER-FREE ENCRYPTION

The durable encrypting scheme known as the one-time pad gets its name from the use of a key once and once only for just one message. It works like this:

Toni, the sender of a sensitive message wakes up one morning and starts shouting out two-digit numbers at random: 56, 34, 01, 92, 27, 11, and so on. These numbers become the key. Toni then assigns a sequential number to each letter of the alphabet: A=01, B=02, C=03, D=04, E=05, and so on.

Next, she encodes the plaintext word "hello," which, in accordance with the preceding sequential numbering of the letters, corresponds to the sequence 08, 05, 12, 12, and 15. She then does a simple modulo-10 addition with no carry, using the key she generated in the preceding. In other words,

$$
\begin{array}{ccccc}
\text{H} & \text{E} & \text{L} & \text{L} & \text{O} \\
08 & 05 & 12 & 12 & 15 \\
+\ 56 & 34 & 01 & 92 & 27 \\
\hline
=\ 54 & 39 & 13 & 04 & 32
\end{array}
$$

This last sequence (54, 39, 13, 04, 32) is the ciphertext, which gets sent to Wolfgang, the intended recipient. Note that the same plaintext letters do not necessarily get encrypted into the same ciphertext symbols (the letter L is both 13 and 04 in this case).

Wolfgang has an exact copy of the key (56, 34, and so on). To decode Toni's message, he does the reverse operation, again with no carry:

$$54 \quad 39 \quad 13 \quad 04 \quad 32$$

$$- \; 56 \quad 34 \quad 01 \quad 92 \quad 27$$

$$= 08 \quad 05 \quad 12 \quad 12 \quad 15$$

$$= H \quad E \quad L \quad L \quad O$$

Generating long keys by "shouting out" long strings of numbers can be impractical. So in modern applications of the one-time pad, computers are often assigned to create the keys. But the result is not truly random: computers' pseudorandom number generators use only 16 (or, in some cases, 32) bits to store their values. The entire space of such values can be searched within a week or so. One remedy is to tweak the pseudorandom number generator by applying an external physical process to generate noise—maybe a sufficiently amplified semiconductor junction of 1/f noise. But that further requires removing the influence of predictable external influences, such as 50–60-Hz noise.

A self-evident shortcoming of the one-time pad is that the key is at least as long as the plaintext being encrypted. To escape cryptanalytic attacks involving statistical analyzes, the key must be used only once. A more serious shortcoming is that the same key is used to both encrypt and decrypt. The sender and the recipient, therefore, need a totally secure opportunity to exchange the key, which is hard to come by when the two are far apart.

An amusing feature of the one-time pad is that a fake key can be created that will "decode" the encrypted document into something quite innocent—an excerpt from the Bible, say, or the Bill of Rights. Alternatively, a fake key could be designed to yield a plausible-looking, but still false, document, thereby fooling people into believing they have cracked the code.[ii]

Symmetric Encryption

Vernam's one-time pad is an example of symmetric encryption, in which the same key is used to both encode and decode a message. Many of the encryption schemes available today are also symmetric, most notably the Data Encryption Standard (DES) (see sidebar, "A Menu of Symmetric Encryption Algorithms").

A MENU OF SYMMETRIC ENCRYPTION ALGORITHMS

In symmetric encryption, the same key is used to encrypt and decrypt a message. Here are the most popular.

The Data Encryption Standard

DES was developed in the 1970s and is still widely used worldwide, although it will be replaced in 2002 by the Advanced Encryption Standard (AES).

Triple DES

Encrypting the already DES-encrypted output with a different output with a different key provides no measurable security, but adding a third round of DES encryption yields a highly secure, albeit slower, algorithm. Most purportedly triple-DES implementations, however, use only two keys: key 1 for the first round of encryption, key 2 for the second round, and key 1 again for the third round.

The International Data Encryption Algorithm

IDEA uses a 128-bit key developed by ETH Zurich, in Switzerland. Its U.S. and European patents are held by Ascom Systec Ltd. of Bern, Switzerland, but noncommercial use is free. IDEA is viewed as a good algorithm for all except the best-funded attacks. It is used in PGP and Speak Freely (a program that allows encrypted digitized voice to be sent over the Internet).

Blowfish

Blowfish is a 64-bit block code having key lengths of 32 to 448 bits. Developed in 1993 by Bruce Schneier of Counterpane Internet Security Inc., San Jose, Calif., it is used in over 100 products and is viewed as one of the best available algorithms.

Twofish

Twofish, also developed by Schneier, is reputedly very strong, and, as one of five candidates for AES, is now being extensively reviewed by cryptanalysts.

RC4

RC4 is a stream cipher of unknown security, designed by Ronald Rivest for RSA Security Inc., Bedford, Mass. It adds the output of a pseudorandom number generator bit by bit to the sequential bits of the digitized plaintext.[iii]

Developed in the 1970s, DES is still popular, especially in the banking industry. It is a block cipher, meaning that it encodes text in fixed-bit blocks using a key whose length is also fixed in length. The alternative, known as stream ciphers, encode the stream of data sequentially without segmenting it into blocks.

After nearly three decades of use, DES is headed for the garbage can. Currently, the United States' National Institute of Standards and Technology (NIST), in Gaithersburg, Maryland, is considering five finalists for an Advanced Encryption Standard (AES) that will replace DES. In all likelihood, the new standard will become nearly as ubiquitous as its predecessor. Unlike DES, however, it will be competing with other algorithms—algorithms that will not suffer from any suspicion that the U.S. government has a back door into the code.

AES will be selected in late 2002. The five contenders are Mars, created by IBM Corp.; RC6, by RSA Laboratories and Ronald Rivest of the Massachusetts Institute of Technology; Rijndael, by two Belgians, Joan Daemen and Vincent Rijmen; Serpent, by Ross Anderson, Eli Biham, and Lars Knudsen, of the UK, Israel, and Norway, respectively; and Twofish, by Bruce Schneier, of Counterpane Internet Security, Inc., and colleagues.

For some encryption algorithms, a plaintext that is repetitive will result in a repetitive ciphertext. This is clearly undesirable because the encrypted output betrays important information about the plaintext. One solution is to encrypt the ciphertext block and add it bit by bit to the sequential bits of the previously encrypted plaintext.

Another problem with symmetric key encryption is that it requires that the sender and recipient of a message have a secure means for exchanging the encryption key. This is clearly difficult when the two parties are far apart, and the problem is compounded every time the keys are updated. Repeated use of the same key creates its own security weakness.

Public Key Encryption

An ingenious scheme that avoids many of the problems of symmetric encryption was proposed in 1976 by Stanford professor Martin Hellman and his graduate student Whitfield Diffie. Their public key encryption scheme, first described in *IEEE Transactions on Information Theory,* also allows the recipient to verify that the sender is who he or she appears to be; and that the message has not been tampered with.

The method works like this: Bob and Alice have a copy of openly available software that implements the public key algorithm. Each directs his or her copy of the software to create a key, or rather, a pair of keys. A file encrypted with one key of a pair can only be decrypted with the other key of that same pair; and one key cannot be mathematically inferred from the other key in the pair.

Bob makes known (by e-mail, by posting to a Web site, or however else he chooses) one of the keys of his pair; this becomes his "public key." Alice does the same. Each retains under tight control the other key in the pair, which is now his or her "private key."

If Bob wants to encrypt a message that only Alice can read, he uses Alice's public key (which is available to anyone); that message can only be decoded by Alice's private key (Figure 19.1).[iv] The reciprocal process (sending an encrypted message from Alice to Bob) is clear. In effect, Bob and Alice can now exchange encrypted files in the absence of a secure means to exchange keys, a major advantage over symmetric encryption.

Sender authentication verifies that the sender is who he or she appears to be. Suppose Bob sends a message to the world after encrypting it with his private key. The world uses Bob's public key to decrypt that message, thereby validating that it could only have come from Bob.

Message authentication, the validation that the message received is an unaltered copy of the message sent, is also easy: Before encrypting an outgoing message, Bob performs a cryptographic hash function on it, which amounts to an elaborate version of a checksum. The hash function compresses the bits of the plaintext message into a fixed-size digest, or hash value, of 128 or more bits. It is extremely difficult to alter the plaintext message without altering the hash value (Figure 19.2).

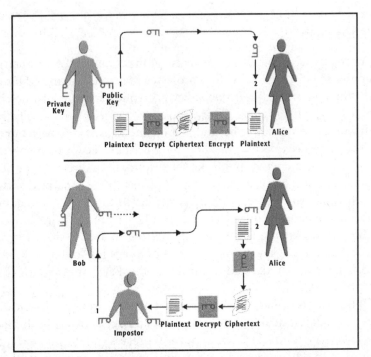

Figure 19.1 In public-key encryption [top], Alice encrypts a message using Bob's public key, and Bob decrypts it using his private key. This scheme allows encrypted files to be sent in the absence of a secure means to exchange keys, a major improvement over symmetric encryption. It's still possible, though, for Alice to receive a public key (or a conventional symmetric key) that ostensibly came from Bob, but that, in fact, belongs to a third party claiming to be Bob—the so-called man-in-the-middle attack (bottom). (©Copyright 2002. IEEE. All rights reserved).

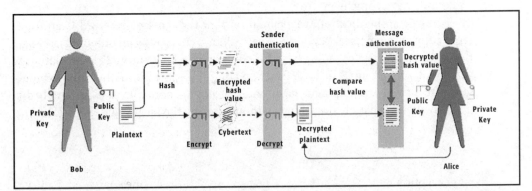

Figure 19.2 Public key encryption allows Alice to verify that a message from Bob actually came from him and that it is unaltered from the original. Here's how: Bob encrypts the hash value with his private key; encrypts the plaintext with Alice's (green) public key; and sends both to her. Alice then decodes the received ciphertext using her own [orange] private key; decodes the hash value using Bob's public key, thereby confirming the sender's authenticity; and compares the decrypted hash value with one that she calculates locally on the just decrypted plaintext, thereby confirming the message's integrity. (©Copyright 2002. IEEE. All rights reserved).

The widely used hash function MD5, developed by Rivest in 1991, hashes a file of arbitrary length into a 128-bit value. Another common hash function is SHA (short for Secure Hash Algorithm), published by the U.S. government in 1995, that hashes a file into a longer, 160-bit value.

Public key encryption has been a part of every Web browser for the last few years. It is used, for example, when sending credit-card information to an on-line vendor or when sending e-mail using the standard S/MIME protocol and a security certificate, which can either be obtained from on-line commercial vendors or created locally using special software.

One drawback of public key encryption is that it is more computationally intensive than symmetric encryption. To cut back on the computing, almost all implementations call on the symmetric approach to encrypt the plaintext and then use public key encryption to encode the local key. The differently encrypted plaintext and key are then both sent to the recipient.

In terms of resistance to brute force cryptanalysis (the exhaustive search of all possible decryption keys) a good 128-bit symmetric encryption algorithm is about as strong as 2304-bit public key algorithm. Realistically, though, the public key should be even longer than that, because the same public and private key pair is used to protect all messages to the same recipient. In other words, although a broken symmetric key typically compromises only a single message, a broken public key pair compromises all messages to a given recipient. To be sure, cracking an encryption key is just one way to get at sensitive data (see sidebar, "Human and Hardware Frailties").

HUMAN AND HARDWARE FRAILTIES

The encryption of material to withstand a brute force attack still leaves many avenues open to invasion. Often, the real weaknesses in security lie in the human tendency to cut corners. It is all too tempting to use easy-to-remember passwords, or keep unencrypted copies of sensitive documents on one's computer, intentionally or otherwise. *Windows*-based computers and many software products, in their quest to be user-friendly, often leave extensive electronic trails across the hard drive. These trails include not only copies of unencrypted files that the user deleted but also passwords and keys typed.

Furthermore, unless each file is encrypted using a different key and/or a different encryption method, an attacker who can somehow read one encrypted file from or to a given person can probably also read many other encrypted files from or to that person.

Cryptanalysts have also been known to exploit the hardware on which the encryption algorithm is used. In 1995, the so-called timing attack became popular. It allowed someone with access to the hardware to draw useful inferences from the precise time it took to encrypt a document using a particular type of algorithm. Public key encryption algorithms such as RSA and Diffie-Hellman are open to such attacks. Other exploitable hardware phenomena include power consumption and RF radiation. It is also possible to assess the electronic paper trail left behind when the hardware is made to fail in the course of an encryption or decryption.

Most of today's commercial e-mail programs, Web browsers, and other Internet applications include some encryption functions. Unfortunately, these schemes are often implemented as an afterthought, by engineers who may be very competent in their respective fields, but have minimal experience in cryptography.

Just like a decent forgery, bad encryption can look like good encryption on the surface. In general, however, "proprietary," "secret," or "revolutionary" schemes that have not withstood the scrutiny of cryptanalysts over time are to be avoided.

One easy test is to attempt to decrypt a file with a different key from the one used for encryption. If the software proudly informs the user that this is the wrong key, that encryption method should be discarded. It means that the encryption key has been stored in some form along with the encrypted file. The cryptanalyst would merely have to keep trying different keys until the software identified the correct one. This is only one of many weaknesses. Given the preceding, the odds favor the person attacking an encrypted file, unless the person being attacked is very knowledgeable in the ways of information security.[v]

Public key encryption is also victim of the uncertainty besetting any cryptographic scheme when the two communicating parties lack a secure channel by which to confirm the other's identity (Figure 19.1). There is, as yet, no technical fix to this problem.

One of the most commonly used public key algorithms is the 24-year-old RSA, named for its creators, Ronald Rivest, Adi Shamir, and Leonard Adleman of the Massachusetts Institute of Technology, Cambridge. Its security derives from the difficulty of factoring large prime integers. At present, a key length of at least 1024 bits is generally held secure enough. However, RSA may be somewhat vulnerable to "chosen plaintext attacks," namely, attacks in which the cryptanalyst already possesses a plaintext file and the corresponding RSA-encrypted ciphertext.

The Diffie-Hellman public key algorithm is used mostly for exchanging keys. Its security rests on the difficulty of computing discrete logarithms in a finite field generated by a large prime number, which is regarded as even harder than factoring large numbers into their prime-number components. The algorithm is generally viewed as secure if long enough keys and proper key generators are used.

By far the most popular public key encryption scheme is PGP, which stands for "pretty good privacy." PGP was created in 1991 by a programmer and activist named Philip Zimmermann as a means of protecting e-mail. After one of his colleagues posted PGP on the Internet, the Department of Justice launched an investigation of Zimmermann, for possible violation of U.S. laws governing export of encryption products. The case against him was eventually dropped in 1996, after which Zimmermann started a company to market PGP. It has since become a mainstream commercial product, sold by Network Associates Inc., of Santa Clara, Calif., although freeware versions continue to be available from the Internet.

Crackdown on Cryptography

What happened to Zimmermann is just one small skirmish in the much wider campaign waged by governments worldwide against cryptography. At issue is whether, and to what extent, persons and organizations should have the ability to encrypt information that the state cannot decipher itself.

Private citizens have legitimate reasons to preserve confidentiality: to protect trade secrets; to prevent legal or medical records from falling into strangers' hands; and to voice dissenting political or religious opinions without retribution. The international group Human Rights Watch, for example, regularly encrypts eye-witness reports of serious abuse, gathered in parts of the globe where the victims may be subject to further reprisals.

From a government's perspective, however, encryption is a double-edged sword: It has honorable purposes, true, but it can also be used to conceal out-and-out criminality. In an effort to keep encryption from gaining ground, many countries have passed laws criminalizing its import, export, and/or use.

To be sure, exactly what constitutes a crime is not always clear; governments have been known to capitalize on the aura of the term "criminal" and apply it to conduct they dislike or consider threatening.

NOTE

The proliferation of encryption has coincided with the explosive growth of the Internet. Nowadays, the man in the street can reach an instant global audience of millions, bypassing the chain of command that rules almost any institution, be that the military, a religious group, or a corporation. In essence, the simultaneous spread of encryption and the Internet has amounted to a transfer of power to the individual.

This turn of events has been viewed differently by different states. An interesting case is the People's Republic of China. There, the outlawed religious sect Falun Dafa has used the Web to great effect to spread its ideology and recruit new members; repeated attempts by the authorities to shut down the group have largely failed. Recently, the government began requiring any company doing business in China to disclose the types of Internet encryption software it uses, as well as the names of employees who use it. It further banned the sale of foreign-designed encryption products. Overseeing the regulations is a newly established body, the State Encryption Management Commission, which is believed to be staffed by China's secret police.

China's unwavering opposition to encryption suggests a more fundamental reason why a government (any government) would want to control the technology: to preserve the ability to exercise censorship. Even enlightened and democratic regimes have topics that are taboo. And when any and all information being exchanged by private citizens can be monitored, it has a chilling effect on dissenting opinions. Conversely, when citizens can communicate freely and privately using encryption, censorship becomes unenforceable. Few sovereign states can accept this loss of control. It's like having two rude guests at one's dinner table who keep whispering in each other's ears.

Encryption, though, is good for business, and that factor is largely responsible for the gradual loosening in the U.S. government's stance on encryption. Until 1996, strong encryption technology was listed as a munition, and until just recently, it fell under the same export restrictions as advanced weaponry. Under concerted pressure from the U.S. business community, which claimed that such controls were reducing sales and choking the growth of e-commerce, the government came out with a revised policy recently that lifts many of the bureaucratic burdens from companies wanting to export encryption. Even so, every encryption product must still undergo a one-time review by the U.S. Commerce Department's Bureau of Export Administration before it can be exported; sales to the so-called terrorist seven (Cuba, Iran, Iraq, Libya, North Korea, Sudan, and Syria) are still excluded. The new stipulation has some cynics wondering if only products with an identifiable weakness will receive an export license.

What's more (although encryption proponents have largely welcomed the relaxation of export rules), another concern has been raised: The same legislation would grant law enforcement new powers, such as the right to present a plaintext in court without disclosing how it was obtained from a suspect's encrypted files. Here the potential for abuse is obvious.

Other Legal Responses

The United States is not alone in backing away from strict encryption bans. What started as a global campaign to limit encryption has splintered into various approaches, with some governments now even encouraging encryption among their respective citizens, as a precaution against snooping by other governments.

Generally speaking, laws pertaining to encryption are quite convoluted and rife with exceptions and qualifications. In Sweden, for instance, encryption importation and use are allowed, and so is its export, except to certain countries; authorities may search someone's premises for a decryption key, but may not compel the person to assist in the investigation by, say, handing over the key to the authorities.

The first international attempt to control encryption was made by the 17-country Coordinating Committee for Multilateral Strategic Export Controls (COCOM), which came together in 1991 to restrict the export of items and data deemed "dangerous" if acquired by particular countries. COCOM members, with the notable exception of the United States, permitted the export of mass-market and public domain cryptography, and restricted export of strong encryption to select countries only. One such item was Global System for Mobile Communications (GSM) cellular telephony,[vi] which has two grades of encryption. Under COCOM, only the lower-grade version could be sent to the restricted countries.

Both grades of encryption have since been broken.

NOTE

In March 1994, Cocom was dissolved, to be replaced the following year by the multilateral Wassenaar Arrangement, which has now been joined by (at last count) 33 countries. Under the nonbinding agreement, countries agreed to restrict the export of mass-market software with keys longer than 64 bits.

The arrangement, administered through a small office in Vienna, Austria, is not a treaty, and so not subject to mandatory review by any country's legislature.

NOTE

But, do such encryption bans work? In a word, no. For one thing, the penalty for using encryption is likely to be far less than the damage caused by disclosing whatever was deemed sensitive enough to warrant encryption. What's more, sophisticated techniques for hiding data, unencrypted or not, are now readily available and extremely hard to detect, so that prosecution of cryptography-ban violations is all but impossible. Who can prove that an innocuous-sounding e-mail message reporting "The temperature in the garage was 86 degrees" really means "Meet me behind Joe's garage on August 6"? Or again, out of tens of millions of digitized images posted to a Usenet electronic bulletin board, who can detect the one image in particular, perhaps of an antique car, that contains a secret message intended for a specific person, who along with millions of unsuspecting others will download that image to his or her computer?

The very existence of the Internet has made it easy to circumvent bans. In most, though not all, countries, a sender can log-on to any public computer connected to the Internet, such as those in public libraries or Internet cafes, and send encryption software anonymously to a recipient, who can also retrieve it anonymously. A would-be user of encryption software can anonymously download it from any of the thousands of Internet servers that openly provide a large collection of programs of this kind.

It may make sense for a country to ban the exportation of something that it alone possesses and that could be used against it. But, it makes no sense for a country to ban the export of what other nations already produce locally. A 2001 survey by the Cyberspace Policy Institute of George Washington University, in Washington, D.C., identified 1,490 encryption products (hardware and software) developed in 79 countries.

The study, published before the latest relaxing of U.S. export laws, states that "on average, the quality of foreign and U.S. products is comparable" and that "in the face of continuing U.S. export controls on encryption products, technology and services, some U.S. companies have financed the creation and growth of foreign cryptographic firms. With the expertise offshore, the relatively stringent U.S. export controls for cryptographic products can be avoided since products can be shipped from countries with less stringent controls."

Nevertheless, in recent years, the war over encryption has moved beyond the mere control of the technology itself. Although encryption proponents may have won the first round, law enforcement and intelligence agencies have responded with a slew of powerful tools for getting at computerized data (encrypted or not). These efforts are in turn being met by ingenious new schemes for hiding and protecting information, including one's identity.

Now, let's look at advanced hacking as part of this chapter's continuing theme of advanced computer forensics. In other words, hack yourself before somebody else does.

ADVANCED HACKING

Today, as enterprisewide networks reach the plant floor and zip data to the far side of the world in a twinkling, and, as the number of computers, personal digital assistants, telephones, and pagers communicating with the network increases, there is a corresponding increase in the opportunities for a critical blunder that would allow an attacker to enter your system. The consequences could be ruinous. According to a recent survey by the Computer Security Institute, the cumulative loss of 297 companies that quantified their losses in 2001 reached $489 million, or about $1.7 million each. Roughly $262 million of that loss was theft of proprietary information—information your competitors want.

One of the best places for plant engineers to learn about network security (see sidebar, "Hack Yourself Before Somebody Else Does") with a peer in information technology (IT), is at the Computer Security Resource Center, a Web site (http://csrc.nist.gov/) established by the National Institute of Standards and Technology (NIST). There you'll find primers that explain security issues and technologies, news about current problems and security initiatives, and downloadable copies of the standards that govern electronic communication with Uncle Sam.

HACK YOURSELF BEFORE SOMEBODY ELSE DOES

How do you test your system to make sure it's as safe as possible? Can you recommend software, hardware, or services that can identify security issues before they become problems? What kind of procedures do you have in place to make sure that the latest patches are applied to Web servers?

The best way to retain your network security is to do frequent security audits, including trying to gain access using easily available hacking tools. In addition, you should ensure that you only run the services you need and only open the ports needed by your network.

Your gateway to the Internet should be a system without any important company data or a hardware solution backed up by a firewall. You should also set up *Windows Update* notification for the server and have a back-up server ready when you need to run the update.

Also, you should always check security bulletins and consider joining "hacking" mailing groups to find out what's happening on "the other side" of computer security. The main thing is to regularly test the security yourself, then you know what to find solutions for.

In addition, one of the most useful items at the site (http://csrc.nist.gov/publications/drafts.html) is the March 2001 draft of the "Self-Assessment Guide for Information Technology Systems," a comprehensive questionnaire that assesses data security from every possible perspective, from cooling fans at the chip to physical security and labeling of back-up disks. Originally developed for the use of U.S. government IT personnel, the questions can teach plant engineers a lot about security and the problems confronting network managers:

- Does building plumbing endanger the system?
- Have you performed a consequence assessment that estimates the degree of harm or loss that could occur?
- Do your emergency exit and reentry procedures ensure that only authorized personnel reenter after fire drills, and so on?
- Do you sanitize media before re-use?
- Do you share incident information and common vulnerabilities with interconnected systems?
- Do you maintain a current list of authorized users and their access?
- Do your security controls detect unauthorized access attempts?

Careful reading and consideration of the questions make it clear that the electronic ganglia tying together the extremities of the modern manufacturing plant are susceptible to attack across many fronts and that security is everyone's business. More than ever, it's vital that plant engineers work effectively with IT to identify potential breaches, shore them up, and train everybody to be security conscious.

Nor is it only NIST that's getting into the act. The National Infrastructure Protection Center (http://www.nipc.gov/) was created by Congress to defend the nation's computer networks by serving as the national focal point for gathering information on threats to critical infrastructures. It is the principal means of facilitating and coordinating the federal government's response to an incident, mitigating attacks, investigating threats, and monitoring reconstitution efforts. The center issues updates about new viruses, Internet frauds, and disruption attempts almost daily. It is located in the FBI's Washington headquarters and maintains its own investigative staff.

Cybersecurity isn't an exclusively local matter, however: A complaint filed by the U.S. Attorney for the Southern District of New York provides an instructive example of the reach of today's e-thieves. The complaint alleged that Oleg Zezov and Igor Yarimaka, residents of Kazakhstan, penetrated the computers of Bloomberg.com, in New York, and demanded $200,000 from the company to tell how they had done it. Bloomberg agreed to pay, but only following a face-to-face meeting in London. There, accompanied by undercover London police officers, Bloomberg met with Zezov and Yarimaka. They repeated their demands, and police arrested them the next day. The United States is now seeking their extradition.

In view of the preceding incident, computer intrusions have more than tripled in the last two years. Who are the people trying to get their hands in your data, and why? Can you fight back by hacking yourself before somebody else does? This part of the chapter continues the theme of advanced computer forensics by providing answers to the previous questions.

Are We a Hacker Nation?

Shadowy, computer-wise predators slip in undetected to steal data, deface Web sites, crash systems, or just look around. Why? Because hacking has become nothing in recent years if not a good career move. Yesterday's hackers are today's security gurus, with more corporations counting on them for protection.

One reason there are so many types of hackers these days is that hacking—at least as manifested in its simpler forms such as Web page defacement and denial-of-service attacks (which overwhelm a site with data to prevent users from accessing it)—has never been easier.

Tools of the Trade

The Internet is filled with Web sites that offer tips and tools for the neophyte hacker. Kids, criminals, and terrorists are some of the people who avail themselves of this information—so more and more intruders are knocking at port doors.

The barrier to entering the hacker world has become very low. If you have a political motivation against wheat farmers and you want to deface their Web page, you could just go on-line and learn how to do it.

Despite tighter Web security and stricter penalties for breaking into systems, hacking attacks have more than tripled in the past two years. The government's Computer Emergency Response Team reported about 5000 cases of corporate hacking in the United States in 1999, more than 17,000 cases in 2000 and over 28,000 in 2001.

And those are just recorded cases; to avoid negative publicity, most companies don't report attacks. The statistics cover network break-ins (which can give a hacker access to data files), Web site vandalism, denial-of-service attacks, and data theft. The FBI estimates that businesses worldwide lost $2.6 trillion in 2001 due to security breaches perpetrated from within the business.

The risks are personal and professional: Hackers can steal passwords and bank account numbers from your home PC or grab trade secrets from your company network. Recently, criminal hackers broke into Microsoft's corporate network and accessed source code for its software (see sidebar, "Future Threat: Advanced Malicious Code in Software").

Signs of the Times

Hacking has definitely changed in the last 40 years. Talk to any hacker over 25, and he's likely to lament the passing of the good old days, when coding was an art form and learning how systems worked was an exercise in persistence. New hackers today are often younger and less skilled than their predecessors, and more likely to focus on showy exploits than the noble pursuit of knowledge, indicate older hackers.

Many old hackers call the Internet generation of hackers *hollow bunnies*—such as gigantic chocolate Easter bunnies *filled with nothing but air*. Ten years ago, hackers respected information and machines, and had to possess knowledge and skills to hack. Now novices use hacking programs without understanding them and are more likely to leave havoc in their wake.

Script kiddies receive the bulk of hacker disdain. These are the graffiti kids who download canned scripts (prewritten hacking programs) for denial-of-service attacks or paint-by-number Web defacement.

The risk here is that an unskilled hacker could release wanton mayhem in your systems. The hacker might download a buggy hacking tool to your network that goes awry, or execute a wrong command and inadvertently damage your machines.

But script kiddies tend to disappear after a year. This is the generation of instant gratification, and if they can't get the hang of *Back Orifice* (a more advanced hacking program), they get bored and move on.

Bigger Threats

Script kiddies may get attention, but experts agree that the most dangerous hackers are the ones who don't make any noise: criminal hackers and cyberterrorists. The truly dangerous people are hacking away in the background, drowned out by the noise and pomp that the script kiddies and denial-of-service packet monkeys have been making.

Hacking has evolved into professional crime. Amateur hackers are falling into the minority, and now the fear is the criminal and the terrorist. These are people like the Russian cracker group who siphoned $20 million from Citibank in 1994 and the mafia boss in Amsterdam who had hackers access police files so he could keep ahead of the law.

In 1997, crime syndicates approached hackers to work for them. Now, with so many easy-to-use hacking tools on the Internet, criminals hardly need hackers to do their dirty work.

But the cyberelement that everyone fears most is one you've yet to see: foreign governments, terrorists, and domestic militia groups hacking for a political cause.

The Department of Defense indicates its systems are probed about 250,000 times a year. It's difficult to tell if probes are coming from enemies seeking military data or from "ankle biters"—harmless hackers on a joyride. Regardless, authorities have to investigate every probe as a potential threat.

The likelihood of obtaining top secret information in this way is small, because classified data is generally stored on machines not connected to the Net. A more problematic assault, would focus on utilities or satellite and phone systems. Ninety-five percent (95%) of U.S. military communications run through civilian phone networks. An attack on these systems could impede military communications.

For example, Navy officials recently reported that hackers broke into a Navy research facility in Washington, D.C., and stole two-thirds of its source code for satellite and missile guidance systems. The Navy indicates that the source code was an "unclassified" older version.

Thus, a large-scale cyberattack is imminent. Members of terrorist groups such as Hezbollah have been educated in Western universities and are capable of developing such attacks in the future—such as a digital 9-11 attack.

Why Hackers Hack

Aside from criminal and political motives, the reasons that hackers hack range from malice and revenge to simple boredom. And, despite the image of hackers as dysfunctional loners, many are drawn to hacking by the sense of community it gives.

Of course, a big part of hacking's attraction is the sense of power that comes from uncovering information you shouldn't possess. A hacker called "Dead Addict" once described the high that comes from discovering valuable information, followed by the low that comes from realizing you can't do anything with it.

For example, one hacker knows a little of that rush. He says that he once broke into a hazardous waste firm and found *pretty evil insider information* that no one was meant to see. Though he didn't act on the information, he did log it for possible use later. Just in case he felt like being socially active.

But many hackers who begin as system voyeurs graduate to more serious activities. It's easy to be lured to the dark side when you get easy gratification messing around with individuals such as for example—AOL users. Most hackers are not old enough to drive a car or vote, but they can exert power over a network.

White Hats

There are a lot of the reasons why hackers' ability to hack into computers fade with age. Life fills their time, and their ethics begin to change. The majority eventually find their interest waning.

You only have three directions to go with hacking: You can keep doing the same old tricks; you can become a real criminal cracker; or you can use those skills wisely to build new software and create a more secure Internet.

Securing the Net is an interest many hackers develop (especially now that employers are hiring them for their skills). They lament that the public never hears about their positive acts, such as patching a hole on their way out of a site and letting the administrator know they fixed it.

Most companies just focus on the fact that you hacked them and want to come after you with a lawsuit. It's made hackers reluctant to help them.

An even sorer point between hackers and vendors is the issue of releasing vulnerability exploits. These are findings about a security problem that hackers (and researchers) post on the Net.

Vendors indicate hackers expose the holes for anyone to exploit, and should instead report them to vendors first so they can fix them. The hacking community frowns on people who don't notify vendors, but when they do, vendors often ignore them. Most software companies won't do anything about a problem until you make it public. Then they have to fix it.

Vendors have a duty to develop secure software. Hackers, on the other hand, force vendors to admit their errors after they've hacked into the vendors' software.. Manufacturers are grossly negligent in selling software that doesn't stand up. What if they were producing cars that were this unsafe? The software they give us is not safe to drive in cyberspace.

Anything that's attached to the Internet is potentially hackable. And, if you're using a *Windows 2000* or *XP* machine, nothing that is on that computer is secure.

Better security is in everyone's best interest, and hackers should play a crucial role in this. The hacker kids who are going to Def Con today are the software architects of tomorrow. The same thing that makes them hackers makes them valuable to employers in the future.

All of this points to the fact that although hackers may be the Internet's greatest annoyance, their warnings are ignored about security at everyone's peril. The network that can't guard against a bored 18-year-old hacking in his or her spare time, can't hope to protect itself from a hostile government or tech-savvy terrorist.

Next, let's look at how digital detectives track hacks. Also, how much does it cost to track a hacker?

ADVANCED TRACKER HACKERS

As the number of computer crimes spirals, the computer forensics experts (a rare breed of security pros) skills are getting ever more precious. These are the data detectives who search for digital clues remaining on computers after malicious (or black-hat) hackers have done their dirty deeds. Cyber sleuths analyze e-mail, Web site records, and hard drive data, looking for clues to the identity of criminals and crackers, much like gumshoes examine crime scenes for fingerprints and stray hairs.

It's not only the number of crimes that's fueling the need for these skills but also the increasing sophistication of criminals. The black-hat community is moving forward at a pace that outstrips the ability of the average system administrator or law enforcement agency. That means that both ebusinesses and law enforcement agencies are paying plenty to find experts to sift through evidence left behind at digital crime scenes.

In other words, security consultants and auditors are well-compensated for their knowledge—especially since the 9-11 attacks. In a recent survey of more than 8,000 IT managers, security consultants, on average, make $27,000 more per year than network administrators. Overall, salaries for all positions grew 22.8% to an average of $80,341 in 2001.

TABLE 19-1 The salary protection racket.

Position	Average salary	Increase from 2000
Security consultants	$98,450	+24%
Security auditors	$87,399	+22.4%
Security administrators	$78,035	+22.7%
System administrators	$75,080	+22.2%
Network administrators	$71,714	+22.8%

The need for computer forensics is growing exponentially. The need is particularly acute at local, state, federal, and military law enforcement agencies that host computer forensics divisions, which are looking for individuals adept at solving hacking and intellectual property cases. And an increasing number of corporations are using computer forensics to resolve internal matters such as fraud, violations of trade secrets, and inappropriate use of company computers.

The job is intense and tedious and requires nerves of steel. Most specialists have years of programming or computer-related experience, strong analytical skills, and the patience to invest days taking apart a computer in search of evidence. And if things keep going the way they are, it probably won't hurt if these experts didn't mind overtime.

Other professional attributes needed to catch a thief, are strong computer science fundamentals, a broad understanding of security vulnerabilities, and strong system administration skills. Cyber sleuths use these skills to seek information to reconstruct how a system was hacked. The number and complexity of intrusions has increased at an alarming rate. Cyber sleuths have been forced to find ways to try to keep up with intruder tools as they have progressed in sophistication.

Experts gather this data and create an audit trail for criminal prosecutions. They search for information that may be encrypted or hidden, along with unallocated disk space. Most cunningly of all, they set traps using vulnerable computers to lure malicious hackers into giving away themselves and their techniques.

Computer forensics specialists must have strong analytic skills and excellent verbal and written communication skills. That's because they're required to document their findings in detail, and they often testify at criminal trials.

The demand is being answered by several educational facilities, including the University of Central Florida, in Orlando, which offers a graduate certificate degree in computer forensics. The International Association of Computer Investigative Specialists, based in Donahue, Iowa, offers certification for computer forensics examiners. Demand for such courses is so high that the association's fall classes are already full. Such courses are helpful for those IT managers or individuals who lack computer programming experience, but who want to make the leap into computer forensics.

Computer forensics specialists caution that IT managers interested in pursuing computer forensics as a career shouldn't expect that just by taking a few courses in the subject, they'll be able to track some of the world's slyest hackers (see sidebar, "The Costs of Tracking a Hacker"). The specialty is a tough discipline in a fast-moving industry that requires highly trained professionals dedicated to continued learning. That's because there's no way to stay ahead of the crooks. White-hat hackers at this point can only try to narrow the gap between themselves and the bad guys—and hope that the black-hat hackers don't get too fastidious when it comes to leaving behind digital footprints.

THE COSTS OF TRACKING A HACKER

It took the intruder less than a minute to break into the university's computer via the Internet, and he stayed less than a half an hour. Yet finding out what he did in that time took researchers, on average, more than 34 hours each.

That inequity—highlighted during the Forensic Challenge, a contest of digital-sleuthing skills whose results were announced recently—underscores the costs of cleaning up after an intruder compromises a network. That damage done in a half an hour would take a company an estimated 34 hours of investigative time and cost about $3,000 if the investigation was handled internally and more than $33,000 if a consultant was called in. And. those are conservative estimates.

Eventually, the members of a loose group of security experts known as the Honeynet Project, would announce the winner of the Forensic Challenge. The contest pitted the reports of 13 amateur and professional cyber sleuths against one another.

Each digital detective used decompilers, data recovery programs and other forensic tools to uncover as much information as possible. The entries consisted of a memo to fictional upper management, a security advisory, and an in-depth analysis of the evidence uncovered by the contestant's digital detective work. The winner of the contest, Thomas Roessler, a student in mathematics at the University of Bonn in Germany, has dabbled in, but not done digital forensics work in the past.

Roessler indicated that it's always amazing how much information you can get out of a system by using rather basic tools. You always miss something.

The contest was made more interesting by the fact that the attack was a real one, captured by one of the several "honeypots" (vulnerable computers connected to the Net and surreptitiously watched) run by the Honeynet Project. In fact, the detectives produced several leads to the identity of the culprit. However, the person responsible would not be prosecuted. Such on-line vandals are extremely common.

The perpetrator represents a very large and common percentage of the black-hat community. It's a threat that everyone faces. Nevertheless, only about 70 to 80% of the so-called black-hat hackers (those who break into computers illegally) have comparable skills to the attacker who breached the computer.

The contest also helped illuminate why securing a computer is more cost effective than hiring consultants to come in and do the detective work afterward. It is a fairly extensive process to take what amounts to a bunch of garbage and build a comprehensive picture of what happened. The costs of such investigations can easily amount to $30,000 per computer.

Companies need to understand the difficulty, and costs, involved. Companies also tend to balk at agreeing to that kind of expense when there is no guaranteed payoff. Hopefully the contest opened the eyes of corporate executives, who all too often want a quick fix.

If you just reinstall the system, do you know if you have plugged the hole that allowed the attacker to get in? Most of the time, such quick fixes just mean the attacker gets another shot at the system. Some computers at the University of Washington have been compromised five times. Multiple intrusions are occurring all over the place.

The Honeynet Project plans to do another contest soon, but it's a question of time. The next project would also focus on either a *Solaris, Windows NT/2000,* or *XP* computer. Getting one would not be a problem, however.

Anonymity in Retrieving System Logs

The 9-11 terrorist attacks have had numerous side effects on national security. One of these is legislation that increases the ability of federal agencies to intercept Internet traffic. Another side effect was the loss of the well-known Web anonymity service hosted by ZeroKnowledge, which turned out not to be related.

Web anonymizers allow people to visit Web sites without disclosing their identity to the owner of the Web site, or even a local administrator who can log the URLs that a user visits. These tools work just as well for a terrorist who wishes to use the Web with anonymity, although using Internet access in a Web cafe, which one the plane hijackers did, works well, too.

Anonymity has its place in a free society, and personal rights and freedoms shouldn't be collateral victims of terrorist attacks. Interestingly, government agencies may also be important users of anonymizers. This part of the chapter explains how anonymization works on the Internet, and why this is important in the face of increasing privacy concerns.

SOURCE ADDRESSES

A source address is an IP address embedded in the header of an IP packet. When the packet is received, the source address becomes the destination address in the reply packet. If you spoof your source address, reply packets wind up going to the address that you've spoofed, and you don't see the results. Worse, spoofing your source address is a lousy technique for anonymity, as most application protocols require a completed TCP connection before exchanging any information.

Something similar to source address spoofing occurs whenever a firewall is between you and the destination network. Most firewalls translate internal addresses into external addresses, most commonly through Network Address Translation (NAT). Another way to rewrite the source address is to connect to a proxy and ask it to connect to the server you want to visit. This capability is built into Web browsers, which permits you to specify the IP address and the proxy you wish to use. If you've configured your Web browser to use a proxy, the Web server sees the address as the source. The proxy relays for you transparently.

Of course, whoever maintains the proxy or firewall has logs of your activity. And the owner of the Web server still has information about you-for example, the type of Web browser you're using, the source IP address, the URL requested, any referring page, as well as the source OS, and sometimes the type of PC.

The Web site's operator can go farther still: A Web designer can include *Javascript* to collect more information about your browser and OS, attaching that to any form data that you return. This information may include your system's real source IP address, which is accessible to *Javascript* programs.

Routing to the Rescue

Surprisingly, the U.S. Navy has researched network anonymity. This research formed the basis for the Freedom Network, and may show up in other systems for anonymity as well.

Suppose that you proxy your Web requests through a third party who promises to keep its logs a secret. You connect to this server via Secure Sockets Layer (SSL) so that anyone sniffing the connection can only see that you're visiting an anonymizer, and not your final destination site, which is encrypted. Sounds like a reasonable solution, but it hasn't worked in the past.

In the early 1990s, a site in Finland, *anon.penet.fi*, provided an anonymous re-mailer. Anonymous e-mailers strip away revealing information from e-mail headers before resending it to your intended destination. That works well as long as the software manages to remove all the headers, and you don't include revealing information in the e-mail you send (for example, including an automatic signature file at the end of your e-mail that, consequently, identifies you).

Penet also supported using aliases, so that the person receiving your e-mail could reply to you without learning your identity. Therefore, Penet had to keep track of the mapping between your anonymous e-mail address and your real one. Penet worked well until authorities stepped in and demanded that Johann Helsingius, Penet's operator, disclose the mapping of a particular e-mail address because it involved information copyrighted by the Church of Scientology.

If the proxy doesn't even know your real source address, how can it successfully relay for you? There have been several approaches to this problem, and one of the most recent (as previously discussed) is Onion Routing.

In Onion Routing, instead of having a single proxy for relaying, there's a network of proxies. Each of these proxies runs the same software, which not only relays your packets but also encrypts them. The first Onion Router chooses a route for your connection, then encrypts your data several times, each time using the public key for one of the routers in its network of routers.

This is where the "onion" comes in. Each layer of encryption resembles the skin of an onion: The Onion Router you've connected to first encrypts your data using the key of the last router in its list of routers—this makes up the innermost layer of the onion. Once this layer of encryption is removed, the packet is sent to its real destination. Then, the first Onion Router adds another layer of encryption. This layer includes the address of the last router in the list, and gets encrypted with the second to last router's key. The next layer gets added, with the address of the second to last router's address, but using the third to last router's key, and so on. There should be at least six routers to ensure confidentiality.

Onion Routing is even more effective if you run one of the routers. Your Onion Router must also be a full participant in the network, so that other Onion Routers can use it. Otherwise, packets coming from your Onion Router will only contain packets from your network, and can reveal your approximate source, even with the content still encrypted.

Onion Routers present another potential problem. An aggressive attacker could monitor the network traffic of every participating Onion Router. This attacker (or snoop) can then track traffic patterns. For example, you send off a request to http://www.fbi.gov via your Onion Router. The snoop sees traffic leaving your Onion Router, bound for another Onion Router, with a certain packet size. The next router sends off a slightly smaller packet and so on, until the final router sends the plaintext packet directly to the real destination. Then the snoop can deduce that this packet came from your network, based on the sizes and the timing of the packets between routers.

Onion Routing defeats this by delaying packets slightly, as well as batching data from several packets. Thus, a snoop cannot make simple deductions about the size and timing of packets. The end user does experience greater latency (delay), but this is the price for greater security.

Onion Routing is only one approach to the problem of network anonymity. AT&T Research (http://www.research.att.com) tried a different approach called "Crowds." The concept behind Crowds is that "Anonymity Loves Company," so the more participants the better. Each Crowd proxy is called a "jondo" (think "John Doe"). Unlike Onion Routing, which relies on layers of encryption, jondos employ secret key encryption with one key per route. This speeds up processing by reducing the amount of time required to handle encryption. As with Onion Routing, state information is required so that the entry and exit points of a route know where to send packets. This information is discarded at the end of each connection, but could be used to track users.

The Freedom Network used an approach similar to Onion Routing. You could either add a plug-in to *Internet Explorer* or patch your Linux kernel so that your system actually becomes an entry point in the network, with sites other than the one run by *ZeroKnowledge* participating as routers. The Freedom Network claims that it decided in spring 2001 to discontinue its service because it wasn't paying for itself.

As of this writing, the Anonymizer (http://www.anonymizer.com) is still up and running today, but functions as a proxy; it also strips identifying information from your requests. Although you can use this service for free, your request will be delayed so that you can read ads encouraging you to pay for the service.

You can also acquire software that acts as a local proxy for Web requests. This software removes the USER-AGENT line, and strips away cookies, which can also be used to track your use of a Web site.

Who Needs It?

The Onion Routing project closed down in January 2000, after processing over 30 million requests. Its home page contains an interesting disclaimer, essentially saying that anyone using the Navy's network should expect their traffic to be monitored—a very chilling statement when one considers the alleged intent of Onion Routing.

Still, government agencies form one of the largest groups of anonymizer users. Anonymizers allow law enforcement to visit Web sites without giving away their identity, or military analysts to collect data without revealing their areas of interest. Such uses of anonymizers are legitimate and actually of value to national security. If only the military and law enforcement used a particular anonymizer, then any visits from that anonymizer would immediately be of interest to someone worried about being investigated.

Anonymizers also have a place for nongovernmental users. While an anonymizer has the potential for misuse-for example, by hiding the identity of visitors to a pornographic site with illegal content—anonymizers have historically had more important and legitimate uses. For example, someone with AIDS could feel free to search the Web without revealing his or her identity. A person on the verge of committing suicide could ask for help, while remaining anonymous, which was one of the actual uses of the original Penet re-mailer. One can only hope that the rush to embrace national security in the United States doesn't have additional casualties—especially ones that actually enhance national security.

Portscans, Probing, and Denial of Service

Pity the poor Intrusion Detection System (IDS)—it has the reputation of an irritating snitch and the track record to prove it. Perhaps no other security device has done its job so well and then been reviled so roundly for doing it.

Designed to sniff out and warn system administrators when hackers are trying to exploit network vulnerabilities or launch Denial-of-Service (DoS) attacks, the original IDSs did their job all too well. That was both bad and good news.

True to vendor promises, first-generation IDSs generated information-traffic patterns on network segments, aberrations in host log files, and so forth, which could indicate whether their systems had been hit with any of the attacks hackers that use to break into critical network resources. This required placing IDSs at key locations on the network, such as at firewalls, switches, routers, Web servers, databases, and other back-end devices further into the enterprise—a straightforward process.

But those IDSs were also overly chatty boxes, renowned for generating mountains of data on traffic passing through networks and on host systems. They cried "Wolf!" too often, reporting false alarms by the droves. Consequently, many systems administrators, overwhelmed by tons of information they couldn't digest or didn't understand, simply dumbed them down or shut them off entirely.

A Bad Idea

The IDS products on the market are now bigger, better, and faster, and offer much more to those charged with protecting network resources. Vendors have, for instance, developed new intrusion-detection methods that go beyond the pattern, or signature-matching, technology that plagued the earlier products with all those false alarms. They have also increased the performance of their devices, which can now keep up with 100Mbit/sec networks. Vendors are also shipping appliance-like IDSs, which simplify their deployment and management. And, they've begun delivering products that combine the best of the two principal types of IDSs into a single offering.

Just as importantly, the number of attacks on networking systems is growing. It's a jungle out there, and network managers need to keep the predators at bay with a variety of security devices, including the IDS.

For example, the nonprofit CERT Coordination Center received reports on 11,071 security incidents in 2001 (the most recent year its incident totals are available). That's comparable to the 10,960 it received in 2000, and the 9,859 incidents logged for 1999.

In June 2001, CERT reported a rise in the number of attempted intrusions using the SubSeven, a Trojan Horse that hackers can install on user PCs to gain complete control over system resources. This activity is most likely related to a new worm that seeks out previously compromised systems that have the SubSeven Trojan Horse installed.

In January 2001, the federal government's National Infrastructure Protection Center (NIPC) warned of a related threat, the W32-Leaves.worm, also thought to permit a remote computer to gain complete control of an infected machine, typically by using Internet Relay Chat (IRC) channels for communications.

The most virulent threat to emerge from the hacker jungle, though, is clearly DoS and Distributed DoS (DDoS) attacks, the number and variety of which have increased dramatically, according to security organizations. Hackers target DoS attacks at devices and networks with Internet exposure, especially e-commerce sites,[vii] according to the NIPC. The goal of such attacks is to incapacitate a device or network with bandwidth (devouring traffic so that external users can't access those resources)—this without hacking password files or stealing sensitive data.

In March 2001, NIPC began investigating a series of organized hacker activities that specifically targeted e-commerce and on-line banking sites. NIPC identified 50 victims in 30 U.S. states that were attacked by organized groups in Eastern Europe (particularly Russia and the Ukraine), that took advantage of vulnerabilities in servers running an unpatched version of Microsoft's *Windows NT* operating system. Once the Eastern European hackers gained access, they downloaded a variety of proprietary data—mostly customer databases and credit-card information. In this case, the intruders didn't use the information maliciously, per se, because they didn't attempt to make purchases with the stolen cards. They did, however, make veiled extortion threats by offering to furnish paid services that would "fix" the unpatched systems.

A Second Look

It's thus time for network professionals who gave up on the IDS a few years ago to go looking again. And, indeed, market research numbers indicate that more and more of them plan to deploy IDSs in the coming years.

Frost & Sullivan, for example, predicts that the market for intrusion detection software will increase from $73.4 million in 2000 to $375.5 million in 2002 and $547.2 million in 2003. Another research house, IDC (http://www.idc. com), paints a slightly rosier picture, saying that the IDS market stands at $461 million in 2002 and will grow to $554.6 million by 2003.

Several developments have moved the IDS back into prominence. These include the fact that IDSs can now keep up with the high-speed transport technologies found in today's networks, the emergence of IDS "appliances," new intrusion-detection methods, better management tools, and a hybrid approach that combines the monitoring of the network- and host-based systems, the two basic types of IDSs, with a single console.

The charge is led by many of the usual vendor suspects—Cisco Systems,[viii] Internet Security Systems (ISS), Intrusion.com , NFR Security, and Symantec-as well as numerous newcomers. The latter list includes CyberSafe, Entercept Security Technologies, and Enterasys Networks.

The market has also spawned a growing number of Managed Security Services Providers (MSSPs) with outsourced offerings that include intrusion-detection capabilities. In this area are Activis, Exodus Communications, OneSecure, NetSolve, RedSiren Technologies, Riptech, and Ubizen.

Moving to Anomaly Tracking

As noted, the developments driving the IDS marketplace are improving organizations' ability to monitor and secure against unwanted attacks, whether intrusions or DoS/DDoS strikes. Arguably, the most critical is the growing use of anomaly-based intrusion detection by vendors of network-based IDSs.

The traditional network-based IDS discovers malicious traffic by detecting the presence of known patterns, a process usually called "signature matching." These systems work much like an antivirus software package (detecting a known "bad" pattern generates an alarm) and effectively discover known patterns.

On the downside, signature-based network IDSs can suffer on two principal accounts. One, they can't see inside encrypted packets—the encryption essentially hides the packet's contents from the IDS, leaving it blind to assaults. Two, hackers often mutate the nature of their attacks, rendering pattern-matching useless. Just as an antivirus package can't protect against a new virus until vendors patch their software, an IDS vendor must update its signature files—and it's not clear how many vendors have figured that out.

The anomaly-based network IDS uses packet sniffing to characterize and track network activities to differentiate between abnormal and normal network behavior. These devices analyze the data transfer among IP devices, permitting them to discern normal traffic from suspicious activity without pattern/signature matching.

These devices don't care about the content of data in a session (as with signature matching). They only care about how a session took place, where the connection was made, what time, how rapid (i.e., is a suspicious connection to one host followed by a suspicious connection to another host?).

With anomaly-based systems, it's important to get a baseline of what "normal" network traffic looks like. The chief difficulty of this approach is how to baseline—to know what's normal traffic as opposed to deviated. Signature-matching should be coupled with anomaly tracking. An anomaly can be compared against a signature, and if the anomaly doesn't show up on multiple probes, you ignore it. Cisco Systems, Enterasys Networks, Lancope, Intrusion. com, ISS, and Recourse Technologies are among the vendors that offer anomaly-based network IDS products.

Faster Systems

Most IDSs on the market now can keep up with 100Mbit/sec Ethernet. Beyond that, they begin to drop packets and become less efficient. When vendors push their IDS offerings beyond 100Mbits/sec, they're only looking at a subset of packets. You can find products that will die in 100Mbit/sec networks. Others players that boast IDSs capable of operating in 100Mbit/sec network environments are Cisco and Enterasys.

One vendor, Top Layer Networks, takes an unusual approach to managing intrusion detection in high-speed networking environments. Its product, the AppSafe 3500 IDS, uses "flow mirroring" to copy each packet of a transmission to a specific port on the AS 3500; each port then distributes the traffic stream to separate IDS systems connected to the AS 3500.

Moving to Appliances

Another trend among IDS products is the network-based IDS appliance. Unlike first-generation IDS products, which required installing and configuring the vendor's intrusion-monitoring software on a PC, these appliances merge hardware and software into a preconfigured unit.

Cisco's Secure IDS, formerly known as the NetRanger, was among the first such appliances, and IDC believes this makes Cisco the current leader in this area. ISS (working with Nokia), Intrusion.com, and NFR Security (formerly Network Flight Recorder), are also moving their IDS products into the appliance category.

The appliance approach makes sense for several reasons. First, it eliminates many of the performance issues involved in installing IDS software on a general-purpose

PC. The IDS software vendor can't optimize its product for every processor and revision of operating system.

Second, the appliance is a controlled environment, built to vendor specifications, so the IDS software can be configured specifically for the application. Appliance-based IDS boxes also eliminate operating system-related concerns, especially in all-Wintel or all-Unix organizations.

Finally, appliance-based IDSs give plug-and-play capabilities to IT departments in multilocation companies, and to service providers. These are especially valuable for deployment in remote offices, where novice end users can handle the physical connections while leaving setup and configuration to centralized IT staff.

Best of Both Worlds

IDS vendors have developed recent products that merge the capabilities of host-and network-based systems into a single management platform. In these environments, a management console works in conjunction with traffic- and log-analysis tools on the network and host IDS systems to provide a correlated view of network activity.

Correlating data from multiple network sources lowers the incidence of false positives and enables network security personnel to view traffic from a higher level. For instance, a single scan of Port 80 on a Web server via a single router probably would not indicate the presence of an attack, but multiple scans across several routers would.

CyberSafe's CentraxICE is one of these "hybrid" IDSs that combine the two capabilities. It teams CyberSafe's own Centrax 3.0 software with Network Ice's ICEpak network-based IDS to monitor traffic on network segments as well as hosts.

Enterasys Networks' Dragon family is similar to that of CyberSafe's product. Symantec's IDS products will soon also offer hybrid host-network IDS capabilities. In addition, Cisco is working with Entercept Security Technologies to add host-based detection to its network-based products.

Although Enterasys sells to enterprises, it's particularly appealing to MSSPs, who need to monitor IDSs distributed not only throughout a network but also throughout multiple customers' networks. Enterasys users include MSSPs such as Riptech, OneSecure, and TrustWave, among others.

Outsourcing Intrusion Detection

Advances in IDS technology notwithstanding, organizations worried about unauthorized intrusions and DoS attacks should also consider outsourcing their intrusion-detection needs. Outsourcing intrusion detection to an MSSP, which monitors customers' IDSs via the Internet, can make sense for several reasons. Not the least of these is cost. Companies with small, limited staff with limited experience in security can benefit greatly from an MSSP. It would typically require five employees, working three eight-hour shifts (with extra staffing for vacations, sickness, and the like), to handle the 24-by-7 needs of an IDS-monitoring program. Forget about the $20,000 for the IDS—an employee costs at least $60,000 a year, and with five employees, you could spend a fortune on training and maintaining security personnel.

Thus, it's important to sit down and perform a Return on Investment (ROI) study. During this process, IT organizations should ask themselves whether they have the expertise to operate critical systems that can cost a business revenue or customer confidence if they're compromised due to hacking or DoS or DDoS attacks.

The MSSPs tout the level of security expertise among their employees, claiming that this expertise enables them to better handle the task of deciphering often arcane IDS logs and alarms that befuddle typical IT employees. There is some truth to this, of course. MSSP Ubizen, for instance, operates and tracks known and emerging security vulnerabilities and exploits and maintains its own database of threats; the information collected gives the analysts in Ubizen's OnlineGuardian service knowledge that few enterprises can afford.

In addition, MSSPs have often deployed tools specifically designed to acquire and correlate information from a wide range of intrusion detection devices and systems. MSSPs Riptech and OneSecure, for example, both indicate that the technology they've developed in this area differentiates them from others in the market.

Riptech, for instance, has spent two years developing proprietary data-mining and correlation software for its Caltarian security service. Caltarian's software permits the company to warn clients of attacks while they're under attack, with recommendations to protect their networks in real time.

So, perhaps one shouldn't pity the IDS after all. No longer an overly chatty box crying "wolf" too often, it now offers network managers an improved set of tools that can finally help them fend off unwanted attacks from insiders and outsiders alike.

Signs of Attempted and Successful Break-ins

Hackers are succeeding more and more in gaining root-privilege control of government computer systems containing sensitive information. Computers at many agencies are riddled with security weaknesses.

When an attacker gets root privileges to a server, he or she essentially has the power to do anything that a systems administrator could do, from copying files to installing software or sniffer programs that can monitor the activities of end users. And, intruders are increasingly doing just that.

The increase in the number of root compromises, denial-of-service attacks, network reconnaissance activities, destructive viruses, and malicious code, coupled with the advances in attack sophistication, pose a measurable threat to government systems.

In 2001, 266 systems at 43 federal agencies suffered root compromises in which intruders took full administrative control of the machines, according to the GSA. That's up from totals of 75 root compromises in 1998 and 221 in 1999. And the government has only a vague idea of what kind of data may have fallen into the wrong hands.

For at least five of the root compromises, officials were able to verify that access had been obtained to sensitive information. But, for the remaining 261 incidents, compromise of any or all information must be assumed. The compromised data involves scientific and environmental studies.

Meanwhile, the U.S. General Accounting Office (GAO), in a report recently released, summarized security audits that have been completed at 35 federal agencies, and indicated it had identified significant security weaknesses at each one. The shortcomings have placed an enormous amount of highly sensitive data at risk of inappropriate disclosure.

The government is going to find itself in "deep, deep trouble" if its IT security procedures aren't improved. If sensitive personal data about U.S. citizens is compromised, Americans are going to wake up angrier then you can possibly imagine.

Many of the thousands of attempts to illegally access federal systems come from abroad. Also, many nations are developing information warfare capabilities as well as adapting cyber crime tools.

Hackers are also exchanging vulnerability information with one another. There is a whole new currency on the Internet that's called the back door. Attackers are trading information about back doors that provide access to different systems.

One step the government could take to increase the security of its systems is to focus more resources on improving education and training. Computer security experts are scarce. They are in short supply, and they are expensive. The average salary is $90,000.

A 1998 directive by ex–President Clinton, ordered all federal agencies to complete a virtual bulletproofing of their IT systems from attack by May 2003. But officials indicate that most agencies are behind in that work, and only a few are doing penetration testing.

Even more alarming, is the fact that many attacks aren't detected. No one knows what was done, and no one has a way of knowing what was done.

Forensics

Threats to an enterprise's information infrastructure can come in a number of unsuspecting forms. Beyond fending off network intrusions and DoS (denial of service) attacks, companies must stave off threats of industrial espionage.

Layoffs are occurring more frequently these days, and when the disgruntled, newly disenfranchised leave, today's technology makes it easy for them to sneak off with trade secrets, research materials, client lists, and proprietary software. Increasingly, cyberthieves are raiding corporate servers, electronically stealing intellectual property, and using e-mail to harass fellow employees, putting companies at risk for liability. The impact on the bottom line alone is cause for concern; the American Society of Industrial Security reports the theft of intellectual property in the United States costs businesses almost $3.6 billion annually.

Constant developments in information technology have posed challenges for those policing cyber crime. For many organizations, identifying, tracking, and prosecuting these threats has become a full-time job.

Specialists in computer forensics must use sophisticated software tools and spend enormous amounts of time to isolate anomalies and detect clues for evidence of a cyber crime or security breach. As previously explained, computer forensics is the equivalent of surveying a crime scene or performing an autopsy on a victim. Clues inadvertently left behind after a cyber crime can often be pieced back together to reveal details of wrongdoing and eventually pinpoint the perpetrator.

Although software tools can identify and document evidence, computer forensics is more than just technology and analysis. Safeguards and forensics methodologies ensure digital evidence is preserved to withstand judicial scrutiny, and, to support civil or criminal litigation should the matter be brought to trial.

Divining Good Forensics

Obtaining a good digital fingerprint of a perpetrator requires that steps be taken to preserve the electronic crime scene. The systematic search for evidence must adhere to basic guidelines to prevent the inadvertent corruption of original data during the course of investigation. Even booting up or shutting down a system runs the risk of losing or overwriting data in memory and temporary files.

The examination will usually begin with a look at the disk drive. Minimal handling preserves its integrity, so any disk investigation should begin by making a copy of the original, using the least intrusive manner available.

Today's forensic software tools, such as DiskSearch Pro and the Law Enforcement Suite from New Technologies, can sniff out storage areas for data that may otherwise go unnoticed. Ambient system data, such as swap files and unallocated disk space, and file "slack" (data padded to the end of files), often hold interesting clues, including e-mail histories, document fragments, Web browsing details, and computer usage timelines.

Be careful to document any inadvertent changes that may occur to the original drive data during data extraction. Complying with the rules of evidence preservation and upholding the integrity of the process, will help withstand any future challenges of admissibility.

Although somewhat trickier than hard drive examination, data communication analysis is another useful forensic tool. Data communication analysis typically includes network intrusion detection, data preservation, and event reconstruction. Isolating suspicious network behavior also requires the use of specialized monitoring software, such as NetProwler from Symantec. Doing so can reveal activities such as unauthorized network access, malicious data-packet monitoring, and any remote system modifications.

Leave It to the Pros

Although today's sophisticated data-recovery tools have become fairly efficient, the process of recovery remains a tedious, labor-intensive task. And no matter how good the tools, the science of computer forensic discovery draws on multiple disciplines.

Forensics demands a skill set often comprised of software engineering and a solid familiarity with binary systems and memory usage, disk geometries, boot records, network systems, and data communications. Principals of cryptography are also important for identifying data encryption and password-protection schemes. And only experience can teach a forensic examiner how to avoid booby traps or an extortionist's logic bomb—items often left to wreak havoc along the path to discovery if not properly dismantled.

For these reasons, it's often wise to leave the process to the professionals. An expert in forensics will be able to quickly isolate the telltale signs of where to look for clues and will better understand data-discovery technologies as they apply to the legal process.

When selecting a forensic examiner, you should have several goals in mind: Your candidate should be familiar with the intricacies of your particular operating systems, know how to protect against data corruption and booby traps, and have a history of court appearances and controls established to deal with evidentiary procedures, such as chain-of-custody.

If you're looking for more information on computer forensics or getting your staff trained on good procedure and practice, there are a number of good resources at your disposal. As storage capacities and network sizes continue to increase, so do the means by which cyberthieves can circumvent security as well as the effort required to bring them to justice. So, start training to detect the signs of suspicious activity today and learn how forensic computer investigation can protect your corporate assets in these dangerous times.

How a Hacker Works

Obviously, knowing how the hacker's mind works is only half of the battle. You must also know your network inside and out, identify its vulnerable points, and take the necessary steps to protect it. This part of the chapter will look at some tips and tools administrators can use to prevent those vulnerabilities.

Diagram Your Network

You should begin by diagramming the topology of your network. You can do this with a sophisticated tool such as Visio, or you can use a less complex tool such as Word. Simpler yet, you can draw it by hand. Once you've diagrammed your network, identify all the machines that are connected to the Internet, including routers, switches, servers, and workstations. Then, evaluate the security precautions in place on those machines. You want to pay close attention to machines that have a public IP address on the Internet, because they're the ones that will be scanned by hackers.

Always-on Means Always-Vulnerable

Currently, the greatest security vulnerability is always-on Internet access using static IP addresses. With always-on access and a static IP, you are a like a big bull's-eye sitting on the Internet waiting to get hit. The question is, once hackers get in your network can they do any damage, or will they be frustrated and move on to the next target? If you have an always-on Internet connection, hopefully you already have a basic security policy and firewall in place on your network. If you have a Web server, mail server, and/or other servers constantly connected to the Internet, your security responsibilities are even greater. Because the Internet is built upon the TCP/IP protocol, many hacker attacks will seek to exploit the TCP ports of these servers with public IP addresses. A number of common ports are scanned and attacked:

- FTP (21)
- Telnet (23)
- SMTP (25)
- DNS (53)
- HTTP (80)
- POP3 (110)
- NNTP (119)
- IMAP (143)
- SNMP (161)

You need to identify whether your servers are utilizing any of these ports because these represent known vulnerabilities.

NOTE

Ways to Protect the Network

There are a number of ways to compensate for these vulnerabilities. First, you can implement firewall filtering. One of the best protections against port attacks is to implement a firewall with dynamic packet-filtering, also called "stateful inspection firewalls." These firewalls open and close ports on an as-needed basis, rather than permanently leaving a port open where it can be identified by one of the hackers' port scans and then exploited. You can also analyze your system log files to track hacker activity. A third option is to install an intrusion-detection program that will do much of the log file examination for you.

Seeing What the Hacker Sees

In addition to protecting against the well-known vulnerabilities, you need to see what the hacker sees when he looks at your network. The best way to do this is to use nmap, a program that gives you a look at your network from a hacker-like perspective. A company called eEye has released a new version of this program for Windows NT (you can download it at: http://www.eeye.com/html/Research/Tools/nmapNT.html). The company also offers an industrial-strength network security scanner called Retina, which helps discover and fix known and unknown vulnerabilities. This is an expensive, yet valuable, product.

You can download the Linux version of nmap at: http://www.insecure.org/nmap/

NOTE

Software Vulnerabilities

Hackers also often exploit software security problems. They take advantage of these behind-the-scenes parts of the software to gain access to your system. Thus, you should take stock of all the software running on your Internet-exposed systems. Go to the Web sites of the vendors that make each of the software packages and bookmark the page that has updates and patches for that software. You'll want to check these sites regularly and always keep your software up-to-date with the latest patches. Some companies even have services that will e-mail you whenever there's a new update or patch.

Security Expert Web Sites

In addition to staying on top of your vendors' security updates and patches, you should also stay current on the security risks and problems that are identified by security experts in the industry. Often, vulnerabilities may become known long before a vendor issues a patch. Therefore, your systems could be vulnerable for a period during which the hackers may know about it, but you don't. Two Web sites that will keep you informed are http://www.L0pht.com and http://www .403-security.org.

Now, let's look at how Internal net saboteurs are being brought to justice. These are the computer forensics problems of the present.

THE PROBLEMS OF THE PRESENT

An IT worker faced federal criminal charges recently in U.S. District Court in Miami for allegedly downloading a virus into his employer's computer system, crashing the network for nearly two full days. This case, which comes a little more than a year after the first federal criminal prosecution of computer sabotage, is just one in a growing number of insider-based network attacks, according to federal law enforcement agents. Another case is getting ready to go to trial in Las Vegas, and yet another was wrapped up with a guilty verdict in New Hampshire (see sidebar, "Insider Accounts").

INSIDER ACCOUNTS

It's a scary indicator of a spiraling economy that in 2001, 4.4 million workers were laid off, according to the U.S Department of Labor. Even scarier is the question of how many of those workers still have active accounts on the networks of their former employers.

So-called ghost accounts, those not closed when workers leave, can include access to mainframes, databases, file servers, intranets, and e-mail. There are also remote access holes with VPN passwords and dial-in accounts. All open "back doors" into a network.

A recent series of high-profile network sabotage cases show that vengeful employees can wreak high-tech havoc. Disgruntled employees are a significant threat. Security experts recommend a combination of procedures, policies, and automation to combat the threat.

Automation is key and is being made available in a class of products known as provisioning software, which can automatically activate and deactivate user accounts. If you are a CIO and are currently using a manual process, fundamentally you have no way to know the process (of deprovisioning) worked. With provisioning software, that is the opposite. You know that the process was completed.

Just, recently, Access360, Novell, and Waveset Technologies announced provisioning products. Business Layers also has a product called *eProvision Day One*.

Access 360 released Version 4.0 of its EnRole provisioning software, which is now integrated with corporate directories to centralize user account information. Novell released its Employee Provisioning System, which is intended to create a single user identity across a corporate network. Waveset Technologies is offering for free its Inactive Account Scanner, which ferrets out dormant accounts.

However, the process must include social engineering. That means teaching employees not to share passwords and administrators not to reactivate closed accounts.

For example, there was one case where a former Coast Guard employee was able to hack into a database using a password given to her by an unsuspecting coworker. The result: A bill of $50,000 and 2,900 staff hours to repair the damage.

The U.S. Secret Service, who splits its focus between protecting heads of state and conducting criminal investigations, is handling twice as many cases that involve insider attacks than occurred in 2001. And the FBI is currently investigating four such cases in New England alone.

Eighty percent (80%) of the cases are from the inside or people who were formerly with an organization. When you conduct an investigation, that's one of the first areas you need to look at now. It's not if you're going to be attacked, but when you're going to be attacked."

Ninety five percent (95%) of the break-ins they're called in to handle are insider-based. An insider attack really gets the attention of the company, because an insider has access to all the critical systems. If they want to do damage, they know how. A company's decision to protect itself isn't just a technology decision. It's a business decision.

Grocer Victimized

In the Miami case previously mentioned, Herbert Pierre-Louis, a hardware engineer who worked in the IT department at Purity Wholesale Grocers, is being charged with computer sabotage for the June 18, 1998, incident at the $2.6 billion national grocery outlet based in Boca Raton, Fla. The Assistant U.S. Attorney indicated the damage was well over the $6,000 waterline that is one of the key factors making this a federal crime.

The FBI warns that this is a time when companies should be particularly cautious. In light of the economy and the downturn and layoffs, companies should pay attention to this. These are not isolated events. They have an awful lot of trust in computer people in these companies.

That's a lesson Omega Engineering's Bridgeport, New Jersey, manufacturing plant learned the hard way. In the summer of 1997, a software timebomb went off in the plant's computer network, systematically eradicating all the programs that ran the company's manufacturing operations. Exacerbating the problem, Omega's only back-up tape was missing. The manufacturing plant was no longer able to manufacture. Company executives, in a 2001 trial in U.S. District Court in Newark, New Jersey, indicated that the company had yet to fully recover. The incident caused $23 million in damages and led to Omega losing its footing in the high-tech instrument and measurement market and the eventual layoff of 90 employees.

Omega's former network administrator was charged with sabotaging the network he helped build. He was found guilty after a four-week trial. The judge later set that verdict aside after a juror told the court she was unsure whether a piece of information she had heard on television news had been factored into her verdict.

The government appealed the judge's ruling, taking its case in front of the Third Circuit Court of Appeals in Philadelphia this past April. A ruling is pending.

The employee was charged under a relatively new statute that made computer sabotage a federal offense if it affected a computer used in interstate commerce and caused more than $5,000 worth of damage to the company over a 12-month span. That was the first federal criminal prosecution of computer sabotage.

Similar Cases Prosecuted

Now that same statute is being used in three other cases. One of those cases charges a network consultant with sabotaging the computer network at one of his clients, Steinberg Diagnostic Medical Imaging in Las Vegas. The consultant is charged with three counts of network intrusion for changing passwords in the network, which locked administrators out of their own system. The Assistant U.S. Attorney notes in the indictment that the consultant allegedly hacked the system on three different days between late February and early March of 2001.

The consultant, working with a partner, had been hired as a subcontractor by the medical imaging company, according to sources close to the investigation. Both the deal and the partnership fell through, and the consultant's partner went to work for Steinberg Diagnostic as a system administrator. The government contends that the consultant attacked the system to gain revenge. The damage had to have added up to at least $5,000 for the consultant to be charged with a federal offense.

In the summer of 2001, a former help desk worker at Bricsnet, a Portsmouth, New Hampshire, application service provider for the construction and design industry, was found guilty on federal charges of network sabotage for hacking into Bricsnet's system after being fired in the fall of 2000. The worker pleaded guilty to breaking into the system twice using a supervisor's password (once the night he was fired and again the next morning) to delete a total of 786 files, change user access levels, and send e-mails to Bricsnet clients saying the company's project center would be temporarily or permanently shut down.

The attack, which was discovered by another Bricsnet employee the next day, cost the company $24,725 in in-house repair costs. Some of the destroyed files could not be restored.

His activities were meant to cause as much damage as possible. It was malicious. And putting a financial number on the loss is misleading. How do you quantify the impact when customers receive these kind of damaging e-mails? You can't put a dollar on that. Would a company pay $24,000 not to have that happen?

Administrators took basic security precautions after firing the worker, who had broken company rules against moonlighting and other activities. They terminated the worker's password, log-on, and user accounts. They also changed the code on their building's keypad and escorted the worker from the building.

There was no sense of foreboding. These steps were routine. Certainly, Bricsnet had an extensive security system in place, but they were always thinking of outside intrusion.

The incident, which the FBI traced back to the worker in less than a week, has changed the way the company evaluates its security needs. Since the attack, Bricsnet has re-evaluated its security system and limited network access.

Bricsnet is acutely aware of the damage a disgruntled employee can cause. People took it personally. For someone you've worked with on a daily basis, it certainly was an element of betrayal for them.

Finally, let's examine the latest outlook for the future. This chapter will end by taking a look at a new breed of hackers: The drive-by hackers.

THE OUTLOOK FOR THE FUTURE

Atlanta-based Internet Security Systems Inc. (ISS) has long had this concern about drive-by hackers. That's right—drive-by hackers.

ISS claims perpetrators can equip their laptops with wireless technology,[ix] sit inconspicuously on a park bench, or in a car, and casually monitor traffic, access applications, and hijack data flowing over someone else's wireless network, unbeknownst to the victim. To combat this threat, which sounds like it could be a plot line from an upcoming James Bond film, ISS recently drew the curtain on wireless local area network (WLAN) security software and consulting practices.

Why create safety for the WLAN? ISS believes enterprises are deploying WLANs with increasing regularity because they are cost-effective and help workers grab knowledge on the go from laptops or personal digital assistants (PDAs). And very little exists in the way of security for wireless networks, as compared to their wired counterparts, LANs?

Gartner Group, it would seem, concurs that wireless networks are in the midst of proliferation. The research firm said 60% of all enterprises in the United States will have deployed a wireless LAN by 2003, an increase from 32% in 2001. Accordingly, ISS indicates that the fact that wireless LANs can easily be accessed by outsiders (friendly or not), means that they need stronger protection.

And, just as perpetrators such as hackers and crackers have done to wired networks, they can assault WLANs through the same methods: unauthorized access points; data interception; denial-of-service (DoS) attacks; peer-to-peer sabotage; and wireless laptops to attacks when they roam to public access points such as airports and hotels.

What is more frightening, ISS claims, is that nontechnical employees, although often victims of attacks, are often unaware of these threats. This ignorance can make the comfort of the firewall a false security blanket.

Most companies have no idea that their networks are wide open to wireless security risks. Employees today are adding their own wireless access points to the backbone of their company's network without the knowledge of their IT and security staffs. With a lack of awareness by the company that an access point has been added and a lack of proper security configuration, these rogue access points can become an intruder's dream back-door into a company's network despite the front-door firewall.

SUMMARY

This chapter introduced numerous solutions to those of you who are in the process of conducting advanced computer forensics through the use of encryption for protection and hacking back with advanced hacker trackers. As previously explained, hackers and crackers are everywhere, but you may think your company's system is too minor for them to notice. Not true. Hackers don't always target specific machines—they scan hundreds with special programs to find any that might be vulnerable to attack. The intruder could be a teen hoping to use your system to launch an attack on a Web site, or a bitter ex-employee looking for payback.

The Internet today is like a walk through a vineyard, with the attackers stopping here and there to pick a grape at their leisure. The feast is seemingly never-ending.

Even a secure company network can be riddled with holes such as badly configured routers that expose data in transit to snoops. Think your firewall will protect you? Not always. Attacks at Microsoft and eBay prove otherwise.

Furthermore, protecting your network against hackers need not be a full-time job. By including a few best practices as part of your organization's daily routine, you can prevent leaks from developing—or at the very least, plug them before the dams break altogether.

Computer forensics provides the methodology for investigating and documenting cyber crimes, so they may be later tried in court. Hiring an expert is costly but necessary to preserve evidence during the legal process.

Also, tools for sifting digital media and detecting network intrusion have become easier to implement, but they still demand a sizeable time commitment and cross-discipline knowledge for most situations. Training is required to secure a crime scene and for procedural litigation.

Conclusions Drawn from Advanced Computer Forensics

- Hackers often break into computers through well-documented holes (they read security alerts, too) when users don't install patches.
- Hackers often enter networks through old computers that are no longer in use. This can happen when administrators forget to disconnect an ex-employee's system from the modem or network.
- An older system is less likely to have the latest security patches installed.
- A shared terminal that's not attached to any one employee is often overlooked when security updates are done.
- Any workstation that's left on and connected to both a modem and the network gives hackers one way to dial into the machine, bypass the firewall, and gain access to the network.
- You encrypt important data on your server, but you neglect to encrypt remote back-ups.
- Hackers can target data on a less-protected off-site machine that stores back-ups.
- Security is an ongoing task. It's not something you install and forget about; it's something you live with.
- Intrusion Detection Systems (IDSs) come in several forms, with the most commonly deployed called "host" and "network" systems. Some experts include the "desktop" IDS in this market, whereas others would also list so-called honeypots and honeynets.
- A host-based IDS is a piece of software that runs on a network-based computer— a Web or application server, for instance. It tracks and analyzes entries in the host system's application and operating system event logs.
- Host-based systems are particularly valuable in monitoring insider threats because they can show when unauthorized personnel attempt to access prohibited data or resources.
- A network-based IDS, which can be software running on a stand-alone PC or on a dedicated appliance, tracks and analyzes the packets that make up network data traffic.

- Network-based IDSs are generally "promiscuous" in that they look at every packet on a network or network segment.
- Network-node IDS systems detect packets headed to a single network node.
- A desktop IDS offers file-level protection. Rather than monitoring network traffic, it examines activity on individual systems, looking for potential attacks on files or registry entries on *Windows* PCs.
- The desktop IDS is also very useful in Trojan Horse detection.
- A honeypot is a system designed to be attacked, with the intent of deception or alerting of intrusion activity.
- Honeypots emulate known vulnerabilities, other systems, or are modified production systems that create "caged" environments.
- A honeynet is a network of production systems, residing behind a firewall, which is designed to be compromised. Once breached, the resulting information gathered during the attack is analyzed to learn about the tools, tactics, and motives of the possible intrusion.

An Agenda for Action in Advanced Computer Forensics

The following is a provisional list of actions for advanced computer forensics. The order is not significant; however, these are the activities for which the research would want to provide a detailed description of procedures, review, and assessment for ease of use and admissibility. A number of these advanced computer forensics topics have been mentioned in passing already:

1. Install patches: Microsoft's *Critical Update Notification* tells you when new patches are available. Be sure to install them on all your PCs.
2. Secure old computers: Inventory your systems, and unplug from the network any that no one uses anymore.
3. If a networked computer is shared, make sure it receives the same security updates as other systems.
4. Encrypt data every place it's stored, including PC hard drives.
5. Do frequent security audits, including trying to gain access using easily available hacking tools.
6. Ensure that you only run the services you need and only open the ports needed by your network.
7. Your gateway to the Internet should be a system without any important company data or a hardware solution backed-up by a firewall.
8. Set up *Windows Update* notification for the server and have a back-up server ready when you need to run the update.

9. Always check security bulletins and consider joining 'hacking' mailing groups to find out what's happening on 'the other side' of computer security.
10. Regularly test the security yourself, then you know what to find solutions for.
11. Make sure no one person is controlling the system front to back.
12. Require every person logging-on to use a password.
13. Assign supervisory rights to as few people as possible.
14. Back-up all systems weekly.
15. Have a strict sign-in/sign-out system for back-up tapes.
16. Always have a current copy of the back-up tape stored remotely.
17. Do back-ups of desktops and laptops as well as servers.
18. Rotate back-up tapes—don't use the same one over and over again.
19. Change passwords every three months.
20. Keep servers in a secured area.
21. Stay up-to-date on software patches.
22. Use intrusion-detection software that alerts you when you are being hit.
23. Make sure two pairs of eyes have checked code before it is entered into the system.
24. Have an information security department (at least one person and then one other for every 1,000 users) that is separate from the IT department and reports directly to the chief information officer.
25. Spend at least 3 to 5% of the IS budget on information security.
26. Train information security personnel to be aware of any employee who shows signs of being troubled or disgruntled, particularly if that employee holds an information-critical position.
27. Beef up security during certain events, such as mergers or downsizings, that could upset workers and cause them to lash out at the company.
28. Monitor the network—set up software that will alert you if the person is working in a different part of the network or at a different time than usual.
29. Scan e-mail to see what's going out of the company, double-check back-up tapes and have someone else do the back-ups if that person is the one in question.
30. Make sure the person in charge of the system is not the same person in charge of the back-up.
31. Have specific policies and punishments built into employee contracts.
32. Make sure critical IS workers are bonded.
33. Change everyone's passwords so he/she can't use them to break into the system.

34. Verify that your back-up tapes are where they should be; make sure the information has been saved correctly and the tape is functioning properly.
35. Do a new back-up.
36. Lock down every system that a terminated employee had access to on the day of termination.
37. Have a new network administrator ready to step into the open position immediately.
38. Go up on the system and check user names and passwords, looking for anything unusual.
39. Make sure every log-on has a password for it.
40. Lock down all the inside doors, such as the file servers, application servers, and mail servers.
41. Look for back-doors on the system, such as *Back Orifice* on *Windows NT.*
42. Make sure there aren't any known vulnerabilities that haven't been patched—the administrator could have left those holes behind so he could get back in.
43. Strengthen your intrusion-detection system.
44. Set a trip wire—software that alerts the administrator to system anomalies, such as the size of a file changing.

ENDNOTES

i   John R. Vacca, *Net Privacy: A Guide to Developing & Implementing an Iron-clad ebusiness Privacy Plan*, McGraw-Hill, 2001.

ii Michael A. Caloyannides, "Encryption Wars: Early Battles," © 2000 IEEE, IEEE Spectrum, 445 Hoes Lane, Piscataway, New Jersey 08855, 2001. *All rights reserved.*

iii Ibid.

iv Ibid.

v   Ibid.

vi John R. Vacca, *i-mode Crash Course*, McGraw-Hill, 2002.

vii John R. Vacca, *Electronic Commerce, Third Edition*, Charles River Media, 2001.

viii John R. Vacca, *High-Speed Cisco Networks: Planning, Design, and Implementation*, CRC Press, 2002.

ix John R. Vacca, *Wireless Broadband Networks Handbook*, McGraw-Hill, 2001.

20 Summary, Conclusions, and Recommendations

Computer forensics may sound like a media-generated catchphrase, but its principle is actually quite simple. Forensics, generally speaking, is investigation of evidence following scientific methods within the regulations of the law. Computer forensics applies those same principles to digital evidence-recovery.

The scope of such digital-evidence salvage operations is enormous, due to many factors, including the global nature of the Internet. To help create cooperation between the United States and other nations, the G8 group (http://www.g8online.org/) of major industrialized nations has proposed six principles for procedures relating to digital evidence, which it defines as *information stored or transmitted in binary form that may be relied on in court:*

1. When dealing with digital evidence, all the standard forensic and procedural principles must be applied.
2. Upon seizing digital evidence, actions taken should not change that evidence.
3. People who access original digital evidence should be trained for the purpose.
4. All activity relating to the seizure, access, storage,[i] or transfer of digital evidence must be fully documented, preserved, and available for review.
5. Individuals are responsible for all actions taken with respect to digital evidence while such evidence is in their possession.
6. Any agency that is responsible for seizing, accessing, storing, or transferring digital evidence is responsible for complying with these principles.[ii]

All computer forensic policy and procedures should be developed from these principles. Not limited to computers in the traditional sense, the field encompasses everything from PDAs to routers, and covers crimes ranging from creating, possessing, and disseminating child pornography to network intrusions. Perpetrators range from 13-year-olds to trained experts paid by rogue nations to infiltrate and steal proprietary information; organization insiders could also perpetrate similar crimes.

SUMMARY

The United States Department of Justice categorizes computers involved in crimes in three ways: contraband, instrumentality, and "mere" evidence. If a network manager discovers contraband (illegal or illegally acquired equipment), he or she should simply turn the matter over to law enforcement.

Computer instrumentality implies that hardware played a significant role in a crime. Within network-related crimes, "innocent" computers are often used as instrumentalities—they are used to commit further crime, either denial of service attacks or by providing a pass thru for the criminal. Law enforcement will often seize computers used as instrumentalities; they must seize them if the crime falls under certain federal statutes.

Computers classified as "mere" evidence are usually not seized. The goal is to acquire the data of evidentiary value from the computer while adhering to computer forensic principles. Before getting into specifics on how this is actually done, let us first examine some policies that should be in place before the need for forensics arises.

Haste Makes Waste

Every business should have a computer security plan, part of which must include collection and preservation of evidence before, during, and after the incident. When formulating all policies regarding computer forensics, a balance must be struck between expediency and following a proper chain of command. It is neither feasible nor desirable for the CIO of a large corporation to be called every time a computer is attacked; at the same time, some oversight is important. Each organization needs to decide how far to proceed up the hierarchy when responding to different levels of attacks.

Because laws will affect corporations differently, and because desktop forensics is extremely important for internal offenses, it is wise to have separate policies for internal attacks and external attacks. A recent study performed jointly by CSI and the National Infrastructure Protection Center arm of the FBI found that a significant number of attacks (81%) came from disgruntled employees (Figure 20.1).[iii]

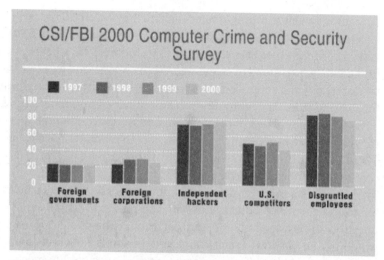

FIGURE 20.1 A joint CSI/FBI study determined that an overwhelming number of desktop attacks (81%) came from disgruntled employees. *(©Copyright 2002. Computer Security Institute. All rights reserved).*

This is not only the case at university-type settings, where public labs are plentiful and security is often lax; but also remains true for all types of organizations. When dealing with internal policies, desktop examination is a crucial element, whether the matter is simple misuse or corporate espionage. Regardless of the reasons, following proper forensic procedures will help establish a legal case.

NOTE

Certain laws exist to provide some privacy to the end user.[iv]

The one most important privacy law for this chapter and book is the Electronic Communication Privacy Act (ECPA), which begins in the United States Code at Title 18, section 2701. The law contains certain provisions that should be incorporated into every policy. For the purposes of this chapter, assume you are dealing with an e-mail system that employs user authentication to verify active employee status. Policy rules regarding an open Internet service provider (wherein anyone can pay and join) are significantly more stringent.

NOTE

One provision of the law, Title 18 USC 2703(f), applies equally to all e-mail providers: A provider of wire or electronic communication services or a remote computing service, upon the request of a governmental entity, shall take all necessary steps to preserve records and other evidence in its possession pending the issuance of a court order or other process."

Law enforcement commonly refers to Title 18 USC 2703(f) as sending an "F-letter" (referencing that the law is section F of the statute) to a provider. Usually such a request will be communicated via telephone first, followed by a letter. A company should immediately take the steps mandated via the phone call, without waiting for the letter's arrival. Under the second part of this section, the records must be preserved for a period of 90 days, and the government has an option to extend this another 90 days. There should be appropriate policies in place to handle this possibility, from the administrative receiving end all the way to placement of the backed-up records. These policies should be created in a partnership among management, computer services personnel, and legal counsel.

How does a manager know if the staff possesses the requisite knowledge to create sound corporate policies on evidence-recovery? This is an extremely difficult question to answer, but one approach might be to determine whom, typically, would not be qualified. The average system administrator usually doesn't have the required knowledge; the Microsoft Certified Systems Engineer (MCSE) test also doesn't include such information. A dedicated network security specialist may or may not have the appropriate knowledge, but this is probably the best place to start looking. That individual, who might be CISSP or SANS certified, will have a fundamental understanding of security issues that a normal system administrator probably would not.

Mapping the Labyrinth

Even though the corporate computer forensics specialist is not a law enforcement officer, he or she will still find merit in following the same forensic procedures. This includes limiting access, photographing the computer screen if information is visible, and, most important, documenting every step. From the moment a computer is recognized as compromised, documenting should begin.

Documentation should hold to a general standard: If someone with comparable knowledge picks up the first examiner's notes, he or she should be able to reach the same conclusion after following each step. Documentation should include the basic "who, what?, when?, and where?" criteria, and also how long each individual spent diagnosing and repairing any problems, which is used to determine damages. The amount of damage may not only influence the involvement of federal investigators but also a resulting federal trial; under U.S. Federal Sentencing Guidelines, damages determine the punishment.

It is essential for companies to keep track of their damages when responding to an intrusion threat for purposes of criminal prosecution. The courts in determining the sentence for an intruder use the costs incurred by a company to detect, repair, and deter future intrusions, including labor costs. Thus, companies are asked to keep track of their costs so that intruders can be effectively prosecuted.

One of the most critical aspects of proper evidence collection is proper shutdown and the creation of a bit stream image of the violated computer. If the computer in question is a Microsoft DOS/*Windows* computer, proper procedure is to pull the plug from the rear of the computer—preferable because normal shutdown procedures may compromise important evidence.

NOTE   *Laptops or machines with an internal, uninterruptible power supply, disconnect the internal UPS or battery before the power cord is pulled. Afterward, the hard drive is usually removed and reinstalled on another machine. The system is booted from a floppy that disallows any attempt to write to the hard drive, and a bit stream image is created via one of a variety of products.*

What imaging software you choose to use is largely a personal preference, provided that it satisfies the criterion of providing complete bit-by-bit imaging. The person performing the imaging procedure must verify the software's ability and accuracy every time a new update is released. Some popular choices (although this author and publisher are not endorsing any) are *Byte Back* (http://www.toolsthatwork .com/byte.shtml), *SafeBack* (http://www.forensics-intl.com/safeback.html), *Fred* (http://www.digitalintel.com/), and *Encase* (http://www.encase.com/html/index. html).

Some popular commercial imaging software may or may not offer forensic capabilities. It may be an option. Just remember that before any software is used, the individual performing the image must verify it. This is done by proper hash testing, discussed later on.

Sealing off the Unix Crime Scene

Unix can be more problematic in response to a forced shutdown that occurs due to power loss. There are several options and opinions within the field regarding how best to handle a Unix box. How the shutdown should be handled will depend on how critical the data on the victimized computer is, among other criteria. Regardless, the first step is, as always, to document the state of the system before touching it. This may include photographing the monitor and the computer. The next step is to collect any possible evidence from RAM, accomplished by using the command line *ps -aux* or *ps -ef* depending on the Unix version.

The individual should look for and be able to recognize any programs that are unauthorized. If any are found, the associated RAM contents should be saved. The method for accomplishing this may vary with the Unix version, but one example is the *gcore* command. A computer forensics specialist should also be familiar with programs such as List Open Files (LSOF), beneficial in isolating trouble spots. It's important to make sure all programs are authentic and updated; intruders may replace commands with their own "trapped" versions.

After RAM documentation, there are several options: One is to sync, halt, reboot, and mount the drives from a CD. One possible danger is that the sync command may have been altered, thus damaging evidence. This procedure also changes the state of the hard drive, which is a possible concern. Another option is simply to pull the power and leave the system in a dirty state. Afterward, the drive can be mounted dirty, and bit stream copies can be created from the original.

A third option is to make a bit stream copy by utilizing the Data Definition *dd* command. This is not a command that can be covered briefly, as it has many options and parameters, such as identifying a data-definition element in a definition list, and converting a file while copying it. It is important that any person using this command is trained to do so.

Truth Serum

No matter what operating system (or program used to create copies) is being utilized, some type of verification software should be part of the forensics equation. The purpose of these programs is to ensure that the copy of the bit stream image of the violated computer is the same as the original. This is accomplished by using mathematical algorithms, called "hash functions," which calculate hash values (also known as checksums, or "fingerprints") based on the original file/image. To be valid, hash functions must meet two primary requirements: The original text may not be determined from the hash function, and they must be collision free—meaning that two different messages cannot produce the same hash value.

A file-hashing utility should always be used to verify the copying of all files or images. The use of the SHA-1 hash is highly recommended. The hash values should be recorded and kept in order, along with such data as when the program was run, who ran it, and what program was used—valuable information for the event reconstruction typical of court cases.

Security Officer's Log: Mission-Critical

Logs create evidence when they capture the actions of an illegal act. What logs an organization chooses to keep, and how long it will keep them, largely depends on available space and average number of entries received. It might see frequent probes—anything from port scans to DNS-version requests on an open system. Although such probes are annoyances that are not even necessarily illegal, it may be important to keep logs of them. If the organization chooses to go to court, such logs will provide a complete picture for a jury.

To keep logs from being destroyed by malicious intrusions, system operators will often output some logs to a printer or a CD-ROM device; this can be an expensive route, but it frequently offers greater security. If utilized, this option should be noted in an organization's policies and procedures, as law enforcement may not automatically think to ask for logs copied in this fashion.

Different versions of Unix have their logs in different areas. Most of the older versions keep logs in /usr/adm, whereas most newer versions use /var/adm or /var/log for storage.

NOTE

One of the primary logs used in computer forensics is syslog, the main system log containing a variety of important messages. This is no secret to hackers, and, hence, is often one of the first logs to be modified. In addition, routers and firewalls can be configured to add messages to the syslog.

A high degree of redundancy exists between syslog's contents and other logs, so they should be checked against each other; log inconsistencies may indicate security breaches.

NOTE

Some popular logs that may prove useful include acct, aculog, lastlog, loginlog, sulog, utmp(x), wtmp(x), void.log, and xferlog. Remember that when any of these logs are copied, a hashing program should be used to ensure proper back-up creation.

Windows NT's three main log files—appevent.evt, secevent.evt, and sysevent.evt are kept in the *percentsystemroot percent\system32\config* directory and are normally viewed using Microsoft's built-in Event Viewer. Various Web and ftp servers will also have their own logs and should be preserved as well. It is important to have a current list of programs and services installed, to have a checklist for log preservation.

Ghosts from the Immediate Past

State tables are another potentially important source of evidence, although their temporary nature makes them difficult to acquire. State tables show actions that take place either in real time or in the immediate past. One of the most popular and powerful is the *netstat* command, which exists in both Unix and Windows NT environments, with different options for each. The *netstat* command "displays network connections, routing tables, interface statistics, masquerade connections, netlink messages, and multicast memberships."

Another temporary log that can sometimes be useful is a system's Address Resolution Protocol (ARP) cache; designed to discover MAC addresses on Ethernet-based networks. MAC addresses do not cross routers. This is important because packets sent over the Internet will not contain the sender's MAC address, but, instead, will have the MAC address of the last router they traversed. If the router is keeping the correct logs, and a packet has only traveled over a few routers, this information may be useful. Both NT and Unix create a temporary cache list of the IP-to-MAC conversions, viewable by using the *arp -a* command.

There are special steps for state table preservation. Not only should they be cut and pasted to a text file but also printing the screen shot is advisable. The log should then be hashed and preserved with other evidence.

Protecting the Evidence

Generally speaking, two separate back-ups of every relevant file and/or image should be made. These files should be hashed along with the original. The media a company chooses to use will depend on size, speed, and cost issues (tapes versus DVD-RAM versus identical hard disk drives, and so on). More important still is the method by which the media are handled. The forensic chain of evidence requires that the person creating the back-ups, along with anyone who touches the media prior to presentation in court, be clearly documented. Obviously, care must also be taken to protect the media from various environmental elements: Preferably, it should be placed in an appropriate container, taped shut, then initialed and dated. This ensures media authenticity after completion of the back-up. Some type of standard tracking method should be used with every piece of evidence.

Costs of Precaution

No summary chapter on computer forensics would be complete without an examination of costs involved. There are two types of costs however: the cost of doing nothing about data-evidence-recovery, and the cost of doing something about it. The most recent CSI/FBI study reported that total losses incurred via data loss, fraud, or abuse for 273 respondents totaled $265,589,940 (see Figure 20.2 for a breakdown).[v]

Personnel costs associated with computer forensics are dependent on several factors, including the number of different operating systems the person is expected to know. Each additional operating system requires additional training. Costs are fluid, and should be taken only as ballpark figures. Training a staffer with preexisting knowledge to be the rough equivalent of an individual in a forensic laboratory may cost around $25,000 for one platform. Costs for materials examination may run from $10 to $400 for one case. The salary level of the examiner will fluctuate with location and experience. It is possible, of course, to hire an outside forensics specialist. The cost for this type of service varies greatly.

There is a wide range of options when it comes to the software itself. The cost of forensic tools may range from no cost for older, basic tools to over $1,500 for one

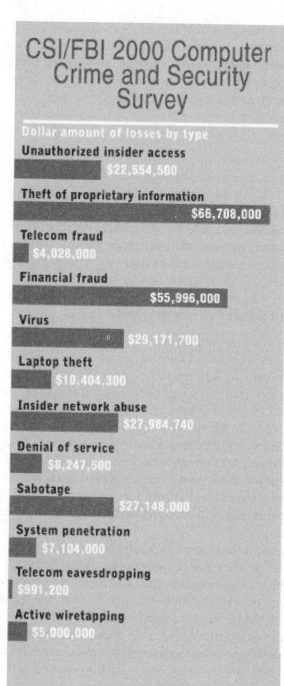

FIGURE 20.2 The 2000 CSI/FBI study totals losses incurred from data loss, fraud, or abuse for 273 respondents at $265,589,940. (@Copyright 2002. Computer Security Institute. All rights reserved).

software package alone. There are also costs for password cracking, both for software and the time necessary on a computer (cost per CPU cycle). It is important to reiterate that every company should keep track of all costs related to the attack, including the amount of time each person spends responding to any damage. Tracking all of these costs is extremely helpful if any court proceedings occur.

Homegrown Salvage Team

Computer forensics is an important part of a larger picture. Every organization should consider forming a Computer Security Incident Response Team (CSIRT, sometimes referred to as a Computer Emergency Response Team, or CERT), if one hasn't already been established.

Incorporating computer forensics into the responsibilities of any CSIRT bolsters organizational security and makes court actions more successful. This can only help create a safer environment for an organization's employees, customers, and business partners.

Computer Forensics to Play Central Role in Terrorist Fight

Computer Forensics begins at home. And for the IT manager, that means the server room, where the Internet has brought not only the promise of a worldwide audience but also the threat of worms, hackers, and cyberterrorism. As the United States mobilizes to shore up security at airports and public gathering spaces and in the country's infrastructure, the IT industry has a central role to play—a role that not only makes business sense but also is important in the unfolding war on terror.

In the same week that the terrorist destruction of the World Trade Center took place, the Nimda worm ran rampant through the Internet. Although there may not be any overt connection between the two events, the continued marauding of worms and viruses across the Net only reinforces a general anxiety about living in an insecure world and a specific feeling that the Net will never be a place where real business can be conducted.

In the past, much of enterprise IT security has been built around firewalls or monitoring products meant to keep the bad guys out. Although that is fine for providing a sense of relief that you avoided the virus that halted the company down the hall, it doesn't do much to solve the problem. That's one of the reasons why there was so much to like in the LaBrea 2.0 worm buster. Not only is it effective in helping you keep your network worm-free but it also stops the propagation of the worm. Of course, the other thing everyone liked was the price, which was free for the download.

The role of computer forensics in the current rush to security cannot be overstated. Before the government rushes to mandate face scanners, fingerprint identification systems, or simply networks to signal when a bad guy might be applying for a crop duster license, there has to be some consideration of the systems that will be required to run these programs. Developing systems that have what appears to be an effective front end, but in reality are porous, is at least partly to blame in the lax airport security programs that had such a horrific result and still do.

Scanning-in lots of data, tapping lots of phones, or opening lots of encrypted e-mail can drown you in data if you don't have some way to collect, sort, and analyze it and alert the security official who needs to know of a breach in process. Too much data is often more dangerous than too little, as overwhelming data can give you a false sense of security.

Where does that system expertise reside? It resides in systems that manage credit-card transactions, phone connection and billing system, and data-management systems. The war on terror will be marked by huge amounts of data, gathered electronically and in person, which will be analyzed to focus on a small group of fanatics. It is telling that President Bush used an attack on financial information as the first salvo in the terror war. The IT sector through computer forensics has a crucial role to play in stopping the terrorists before they can strike again.

CONCLUSIONS

The federal government can report in exacting detail the number of bank robberies committed in any given year. But when it comes to computer crimes against government agencies, it's close to clueless.

Government officials estimate that only 20% of such incidents are being reported because individual agencies either don't have the technical sophistication to discover the crimes or want to keep bad news quiet. It's for those reasons that the 155 root compromises of federal computers reported in 2000 likely represent a fraction of the actual number.

Computer compromises are a serious issue. Agencies fear the unwelcome attention computer crime reports bring and often lack the money and tools needed to detect IT security breaches.

In addition, there's an ingrained reluctance on the part of agencies to work together to combat computer crimes. There is no culture of collaboration in the federal government.

During the first three months of 2001, the Federal Computer Incident Response Center (FedCIRC), the government's central crime data repository, recorded 55 root compromises at civilian nondefense federal agencies, which put it on pace to exceed the year 2000's total. That would result in an increase in the number of such intrusions for the third straight year.

A root compromise occurs when an intruder gains systems administration privileges on a network, giving the attacker the ability to do things such as copy documents, alter data, or plant malicious code. Still, security analysts said it's impossible to gauge just what the first-quarter increase recorded by FedCIRC (http://www.fedcirc.gov/) means. FedCIRC doesn't know whether they're seeing a change in the rate of reporting, the rate of detection, or the rate of penetration.

For its part (prior to the 9-11 attacks), the Bush administration had begun to take steps to improve compliance by federal agencies in reporting and responding to security breaches, including a recommendation that FedCIRC's annual funding be boosted 38%, from $8 million to $11 million. Agencies are already required by law to report breaches to FedCIRC as a result of the Government Security Reform Act approved in 2000.

Federal agencies have repeatedly been faulted by the General Accounting Office for poor security practices—the 9-11 attacks and the recent issuance of educational visas to the dead terrorists have bore that out. The GAO has conducted penetration testing against various government systems. For example, it said in a report recently released that it found significant security weaknesses at all of the 24 agencies where it conducted audits of IT security readiness. Improving security procedures needs to be a priority within the Bush administration, and from some of the early indications in the budget, it is going to be.

Cost of Computer Crime Exploding

According to results of the 2002 Computer Crime and Security Survey recently released, intellectual property theft and security breaches are on the rise while the costs of those intrusions are skyrocketing. Conducted by the Computer Security Institute of San Francisco and the FBI, the survey of 649 security administrators from industry, government, and academia shows that 86% of respondents reported security breaches in 2002"s survey, and 27% reported intellectual property theft, up from 21% in 2001.

But the survey also shows that the cost of that theft is exploding. Although only 35 respondents could quantify the financial losses associated with intellectual property theft, that number added up to more than $262 million. The amount is up from almost $78 million in 2001 and $31 million in 1998. In total, 297 respondents said losses from all types of security breaches cost more than $488 million. That means theft of intellectual property accounts for 41% of all losses tabulated in the survey, despite the fact that such a small number of companies could quantify it.

Companies are figuring out how to protect their financial data, customers" credit information, and personnel records. The problem is many companies aren't aware that they should be protecting the information that fuels their businesses—such as marketing plans, source codes, and research information. You lock up rooms so people can't steal laptops; but, if your company is based on information and information systems that can't be secured, then you're in line to lose your cash crop.

Industrial espionage is giving way to information age espionage. It used to be that if you wanted information on your competition, you would turn to an insider. You bribed them. You blackmailed them. But why risk someone getting caught when you can just hack in and take what you need? The survey also points to several other aspects of computer security that are on the rise:

- Forty-one percent (41%) of respondents reported outside system penetration. That number is up from 21% in 1998.
- Thirty-nine percent (39%) detected denial-of-service attacks. That number is up from 25% in 1999 and 28% in 2001.
- In 2000, 249 people were able (and willing) to quantify financial losses. That number totaled $265 million.
- Thirty-seven percent (37%) of respondents reported security breaches to law enforcement agencies. That's up from 18% in 1998 and 26% in 2001.

Industry analysts and corporate users agree that more administrators should be focused on protecting their valuable proprietary information. Companies that collect credit card numbers and personal information about people take on that security responsibility. What they're not doing is protecting their own information, records, plans, and technologies.

For some IT administrators, getting the message through to upper management is another problem. It's not that upper management doubts the information's value, but, rather, that upper management feels that there isn't enough threat to warrant any significant attention. Once management buys into the importance of protecting information, it's another matter to put a strong security plan in place.

Companies developing a new drug or a new widget may understand how sensitive that product information is, but they find it hard to protect. It's the core of what they're doing, so it requires access from a whole lot of people for a lot of reasons. It's difficult to enforce protection of information while still letting people at the information.

The survey trends are unnerving. It's clearly a dangerous world, and has been—and will continue for years to come—possibly even get worse, given the widespread deployment of computer forensics and security technologies. And it's costing American businesses billions.

RECOMMENDATIONS

Details of the recent arrest of U.S. Federal Bureau of Investigation Special Agent Robert P. Hanssen for espionage highlight the need for increasingly sophisticated computer forensic imaging and analysis tools and methodologies for their proper use. The FBI conducted a search of Mr. Hanssen's briefcase in 2001 and found a "computer memory card," from which they were able to retrieve a digital copy of a note Mr. Hanssen wrote to his Russian handlers in 2000. The digital copy was made in the off-limits room Hanssen kept in his basement—the one with two computers that authorities believe he used to maintain his own spy operation.

Few of us will ever be in as tense a situation as the one the FBI faced recently with Mr. Hanssen and the "computer memory card" or the off-limits room in the basement. Mess that up from an evidence-handling perspective and a major international espionage case could evaporate. But, no matter where you work in the computer security field, you may one day find yourself faced with a tough investigative challenge, looking for the right tools to accomplish an incredibly important job, facing near impossible deadlines—and always with the thought in the back of your mind that if you mess something up, life as you know it could change drastically.

The need for technical investigative capabilities has been growing steadily with the proliferation of computers in the workplace. And the discipline of computer forensics has emerged to meet that need. But computers being what they are, it takes a computer and a robust set of applications to analyze another computer in such a manner that the results of the analysis are thorough, sound, unbiased, and repeatable. That's where the various developers and vendors of computer forensic analysis software come in. Each developer has his or her own unique perspective on the needs of the investigative community and his or her own approach as to how to meet those needs. But few have started the software-development process with a well-stated computer forensic analysis requirements document.

What tasks must computer forensic analysis software be able to accomplish? And how can you measure the performance of various tools against one another without a well-defined requirements definition? The speed of a forensic analysis tool is of little consequence if it is not also thorough, unbiased, and forensically sound; so speed alone cannot be the primary consideration. And the knowledge, skills, and experience of the analyst at the keyboard can also play a significant factor in the performance of a tool, when no thorough requirements document exists.

This final recommendations chapter is concerned with how to conduct a relevant and meaningful review of computer-forensic-analysis software tools. Let's start with a requirements definition.

With more practitioners involved in stating requirements and designing tests, the tests will be more relevant to the computer forensics community. And, hopefully, where tools fall short of meeting requirements, developers will take the results to their labs and work to improve the tools. So, it is the intent of this recommendations part of the chapter to initiate discussion and solidify the various computer forensics requirements.

Requirements Definition

Let's begin this look at requirements by identifying certain capabilities that a forensic examiner needs, based on tasks the examiner must perform to complete a thorough, unbiased, and forensically sound examination of computer media. The requirements definition is not intended to mandate specific procedures or to endorse certain products. It is also not intended to mandate that any specific software tool be used in any specific set of circumstances. Where possible, the requirements definition is also media independent, operating system independent, file system independent, and hardware platform independent.

This requirements definition also takes into account the fact that law enforcement officers have different requirements than corporate security/investigations personnel. Whereas law enforcement officers typically have legal authority to seize computer systems as evidence in criminal cases, corporate security/investigations personnel are typically involved in civil cases and rarely have authority to seize equipment. But corporate security/investigations personnel typically have some authority to preview systems, determine which ones may have relevant evidence, and preserve evidentiary images of systems deemed to contain relevant evidence. Likewise, where the law enforcement officer may remove evidence to a lab environment for analysis, the corporate security officer will typically remove only evidentiary images of media, leaving the original media on-site.

At a fairly fundamental level, the forensic analysis toolbox needs certain capabilities. For instance, you must be able to complete forensically sound searches of computer media at both the logical and physical levels of the media. That requirement exists because certain data in the logical file system may not be readily available or readable at the physical level. As an example, much of the Windows registry is written physically to disk in binary form, but is readable logically with a tool such as REGEDIT.EXE. Adobe Acrobat portable document format (.PDF) files are, likewise, physically written to disk in a manner that obscures the textual content of the document. Compressed files, encrypted files, and other "special" files written physically to disk in a format other than text format, likewise, will not show their real content at the physical level.

A search of computer media at the physical level also might miss plain text words in a document, if the document is fragmented physically on disk and the word of interest is partially contained at the end of one sector and the beginning of a noncontiguous sector. Only a logical search of the file system can ensure that relevant text contained in logical files fragmented physically on disk is found, because a logical search can account for fragmentation.

This requirements definition also sets forth minimum requirements for functionality taking into account a wide variety of technical, logistical, and legal circumstances. The "Identify–Preserve–Analyze–Report" model continues to serve to describe the overall process investigators use to conduct an investigation involving computer-based evidence. An investigator at a crime scene must be able to identify computer systems or media possibly containing digital evidence relevant to the case. If a crime scene contains computers, and investigators leave the scene without them (or without forensically sound evidentiary images of them), then the process ends and no analysis or reporting can take place. Any evidence on the media is possibly lost.

Once an investigator identifies the systems or media possibly containing data of an evidentiary nature, he or she must properly preserve their digital contents in a forensically sound manner. After preserving the evidence, an investigator will conduct some series of examinations (analyze) of the data on the media to extract from it relevant information. After identifying relevant media, preserving appropriate evidentiary images of the media, and conducting a thorough, unbiased, and forensically sound examination of the media, the investigator will report the results of their efforts in some fashion.

The capabilities an examiner requires in any one step of the process may sometimes overlap with capabilities required in other steps. Essentially, without the capability to do each of these functions, an investigator might not have in his or her toolkit the requisite tools necessary to accomplish a thorough, unbiased examination of media, finding all relevant and potentially incriminating or exculpatory evidence on the media under examination. But it is recommended that the following capabilities be useful as a starting point to develop a set of minimum requirements:

1. An investigator requires a capability to simultaneously preview a large number of systems on-site to determine which ones contain relevant evidence.
2. An investigator requires the capability to conduct a search at the physical level of the target media, ignoring operating system and file system logical structures, and searching from sector 0 to the end of the media regardless of the logical content.
3. The search tool must be able to reliably report the physical location on the media where responsive data were found.
4. An investigator requires the capability to conduct a thorough, read-only search at the logical level of the target media.
5. An investigator requires an ability to generate a listing of all logical files in a file system.
6. An investigator requires an ability to search the contents of the regular files in a file system without changing either the data in the file or any date/time data recorded by the operating system about the file.

7. An investigator requires an ability to identify and process special files.
8. Investigators require the capability to recover pertinent deleted files or portions thereof that have not been overwritten.
9. Investigators require the capability to make forensically sound images of a wide variety of media.
10. Investigators require the capability to restore forensic images to suitable media.
11. Investigators require the capability to perform a sector-by-sector comparison of two pieces of media to determine where they differ.
12. Investigators require the capability to thoroughly document their investigative activities and succinctly document the data recovered from a piece of media that are relevant to the allegations under investigation.

Simultaneously Preview a Large Number of Systems on Site

In some situations, identifying which computers or media at a scene may contain information or data of evidentiary value is fairly straightforward. The hacked Web server, a compromised file server, a firewall, or other networked devices may be, due to the nature of the investigation, an obvious system to preserve. But, in other cases, particularly where the allegation concerns activities of insiders, it may not be so easy to determine which systems contain information of evidentiary value. In cases where an office has multiple computers, and a subset of those computers might contain relevant evidence, then seizing or imaging all the computers at that site could be a tremendous waste of vital resources.

In most cases, an initial search at the physical level of the media may be sufficient to determine if a specific computer system or piece of media contains relevant information and should be imaged/preserved for further, more detailed analysis. However, keep in mind that a fruitless search at the physical level may have actually missed relevant information for a wide variety of reasons, including that relevant keywords in logical files may be physically fragmented on disk; relevant files may be compressed or encrypted; or relevant files may be otherwise encoded or obscured. So, the investigator must decide, based on the circumstances of the case, whether a fruitless search at the physical level of the media is sufficient to exclude the media from further processing. Previewing computer media has two subcomponent requirements: a validated read-only methodology and a controlled boot process.

Validated Read-only Methodology

For previewing media on scene, an investigator requires a capability to preview media using tools and methodologies that have been tested under various circumstances and validated not to make changes to the original media. Otherwise, the preview process itself may taint the evidence by changing pertinent date/time stamps on files or otherwise modifying data on the target media. Unintentionally modifying date/time stamps in particular could unnecessarily complicate the evidence-analysis process.

Controlled Boot Process

For previewing media on scene, an investigator requires a boot process that can be precisely controlled. Whether the preview process will be done via a remote connection to a computer system or will be executed locally on the system, the investigator must know exactly what the boot process is, ensure that the boot process used does not make changes to any of the data on the media to be previewed, and ensure that the preview tools and methodologies are forensically sound.

The preview process itself can be conducted several ways, including either remotely or locally. A local preview of media involves using a controlled boot process to boot the suspect machine and conduct a review of the system locally. If the entire process can be contained on floppy diskette or bootable CD-ROM, this could allow as many simultaneous iterations as there are suspect systems to be previewed. But the local preview process must not make changes to the media being previewed.

Like a local preview, a remote preview must be conducted in such a manner that it does not make changes to the media being previewed. If the investigator uses a tool with a remote preview capability, they will actually boot two computers: the one housing the media to be previewed and the one from which the preview will be accomplished. Using a remote preview capability may limit the number of simultaneous iterations that can be conducted because it requires more hardware; but, in cases where only a few systems need to be previewed, a remote capability could be very useful. Typically, remote previewing involves connecting two computers via a parallel port, com port, video port, or other port, running a "server" version of an application on the machine to be previewed, and running a "client" version of the software on the machine from which the preview is conducted. No matter the exact mechanism used, the preview process must be forensically sound, and must not make changes to the media being previewed.

Conduct a Search at the Physical Level of the Target Media

A physical search of the media essentially searches all logical files, file slack, free or unallocated space, and all space on the media outside any logical data areas. The search tool must have the ability to use both ASCII and UNICODE character sets. Some operating systems write documents and other files to disk using printable and nonprintable ASCII characters. But other operating systems can use the UNICODE character set as well as the ASCII character set. A search for a word using the ASCII character set will not find that word if it is written to disk using the UNICODE character set. So an investigator requires a search tool that can use both character sets in its searches. Preferably, a single pass through the media will search using both character sets simultaneously.

The search tool must be capable of searching all sectors of the physical media. If the tool cannot see and search all sectors of the media, the resultant search may not be thorough enough to establish that evidence either does or does not reside on the media.

The search tool must be capable of using a keyword list. Tools that require separate passes through the media to search for each keyword would unnecessarily constrain the investigator in terms of both time and efficiency, especially when searching one of today's 80GB and larger hard drives. The keyword list must be able to include regular ASCII text as well as hexadecimal notations. Some file type headers and all binary files will contain nonprintable ASCII characters. Hexadecimal notation is the best way to search for this type of data.

Report the Physical Location on the Media

This report could use either the cylinder-head-sector (CHS) or logical block addressing (LBA) address of the responsive data. In the best case, even though a physical search is conducted, the search tool may be able to determine whether the keyword resides in a logical file on the media, file slack, free space, or areas of the media outside the logical data area.

The search tool must be able to show results in context. Rarely is a keyword or phrase so unique to an investigation that its mere presence on a piece of media indicates the media contains data of evidentiary value. The investigator must be able to discern the context within which a word or phrase resides on the media to determine whether the context is relevant to the investigation. So, the search tool must be capable of displaying some amount of data that resides on disk immediately prior to the keyword and some amount of data that resides on disk immediately after the keyword. Otherwise, the investigator must use a hex editor to preview each sector containing the key word to determine whether it actually contains relevant data.

An investigator also requires the ability to calculate a hash of the physical media. The hash process must take into account every bit of every byte of every sector on the media, from sector 0 to the last physical sector, regardless of whether any specific sector is included in any logical volume on the media. In most cases, the minimum standard is the 32-bit cyclic redundancy check (CRC) algorithm. But for hard drives, the 128-bit message digest 5 (MD5) algorithm is preferred.

Conduct a Thorough Read-only Search

A search of the logical file space is likely to require less time than a search of the physical media, but likely will not search every sector of the media. If an investigator begins with a logical search to preview media, and that search produces no relevant results, the investigator may have to follow up with a search of the physical media to ensure a thorough search. And if the search tool used on one logical partition does not understand the file system formatting of another partition on the media, then a different search tool must be used on the other partition. For instance, a hard drive may be partitioned and formatted to boot multiple operating systems, each using a different file system. That may require several logical level search tools if no one tool understands all the file systems on the media.

As with the physical level search, the search tool must have the ability to use both ASCII and UNICODE character sets. This is for exactly the same reasons as previously stated, on searching at the physical level.

The search tool must be capable of searching all sectors within the logical boundaries of the file system. If the tool cannot see and search all sectors of the file system, the resultant search may not be thorough enough to establish that the evidence either does or does not reside on the media. And for reasons already stated, the search tool must be able to use a keyword list.

Generate a Listing of All Logical Files

This listing must include not only all the regular files in a file system but also all files with special attributes, such as hidden files, read-only files, system files, executable files, directories, links to files, device files, and so on. And, the tool that creates this list must be able to write the list of files to appropriate media, whether that is a network accessible volume, a local hard drive not under investigation, or some appropriate removable media connected to the analysis machine. Preferably, the tool that generates the list of files would not allow the list to be written to the media being searched.

In addition, an investigator requires an ability to generate a listing of all the date/time stamps an operating system may store in relation to each file in the file system. Some operating systems store various dates and times in relation to the files in the file system. Those dates/times may include Date/Time Last Modified, Date/Time Last Accessed, or Date/Time Created. Not all operating systems record all date/time combinations. But if an operating system records any date/time stamp data in relation to files in a file system, the tool must list all date/time data available.

Furthermore, an investigator requires the ability to identify and generate a listing of all deleted files in the file system. Various operating systems handle deleting files in various ways, so the specific capability of a tool will be dependent on the file system the tool is examining, but to some degree, all file systems have a way of at least identifying that a file once existed in a certain space.

Search the Contents of the Regular Files

Searching the contents of the regular files is a particularly important requirement for the search tool. If the search tool opens a regular file to search its contents for a keyword, and that process changes either the file contents or a date/time stamp maintained by the operating system about the file, then the investigator may have to restore an image of the media to get back to the original file contents or date/time stamps. Some search tools that operate at the logical level of the media do not quite meet this requirement, because most operating systems keep a Date/Time Last Accessed timestamp and will attempt to update this stamp when the search tool opens or closes the file.

It is particularly important to test search tools under very controlled conditions to ensure they actually meet this requirement. If a search tool, in fact, allows the operating system to update Date/Time Last Accessed when the tool runs, then the investigator must take steps to preserve those date/time stamps prior to using the search tool.

An investigator also needs the capability to validate file types where applicable using known header-extension pairs, and to hash all the logical files using a recognized and appropriate hashing algorithm. In most cases, the minimum standard at a file level is the CRC algorithm. But for very large files, the MD5 algorithm is preferred.

Ability to Identify and Process Special Files

Special files are in a format in which their contents are either not written to disk or not maintained internally in a readily readable, searchable format. "Special files" include encrypted, compressed, or password-protected files; steganographic carrier files; graphics files, video files and audio files; .PDF format files; executable files or binary data files; files housing e-mail archives and/or active email content; swap files or virtual memory files; and other such file formats that obscure their plain text content. Some password-protected files can be processed in a manner to remove or expose the password. Other types of special files, such as encryption or steganography, may require a more dedicated effort to bypass the security mechanisms.

Recover Pertinent Deleted Files

Recovering pertinent deleted files would logically include a capability to identify and search all file slack. This would also include identifying and searching all free (unallocated) space, identifying relevant file headers in free space, identifying deleted directories in free space, including directory entries for deleted files, and recovering deleted directory entries as well as all pertinent deleted files that are not overwritten

Make Forensically Sound Images

Once the preview process has identified that certain systems or media contain information relevant to the issues at hand, an investigator must have tools capable of making forensically sound images of those systems or media. The criteria for "forensically sound" media images is fairly straightforward: The image must include a true, validated copy of every bit of every byte contained on the media, without regard to media contents, from the absolute beginning of the media to the end of the physical device.

The exact mechanism by which that data is retrieved from the "evidence" media, stored in an image file, and validated will vary. But the image file must contain validated copies of all data from the original media. In today's world of smartcards and "computer memory cards," where cameras can store hundreds of pictures on memory cards (where these cards can supply memory to portable or handheld devices), the investigators are faced with an ever-widening variety of media. Today's media is outdated tomorrow. New imaging and analysis tools must keep apace.

Restore Forensic Images to Suitable Media

Where the functionality of an application is the issue, merely analyzing the files comprising the application at a physical or logical level may not be enough to satisfy the questions. This requirement stems from a need to be able to run applications installed on drives that have been preserved as evidence. For instance, in a fraud investigation, if an investigator needs to print reports from a large financial application installed on a drive, that she or he has imaged, and she or he no longer has access to the original drives, she or he may need to restore the image to run the application to print the reports. Today's large applications rely on installation processes that do more than just copy the application files to the media. So, running the application in its installed environment may be necessary. This cannot currently be done from within the image files, so the image must be restored.

Perform a Sector-by-Sector Comparison

To verify that one piece of media is an identical copy of another, investigators typically use media hashes of some type. But where two pieces of media are thought to be identical copies of each other, but hash differently, it must be possible to compare sector-by-sector. In most cases, simply knowing that two pieces of media have different hashes will not give you an indication of where on the media the difference occurs. And this capability would be especially useful when an investigator must restore an image of a piece of media to a dissimilar piece of media. This tool could verify that any differences between the original and the copy are merely sectors filled with hashes and are accounted for by geometry differences only.

Thoroughly Document Investigative Activities

Thoroughly documenting investigative activities would preferably be an automated part of the forensic analysis software. If the software is self-documenting and certain reports are automatically generated for the user, based on the results of exercising the capabilities of the software, this could help make reporting results much simpler.

Now that we've looked at computer forensics requirements definitions, let's look at digital evidence standards and principles. This next part of the chapter recommends the establishment of computer forensics standards for the exchange of digital evidence between sovereign nations and is intended to elicit constructive discussion regarding digital evidence.

Standards and Principles of Digital Evidence

The latter part of the 20th century was marked by the electronic transistor and the machines and ideas made possible by it. As a result, the world changed from analog to digital. Although the computer reigns supreme in the digital domain, it is not the only digital device. An entire constellation of audio, video, communications, and photographic devices are becoming so closely associated with the computer as to have converged with it.

From a law enforcement perspective, more of the information that serves as currency in the judicial process is being stored, transmitted, or processed in digital form. The connectivity resulting from a single world economy in which the companies providing goods and services are truly international has enabled criminals to act transjurisdictionally with ease. Consequently, a perpetrator may be brought to justice in one jurisdiction while the digital evidence required to successfully prosecute the case may reside only in other jurisdictions.

This situation requires that all nations have the ability to collect and preserve digital evidence for their own needs as well as for the potential needs of other sovereigns. Each jurisdiction has its own system of government and administration of justice, but in order for one country to protect itself and its citizens, it must be able to make use of evidence collected by other nations.

Although it is not reasonable to expect all nations to know about and abide by the precise laws and rules of other countries, a means that will allow the exchange of evidence must be found. This part of the chapter defines the technical aspects of these exchanges.

Standards

To ensure that digital evidence is collected, preserved, examined, or transferred in a manner that safeguards the accuracy and reliability of the evidence, law enforcement and forensic organizations must establish and maintain an effective quality system. Standard Operating Procedures (SOPs) are documented quality-control guidelines that must be supported by proper case records and use broadly accepted procedures, equipment, and materials.

Standards and Criteria

All agencies and/or organizations that seize and/or examine digital evidence must maintain an appropriate SOP document. All elements of an organization's policies and procedures concerning digital evidence must be clearly set forth in this SOP document, which must be issued under the agency's management authority.

The use of SOPs is fundamental to both law enforcement and forensic science. Guidelines that are consistent with scientific and legal principles are essential to the acceptance of results and conclusions by courts and other agencies. The development and implementation of these SOPs must be under an organization's management authority.

Management must review the SOPs on an annual basis to ensure their continued suitability and effectiveness. Rapid technological changes are the hallmark of digital evidence, with the types, formats, and methods for seizing and examining digital evidence changing quickly. To ensure that personnel, training, equipment, and procedures continue to be appropriate and effective, management must review and update SOP documents annually.

Procedures used must be generally accepted in the field or supported by data gathered and recorded in a scientific manner. Because a variety of scientific procedures may validly be applied to a given problem, standards and criteria for assessing procedures need to remain flexible. The validity of a procedure may be established by demonstrating the accuracy and reliability of specific techniques. In the digital evidence area, peer review of SOPs by other organizations may be useful.

The organization must maintain written copies of appropriate technical procedures. Procedures should set forth their purpose and appropriate application. Required elements such as hardware and software must be listed and the proper steps for successful use should be listed or discussed. Any limitations in the use of the procedure or the use or interpretation of the results should be established. Personnel who use these procedures must be familiar with them and have them available for reference.

The organization must use hardware and software that is appropriate and effective for the seizure or examination procedure. Although many acceptable procedures may be used to perform a task, considerable variation among cases requires that personnel have the flexibility to exercise judgment in selecting a method appropriate to the problem.

Hardware used in the seizure and/or examination of digital evidence should be in good operating condition and be tested to ensure that it operates correctly. Software must be tested to ensure that it produces reliable results for use in seizure and/or examination purposes.

All activity relating to the seizure, storage, examination, or transfer of digital evidence must be recorded in writing and be available for review and testimony. In general, documentation to support conclusions must be such that, in the absence of the originator, another competent person could evaluate what was done, interpret the data, and arrive at the same conclusions as the originator.

The requirement for evidence reliability necessitates a chain of custody for all items of evidence. Chain-of-custody documentation must be maintained for all digital evidence.

Case notes and records of observations must be of a permanent nature. Handwritten notes and observations must be in ink, not pencil, although pencil (including color) may be appropriate for diagrams or making tracings. Any corrections to notes must be made by an initialed, single strikeout; nothing in the handwritten information should be obliterated or erased. Notes and records should be authenticated by handwritten signatures, initials, digital signatures, or other marking systems.

Any action that has the potential to alter, damage, or destroy any aspect of original evidence must be performed by qualified persons in a forensically sound manner. As discussed in the preceding standards and criteria, evidence has value only if it can be shown to be accurate, reliable, and controlled. A quality forensic program consists of properly trained personnel and appropriate equipment, software, and procedures to collectively ensure these attributes.

Finally, now that the establishment of computer forensics standards has been made, it is time to recommend some auditing techniques. The following auditing techniques are based on how to audit your internal computer forensics and Internet security policies.

Computer Forensics Auditing Techniques

Companies that believe their networks and the Internet can be completely protected by a phalanx of add-on computer forensics and security products may be in for a rude awakening. Underlying vulnerabilities, embedded and unseen many layers down in network infrastructures and the Internet, may be unwitting invitations to even moderately skilled attackers.

Computer forensics and security-auditing companies can give a company expert analysis of obscure but potentially devastating loopholes, along with estimates of cost versus risk for each of many possible approaches to address them—and a basis for deciding whether spending a little more money up front will save much more in the long run. So, without further ado, this last part of the chapter makes some recommendations into how computer forensic and security auditors go through a network and what steps are necessary for companies to lock down their networks—especially the ones that are connected to the Internet.

How to Audit Your Network and Internet Security Policies with Computer Forensics Techniques

The Internet has allowed businesses to communicate in new and strategic ways with various types of people and organizations. Thus, system administrators do not have to argue for an Internet connection anymore. Instead, they have to fight for the resources to secure it. Auditing your Internet and network security with computer-forensics techniques is a responsibility that should be frequently revisited and improved, and you should not hesitate in dedicating resources to security when you find shortcomings.

The Internet Octopus

Over the years, you have added feature upon feature to your Internet and network connections. As the needs have changed, you have found yourself needing more robust services, faster connections, and more flexibility in what can be done. In the beginning, services such as simple POP3-style e-mail and Web access were the extent of an Internet connection. Today, you have site-to-site VPNs; client-side and home-user VPNs; streaming media; Web-based training; company Web sites; Internet applications; e-commerce;[vi] and business-to-business extranets. During all these changes in the last few years, you have probably changed IT personnel, Internet platforms, and network connections at least once in your organizations. This scenario makes it easy to have some unforeseen, yet preventable, exposures.

Any network connection to the Internet is vulnerable to exploitation. The most basic vulnerability that all network connections face is that they could be made unavailable and bring down mission-critical services with them. Today, you are finding more intelligent defenses against attacks, such as denial of service attacks (see sidebar, "How DoS Attacks Work"), as routers and other devices can be set to verify source addresses and ignore packets if they are bogus or carry a suspicious pattern. However, beyond the DoS category of vulnerabilities, there are always the standard concerns of open ports, easy passwords, unsecured routers, and unknown "features" that any Internet device may have.

HOW DOS ATTACKS WORK

The main thing that makes DoS attacks so hard to fend off is that, at least on the surface, they look like valid traffic. The basic difference between legitimate visits and attacks is the intent—along with the volume, frequency, and source of the traffic. Normal traffic to a mail server might come in spurts and waves, but an attack against sendmail entails a barrage of messages in close proximity—so close that the service cannot keep up with the volume and crashes or hangs. In fact, a DoS attack will likely bring the system itself to a halt. If the server doesn't run out of swap space, it will probably run out of process space or network connections. It's also likely to suffer from network congestion problems. In addition to the difficulty of differentiating attacks from normal traffic, it is hard to effectively slow down or control the traffic comprising the attack.

DoS attacks are cheaper to launch than to deal with. The effort involved in launching attack is almost always minimal compared to the effort involved in fending off or recovering from the attack.

DoS attacks are hard to characterize because what they have in common is their overall effect, not the technique by which they're carried out. DoS attacks can seek to flood a network with traffic or to modify a router's configuration. The goal of both methods is to deny legitimate users access. The various means of achieving that goal have little in common. Typical DoS attacks involve:

- Jamming networks
- Flooding service ports
- Misconfiguring routers or other critical devices

Efforts to flood a network, for example, can block or slow all communication between servers and clients, making it difficult or impossible for any work to be done. Excessive traffic to a specific service port on a server, on the other hand, might make that service or server unusable.

In a DoS attack against sendmail, hundreds of thousands of messages can be sent in a short period of time; a normal load might only be 100 or 1,000 messages an hour. If a DoS attack is noticed in time, a service can be shut down while the organization rides out the attack. That cannot always be done without repercussions, though. Attacks against sendmail might not make the front page, but downtime on major Web sites will. For companies whose reputation depends on the reliability and accuracy of their Web-based transactions, a DoS attack can be a major embarrassment and a serious threat to business.

SYN Floods

DoS attacks do not always involve a deluge of service requests. Some involve the disabling of a critical component. If an attacker crashed or changed the configuration of a company's firewall, for example, the company would likely be isolated until someone brought the system back on-line or routed traffic through another system. In fact, the recent DoS attack on Microsoft involved interference with the routers that provide access to the company's Web sites.

Even more insidious than overwhelming a system with legitimate requests is flooding a system with requests falsified in such a way that the server expends more resources trying to validate or complete connections than it would setting up legitimate connections.

One well-known attack of this type is the SYN flood. A SYN (SYN stands for synchronize or start) is a request that's sent to a server when establishing a network connection (when someone issues a telnet request). In a normal sequence, the server replies with a SYN ACK (an acknowledgment) and the client then sends an ACK in response to the SYN ACK. This orderly handshaking establishes a connection and is called the TCP three-way handshake.

The server keeps track of incomplete connections by maintaining a queue: a kernel data structure of limited size that's dedicated to keeping track of connections. When the ACK from the client isn't returned, the incomplete connection sits in the queue until it times out. Because ACKs are normally returned in a matter of milliseconds, a connection that takes minutes to expire occupies space in the queue for a relatively long time. Given enough malformed SYNs, the kernel data structures are used up faster than they can be released, and no additional connections can be made. The pending connections, referred to as being half-open, block proper connections from being initiated.

Why are the ACKs not returned? Generally, connection requests sent in SYN floods contain bogus source addresses. TCP SYN floods are sent with random source addresses. Therefore, when the server replies to a SYN with its SYN ACK, it sends it to a nonexistent system, or one that didn't make the initial request and isn't waiting for it.

Though most DoS attacks are deliberate, some are merely a side effect of some other form of abuse or carelessness. A small minority may actually be the result of honest mistakes. When an undergraduate at a major university took it upon himself to mirror a newsgroup on a departmental server, he probably had no idea that the number of visitors would cripple the system so it could no longer be used by the researchers for scientific computation. Similarly, the individual who used an e-mail address associated with one of his employers as a reply address in his spam probably only meant to hide his real address. The fact that the hundred thousand or so bounced messages that a server processed nearly brought the flow of legitimate e-mail to a standstill may or may not have crossed his mind.

DoS Versus DDoS

A variation on the basic DoS attack is the distributed denial of service (DDoS) attack. A DDoS attack is launched from a variety of sites, making it more difficult to detect and block. DDoS attacks are considerably harder to combat because blocking a single IP address or network will not stop them. The traffic can derive from hundreds or even thousands of individual systems; sometimes the users are not even aware that their computers are part of the attack.

A program may have been planted on their systems as part of a virus.

NOTE

The potentially unintentional attacks described in the preceding are more like DDoS attacks than normal DoS attacks, simply because the bounces could derive from as many different sources as the original e-mail was sent to. Some DoS attacks can be squelched while in progress by blocking the particular site from which the attack is launched (at your company's firewall). By blocking a particular IP address, network address, or service port combination, you can keep the offensive traffic from reaching your server—but only if you recognize the attack in time to prevent it from fully compromising your server(s). Unfortunately, most attackers are cleverer than that, and use falsified addresses or launch their attacks from so many locations that it's impossible to discern the source.

Detection of DoS attacks depends on the requests being sent at regular intervals. If the messages are all from the same site, are the same size, or have some other characteristic in common, you may be able to build a filter that blocks messages that match the pattern. The problem with this approach is that it's not possible to determine what the pattern will be, and, during an attack, it may be difficult to respond coolly and decisively. Increasingly, products are incorporating detection of attacks, such as filters that look for patterns of activity that correspond to various attack methodologies. Eventually, packet headers may be encrypted so source addresses cannot be falsified.

Some preventative measures might involve pacing a service so it never processes enough requests in a short period of time to overwhelm a service. These choke points are often established on routers and might, for example, limit ICMP requests (as would be used in a Ping of Death attack).

Preventative measures have been slow to evolve because DoS attacks are so diverse and hard to predict. Nevertheless, some effective measures, such as smart filtering on Cisco routers,[vii] are being developed.

One of the most effective safeguards against DoS attacks is simple redundancy. If your primary router or firewall can be brought down, have a back-up on hand. Also, be ready to rebuild from back-up or hot spares as needed. There's no substitute for being prepared for an attack—even if the playing field is wide open. A staff that runs through fire drills to prepare itself has a chance of surviving an attack without a major outage.

Many organizations have grown their Internet set of features across multiple devices or possibly multiple network connections—a firewall for Web and mail traffic, a VPN appliance for remote connections, a different firewall for a business-to-business relationship that may exist, or other possible combinations of lines and devices that can push Internet vulnerabilities beyond control. These services can even be distributed across multiple Internet connections or across multiple Internet service providers. Regardless of the number of devices that are on the Internet, each has different services that can be potentially exploited. You can see how an enterprise environment such as this could quickly become difficult to manage from a security standpoint.

What You Can Do

There are a number of things you can do to keep your network connections secure and to keep business running as usual. One of the easiest measures you can take is to clean things up:

- Verify that there are no accounts for terminated employees.
- Check for any manufacturer or service provider default passwords that may be easily known or guessed.
- Verify that any "temporary" services or open ports are disabled.
- Beware of potential internal threats.
- Have the mindset of "deny all except that which is explicitly stated in the rule set."

After this basic housekeeping is completed, it's important to perform a "Vulnerability Chain Assessment" with your computer forensics tools on your own. This will allow you to gauge the entire scope of an Internet and network security policy. A Vulnerability Chain Assessment tells administrators what is affected by what and who potential perpetrators could be.

All the items listed below have vulnerabilities—some of which are beyond your control. For each item, consider the potential vulnerabilities that could cause an interruption of service:

- Internet (outside of your router): Internet being unavailable from your carrier or region, phone line cut, denial of service, and so on.
- Internet line: physical disconnection—via a perpetrator or the carrier.
- Internet router: ISP configuration may have well-known default passwords; this could reroute all incoming mail, shut down an interface, or adversely affect performance by some other means.
- Internet/external network: If this segment is a managed device (hub, switch, or other), it could be falsely managed to disable ports or could be affected by the failure of device.
- VPN appliance and firewall: security compromise, stale VPN accounts or vendor default account, unwanted services, failure of device, and so on.
- Internal network: failure of any internal device, internal security threats on interior devices to the Internet, and the like.

Obtain Peace of Mind

One thing you can do to bring some validity to your efforts is to get an external opinion of your Internet and network security. You can obtain this opinion via:

- A formal Internet and network security audit from a person or organization with CISA and computer forensics certification.
- A third-party piece of computer forensic auditing software or OEM-provided tool to examine security issues.
- A professional hacker trying to compromise an Internet presence.

The professional hacker approach is recommended, but you have to be careful. These types of companies need to be true DEF CON followers and really know their stuff. You want a professional hacker to do more than call vendors asking for passwords and back-door methods.

Many general IT vendors offer intrusion detection or an Internet exposure analysis. These third-party computer forensic examinations can yield beneficial information to solidify a security strategy. One of the benefits provided is when they attempt to exploit vulnerabilities (although they will not actually destroy data or compromise systems) and demonstrate how much damage they could do by how far they're able to get in. It's a wonderful feeling to present management with a report saying that this external group is impressed with the security of your Internet presence.

Appendix A

Frequently Asked Questions

WHAT IS COMPUTER FORENSICS?

Computer forensics is the collection, preservation, analysis, and court presentation of computer-related evidence.

WHY COMPUTER FORENSICS?

The vast majority of documents now exist in electronic form. No investigation involving the review of documents, either in a criminal or corporate setting, is complete without including properly handled computer evidence. Computer forensics ensures the preservation and authentication of computer data, which is fragile by its nature and can be easily altered, erased, or subject to claims of tampering without proper handling. Additionally, computer forensics greatly facilitates the recovery and analysis of deleted files and many other forms of compelling information normally invisible to the user.

WHAT IS DATA RECOVERY?

Data recovery is the process of retrieving deleted or inaccessible data from failed electronic storage media such as computer hard disk drives, removable media, optical devices, and tape cartridges. Your data can become inaccessible due to a software problem, computer virus, mechanical or electrical malfunction, or a deliberate human act. Regardless of the cause of your data loss, your experienced technicians should be able to successfully recover lost data 80 to 85% of the time.

How Long Does Data Recovery Take?

Standard Data Recovery

Most recoveries will be completed in 2–5 days.

Expedited Data Recovery

If you should need this service, you need a dedicated technician assigned to your drive within 4 hours of the time that you send in your hard disk. This process will normally cut your turnaround time in half.

Emergency Data Recovery

If your situation is critical, you will need to make arrangements for a technician to be available who will be assigned to work on your recovery until complete. The goal here is to return your data to you within three to five working days. However, because of the complexity of data recovery, there will be times when it will take longer.

ARE THERE INSTANCES WHERE DATA CANNOT BE RECOVERED?

Yes. There are instances where the damage to the hard drive is so severe that data recovery is not possible. This usually occurs when the read/write heads actually "crash" and gouge the magnetic storage media to the point where the data is destroyed.

However, in a number of cases, data recovery was possible at the time the damage first occurred, but the data became unrecoverable through the use of commercial-recovery software. This software is designed to recover data from working drives. If your drive has experienced a mechanical or electrical failure, the use of recovery software can cause permanent loss of your data.

What Can I Do to Protect My Data and Minimize My Chances of Losing Data?

The adage in the industry is not "if my drive fails," but, rather, "when my drive fails." Although your hard drive has many electronic components, it also has moving parts. Over time, these mechanical components can fail as the result of use.

Avoid Heat and Vibration

All drive components, both electronic and mechanical, are sensitive to heat and vibration. Keep your computer in a dry, controlled environment that is clean and dust-free. Set up your computer in an area with little traffic to ensure that it does not get bumped. Heat and/or vibration are two of the leading causes of hard drive failure. Also, beware of static.

Back-Up Your Data

The surest way to avoid data loss, even if your hard drive fails, is to back-up your data. If you don't have a tape back-up device or network drive at your fingertips, back-up your most important files to a floppy disk at least once a week.

To Avoid Premature Drive Failure, Run Scandisk

Scandisk examines your hard disk for logical inconsistencies and damaged surfaces. Run it every two or three weeks just to be safe. It is important to save any changes to a floppy until you are sure that the changes you are about to make will not adversely affect your hard drive.

Run Defrag Frequently

Files will most likely not be stored in adjacent clusters. Defrag rearranges the data on your hard disk so that each file is stored in a set of contiguous clusters. This is essential for data recovery because success is more likely when the damaged file's clusters are adjacent to each other.

Antivirus Software

Use antivirus software and update it at least four times a year. Also, use an uninterrupted power supply (UPS).

In the event of a surge of electricity, black out, brown out, or lightning strike, a UPS can protect your system from electrical damage. A UPS is also a back-up power source that keeps your computer running for a short period of time, giving you the opportunity to properly save your work and shut down, avoiding a potential data loss.

Be Cautious When Using Recovery Utilities

Use diagnostic and repair utilities with caution. Verify that your utility software is compatible with your operating software. Never use file-recovery software if you suspect an electrical or mechanical drive failure. Always make an undo disk when you allow a utility to make changes to your hard drive.

Floppy Disks

Never buy bargain-basement disks. Recommended are 3.5" pre-formatted high-density disks. Store your disks in a cool, dry, dust-free environment—not, for example, in a shirt-pocket, book bag, or briefcase, unless they are inside a diskette container of some kind.

Back-up your disks on a regular basis. This means copying files from one floppy disk to another—don't just rename a file on the same disk!

Save information as you type, say every 10 minutes. (If you are working on your own machine, set the "automatic save" feature of your word processor.) Do not type for 3 hours straight and expect to be able to save information to your disk. It is possible you have typed too much information for the floppy disk to store.

Diligent maintenance such as antivirus scanning, sensible back-up procedures, off-site storage of mission-critical data, together with knowledge of your limitations, should prevent you from becoming one of the many casualties of data loss. If you suffer a data loss, contact a data-recovery expert immediately. The most important thing is to not attempt any repairs yourself. Trust your data to Data Recovery Group engineers who have the experience, expertise, and tools to recover your data without damaging your system.

How Do I Ship My Hard Drive?

It is extremely important that your hard drive is packaged carefully—to avoid any additional damage during shipment. Only your drive is required for data recovery.

Packaging the Hard Drive

Wrap the hard drive in an antistatic material. If an antistatic bag is not available, a freezer bag will suffice. It is recommended that you ship the drive in its original manufacturer's packaging. If this is not possible, pack the hard drive in a sturdy corrugated cardboard box twice the size of the drive, with heavy foam padding, bubble wrap, or other antivibration materials. Do not use Styrofoam peanuts as they attract static electricity. Be sure the padding material is at least two inches thick around the drive.

Water-Damaged Hard Drives

If your drive has suffered water damage, please do not dry it. Enclose the drive along with a damp sponge in a sealed plastic bag to prevent it from drying out.

Controller Boards

When recovering from older models, you may need to send the controller along with the drive. Please remove the controller carefully, enclose in antistatic material, and ship it along with the drive.

Other

Please package all other types of media, following the guidelines in the preceding for a typical hard drive.

Locations

Ship the drive directly to the recovery facility nearest you: It is recommended that you ship via UPS or Federal Express domestically and DHL internationally, using next-day service. If you elect to use another carrier, it is suggested that you use an overnight service. Also, if you have any special shipping considerations, questions, or concerns, please contact your overnight carrier.

How Do I Get My Data Back?

If your drive is repairable, the repair will be completed and your data returned to you on your original drive. When your data is recovered and your drive is not re-pairable, there are many different ways to return your data, including a new drive, magnetic tapes, Zip cartridges, or CD-ROM.

Appendix
B
Computer Forensics Resources

Disclaimer!

This author and publisher do not endorse the contents of the links on this site. They are offered as resources that other systems security and forensics professionals have found helpful.

GENERAL FORENSICS RESOURCES

AccessData (http://www.accessdata.com/)

Known best for their *Password Recovery* Toolkit. AccessData's site offers information about this and other security-related tools and you will find several free tools here. Also, you will find several articles and links regarding cryptography and related subjects.

Digital Intelligence, Inc. (http://www.digitalintel.com/)

Digital Intelligence designs and builds computer forensic software and hardware. They also offer free forensic utility software for law enforcement.

Fred Cohen & Associates (ForensiX) [http://all.net/]

This site is full of network security and information warfare articles and white papers. Fred Cohen is one of the most recognized, respected, and requested names in information protection today. Mr. Cohen has created a comprehensive forensic examination tool called *ForensiX* for the Linux platform. Information about *ForensiX* is provided on this site.

Guidance Software (http://www.guidancesoftware.com/html/index.html)

The creators of the popular GUI-based forensic tool EnCase. Besides information regarding their EnCase forensic tool, there is a bulletin board with a number of forums relating to their products and computer forensics.

High-Tech Crime Investigation Association (http://htcia.org/)

Association that promotes the exchange of data and ideas about methods relating to investigations and security among its membership.

International Association of Computer Investigative Specialists (http://cops.org/)

IACIS is an international, volunteer nonprofit corporation composed of law enforcement professionals dedicated to education in the field of forensic computer science.

ILook's Home Page (http://www.spnc.demon.co.uk/ilook/ilook.htm)

ILook Image Investigator© is a forensic software tool. It is designed to allow an investigator to access the partition file system(s) on forensic images created by many of the best known forensic imaging systems.

Maresware–Danny Mares (http://www.dmares.com/)

Danny Mares has been authoring computer forensic tools for law enforcement for many years. This site provides access to all his tools as well as a number of articles and papers relating to computer forensics. Information regarding Danny Mares computer forensic training can also be found on this site.

NTI–Computer Evidence Leaders (http://www.forensics-intl.com/)

NTI has a comprehensive suite of computer forensic tools that have been used by law enforcement for many years. There are also many good articles concerning technical and legal issues surrounding computer forensics.

Porcupine.org (http://www.porcupine.org/wietse/)

Site provided by Wietse Zweitze Venema, which provides tools and white papers focused primarily on post-mortem analysis of computer break-ins.

Sydex WWW Home Page (http://www.sydex.com/)

Recently bought by NTI, Inc., this is the home of one of the most used Imaging tools, Safeback. Also tools for imaging and analyzing diskettes, TeleDisk, AnaDisk, and CopyQM can be found here.

The Cornoner's Toolkit (http://www.fish.com/tct/)

The Coroner's Toolkit (TCT) is a collection of tools that are either oriented toward gathering or analyzing forensic data on a Unix system.

TUCOFS (http://www.tucofs.com/tucofs.htm)

The TUCOFS Web site is a great resource of computer forensics resources and tools.

USSS&IACP Digital Evidence Best Practices. (http://www.infowar.com/law/00/e-evidence/e-evidence.shtml)

The on-line version of IACP & USSS's—*Best Practices for Seizing Electronic Evidence* booklet.

WetStone Technologies, Inc. (http://www.wetstonetech.com/)

WetStone Technologies is a developer of information security technologies. This site includes some excellent technical papers concerning advancing crime scene computer forensics, timelining computer evidence, using smart cards, and digital signatures to preserve electronic evidence among others.

COMPUTER CRIME

Terrorism Issues Page (http://www.cdt.org/policy/terrorism/)

The Center for Democracy and Technology works to promote democratic values and constitutional liberties in the digital age. With expertise in law, technology, and policy, CDT seeks practical solutions to enhance free expression and privacy in global communications technologies. CDT is dedicated to building consensus among all parties interested in the future of the Internet and other new communications media.

FILE FORMATS AND EXTENSIONS

File Extensions (http://filext.com/)

File extensions are often used to determine the program that created the file. Although there is no guarantee that users will not rename files and/or associate odd extensions with particular programs, this site lists some fairly standard associations.

What Is. . .Every File Format in the World (http://whatis.techtarget.com/Flat_Files/WhatIs_File_Format_A/0,281899,,00.html)

This is a list of file name extensions or suffixes that indicate the format or usage of a file and a brief description of that format.

Wotsit's Format (http://www.wotsit.org/)

This site contains file format information, including header/foot signatures, on hundreds of different file types and all sorts of other useful programming information: algorithms, source code, specifications, and so on.

CRYPTOGRAPHY AND STEGANOGRAPHY

Counterpane Labs (http://www.counterpane.com/labs.html)

An outstanding site about cryptography containing numerous technical papers about the subject. Free tools can also be found here. Counterpane Labs is the research arm of Counterpane Internet Security, Inc. Counterpane Internet Security, Inc. offers leading-edge expertise in the fields of 24x7 intrusion detection and prevention, preemptive threat discovery, forensic research, and organizational IT systems analysis.

Steganalysis—Attacks Against Steganography and Watermarking—Countermeasures (http://www.jjtc.com/Steganalysis/)

An excellent site about steganography and steganalysis. Includes white papers on steganalysis and countermeasures among other things.

CAUTION

Warning

URLs are subject to change without notice!

Appendix C

Links to Computer Forensics and Related Law Enforcement Web Pages

NOTE

Disclaimer!

This author and publisher do not endorse the contents of the links in this appendix. They are offered as resources that other systems security and forensics professionals have found helpful.

LAW ENFORCEMENT LINKS

Computer Crimes Criminal Justice Links

(http://www.co.pinellas.fl.us/bcc/juscoord/ecomputer.htm)

Computer and Internet Security Resources

(http://www.virtuallibrarian.com/legal/)

Criminal Justice Institute

(http://www.mitretek.org/business_areas/justice/cjiti/cjiti.html)

Criminal Justice Links

(http://www.fsu.edu/~crimdo/forensics.html)

Forensic Science & Law Enforcement Links

(http://www.ssc.msu.edu/~forensic/links.html)

The HIT Law Enforcement Connection

(http://members.aol.com/JetTroop/police.html)

Internet Resources on Technology Law

(http://www.bitlaw.com/)

Ira Wilsker's Law Enforcement Sites on the Web

(http://www.ih2000.net/ira/ira.htm)

Law Enforcment Guide to the World Wide Web

(http://www.leolinks.com/)

Legal and Court-Related Sites

(http://www.ih2000.net/ira/legal.htm)

Mega Links in Criminal Justice

(http://faculty.ncwc.edu/toconnor/)

The Police Officer's Internet Directory

(http://www.officer.com/)

Web of Justice Links

(http://www.co.pinellas.fl.us/bcc/juscoord/explore.htm)

What's on the Internet for Legal and Law Enforcement Personnel

(http://www.knock-knock.com/forensic.htm)

ORGANIZATIONS

High-Tech Crime Cops

(http://www.HighTechCrimeCops.org/)

High-Technology Crime Investigation Association

(http://htcia.org/)

International Association of Computer Investigative Specialists

> (http://www.cops.org/)

MAILING LISTS

High-Tech Crime Cops List

> (http://groups.yahoo.com/subscribe.cgi/htcc)

USDOJ GUIDELINES FOR SEARCHING & SEIZING COMPUTERS

Main Table of Contents

> (http://www.usdoj.gov/criminal/cybercrime/search_docs/toc.htm)

Update to USDOJ Guidelines

> (http://www.usdoj.gov/criminal/cybercrime/supplement/ssgsup.htm)

COMPUTER FORENSIC AND SECURITY SOFTWARE AVAILABLE FREE OF CHARGE TO LAW ENFORCEMENT AGENCIES

New Technologies, Inc.

> (http://www.forensics-intl.com/download.html)

MISCELLANEOUS

Berryhill Computer Forensics

> (http://www.computerforensics.com/index.htm)

Computer Expert and Computer Forensics Consultant_ Judd Robbins:

> (http://www.knock-knock.com/jr.htm)

Computer Forensics—NTI Training and Tools:

> (http://secure-data.com/intro.html)

Computer Forensics Expert Witness Network

(http://computerforensics.net/)

Computer Forensics FAQ

(http://www.surveil.com/frequent.htm)

Computer Forensics Ltd., UK

(http://www.computer-forensics.com/welcome.html)

Computer Forensics On-line

(http://www.shk-dplc.com/cfo/)

Florida Association of Computer Crime Investigators

(http://facci.org/)

Forensic Computing–Journal–Authoritative Comment

(http://www.forensic-computing.com/welcome.html)

The Risk Advisory Group Limited – Investigations

(http://www.riskadvisory.net/index.html)

CCIPS Searching and Seizing Computers

(http://www.usdoj.gov/criminal/cybercrime/searching.html)

FDIC: Law, Regulations, Regulated Acts–Miscellaneous Statutes and Regulations netForensics Home Page

(http://www.fdic.gov/regulations/laws/rules/8000-900.html)

INFOWAR, INFO-SEC PORTAL, INFORMATION WARFARE & SECURITY GLOBAL CLEARINGHOUSE,

Cyber crime Reporting

(http://www.infowar.com/)

FOCUS on Incident Handling: An Introduction to the Field Guide for Investigating Computer Crime

[http://www.securityfocus.com/focus/ih/articles/crimeguide1.html]

FOCUS on Incident Handling: Overview of a Methodology for the Application of Computer Forensics

[http://www.securityfocus.com/focus/ih/articles/crimeguide2.html]

FOCUS on Incident Handling: Digital Media Forensics

[http://www.securityfocus.com/focus/ih/articles/dforensics.html]

FOCUS on Intrusion Detection: Know Your Enemy: A Forensic Analysis

[http://www.securityfocus.com/focus/ih/articles/foranalysis.html]

SMO: Legal Reporter 06/00

[http://www.securitymanagement.com/library/000873.html]

Warning

URLs are subject to change without notice!

More Computer Forensics Cases

Claims of six-figure salaries earned without ever leaving the bedroom. A hearty supply of free computer hardware and a never-ending e-mail inbox full of victims. Credit-card accounts fished from fake porn sites, or clever e-mails promising "You've Got Pictures" that ask for AOL user names and passwords. What do computer criminals do all day? Work the system—and reap the rewards.

So, what's been the result? Fraud and credit-card theft have run rampant on the Internet, and in-house corporate thieves abound. The following are some additional computer forensics case studies for your reading enjoyment, shock value, and horror.

CASE STUDY 1: LOST FILES

A set of *Word*, *Excel*, and *Project* files that was created over 18 months relating to a project currently under construction has been maliciously deleted by a departing employee. The PC was not backed up. The action was discovered 3 days later and the IT group endeavored to locate and restore the files. They were unsuccessful. Management is assessing the options available. They are time consuming and expensive. Some data cannot be rekeyed in because the source data is missing. The IT manager contacts a computer forensics firm. The firm finally restores the entire project directory within 4 days from first contact.

CASE STUDY 2: CORRUPTED FILES

Files relating to a multimillion tender on a sales/marketing PC have been found to be corrupted. The PC was not on the network and not backed up. The IT group advises that the data is gone forever. The tender closes at the end of the month, which is only 12 days away. Management is assessing the options available. The only option appears to be to withdraw from the tender process. Their hardware supplier recommends an inquiry to a computer forensics data-recovery firm. The firm received the hard disk at 4:00 P.M. on Friday and had a CD-ROM containing the draft tender response, worksheets, subcontractor quotations, graphics files, and peripheral material on the client's premises by 11:00 A.M. on the following Monday.

CASE STUDY 3: DISAPPEARING FILES

The debtors module of an accounting package has somehow disappeared from the accounting PC. The software-support company is unable to locate the files and the back-up tapes do not restore correctly. The software-support company suggests that the data be rekeyed in—a massive task. Management is assessing the options available. They are time consuming and expensive. The distributor of the software recommends contact be made with a computer forensics firm. The firm finally restored the faulty data in time for the complete end-of-month statement run.

CASE STUDY 4: COMPUTER FORENSICS

The founder and majority shareholder of a consultancy business sold his interest to a multinational communications corporation. The contract of sale contained restraint clauses, prohibitions on the removal of confidential information, and nonsolicitation of staff and client clauses. After about a year, the client—the multinational—became suspicious that he was acting in breach of contract. A computer forensics firm was asked to investigate. At the outset, the firm suggested that the individual's desktop and laptop computer be recovered to copy the hard disks and analyze their content. Within an encrypted file on his desktop, the firm found a draft business plan for a new enterprise that would compete with his former business. On his laptop, in a deleted file that was restored, the firm recovered details of key clients and revenue streams. It was possible to demonstrate that information had been updated within these files after he had left the company, but before he had returned the computer. Taken together, the evidence was sufficient to initiate criminal proceedings.

CASE STUDY 5: FORENSIC ACCOUNTING

A multinational manufacturer reported significant losses in the company's distribution division. It was not clear whether this was simply a result of an inequitable transfer pricing policy within the group or whether the company had been defrauded. Accountants from a computer forensics firm set out to investigate how the losses had been incurred, reconstructing incomplete records and unraveling a confusing series of transactions. They discovered that other companies within the group had transferred products to the division at over market value to maintain their own profitability. More disturbingly, the division had sold on much of its product at inexplicably low prices to a number of key customers. The business manager was dismissed after the computer forensics firm discovered that he had concealed ownership interests in some of these customers and evidence came to light indicating that he had accepted kickback payments. Poor and missing records prevented legal action from being commenced. In the following period, the division is now on track to report profits following tighter controls over transfer pricing and sales invoicing.

CASE STUDY 6: CORPORATE INVESTIGATION INTO PC PORNOGRAPHY

A computer forensics team was contracted to assist in an investigation for an organization that suspected an employee of downloading and storing inappropriate material on a company PC. A computer forensics team visited the site and, using correct forensic procedures, created an image of the hard drive of the suspect PC. The team was then able to recover a large amount of inappropriate material from the PC in a forensically sound manner, including files that had been deleted, renamed, and hidden in an attempt to disguise their true nature. Using this evidence and the report the team produced, the client was able to take the appropriate action against the employee.

CASE STUDY 7: DATA RECOVERY

A computer forensics team was asked to assist an organization that had lost data as a result of a computer virus. The affected laptops were with field personnel and away from the central office when the virus was introduced. Consequently, the data collected over this period had not been backed up. The affected machines were brought to the team's secure laboratory, and, using forensic recovery techniques, they were able to image data from the affected machines, recover all of the data that had been stored since the machines had last been backed up, and eliminate the virus.

CASE STUDY 8: INDUSTRIAL ESPIONAGE

A computer forensics team was asked to assist in a case where it was suspected that industrial espionage had taken place through the computer system. It was suspected that a number of techniques had been used to plant spyware (remote control and covert information-gathering programs) on a network. After carrying out a preliminary on-site analysis, the team removed a number of suspect machines to their secure laboratory for further analysis. A number of machines had been compromised after employees had opened e-mail attachments that contained Trojan Horse programs (programs that are disguised as common files but actually contain malicious code). Unfortunately, these had been missed by the organization's antivirus measures. As an added service, the team's security engineers were able to offer advice and assistance in reconfiguring antivirus and firewall products to minimize the chance of a repeat occurrence.

CASE STUDY 9: FAMILY MEMBERS BOLT

Family members bolt, take the IT department, the product design; sabotage the originals, and go into competition. A family-owned product manufacturer and designer on the verge of being bought for many millions of dollars found most of its designs missing after the departure of key managers and designers. A program used for deep file destruction had been implemented to destroy both product designs and evidence of the procedure itself. An outside computer forensics consultant is brought in to recover designs and overwrites evidence instead. A computer forensics team is then brought in and discovers remnants of file destruction utility, and data patterns consistent with sabotage by the same utility. The suspects finally admitted to the use of the utility.

CASE STUDY 10: FORMER EMPLOYER

A former employer claims a competitor's new hire has stolen designs for manufacture. An individual working for a biomaterials firm gained employment with a competing firm. The individual had used several dozen diskettes for storage at the old firm, and then used the same diskettes for new storage at the new firm. The previous employer claimed that the individual took designs to the new employer on diskettes. A computer forensics team was engaged to demonstrate employee's innocence. The original firm finally settled out of court.

CASE STUDY 11: GOODS LEFT TO ROT

Goods were left to rot while documents were allegedly backdated. A computer forensics team was hired to check the results of a police report that suggested the client's guilt. The client's attorney was advised as to the potential veracity of the claim. Inconsistencies in the police report were discovered, and the sentence was mitigated.

CASE STUDY 12: MANAGERS START NEW COMPANY

Managers start a new company in the very offices of their employers; computers and back-ups disappear. A foreign branch of the entertainment arm of a multinational conglomerate suspect that key managers had been attempting to incorporate company intellectual assets into a competing product line. Once the suspects believed they were under suspicion, the relevant office computers were reported as stolen. Data back-ups were reported as missing. Under pressure, the original computers were found and produced by a computer expert among the suspect group, but with large amounts of data missing. A computer forensics team was hired to investigate. Unequivocal evidence of illegal activities was produced from the remains of files on the computers in question.

CASE STUDY 13: FAMILY MEMBER STEALS CLIENTS

A member of a family-run communications business left the company. While denying it, the individual started a business in direct competition with the family business. The individual's computer was identified as an asset of the original company. The individual claimed that no company information was on the computer. A computer forensics team was hired to test the claim. Although the computer had been completely deleted, reformatted, and had entirely new operating systems and applications installed on it, the original database entries were, nonetheless, uncovered. The individual also claimed innocence up until the moment that the team experts were seen awaiting a call into the courtroom. The individual then admitted the wrongdoing and settled.

CASE STUDY 14: ERASED E-MAIL

A private investigation firm was purchased, with a covenant by the previous owners not to compete. Within weeks, suspicion arose that the covenant was not being respected, and that files and media that had been turned over had data removed. A computer forensics team was hired to look into the matter. Thousands of files were turned up by the investigation, showing a violation of the covenant.

CASE STUDY 23: FORMER EMPLOYEE CLAIMS

A former employee claims he never took any information with him when he left. The firm suspected the former employee of absconding with proprietary information. Under court order, the individual turned over a laptop computer, with no obvious data related to the case. A forensic inspection by a computer forensics team revealed enough relevant data to print two entire reams of documents. The suspect finally settled.

CASE STUDY 24: EX-PARTNER CLAIMS

A partner in an information technology firm left and went into his own business. The individual was accused of taking proprietary documents on his laptop. The individual also produced the laptop, along with the claim that, although there were missing documents, none were relevant to the claims. Additionally, the individual claimed that a prolific virus had destroyed the documents. A computer forensics team was hired and was able to show fabrication of evidence, upon which the individual then admitted wrongdoing in a deposition. The individual was then sanctioned.

CASE STUDY 25: FORMER MANAGER

A manager of a Big 10 consulting firm went to work for a competitor. Under court order, the competitor provided a diskette that had gone with the individual to the new firm. Finally, a computer forensics team was hired to inspect said diskette. Although it was damaged, deleted and overwritten, evidence of illegal customer lists and the lists themselves were discovered on the diskette.

On the CD-ROM

The following forensic tools, demos, and presentations are included on the accompanying CD-ROM.

Please visit the Web sites for exact system requirements, FAQs, updates, ordering information, licenses and links to other tools and sources. The information contained on the CD-ROM is the property of the respective developers. It may not be distributed without their permission. Inquiries regarding the software contained on the CD-ROM should be directed to the developers of the products. In addition, please review the publisher's disclaimer at the beginning of the book.

The Forensics Challenge Partition Images (also see case study in text)
http://project.honeynet.org/challenge/
Sponsored by the HoneyNet Project
http://project.honeynet.org/

Partition Images from The Forensics Challenge, real images of hacked computers and complete forensics analysis. The Forensic Challenge is an effort to allow incident handlers around the world to all look at the same data—an image reproduction of the same compromised system—and to see who can dig the most out of that system and communicate what they've found in a concise manner. This is a nonscientific study of tools, techniques, and procedures applied to postcompromise incident handling.

FW-1 Specific Network Intrusion Detector
Lance Spitzner
http://www.enteract.com/~lspitz/intrusion.html

This paper discusses how you can detect scans, probes, and unauthorized activity using your FW-1 firewall and a simple script, which I call *alert.sh*. This tool is written specifically for UNIX systems and has been tested with Linux, Solaris, and Nokia platforms and FW-1. There are two different version of this script you can download. If you are running FW-1 version 4.1 or below, you want to download and use alert.sh ver 1.4.5. If you are running FW-1 NG (Next Generation), you want to download and use alert.sh ver 2.1.1

RecoverNT v3.5
Recover98 v3.5
FILERECOVERYfor Windows v2.1
PHOTORECOVERY for Digital Media 1.5
LC Technology International, Inc.
28100 US Hwy 19 North, Suite 203
Clearwater, FL 3371
727-449-0891
http://www.lc-tech.com
info@lc-tech.com

Over 75 percent of data loss is accidental or caused by user error, and now more than ever, businesses today rely on their data for day-to-day operations. FILERECOVERY gives you support for all current Microsoft operating systems. RecoverNT and Recover98 both support all current Microsoft operating systems. PhotoRecovery recovers deleted images from digital media and supports all current Microsoft operating systems.

Free Hex Editor v1.1
Raihan Kibria
http://www.kibria.de/frhed.html

Frhed (free hex editor) is a free binary file editor for all 32-bit Windows releases, like 95/98/Me/NT/2000/XP (it also runs under Win 3.11 with Win32s). It is open-sourced and comes with C++ source code. Features include search & replace for any combination of binary and text data, file comparison, bit manipulation, customizable display colors and font size, ANSI or OEM character set, cut & paste, bookmarking and more.

The Coroner's Toolkit (TCT)
Dan Farmer and Wietse Venema
http://www.fish.com/tct/
http://www.porcupine.org/forensics/

TCT is a collection of programs by for a post-mortem analysis of a UNIX system after break-in. Notable TCT components are the grave-robber tool that captures information, the ils and mactime tools that display access patterns of files dead or alive, the unrm and lazarus tools that recover deleted files, and the findkey tool that recovers cryptographic keys from a running process or from files. The Coroner's Toolkit is a collection of tools designed to assist in a forensic examination of a computer. It is primarily designed for Unix systems, but it can some small amount of data collection & analysis from non-Unix disks/media.

WinHex 10.45
X-Ways Software Technology AG
Carl-Diem-Str. 32
32257 Bünde
Germany
http://www.x-ways.com

An advanced tool for everyday and emergency use: Inspect or repair all kinds of files, recover deleted files or lost data from corrupt hard drives or digital camera cards. This hex editor grants access to data other programs hide from you.

Protect2000 Security Suite (Product Presentation)
Computer Security Products Inc.
5770 Hurontario Street, Suite 700
Mississauga, Ontario L5R 3G5
905-568-8900
http://. www.TandemSecurity.com

Uses sophisticated modeling techniques to define and manage network wide security policy on Compaq NonStop Himalaya Servers. Protect2000 includes *Auditview* for Windows(Safeguard audit reporting tool), *Alert-plus*, and *Tandem Security Analyzer* (TSA-security review and recommendations) that are all bundled into the Protect2000 interface which itself handles user, policy and object management.

TCPurify 0.9.6
Ethan Blanton
http://irg.cs.ohiou.edu/~eblanton/index.html

TCPurify is a packet sniffer/capture program similar to tcpdump, but with much reduced functionality. What sets TCPurify apart from other, similar programs is its focus on privacy. TCPurify is designed from the ground up to protect the privacy of users on the sniffed network as much as possible.

Mazu Enforcer (Product Presentation)
Mazu Networks
125 CambridgePark Drive
Sixth Floor
Cambridge, MA 02140
Ph: 617.354.9292
Fax: 617.354.9272
http://www.mazunetworks.com

This dynamic video demonstration shows the Mazu *Enforcer* in action, from a user's perspective, as it is used for DDoS Attack detection, mitigation and detailed traffic analysis. The screens show the *Enforcer's* own Graphical User Interface used for management, administration, and configuration of the Mazu Enforcer.

Glossary of Terms and Acronyms

2600 A "hacker" organization whose main product is 2600 magazine. This publication has (at times) been considered the premier hacker print product.

8lgm Eight (8) Little Green Men "hacker" group that compiles and distributes security tips.

Abuse of privilege Formal nomenclature for user action(s) not in accordance with organizational policy or law. Actions falling outside, or explicitly proscribed by, acceptable use policy.

Acceptable level of risk A judicious and carefully considered assessment by the appropriate authority that a computing activity or network meets the minimum requirements of applicable security directives. The assessment should take into account the value of assets; threats and vulnerabilities; countermeasures; and operational requirements.

Acceptable use policy (AUP) DoD nomenclature for documented standards and/or guidance on usage of information systems and networked assets.

Accountability The principle that individuals using a facility or a computer system must be identifiable. With accountability, violations or attempted violations of system security can be traced to individuals who can then be held responsible.

Accuracy DoD parlance for the notion that information has been maintained and transferred in such a way as to be inviolate (the information has been protected from being modified or otherwise corrupted either maliciously or accidentally). Accuracy protects against forgery or tampering. Typically invoked as a synonym for integrity.

Acme of skill To subdue an adversary without killing him.

Active attack A form of attack in which data is actually modified, corrupted, or destroyed.

Adapter A device that serves as an interface between the system unit and a device attached to it, such as a SCSI Adapter. Often synonymous with expansion card or board. Can also refer to a special type of connector.

Advanced WWWCount Counter Full-featured advanced counter that is highly customizable allowing you to change digit formats, colors, time, and adjustable data counts.

Ambient data This is a forensic term that describes, in general terms, data stored in nontraditional computer storage areas and formats. The term was coined in 1996 to help students understand computer-evidence-processing techniques that deal with evidence not stored in standard computer files, formats, and storage areas. The term is now widely used in the computer forensics community and it generally describes data stored in the Windows swap file, unallocated space, and file slack.

Anomaly detection A label for the class of intrusion-detection tactics that seek to identify potential intrusion attempts by virtue of their being (presumably) sufficiently deviant (anomalous) in comparison with expected or authorized activities. Phrased another way, anomaly detection begins with a positive model of expected system operations and flags potential intrusions on the basis of their deviation (as particular events or actions) from this presumed norm.

Anonymous FTP Allows visitors to upload and/or download predetermined files from designated directories without usernames or passwords. For example, distribute your latest software package by allowing visitors to download it through anonymous FTP. This is different than a regular FTP account

Antivirus Software that detects, repairs, cleans, or removes virus-infected files from a computer.

Application A more technical term for program.

Application gateway One form of a firewall in which valid application-level data must be checked or confirmed before allowing a connection. In the case of an ftp connection, the application gateway appears as a ftp server to the client and a ftp client to the server.

ASIM (Automated Security Incident Measurement) Current DoD automated security tool that monitors network traffic, collects information on targeted unit networks, and detects unauthorized network activity.

Assurance A measure of confidence that the security features and architecture of an information system or network accurately reflect and enforce the given security policy.

Asynchronous attacks Attacks that take advantage of dynamic system actions—especially by exploiting an ability to manipulate the timing of those actions.

Attack   With specific regard to IW—a specific formulation or execution of a plan to carry out a threat. An attempt to bypass security controls on a computer. An active attack alters data. A passive attack releases data. Whether an attack will succeed depends on the vulnerability of the computer system and the effectiveness of existing countermeasures.

Attitudes   Positively or negatively learned orientations toward something or someone that have a tendency to motivate an individual or group toward some behavior. Experienced soldiers, for example, have negative attitudes toward slovenliness.

Audit trail   In computer security systems, a chronological record of when users log-in, how long they are engaged in various activities, what they were doing, and whether any actual or attempted security violations occurred. An automated or manual set of chronological records of system activities that may enable the reconstruction and examination of a sequence of events and/or changes in an event.

AUP   Acronym for acceptable use policy.

Autoresponders   Sends an automated e-mail response to incoming mail sent to a specific address. For instance, you can have your visitors send an e-mail to 'info@yourdomain.com' to get an e-mail explaining your latest product, or automatically reply to orders with a prewritten 'thank you' e-mail message.

Back door   A hole in the security of a computer system deliberately left in place by designers or maintainers. Synonymous with trap door. A hidden software or hardware mechanism used to circumvent security controls. A breach created intentionally for the purpose of collecting, altering, or destroying data.

Bandwidth   Bandwidth is the sum of all the data transferred from and to your Web site, including e-mail, Web pages, and images. See "Monthly Traffic."

Bank   The collection of memory chips or modules that make up a block of memory. This can be 1, 2 or 4 chips. Memory in a PC must always be added or removed in full-bank increments.

Basic PSYOP Study (BPS)   A detailed background document that describes the PSYOP-relevant vulnerabilities, characteristics, insights, and opportunities that are known about a specific country susceptible to exploitation.

Battlefield visualization   The process whereby the commander develops a clear understanding of the current state with relation to the enemy and environment, envisions a desired end-state that represents mission accomplishment, and then subsequently visualizes the sequence of activity that moves the commander's force from its current state to the end-state.

Battlespace   The field of military operations circumscribed by the aggregate of all spatial (geographic range, altitude) and virtual (communicational connectivity) dimensions in which those operations are realized. This is a generic term connoting no limitation to the geographical constraints suggested by the term "battlefield." Components are determined by the maximum capabilities of friendly and enemy forces to acquire and dominate each other by fires and maneuver and in the electromagnetic spectrum.

Between-the-lines-entry   Access that an unauthorized user gets, typically by tapping the terminal of a legitimate user that is inactive at the time.

BIOS   The part of the operating system that provides the lowest level interface to peripheral devices. The BIOS is stored in the ROM on the computer's motherboard.

BLOB   Binary Large Object, used to describe any random large block of bits, usually a picture or sound file; can be stored in a database but normally not interpretable by a database program. Can be used as a mild hacker threat (mailbomb) when mailed. Can also be used to hide malicious logic code.

Blue box devices   Gadgets created by crackers and phone hackers ("phreakers") to break into the telephone system and make calls bypassing normal controls and/or billing procedures.

BMC4I   Battle(-space) Management Command, Control, Communications, and Intelligence. Briefly stated, the overall label for those components and processes comprising the "nervous system" of a modern military force in a theater of operations. The planning, tasking, and control of the execution of missions through an architecture of sensors, communications, automation, and intelligence support.

Boot   To start up your computer. Because the computer gets itself up and going from an inert state, it could be said to lift itself up "by its own bootstraps"—this is where the term 'boot' originates.

Boot disk   The magnetic disk (usually a hard disk) from which an operating system kernel is loaded (or "bootstrapped"). MS-DOS and Microsoft ® Windows® can be configured (in the BIOS) to try to boot off either floppy disk or hard disk, in either order (and on some modern systems even from CD or other removable media). A special floppy boot disk (often called a "System Rescue Disk") can be created, which will allow your computer to boot even if it cannot boot from the hard disk.

Boot Record   Once the BIOS determines which disk to boot from, it loads the first sector of that disk into memory and executes it. Besides this loader program, the Boot Record contains the partition table for that disk. If the Boot Record is damaged, it can be a very serious situation!

Bootstrap   To load and initialize the operating system on a computer. Often abbreviated to boot.

Bulletin Board   Web-based message forum where visitors can read, post, and reply to messages or questions left by other visitors.

Bus   A set of conductors (wires or connectors in an integrated circuit) connecting the various functional units in a computer. There are busses both within the CPU and connecting it to external memory and peripheral devices. The bus width (i.e., the number of parallel connectors) is one factor limiting a computer's performance.

C2   Acronym for command and control.

C2 attack   Sometimes written "C2-attack." Abbreviation for command-and-control attack. Any action against any element of the enemy's command and control system.

C2 protect   Abbreviation for command-and-control protect.

C2 Counterwar   Presumed synonym for command-and-control counterwar.

C2W   Acronym for command-and-control warfare.

C3   Acronym for command, control, and communications.

C3I   Acronym for command, control, communications, and intelligence.

C4I   Acronym for command, control, communications, computers, and intelligence.

C4ISR   Acronym for command, control, communications, computer intelligence, surveillance, and reconnaissance.

Card   A circuit board that is usually designed to plug into a connector or slot. See also adapter.

Cache   (Internet Browser)—The files and graphics saved locally from Web sites you have previously visited.

Center of gravity   A term commonly encountered that connotes a component or feature of a given system (an adversary's deployed instrumentality) that is critical to either (a) the viability of that given system and/or (b) the viability of the supersystem within which that given system is a participating component.

CERT   Acronym for computer emergency response team. Supports others in enhancing the security of their computing systems; develops standardized set of responses to security problems; provides a central point of contact for information about security incidents; and assists in collecting and disseminating information on issues related to computer security, including information on configuration, management, and bug fixes for systems.

CGI-BIN CGI stands for "common gateway interface." It's simply a way for your visitor's computer to communicate with programs, such as shopping-cart scripts, on your server. The CGI-BIN is a special directory where you store executable programs, such as shopping-cart scripts and counters, on the server. If you don't have access to a CGI-bin directory, you can't run programs (scripts) on your Web site.

Cgie-mail Allows you to custom-build e-mail results from a Web page form, much like a mail merge letter.

CIP Acronym for critical infrastructure protection.

Click To click an item means to point to it with the screen pointer, and then press quickly and release the left mouse button at once.

Cluster Windows allocates space to files in units called "clusters." Each cluster contains from 1 to 64 sectors, depending on the type and size of the disk. A cluster is the smallest unit of disk space that can be allocated for use by files.

CMOS A part of the motherboard that maintains system variables in static RAM. It also supplies a real-time clock that keeps track of the date, day and time. CMOS Setup is typically accessible by entering a specific sequence of keystrokes during the POST at system start-up.

Cold boot Starting or restarting a computer by turning on the power supply. See also warm boot.

Computer evidence Computer evidence is quite unique when compared to other forms of "documentary evidence." Unlike paper documentation, computer evidence is fragile and a copy of a document stored in a computer file is identical to the original. The legal 'best evidence' rules change when it comes to the processing of computer evidence. Another unique aspect of computer evidence is the potential for unauthorized copies to be made of important computer files without leaving behind a trace that the copy was made. This situation creates problems concerning the investigation of the theft of trade secrets (client lists, research materials, computer-aided design files, formulas, and proprietary software).

Computer Forensics Computer Forensics deals with the preservation, identification, extraction, and documentation of computer evidence. The field is relatively new to the private sector but it has been the mainstay of technology-related investigations and intelligence gathering in law enforcement and military agencies since the mid-1980s. Like any other forensic science, computer forensics involves the use of sophisticated technology tools and procedures, which must be followed to guarantee the accuracy of the preservation of evidence and the accuracy of results concerning computer-evidence processing. Typically, computer forensic tools exist in the form of computer software.

Computer forensic specialists guarantee accuracy of evidence-processing results through the use of time-tested evidence-processing procedures and through the use of multiple software tools, developed by separate and independent developers. The use of different tools that have been developed independently to validate results is important to avoid inaccuracies introduced by potential software design flaws and software bugs. It is a serious mistake for a computer forensics specialist to put "all of their eggs in one basket" by using just one tool to preserve, identify, extract, and validate the computer evidence. Cross-validation through the use of multiple tools and techniques is standard in all forensic sciences. When this procedure is not used, it creates advantages for defense lawyers who may challenge the accuracy of the software tool used and thus the integrity of the results. Validation through the user of multiple software tools, computer specialists, and procedures eliminates the potential for errors and the destruction of evidence.

Computer investigations Computer investigations rely on evidence stored as data and the timeline of dates and times that files were created, modified, and/or last accessed by the computer user. Timelines of activity can be especially helpful when multiple computers and individuals are involved in the commission of a crime. The computer forensics investigator should always consider timelines of computer usage in all computer-related investigations. The same is true in computer security reviews concerning potential access to sensitive and/or trade secret information stored in the form of computer files.

Context menu Also called a "context-sensitive menu," or a "shortcut menu," a context menu includes the commands that are commonly associated with an object on the screen. To activate an itme's context menu, point to it with the screen pointer, then press and release the right mouse button once.

Cookies (Internet Browser)—Holds information on the times and dates you have visited Web sites. Other information can also be saved to your hard disk in these text files, including information about on-line purchases, validation information about you for members-only Web sites, and more.

CPU Stands for central processing unit, a programmable logic device that performs all the instruction, logic, and mathematical processing in a computer.

Crash A sudden, usually drastic failure. Can be said of the operating system or a particular program when there is a software failure. Also, a disk drive can crash because of hardware failure.

Cross-linked files Two files that both refer to the same data.

Customizable missing docs page By placing a file in your main directory called missing.html, you will be able to provide a customized page to any browser that requests a file that does not exist on your server. You can use it to steer visitors to your front page, so you don't lose them if they click on a bad link somewhere.

CyberCash©   Used for secure processing of credit-card transactions. It actually takes the payment information and sends it via the banking gateways to obtain real-time approvals for credit cards and checks.

Data   Representation of facts, concepts, or instructions in a formalized manner suitable for communication, interpretation, or processing by humans or by automatic means. Any representations such as characters or analog quantities to which meaning is or might be assigned. A representation of facts, concepts, or instructions suitable for communication, interpretation, or processing by humans or computers.

Data-driven attack   A form of attack that is encoded in innocuous seeming data that is executed by a users or other software to implement an attack. In the case of firewalls, a data-driven attack is a concern because it may get through the firewall in data form and launch an attack against a system behind the firewall.

Datum   Any numerical or geometrical quantity or set of such quantities which may serve as reference or base for other quantities. Where the concept is geometric, the plural form is "datums" in contrast to the normal plural "data."

DBA   Acronym for dominant battlespace awareness.

DBK   Acronym for dominant battlespace knowledge.

Deception   Those measures designed to mislead the enemy by manipulation, distortion, or falsification of evidence to induce him or her to react in a manner prejudicial to his or her interests.

Decision   In an estimate of the situation, a clear and concise statement of the line of action intended to be followed by the commander as the one most favorable to the successful accomplishment of the mission.

Defense information infrastructure (DII)   A label for the composite information assets of DoD (the American defense establishment).

Defensive counterinformation   Actions protecting the military information functions from the adversary.

Defragment   As modern file systems are used and files are deleted and created, the total free space becomes split into smaller noncontiguous blocks. Eventually new files being created, and old files being extended, cannot be stored each in a single contiguous block but become scattered across the file system. This degrades performance as multiple seek operations are required to access a single fragmented file. Defragmenting consolidates each existing file and the free space into a contiguous group of sectors. Access speed will be improved due to reduced seeking. A nearly full disk system will fragment more quickly. A disk should be defragmented before fragmenting reaches 10%.

Degradation of service   Any reduction (with respect to norms or expectations) in service processes' reaction or response time, quantitative throughput, or quality parameters. This term is often used to denote the general set of service(s) impairment(s) that at the extreme (total degradation to a "zero state" with respect to the given parameters) constitutes an absolute denial of service. Note that (owing to operational constraints such as "time before timing out" settings) a disruptive tactic capable of only degrading service(s) may result in a complete denial of said service(s) from the perspective of the end user(s).

Denial of service   Action(s) that prevent any part of an AIS from functioning in accordance with its intended purpose. Denial of service attacks may include denying services or processes limited to one host machine. However, the term is most often invoked to connote action against a single host (or set of hosts), which results in the target's inability to perform service(s) for other users— particularly over a network. One may consider denial of service to be the extreme case of degradation of service in which one or more normal functional parameters (response, throughput) get "zeroed out," at least as far as the end user is concerned. It is important to note that "denial" is delineated with respect to whether the normal end user(s) can exploit the system or network as expected. Seen in this light, "denial" (like "degradation") is descriptive of a functional outcome, and is not, therefore, definitive with respect to cause(s) (tactics effecting said result). Forms of attack not geared to "denial" per se may lead to "denial" as a corollary effect (when a system administrator's actions in response to an intrusion attempt lead to a service outage). As such, "denial of service" is not a good criterion for categorizing attack tactics.

Denial time   The average length of time that an affected asset is denied to the organization. The temporal extent of operational malaise induced by a denial of service attack.

DII   Acronym for defense information infrastructure.

Direct information warfare   Changing the adversary's information without involving the intervening perceptive and analytical functions.

Directed-energy protective measures   That division of directed-energy warfare involving actions taken to protect friendly equipment, facilities, and personnel to ensure friendly effective uses of the electromagnetic spectrum that are threatened by hostile directed-energy weapons and devices.

Directory   This is an index into the files on your disk. It acts as a hierarchy, and you will see the directory represented in Windows looking like manila folders.

Disk space Disk space is the amount of storage space you're allocated to use on the server, also server space and Web space. The more disk space you have, the bigger your Web site can be. It's used to store everything related to your Web site such as your regular html files, images, multimedia files, anonymous ftp files, POP mail messages, CGI scripts, and any other files that make up your Web site.

DMA Stands for direct access memory. DMA is a fast way of transferring data within a computer. Most devices require a dedicated DMA channel (so the number of DMA channels that are available may limit the number of peripherals that can be installed).

Domain name registration A domain name is a textual address that is a unique identifier for your Web site that corresponds to your site's numerical Internet Protocol (IP) address, and is usually related to your business, such as www.acmecatapults.com.

DRAM Dynamic random access memory (see also SDRAM). A type of memory used in a PC for the main memory (such as your "32 Mbytes of RAM"). "Dynamic" refers to the memory's memory of storage—basically storing the charge on a capacitor. Specialized types of DRAM (such as EDO memory) have been developed to work with today's faster processors.

Driver A program designed to interface a particular piece of hardware to an operating system or other software.

DOS Disk operating system. Usually used as an abbreviation for MS-DOS, a microcomputer operating system developed by Microsoft.

Economic info-warfare/economic information warfare The application of IW tactics to leverage one's interests in the economic realm. A subclassification of IW.

Economic warfare Aggressive use of economic means to achieve national objectives.

EIDE Stands for enhanced integrated drive electronics. A specific type of attachment interface specification that allows for high-performance, large-capacity drives. See also IDE.

Electromagnetic intrusion The intentional insertion of electromagnetic energy into transmission paths in any manner, with the objective of deceiving operators or causing confusion.

Electronic warfare Any military action involving the use of electromagnetic and directed energy to control the electromagnetic spectrum or attack the enemy. Also called EW.

Electronics intelligence (ELINT) Technical and geolocation intelligence derived from foreign noncommunications, electromagnetic radiations emanating from sources other than nuclear detonations or radioactive sources.

Electronics security The protection resulting from all measures designed to deny unauthorized persons information of value that might be derived from their interception and study of noncommunications electromagnetic radiations (radar). This term is also (more loosely) used to connote the topical area or task specialization focusing on achieving this type of protection.

Electro-optical intelligence (ELECTRO-OPTINT) Intelligence other than signals intelligence derived from the optical monitoring of the electromagnetic spectrum from ultraviolet (0.01 micrometers) through far infrared (1,000 micrometers).

ELINT Acronym for electronics intelligence.

E-mail accounts (POP3) These are your e-mail boxes on a server that can be accessed directly to retrieve your mail using such programs as Outlook Express and Netscape Mail. Each POP3 has its own password to ensure privacy, so each of your employees could have their own e-mail address.

E-mail aliases Your main POP account for your domain allows the system to capture any name that may be sent to your domain name. This means as long as the @yourdomain.com is proper, any name in front of it will be delivered to your main POP account. Each alias can be forwarded or redirected to any other address of your choice.

E-mail forwarding Any e-mail address at your domain may be configured to forward to any other real internet e-mail address. For example, sales@yourname.com can forward to you@aol.com if you like.

E-mail mini mailing lists Use it to send your customers news and updates about your product or services without e-mailing each one separately. Visitors can add themselves to your list or take themselves off automatically. You send one e-mail and it goes to every e-mail address on the list. The system is capable of multiple lists, each of which can handle up to 1,000 e-mail addresses and outgoing messages up to 75K each.

Entrapment The deliberate planting of apparent flaws in a system for the purpose of detecting attempted penetrations.

essential elements of friendly information Key questions likely to be asked by adversary officials and intelligence systems about specific friendly intentions, capabilities, and activities, so they can obtain answers critical to their operational effectiveness.

Executable A binary file containing a program in machine language that is ready to be executed (run). MS-DOS and Windows machines use the filename extension ".exe" for these files.

Extract To extract is to return a compressed file to its original state. Typically, to view the contents of a compressed file, you must extract it first.

Expansion card   An integrated circuit card that plugs into an expansion slot on a motherboard to provide access to additional peripherals or features not built into the motherboard. See also adapter.

FDISK   The disk-partitioning program used in DOS and several other operating systems to create the master boot record and allocate partitions for the operating system's use.

File   A collection of data grouped into one unit on a disk.

File allocation table   (FAT or FAT32) DOS uses the FAT to manage the disk data area. The FAT tells DOS which portions of the disk belong to each file. The FAT links together all of the clusters belonging to each file, no matter where they are on disk. The FAT is a critical file: You should be sure to back it up regularly. FAT32 is a newer type of FAT, which was designed to handle large hard disks. The older FAT (FAT16) can only support partitions up to two gigabytes in size. FAT32 can handle partitions that are thousands of gigabytes.

File slack   File slack potentially contains randomly selected bytes of data from computer memory. This happens because DOS/Windows normally writes in 512 byte blocks called "sectors." Clusters are made up of blocks of sectors. If there is not enough data in the file to fill the last sector in a file, DOS/Windows makes up the difference by padding the remaining space with data from the memory buffers of the operating system. This randomly selected data from memory is called "RAM Slack" because it comes from the memory of the computer. RAM Slack can contain any information that may have been created, viewed, modified, downloaded, or copied during work sessions that have occurred since the computer was last booted. Thus, if the computer has not been shut down for several days, the data stored in file slack can come from work sessions that occurred in the past.

File system   A system for organizing directories and files, generally in terms of how it is implemented in the disk-operating system.

Firewall   A metaphorical label for a set of hardware and software components protecting system resources (servers, LANs) from exogenous attack via a network (from Internet users) by intercepting and checking network traffic. The "mix" of hardware and software accomplishing firewall operations can vary. For LAN installations of any size, the typical approach is to install one or more computers "positioned" at critical junctures (gateways) and dedicated to the firewall functions. It is typically the case that such installations are configured such that all external connections (modems, ports) are "outside" the firewall (with respect to its domain of protection), or at least "abut" it on its "external face." The firewall's own "internal" connection into the protected domain is typically the focus of monitoring functions. A system or combination of systems that enforces a boundary between two or more networks. Gateway that limits access between networks in accordance with local security policy. The typical firewall is an inexpensive micro-based Unix box kept clean of critical data, with a bunch of modems and public network ports on it but just one carefully watched connection back to the rest of the cluster.

Firewall machine   A specific computer dedicated to effecting a firewall.

Firmware   Software contained in a read-only memory (ROM) device.

First-wave war(fare)   The term for the mode or character of war(fare) exemplified in primitive, pastoral, and agricultural societies and dating from prehistory.

Fishbowl   A defensive IW tactic in which a suspicious or unauthorized user is permitted to continue established access to the protected system or network, but whose interactions with that system or network are (all unknown and unapparent to the subject) "encapsulated" within a secure domain of operations (rerouted to an isolated computer; redirected to a dummy environment simulating an actual server) so that IW defenders can observe and analyze the user's intentions, tactics, and/or identity. To contain, isolate, and monitor an unauthorized user within a system in order to gain information about the user.

Fog of war   The aggregate of factors that reduce or preclude situational certainty in a battlespace.

Fork bomb   A disruptive piece of code directed toward a Unix-based system that causes runaway "forking" (splitting or replication) of operating system processes to degrade or (if saturation is achieved) deny that target system's operations. Code that can be written in one line of code on any Unix system; used to recursively spawn copies of itself, explode, and eventually eat all the process table entries and effectively locks up the system.

Folder   Commonly used as a standard Windows 95/98/NT term, equivalent to the Windows 3.x term directory.

FORMAT   The DOS format program that performs high-level formatting on a hard disk, and both high- and low-level formatting on a floppy disk.

Formmail   Use Formmail to e-mail the contents of forms on your Web pages to you when a visitor fills it out.

Fragmentation   The state of having a file scattered around a disk in pieces rather than existing in one contiguous area of the disk. Fragmented files are slower to read than unfragmented files.

Free for all links page   Allows visitors to add links to any Web site onto the list, categorized by subject.

Friction (of war)   The aggregate of factors and events that reduce or degrade operational efficiency (and, hence, effectiveness) in the "real world" of war-making. The label is a metaphorical allusion to the sort of "heat loss" that is an inescapable part of physical–mechanical systems.

FrontPage extensions   FrontPage is Microsoft's simple Web-page editor designed for nonprogrammers. It includes many of its own scripts and special effects, but to use them, you have to install the FrontPage "extensions" on your Web site. You should either plan to use CGI-based applications or FrontPage. FrontPage does not provide the ability to edit or maintain files in your home directory and does not upload in true ascii.

FTP Account   Used to upload and download files to and from your Web site. You have unlimited access to your account 24 hours a day. You'll need to have FTP client software.

Global information environment   All individuals, organizations, or systems, most of which are outside the control of the military or national command authorities, that collect, process, and disseminate information to national and international audiences.

Guestbook   Visitors sign-in to your Web site, leaving a message to let you know what they thought of your site.

Hacker   The label "hacker" has come to connote a person who deliberately accesses and exploits computer and information systems to which he or she has no authorized access. Originally, the term was an accolade for someone highly motivated to explore what computers could do and/or the limits of his or her technical skills (especially in programming). "A great hack" was a common compliment for an especially cunning or innovative piece of software code. The term "cracker" was then reserved for people intruding into computer or information systems for the thrill of it (or worse). Over time, "cracker" faded from usage and "hacker" came to subsume its (unfortunate) connotations.

Head   A small electromagnetic device inside a drive that reads, writes, and erases data on the drive's media.

Hijacking   A term (typically applied in combination with another) to connote action to usurp activity or interactions in progress. Most commonly used for those tactics that allow an intruder to usurp an authorized user's session for his or her own ends.

History   (Internet Browser)—Stores the internet addresses (URLs) of the Web sites you have visited.

Heat Sink   A mass of metal attached to a chip carrier or socket for the purpose of dissipating heat.

Hyperwar   A term (attributed to "Air Force planners") describing the notion that "war is becoming unimaginably and unmanageably fast."

I2WAR   Acronym for infrastructural and information warfare.

I/O Port   I/O stands for input/output. I/O is the communication between a computer and its user, its storage devices, other computers (via a network), or the outside world. The I/O port is the logical channel or channel endpoint in an I/O communication system.

I&W   Acronym for indications and warnings. This is a sort of catch-all label for any and all data signifying an operant or potential threat. Typically, "indications and warnings" connotes a summarization or fusion of raw data into a synopsis of current threat condition(s) (a report from an intel unit).

I&W/TA   Acronym for "indications and warnings or threat assessment.".This label is occasionally used to connote the summarization of incoming data with respect to threat conditions (extant or predicted).

IBW   Acronym for information-based warfare. Acronym for intelligence-based warfare.

IDE   Stands for integrated drive electronics. Describes a hard disk with the disk controller integrated within it. See also EIDE.

IDS   Acronym for intrusion-detection system.

IDW   Acronym for information-dominance warfare.

IEW   Acronym for intelligence and electronic warfare.

Indications and warning(s) (I&W)   Those intelligence activities intended to detect and report time-sensitive intelligence information on foreign developments that could involve a threat to the United States or allied military, political, or economic interests or to U.S. citizens abroad. It includes forewarning of enemy actions or intentions; the imminence of hostilities; insurgency; nuclear or non-nuclear attack on the United States, its overseas forces, or allied nations; hostile reactions to U.S. reconnaissance activities; terrorists' attacks; and other similar events.

Indirect information warfare   Changing the adversary's information by creating phenomena that the adversary must then observe and analyze.

Industrial warfare   The term for the class or character of war or warfare exemplified from the 18th century through to the present. Synonymous with second-wave war(fare).

Information   Facts, data, or instructions in any medium or form. The meaning that a human assigns to data by means of the known conventions used in their representation. In intelligence usage, unevaluated material of every description that may be used in the production of intelligence.

Information age   A label generally used to connote the present or prospective era in which information technology (IT) is the dominant technical artifacture. The future time period when social, cultural, and economic patterns will reflect the decentralized,

and command, control, communications, computers, and intelligence (C4I) to acquire and assimilate information needed to effectively employ our own forces to dominate and neutralize adversary forces. It includes the capability for near-real-time awareness of the location and activity of friendly, adversary, and neutral forces throughout the battlespace; and a seamless, robust C4I network linking all friendly forces that provides common awareness of the current situation.

Information system(s) (INFOSYS) The entire infrastructure, organization, personnel, and components that collect, process, store, transmit, display, disseminate, and act on information.

Information systems security A synonym for INFOSEC. Protection of information systems against unauthorized access to or modification of information, whether in storage, processing, or transit and against the denial of service to authorized users.

Information systems warfare (ISW) The subcategory of information warfare (IW) aimed at leveraging media, channels, and vehicles of information transfer and/or processing to tactical and strategic advantage.

Information terrorism An ill-defined term (as yet) invoked to connote cyberspace mischief undertaken with intentions or ramifications analogous to the fear-inducing physical attacks one associates with terrorist activity.

Information transport That element of IW activities that involves moving data from points of collection to points of storage or use. The speed with which this is done affects the timelines of the data availability and, therefore, the responsiveness of the organization to situations. Transport considerations must be viewed within the overall information warfare perspective, because the same efficiency that facilitates rapid message and data transportation may also be used by a competitor to download proprietary databases in seconds or minutes.

Information war Activities intertwined with, and superimposed on, other military operations, exploiting data and information in support of traditional military tasks such as command-and-control.

Information warfare (abbreviated IW) The broad class of activities aimed at leveraging data, information, and knowledge in support of military goals. Subcategories of information warfare can be differentiated into two general classes: (a) those aimed at leveraging the vehicles of information transfer or processing (information systems warfare— ISW); and (b) those aimed at leveraging the informative content or effect of such systems.

IRQ Stands for interrupt request. IRQ is the name of the hardware interrupt signals that PC peripherals (such as serial or parallel ports) use to get the processor's attention. Because interrupts usually cannot be shared, devices are assigned unique IRQ addresses that enable them to communicate with the processor. Peripherals that use interrupts include LAN adapters, sound boards, scanner interfaces, and SCSI adapters.

Java chat Rooms   Real-time chat via a Java applet that allows visitors to your Web site to engage in live discussion with you or with each other. You can provide it just for fun, or use it to interact with your customers in real-time.

Jumper   A small, plastic-covered metal clip that slips over two pins protruding from a circuit board. When in place, the jumper connects the pins electronically and closes the circuit, turning it "on."

Kernel   An essential part of the operating system, responsible for resource allocation, low-level hardware interfaces, security, and more.

Key communicator   An individual or group having the economic, social, or political power to persuade the individuals or groups with which he or she interacts to change or reinforce existing opinions, emotions, attitudes, and behaviors.

Keystroke monitoring   A form of user surveillance in which the actual character-by-character traffic (that user's keystrokes) are monitored, analyzed, and/or logged for future reference. A specialized form of audit trail software, or a specially designed device, that records every key struck by a user and every character of the response that the host computer returns to the user.

Knowledge   The state or mechanism(s) ascribed to a system to explain complex mediation between effective acquisition of data from, and effective action in, an operational environment. This approach to knowledge explicitly ties it to the processes of both education and inaction with respect to the given operational environment, and, hence, links it to one or more specific actors in that given domain. These connections explain the IW literature's claims that knowledge is active and must be possessed if it is to exist— let alone be useful.

Knowledge-based warfare   Knowledge-based warfare is the ability of one side to obtain essential and key elements of truth while denying these same elements of truth to the other side. The key attributes of knowledge-based warfare are timely, high fidelity, comprehensive, synthesized, and visual data. The end game is a complete pictorial representation of reality that the decision maker can tune to his or her unique needs at any given time. This picture must include both blue and red data, although this ACTD concentrates on the provision of blue data only.

Knowledge dominance   In warfare, an operational advantage (vis a vis an adversary) in exploiting information to guide effective action. This is the goal of information dominance.

Knowledge war   A synonym for IW or third-wave war.

Leapfrog attack Any form of intrusion or attack accomplished by exploitation of data or information obtained on a site or server other than the attack's target.

Letter bomb/letterbomb Malicious or disruptive code delivered via an e-mail message (and/or an attachment to said message). A piece of e-mail containing live data intended to do malicious things to the recipient's machine or terminal. Under UNIX, a letterbomb can also try to get part of its contents interpreted as a shell command to the mailer. The results of this could range from silly to tragic.

Logic bomb The term for a mischievous or destructive piece of software (virus, Trojan horse which lies resident on the victim computer or system until triggered by a specific event (onset of a predetermined date or set of system conditions).

Lost cluster chain This is a cluster on disk that is not registered as free, but does not have any known data in it.

Mail bomb/mailbomb Unlike logic bomb (a thing), mail bomb is a verb used to connote deliberately deluging a target system or host with e-mail messages for purposes of harassment, degradation of service, or even denial of service.

Mail storm/mailstorm What the target system or users see when being mail bombed. Any large amount of incoming e-mail sufficient to disrupt or bog down normal local operations. What often happens when a machine with an Internet connection and active users reconnects after extended downtime—a flood of incoming mail that brings the machine to its knees.

Majordomo list This is a very flexible tool for allowing your clients to interact with each other by e-mail. In simple terms, it is an interactive e-mail discussion group that allows all subscribers to send and receive messages to and from everyone on the list through e-mail, sort of like an e-mail chat room, but not in real time. Majordomo lists usually focus on a particular topic of common interest, such as dried flower arranging, forensics, or anything that people can share information or talk about. There are many configurable features including automatic subscribe and unsubscribe and much more. Each list can e-mail up to 1500 e-mails per day.

MASINT Acronym for measurement and signature intelligence.

Measurement and signature intelligence Scientific and technical intelligence obtained by quantitative and qualitative analysis of data (metric, angle, spatial, wavelength, time dependence, modulation, plasma, and hydromagnetic) derived from specific technical sensors for the purpose of identifying any distinctive features associated with the source, emitter, or sender and to facilitate subsequent identification and/or measurement of the same.

MEII Acronym for minimum essential information infrastructure.

Message   Any thought or idea expressed briefly in a plain or secret language and prepared in a form suitable for transmission by any means of communication.

MIE   Acronym for military information environment.

Military deception   Actions executed to deliberately mislead adversary military decision makers as to friendly military capabilities, intentions, and operations, thereby causing the adversary to take specific actions (or inactions) that will contribute to the accomplishment of the friendly mission.

Military information environment (MIE)   The environment contained within the global information environment, consisting of information systems and organizations (friendly and adversary, military and nonmilitary) that support, enable, or significantly influence a specific military operation.

Military information function   Any information function supporting and enhancing the employment of military forces.

Military technical revolution (MTR)   A term from Soviet military theorization of the late 1970s. It denotes the phenomenon of extreme transformations in warfare occurring as a result of the exploitation of technology. The Soviets saw the operational and organizational innovations resulting from the exploitation of the technology as defining a military technical revolution.

Minimum essential information infrastructure (MEII)   A label for the least set of own-force information assets that can serve to support a given mission or operation.

Mirror image back-ups   Mirror image back-ups (also referred to as bit stream back-ups) involve the back-up of all areas of a computer hard disk drive or another type of storage media (Zip disks, floppy disks, Jazz disks, etc.). Such mirror image back-ups exactly replicate all sectors on a given storage device. Thus, all files and ambient data storage areas are copied. Such back-ups are sometimes referred to as "evidence grade back-ups" and they differ substantially from standard file back-ups and network server back-ups.

Misuse detection   The class of intrusion-detection tactics that proceed on the presumption that problematical intrusions (attacks) can be positively characterized, and that detection of their characteristic profile is sufficient for identifying potential threats.

Mockingbird   A computer program or process that mimics the legitimate behavior of a normal system feature (or other apparently useful function) but performs malicious activities once invoked by the user.

Monthly traffic (bandwidth)   Your monthly traffic is the sum of outward-bound or inward-bound Web pages, files, e-mail, and anonymous FTP traffic. Each time a Web page, image, audio, video, and other elements of your Web site is accessed by your visitor, traffic is generated.

Motherboard   The "heart" of your PC—it handles system resources (IRQ lines, DMA channels, I/O locations), as well as core components such as the CPU, and all system memory. It accepts expansion devices such as sound and network cards, and modems.

mSQL database   A database engine used for accessing individual records.

MTR   Acronym for military technical revolution.

National Information Infrastructure (NII)   A general label for the composite network of data or information systems and connectivity channels that serve as the foundation for U.S. economic, political, and military operations.

Navigation warfare (NAVWAR)   A term for activities directed toward disrupting, degrading, or denying the adversary's capabilities for geographical location, tracking, and control (navigation) based on such capabilities. This term is currently used specifically to connote those EW and IW (counter-) measures involving the Global Positioning System (GPS) network of satellites and/or terrestrial or airborne or shipborne receivers.

Netwar   A synonym for cyberwar.

Network spoofing   In network spoofing, a system presents itself to the network as though it were a different system (system A impersonates system B by sending B's address instead of its own). The reason for doing this is that systems tend to operate within a group of other "trusted" systems. Trust is imparted in a one-to-one fashion; system A trusts system B (this does not imply that system B trusts system A). Implied with this trust is that the system administrator of the trusted system is performing his or her job properly and maintaining an appropriate level of security for his or her system. Network spoofing occurs in the following manner: if system A trusts system B and system C spoofs (impersonates) system B, then system C can gain otherwise denied access to system A.

Network worm   A worm that migrates across platforms over a network by copying itself from one system to another by exploiting common network facilities, resulting in execution of the (replicated) worm on that system and potentially others.

NII   Acronym for National Information Infrastructure.

NTFS   Windows NT file system.

Offensive counterinformation   Actions against the adversary's information functions.

On-line training courses   Receive unlimited access to over 180 course offerings via your Web browser by DPEC. Unlimited access is provided at no extra charge to E-Corporate (electronic corporate) account holders.

OODA loop (also O-O-D-A loop)   Observation, orientation, decision, action loop. Taken to describe a single iteration of the cycle proceeding from data acquisition, through information integration and decision making, to inaction of a response. Disruption or other damage to the OODA loop is a common way of portraying the goal and/or main effect of IW.

OOTW   Acronym for operations other than war (missions carried out by the military that lie outside the scope of what is conventionally termed "war"). Examples include humanitarian and police actions.

Open-source intelligence (OSINT)   Information of potential intelligence value that is available to the general public.

Operational intelligence   Intelligence that is required for planning and conducting campaigns and major operations to accomplish strategic objectives within theaters or areas of operations.

Operations security (OPSEC)   A process of identifying critical information and subsequently analyzing friendly actions attendant to military operations and other activities.

Opinion   A view, judgment, or appraisal formed in the mind about a particular matter or particular matters. It may also be said to be an intellectually defined judgment of what is true for the individual or group. It may be more influenced by attitudes than facts.

Orientation   An interactive process of many-sided implicit cross-referencing projections, empathies, correlations, and rejections that shapes and is shaped by the interplay of genetic heritage, cultural tradition, previous experiences, and unfolding circumstances.

OSINT   Acronym for open-source intelligence.

Packet sniffer   A device or program that monitors the data traveling between computers on a network.

packet sniffing   Packet sniffing is a technique in which attackers surreptitiously insert a software program at remote network switches or host computers. The program monitors information packets as they are sent through networks and sends a copy of the information retrieved to the hacker. By picking up the first 125 keystrokes of a connection, attackers can learn passwords and user identifications, which, in turn, they can use to break into systems.

Partition   A logical section of a disk. Each partition normally has its own file system.

Partition table   A 64-byte data structure that defines the way a PC's hard disk is divided into logical sectors known as partitions. The partition table describes to the operating system how the hard disk is divided. Each partition on a disk has a corresponding entry in the partition table. The partition table is always stored in the first physical sector of a disk drive.

Passive attack   A form of attack in which data is released (captured or obtained) from the target system. Attack that does not result in an unauthorized state change, such as an attack that only monitors and/or records data.

Passive threat   The threat of unauthorized disclosure of information without changing the state of the system. A type of threat that involves the interception, not the alteration, of information.

Password cracking/password theft   Password cracking is a technique used to surreptitiously gain system access by using another users account. Users often select weak password. The two major sources of weakness in passwords are easily guessed passwords based on knowledge of the user (wife's maiden name) and passwords that are susceptible to dictionary attacks (brute-force guessing of passwords using a dictionary as the source of guesses). Password cracking and theft is a technique in which attackers try to guess or steal passwords to obtain access to computer systems. Attackers have automated this technique; rather than attackers trying to guess legitimate users' passwords, computers can very efficiently and systematically do the guessing. For example, if the password is a dictionary word, a computer can quickly look up all possibilities to find a match. Complex passwords comprised of alphanumeric characters are more difficult to crack. However, even with complex passwords, powerful computers can use brute force to compare all possible combinations of characters until a match is found.

Password sniffing   A form of sniffing that entails sampling specific portions of the data stream during a session (collecting a certain number of initial bytes where the password can be intercepted in unencrypted form on common Internet services) so as to obtain password data that can then be exploited.

Path   A location of a file. The path consists of directory or folder names, beginning with the highest-level directory or disk name and ending with the lowest-level directory name. A path can identify a drive (e.g. C:\), a folder (e.g. C:\Temp), or a file (e.g., C:\Windows \ftp.exe).

Penetration   With regard to IW: A successful attack—the ability to obtain unauthorized (undetected) access to files and programs or the control state of a computer system.

Penetration signature   The description of a situation or set of conditions in which a penetration could occur or of system events which in conjunction can indicate the occurrence of a penetration in progress.

Perception   The process of evaluating information that has been received and classified by the five physical senses (vision, hearing, smell, taste, and touch) and interpreted by criteria of the culture and society.

Perception management   Actions to convey and/or deny selected information and indicators to foreign audiences to influence their emotions, motives, and objective reasoning; and to intelligence systems and leaders at all levels to influence official estimates, ultimately resulting in foreign behaviors and official actions favorable to the originator's objectives. In various ways, perception management combines truth projection, operations security, cover and deception, and psychological operations.

Peripheral   Any part of a computer other than the CPU or working memory (RAM and ROM). For example, disks, keyboards, monitors, mice, printers, scanners, tape drives, microphones, speakers, and other such devices are peripherals.

Phracker   Individual who combines phone phreaking with computer hacking. Formed by a play on both phreaker and hacker.

Phreak/phone phreak   A term for hacking or cracking-type exploitation directed at the telephone system (as opposed to the data communications networks). When the intrusion or action involves both telephone and data communications networks, that portion of the intrusion activity directed toward manipulating the telephone system is typically called phreaking.

Phreaker   Individual fascinated by the telephone system. Commonly, an individual who uses his or her knowledge of the telephone system to make calls at the expense of another.

Plug-and-Play (PnP)   A hardware and software specification developed by Intel that allows a PnP system and a PnP adapter to configure automatically. PnP cards generally have no switches or jumpers, but are configured via the PnP system's BIOS or with supplied software for non-PnP computers.

POST   Stands for power-on self test. Each time a PC initializes, the BIOS executes a series of tests collectively known as the POST. The test checks each of the primary areas of the system, including the motherboard, video system, drive system, and keyboard, and ensures that all components can be used safely. If a fault is detected, the POST reports it as an audible series of beeps or a hexadecimal code written to an I/O port.

RAM   Random Access Memory (see also DRAM, SDRAM). A data-storage device for which the order of access to different locations does not affect the speed of access. This is in contrast to magnetic disk or magnetic tape where it is much quicker to access data sequentially because accessing a nonsequential location requires physical movement of the storage medium rather than just electronic switching. The most common form of RAM in use today is built from semiconductor integrated circuits, which can either be static (SRAM) or dynamic (DRAM).

together. Servers run special software called "Web server software," which enables them to receive requests and deliver files to other computers across the Internet.

Server side includes (SSI)   Allows the server to understand and respond to special page commands. As an example, if you had a footer you wanted on all your pages that may change from time to time, you can create a text file with the desired footer and place it in your document. On each page you put a simple include to read the file and place it at the bottom of the desired pages. Then changing the footer on all your pages would be just as simple as changing the one text file.

Session hijacking   Taking over an authorized user's terminal session, either physcially when the user leaves his or her terminal unattended, or electronically when the intruder carefully connects to a just-disconnected communications line.

Shared situation awareness (SSA)   The collective perception, comprehension, and projection of environmental elements among a set of actors.

Shopping cart   Keeps track of what your customers have ordered on-line as they add and remove items. When a customer is ready to check-out, the program tallies the order for processing and takes their credit card and other information.

SIGINT   Acronym for signals intelligence.

Signal   As applied to electronics, any transmitted electrical impulse.

Signal security (SIGSEC)   A generic term that includes both communications security and electronic security.

Signals intelligence (SIGINT)   A category of intelligence comprising—either individually or in combination—all communications intelligence, electronics intelligence, and foreign instrumentation signals intelligence, however transmitted.

SIGSEC   Acronym for signal security.

Simple counter   Graphical count of visitors to your Web site, which appears on your Web page.

Site submission   Submits your site information to a database of over 1600 search engines, link engines, and directories.

Situation awareness (SA)   Sometimes termed "situational awareness." The perception of the elements in the environment within a volume of time and space, the comprehension of their meaning, and the projection of their status in the near future. This term is broadly used to denote the state of awareness that a subject (operator; pilot) has in the course of a task at a given point in time. As such, it connotes a degree of orientation to those circumstances at that point in time— particularly those that are germane to the task itself. The term is also (more loosely) used to connote such a state of awareness or orientation with respect to multiple actors and/or organizational units. As such, the notion of situation awareness maps straightforwardly onto the "Orientation" phase of the OODA Loop.

Slot   A physical connector on a motherboard to hold an expansion card, SIMM, DIMM, or a processor card in place.

Sniff / sniffing   The act of surreptitiously monitoring data streams so as to intercept and capture exploitable information.

Sniffer   A tool used to intercept potentially exploitable data from the traffic on a network. A program to capture data across a computer network. Used by hackers to capture user-ID names and passwords. Software tool that audits and identifies network traffic packets.

Social engineering   A term for personal (social) tactics employed in support of attempts to achieve unauthorized access to a computer/information system. This is something of a catch-all category for any tricks used to obtain the intended access or to obtain information critical to achieving that access.

Socket   A receptacle, usually on a motherboard, that processors or chips can be inserted into.

SOS   Acronym for system of systems.

Spam   The act of bombarding a target (system, Usenet news group, set of e-mail addresses) with sufficient volume of data (or a volume of sufficiently massive data items) such that degradation or even denial of service is achieved. This term is also pejoratively applied to describe the perceived harassment of receiving profligately broadcast data (junk e-mail advertising). To crash a program by overrunning a fixed-site buffer with excessively large input data. Also, to cause a person or newsgroup to be flooded with irrelevant or inappropriate messages.

Spectrum management   Planning, coordinating, and managing joint use of the electromagnetic spectrum through operational, engineering, and administrative procedures, with the objective of enabling electronic systems to perform their functions in the intended environment without causing or suffering unacceptable interference.

System registry   The system configuration files used by Windows 95, 98, and NT to store settings about user preferences, installed software, hardware and drivers, and other settings required for Windows to run correctly. The system updates the registry every time you add new hardware or a new program to your system. When the registry becomes "broken," it can cause serious system problems.

Tactical internet   A battlefield communication system networked together using commercially based internet protocols.

TECHINT   Acronym for technical intelligence.

Technical attack   An attack that can be perpetrated by circumventing or nullifying hardware and software protection mechanisms, rather than by subverting system personnel or other users.

Technical intelligence (TECHINT)   Intelligence derived from exploitation of foreign materiel, produced for strategic, operational, and tactical level commanders. Technical intelligence begins when an individual service member finds something new on the battlefield and takes the proper steps to report it. The item is then exploited at succeedingly higher levels until a countermeasure is produced to neutralize the adversary's technological advantage. (DOD Dictionary of Military Terms)

Telnet account   Telnet allows real-time access to the command line of your server (similar to the C:\ prompt in DOS) to run programs and install and configure scripts. Most cgi scripts can be installed without Telnet unless you need it for debugging purposes.

Terminal hijacking   Allows an attacker on a certain machine to control any terminal session that is in progress. A attack hacker can send and receive terminal I/O while a user is on the terminal.

Terminator   Most commonly found in relation to a SCSI chain, this functions to prevent the reflection or echoing of signals that reach the ends of the SCSI bus. Usually terminators are hardware circuits or jumpers.

Third-wave war(fare)   A synonym for IW or knowledge war The allusion is to Toffler's "Third Wave" of economic activity, which concentrates on information and knowledge as raw material and product. This three-tiered economic or political model was a major influence on the DOD thinkers whose work led to today's interest in IW.

Time bomb   A logic bomb that is specifically triggered by a temporal event (a predetermined date/time). A logic bomb that is triggered by reaching some preset time, either once or periodically. A variant of the Trojan horse in which malicious code is inserted to be triggered later.

TRANSEC   Acronym for transmission security (communications security).

Trap door   A hidden software or hardware mechanism used to circumvent security control.

Trojan horse   A Trojan horse is an independent program that, when called by an authorized user, performs a useful function, but also performs unauthorized functions, often usurping the privileges of the user.

Troll   The act of subverting a forum by deliberately posting provocative (especially provocatively stupid) messages with the intention of distracting others into response.

Unallocated file space Unallocated file space and file slack are both important sources of leads for the computer forensics investigator. The data-storage area in a factory-fresh hard disk drive typically contains patterns of sectors that are filled with patterns of format characters. In DOS and Windows-based computer systems, the format pattern for a floppy diskette usually consists of binary data in the form of hex F6s. The same format pattern is sometimes used in the format of hard disk drives, but the format patterns can consist of essentially any repeat character as determined by the factory test machine that made the last writes to the hard disk drive. The format pattern is overwritten as files and subdirectories are written in the data area.

Unzip To unzip is to extract (see extract) a Zip archive.

UUencode Many file formats are 8-bit (also called binary), which means that the basic unit of information—a byte—comprises 8 on/off signals. E-mail, however, is a 7-bit (or text) medium, preventing the transfer of 8-bit data. UUencoding compensates for this restriction by converting 8-bit data to 7-bit data. UUencode accomplishes this by joining all of the file's bits together into a single stream, and then dividing the stream into 7-bit chunks. The data are then e-mailed and received by someone who must UUdecode it.

Vandal As contrasted with crackers and criminals in a tripartite taxonomy of cyberspace intruders, this term is used to denote anyone whose goal is to destroy information and/or information systems in the course of their intrusion attempts.

Video adapter An expansion card or chip set built into a motherboard that provides the capability to display text and graphics on the computer's monitor. If the adapter is part of an expansion card, it also includes the physical connector for the monitor cable. If it is a chip set on the motherboard, the video connector will be on the motherboard also.

Virtual battlespace The ether occupied by communications impulses, databases, and computer codes. In this usage, the term is synonymous with cyber medium, cyberspace, and infosphere.

Virtual realm A synonym for information realm or cyberspace.

Virus The generic label for a unary set of code that is designed to operate so as to cause mischief or other subversive effect in a target computer system.

Vulnerability With specific regard to IW—a known or suspected flaw in the hardware or software or operation of a system that exposes the system to penetration or its information to accidental disclosure.

War An event characterized by the open, total, and (relatively) unrestricted prosecution of warfare by lethal means. As such, war is not synonymous with warfare.

War dialer   A cracking tool, a program that calls a given list or range of numbers and records those that answer with handshake tones (and so might be entry points to computer or telecommunications systems).

Warfare   The set of all lethal and nonlethal activities undertaken to subdue the hostile will of an adversary or enemy. The distinction between this and war ties into the delineation of information warfare as an activity, which could or should be conducted outside the situational frame of war itself.

Warm boot   Rebooting a system by means of a software command as opposed to turning the power off and on. See also cold boot.

Wizard   A wizard is a series of dialog boxes that guides you step by step through a procedure.

Web-based Telnet   Invoke a telnet session directly from your web browser. There's no need for any other applications or software.

Windows swap files   Windows swap files are relied on by Windows, Windows 95, and Windows 98 to create "virtual memory" (using a portion of the hard disk drive for memory operations). The storage area is important to the computer forensics specialist for the same reason that file slack and unallocated space are important (large volumes of data exist for which the computer user likely has no knowledge). Windows swap files can be temporary or permanent, depending on the version of Windows involved and settings selected by the computer user. Permanent swap files are of more interest to a computer forensics specialist because they normally store larger amounts of information for much longer periods of time.

World-Wide Web   The World-Wide Web, or WWW, is the part of the Internet that you're using to view a particular Web page. The Web is just a set of protocols, or standards, for transferring data from one computer to another; just one aspect of the Internet, but by far the most popular. Telnet, FTP, Veronica, and Archie are some other Internet data-transfer protocols. Without protocols, computers wouldn't be able to communicate with or understand each other.

Worm   A class of mischievous or disruptive software whose negative effect is primarily realized through rampant proliferation (via replication and distribution of the worm's own code). Replication is the hallmark of the worm. Worm code is relatively host-independent, in that the code is self-contained enough to migrate across multiple instances of a given platform, or across multiple platforms over a network (network worm). To replicate itself, a worm needs to spawn a process; this implies that worms require a multitasking operating system to thrive. A program or executable code module that resides in distributed systems or networks. It will replicate itself, if necessary, in order to exercise as much of the systems' resources as possible for its own processing. Such resources may take the form of CPU time, I/O channels, or system memory. It will replicate itself from machine to machine across network connections, often clogging networks and computer systems as it spreads.

Zip   To zip (notice the lower case z) a file is to compress it into an archive so that it occupies less disk space.

Zip archive   An archive of one or more Zip-compressed files. When used as a noun, Zip is typically capitalized. Compressed files can come in many formats besides Zip.

Zip file   A Zip archive that Windows presents as a single file. In general, the contents cannot be accessed unless the archive is decompressed, except when you are running Zip-Magic 2000.

Index

Note: Italized numbers refer to figures.

Norton Utilities, 80
notebooks, 157
Novell, 594
NSA (See National Security Agency)
NSA Headquarters, 395
NSA IW games, 394–96
NTI's Filter_I™ software, 43
ntpd, 195
NTP Version 4, 193, 195
NT servers vulnerability check tool, 522
NTT DoCoMo, 471
nuclear arms, 313–15, 362
Nuclear Emergency Search Team (NEST), 364
nuclear weapons disappearance, 364
Nutrasweet, 196, 198

O

object code, 264
Observation, Orientation, Decision, Action (OODA)
    loop, 292
O'Connor verses Ortega, 480 U.S., 709 (1987), 156
Office of Personnel Management, 343
off-line back-ups, 106
Oklahoma City bombing, 301, 305–06, 309–10
OLDS, 111
Oleg Zezov, 570
Oliver North, 49, 224
Omar Bakri Mohammed, 328
Omega Engineering's Bridgeport manufacturing
    plant, 595–96
OneSecure, 585, 587–88
one-time pad, 557–59
Onion Router project, 414–15, 581–82
on-line conversations, 408
on-line databases, 531
On-line extortion, 350
on-site service, 10
Open Profiling Standard (OPS), 530
open-source encryption software, 417
Operation Desert Storm, 293, 439
Operation El Dorado Canyon, 304
operations other than war (OOTW), 513
Operations Security (OPSEC), 290–91
OPLAN, 3600, 287
optical networking, 281
Oracle Corp., 201, 247
Order of Volatility, 127–28, 131
organized hacker activities, 584
OS/COMET, 433–34
Osama bin Laden
    9-11 attack, 337, 366
    al Qaeda group, 327, 367

Osama bin Laden *(continued)*
    Ali Mohamed, 366–67
    attack planning via Internet, 325, 373
    bin Laden associates, 334
    communiqués, 327
    dead drop information, 443
    double walls of security, 370
    encryption, 334, 373
    groups financed, 369
    interviews, 325
    Khalfan Khamis Mohamed, 367
    Ladenese Epistle, 328–29
    Mamdouh Mahmud Salim, 367
    Mohamed Rashed Daoud al-Owali, 367–68
    bin Laden organization, 356
    recruitment, 370
    terrorist profile, 334
    U.S. embassies in East Africa, 343, 366
    USS Cole, 363, 366
    Wadih el-Hage, 367–68
Outlook, 166, 373, 452
Outlook Express, 166, 373, 452
outside service providers, 294
outsourcing intrusion detection, 587–88

P

Pacific Command, 281
packet data, 476–77
packet sniffers, 448
Page Files, 49
PAGEFILE.SYS, 49
paging mode, 476
Palestine Information Center, 328
Palestine site, 328
Palestinian Hamas site, 262
Palestinian Islamic Jihad's command and control
    system, 325
Palestinian supporters, 350, 352, 418
paper documents, 185–86
paper trail, 123, 185, 412–13
Partition Magic™, 153
passwords, 299, 388, 396
past event reconstruction action agenda, 216–17
past event reconstruction conclusions, 216
Paul Fromm, 330
Paul Mace Software, 145
PBX equipment, 67
PC PhoneHome, 47
Penet re-mailer, 581, 583
pen register devices, 450
Pentagon, 268, 288, 295, 330, 346, 371
Pentaguard, 573
Penthouse, 347